JORDAN MECHNER
REPLAY
MEMOIR OF AN UPROOTED FAMILY

:01
First Second
New York

Many place names of the former Austro-Hungarian Empire
have changed since my grandfather's youth, and since he wrote his
memoir in the 1970s. In the sections of this book that are in his voice,
I've retained the names he knew those places by.

—JM

First Second

Published by First Second
First Second is an imprint of Roaring Brook Press,
a division of Holtzbrinck Publishing Holdings Limited Partnership
120 Broadway, New York, NY 10271
firstsecondbooks.com

Library of Congress Control Number: 2023908167

Our books may be purchased in bulk for promotional, educational, or business use. Please
contact your local bookseller or the Macmillan Corporate and Premium Sales Department at
(800) 221-7945 ext. 5442 or by email at MacmillanSpecialMarkets@macmillan.com.

First edition, 2024
Edited by Mark Siegel and Tess Banta
Cover design by Sunny Lee
Interior book design by Casper Manning
Production editing by Starr Baer

Previously published in French under the title *Replay: Mémoires d'une famille*.

Drawn in Procreate on an iPad Pro, and on A4 paper using Pigma Micron black ink pen and
Pentel brush pen. Colored in Procreate. Lettered with a custom font created from the artist's
handwriting. My Underwood typewriter font created by Michael Tension.

Printed in China

ISBN 978-1-250-87375-0 (hardcover)
1 3 5 7 9 10 8 6 4 2

Don't miss your next favorite book from First Second!
For the latest updates go to firstsecondnewsletter.com and sign up for our enewsletter.

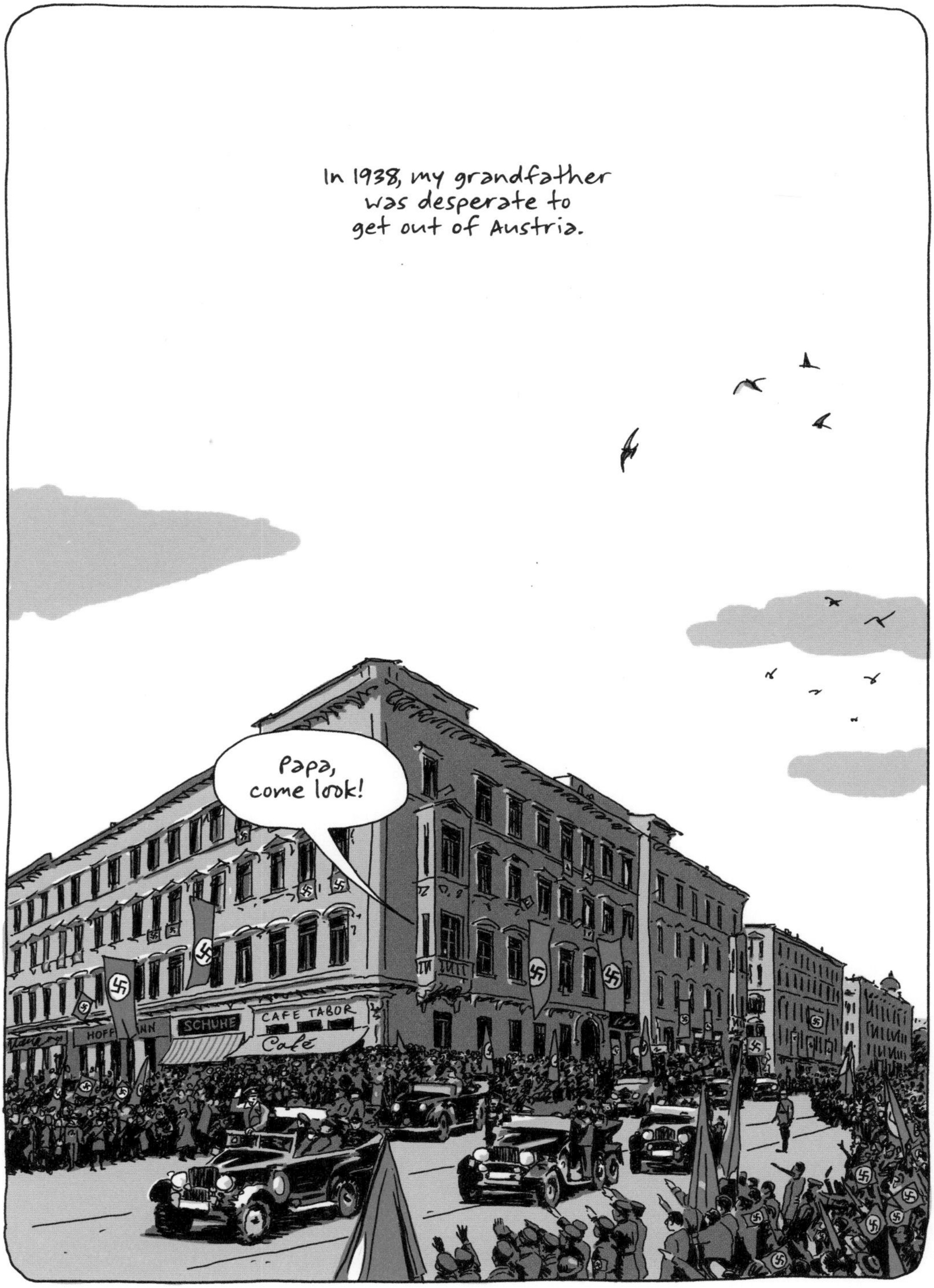
In 1938, my grandfather was desperate to get out of Austria.
Papa, come look!
SCHUHE
CAFE TABOR
Café

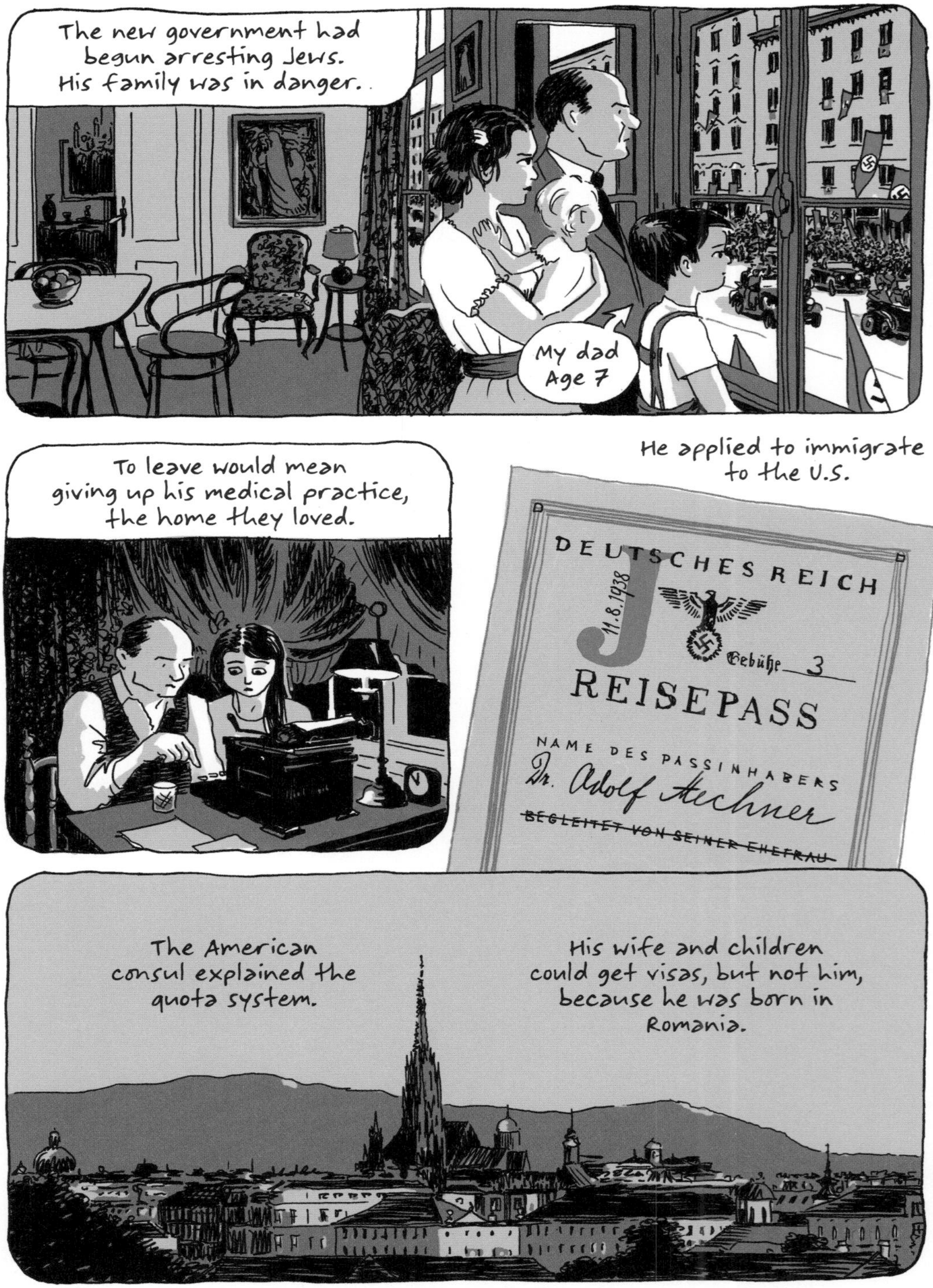
The new government had begun arresting Jews. His family was in danger.
My dad Age 7
To leave would mean giving up his medical practice, the home they loved.
He applied to immigrate to the U.S.
DEUTSCHES REICH
J
11.8.1938
Gebühr 3
REISEPASS
NAME DES PASSINHABERS
Dr. Adolf Aechner
~~BEGLEITET VON SEINER EHEFRAU~~
The American consul explained the quota system.
His wife and children could get visas, but not him, because he was born in Romania.

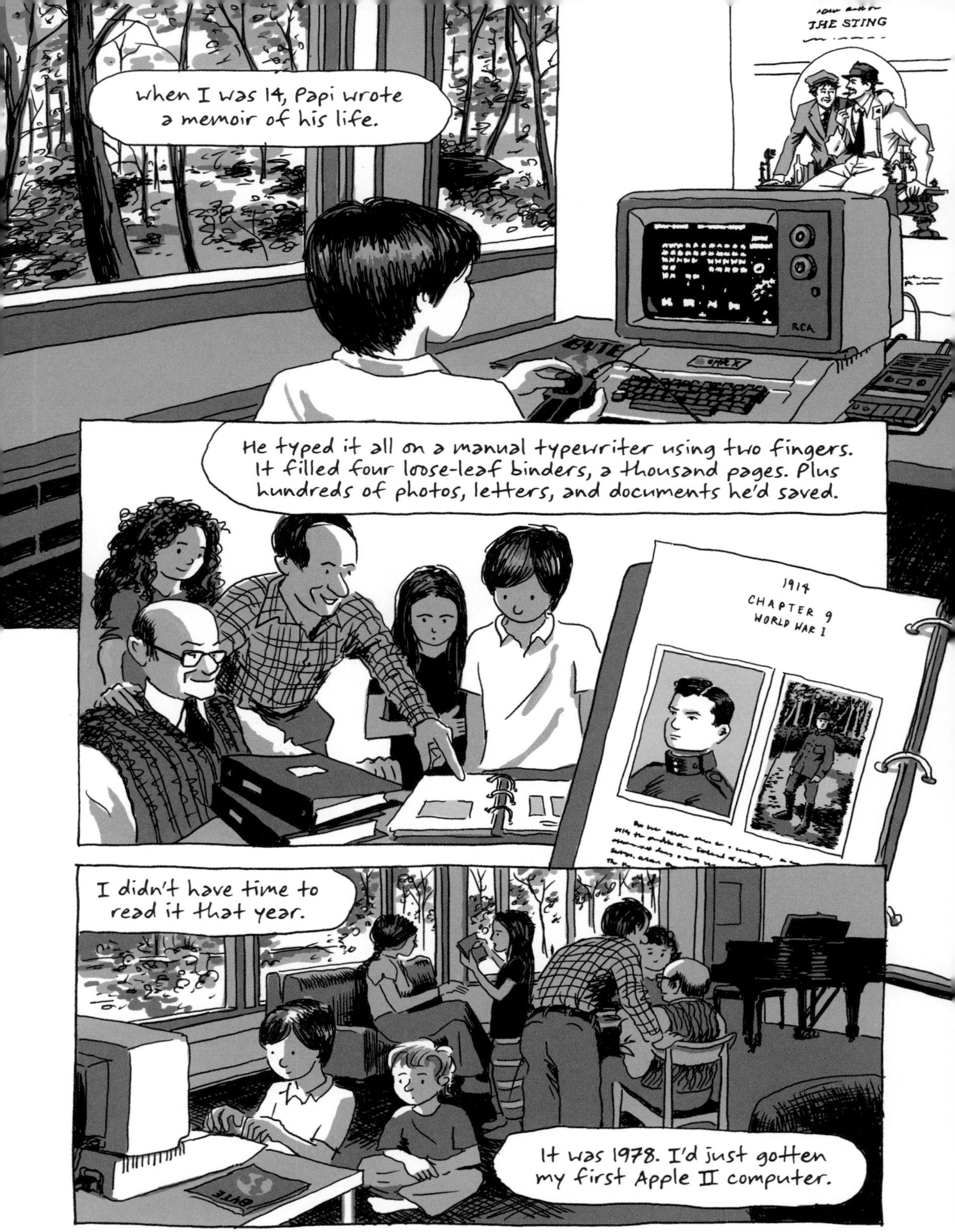

THE STING
When I was 14, Papi wrote a memoir of his life.
BYTE
RCA
He typed it all on a manual typewriter using two fingers. It filled four loose-leaf binders, a thousand pages. Plus hundreds of photos, letters, and documents he'd saved.
1914
CHAPTER 9
WORLD WAR I
I didn't have time to read it that year.
It was 1978. I'd just gotten my first Apple II computer.
BYTE

Wahr spricht, wer Schatten spricht.
—Paul Celan

Chapter 1

Leaving

Adolf and Franz Mechner
Paris, October 1938

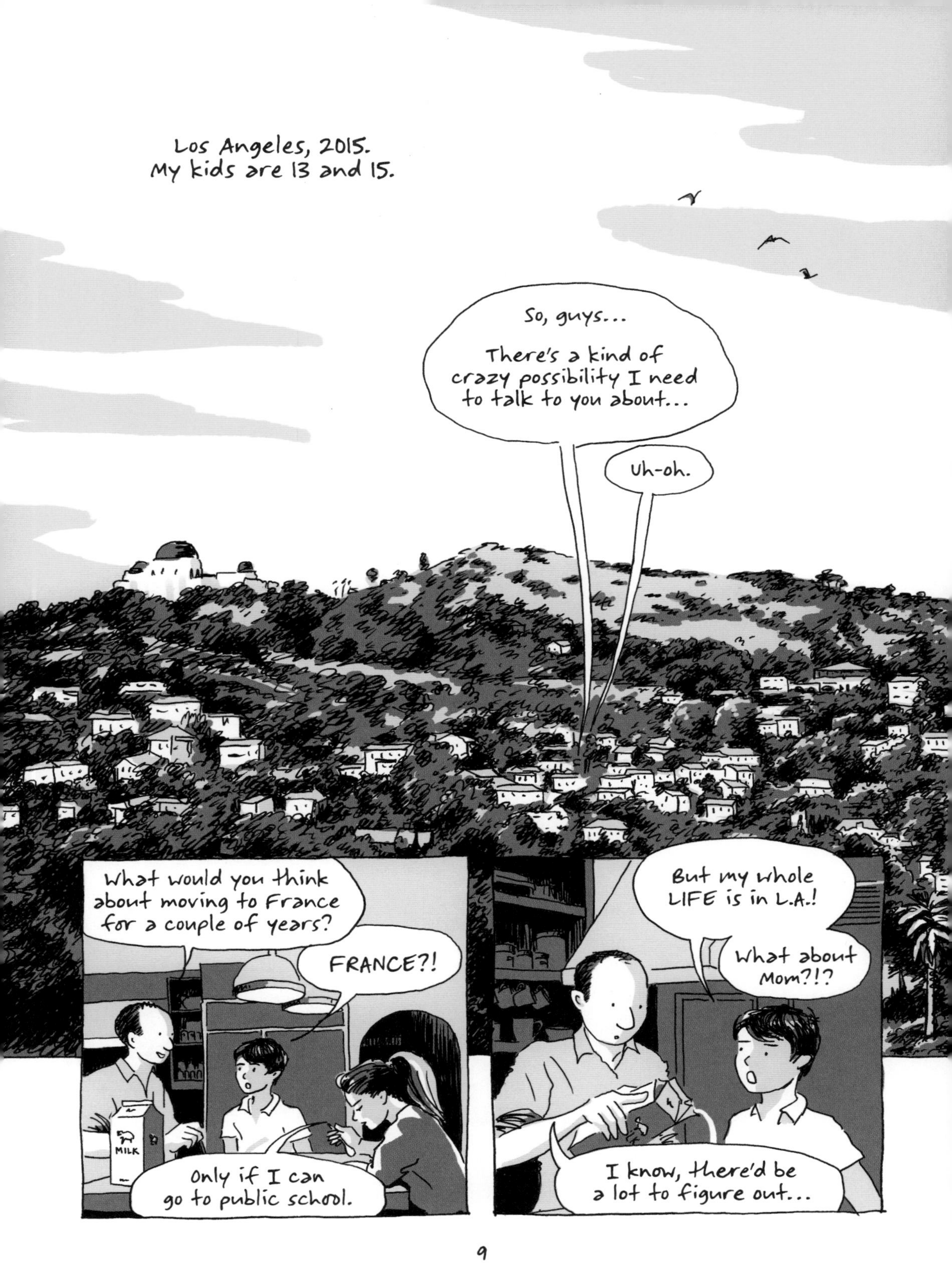
Los Angeles, 2015.
My kids are 13 and 15.
So, guys...
There's a kind of crazy possibility I need to talk to you about...
Uh-oh.
What would you think about moving to France for a couple of years?
FRANCE?!
Only if I can go to public school.
But my whole LIFE is in L.A.!
What about Mom?!?
I know, there'd be a lot to figure out...

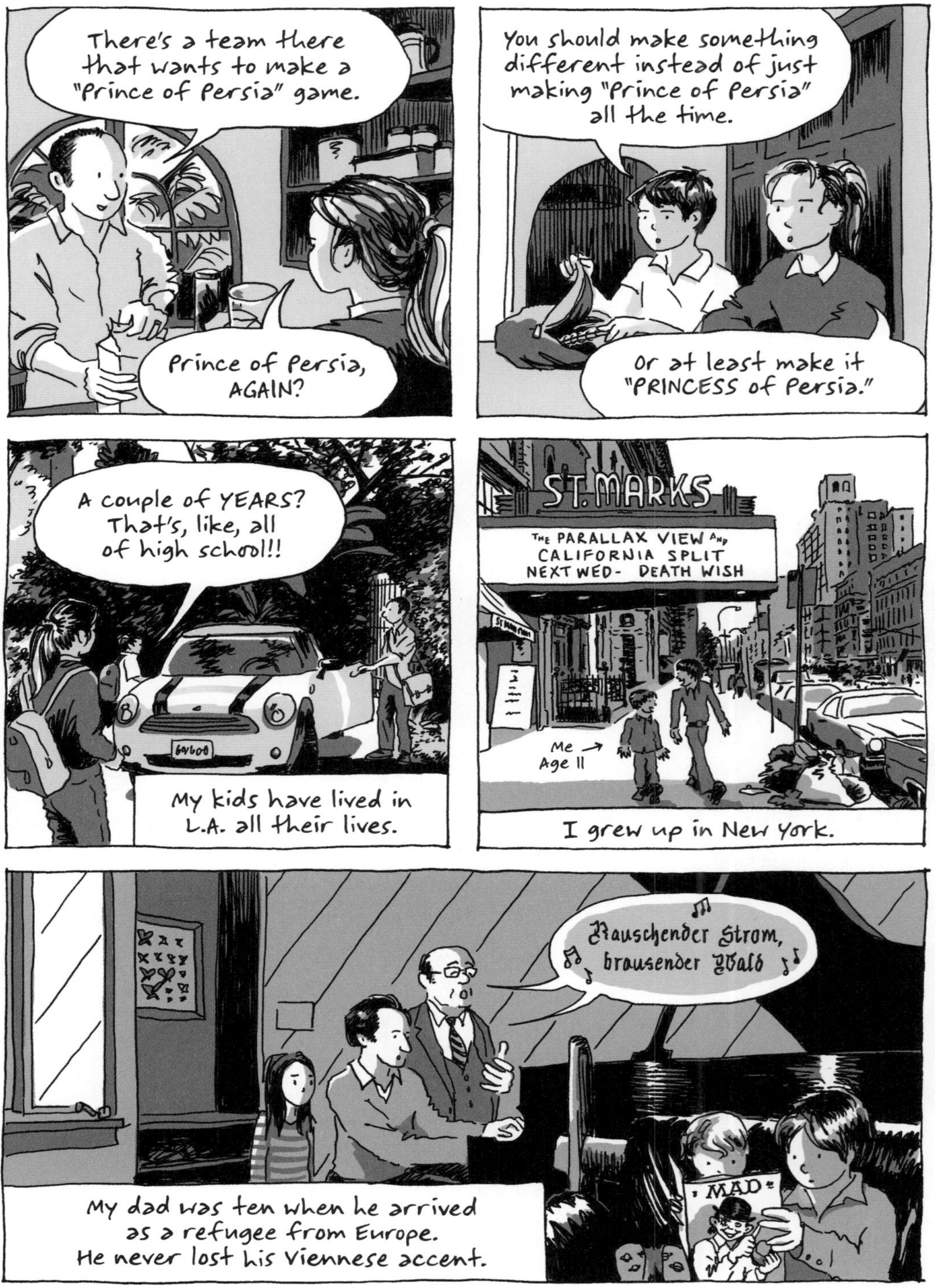

There's a team there that wants to make a "Prince of Persia" game.
Prince of Persia, AGAIN?
You should make something different instead of just making "Prince of Persia" all the time.
Or at least make it "PRINCESS of Persia."
A couple of YEARS? That's, like, all of high school!!
My kids have lived in L.A. all their lives.
ST. MARKS
THE PARALLAX VIEW AND
CALIFORNIA SPLIT
NEXT WED- DEATH WISH
Me →
Age 11
I grew up in New York.
Rauschender Strom, brausender Wald
MAD
My dad was ten when he arrived as a refugee from Europe. He never lost his Viennese accent.

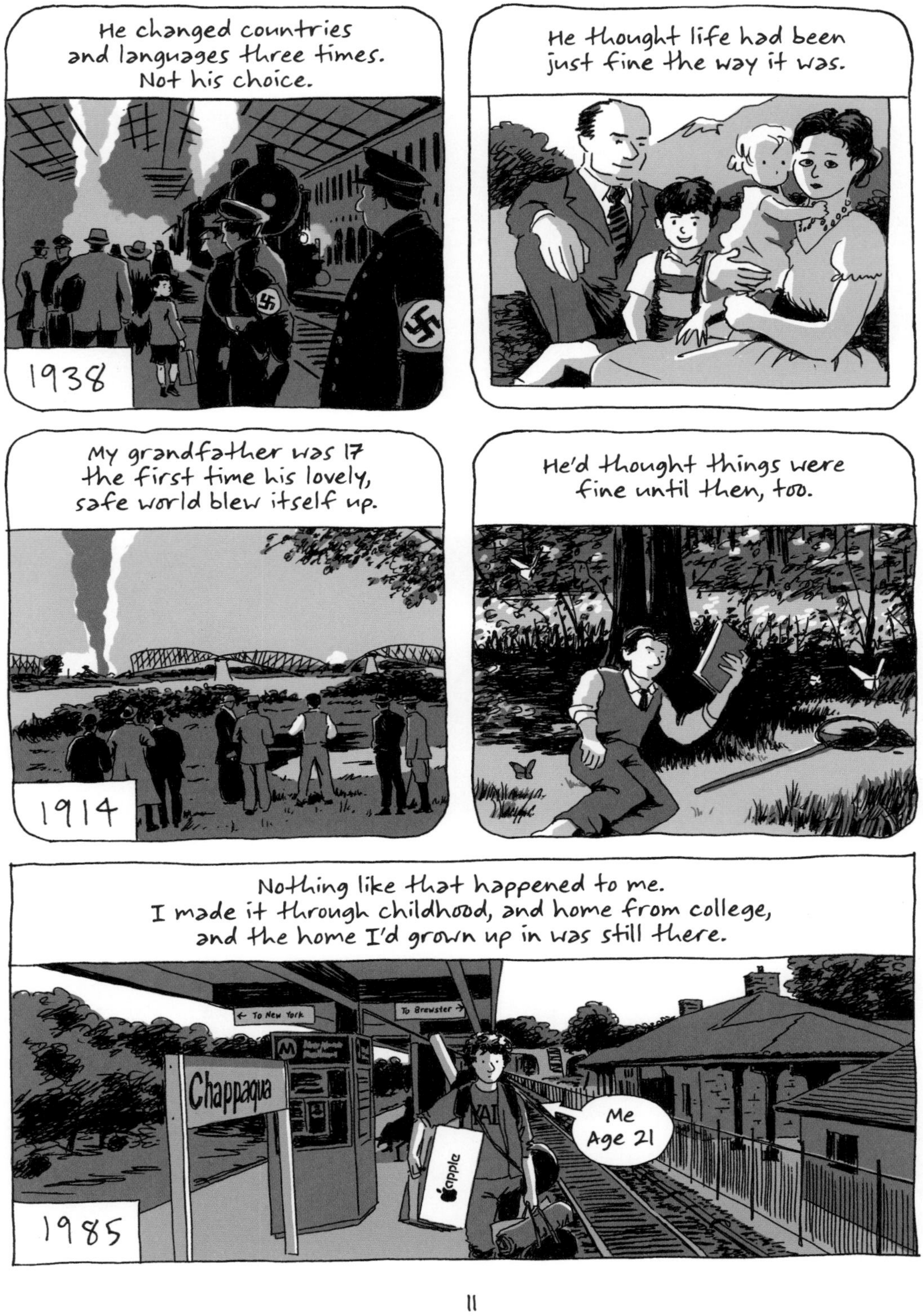
He changed countries and languages three times. Not his choice.
1938
He thought life had been just fine the way it was.
My grandfather was 17 the first time his lovely, safe world blew itself up.
1914
He'd thought things were fine until then, too.
Nothing like that happened to me. I made it through childhood, and home from college, and the home I'd grown up in was still there.
← To New York
To Brewster →
Chappaqua
apple
Me Age 21
1985

The Prince

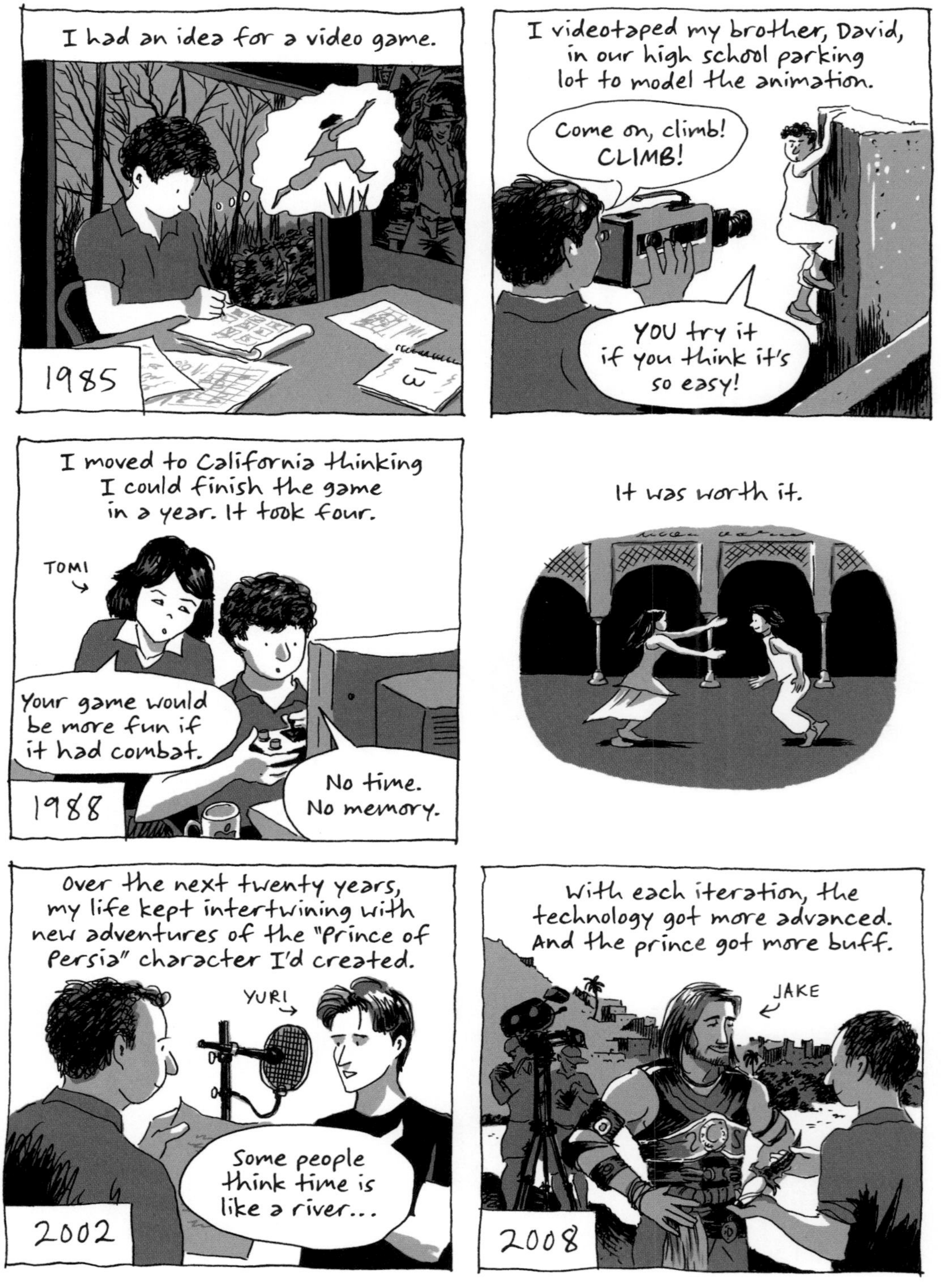
I had an idea for a video game.
1985
I videotaped my brother, David, in our high school parking lot to model the animation.
Come on, climb! CLIMB!
YOU try it if you think it's so easy!
I moved to California thinking I could finish the game in a year. It took four.
TOMI
Your game would be more fun if it had combat.
No time. No memory.
1988
It was worth it.
Over the next twenty years, my life kept intertwining with new adventures of the "Prince of Persia" character I'd created.
YURI
Some people think time is like a river...
2002
With each iteration, the technology got more advanced. And the prince got more buff.
JAKE
2008

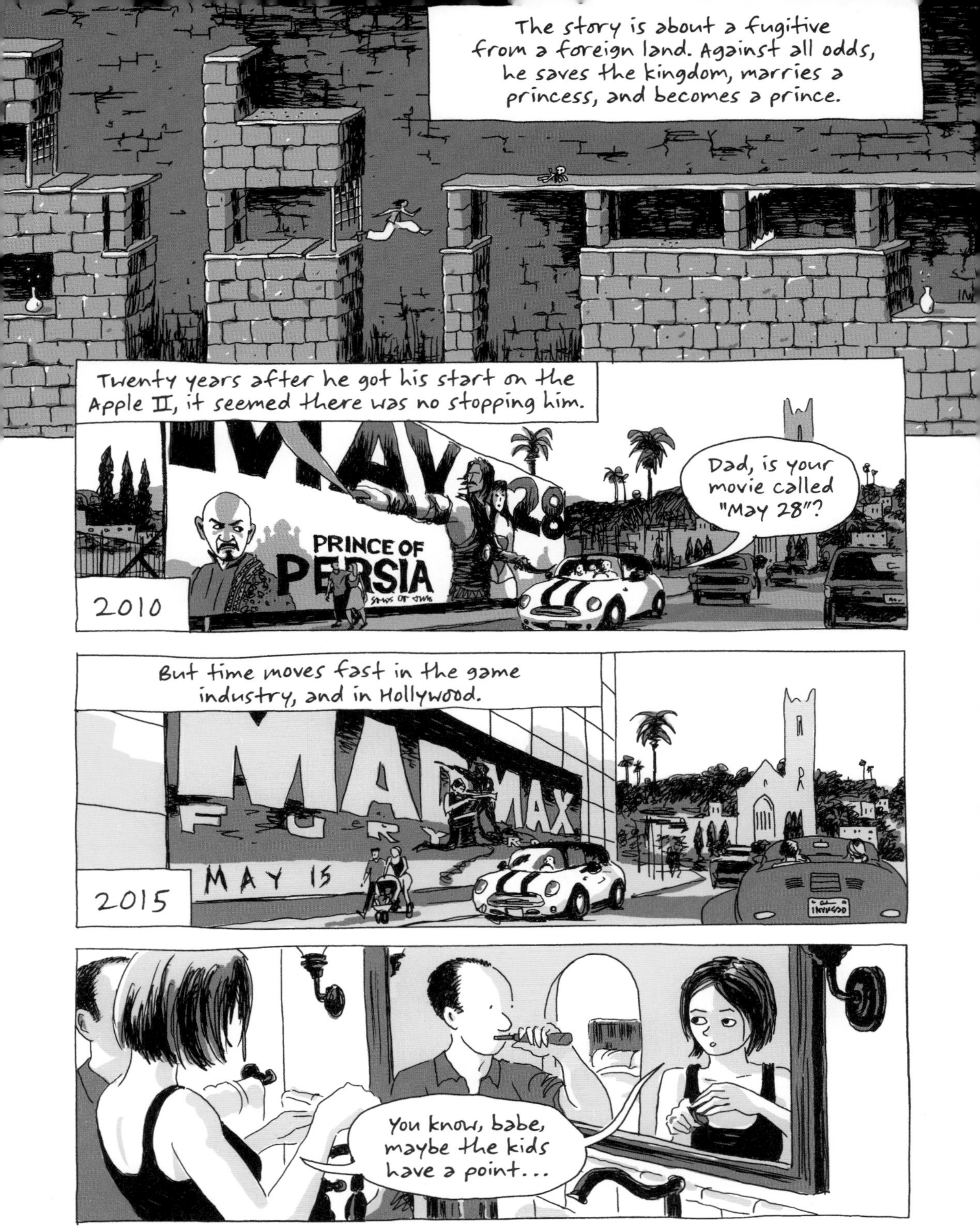
The story is about a fugitive from a foreign land. Against all odds, he saves the kingdom, marries a princess, and becomes a prince.
Twenty years after he got his start on the Apple II, it seemed there was no stopping him.
MAY 28
PRINCE OF PERSIA
Dad, is your movie called "May 28"?
2010
But time moves fast in the game industry, and in Hollywood.
MAD MAX
FURY
MAY 15
2015
You know, babe, maybe the kids have a point...

Open World

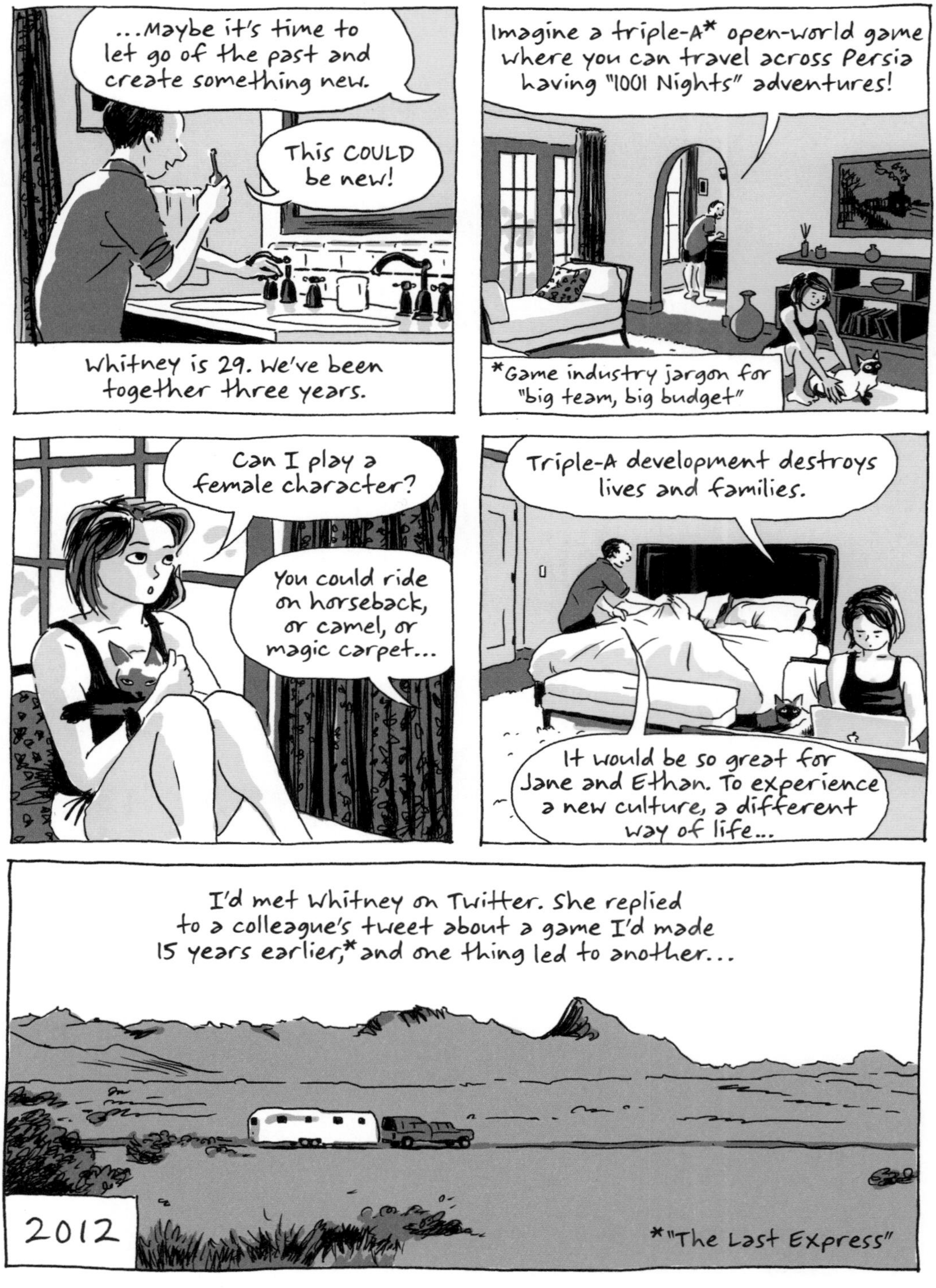
...Maybe it's time to let go of the past and create something new.
This COULD be new!
Whitney is 29. We've been together three years.
Imagine a triple-A* open-world game where you can travel across Persia having "1001 Nights" adventures!
*Game industry jargon for "big team, big budget"
Can I play a female character?
You could ride on horseback, or camel, or magic carpet...
Triple-A development destroys lives and families.
It would be so great for Jane and Ethan. To experience a new culture, a different way of life...
I'd met Whitney on Twitter. She replied to a colleague's tweet about a game I'd made 15 years earlier,* and one thing led to another...
2012
*"The Last Express"

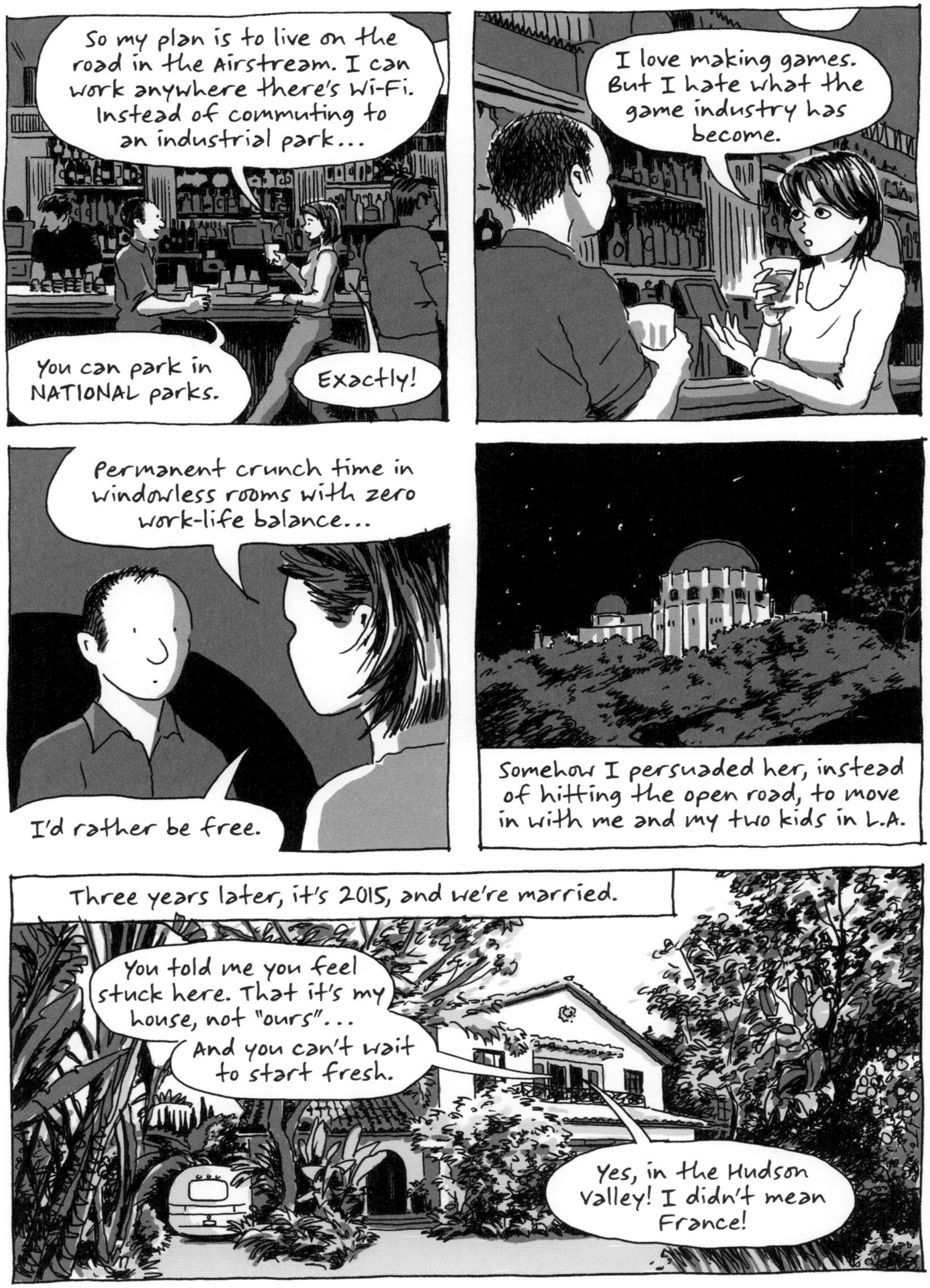
So my plan is to live on the road in the Airstream. I can work anywhere there's Wi-Fi. Instead of commuting to an industrial park...
You can park in NATIONAL parks.
Exactly!
I love making games. But I hate what the game industry has become.
Permanent crunch time in windowless rooms with zero work-life balance...
I'd rather be free.
Somehow I persuaded her, instead of hitting the open road, to move in with me and my two kids in L.A.
Three years later, it's 2015, and we're married.
You told me you feel stuck here. That it's my house, not "ours"...
And you can't wait to start fresh.
Yes, in the Hudson Valley! I didn't mean France!

Cousins

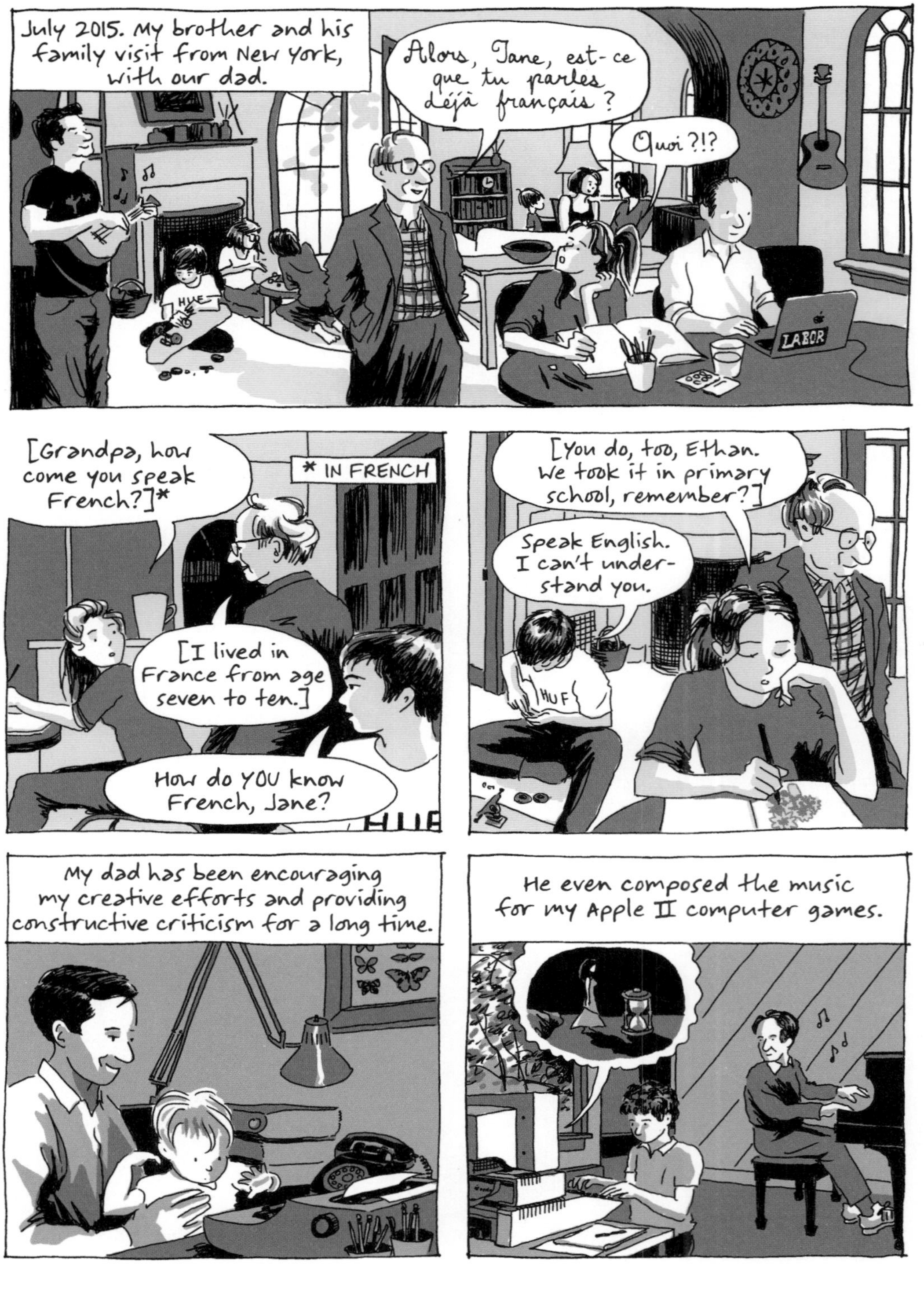
July 2015. My brother and his family visit from New York, with our dad.
Alors, Jane, est-ce que tu parles déjà français ?
Quoi ?!?
[Grandpa, how come you speak French?]*
* IN FRENCH
[I lived in France from age seven to ten.]
How do YOU know French, Jane?
[You do, too, Ethan. We took it in primary school, remember?]
Speak English. I can't under-stand you.
My dad has been encouraging my creative efforts and providing constructive criticism for a long time.
He even composed the music for my Apple II computer games.
LABOR
HUF

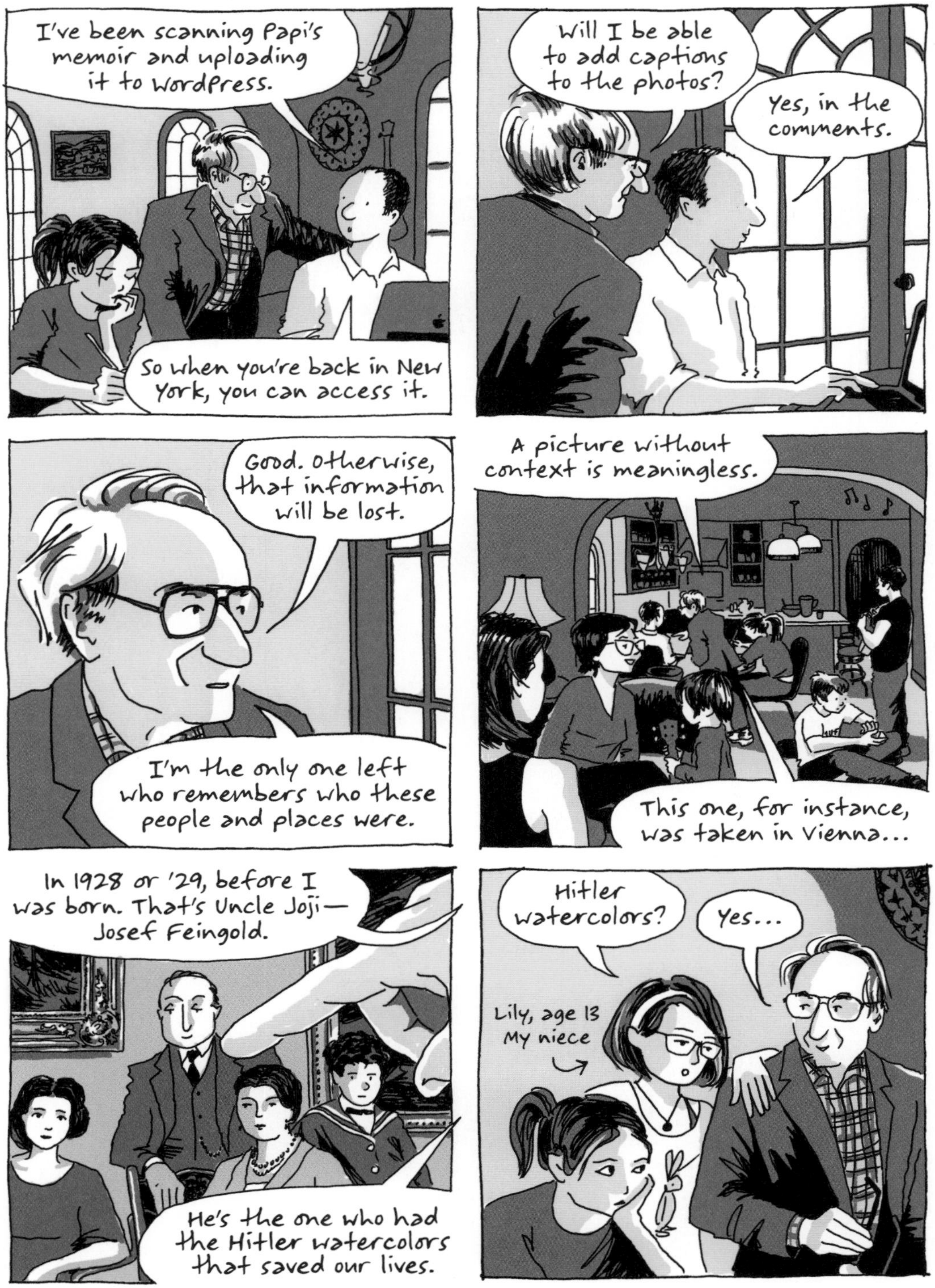
I've been scanning Papi's memoir and uploading it to WordPress.
So when you're back in New York, you can access it.
Will I be able to add captions to the photos?
Yes, in the comments.
Good. Otherwise, that information will be lost.
I'm the only one left who remembers who these people and places were.
A picture without context is meaningless.
This one, for instance, was taken in Vienna...
In 1928 or '29, before I was born. That's Uncle Joji—Josef Feingold.
He's the one who had the Hitler watercolors that saved our lives.
Hitler watercolors?
Yes...
Lily, age 13
My niece

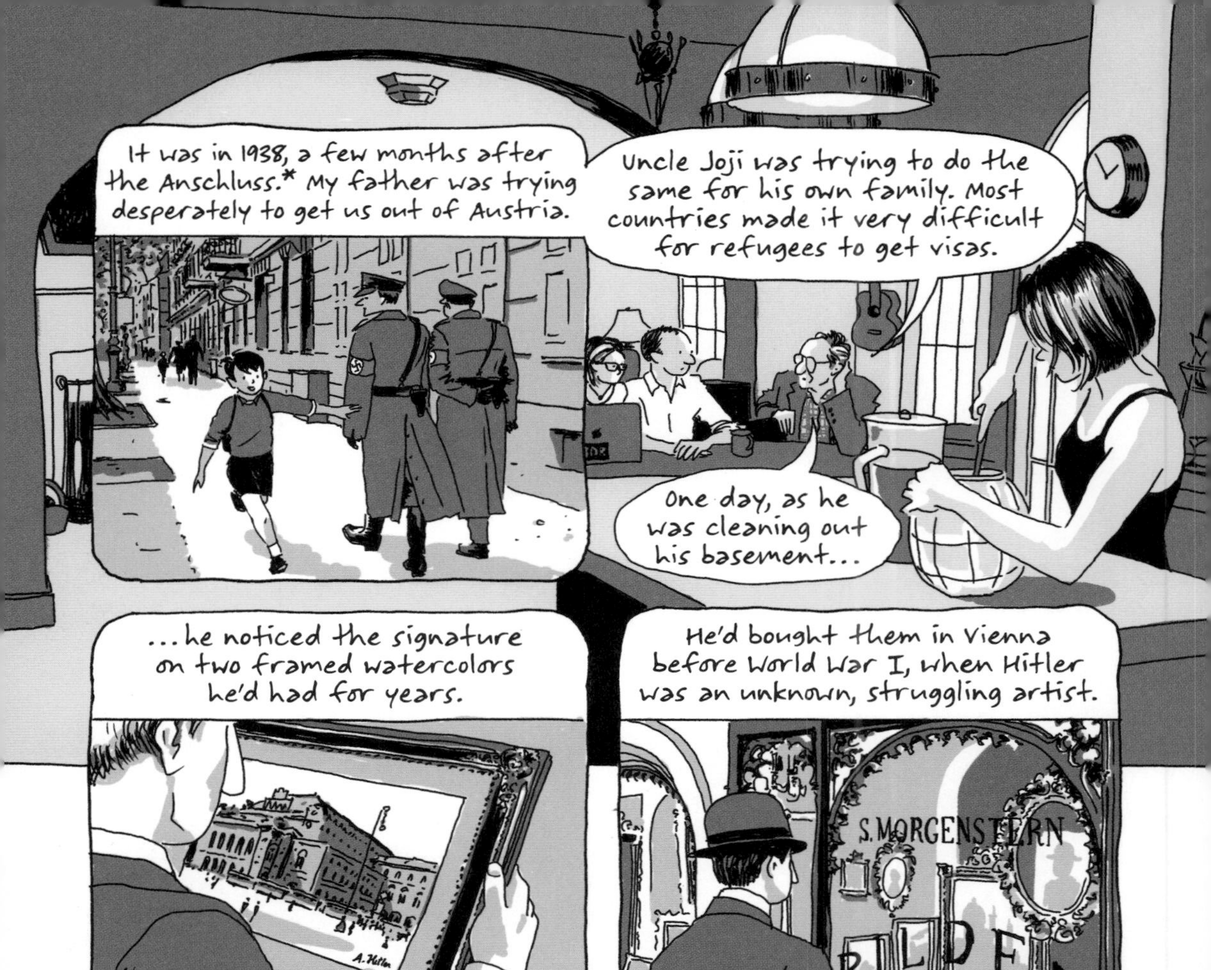
It was in 1938, a few months after the Anschluss.* My father was trying desperately to get us out of Austria.
Uncle Joji was trying to do the same for his own family. Most countries made it very difficult for refugees to get visas.
One day, as he was cleaning out his basement...
...he noticed the signature on two framed watercolors he'd had for years.
He'd bought them in Vienna before World War I, when Hitler was an unknown, struggling artist.
S.MORGENSTERN
BILDER
RAHMEN
Was Hitler good?
Well, he didn't get into the art academy. But Uncle Joji must have liked his work.
He showed the paintings to a Nazi dignitary. Within a week, he and his wife and son had visas for France.

*Annexation of Austria into the German Reich

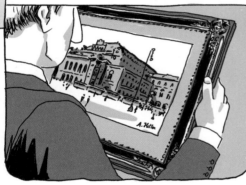

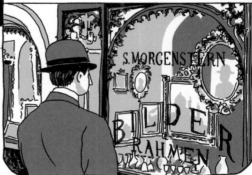

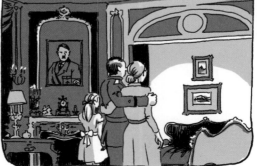

Once Uncle Joji was settled in France, he wrote to my parents with a plan to bring us there, too.

Who's the pretty one next to Uncle Joji?

That's Lisa! My mother's younger sister.

She made it to Paris, too, with the help of two other Feingold cousins... Suzanne and Raymond.

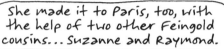

See, Lily, it's good to have cousins in France!

Yes, we had a big family...

Over a hundred cousins on my mother's side alone. Feingolds, Zieglers...

Of course, most of these family branches were wiped out.

It's good you're putting these pictures online. Otherwise, they'd just end up in a closet somewhere and eventually get thrown out.

Moving Energy

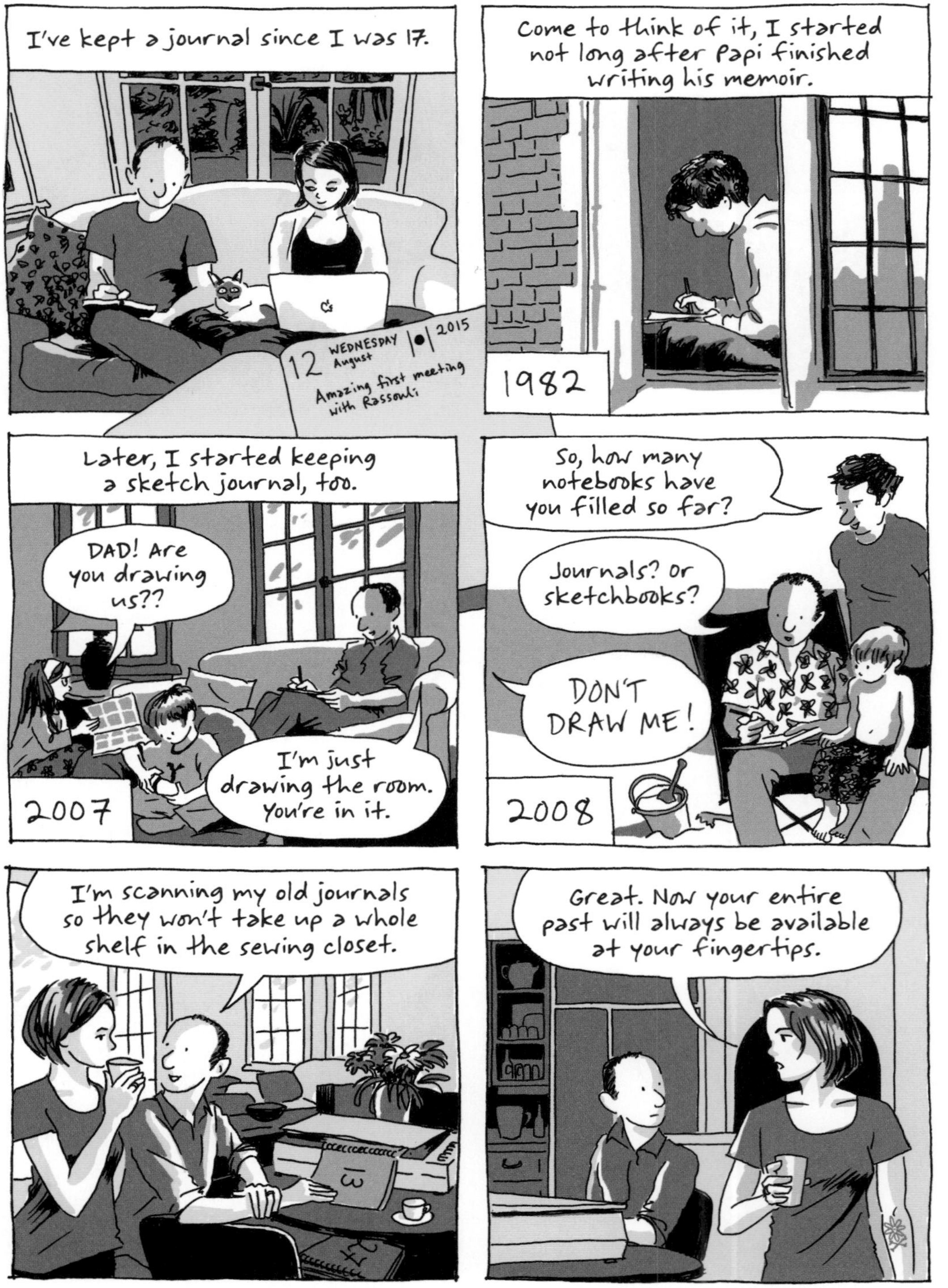

I've kept a journal since I was 17.
12 WEDNESDAY August 2015
Amazing first meeting with Rassouli
Come to think of it, I started not long after Papi finished writing his memoir.
1982
Later, I started keeping a sketch journal, too.
DAD! Are you drawing us??
I'm just drawing the room. You're in it.
2007
So, how many notebooks have you filled so far?
Journals? or sketchbooks?
DON'T DRAW ME!
2008
I'm scanning my old journals so they won't take up a whole shelf in the sewing closet.
Great. Now your entire past will always be available at your fingertips.

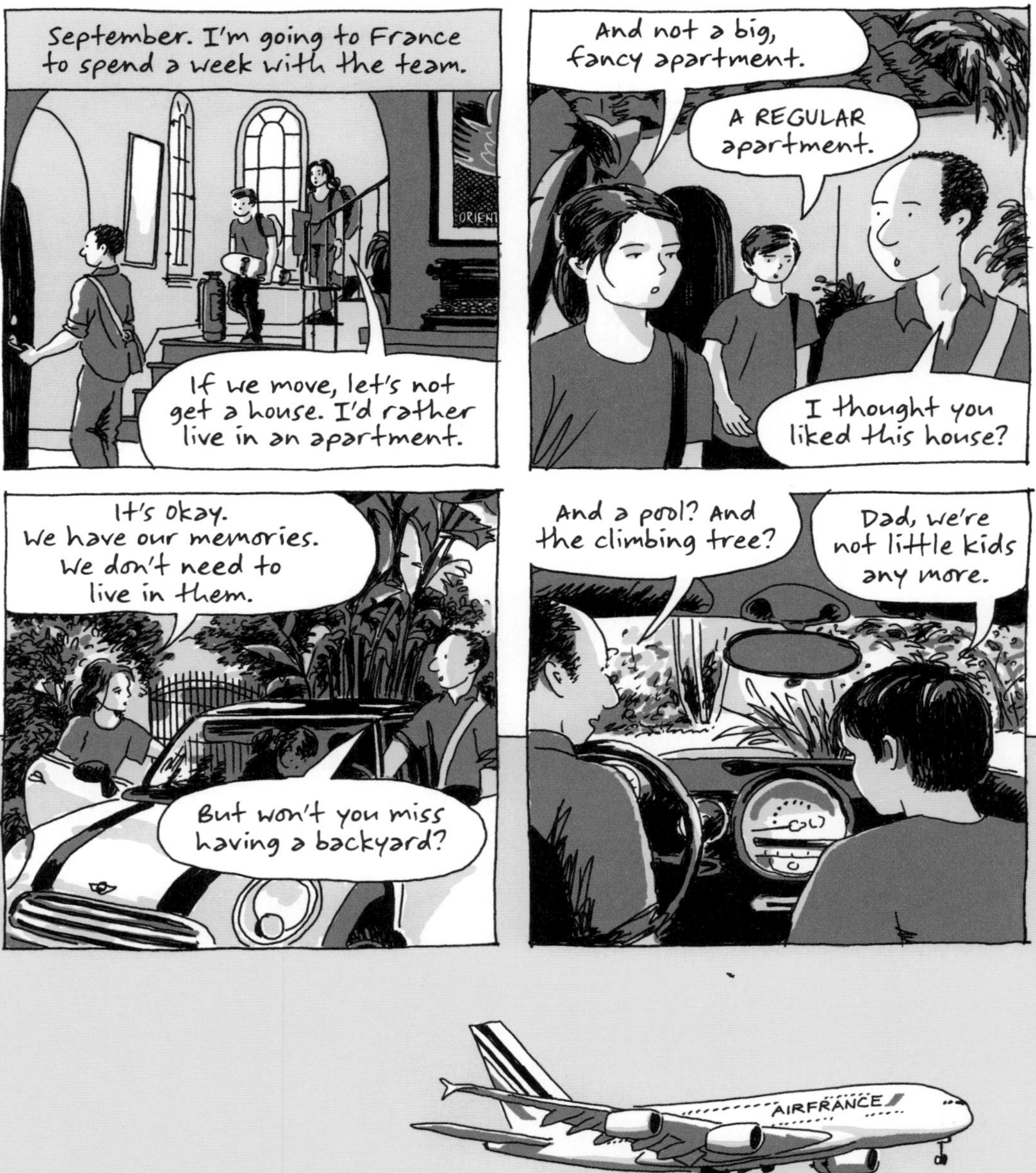
September. I'm going to France to spend a week with the team.
ORIENT
If we move, let's not get a house. I'd rather live in an apartment.
And not a big, fancy apartment.
A REGULAR apartment.
I thought you liked this house?
It's okay. We have our memories. We don't need to live in them.
But won't you miss having a backyard?
And a pool? And the climbing tree?
Dad, we're not little kids any more.

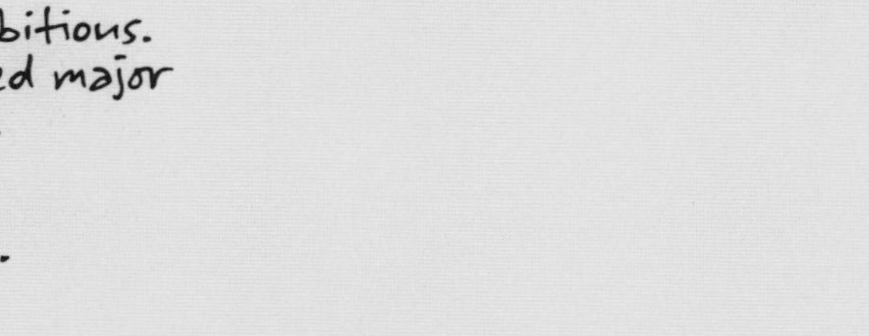
AIRFRANCE

Our game concept is ambitious.
To move forward, we'll need major financial backing.

This is pitch week.

Precipice

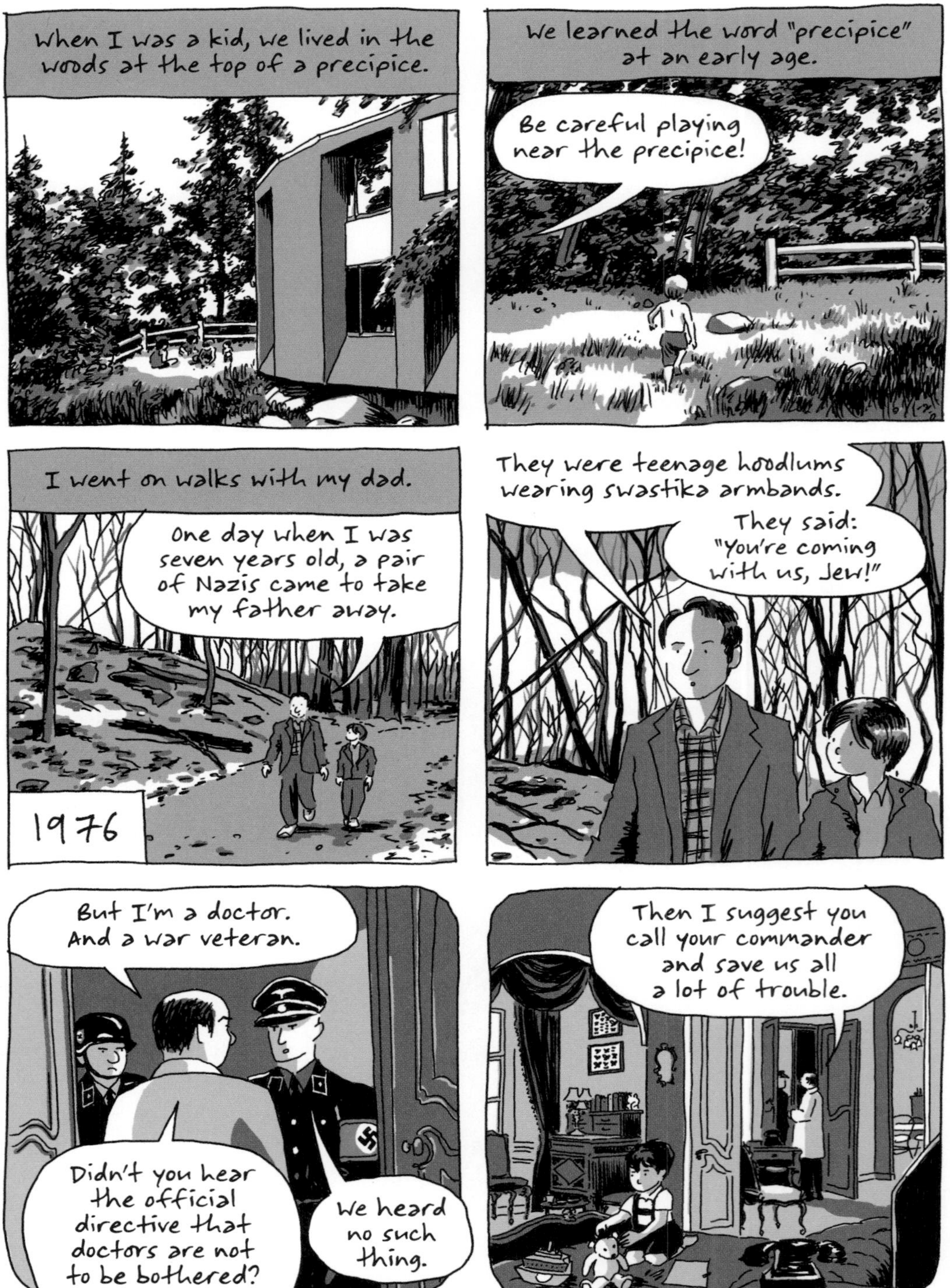
When I was a kid, we lived in the woods at the top of a precipice.
We learned the word "precipice" at an early age.
Be careful playing near the precipice!
I went on walks with my dad.
One day when I was seven years old, a pair of Nazis came to take my father away.
1976
They were teenage hoodlums wearing swastika armbands.
They said: "You're coming with us, Jew!"
But I'm a doctor. And a war veteran.
Didn't you hear the official directive that doctors are not to be bothered?
We heard no such thing.
Then I suggest you call your commander and save us all a lot of trouble.

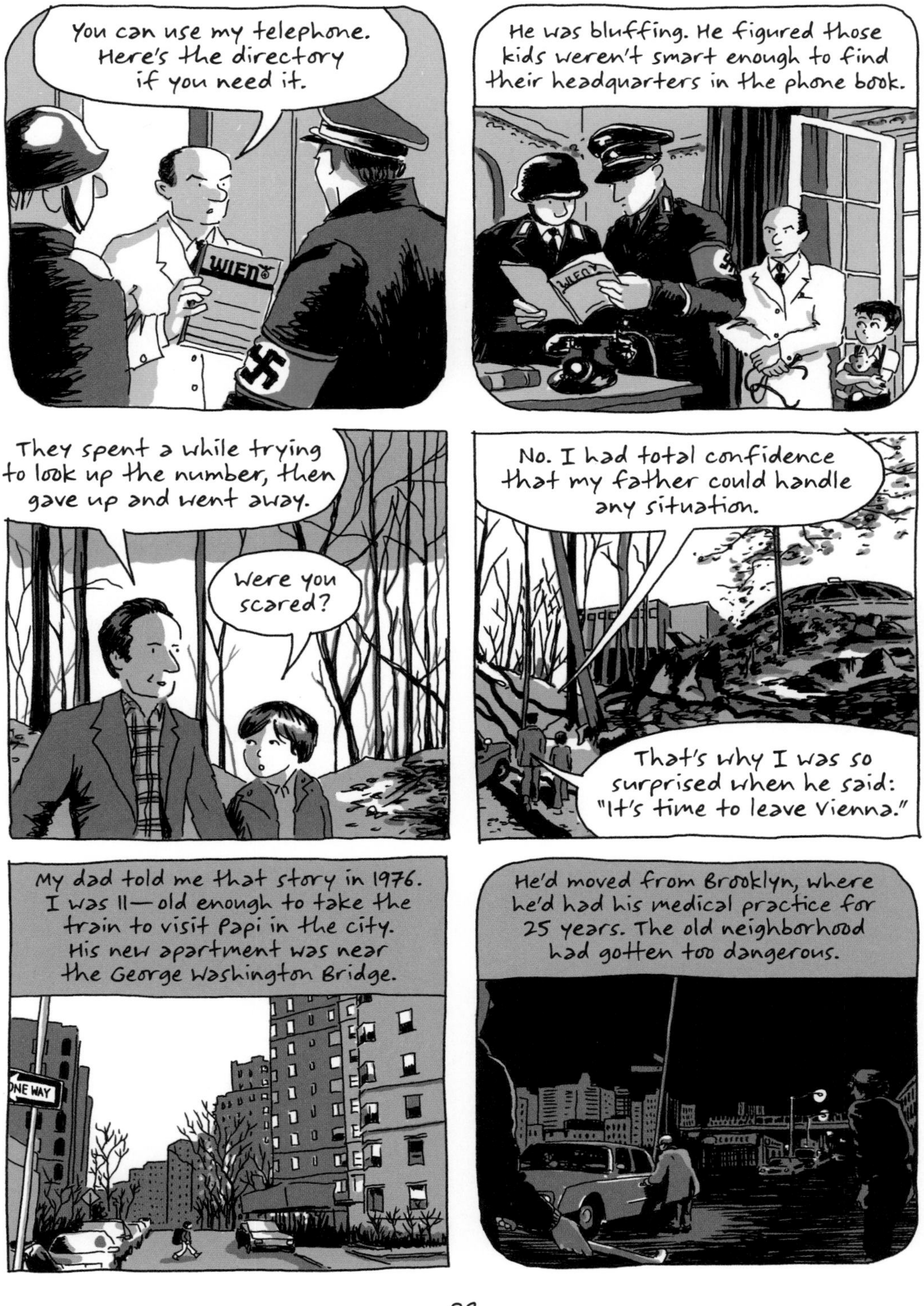
You can use my telephone. Here's the directory if you need it.
WIEN
He was bluffing. He figured those kids weren't smart enough to find their headquarters in the phone book.
They spent a while trying to look up the number, then gave up and went away.
Were you scared?
No. I had total confidence that my father could handle any situation.
That's why I was so surprised when he said: "It's time to leave Vienna."
My dad told me that story in 1976. I was 11—old enough to take the train to visit Papi in the city. His new apartment was near the George Washington Bridge.
ONE WAY
He'd moved from Brooklyn, where he'd had his medical practice for 25 years. The old neighborhood had gotten too dangerous.

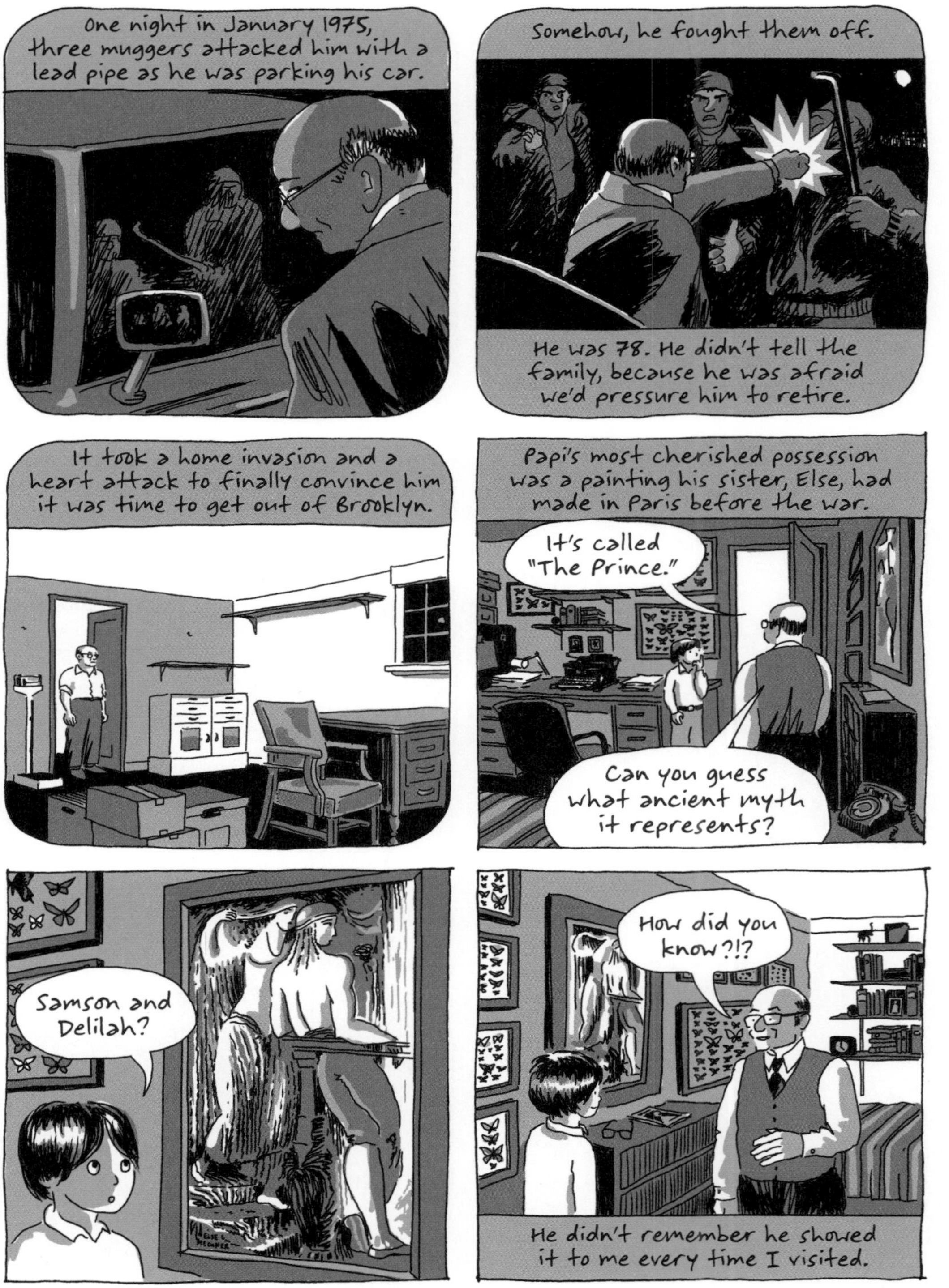
One night in January 1975, three muggers attacked him with a lead pipe as he was parking his car.
Somehow, he fought them off.
He was 78. He didn't tell the family, because he was afraid we'd pressure him to retire.
It took a home invasion and a heart attack to finally convince him it was time to get out of Brooklyn.
Papi's most cherished possession was a painting his sister, Else, had made in Paris before the war.
It's called "The Prince."
Can you guess what ancient myth it represents?
Samson and Delilah?
How did you know?!?
He didn't remember he showed it to me every time I visited.

Mediterranean

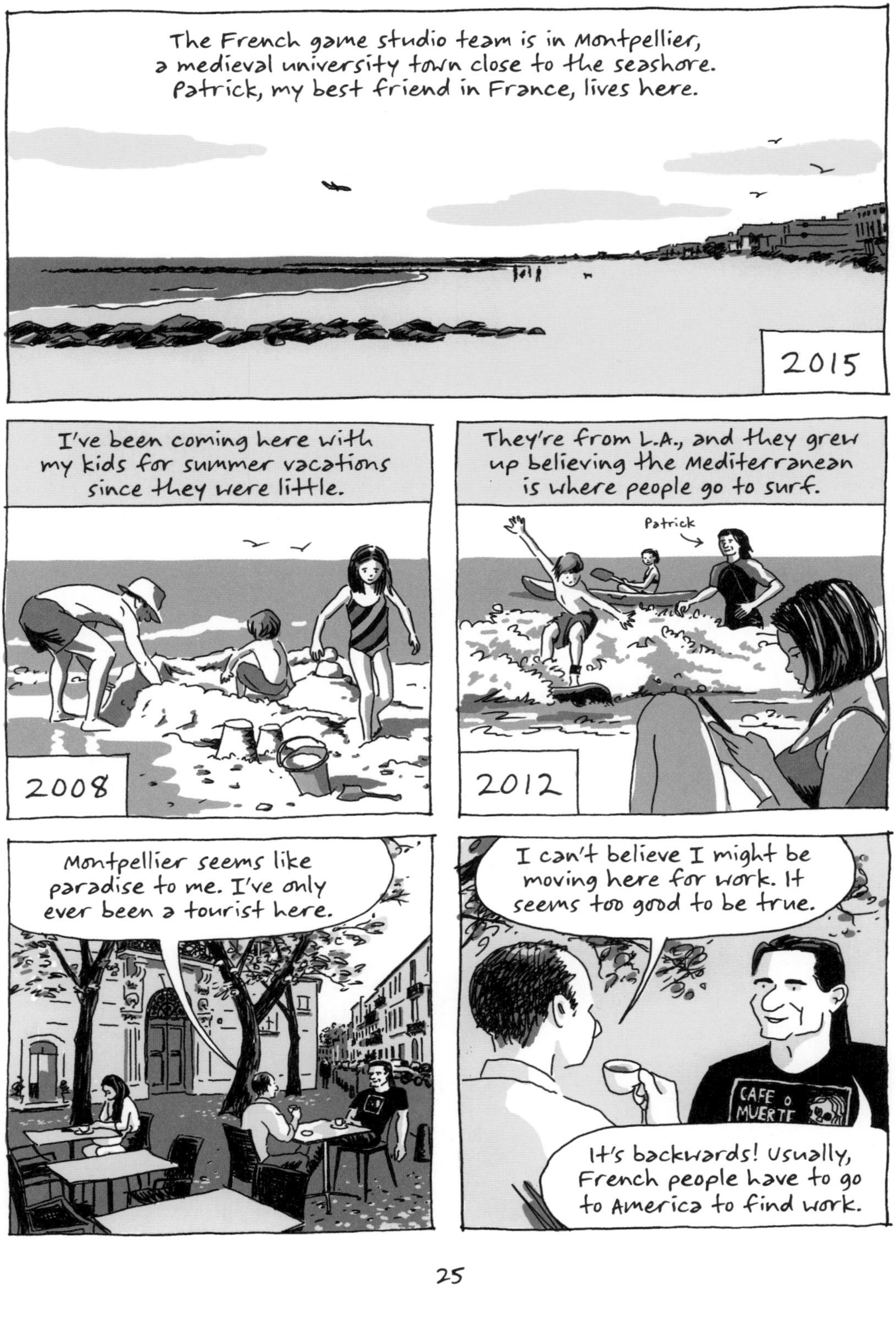
The French game studio team is in Montpellier, a medieval university town close to the seashore. Patrick, my best friend in France, lives here.
2015
I've been coming here with my kids for summer vacations since they were little.
2008
They're from L.A., and they grew up believing the Mediterranean is where people go to surf.
Patrick
2012
Montpellier seems like paradise to me. I've only ever been a tourist here.
I can't believe I might be moving here for work. It seems too good to be true.
CAFE o MUERTE
It's backwards! Usually, French people have to go to America to find work.

Making Games, Then...

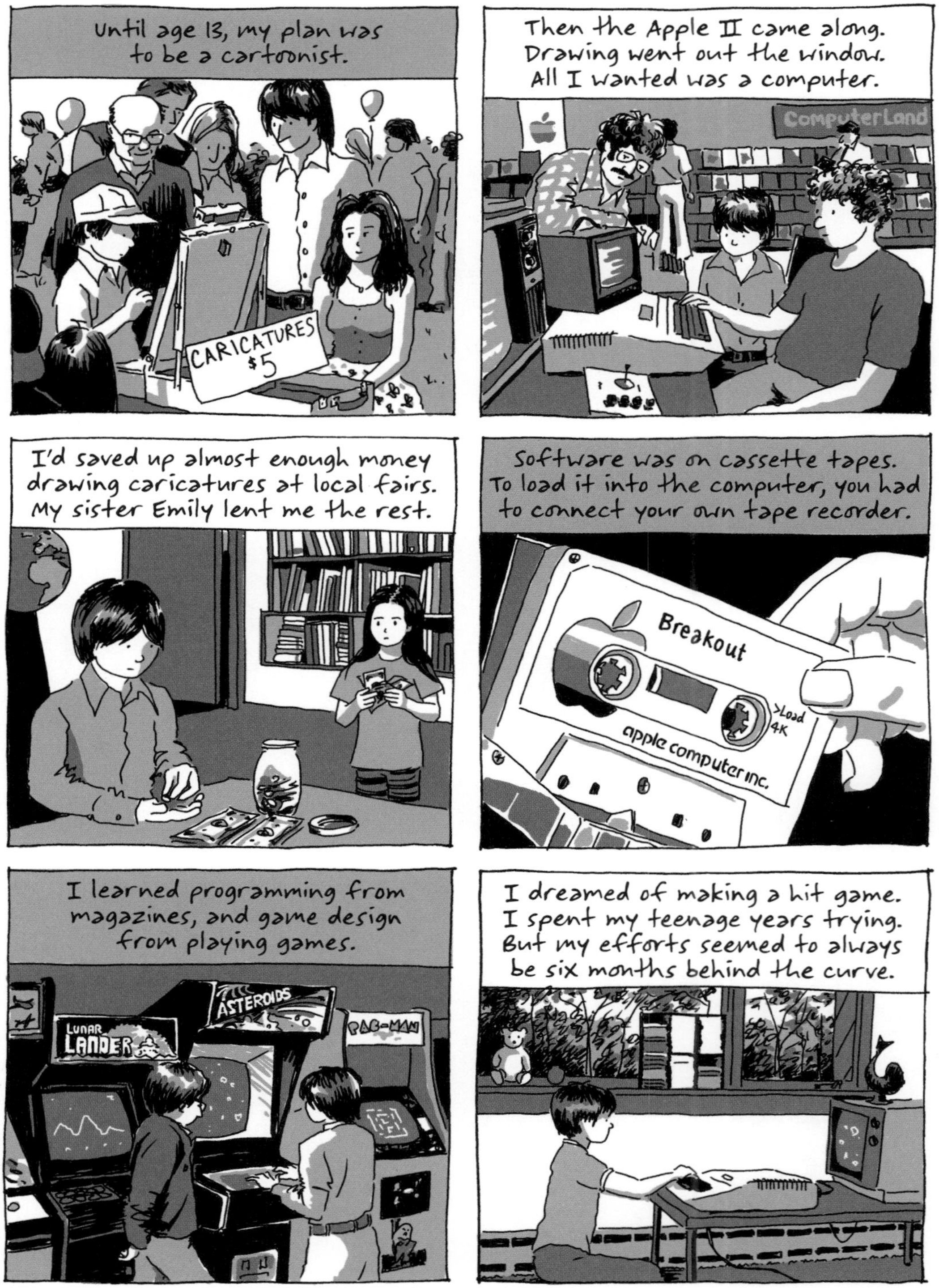
Until age 13, my plan was to be a cartoonist.
CARICATURES $5
Then the Apple II came along. Drawing went out the window. All I wanted was a computer.
ComputerLand
I'd saved up almost enough money drawing caricatures at local fairs. My sister Emily lent me the rest.
Software was on cassette tapes. To load it into the computer, you had to connect your own tape recorder.
Breakout
>Load 4K
apple computer inc.
I learned programming from magazines, and game design from playing games.
LUNAR LANDER
ASTEROIDS
PAC-MAN
I dreamed of making a hit game. I spent my teenage years trying. But my efforts seemed to always be six months behind the curve.

...and Now

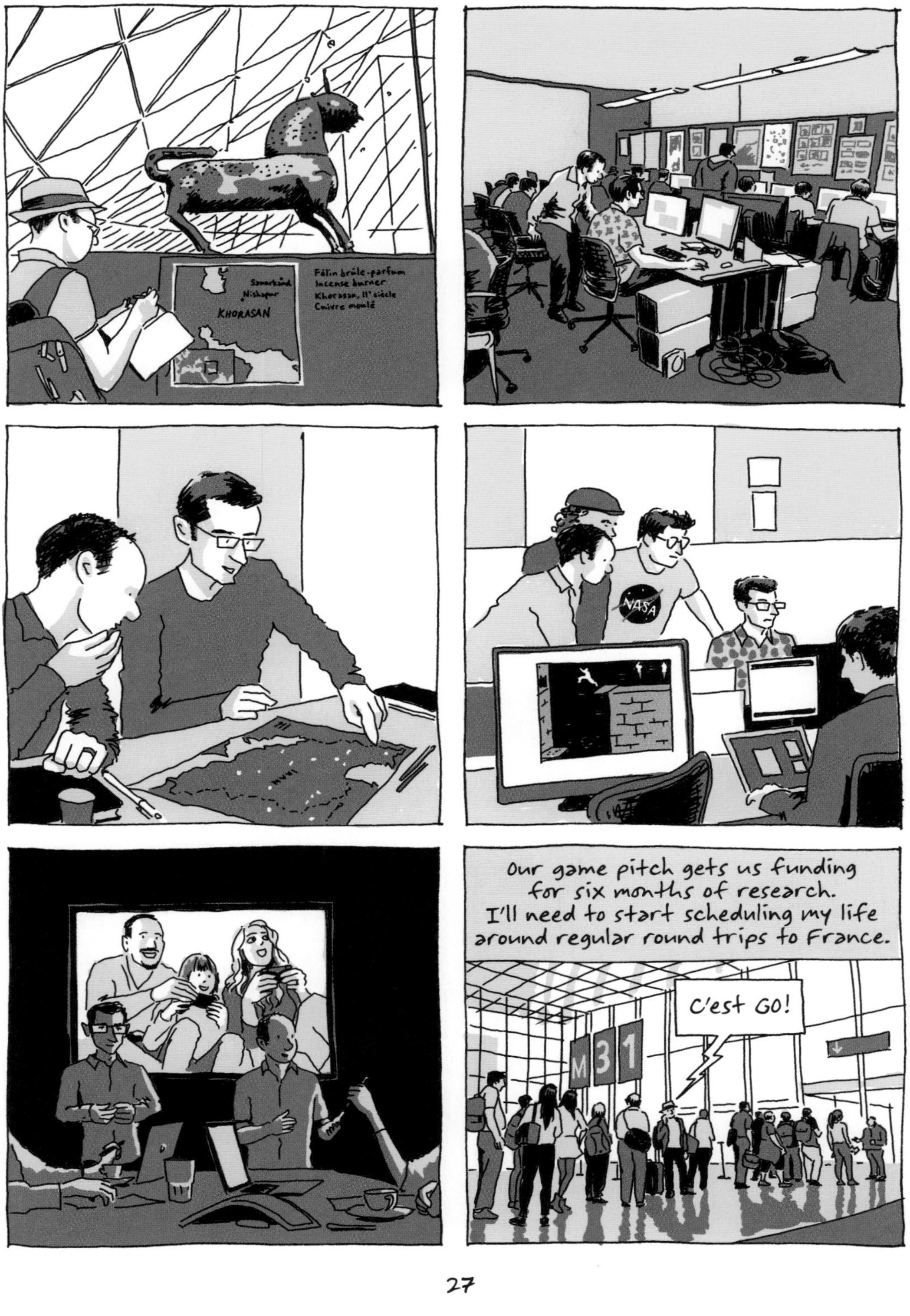
Samarkand
Nishapur
KHORASAN
Félin brûle-parfum
Incense burner
Khorasan, 11e siècle
Cuivre moulé
NASA
Our game pitch gets us funding for six months of research. I'll need to start scheduling my life around regular round trips to France.
C'est GO!
M31

Family Room

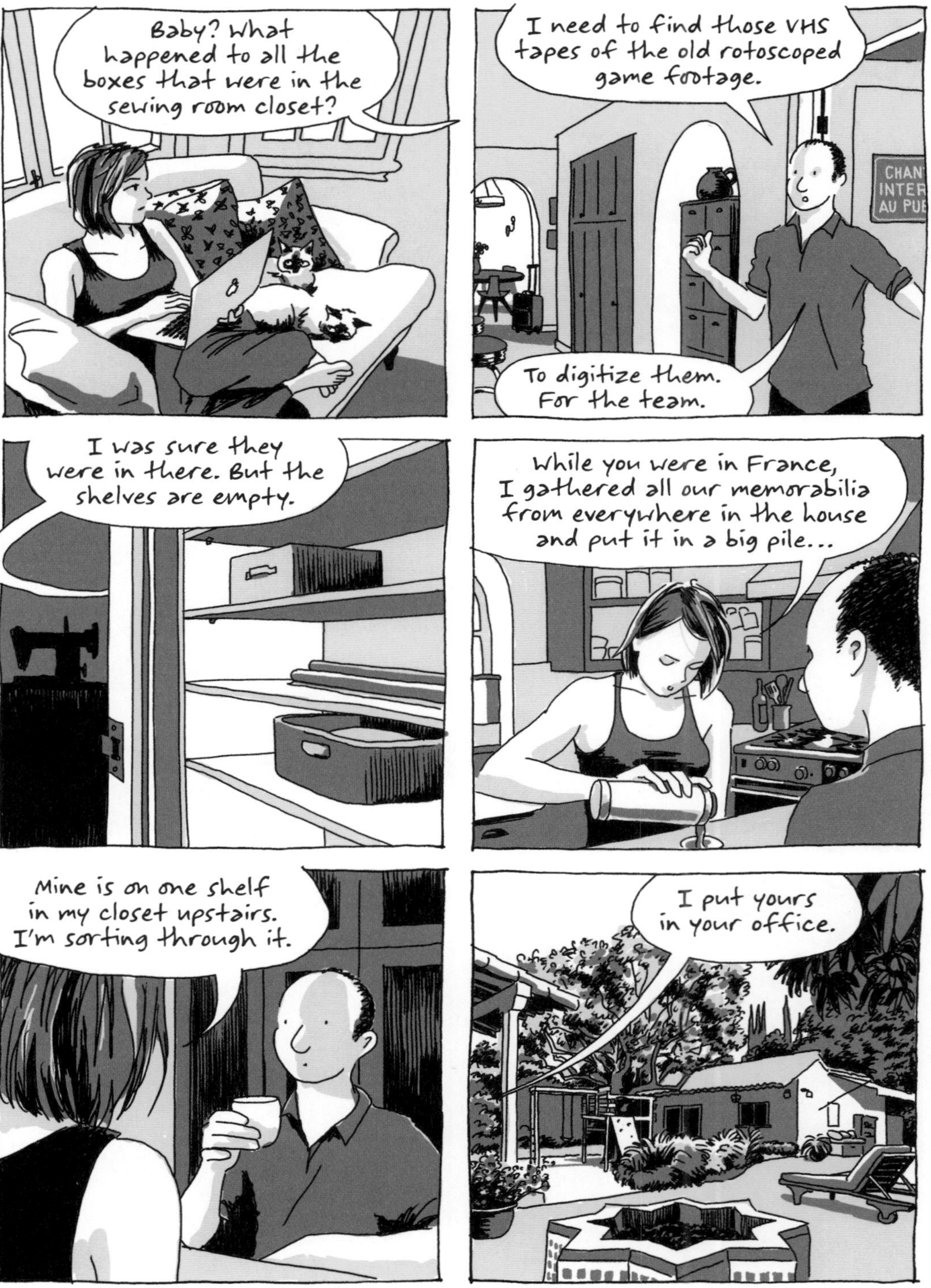
Baby? What happened to all the boxes that were in the sewing room closet?
I need to find those VHS tapes of the old rotoscoped game footage.
To digitize them. For the team.
I was sure they were in there. But the shelves are empty.
While you were in France, I gathered all our memorabilia from everywhere in the house and put it in a big pile...
Mine is on one shelf in my closet upstairs. I'm sorting through it.
I put yours in your office.

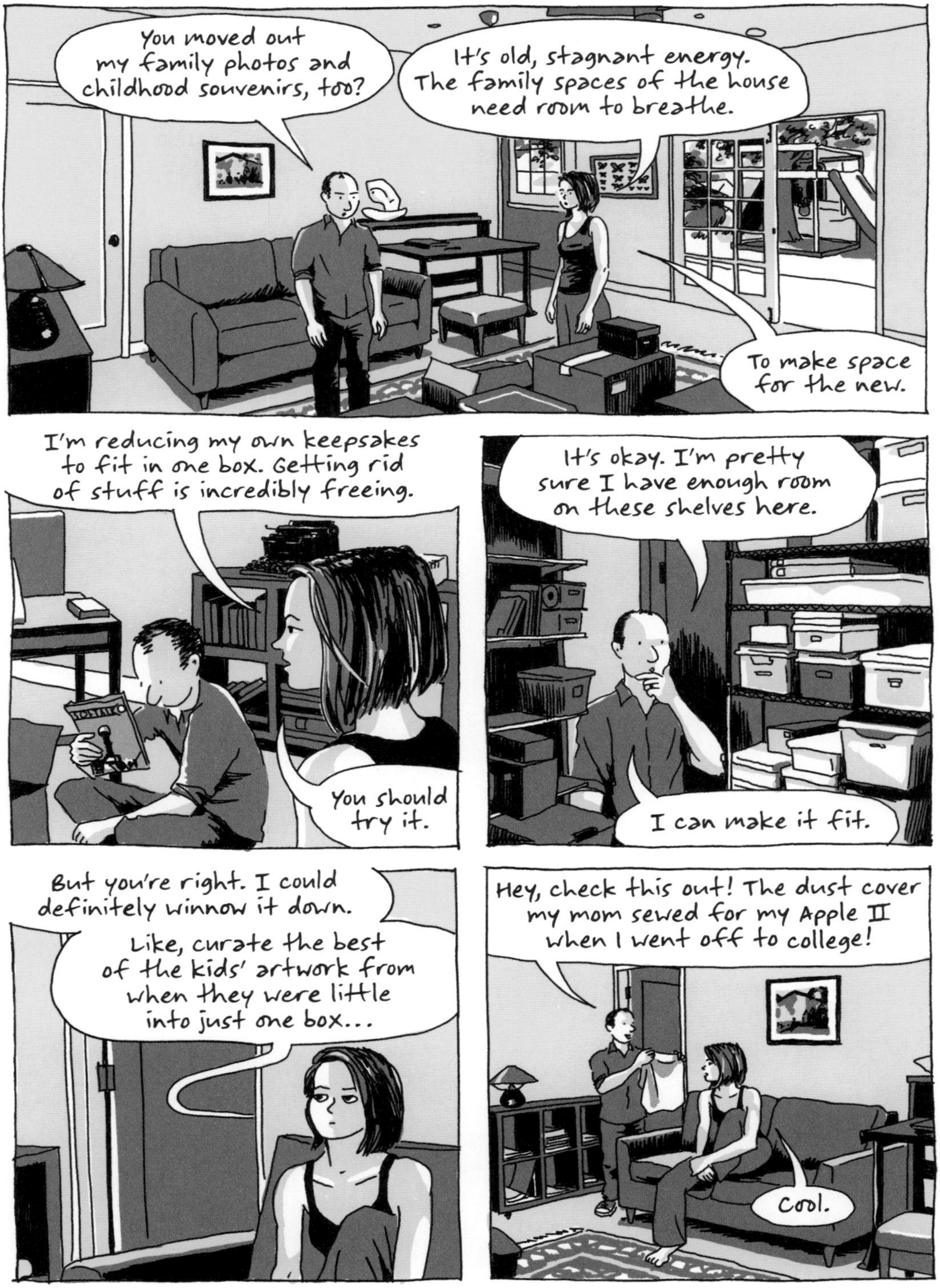
You moved out my family photos and childhood souvenirs, too?
It's old, stagnant energy. The family spaces of the house need room to breathe.
To make space for the new.
I'm reducing my own keepsakes to fit in one box. Getting rid of stuff is incredibly freeing.
You should try it.
It's okay. I'm pretty sure I have enough room on these shelves here.
I can make it fit.
But you're right. I could definitely winnow it down.
Like, curate the best of the kids' artwork from when they were little into just one box...
Hey, check this out! The dust cover my mom sewed for my Apple II when I went off to college!
Cool.

Making Games, Then...

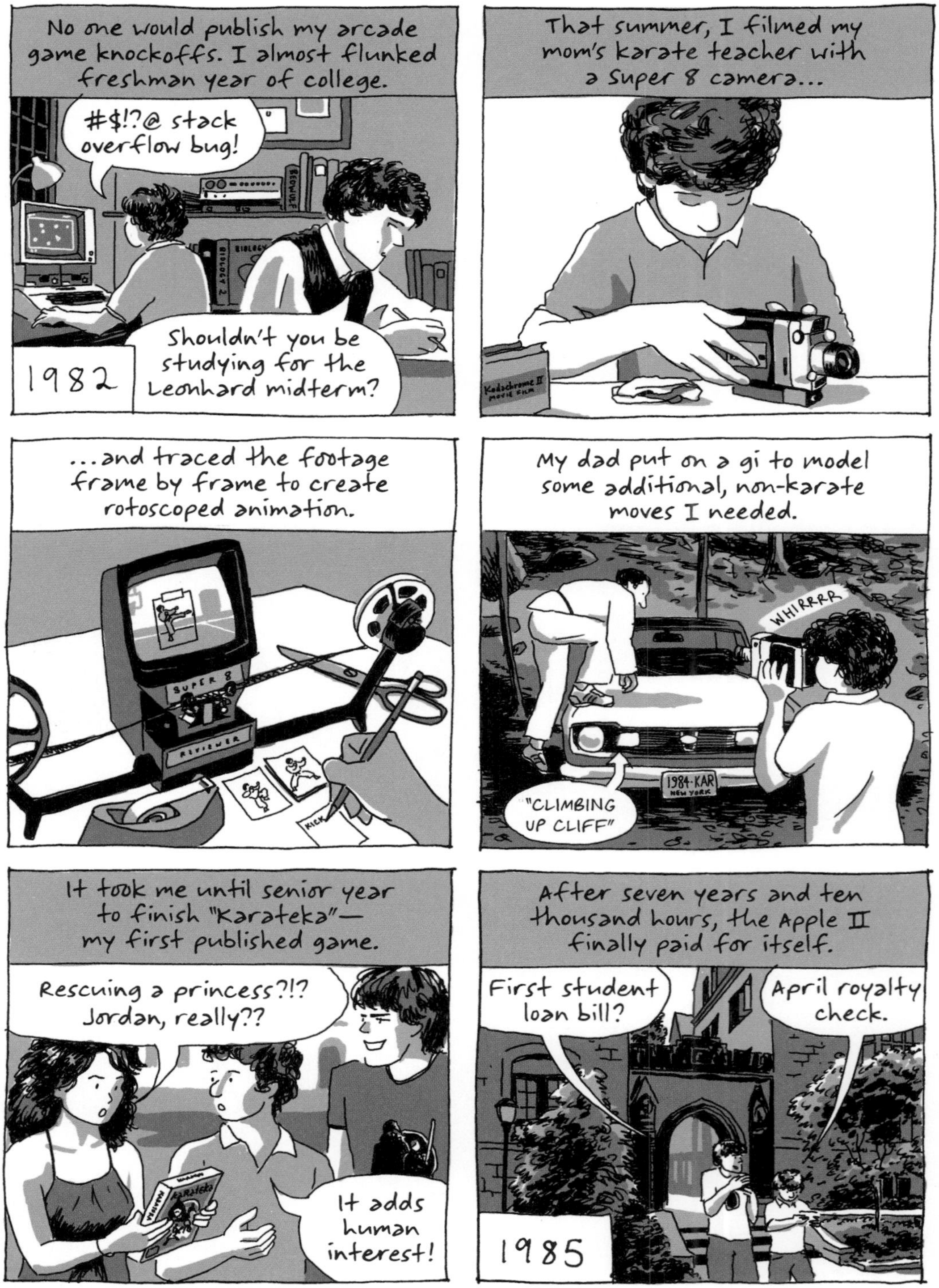

No one would publish my arcade game knockoffs. I almost flunked freshman year of college.
#$!?@ stack overflow bug!
Shouldn't you be studying for the Leonhard midterm?
1982
That summer, I filmed my mom's karate teacher with a Super 8 camera...
Kodachrome II
...and traced the footage frame by frame to create rotoscoped animation.
SUPER 8
KICK
My dad put on a gi to model some additional, non-karate moves I needed.
WHIRRRR
1984-KAR NEW YORK
"CLIMBING UP CLIFF"
It took me until senior year to finish "Karateka"— my first published game.
Rescuing a princess?!? Jordan, really??
It adds human interest!
After seven years and ten thousand hours, the Apple II finally paid for itself.
First student loan bill?
April royalty check.
1985

. . . and Now

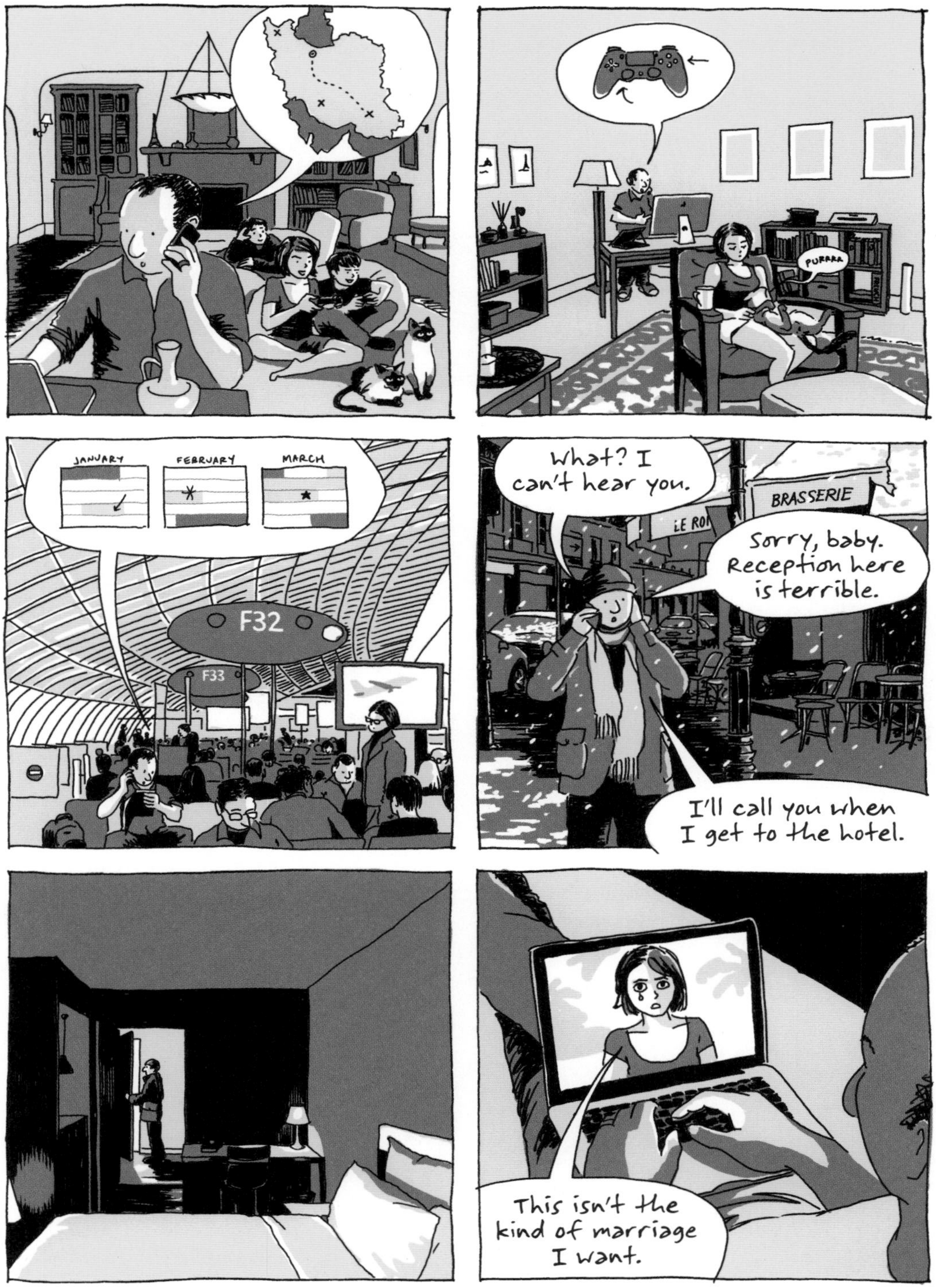

PURRR
JANUARY
FEBRUARY
MARCH
F32
F33
What? I can't hear you.
BRASSERIE
Sorry, baby. Reception here is terrible.
I'll call you when I get to the hotel.
This isn't the kind of marriage I want.

Downsizing

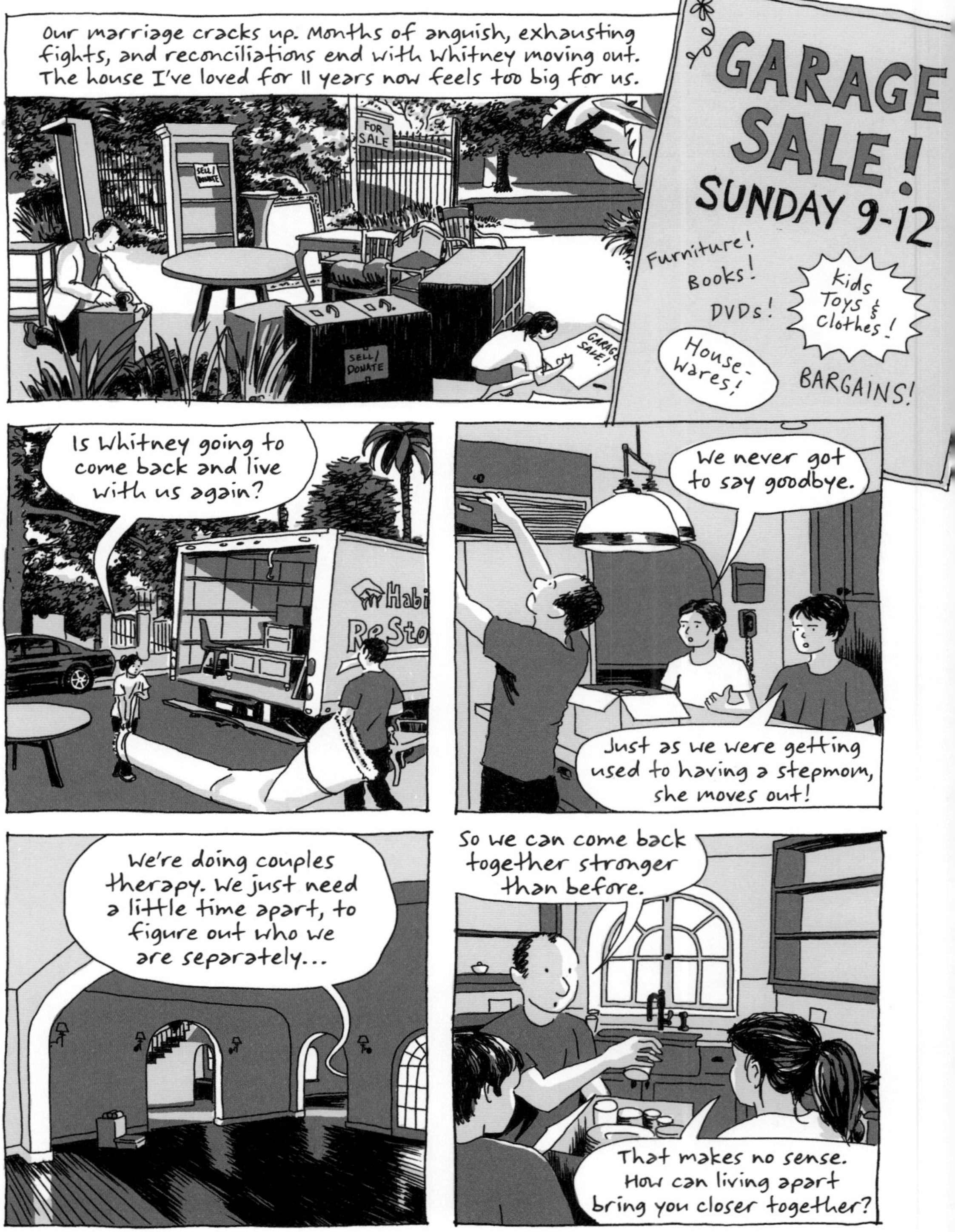

Our marriage cracks up. Months of anguish, exhausting fights, and reconciliations end with Whitney moving out. The house I've loved for 11 years now feels too big for us.
FOR SALE
SELL/ DONATE
SELL/ DONATE
GARAGE SALE!
GARAGE SALE! SUNDAY 9-12
Furniture!
Books!
DVDs!
Kids Toys & Clothes!
House-Wares!
BARGAINS!
Is Whitney going to come back and live with us again?
Habi
ReSto
We never got to say goodbye.
Just as we were getting used to having a stepmom, she moves out!
We're doing couples therapy. We just need a little time apart, to figure out who we are separately...
So we can come back together stronger than before.
That makes no sense. How can living apart bring you closer together?

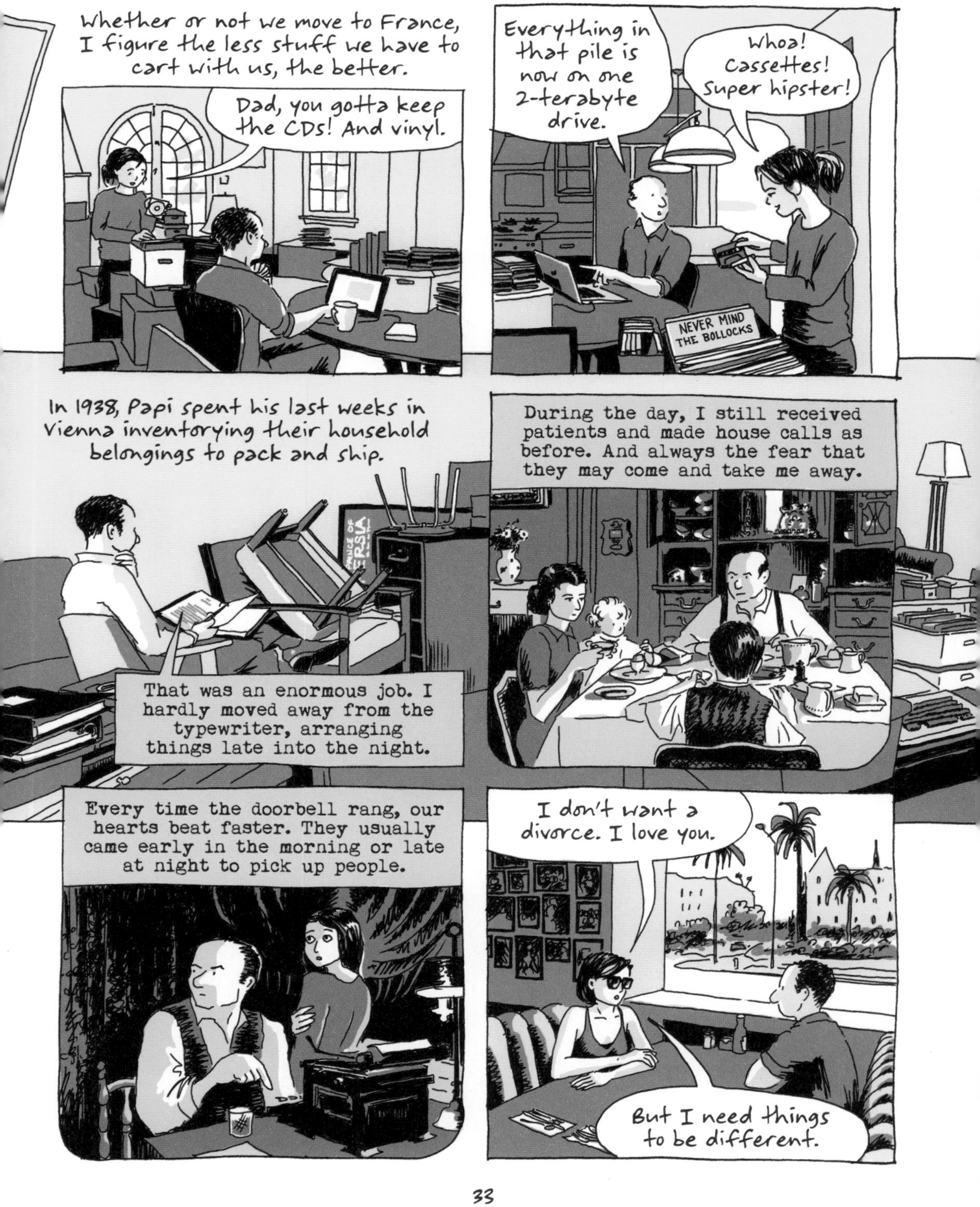
Whether or not we move to France, I figure the less stuff we have to cart with us, the better.
Dad, you gotta keep the CDs! And vinyl.
Everything in that pile is now on one 2-terabyte drive.
Whoa! Cassettes! Super hipster!
NEVER MIND THE BOLLOCKS
In 1938, Papi spent his last weeks in Vienna inventorying their household belongings to pack and ship.
That was an enormous job. I hardly moved away from the typewriter, arranging things late into the night.
During the day, I still received patients and made house calls as before. And always the fear that they may come and take me away.
Every time the doorbell rang, our hearts beat faster. They usually came early in the morning or late at night to pick up people.
I don't want a divorce. I love you.
But I need things to be different.

French Connection

On the way back to L.A. from a workshop with the team in France, I stop in New York to visit my dad.

He's 84. If this game project goes forward, we'll be separated by an ocean.

There's something about our family story that's always confused me...

Why did Papi take only you with him to Paris in 1938?

Well, my parents wanted to immigrate to America. Not France.

My father was the one in the most immediate danger. He needed to get out of Austria any way he could.

They figured if my mother stayed in Vienna, she'd get her U.S. visa within a few weeks.

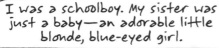

I was a schoolboy. My sister was just a baby—an adorable little blonde, blue-eyed girl.

My mother didn't think the Nazis would bother the two of them.

Look, Franzi, that's the Black Forest.

It's not black. It's green!

Passports, bitte...

You're Jewish?

Yes. Destination Havana, Cuba. Here are our papers—boat tickets, visas...

Why Cuba?

Cuba was one of the few countries that welcomed Jewish refugees in 1938. Uncle Joji paid the fee.

For me, it was a great adventure, traveling with my father, having him all to myself. I was in heaven.

Our plan was to spend one week in Paris with Lisa and our cousins, then take the boat to Havana.

Or rather, I thought that was the plan. Until the night my father left.

PLEASE PAPA DON'T GO!

TAKE ME WITH YOU!

He sailed to Cuba without me.

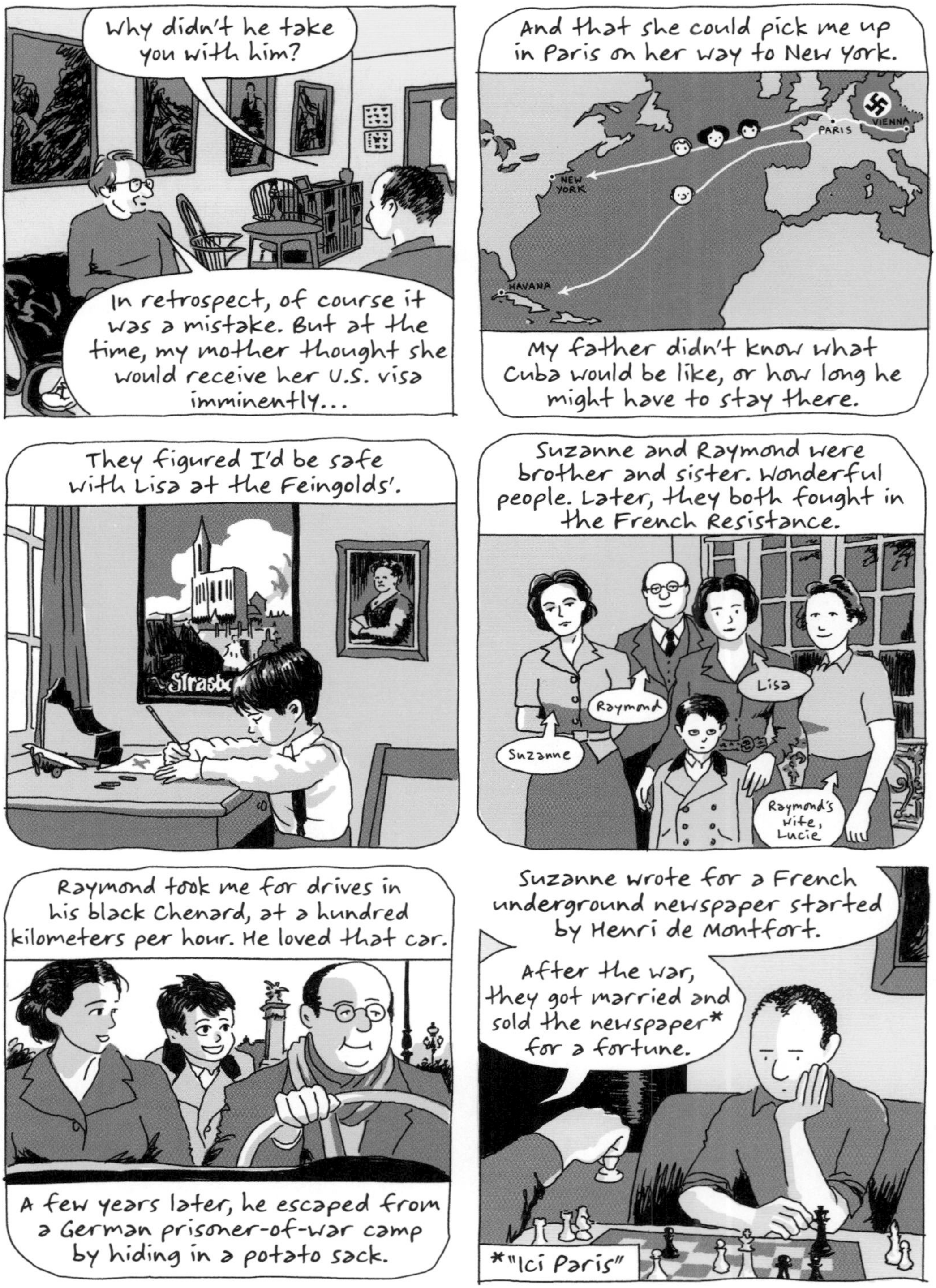
Why didn't he take you with him?
In retrospect, of course it was a mistake. But at the time, my mother thought she would receive her U.S. visa imminently...
And that she could pick me up in Paris on her way to New York.
NEW YORK
PARIS
VIENNA
HAVANA
My father didn't know what Cuba would be like, or how long he might have to stay there.
They figured I'd be safe with Lisa at the Feingolds'.
Suzanne and Raymond were brother and sister. Wonderful people. Later, they both fought in the French Resistance.
Raymond
Lisa
Suzanne
Raymond's wife, Lucie
Raymond took me for drives in his black Chenard, at a hundred kilometers per hour. He loved that car.
A few years later, he escaped from a German prisoner-of-war camp by hiding in a potato sack.
Suzanne wrote for a French underground newspaper started by Henri de Montfort.
After the war, they got married and sold the newspaper* for a fortune.
*"Ici Paris"

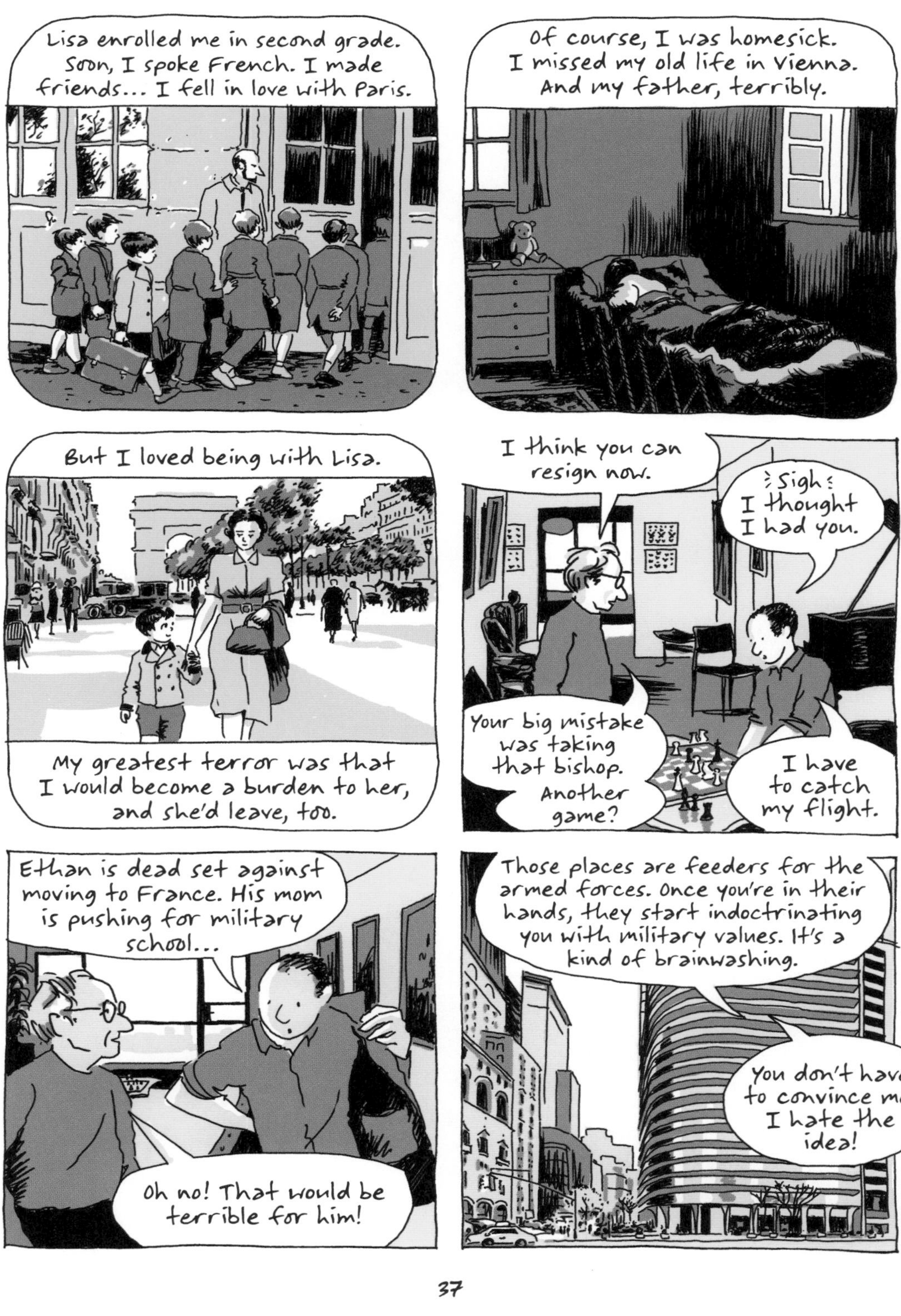

Lisa enrolled me in second grade. Soon, I spoke French. I made friends... I fell in love with Paris.
Of course, I was homesick. I missed my old life in Vienna. And my father, terribly.
But I loved being with Lisa.
My greatest terror was that I would become a burden to her, and she'd leave, too.
I think you can resign now.
Sigh
I thought I had you.
Your big mistake was taking that bishop. Another game?
I have to catch my flight.
Ethan is dead set against moving to France. His mom is pushing for military school...
Oh no! That would be terrible for him!
Those places are feeders for the armed forces. Once you're in their hands, they start indoctrinating you with military values. It's a kind of brainwashing.
You don't have to convince me. I hate the idea!

April 2016.
We pitch the vision we've spent six months developing.
A game that will take three years, several hundred people, and an eight-figure budget to bring to life.

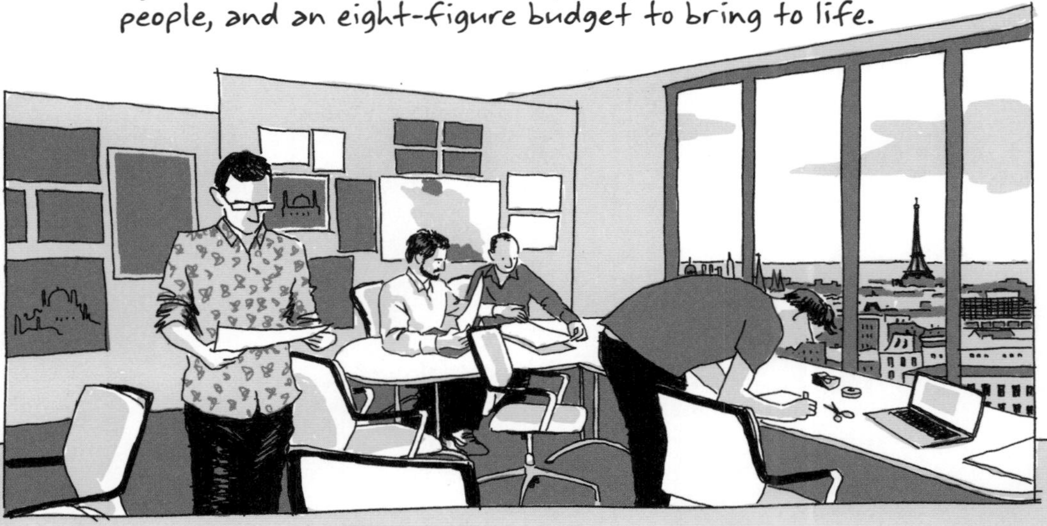

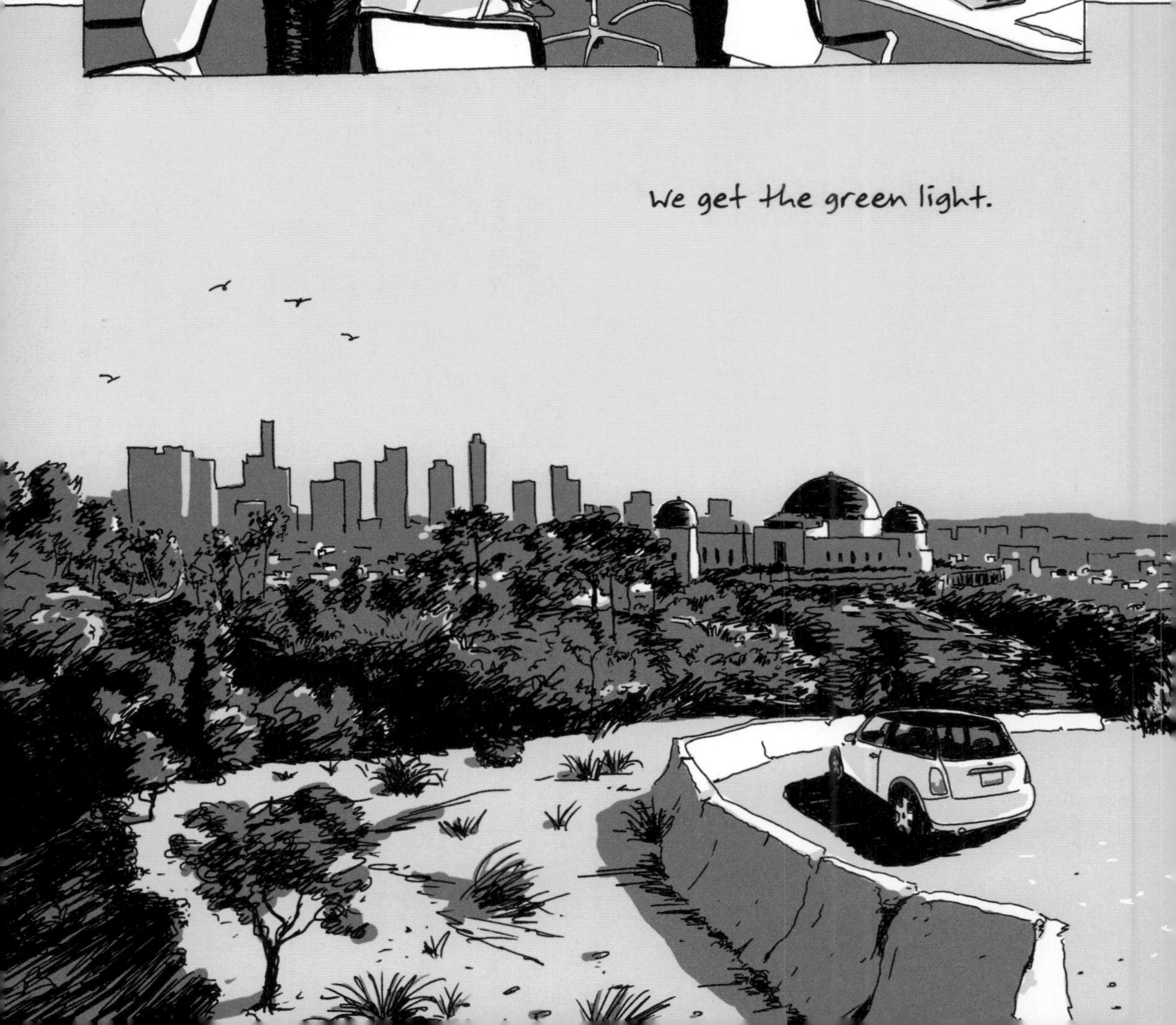
We get the green light.

Chapter 2

Transit

Adolf Mechner
Havana, November 1938

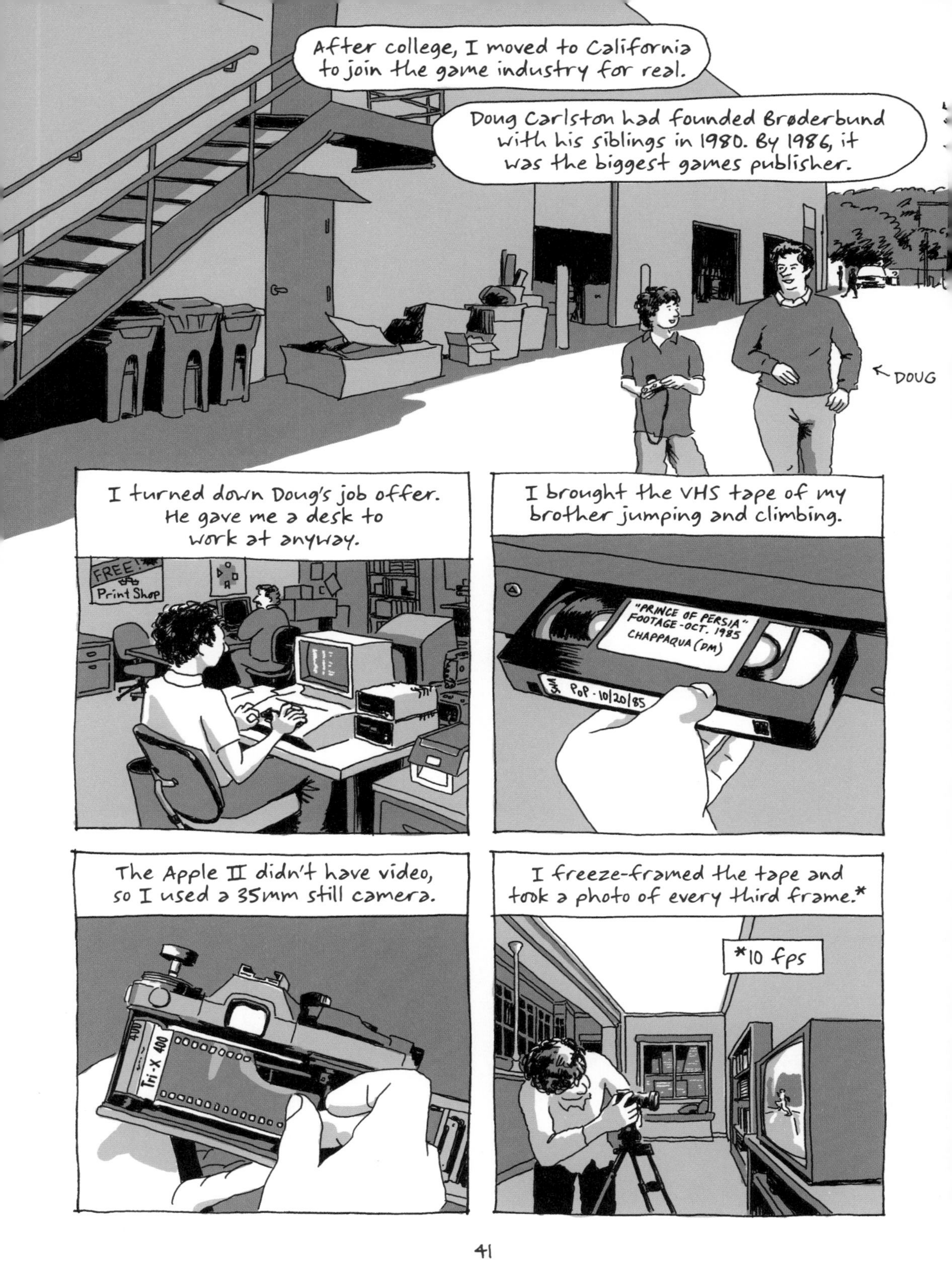
After college, I moved to California to join the game industry for real.
Doug Carlston had founded Brøderbund with his siblings in 1980. By 1986, it was the biggest games publisher.
DOUG
I turned down Doug's job offer. He gave me a desk to work at anyway.
FREE! Print Shop
I brought the VHS tape of my brother jumping and climbing.
"PRINCE OF PERSIA" FOOTAGE - OCT. 1985 CHAPPAQUA (DM)
PoP - 10/20/85
The Apple II didn't have video, so I used a 35mm still camera.
Tri-X 400
I freeze-framed the tape and took a photo of every third frame.*
*10 fps

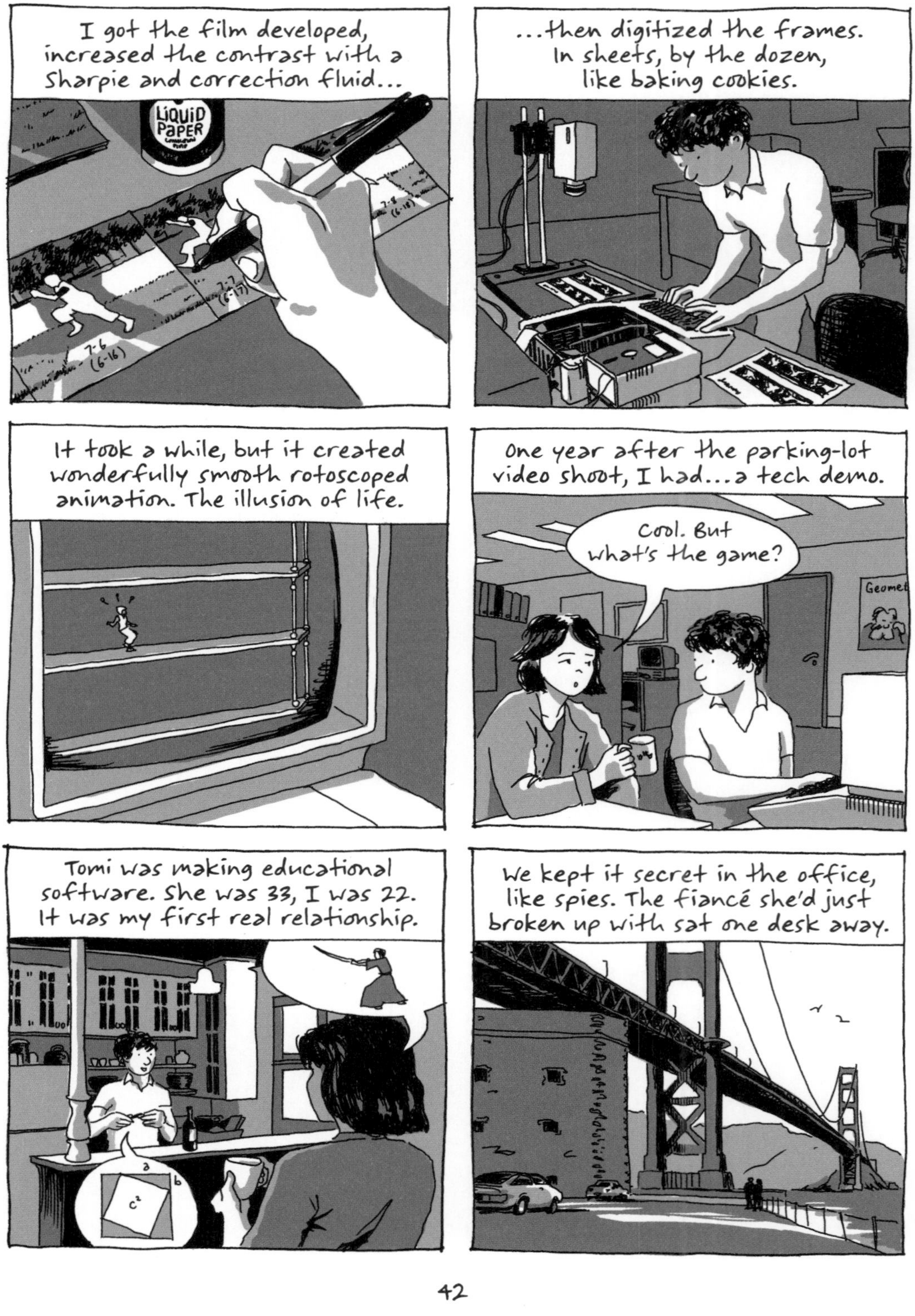

I got the film developed, increased the contrast with a Sharpie and correction fluid...
LIQUID PAPER
7-8 (6-18)
7-7 (6-17)
7-6 (6-16)
...then digitized the frames. In sheets, by the dozen, like baking cookies.
It took a while, but it created wonderfully smooth rotoscoped animation. The illusion of life.
One year after the parking-lot video shoot, I had... a tech demo.
Cool. But what's the game?
Tomi was making educational software. She was 33, I was 22. It was my first real relationship.
We kept it secret in the office, like spies. The fiancé she'd just broken up with sat one desk away.

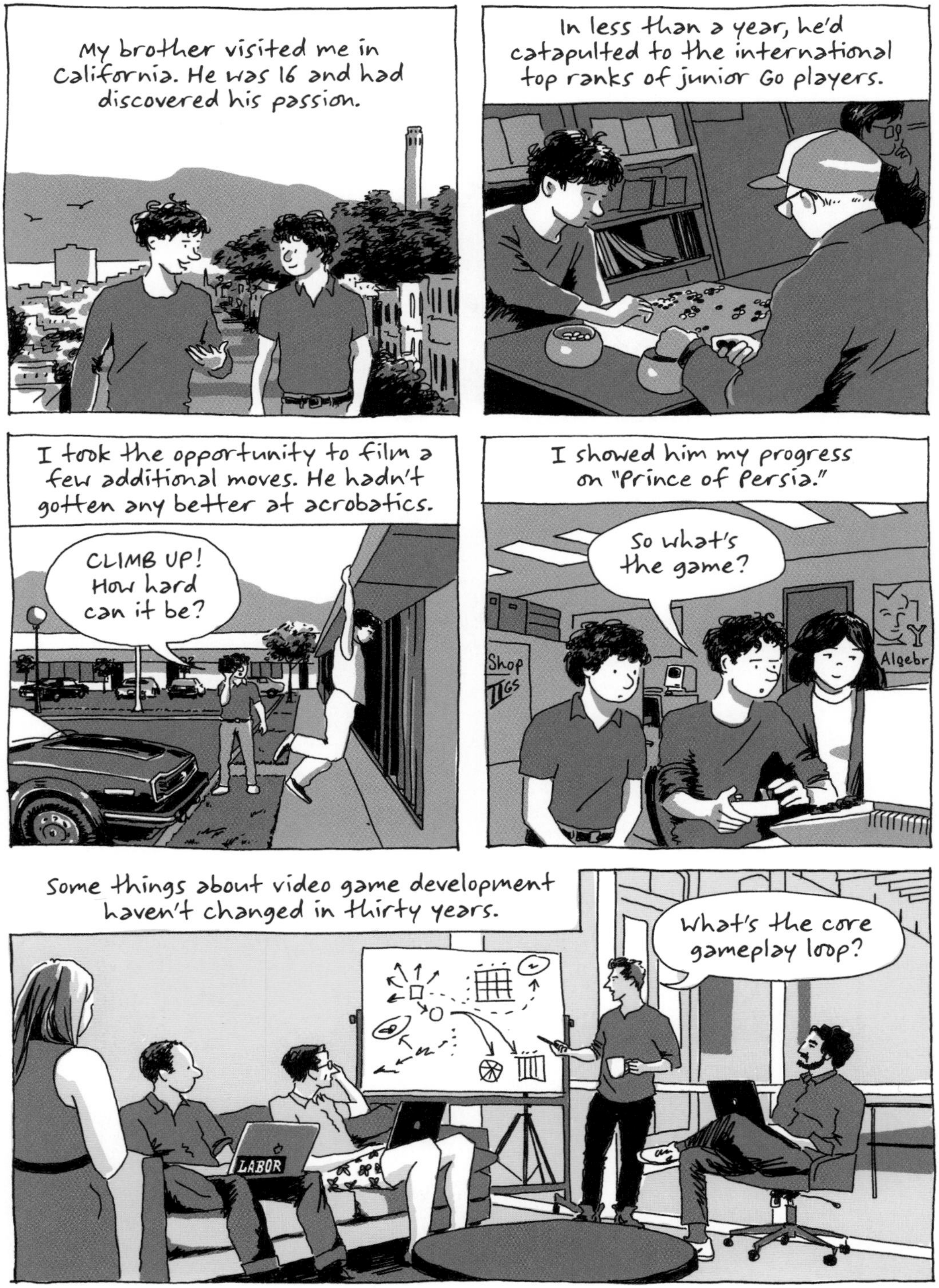
My brother visited me in California. He was 16 and had discovered his passion.
In less than a year, he'd catapulted to the international top ranks of junior Go players.
I took the opportunity to film a few additional moves. He hadn't gotten any better at acrobatics.
CLIMB UP! How hard can it be?
I showed him my progress on "Prince of Persia."
So what's the game?
Shop
IIGS
Algebr
Some things about video game development haven't changed in thirty years.
What's the core gameplay loop?
LABOR

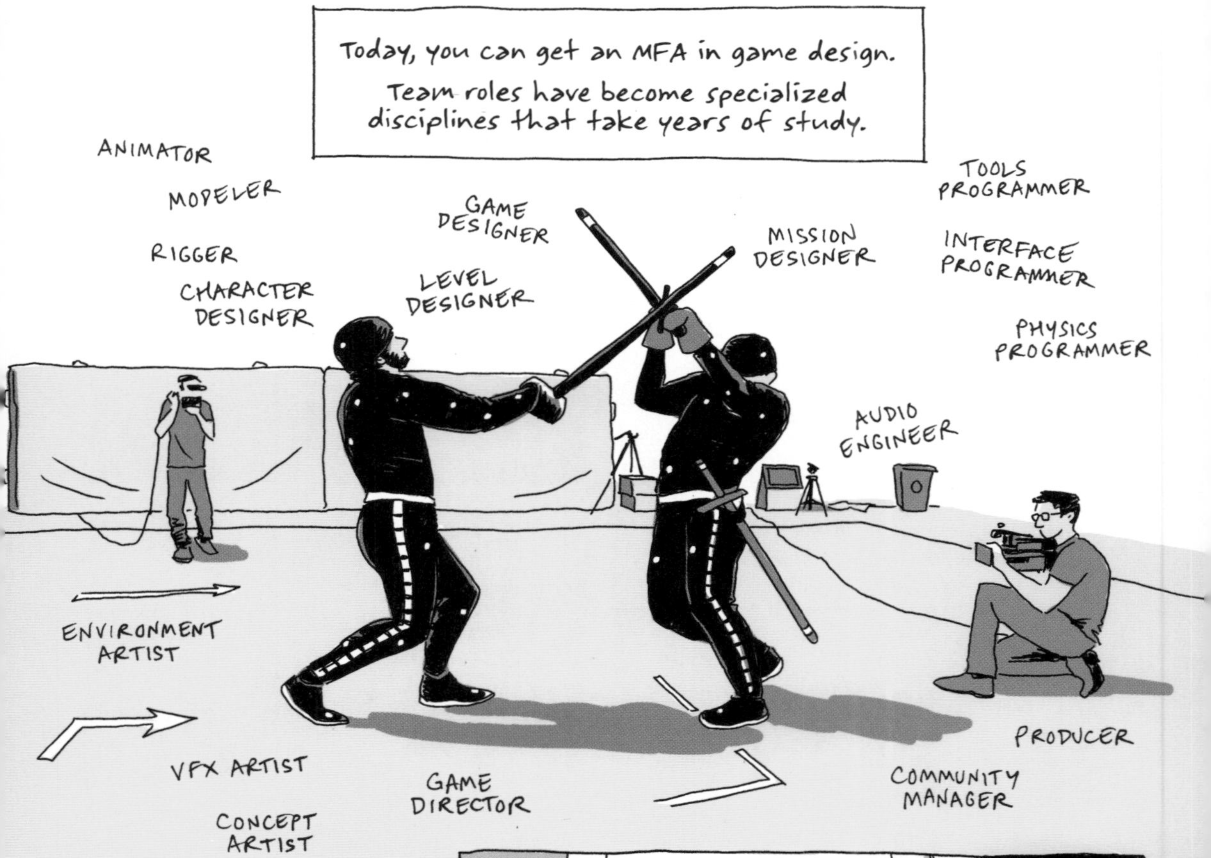

Today, you can get an MFA in game design.
Team roles have become specialized disciplines that take years of study.
ANIMATOR
MODELER
RIGGER
CHARACTER DESIGNER
GAME DESIGNER
LEVEL DESIGNER
MISSION DESIGNER
TOOLS PROGRAMMER
INTERFACE PROGRAMMER
PHYSICS PROGRAMMER
AUDIO ENGINEER
ENVIRONMENT ARTIST
VFX ARTIST
CONCEPT ARTIST
GAME DIRECTOR
COMMUNITY MANAGER
PRODUCER

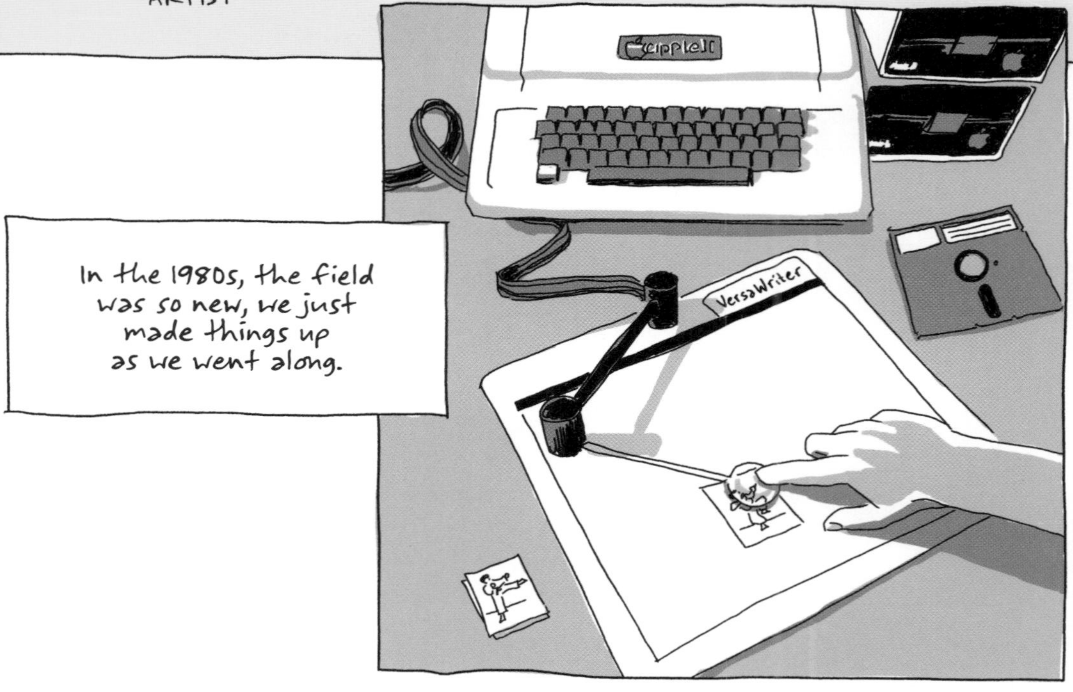

In the 1980s, the field was so new, we just made things up as we went along.
apple][
VersaWriter

I'd been making games for about ten years when I wrote my first "what I've learned" list.

#10 still keeps me awake at night.

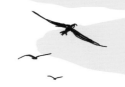

TEN TIPS FOR GAME DEVELOPERS

1. Prototype and test key game elements as early as possible.
2. Build the game in incremental steps. Don't make grand design documents.
3. As you go, continue to strengthen what's strong and cut what's weak.
4. Be open to the unexpected. Make the most of serendipity.
5. Be prepared to sell your project at every stage along the way.
6. The moment when the game first becomes playable is the moment of truth. Don't be surprised if it isn't as much fun as you expected.
7. Listen to the voice of criticism. It's always right. (You just have to figure out in what way.)
8. Your original vision is not sacred. It's just a first draft.
9. When you discover what the heart of the game is, protect it to the death.
10. Nobody knows what will succeed.

ALIGOT SAUCISSE
Aveyron
Traiteur

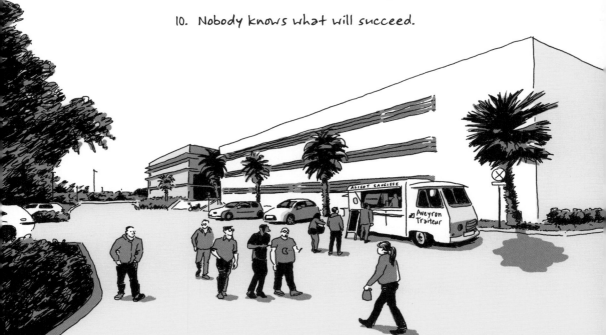

Lost in Translation

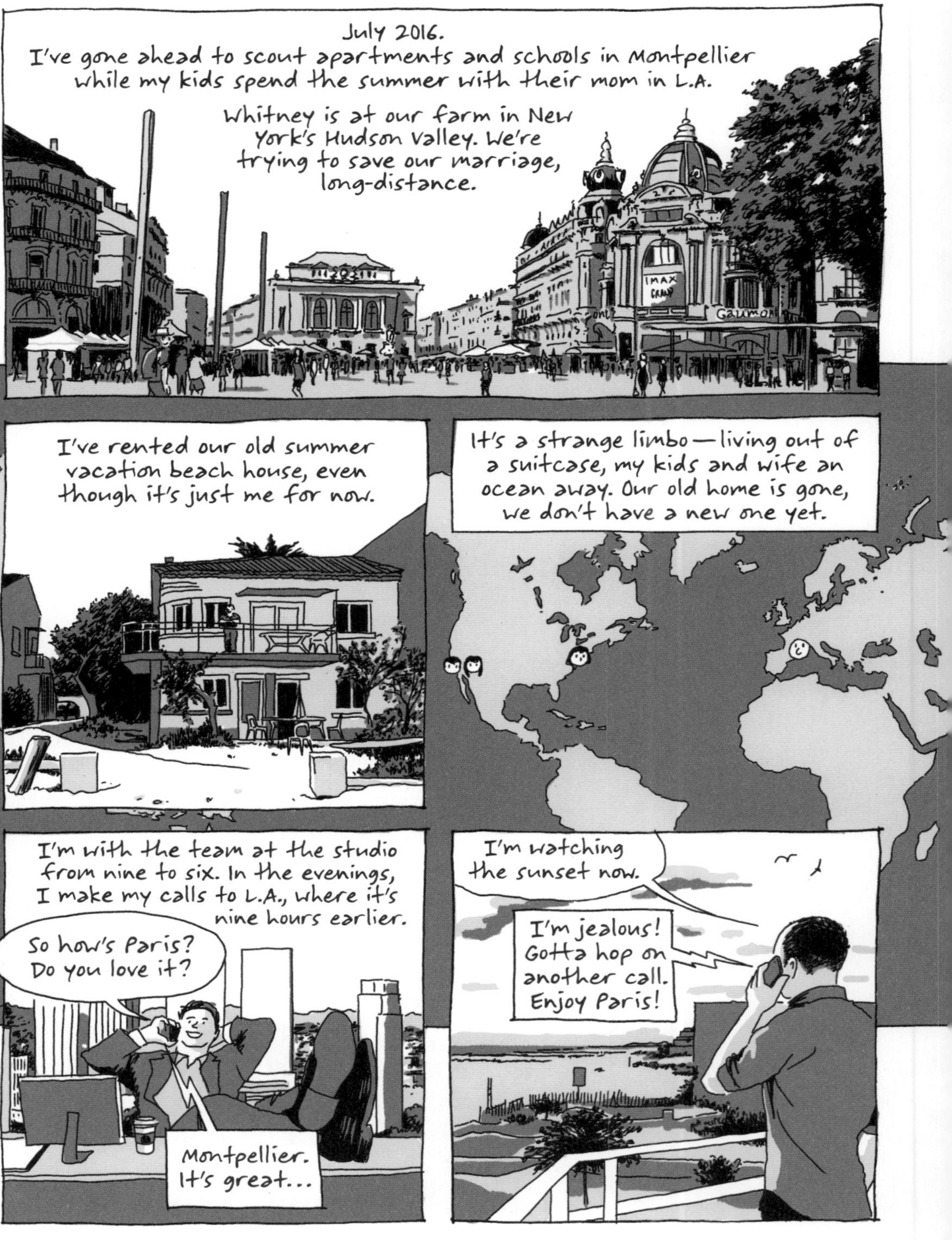
July 2016.
I've gone ahead to scout apartments and schools in Montpellier while my kids spend the summer with their mom in L.A.
Whitney is at our farm in New York's Hudson Valley. We're trying to save our marriage, long-distance.
IMAX
Gaumont
I've rented our old summer vacation beach house, even though it's just me for now.
It's a strange limbo—living out of a suitcase, my kids and wife an ocean away. Our old home is gone, we don't have a new one yet.
I'm with the team at the studio from nine to six. In the evenings, I make my calls to L.A., where it's nine hours earlier.
So how's Paris? Do you love it?
Montpellier. It's great...
I'm watching the sunset now.
I'm jealous! Gotta hop on another call. Enjoy Paris!

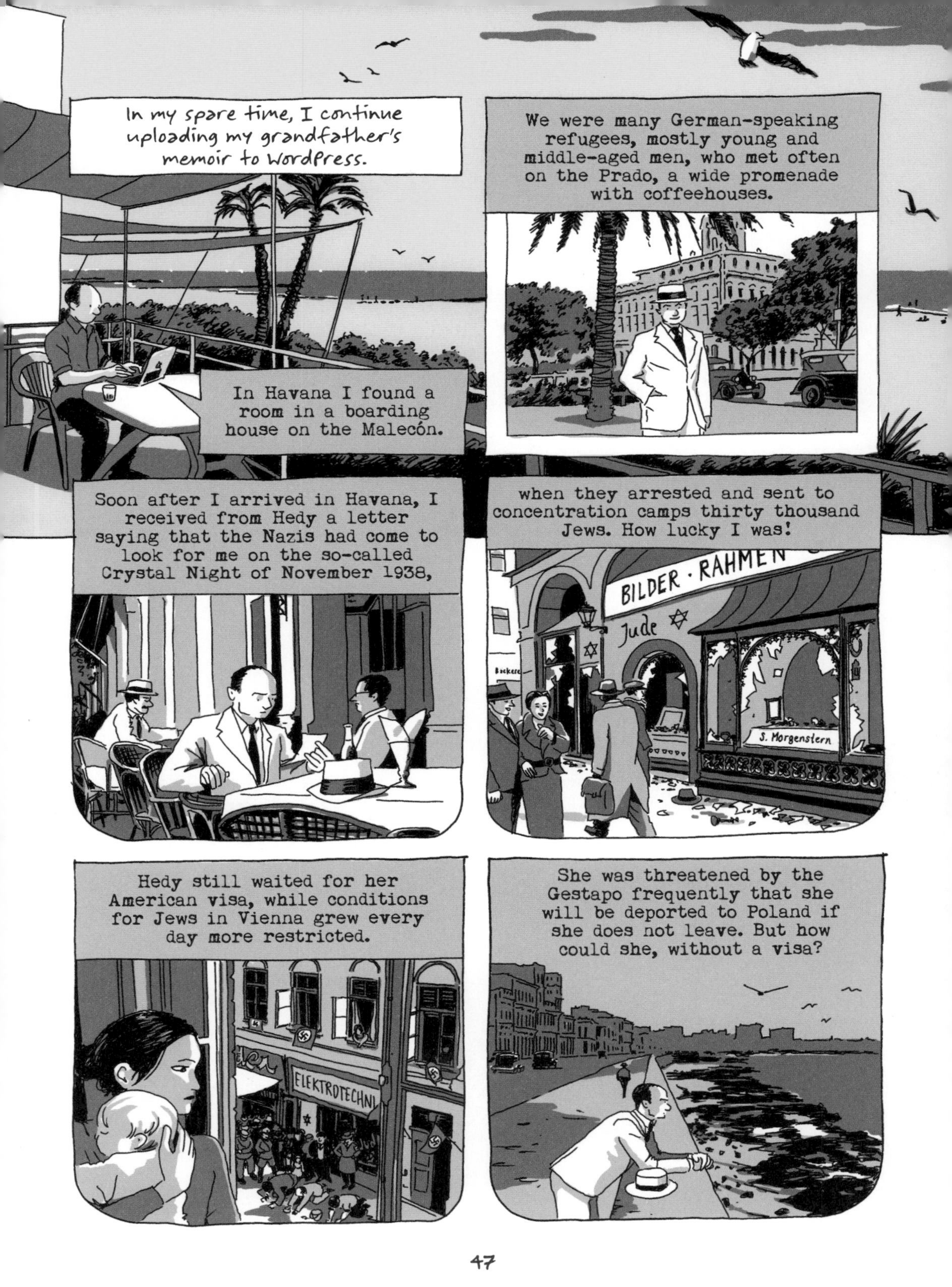
In my spare time, I continue uploading my grandfather's memoir to WordPress.
In Havana I found a room in a boarding house on the Malecón.
We were many German-speaking refugees, mostly young and middle-aged men, who met often on the Prado, a wide promenade with coffeehouses.
Soon after I arrived in Havana, I received from Hedy a letter saying that the Nazis had come to look for me on the so-called Crystal Night of November 1938,
when they arrested and sent to concentration camps thirty thousand Jews. How lucky I was!
BILDER · RAHMEN
Jude
S. Morgenstern
Hedy still waited for her American visa, while conditions for Jews in Vienna grew every day more restricted.
ELEKTROTECHNI
She was threatened by the Gestapo frequently that she will be deported to Poland if she does not leave. But how could she, without a visa?

Immigration

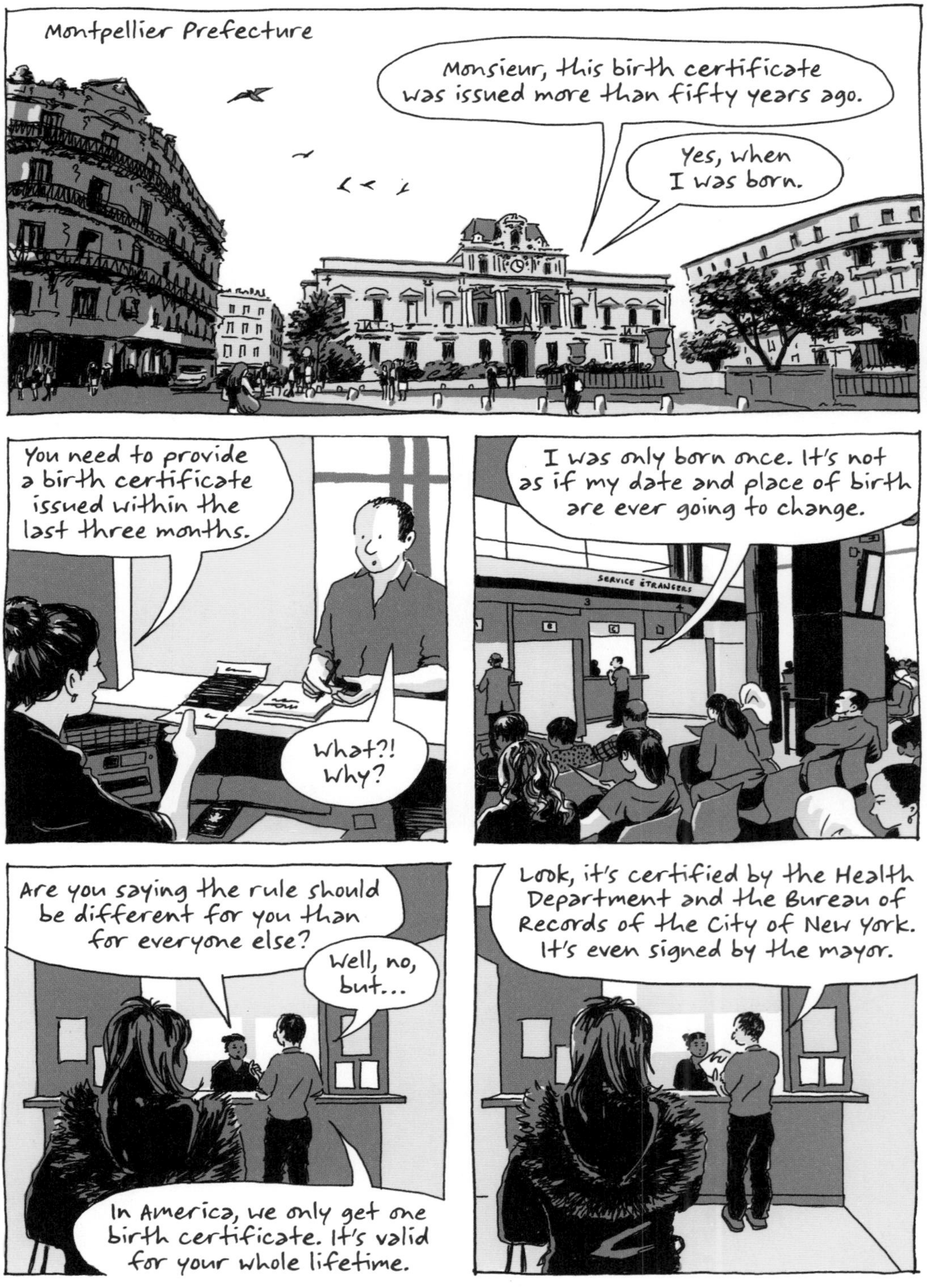

Montpellier Prefecture
Monsieur, this birth certificate was issued more than fifty years ago.
Yes, when I was born.
You need to provide a birth certificate issued within the last three months.
What?! Why?
I was only born once. It's not as if my date and place of birth are ever going to change.
SERVICE ÉTRANGERS
Are you saying the rule should be different for you than for everyone else?
Well, no, but...
In America, we only get one birth certificate. It's valid for your whole lifetime.
Look, it's certified by the Health Department and the Bureau of Records of the City of New York. It's even signed by the mayor.

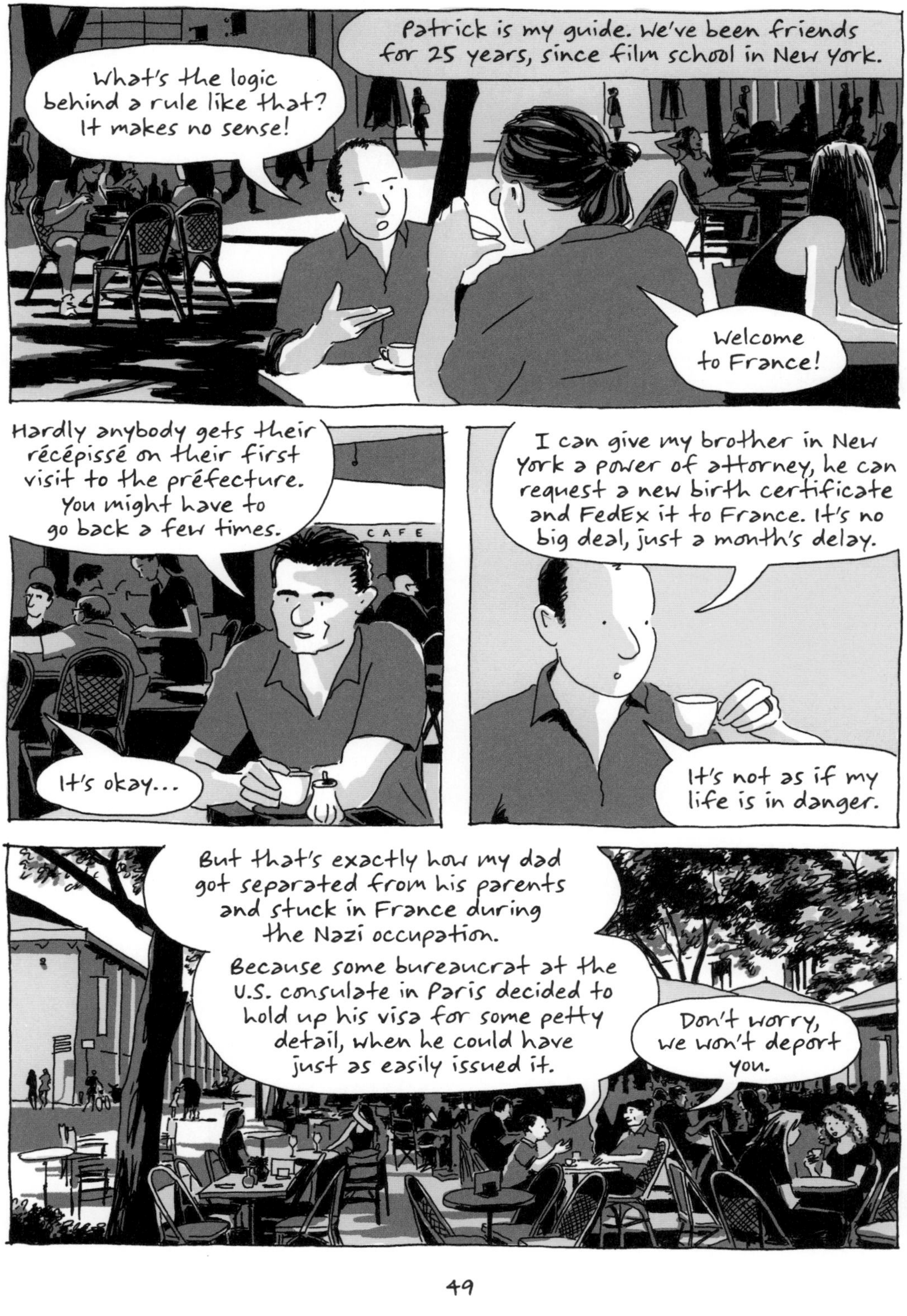
Patrick is my guide. We've been friends for 25 years, since film school in New York.
What's the logic behind a rule like that? It makes no sense!
Welcome to France!
Hardly anybody gets their récépissé on their first visit to the préfecture. You might have to go back a few times.
CAFE
It's okay...
I can give my brother in New York a power of attorney, he can request a new birth certificate and FedEx it to France. It's no big deal, just a month's delay.
It's not as if my life is in danger.
But that's exactly how my dad got separated from his parents and stuck in France during the Nazi occupation.
Because some bureaucrat at the U.S. consulate in Paris decided to hold up his visa for some petty detail, when he could have just as easily issued it.
Don't worry, we won't deport you.

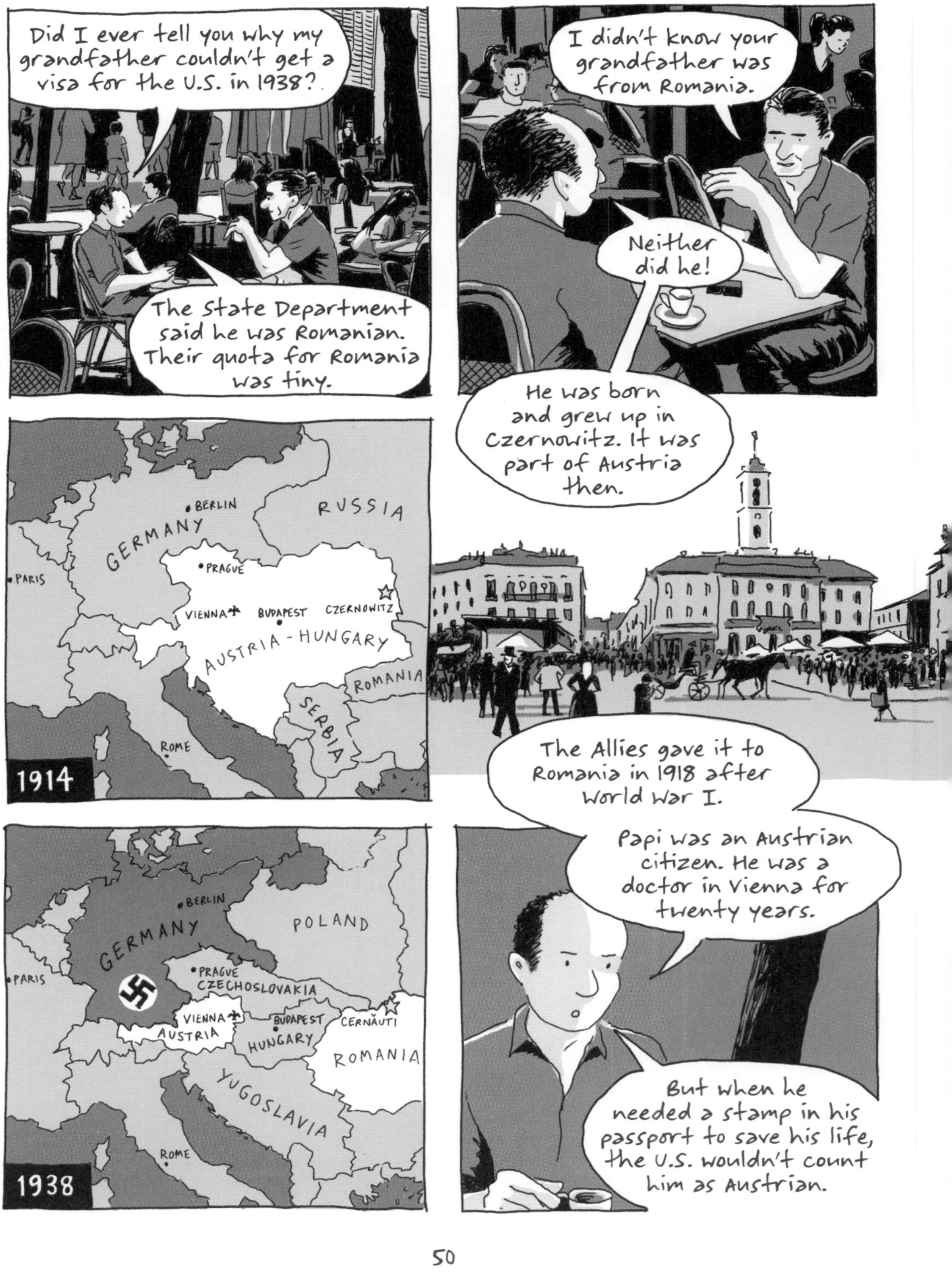
Did I ever tell you why my grandfather couldn't get a visa for the U.S. in 1938?
The State Department said he was Romanian. Their quota for Romania was tiny.
I didn't know your grandfather was from Romania.
Neither did he!
He was born and grew up in Czernowitz. It was part of Austria then.
BERLIN
RUSSIA
GERMANY
PRAGUE
PARIS
VIENNA
BUDAPEST
CZERNOWITZ
AUSTRIA-HUNGARY
ROMANIA
SERBIA
ROME
1914
The Allies gave it to Romania in 1918 after World War I.
Papi was an Austrian citizen. He was a doctor in Vienna for twenty years.
BERLIN
POLAND
GERMANY
PRAGUE
CZECHOSLOVAKIA
PARIS
VIENNA
AUSTRIA
BUDAPEST
HUNGARY
CERNĂUTI
ROMANIA
YUGOSLAVIA
ROME
1938
But when he needed a stamp in his passport to save his life, the U.S. wouldn't count him as Austrian.

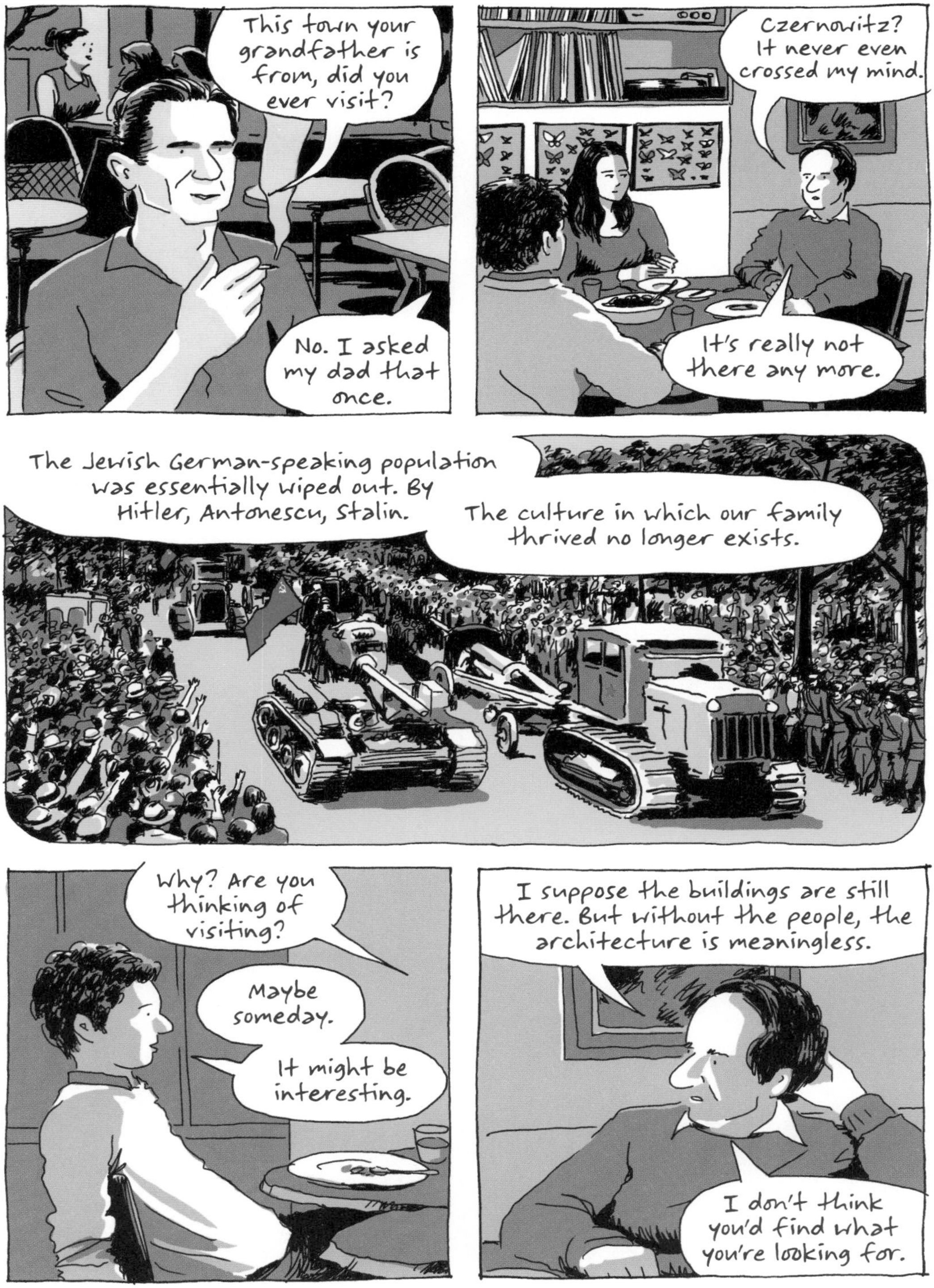
This town your grandfather is from, did you ever visit?
No. I asked my dad that once.
Czernowitz? It never even crossed my mind.
It's really not there any more.
The Jewish German-speaking population was essentially wiped out. By Hitler, Antonescu, Stalin.
The culture in which our family thrived no longer exists.
Why? Are you thinking of visiting?
Maybe someday.
It might be interesting.
I suppose the buildings are still there. But without the people, the architecture is meaningless.
I don't think you'd find what you're looking for.

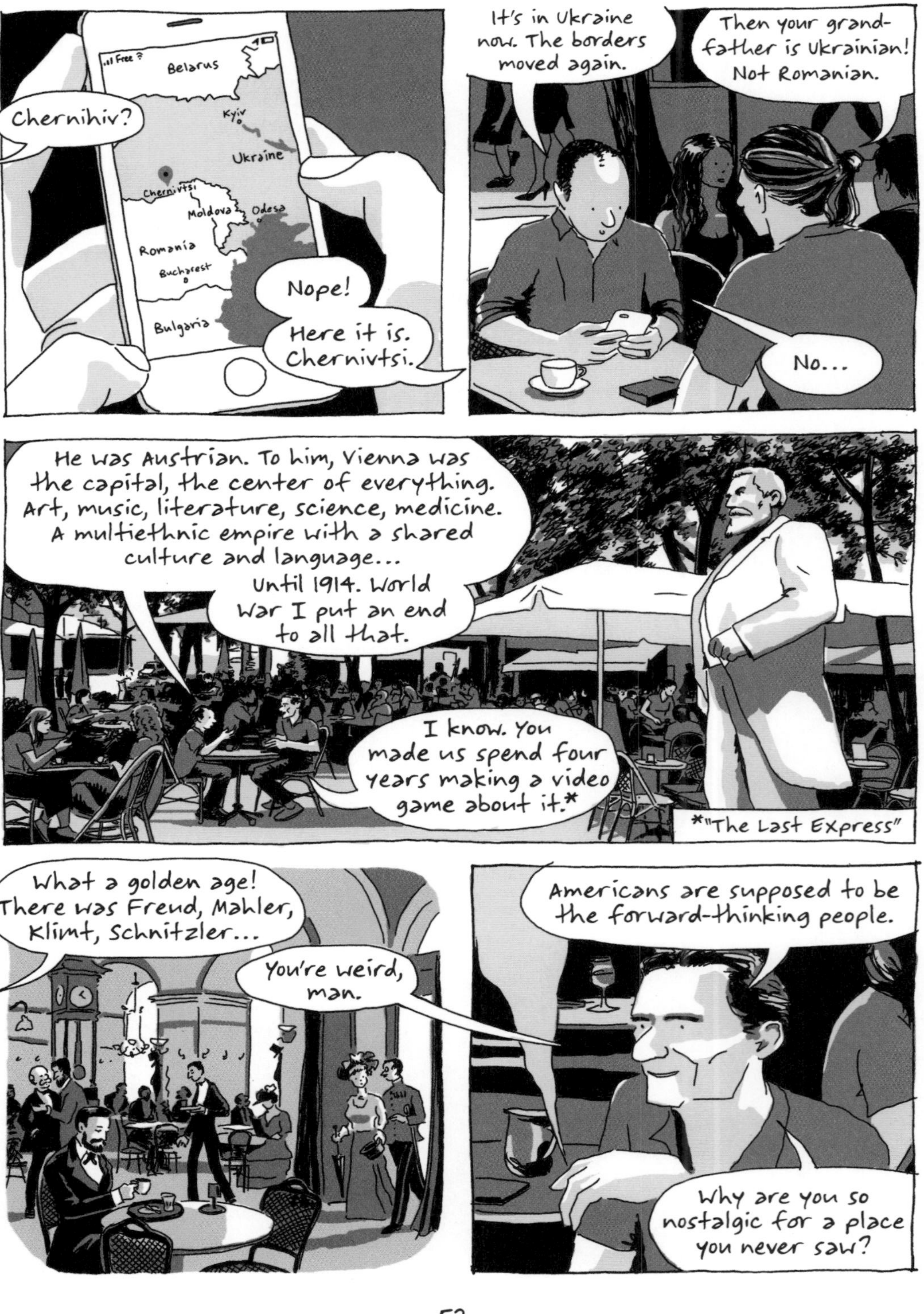

Belarus
Kyiv
Ukraine
Chernivtsi
Moldova
Odesa
Romania
Bucharest
Bulgaria
Chernihiv?
Nope!
Here it is. Chernivtsi.
It's in Ukraine now. The borders moved again.
Then your grand-father is Ukrainian! Not Romanian.
No...
He was Austrian. To him, Vienna was the capital, the center of everything. Art, music, literature, science, medicine. A multiethnic empire with a shared culture and language...
Until 1914. World War I put an end to all that.
I know. You made us spend four years making a video game about it.*
*"The Last Express"
What a golden age! There was Freud, Mahler, Klimt, Schnitzler...
You're weird, man.
Americans are supposed to be the forward-thinking people.
Why are you so nostalgic for a place you never saw?

An Ocean Apart

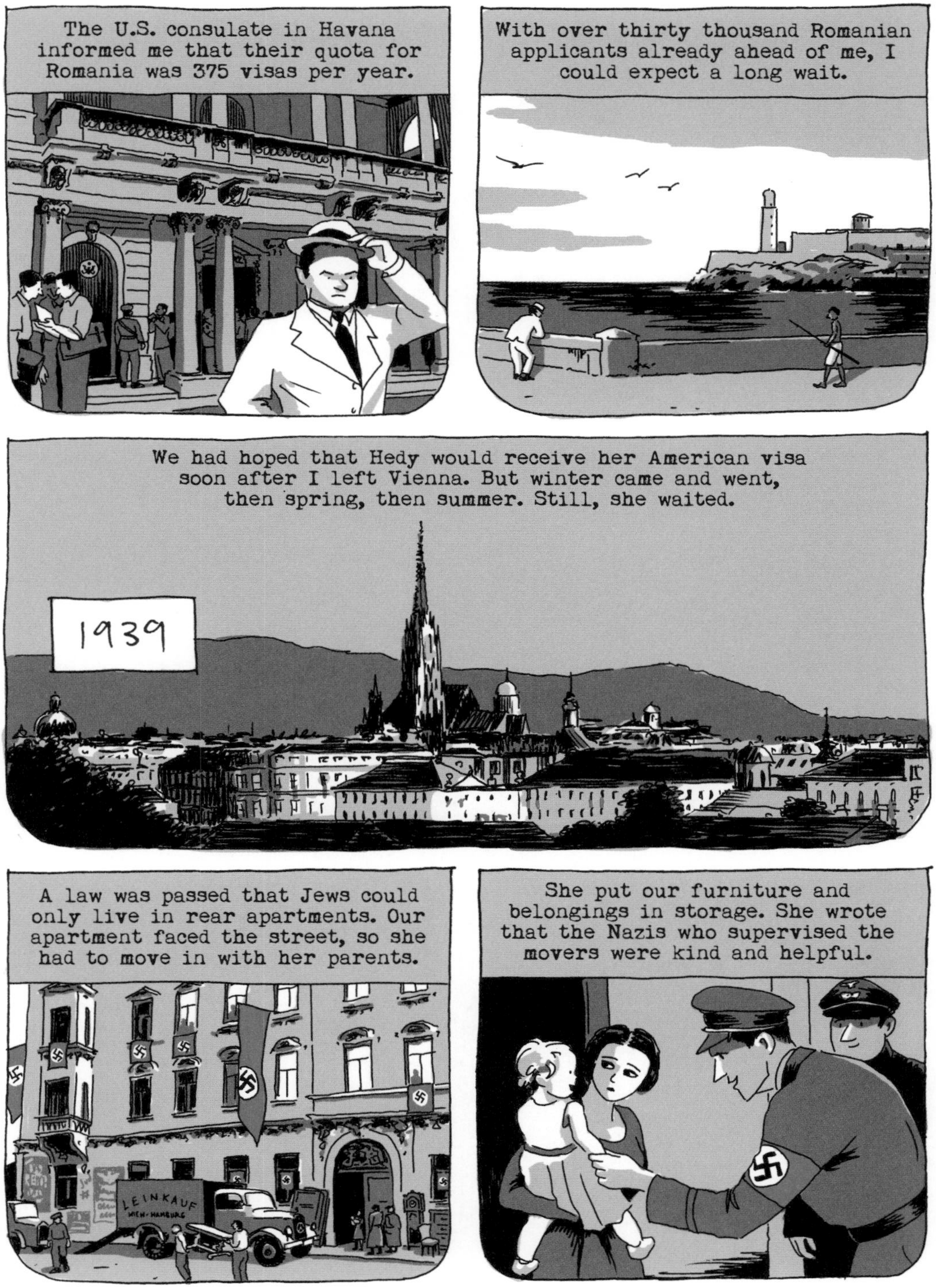
The U.S. consulate in Havana informed me that their quota for Romania was 375 visas per year.
With over thirty thousand Romanian applicants already ahead of me, I could expect a long wait.
We had hoped that Hedy would receive her American visa soon after I left Vienna. But winter came and went, then spring, then summer. Still, she waited.
1939
A law was passed that Jews could only live in rear apartments. Our apartment faced the street, so she had to move in with her parents.
LEINKAUF
She put our furniture and belongings in storage. She wrote that the Nazis who supervised the movers were kind and helpful.

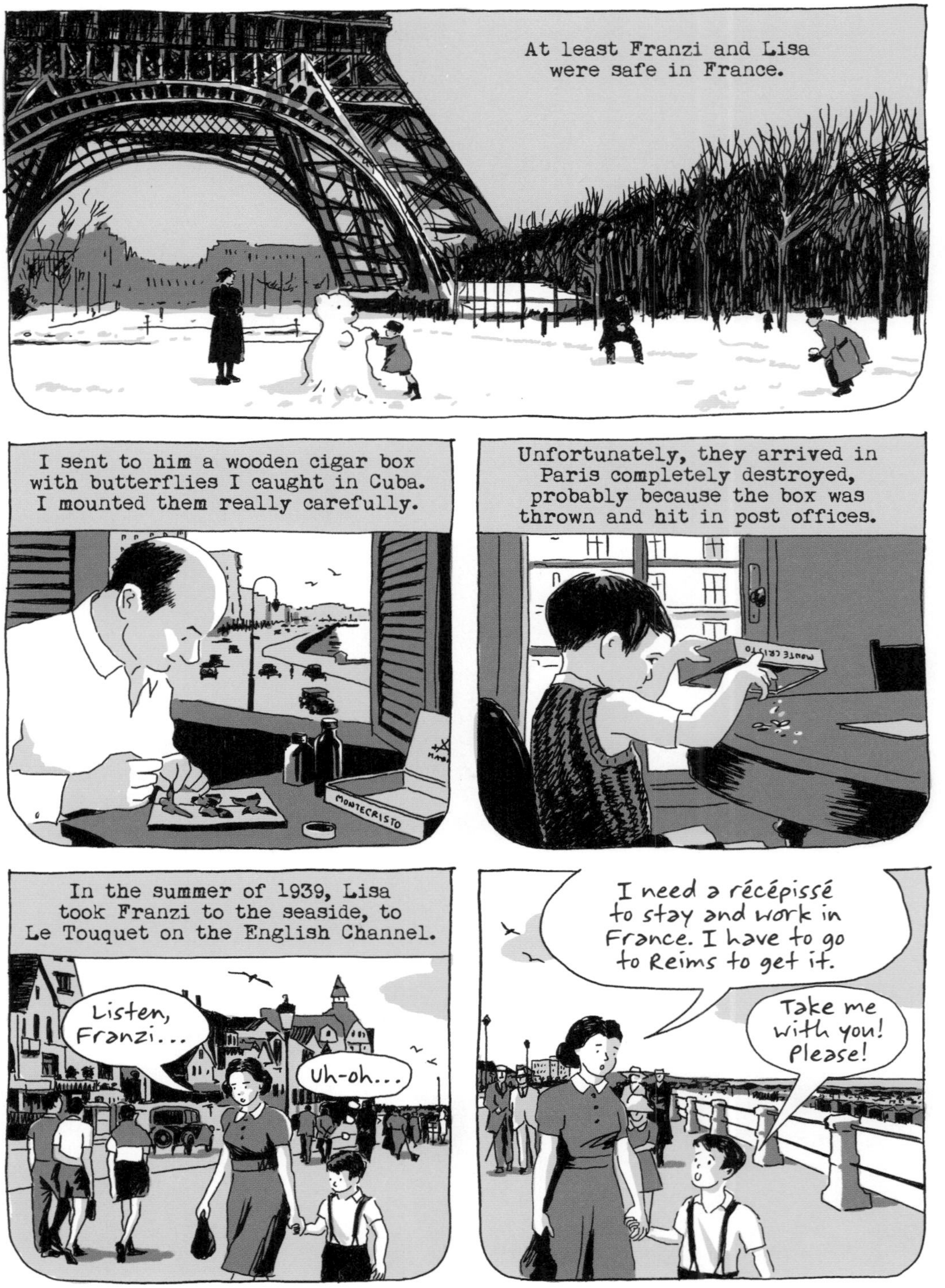
At least Franzi and Lisa were safe in France.
I sent to him a wooden cigar box with butterflies I caught in Cuba. I mounted them really carefully.
MONTECRISTO
Unfortunately, they arrived in Paris completely destroyed, probably because the box was thrown and hit in post offices.
MONTE CRISTO
In the summer of 1939, Lisa took Franzi to the seaside, to Le Touquet on the English Channel.
Listen, Franzi...
Uh-oh...
I need a récépissé to stay and work in France. I have to go to Reims to get it.
Take me with you! Please!

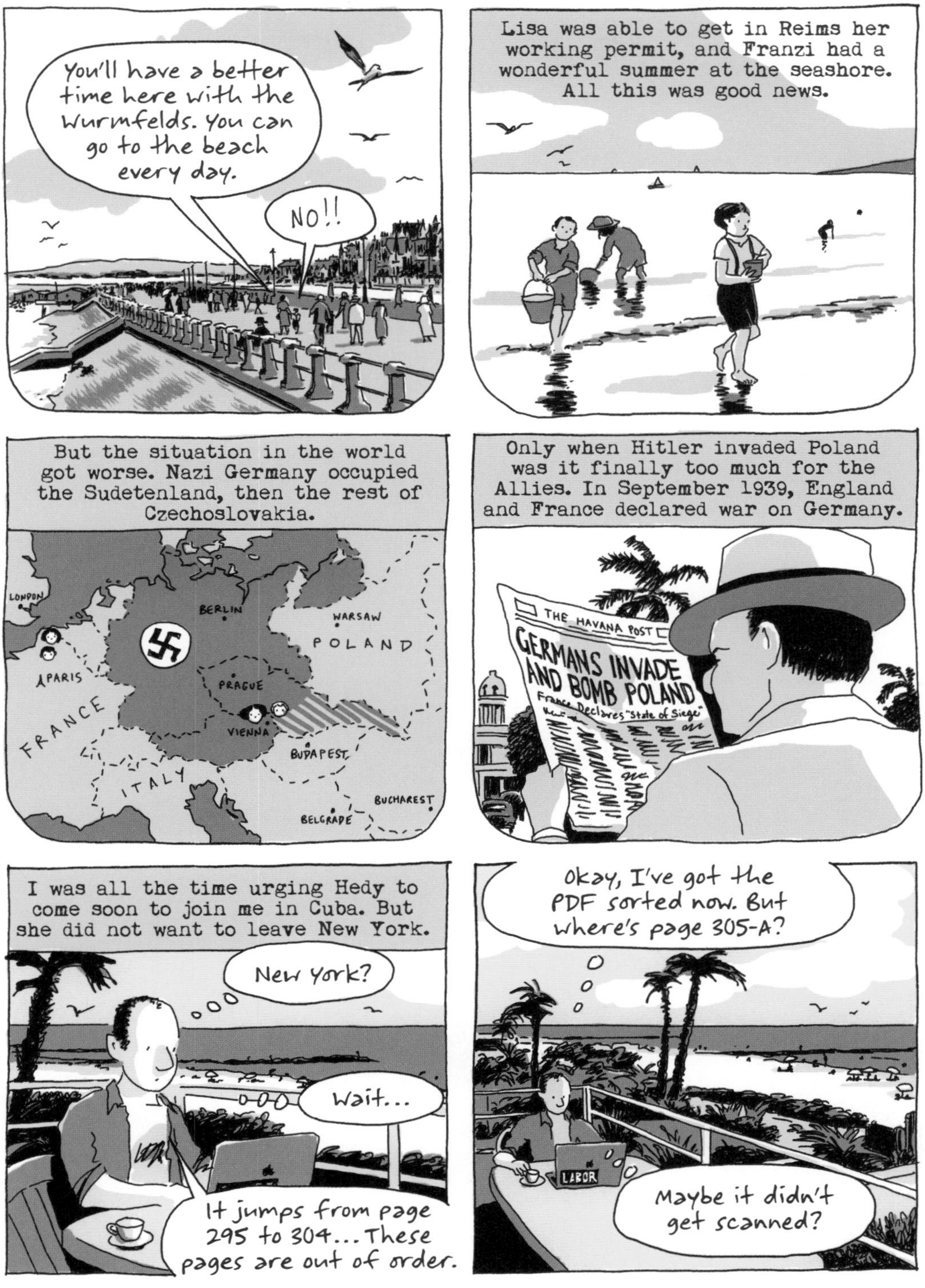
You'll have a better time here with the Wurmfelds. You can go to the beach every day.
NO!!
Lisa was able to get in Reims her working permit, and Franzi had a wonderful summer at the seashore. All this was good news.
But the situation in the world got worse. Nazi Germany occupied the Sudetenland, then the rest of Czechoslovakia.
LONDON
BERLIN
WARSAW
POLAND
PARIS
PRAGUE
FRANCE
VIENNA
BUDAPEST
ITALY
BUCHAREST
BELGRADE
Only when Hitler invaded Poland was it finally too much for the Allies. In September 1939, England and France declared war on Germany.
THE HAVANA POST
GERMANS INVADE AND BOMB POLAND
France Declares "State of Siege"
I was all the time urging Hedy to come soon to join me in Cuba. But she did not want to leave New York.
New York?
Wait...
It jumps from page 295 to 304... These pages are out of order.
Okay, I've got the PDF sorted now. But where's page 305-A?
LABOR
Maybe it didn't get scanned?

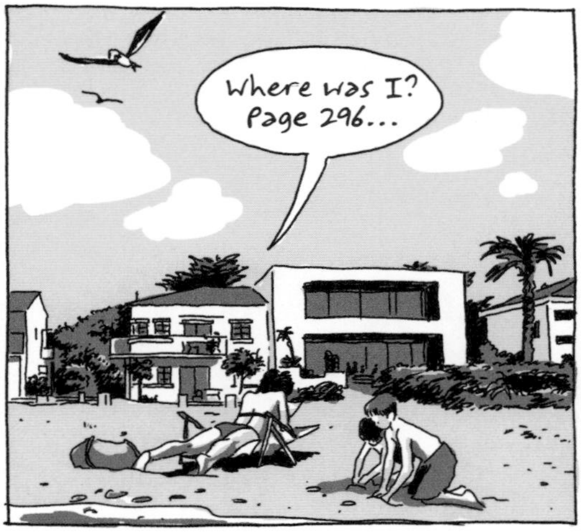
Where was I?
Page 296...

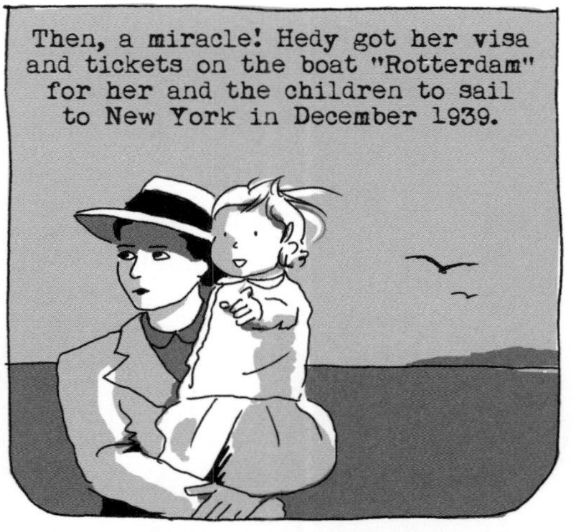
Then, a miracle! Hedy got her visa and tickets on the boat "Rotterdam" for her and the children to sail to New York in December 1939.

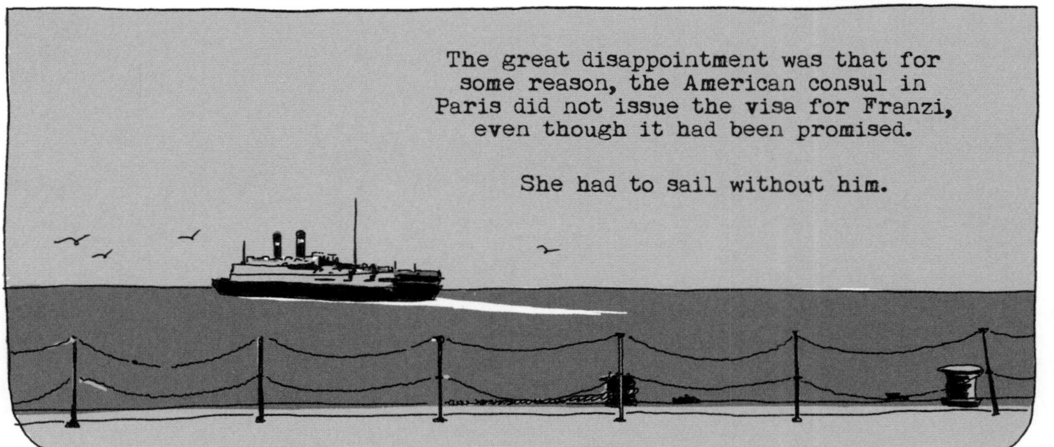
The great disappointment was that for some reason, the American consul in Paris did not issue the visa for Franzi, even though it had been promised.
She had to sail without him.

It was a huge relief to me when Hedy and Johanna arrived safely in New York. Our worry now was to get Franzi and Lisa out of Europe.

I had at least the comfort that in Le Touquet they were far from the battle zone, with the Maginot Line and the entire French army between them and Hitler.

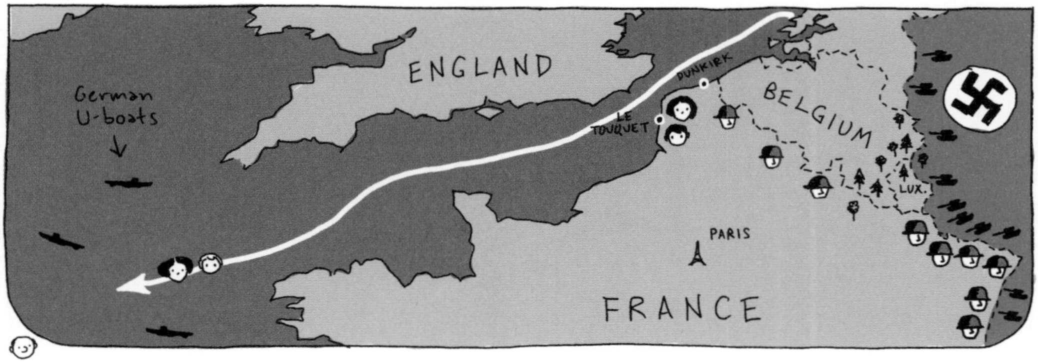
ENGLAND
German U-boats
DUNKIRK
LE TOUQUET
BELGIUM
LUX.
PARIS
FRANCE

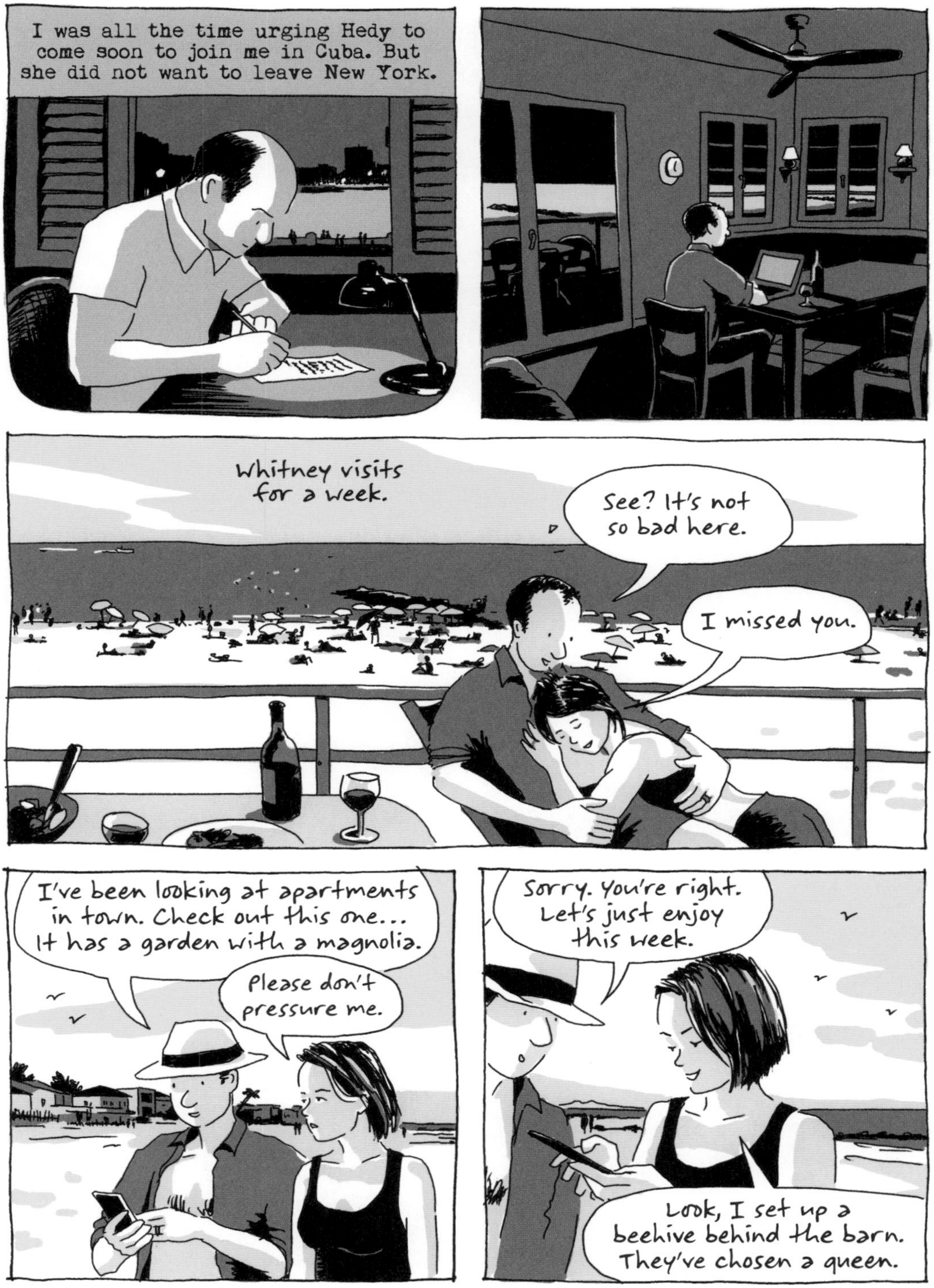

I was all the time urging Hedy to come soon to join me in Cuba. But she did not want to leave New York.
Whitney visits for a week.
See? It's not so bad here.
I missed you.
I've been looking at apartments in town. Check out this one... It has a garden with a magnolia.
Please don't pressure me.
Sorry. You're right. Let's just enjoy this week.
Look, I set up a beehive behind the barn. They've chosen a queen.

Sustainable

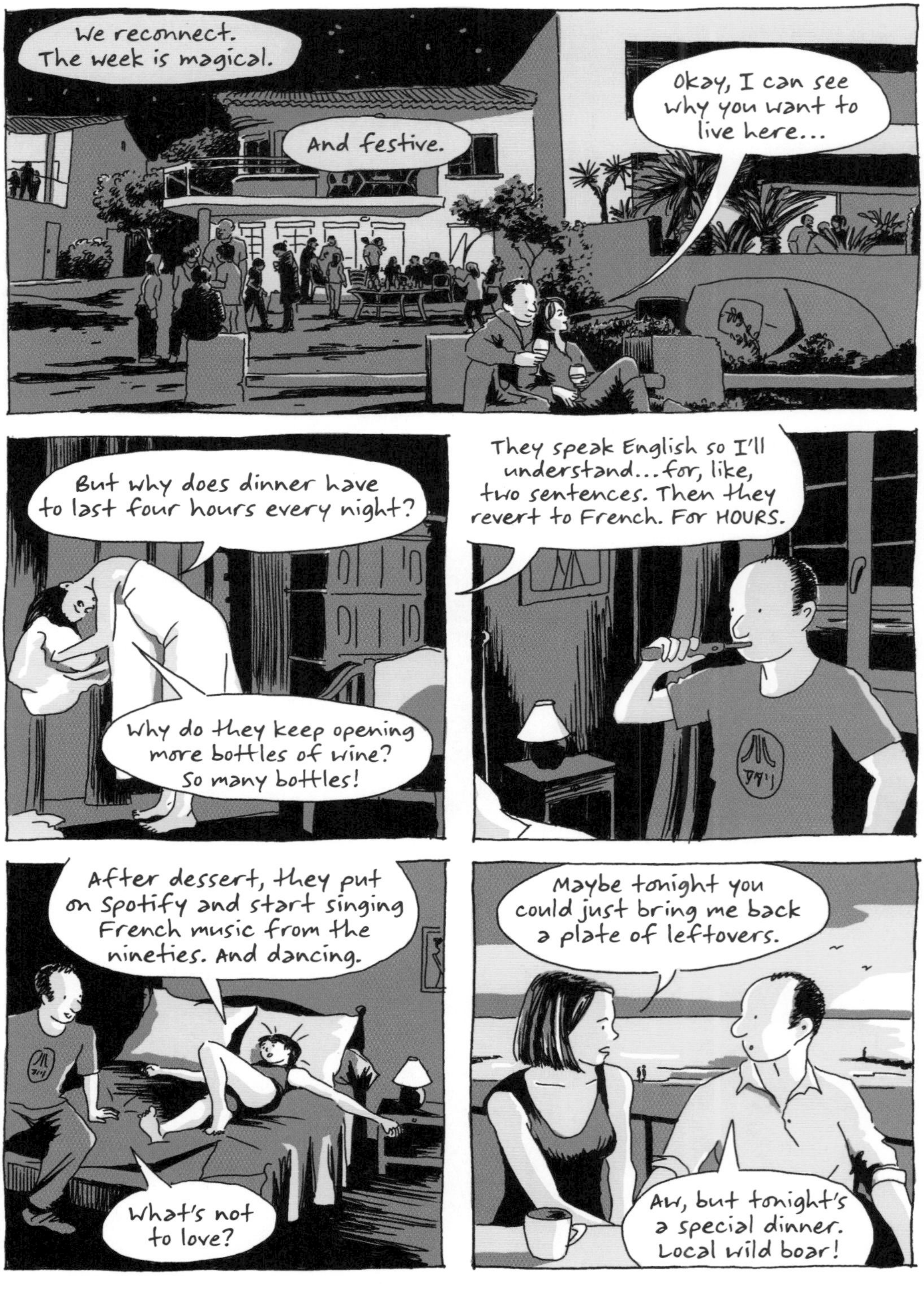
We reconnect. The week is magical.
And festive.
Okay, I can see why you want to live here...
But why does dinner have to last four hours every night?
Why do they keep opening more bottles of wine? So many bottles!
They speak English so I'll understand... for, like, two sentences. Then they revert to French. For HOURS.
After dessert, they put on Spotify and start singing French music from the nineties. And dancing.
What's not to love?
Maybe tonight you could just bring me back a plate of leftovers.
Aw, but tonight's a special dinner. Local wild boar!

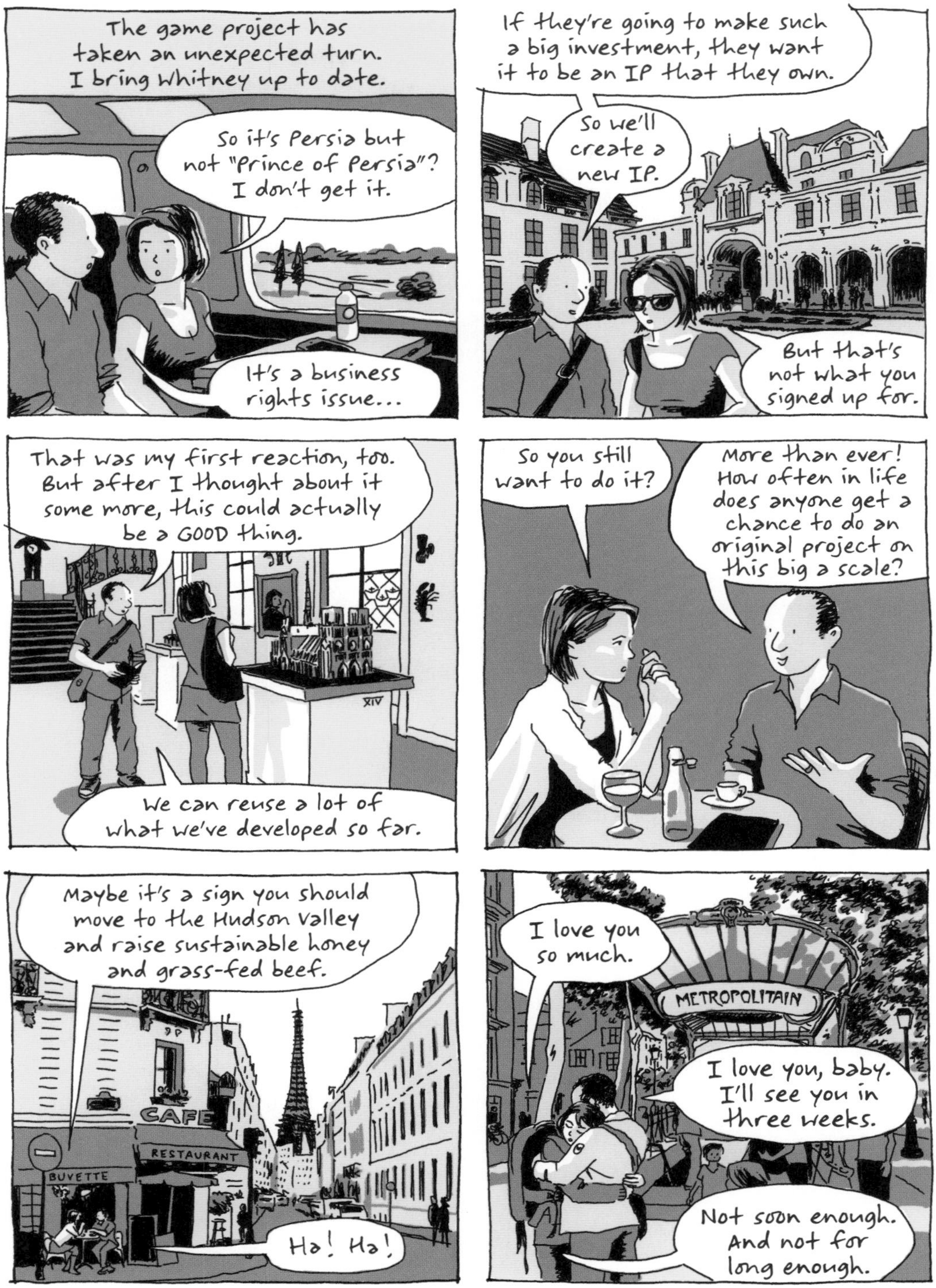

The game project has taken an unexpected turn. I bring Whitney up to date.
So it's Persia but not "Prince of Persia"? I don't get it.
It's a business rights issue...
If they're going to make such a big investment, they want it to be an IP that they own.
So we'll create a new IP.
But that's not what you signed up for.
That was my first reaction, too. But after I thought about it some more, this could actually be a GOOD thing.
XIV
We can reuse a lot of what we've developed so far.
So you still want to do it?
More than ever! How often in life does anyone get a chance to do an original project on this big a scale?
Maybe it's a sign you should move to the Hudson Valley and raise sustainable honey and grass-fed beef.
CAFE
RESTAURANT
BUVETTE
Ha! Ha!
I love you so much.
METROPOLITAIN
I love you, baby. I'll see you in three weeks.
Not soon enough. And not for long enough.

Spiral

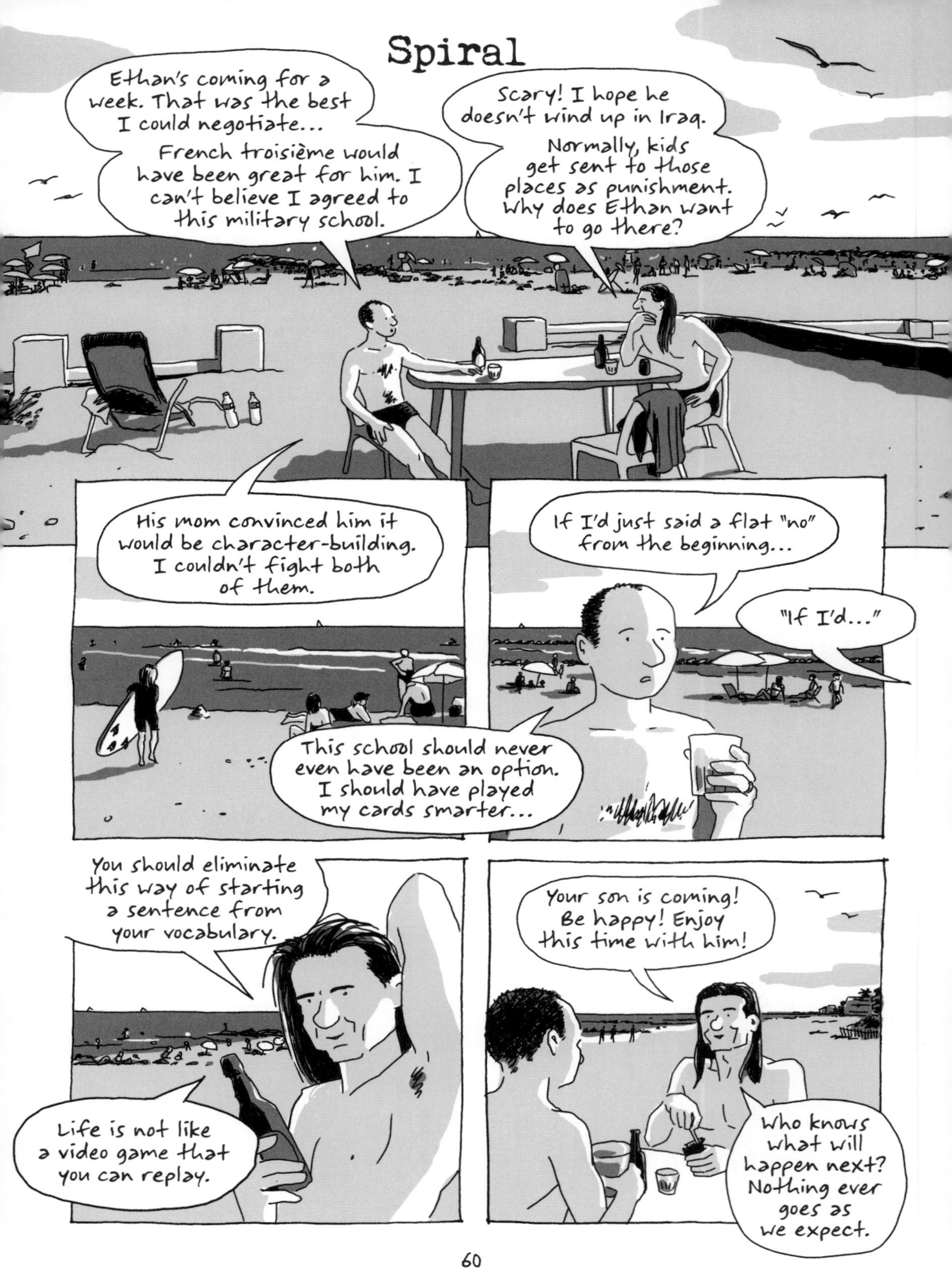

Ethan's coming for a week. That was the best I could negotiate...
French troisième would have been great for him. I can't believe I agreed to this military school.
Scary! I hope he doesn't wind up in Iraq.
Normally, kids get sent to those places as punishment. Why does Ethan want to go there?
His mom convinced him it would be character-building. I couldn't fight both of them.
If I'd just said a flat "no" from the beginning...
"If I'd..."
This school should never even have been an option. I should have played my cards smarter...
You should eliminate this way of starting a sentence from your vocabulary.
Life is not like a video game that you can replay.
Your son is coming! Be happy! Enjoy this time with him!
Who knows what will happen next? Nothing ever goes as we expect.

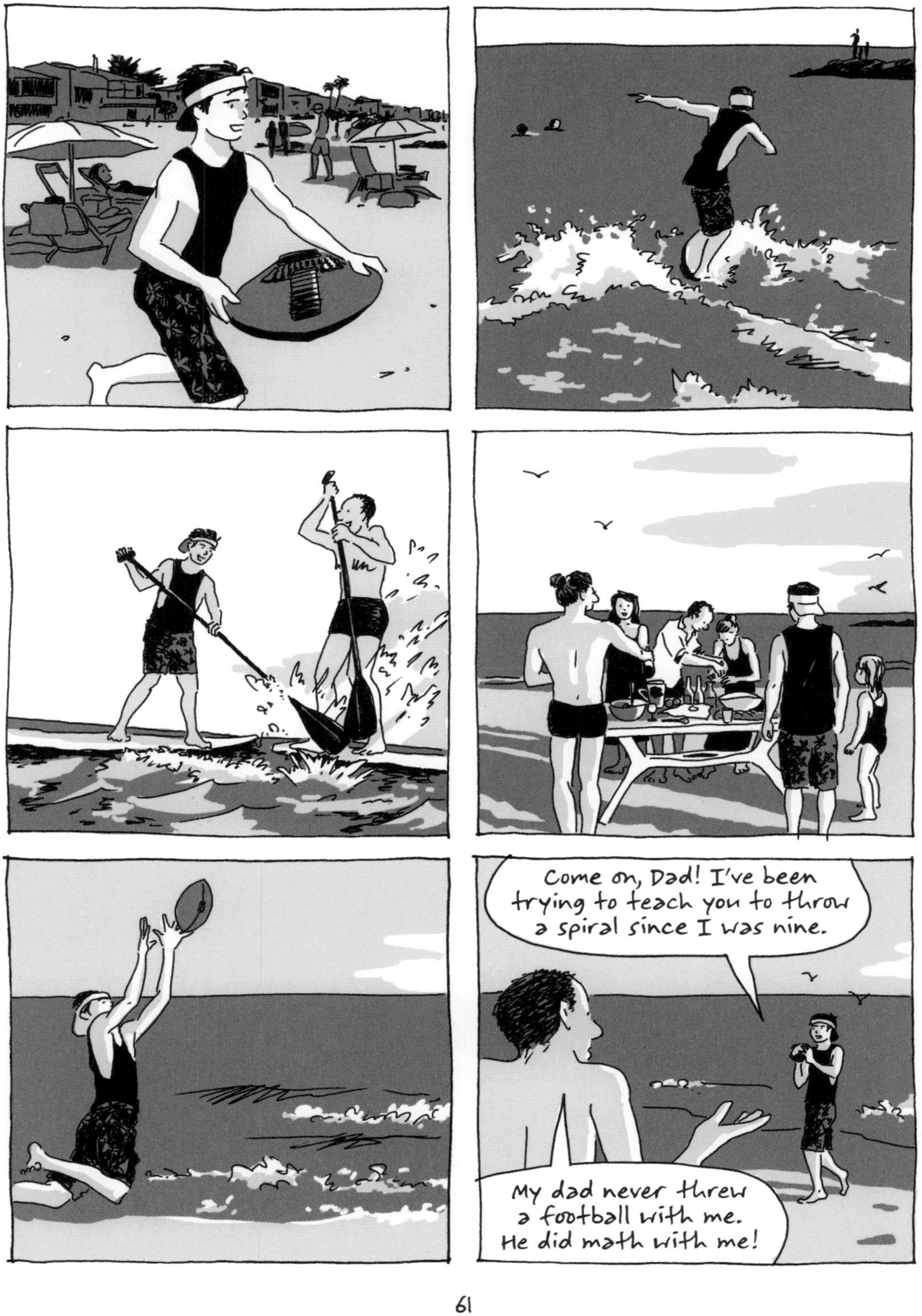
Come on, Dad! I've been trying to teach you to throw a spiral since I was nine.
My dad never threw a football with me. He did math with me!

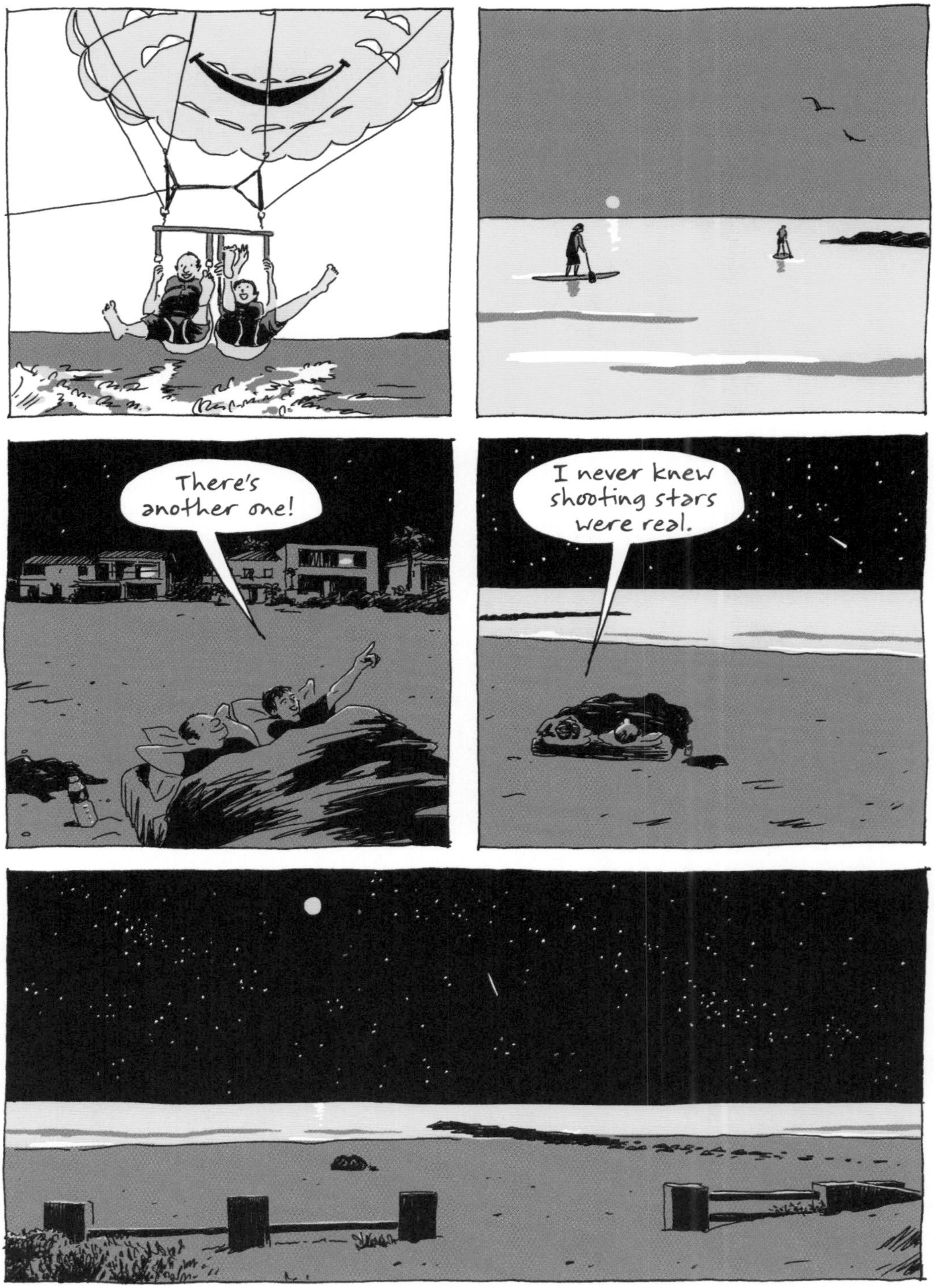
There's another one!
I never knew shooting stars were real.

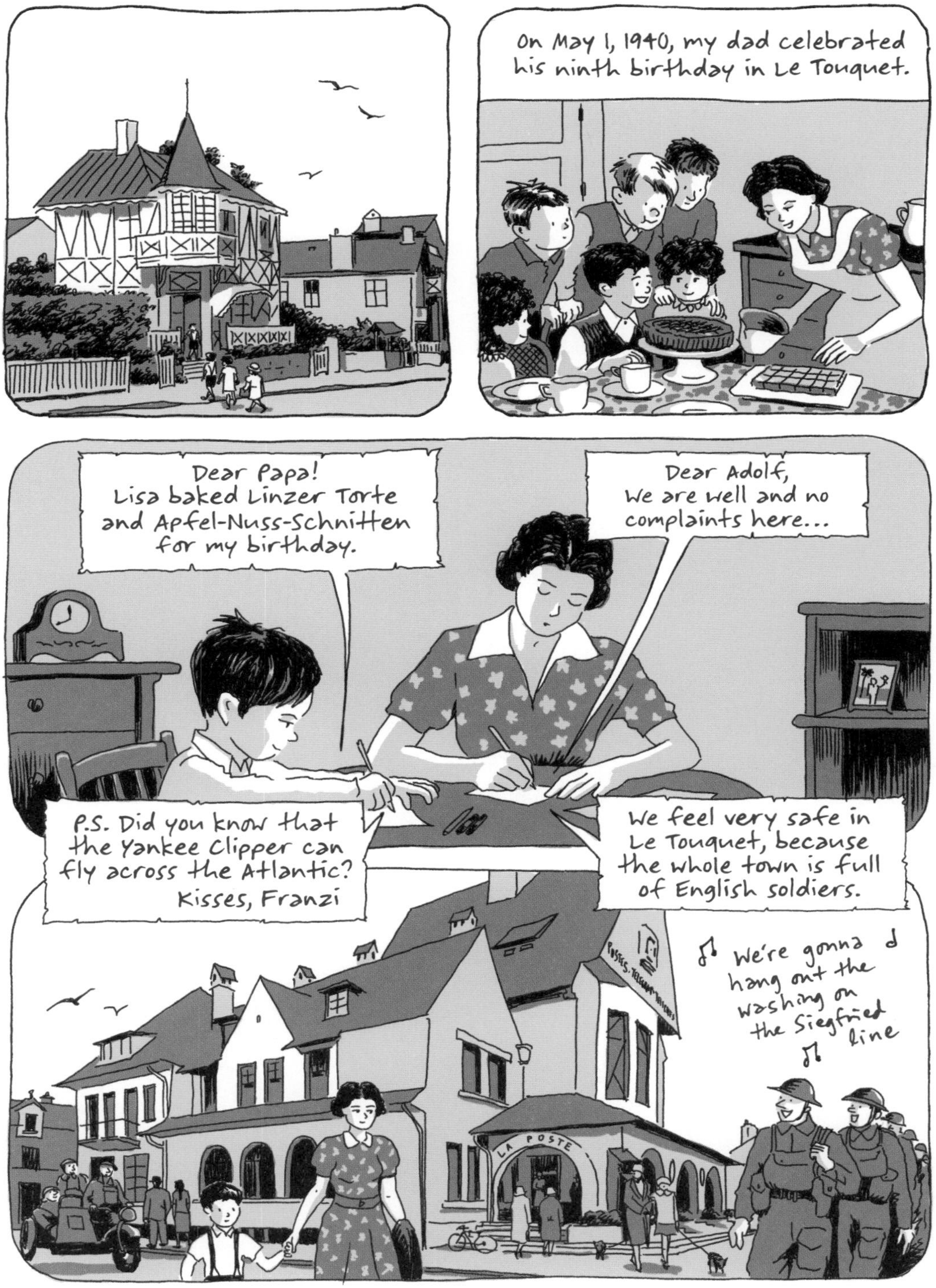
On May 1, 1940, my dad celebrated his ninth birthday in Le Touquet.
Dear Papa! Lisa baked Linzer Torte and Apfel-Nuss-Schnitten for my birthday.
Dear Adolf, We are well and no complaints here...
P.S. Did you know that the Yankee Clipper can fly across the Atlantic? Kisses, Franzi
We feel very safe in Le Touquet, because the whole town is full of English soldiers.
We're gonna hang out the washing on the Siegfried line
LA POSTE

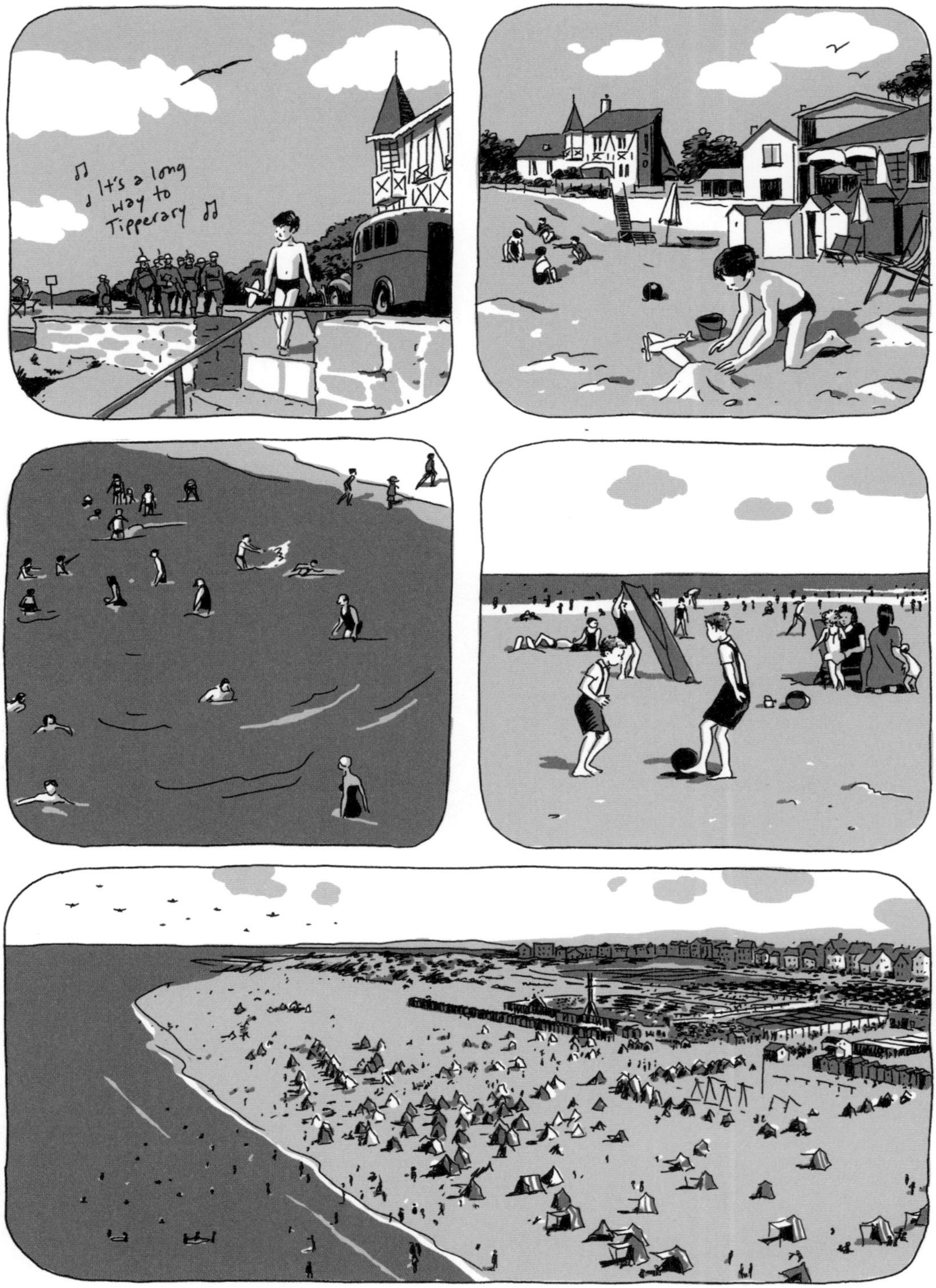
♫ It's a long way to Tipperary ♫

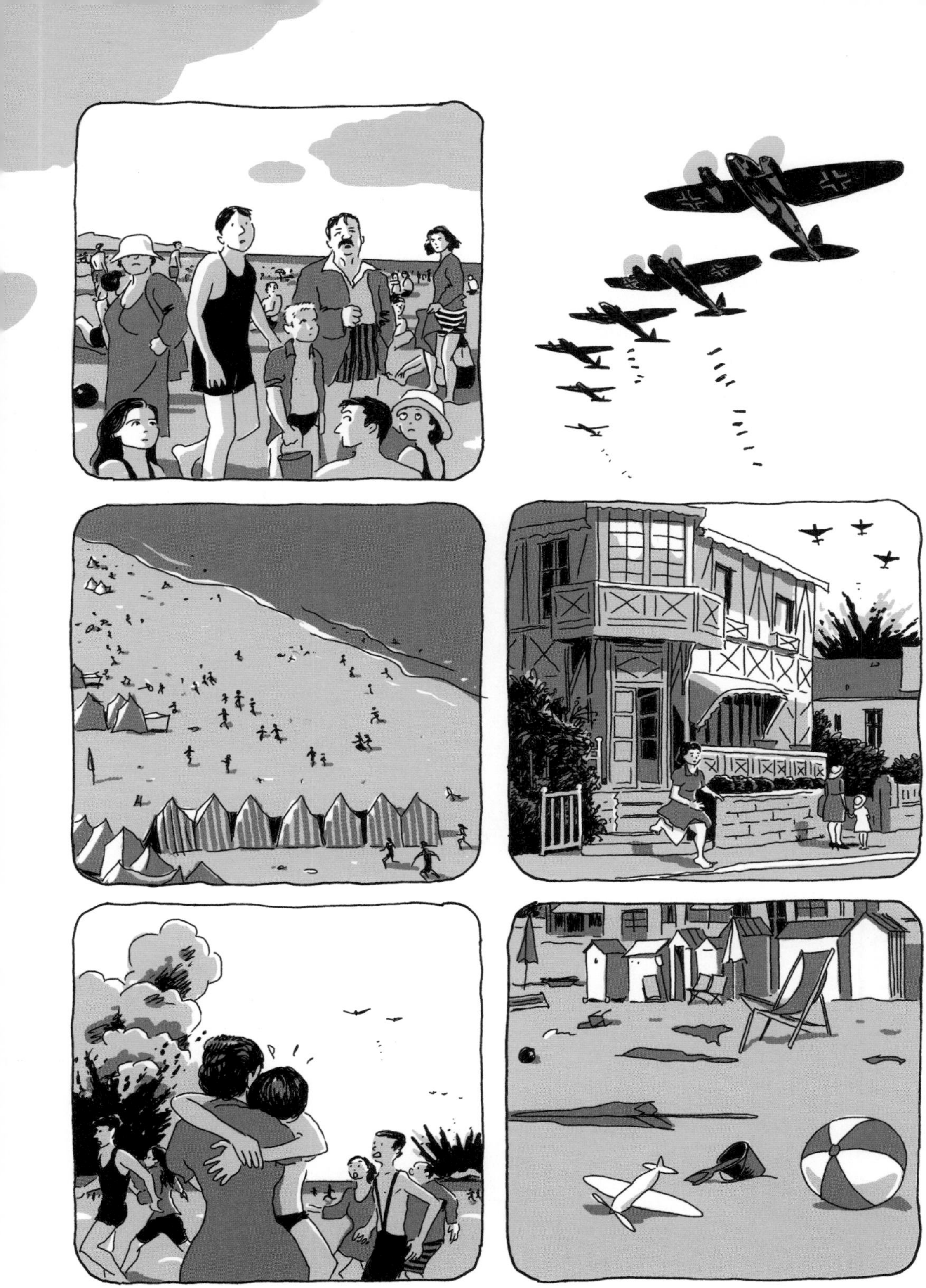

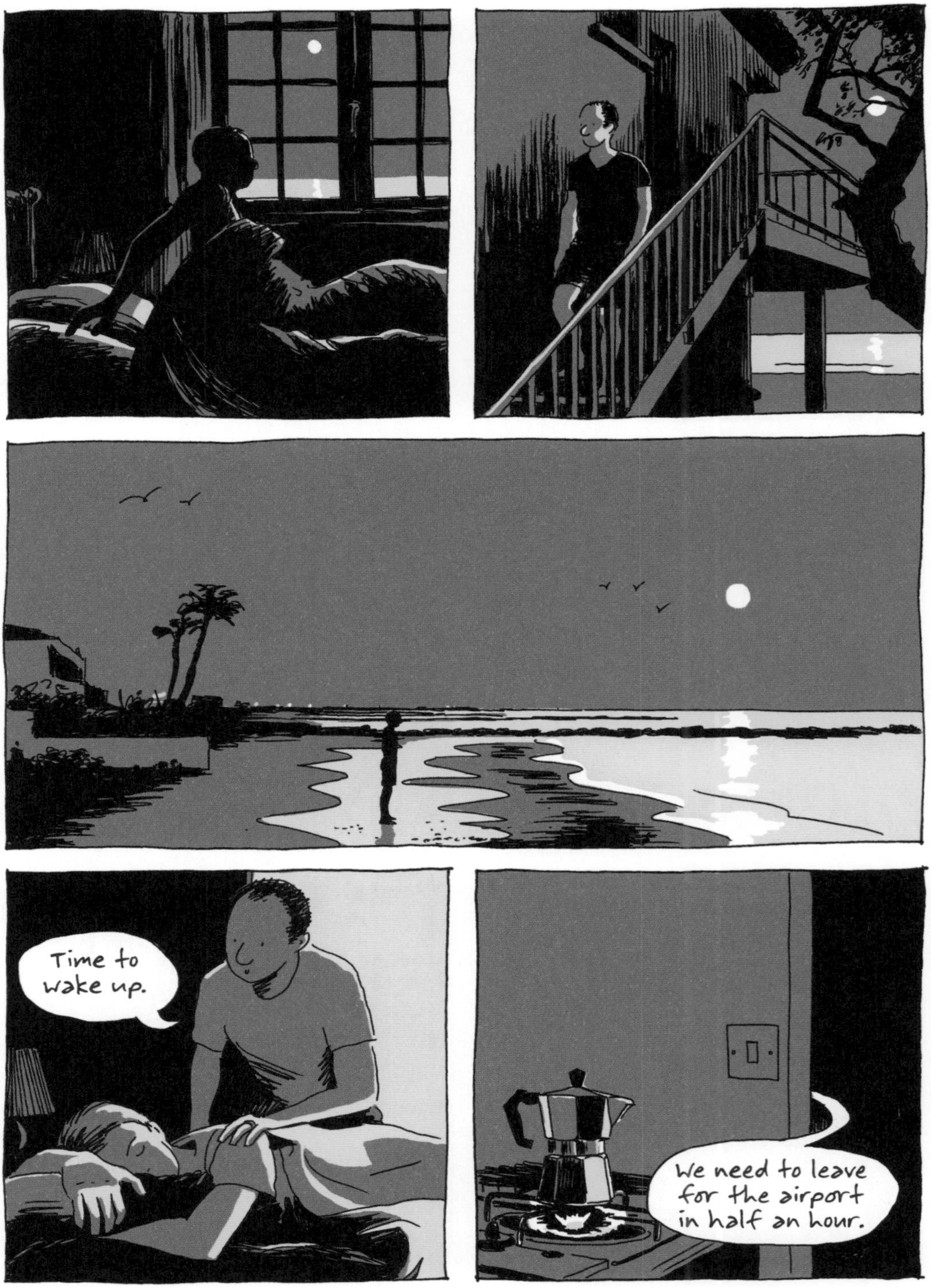
Time to wake up.
We need to leave for the airport in half an hour.

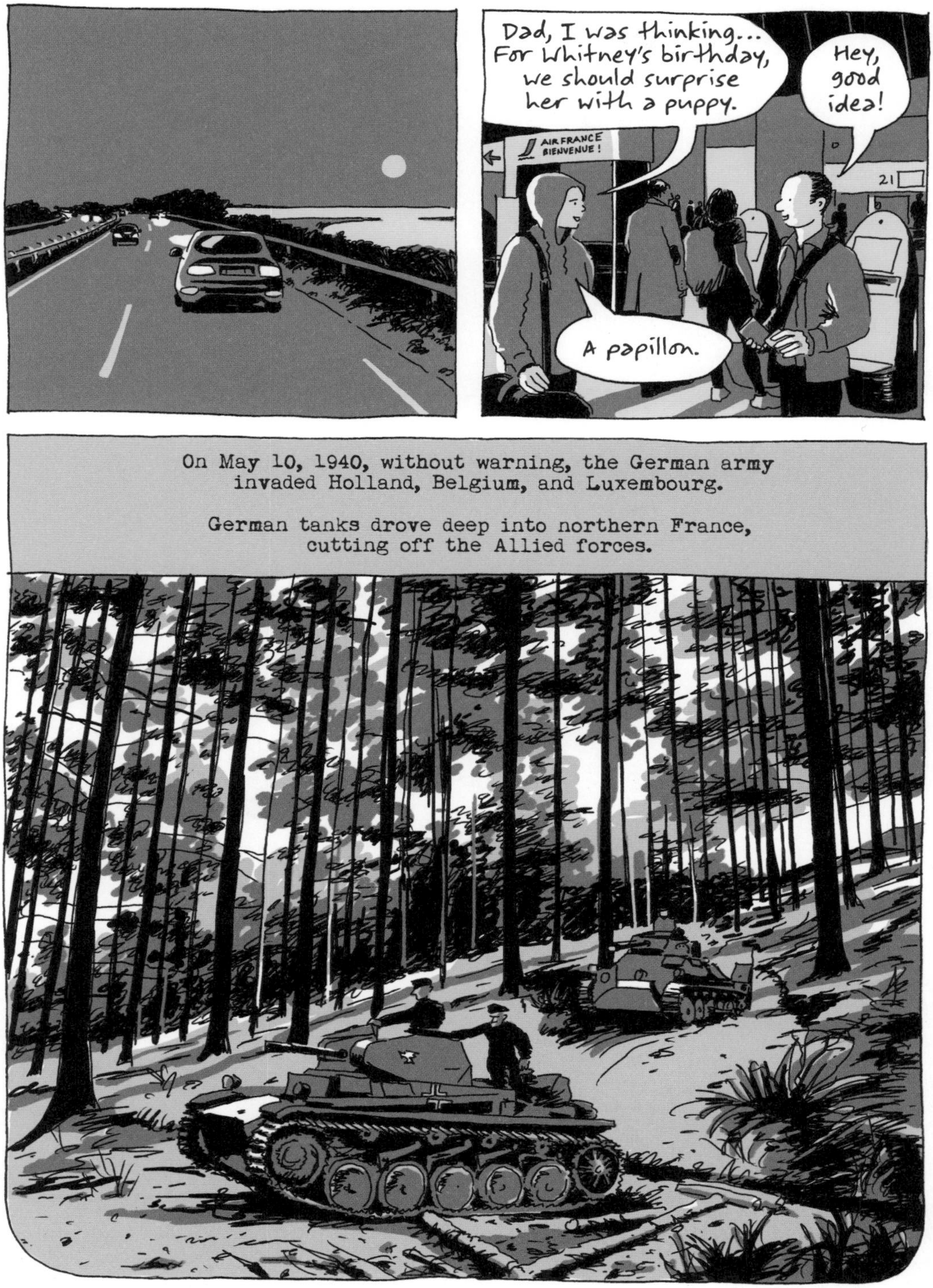
Dad, I was thinking... For Whitney's birthday, we should surprise her with a puppy.
Hey, good idea!
AIR FRANCE BIENVENUE !
21
A papillon.
On May 10, 1940, without warning, the German army invaded Holland, Belgium, and Luxembourg.
German tanks drove deep into northern France, cutting off the Allied forces.

Lisa and Franzi had no warning, either.

I in Cuba, and Hedy in New York, went through days of agony, studying the map and hoping they had been able to escape in time.

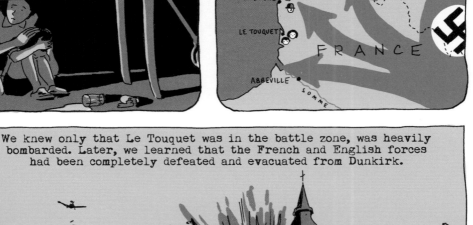

DUNKIRK
CALAIS
BELGIUM
BOULOGNE
LE TOUQUET
FRANCE
ABBEVILLE
SOMME

We knew only that Le Touquet was in the battle zone, was heavily bombarded. Later, we learned that the French and English forces had been completely defeated and evacuated from Dunkirk.

Lisa and Franzi were, of course, unable to write to us.

For months afterward, we did not know whether they were still alive.

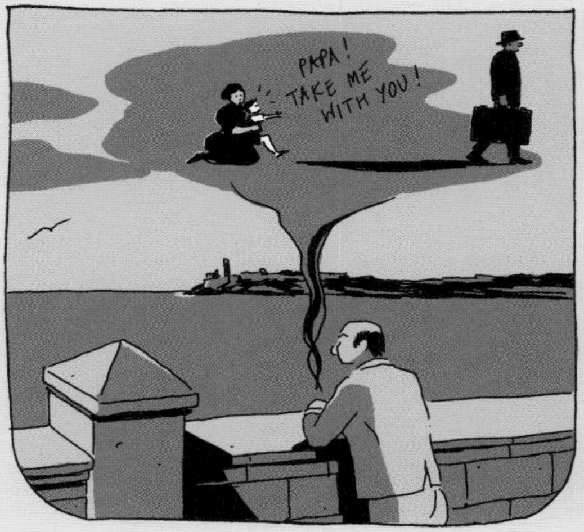
PAPA! TAKE ME WITH YOU!

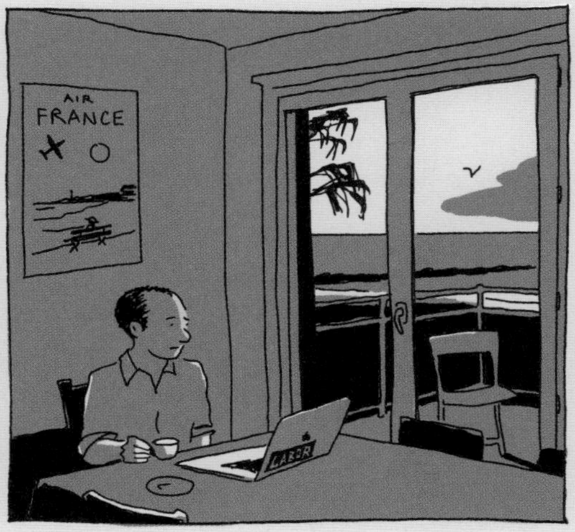
AIR FRANCE

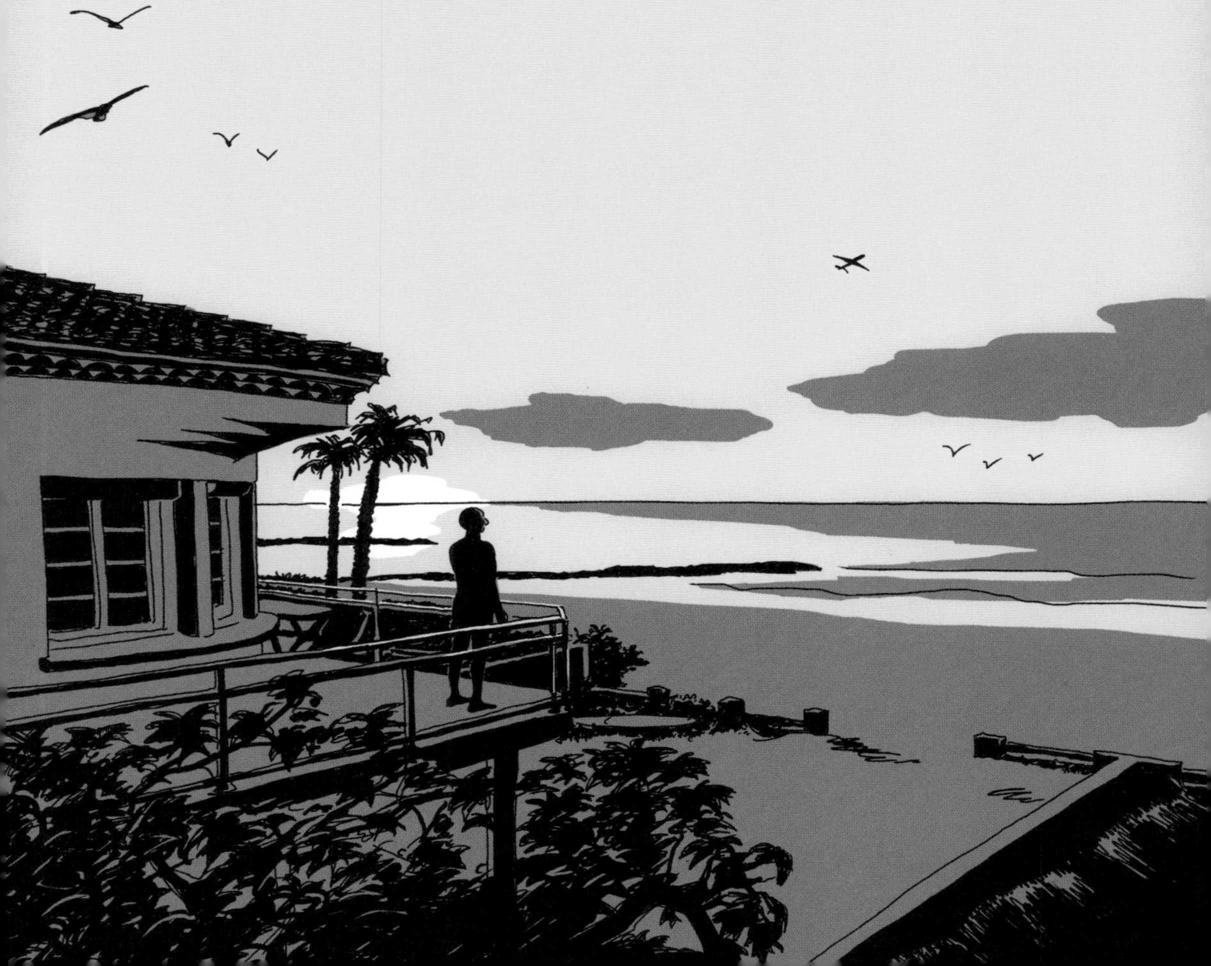

Chapter 3

Reuniting

Hedy, Johanna, and Adolf Mechner
Havana, October 1940

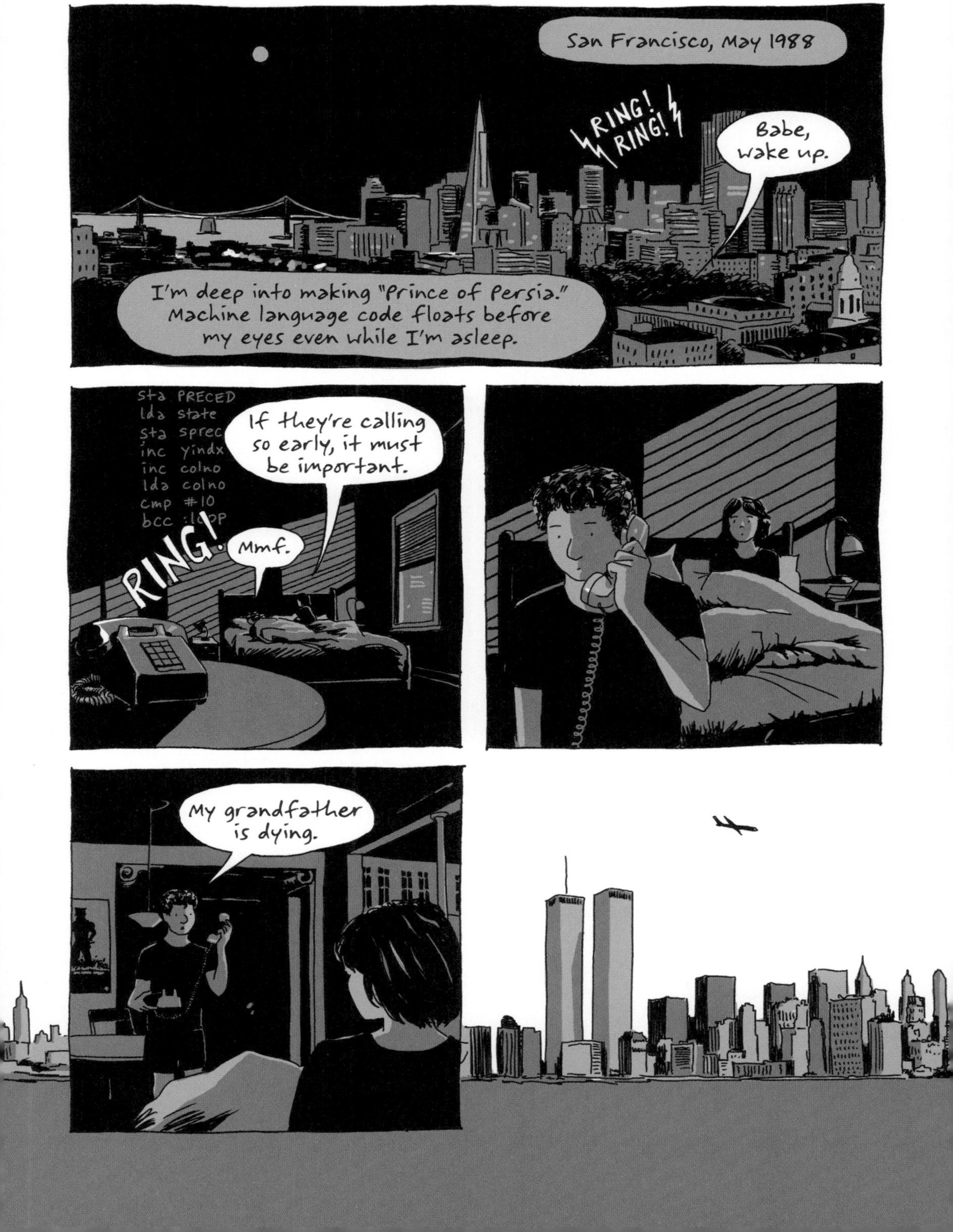
San Francisco, May 1988
RING! RING!
Babe, wake up.
I'm deep into making "Prince of Persia." Machine language code floats before my eyes even while I'm asleep.
sta PRECED
lda state
sta sprec
inc yindx
inc colno
lda colno
cmp #10
bcc
RING!
Mmf.
If they're calling so early, it must be important.
My grandfather is dying.

Already Dead

My dad played the funeral march from Beethoven's "Eroica" symphony at Papi's memorial, as he'd wanted.

I stayed in New York a few days. It wasn't so often that the whole family got together.

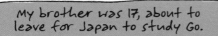

My brother was 17, about to leave for Japan to study Go.

I wish I'd known Papi better before he got senile.

You were too young.

Neither of you knew him when he was his full self.

What was that joke he always told? A man goes to the doctor to get his cane shortened...

"Okay, so we will cut off three inches here from the bottom..."

"No, Doctor! The bottom is fine. It is the top that is too high!"

Ha ha

Ha

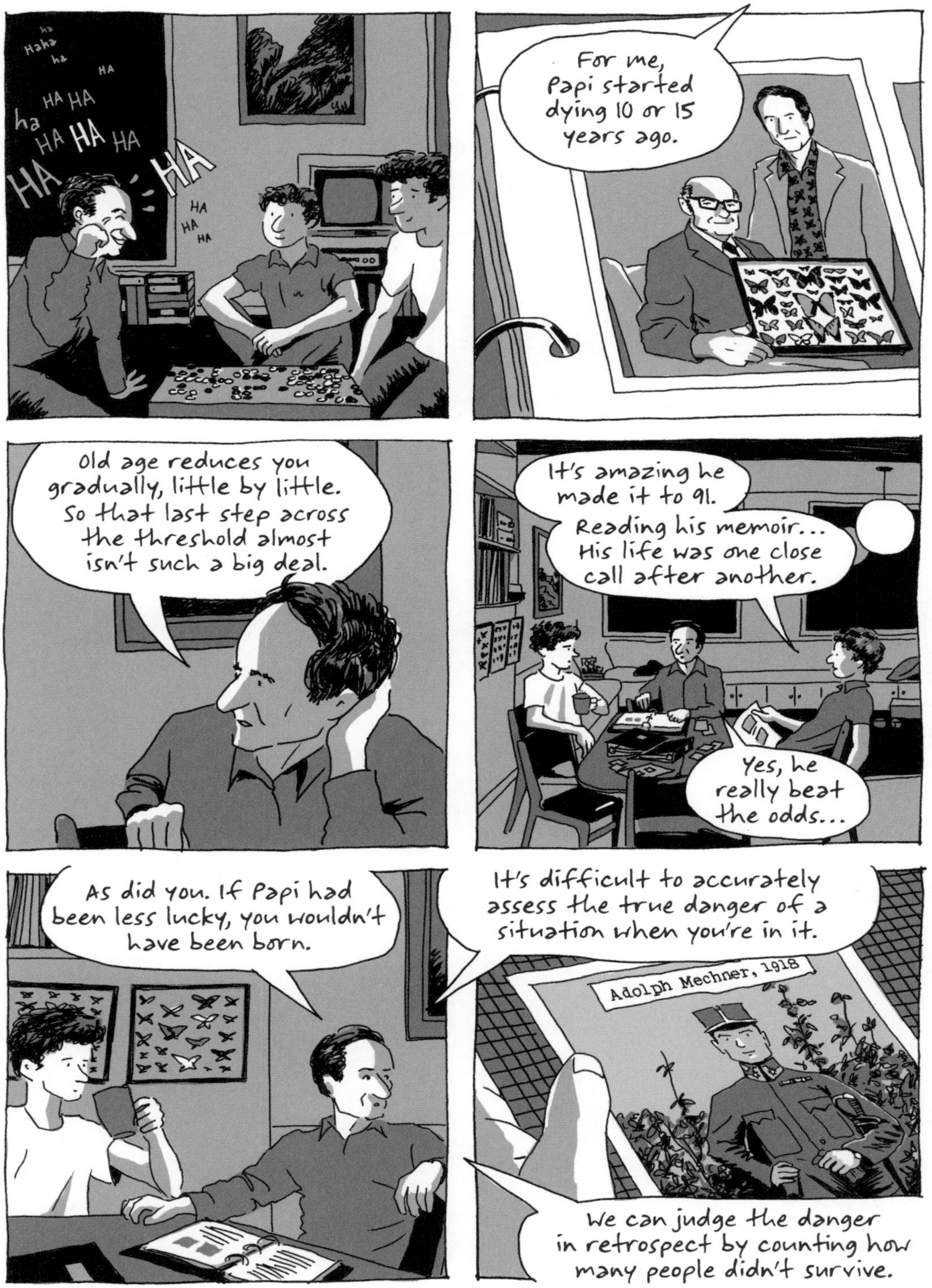
ha
Haha
ha
HA
ha HA HA
HA HA HA
HA HA
HA
HA
HA
HA
For me, Papi started dying 10 or 15 years ago.
Old age reduces you gradually, little by little. So that last step across the threshold almost isn't such a big deal.
It's amazing he made it to 91.
Reading his memoir... His life was one close call after another.
Yes, he really beat the odds...
As did you. If Papi had been less lucky, you wouldn't have been born.
It's difficult to accurately assess the true danger of a situation when you're in it.
Adolph Mechner, 1918
We can judge the danger in retrospect by counting how many people didn't survive.

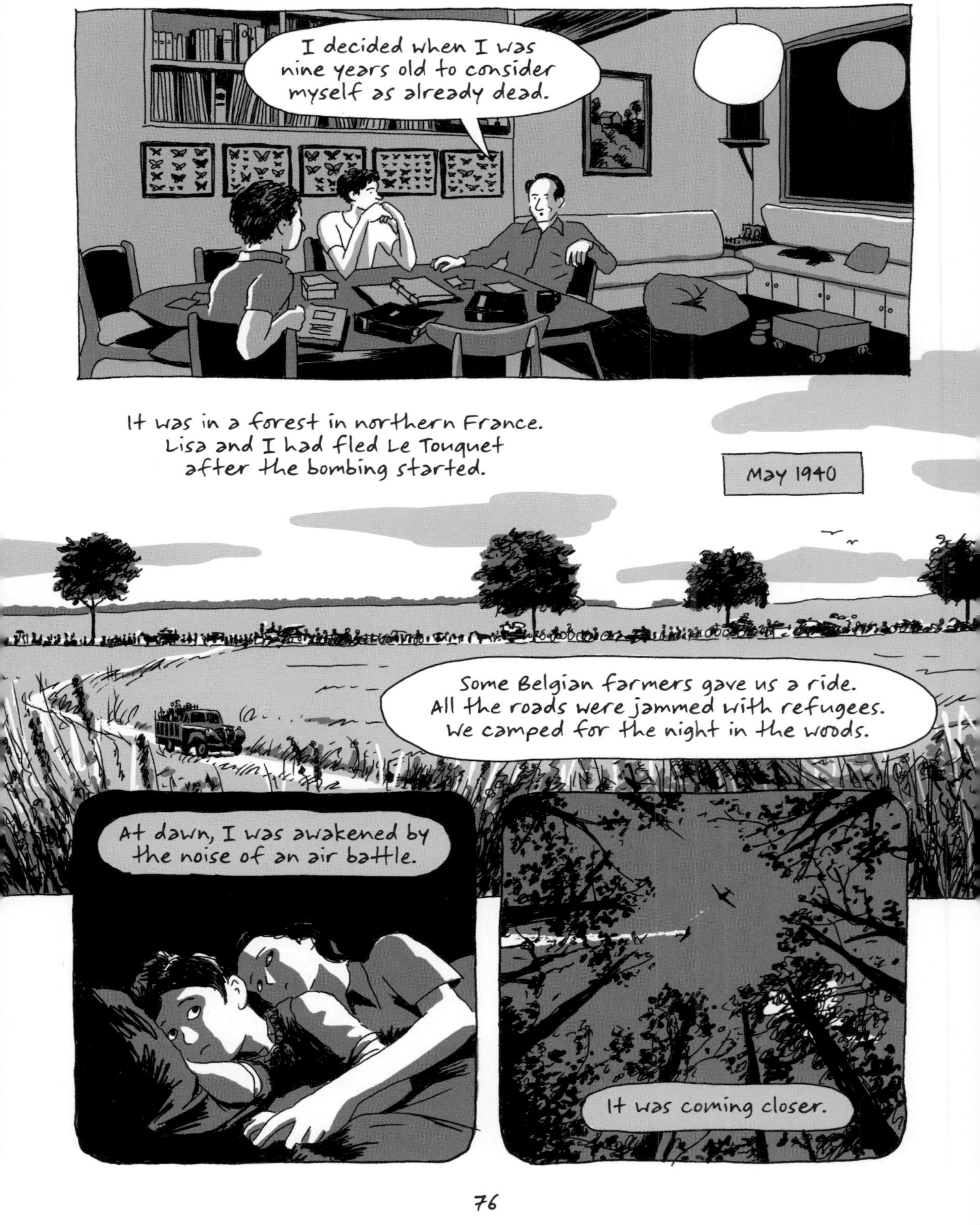

I decided when I was nine years old to consider myself as already dead.
It was in a forest in northern France. Lisa and I had fled Le Touquet after the bombing started.
May 1940
Some Belgian farmers gave us a ride. All the roads were jammed with refugees. We camped for the night in the woods.
At dawn, I was awakened by the noise of an air battle.
It was coming closer.

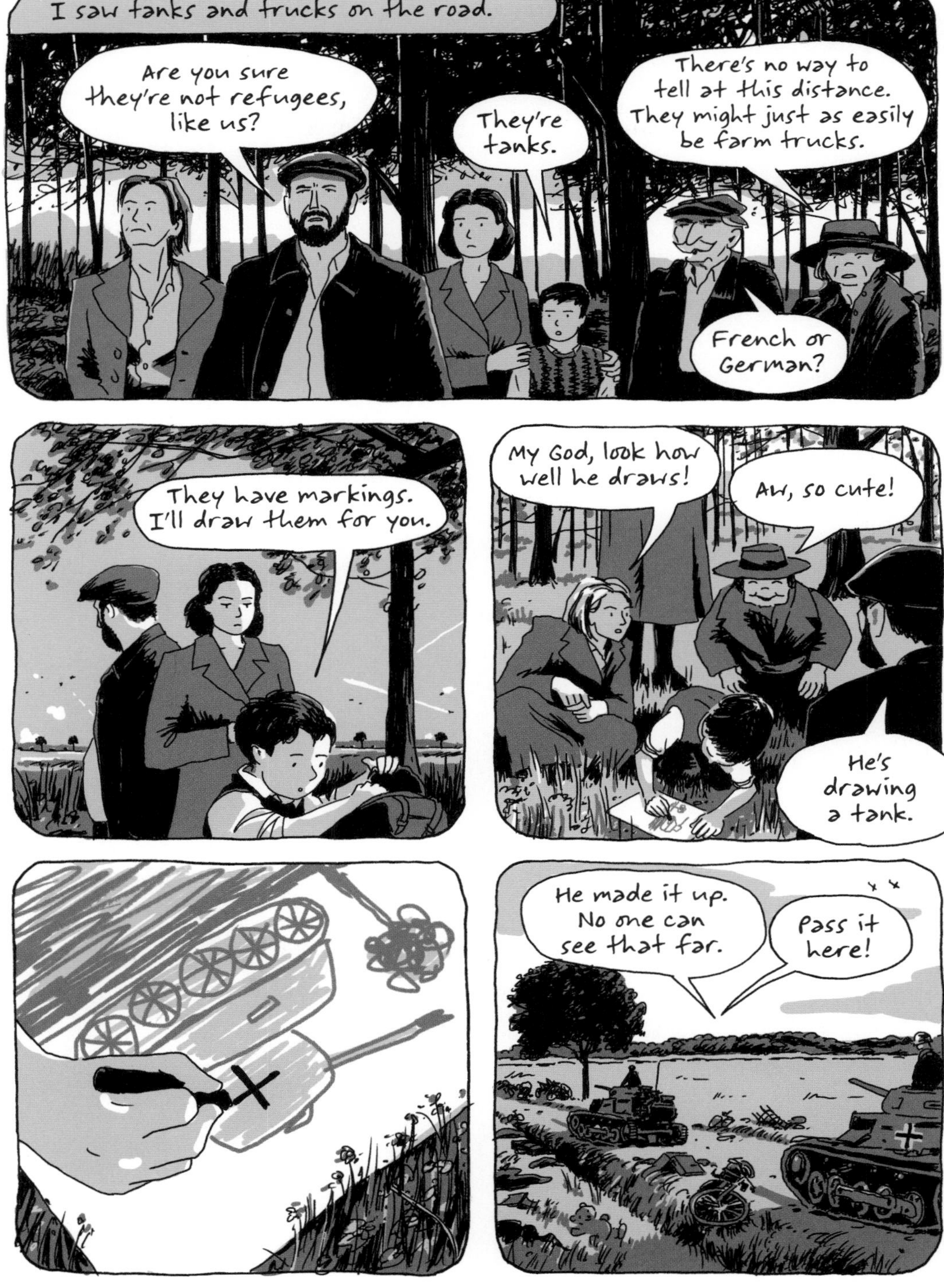
I saw tanks and trucks on the road.
Are you sure they're not refugees, like us?
They're tanks.
There's no way to tell at this distance. They might just as easily be farm trucks.
French or German?
They have markings. I'll draw them for you.
My God, look how well he draws!
Aw, so cute!
He's drawing a tank.
He made it up. No one can see that far.
Pass it here!

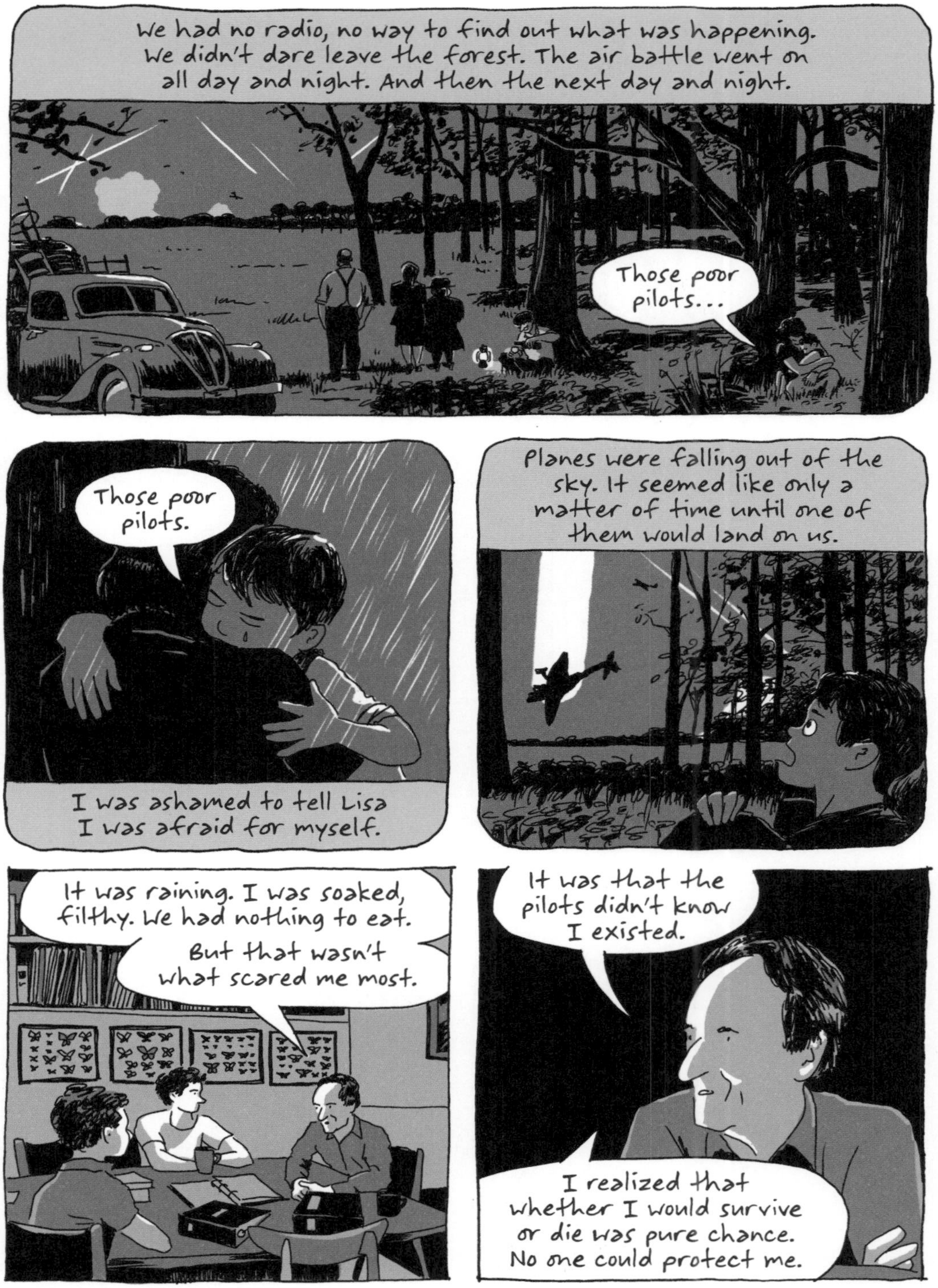
We had no radio, no way to find out what was happening. We didn't dare leave the forest. The air battle went on all day and night. And then the next day and night.
Those poor pilots...
Those poor pilots.
I was ashamed to tell Lisa I was afraid for myself.
Planes were falling out of the sky. It seemed like only a matter of time until one of them would land on us.
It was raining. I was soaked, filthy. We had nothing to eat.
But that wasn't what scared me most.
It was that the pilots didn't know I existed.
I realized that whether I would survive or die was pure chance. No one could protect me.

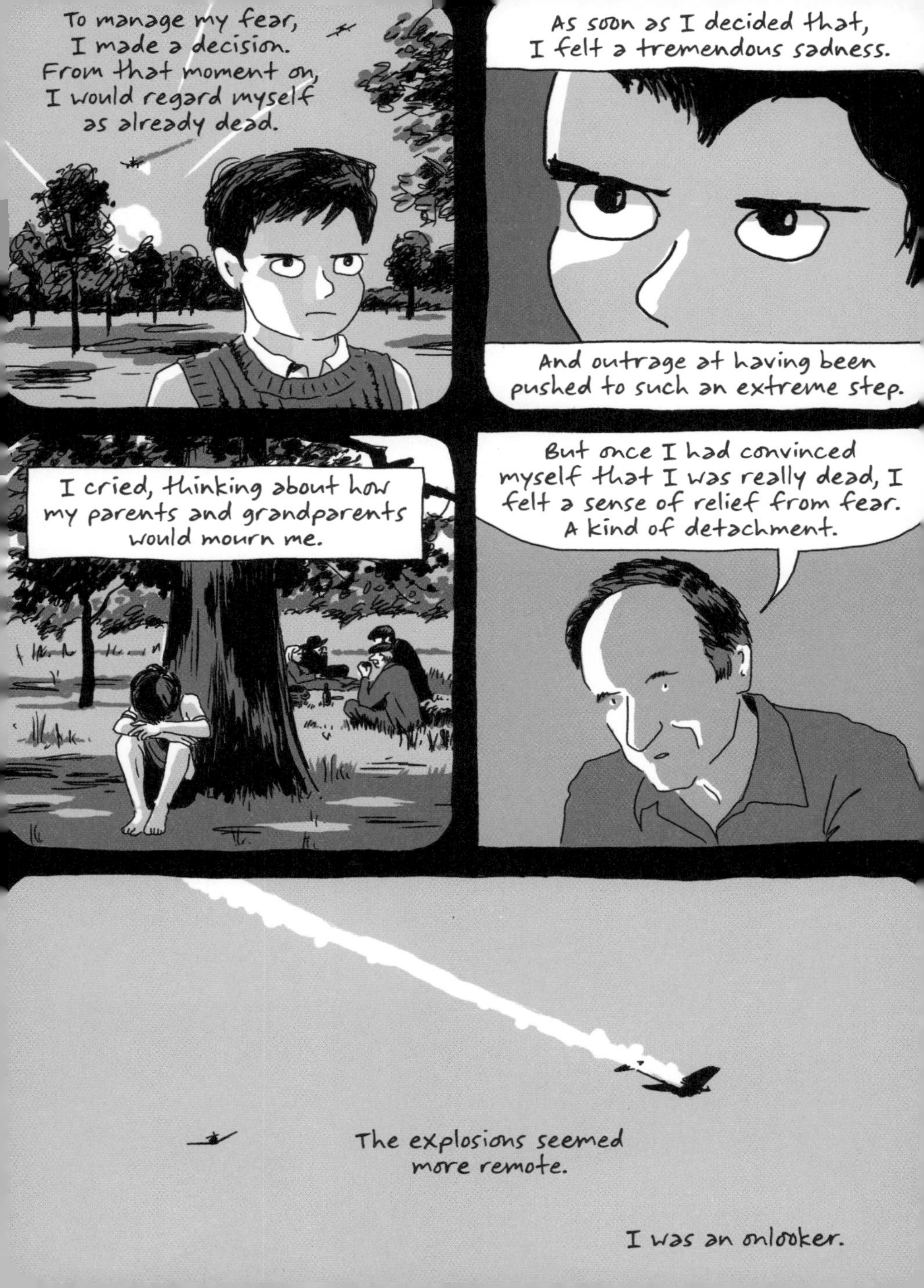
To manage my fear, I made a decision. From that moment on, I would regard myself as already dead.
As soon as I decided that, I felt a tremendous sadness.
And outrage at having been pushed to such an extreme step.
I cried, thinking about how my parents and grandparents would mourn me.
But once I had convinced myself that I was really dead, I felt a sense of relief from fear. A kind of detachment.
The explosions seemed more remote.
I was an onlooker.

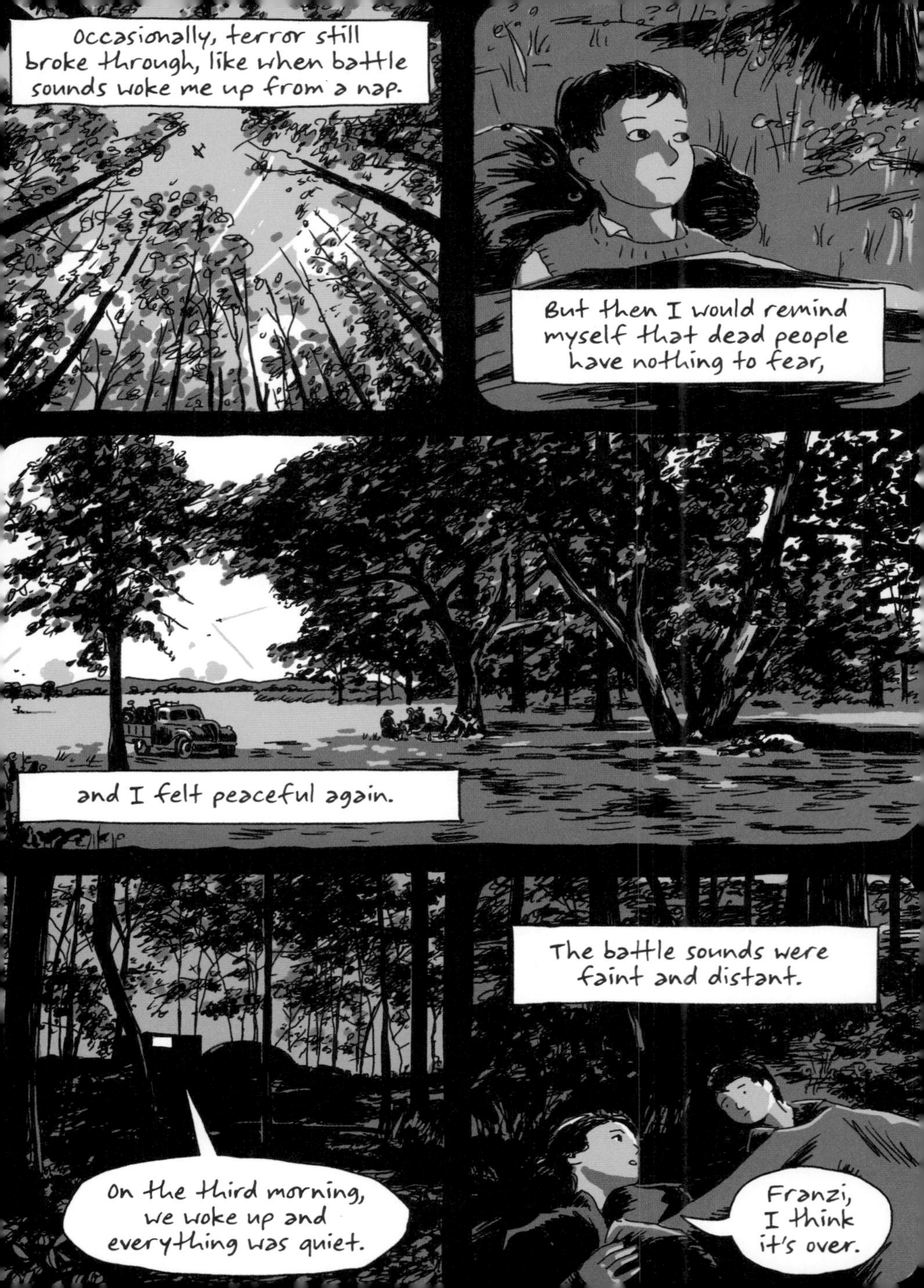
Occasionally, terror still broke through, like when battle sounds woke me up from a nap.
But then I would remind myself that dead people have nothing to fear,
and I felt peaceful again.
On the third morning, we woke up and everything was quiet.
The battle sounds were faint and distant.
Franzi, I think it's over.

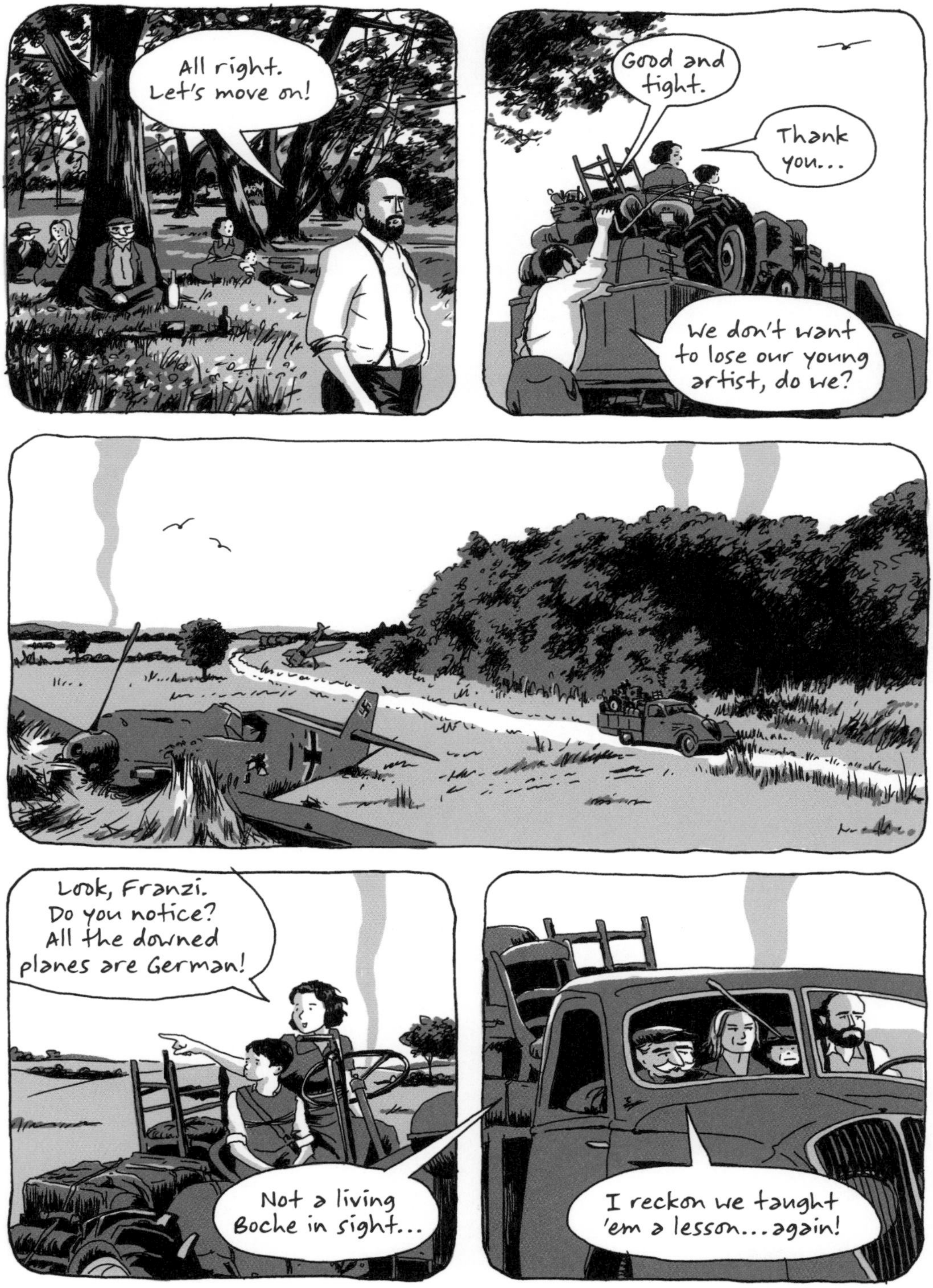
All right. Let's move on!
Good and tight.
Thank you...
We don't want to lose our young artist, do we?
Look, Franzi. Do you notice? All the downed planes are German!
Not a living Boche in sight...
I reckon we taught 'em a lesson... again!

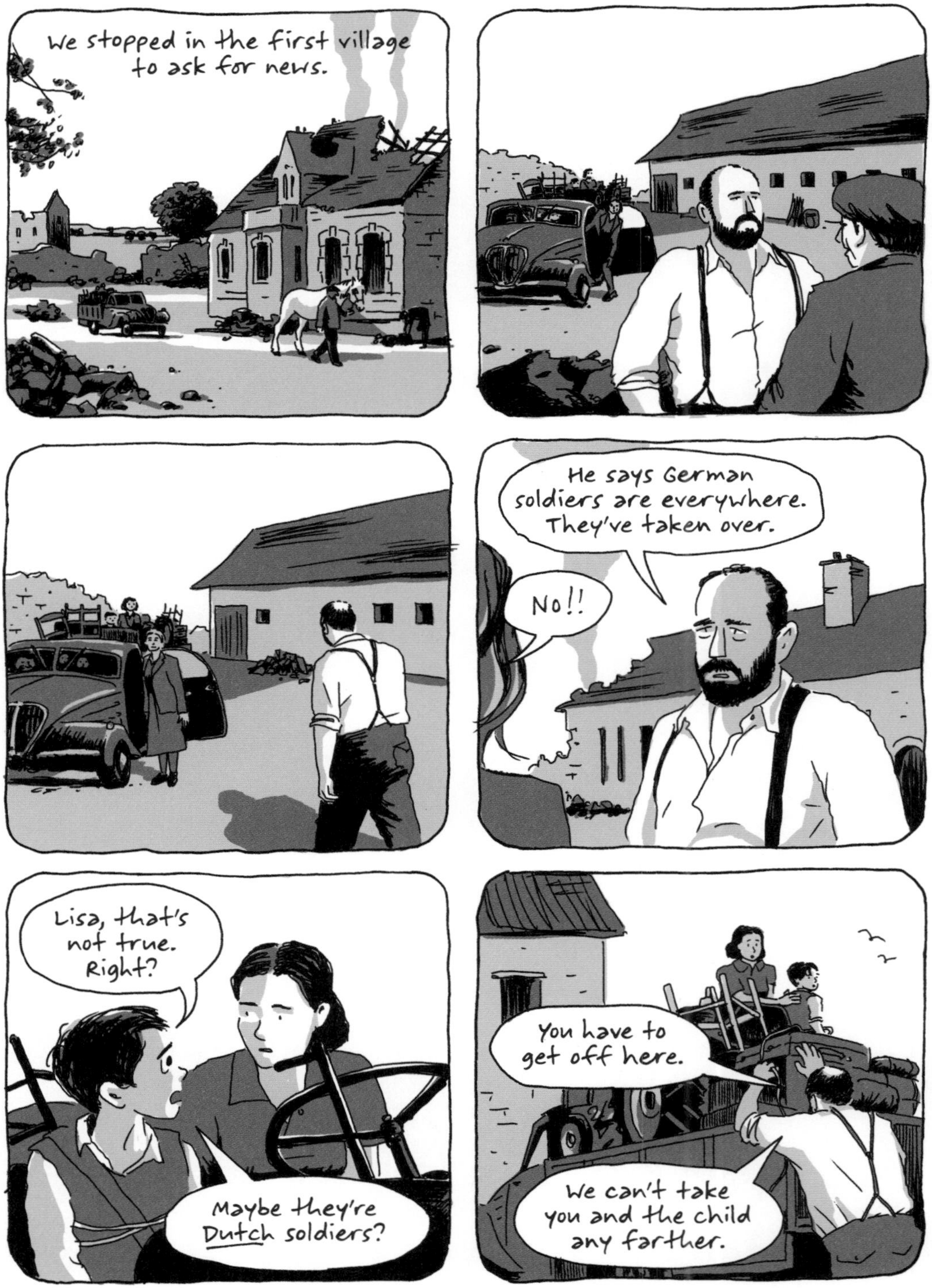
We stopped in the first village to ask for news.
He says German soldiers are everywhere. They've taken over.
No!!
Lisa, that's not true. Right?
Maybe they're Dutch soldiers?
You have to get off here.
We can't take you and the child any farther.

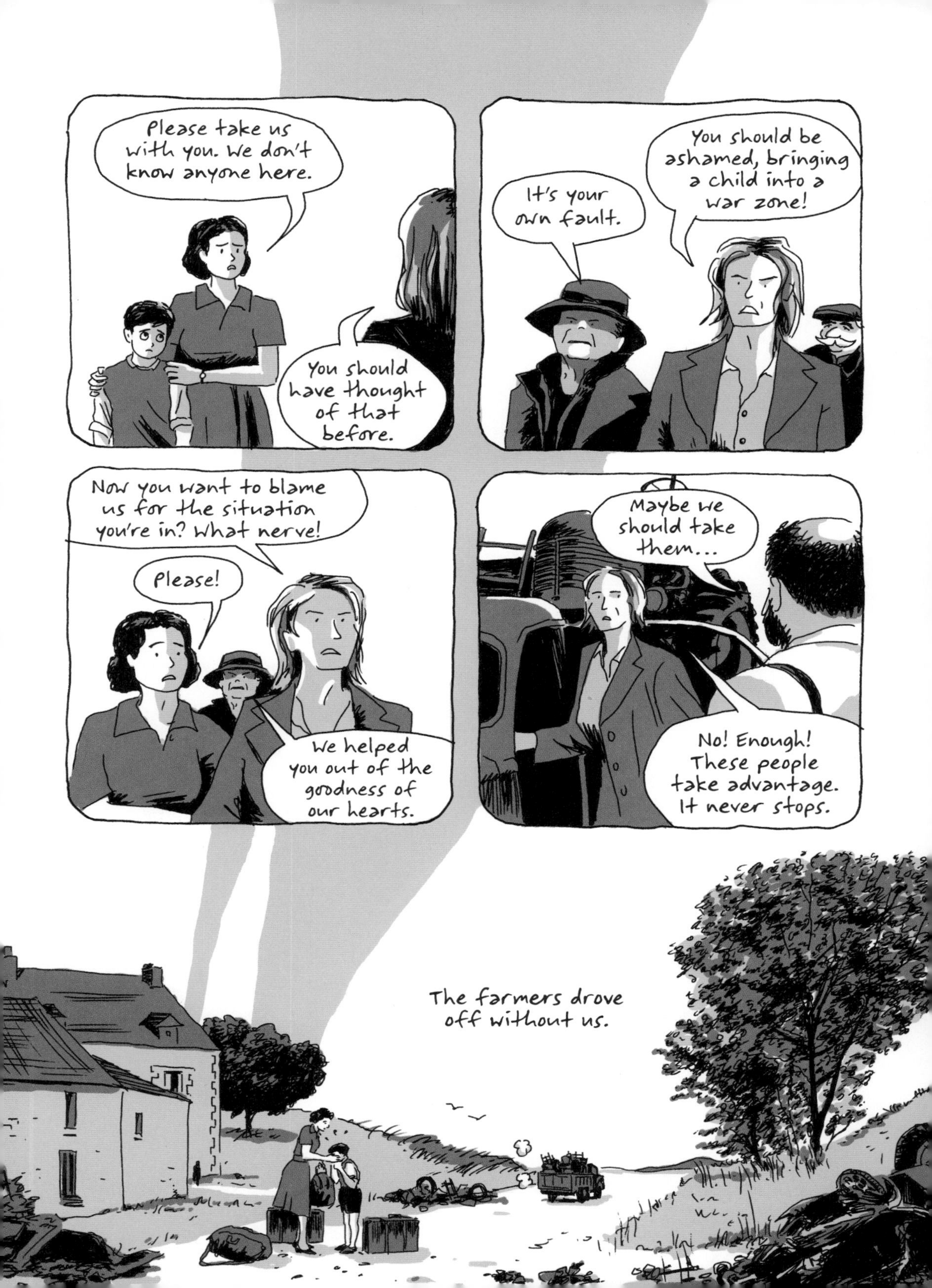
Please take us with you. We don't know anyone here.
You should have thought of that before.
It's your own fault.
You should be ashamed, bringing a child into a war zone!
Now you want to blame us for the situation you're in? What nerve!
Please!
We helped you out of the goodness of our hearts.
Maybe we should take them...
No! Enough! These people take advantage. It never stops.
The farmers drove off without us.

Soldiers

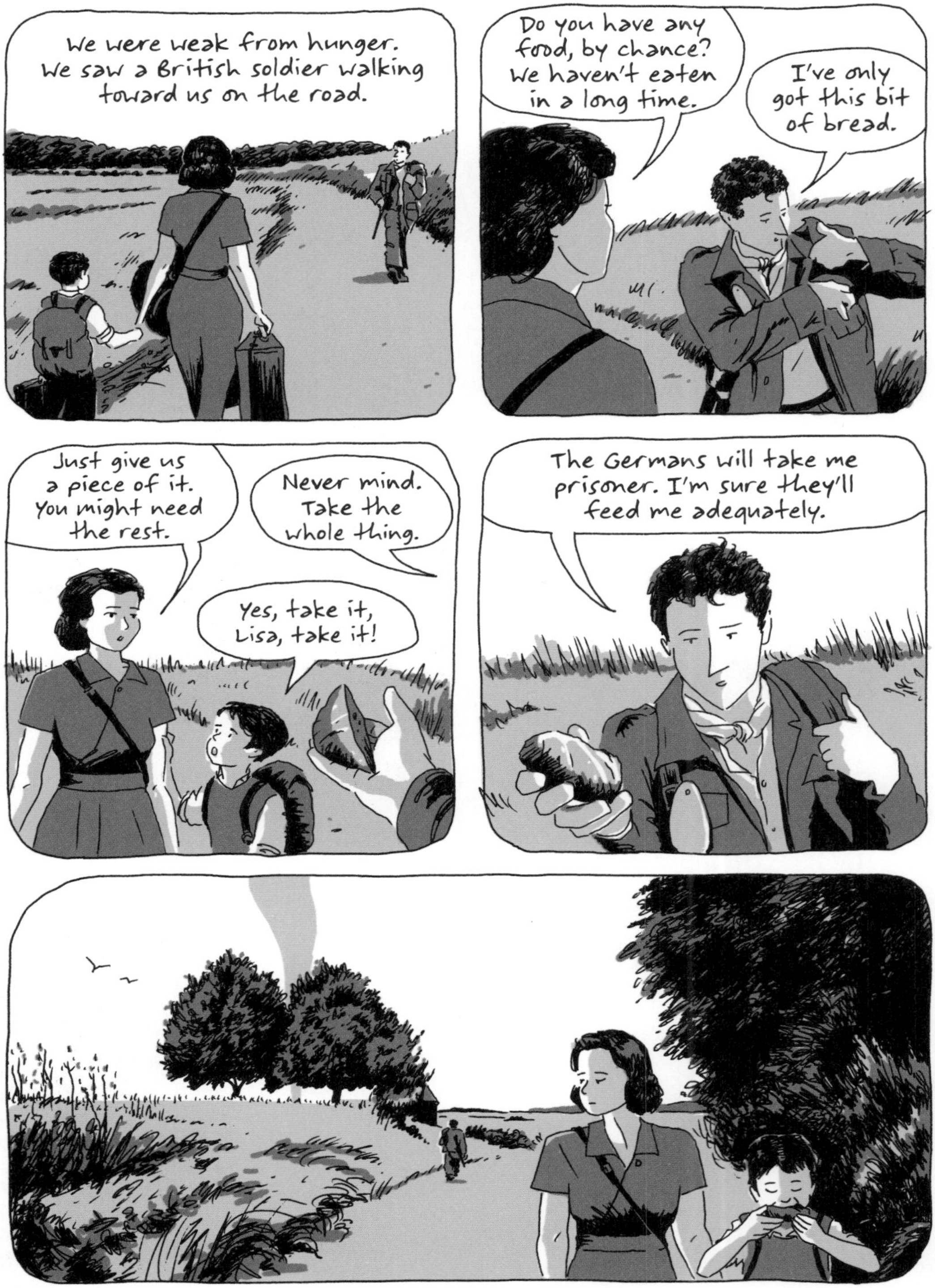

We were weak from hunger. We saw a British soldier walking toward us on the road.
Do you have any food, by chance? We haven't eaten in a long time.
I've only got this bit of bread.
Just give us a piece of it. You might need the rest.
Never mind. Take the whole thing.
Yes, take it, Lisa, take it!
The Germans will take me prisoner. I'm sure they'll feed me adequately.

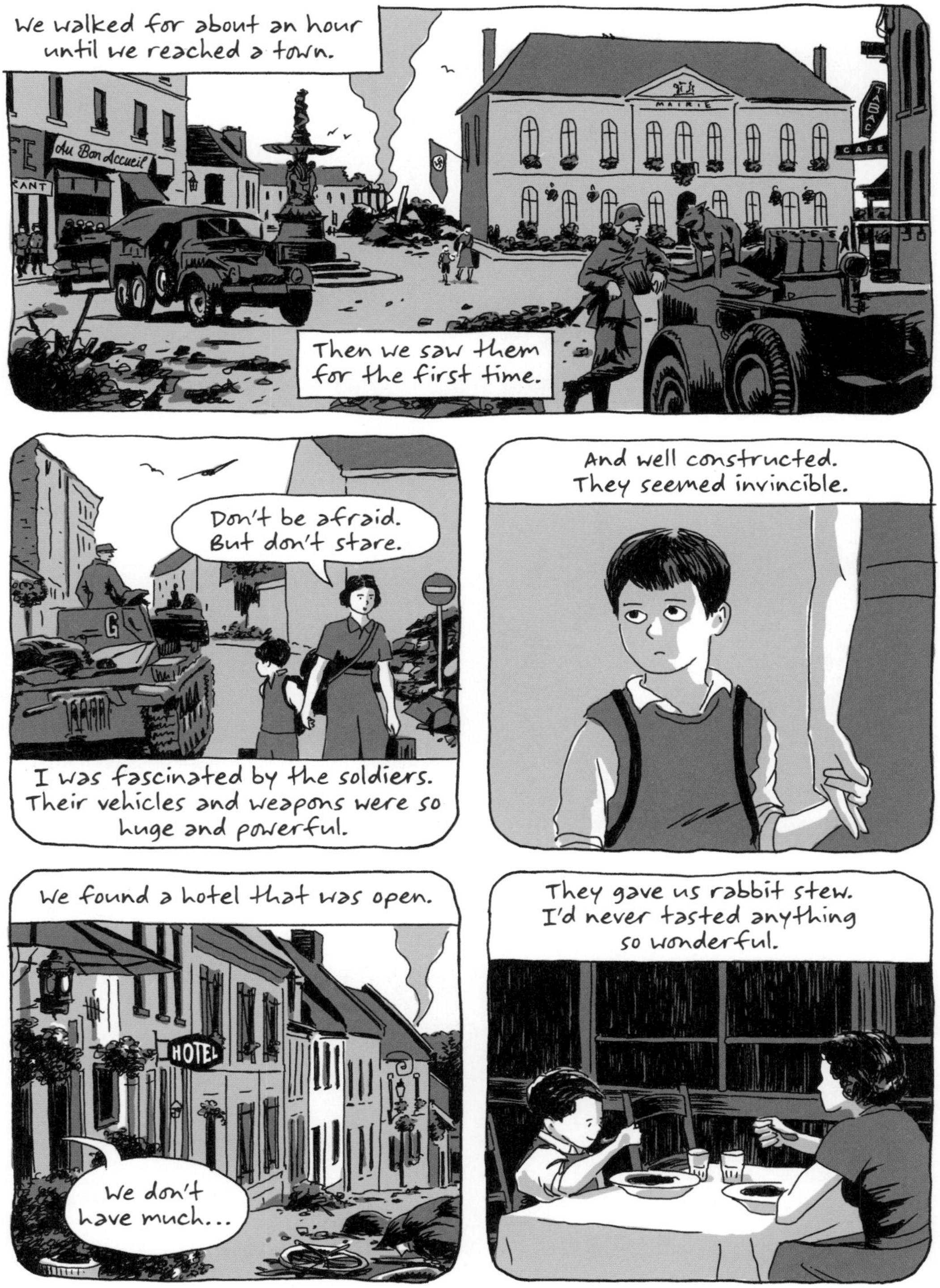
We walked for about an hour until we reached a town.
Au Bon Accueil
MAIRIE
TABAC
CAFE
Then we saw them for the first time.
Don't be afraid. But don't stare.
I was fascinated by the soldiers. Their vehicles and weapons were so huge and powerful.
And well constructed. They seemed invincible.
We found a hotel that was open.
HOTEL
We don't have much...
They gave us rabbit stew. I'd never tasted anything so wonderful.

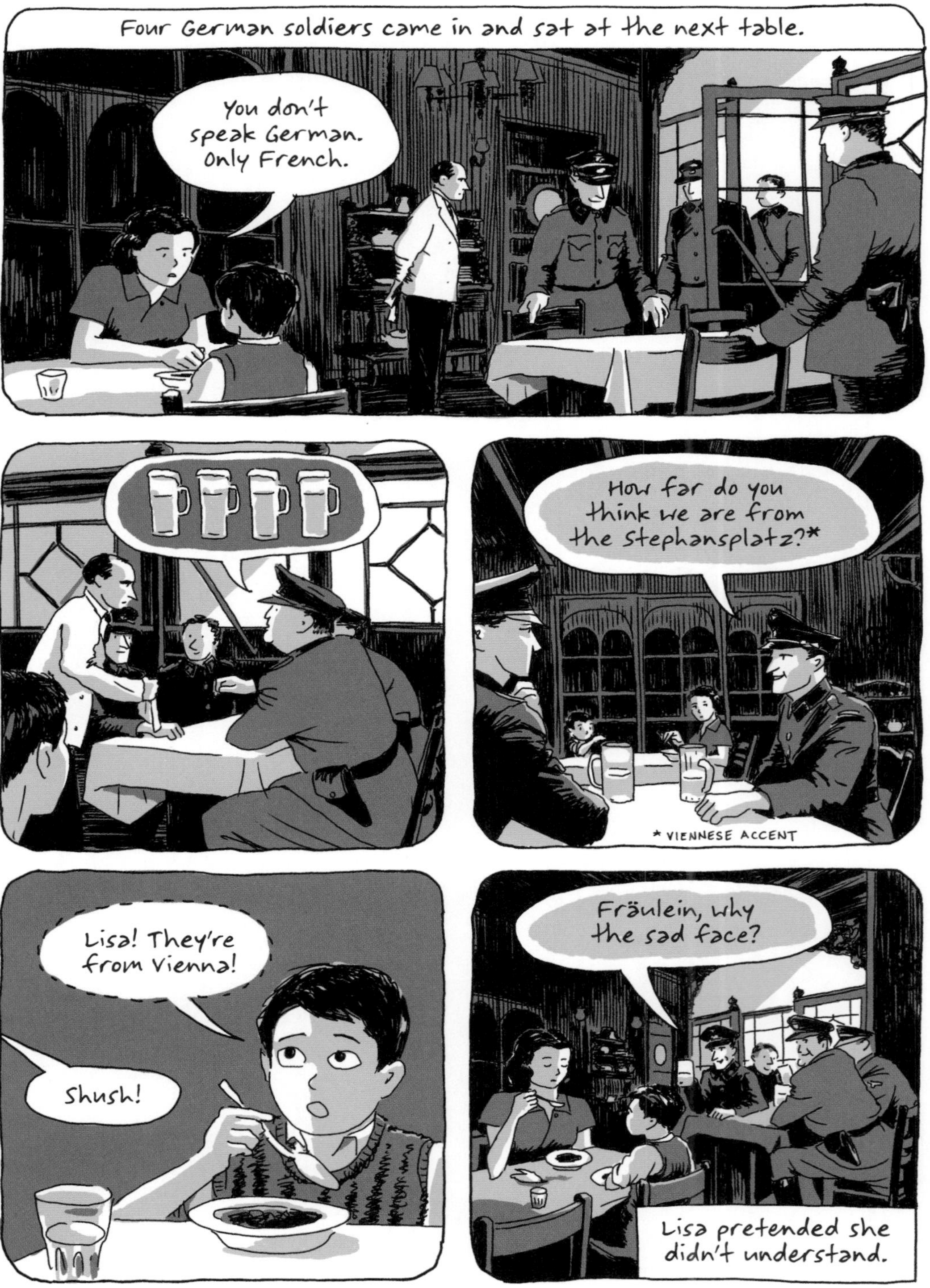
Four German soldiers came in and sat at the next table.
You don't speak German. Only French.
How far do you think we are from the Stephansplatz?*
* VIENNESE ACCENT
Lisa! They're from Vienna!
Shush!
Fräulein, why the sad face?
Lisa pretended she didn't understand.

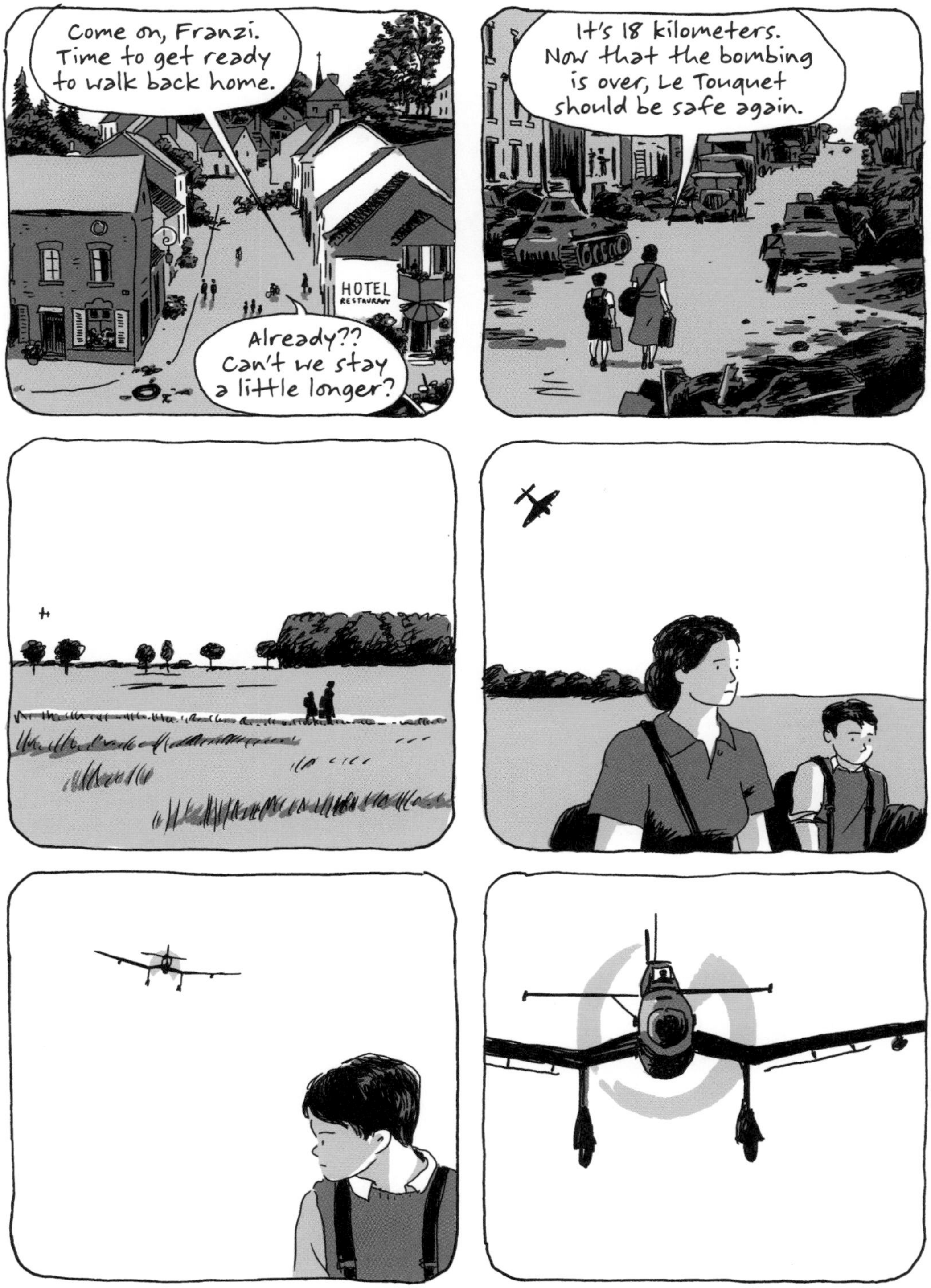
Come on, Franzi. Time to get ready to walk back home.
HOTEL
RESTAURANT
Already?? Can't we stay a little longer?
It's 18 kilometers. Now that the bombing is over, Le Touquet should be safe again.

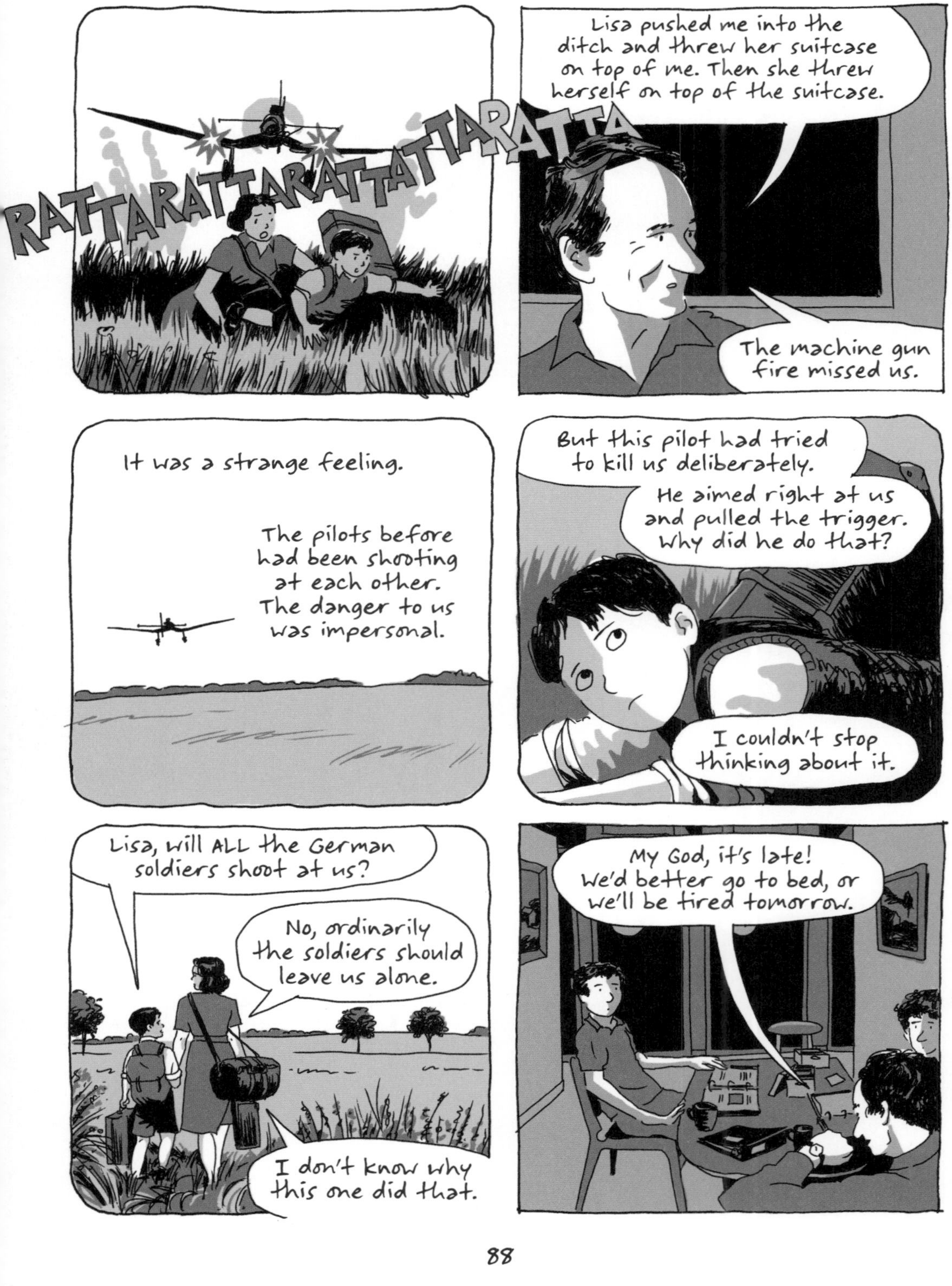
RATTARATTARATTATTARATTA
Lisa pushed me into the ditch and threw her suitcase on top of me. Then she threw herself on top of the suitcase.
The machine gun fire missed us.
It was a strange feeling.
The pilots before had been shooting at each other. The danger to us was impersonal.
But this pilot had tried to kill us deliberately.
He aimed right at us and pulled the trigger. Why did he do that?
I couldn't stop thinking about it.
Lisa, will ALL the German soldiers shoot at us?
No, ordinarily the soldiers should leave us alone.
I don't know why this one did that.
My God, it's late! We'd better go to bed, or we'll be tired tomorrow.

Archives

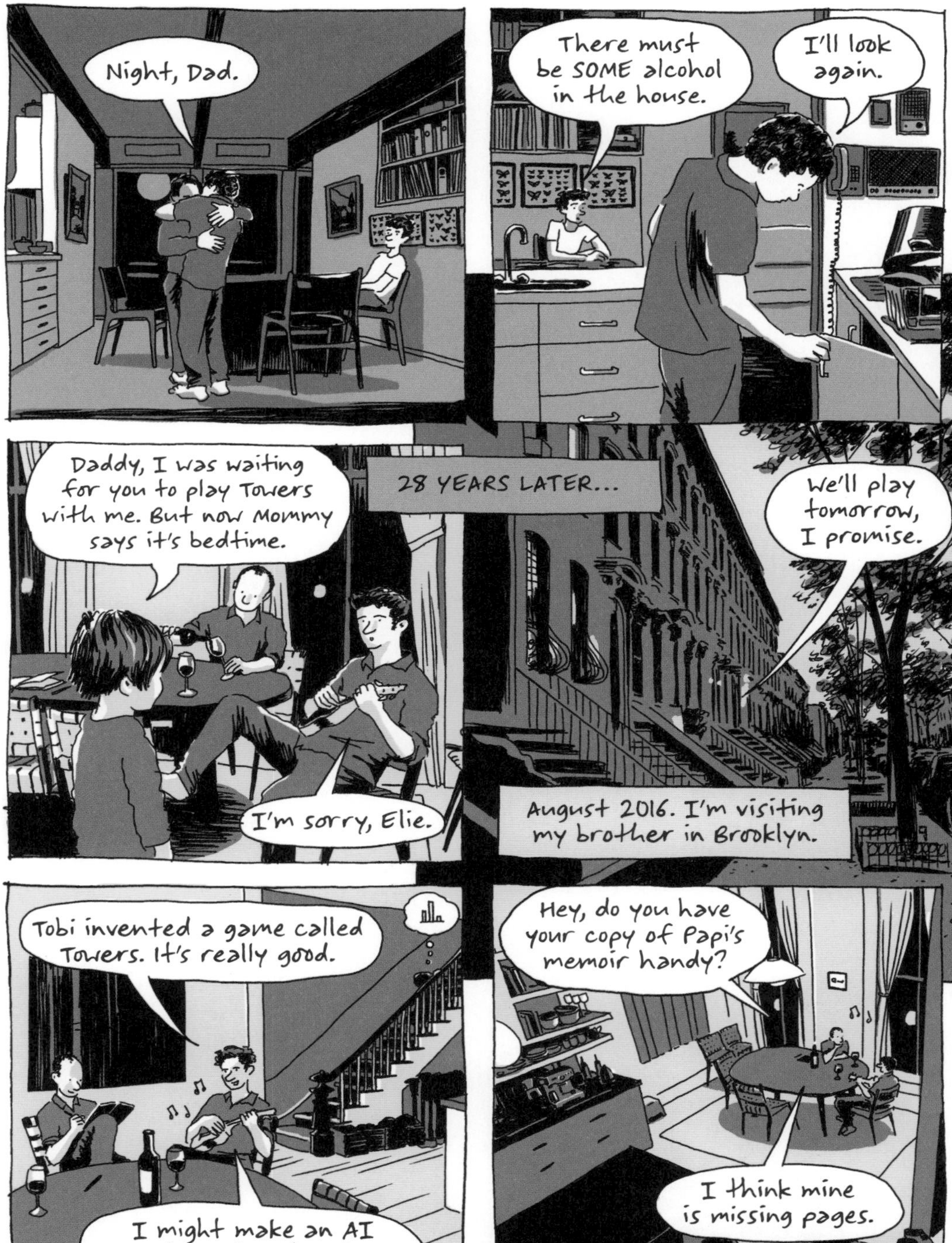
Night, Dad.
There must be SOME alcohol in the house.
I'll look again.
Daddy, I was waiting for you to play Towers with me. But now Mommy says it's bedtime.
I'm sorry, Elie.
28 YEARS LATER...
We'll play tomorrow, I promise.
August 2016. I'm visiting my brother in Brooklyn.
Tobi invented a game called Towers. It's really good.
I might make an AI agent to play it, using a Monte Carlo algorithm.
Hey, do you have your copy of Papi's memoir handy?
I think mine is missing pages.

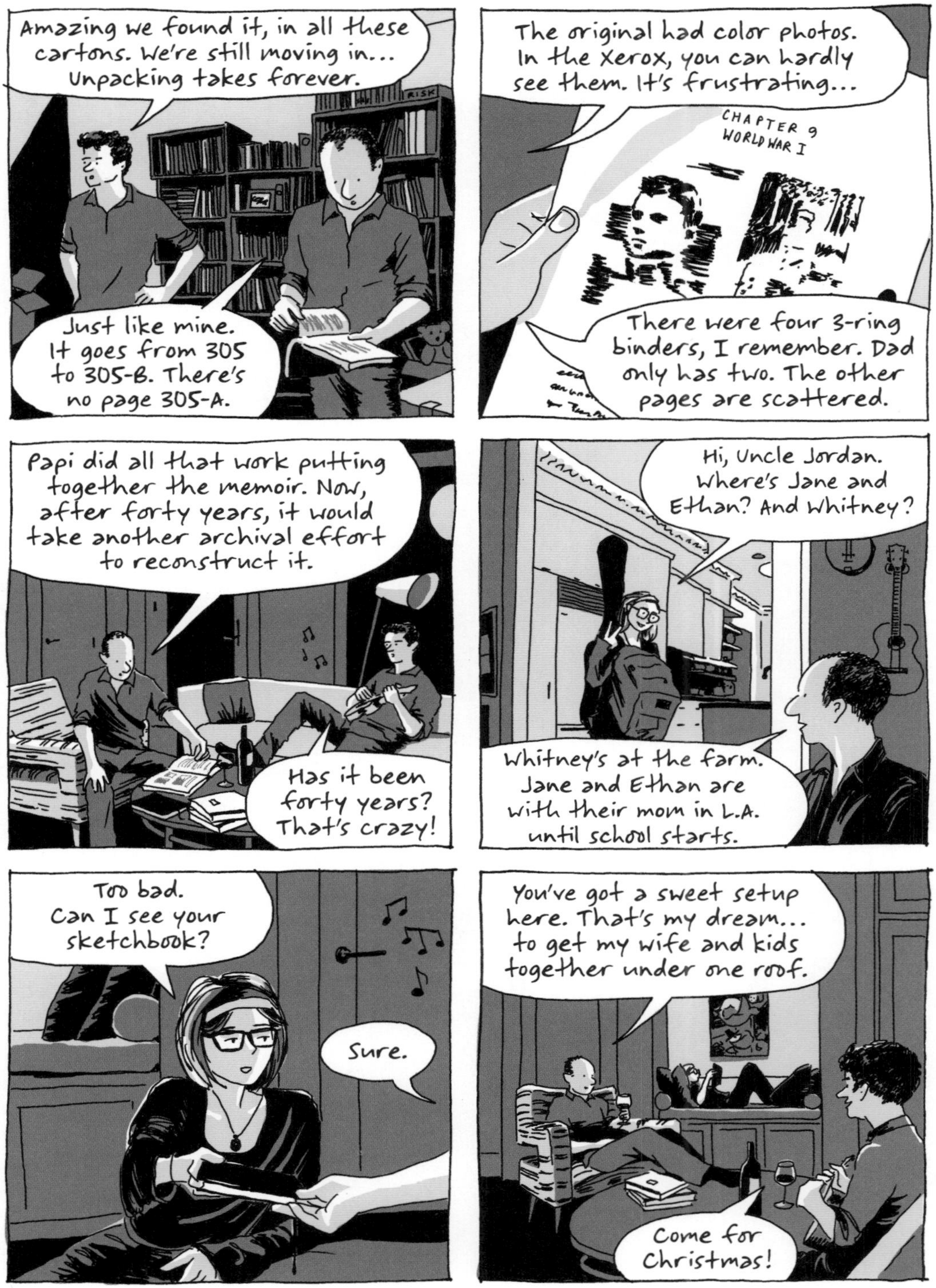
Amazing we found it, in all these cartons. We're still moving in... Unpacking takes forever.
RISK
Just like mine. It goes from 305 to 305-B. There's no page 305-A.
The original had color photos. In the Xerox, you can hardly see them. It's frustrating...
CHAPTER 9
WORLD WAR I
There were four 3-ring binders, I remember. Dad only has two. The other pages are scattered.
Papi did all that work putting together the memoir. Now, after forty years, it would take another archival effort to reconstruct it.
Has it been forty years? That's crazy!
Hi, Uncle Jordan. Where's Jane and Ethan? And Whitney?
Whitney's at the farm. Jane and Ethan are with their mom in L.A. until school starts.
Too bad. Can I see your sketchbook?
Sure.
You've got a sweet setup here. That's my dream... to get my wife and kids together under one roof.
Come for Christmas!

Moving Van

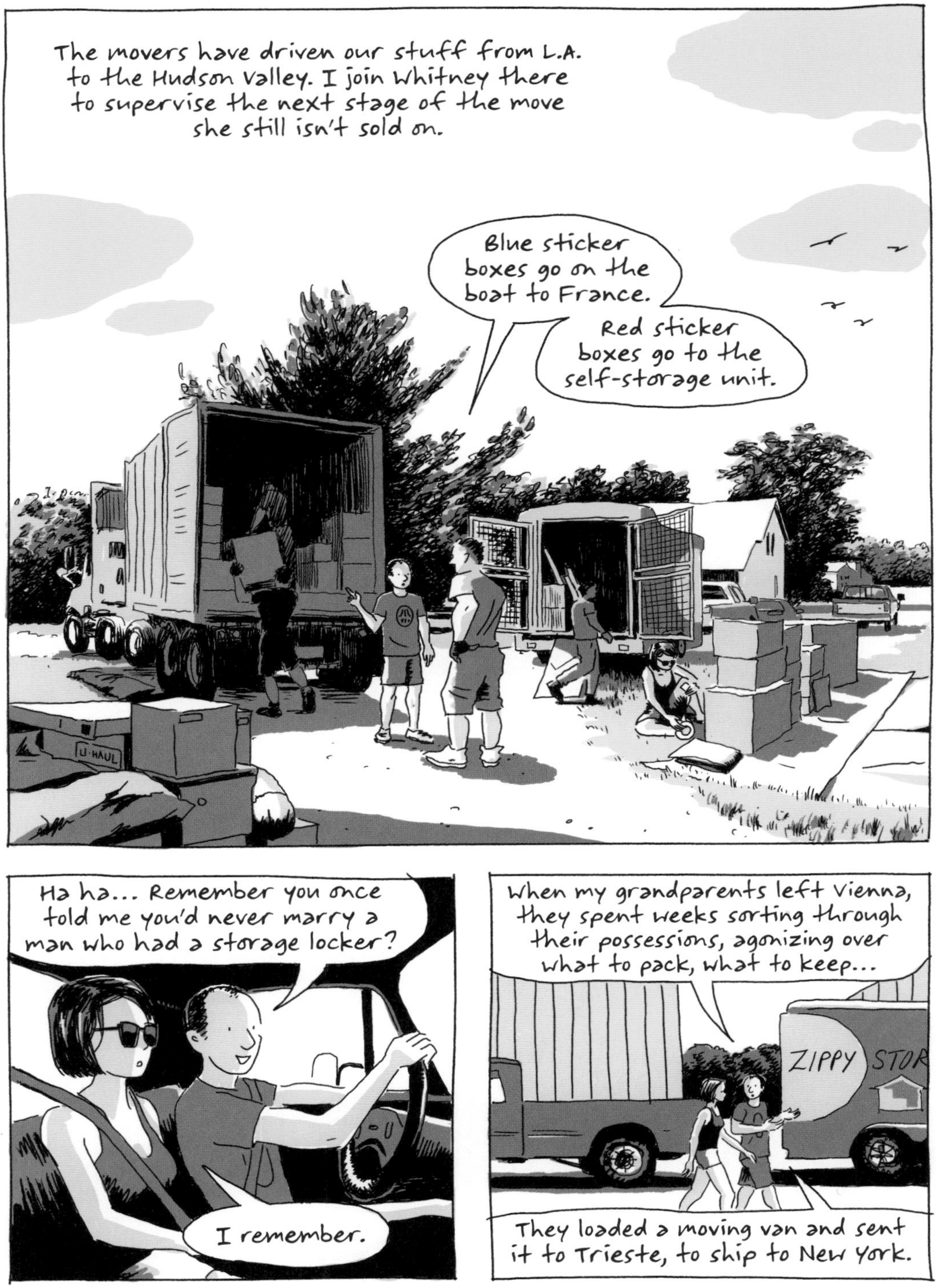

The movers have driven our stuff from L.A. to the Hudson Valley. I join Whitney there to supervise the next stage of the move she still isn't sold on.
Blue sticker boxes go on the boat to France.
Red sticker boxes go to the self-storage unit.
U-HAUL
Ha ha... Remember you once told me you'd never marry a man who had a storage locker?
I remember.
When my grandparents left Vienna, they spent weeks sorting through their possessions, agonizing over what to pack, what to keep...
ZIPPY
STOR
They loaded a moving van and sent it to Trieste, to ship to New York.

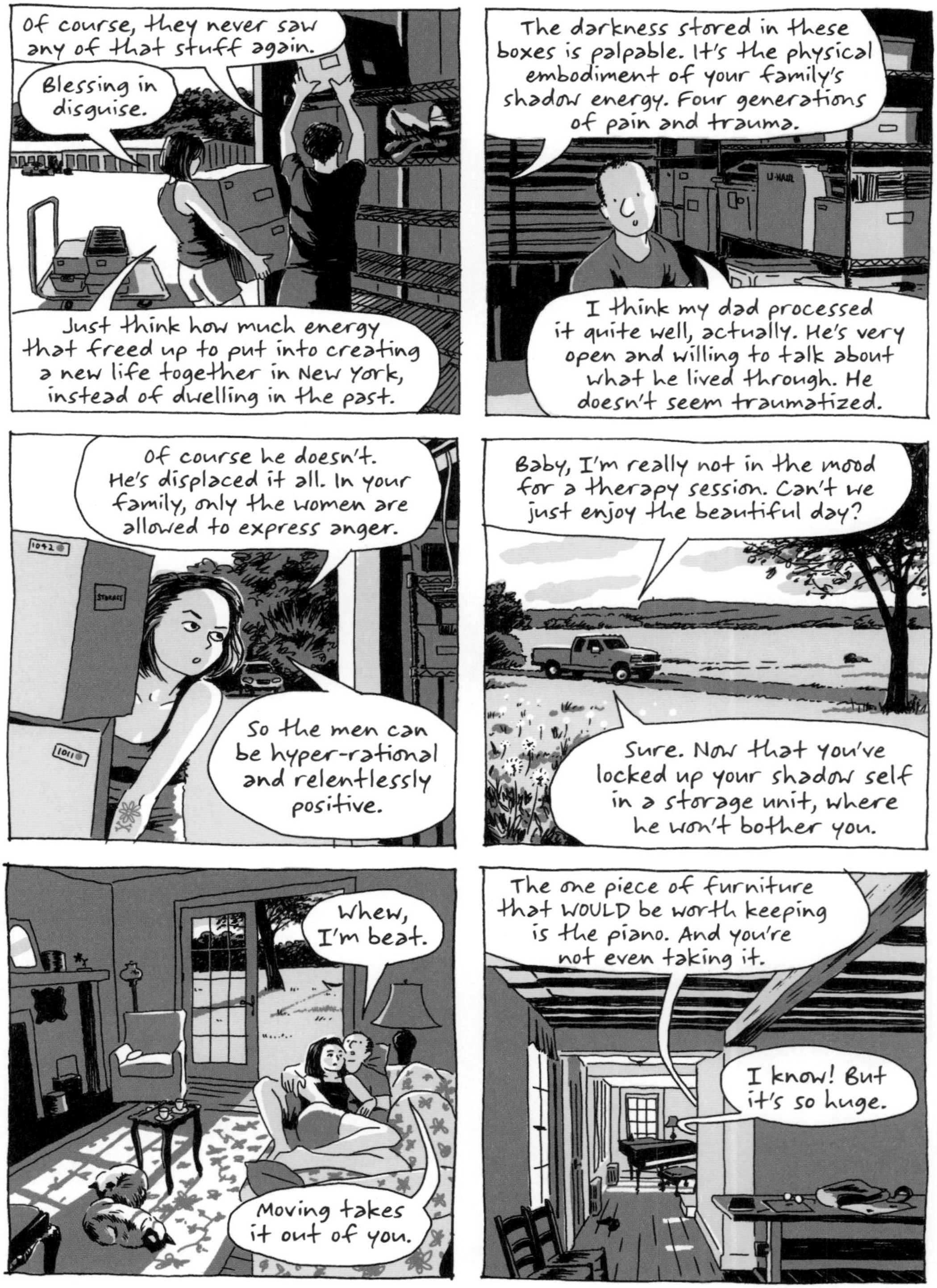
Of course, they never saw any of that stuff again.
Blessing in disguise.
Just think how much energy that freed up to put into creating a new life together in New York, instead of dwelling in the past.
The darkness stored in these boxes is palpable. It's the physical embodiment of your family's shadow energy. Four generations of pain and trauma.
I think my dad processed it quite well, actually. He's very open and willing to talk about what he lived through. He doesn't seem traumatized.
Of course he doesn't. He's displaced it all. In your family, only the women are allowed to express anger.
So the men can be hyper-rational and relentlessly positive.
Baby, I'm really not in the mood for a therapy session. Can't we just enjoy the beautiful day?
Sure. Now that you've locked up your shadow self in a storage unit, where he won't bother you.
Whew, I'm beat.
Moving takes it out of you.
The one piece of furniture that WOULD be worth keeping is the piano. And you're not even taking it.
I know! But it's so huge.

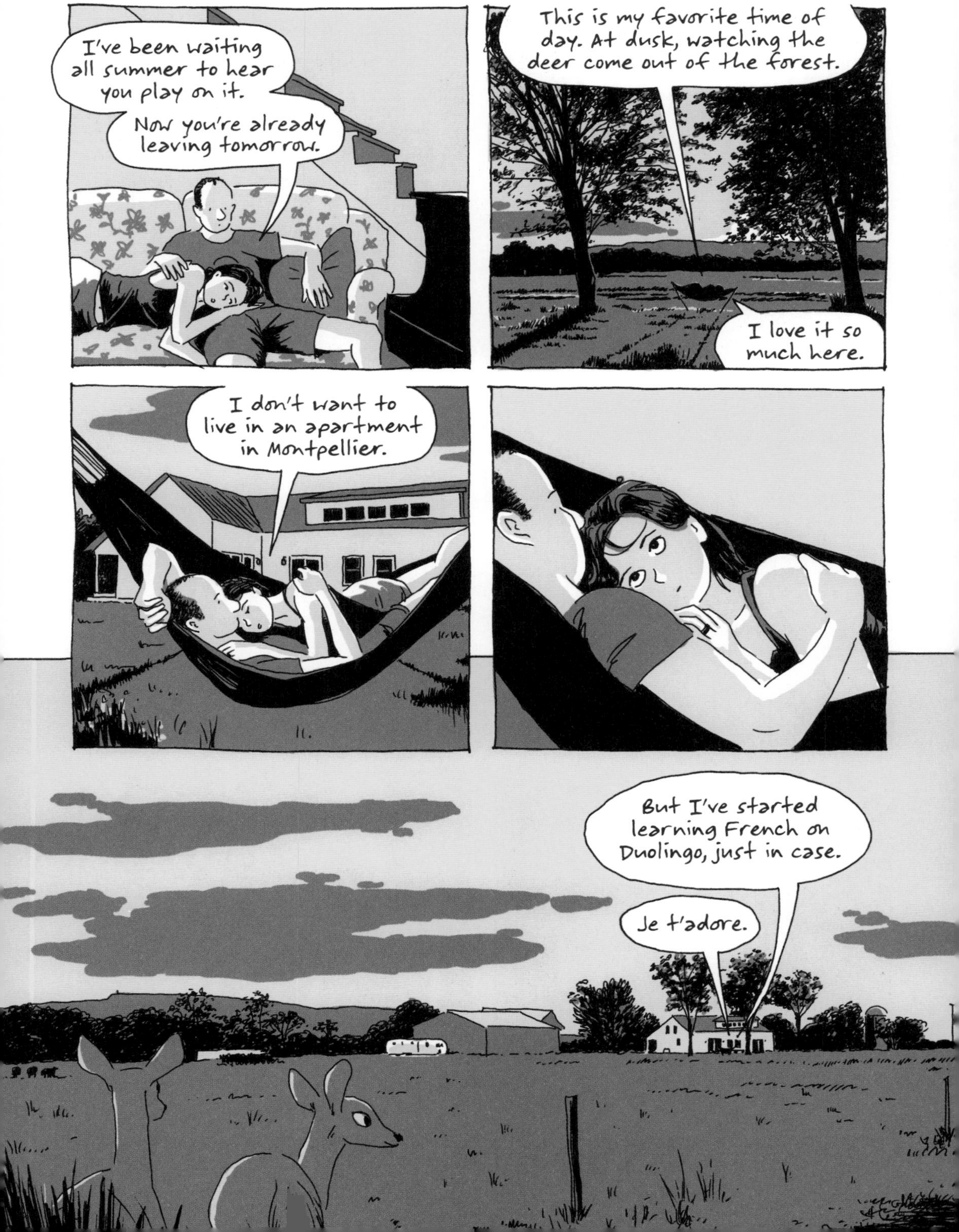
I've been waiting all summer to hear you play on it.
Now you're already leaving tomorrow.
This is my favorite time of day. At dusk, watching the deer come out of the forest.
I love it so much here.
I don't want to live in an apartment in Montpellier.
But I've started learning French on Duolingo, just in case.
Je t'adore.

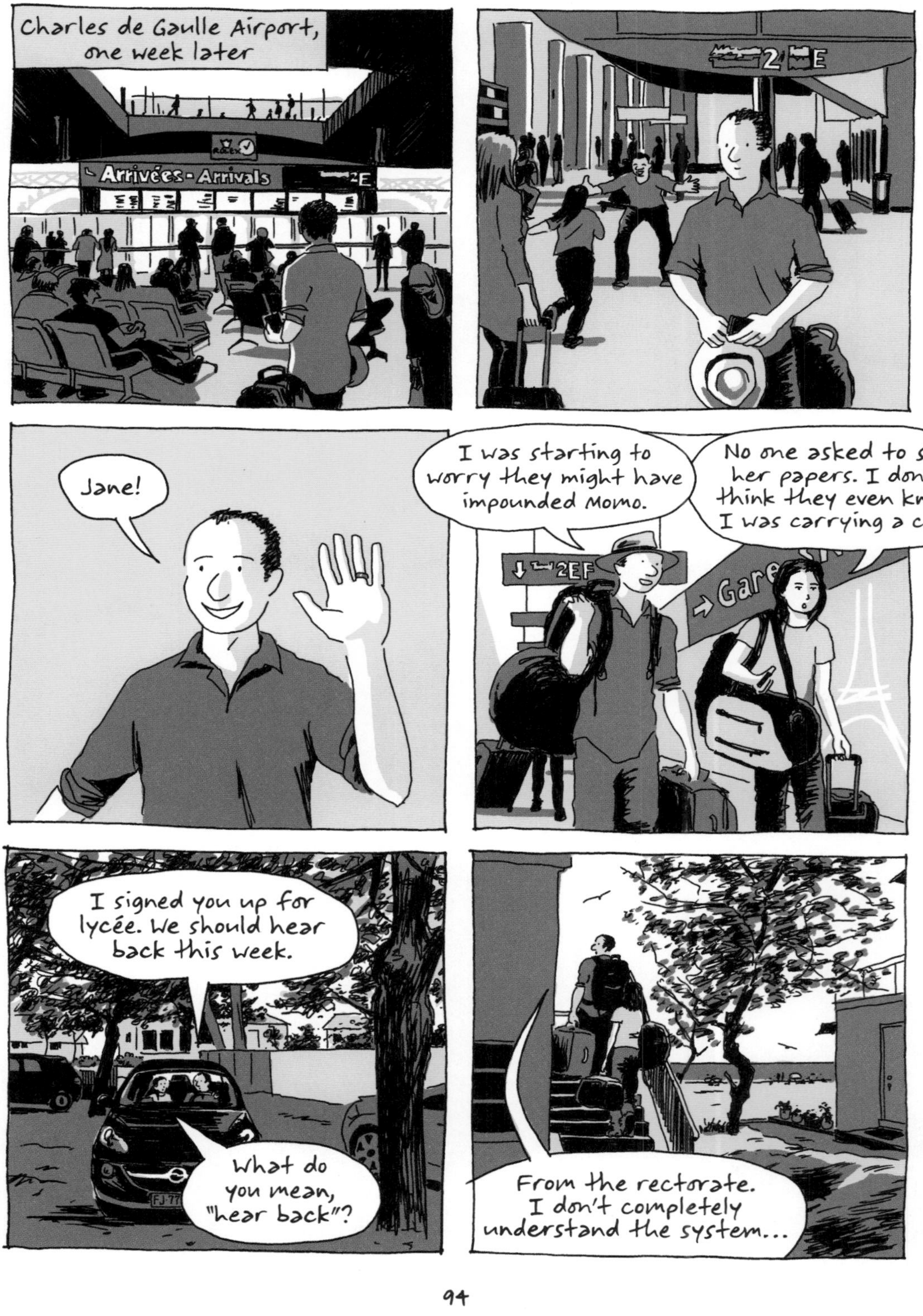
Charles de Gaulle Airport, one week later
Arrivées - Arrivals
2E
2E
Jane!
I was starting to worry they might have impounded Momo.
No one asked to see her papers. I don't think they even knew I was carrying a cat.
2EF
Gare
I signed you up for lycée. We should hear back this week.
What do you mean, "hear back"?
From the rectorate. I don't completely understand the system...

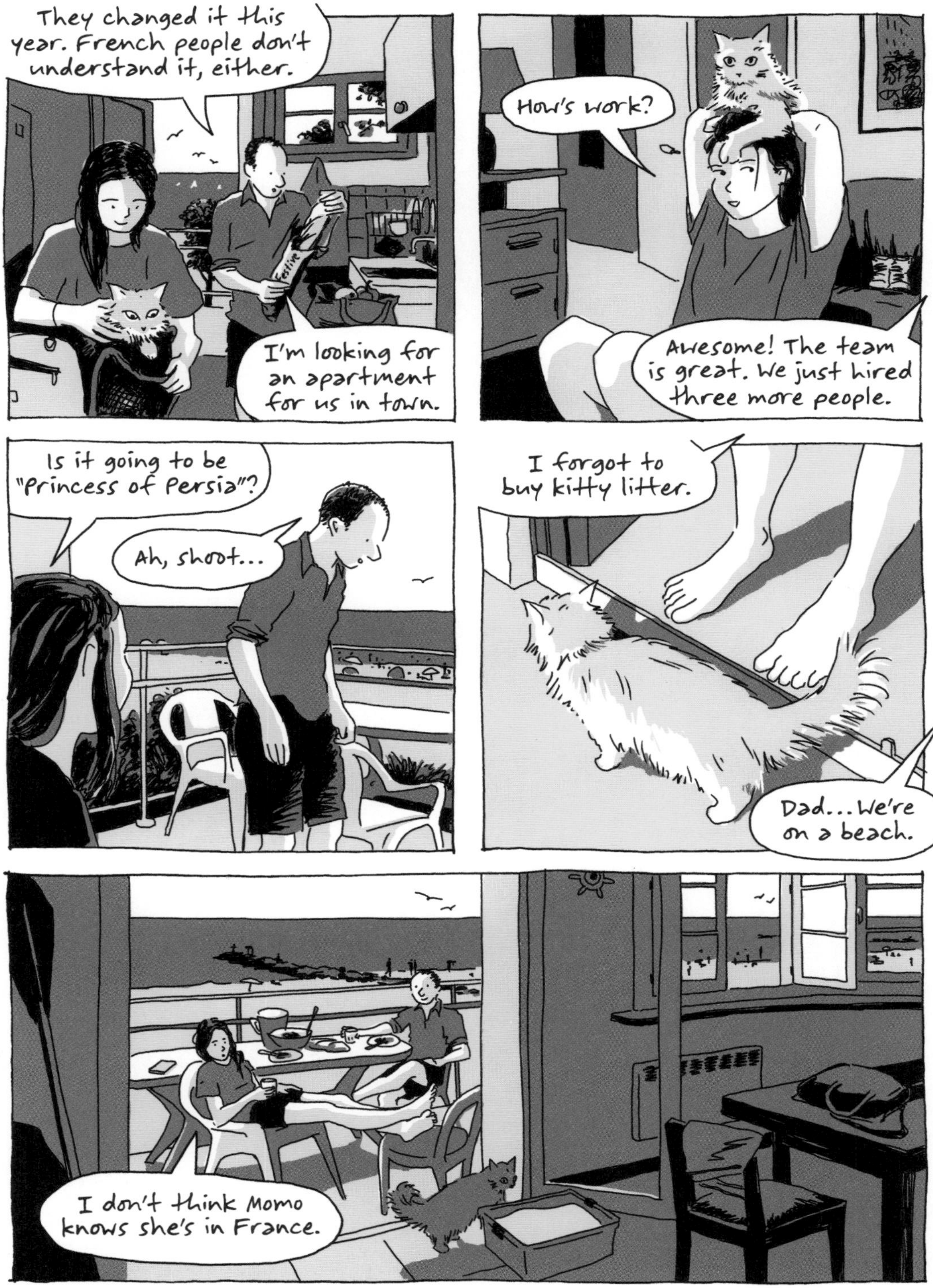
They changed it this year. French people don't understand it, either.
Festive
I'm looking for an apartment for us in town.
How's work?
Awesome! The team is great. We just hired three more people.
Is it going to be "Princess of Persia"?
Ah, shoot...
I forgot to buy kitty litter.
Dad... We're on a beach.
I don't think Momo knows she's in France.

Companion

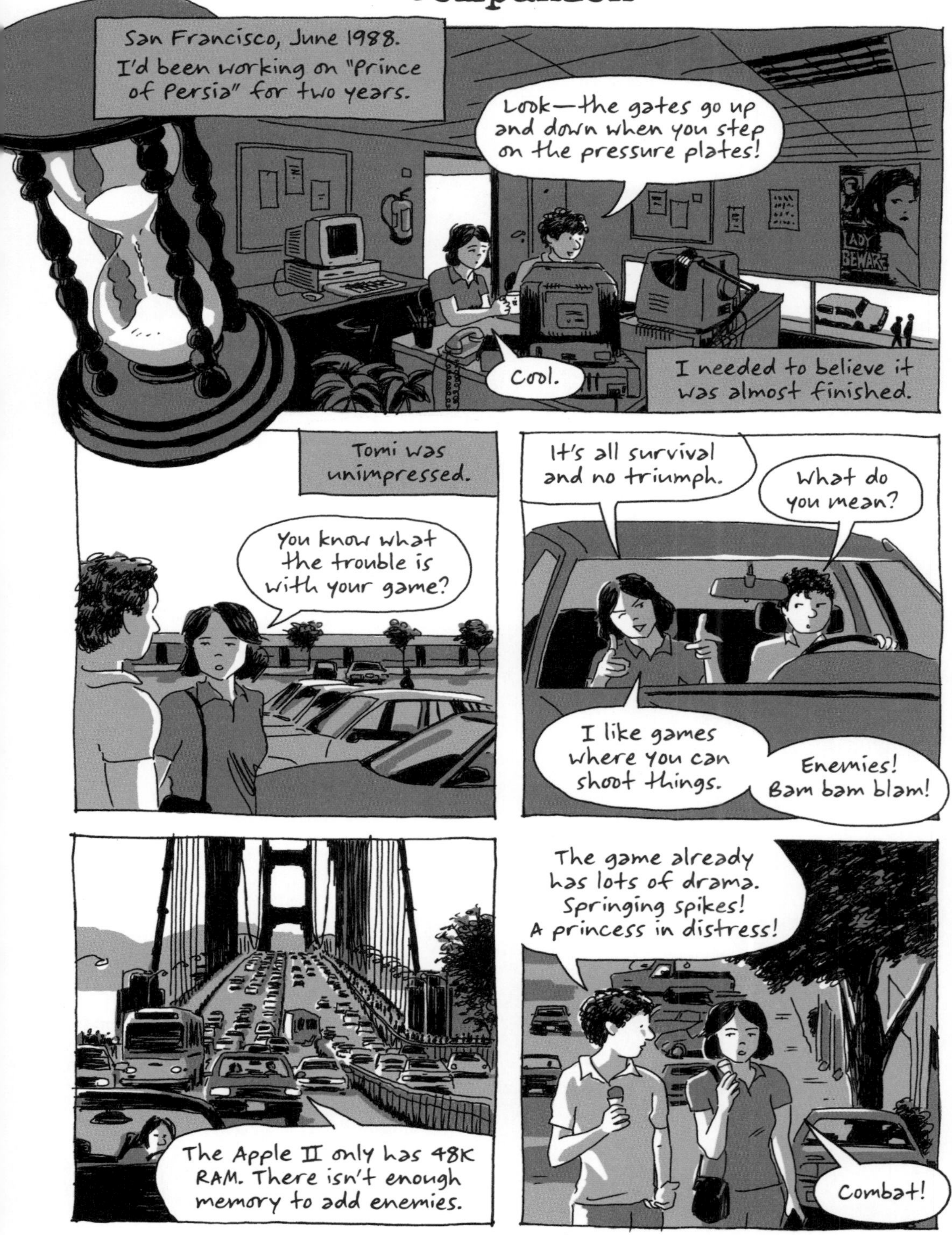
San Francisco, June 1988.
I'd been working on "Prince of Persia" for two years.
Look—the gates go up and down when you step on the pressure plates!
Cool.
I needed to believe it was almost finished.
Tomi was unimpressed.
You know what the trouble is with your game?
It's all survival and no triumph.
What do you mean?
I like games where you can shoot things.
Enemies! Bam bam blam!
The Apple II only has 48K RAM. There isn't enough memory to add enemies.
The game already has lots of drama. Springing spikes! A princess in distress!
Combat!

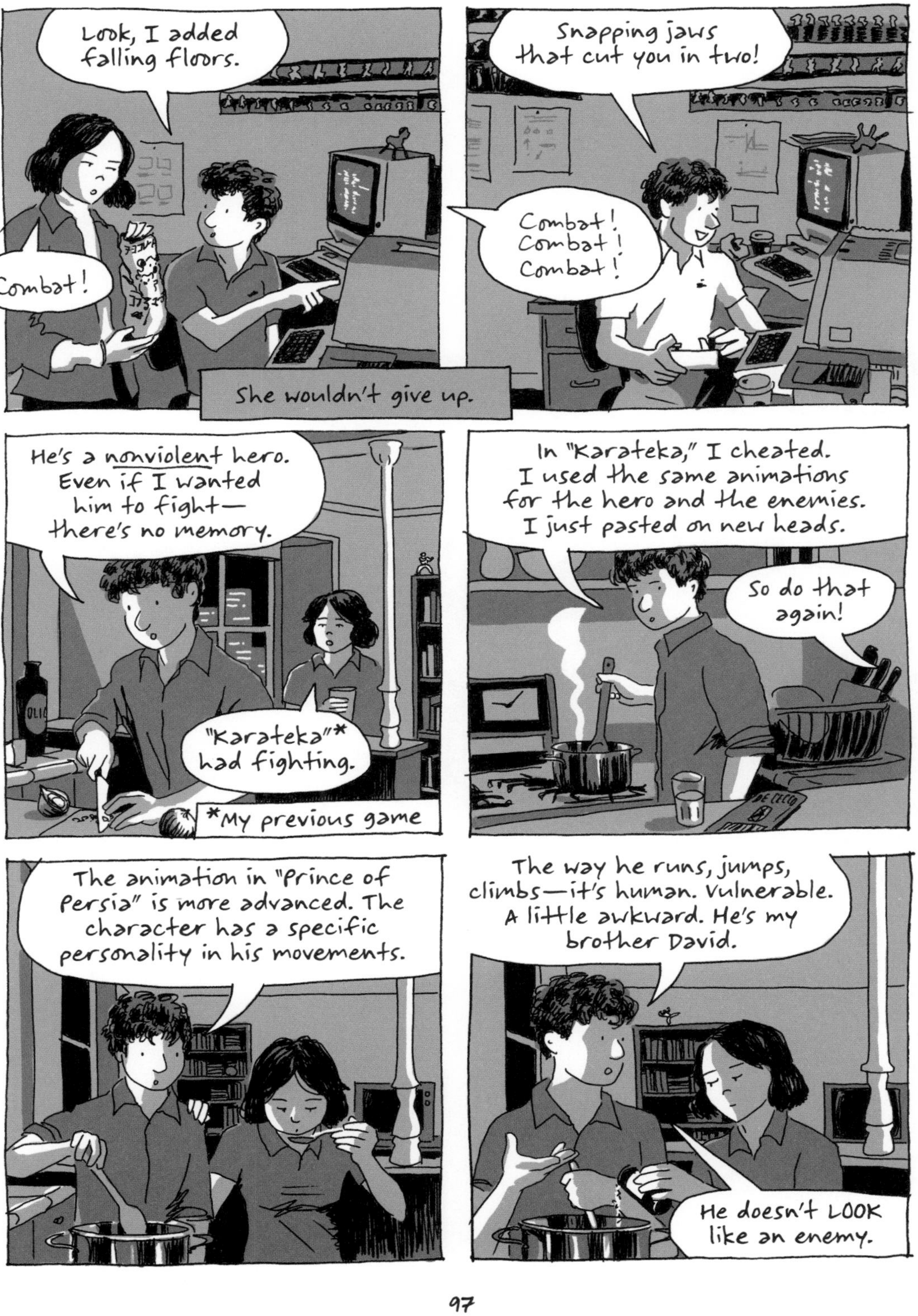
Look, I added falling floors.
Combat!
She wouldn't give up.
Snapping jaws that cut you in two!
Combat! Combat! Combat!
He's a nonviolent hero. Even if I wanted him to fight— there's no memory.
"Karateka"* had fighting.
*My previous game
In "Karateka," I cheated. I used the same animations for the hero and the enemies. I just pasted on new heads.
So do that again!
The animation in "Prince of Persia" is more advanced. The character has a specific personality in his movements.
The way he runs, jumps, climbs—it's human. Vulnerable. A little awkward. He's my brother David.
He doesn't LOOK like an enemy.

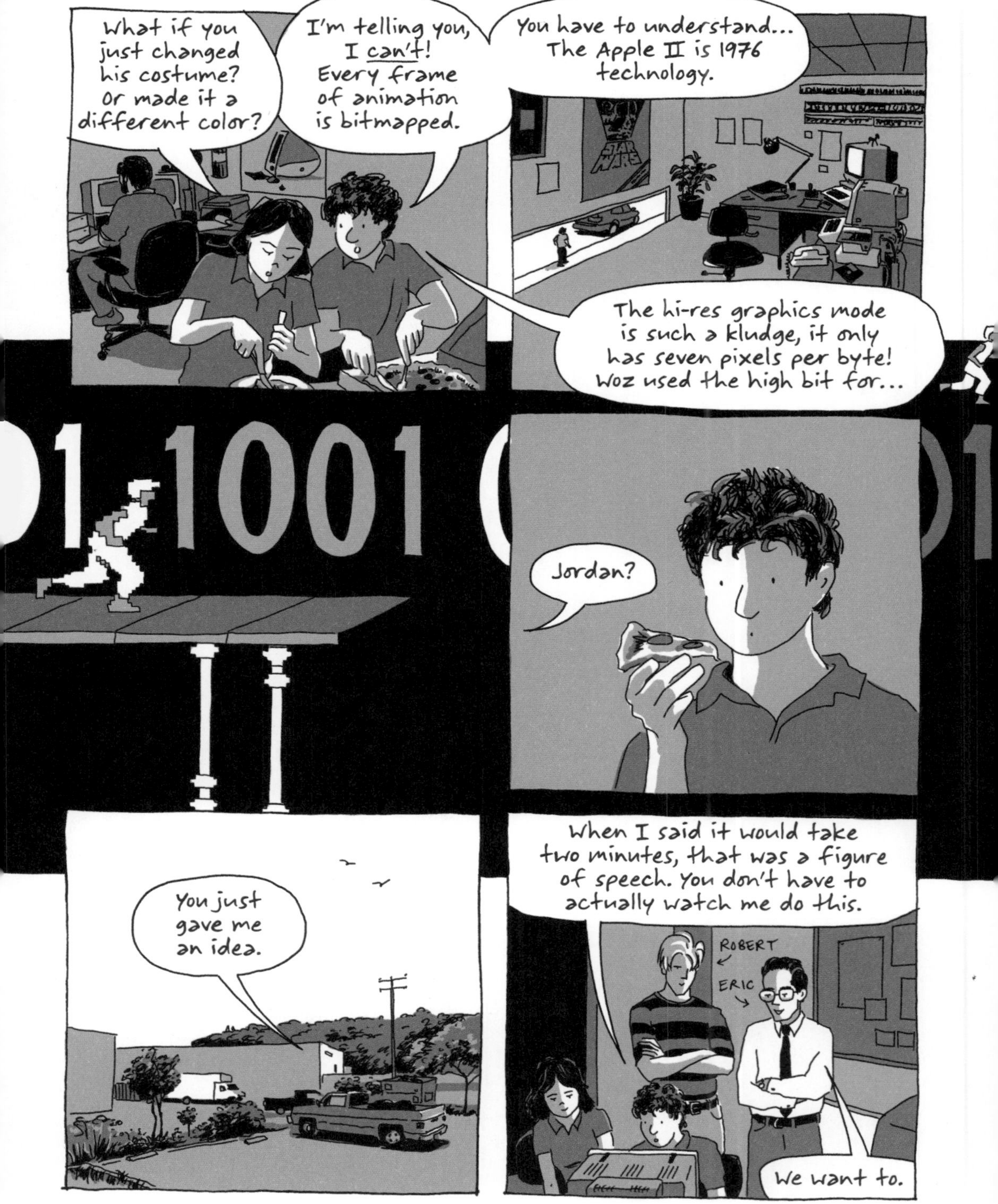
What if you just changed his costume? Or made it a different color?
I'm telling you, I can't! Every frame of animation is bitmapped.
You have to understand... The Apple II is 1976 technology.
STAR WARS
The hi-res graphics mode is such a kludge, it only has seven pixels per byte! Woz used the high bit for...
1 1001
Jordan?
You just gave me an idea.
When I said it would take two minutes, that was a figure of speech. You don't have to actually watch me do this.
ROBERT
ERIC
We want to.

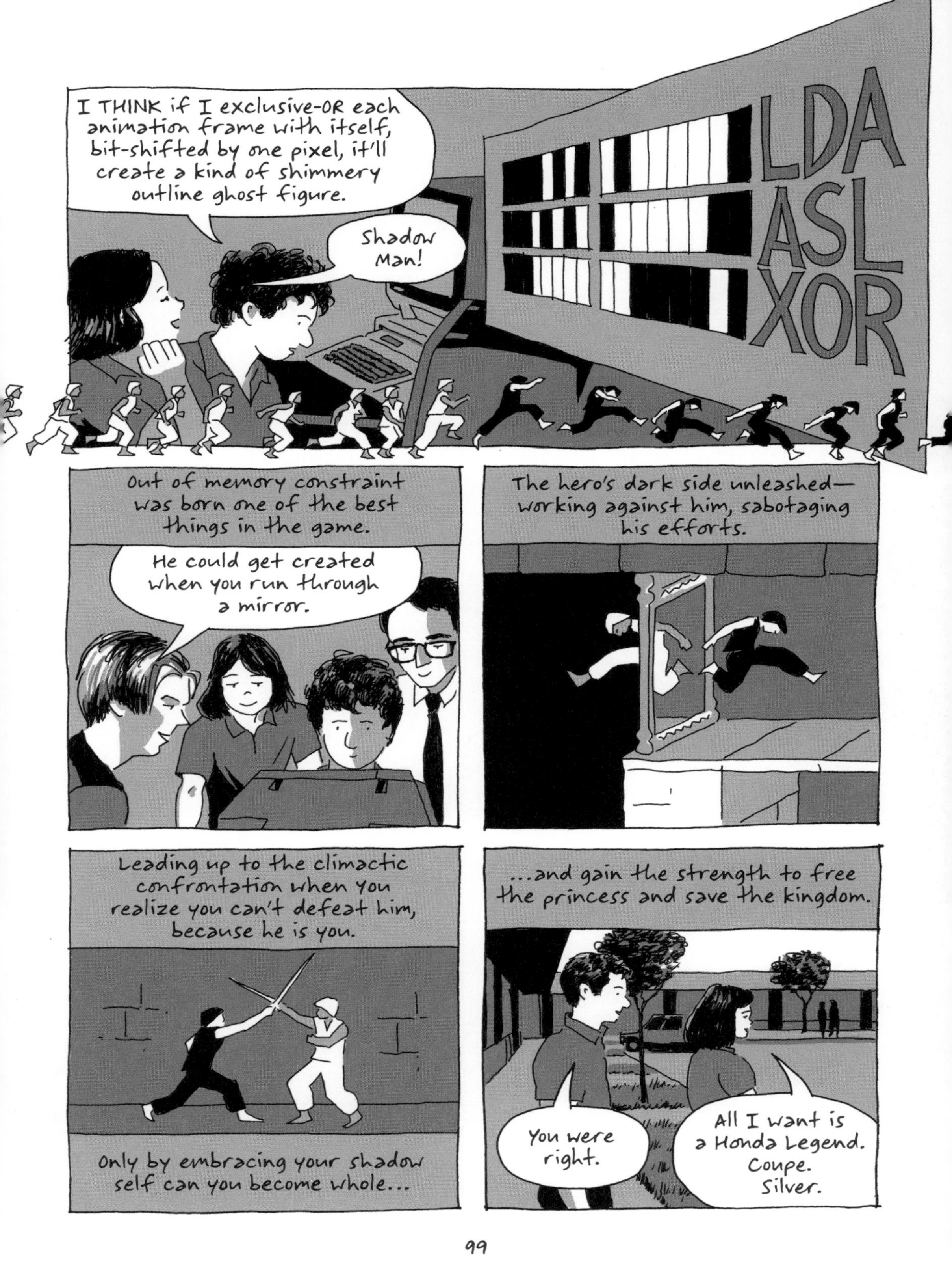
I THINK if I exclusive-OR each animation frame with itself, bit-shifted by one pixel, it'll create a kind of shimmery outline ghost figure.
Shadow Man!
LDA
ASL
XOR
Out of memory constraint was born one of the best things in the game.
He could get created when you run through a mirror.
The hero's dark side unleashed— working against him, sabotaging his efforts.
Leading up to the climactic confrontation when you realize you can't defeat him, because he is you.
Only by embracing your shadow self can you become whole...
...and gain the strength to free the princess and save the kingdom.
You were right.
All I want is a Honda Legend. Coupe. Silver.

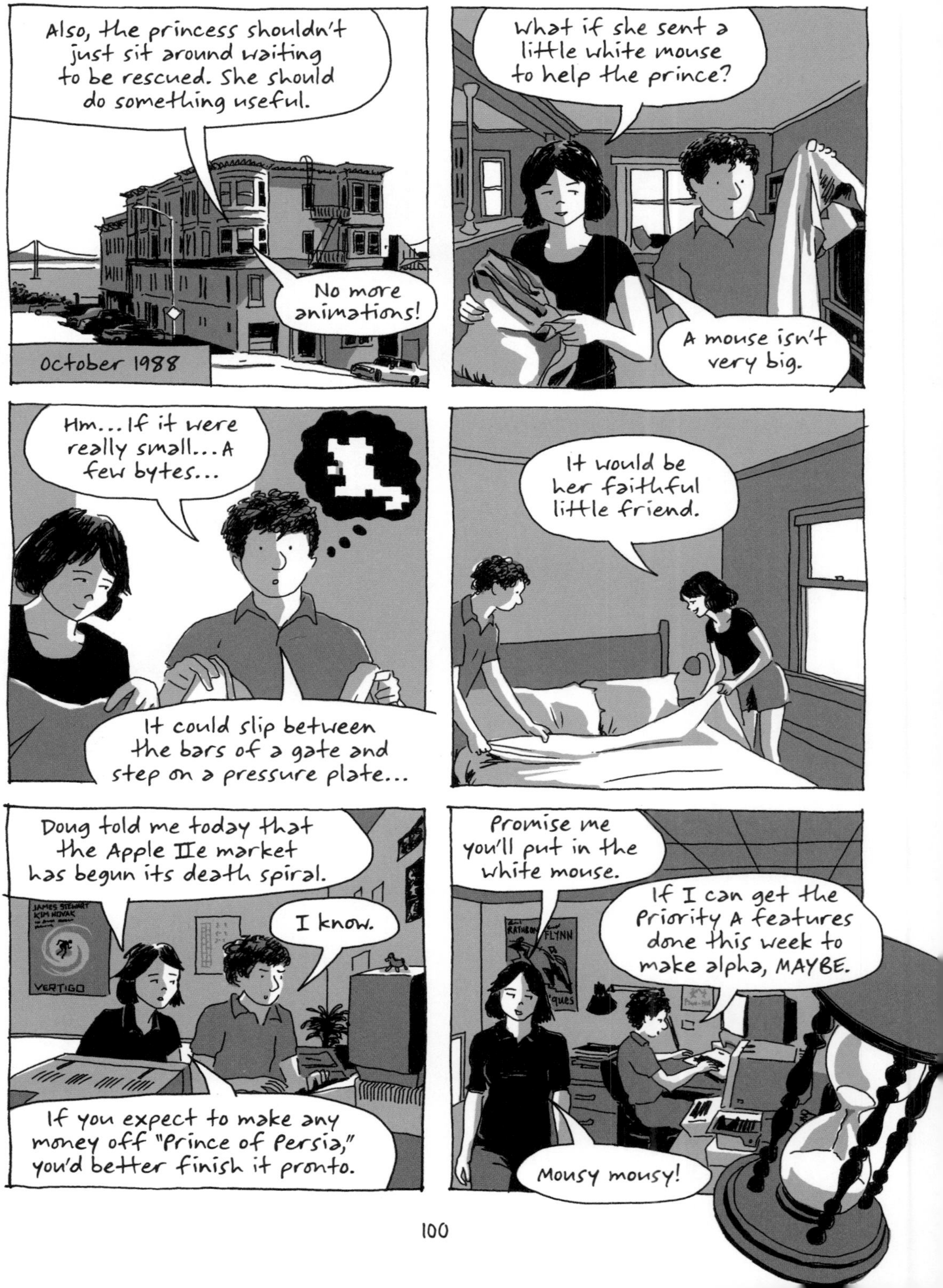
Also, the princess shouldn't just sit around waiting to be rescued. She should do something useful.
No more animations!
October 1988
What if she sent a little white mouse to help the prince?
A mouse isn't very big.
Hm... If it were really small... A few bytes...
It could slip between the bars of a gate and step on a pressure plate...
It would be her faithful little friend.
Doug told me today that the Apple IIe market has begun its death spiral.
I know.
If you expect to make any money off "Prince of Persia," you'd better finish it pronto.
VERTIGO
Promise me you'll put in the white mouse.
If I can get the Priority A features done this week to make alpha, MAYBE.
Mousy mousy!

Storybook

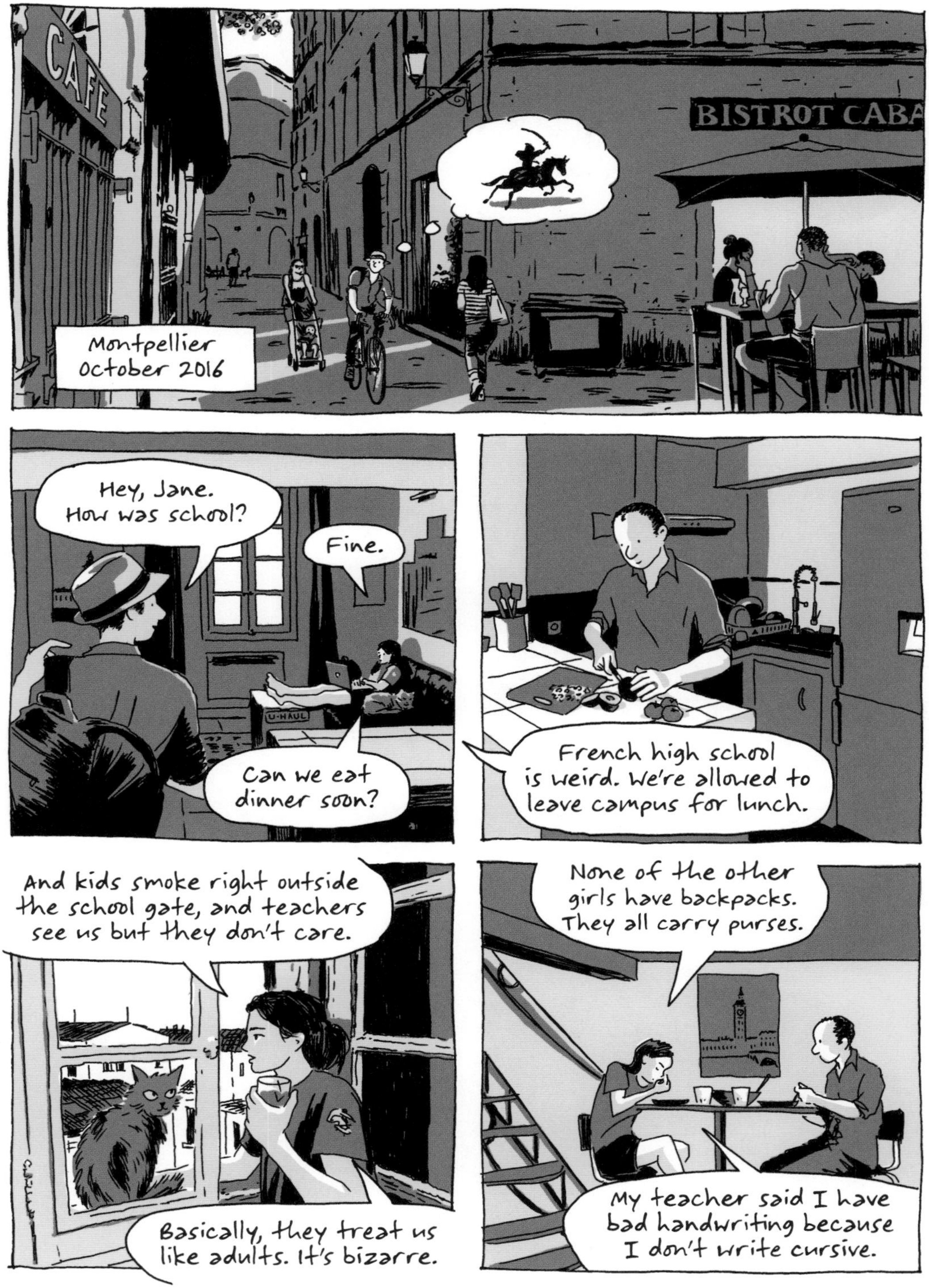
CAFE
BISTROT CABA
Montpellier
October 2016
Hey, Jane.
How was school?
Fine.
U-HAUL
Can we eat
dinner soon?
French high school
is weird. We're allowed to
leave campus for lunch.
And kids smoke right outside
the school gate, and teachers
see us but they don't care.
Basically, they treat us
like adults. It's bizarre.
None of the other
girls have backpacks.
They all carry purses.
My teacher said I have
bad handwriting because
I don't write cursive.

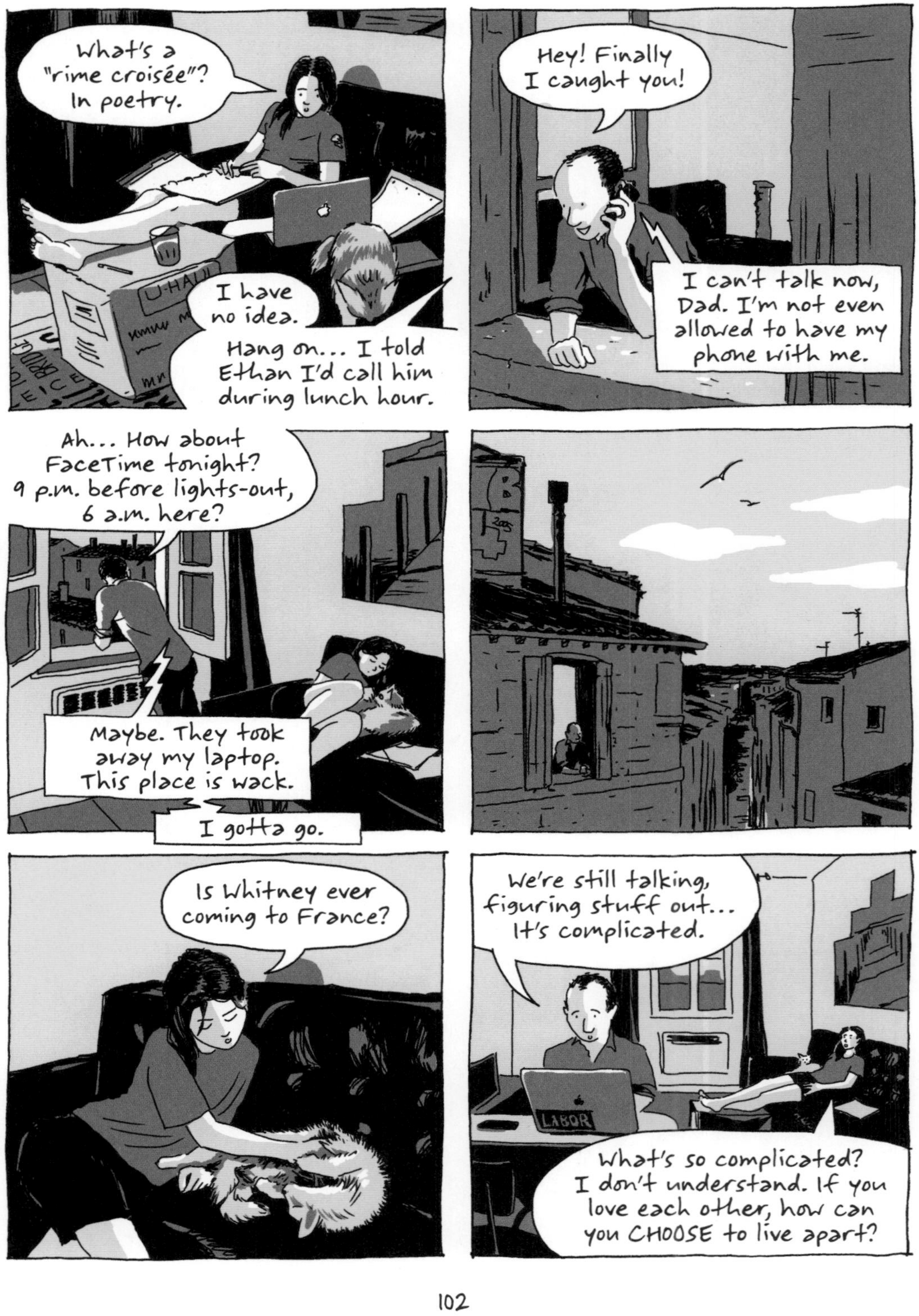
What's a "rime croisée"? In poetry.
I have no idea.
Hang on... I told Ethan I'd call him during lunch hour.
Hey! Finally I caught you!
I can't talk now, Dad. I'm not even allowed to have my phone with me.
Ah... How about FaceTime tonight? 9 p.m. before lights-out, 6 a.m. here?
Maybe. They took away my laptop. This place is wack.
I gotta go.
Is Whitney ever coming to France?
We're still talking, figuring stuff out... It's complicated.
What's so complicated? I don't understand. If you love each other, how can you CHOOSE to live apart?

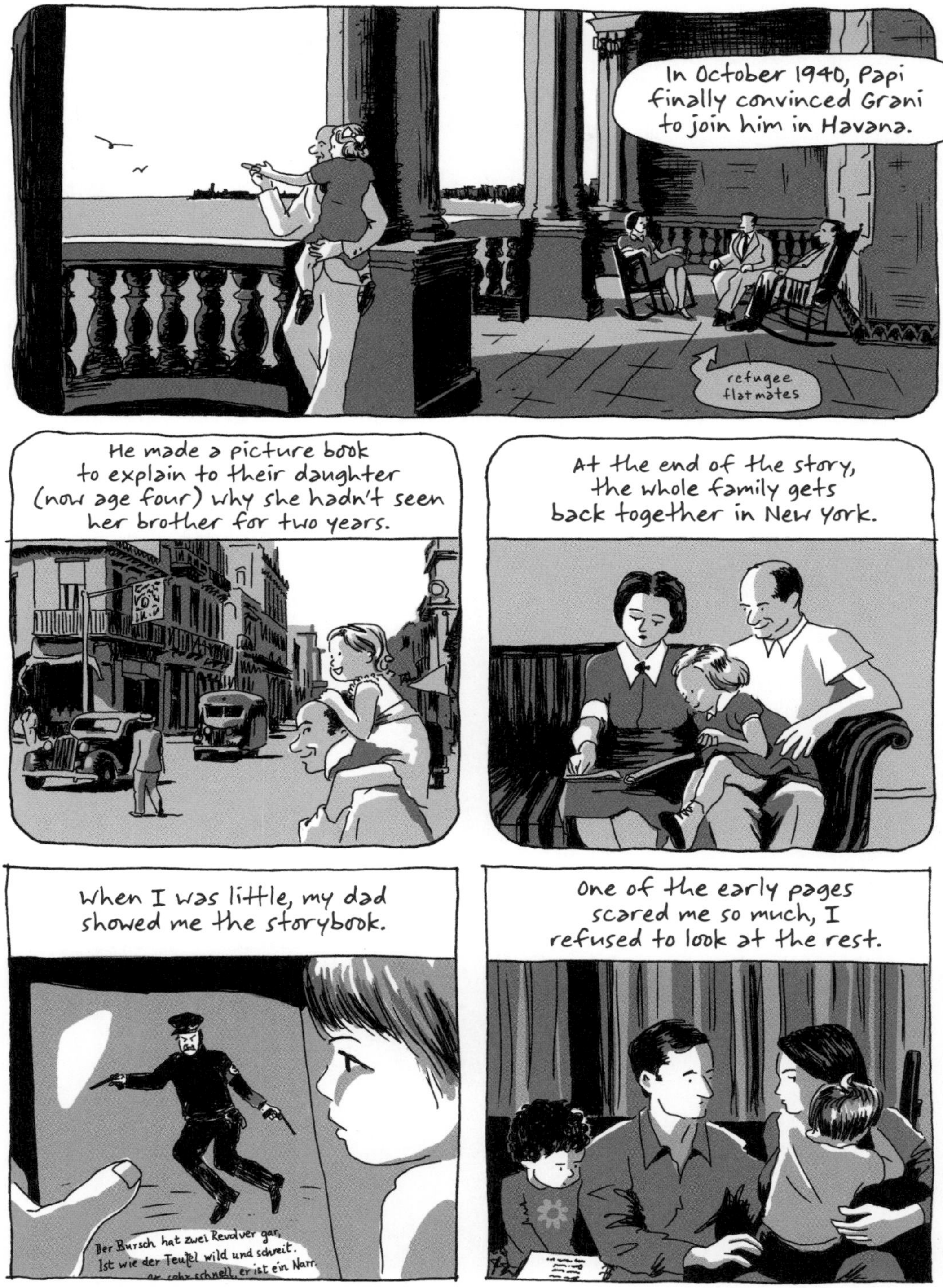

In October 1940, Papi finally convinced Grani to join him in Havana.
refugee flatmates
He made a picture book to explain to their daughter (now age four) why she hadn't seen her brother for two years.
At the end of the story, the whole family gets back together in New York.
When I was little, my dad showed me the storybook.
Der Bursch hat zwei Revolver gar,
Ist wie der Teufel wild und schreit.
One of the early pages scared me so much, I refused to look at the rest.

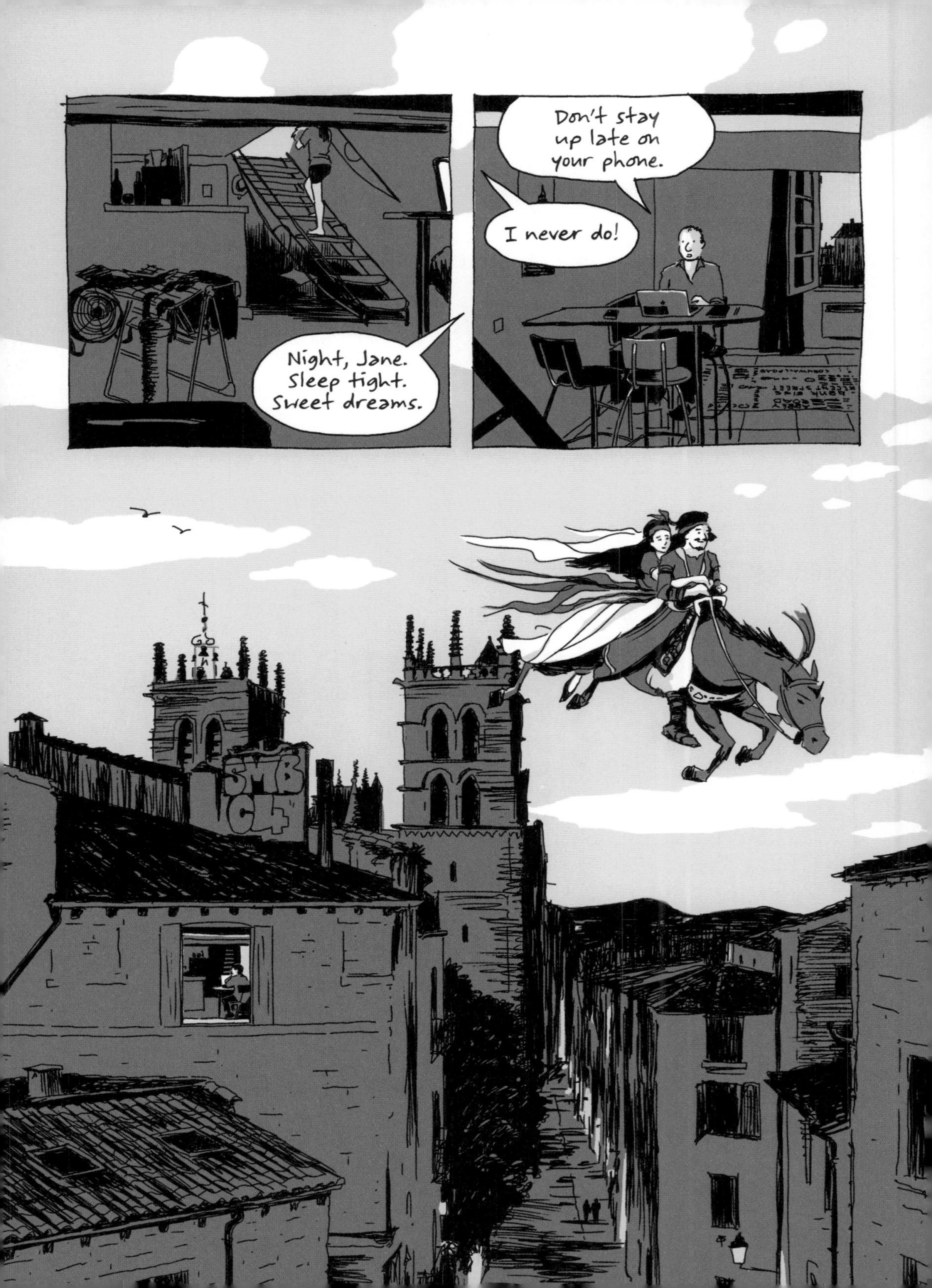

Night, Jane. Sleep tight. Sweet dreams.
Don't stay up late on your phone.
I never do!
SMB C4

Chapter 4

Goodbye to All That

Adolf Mechner, age 15
Czernowitz, 1912

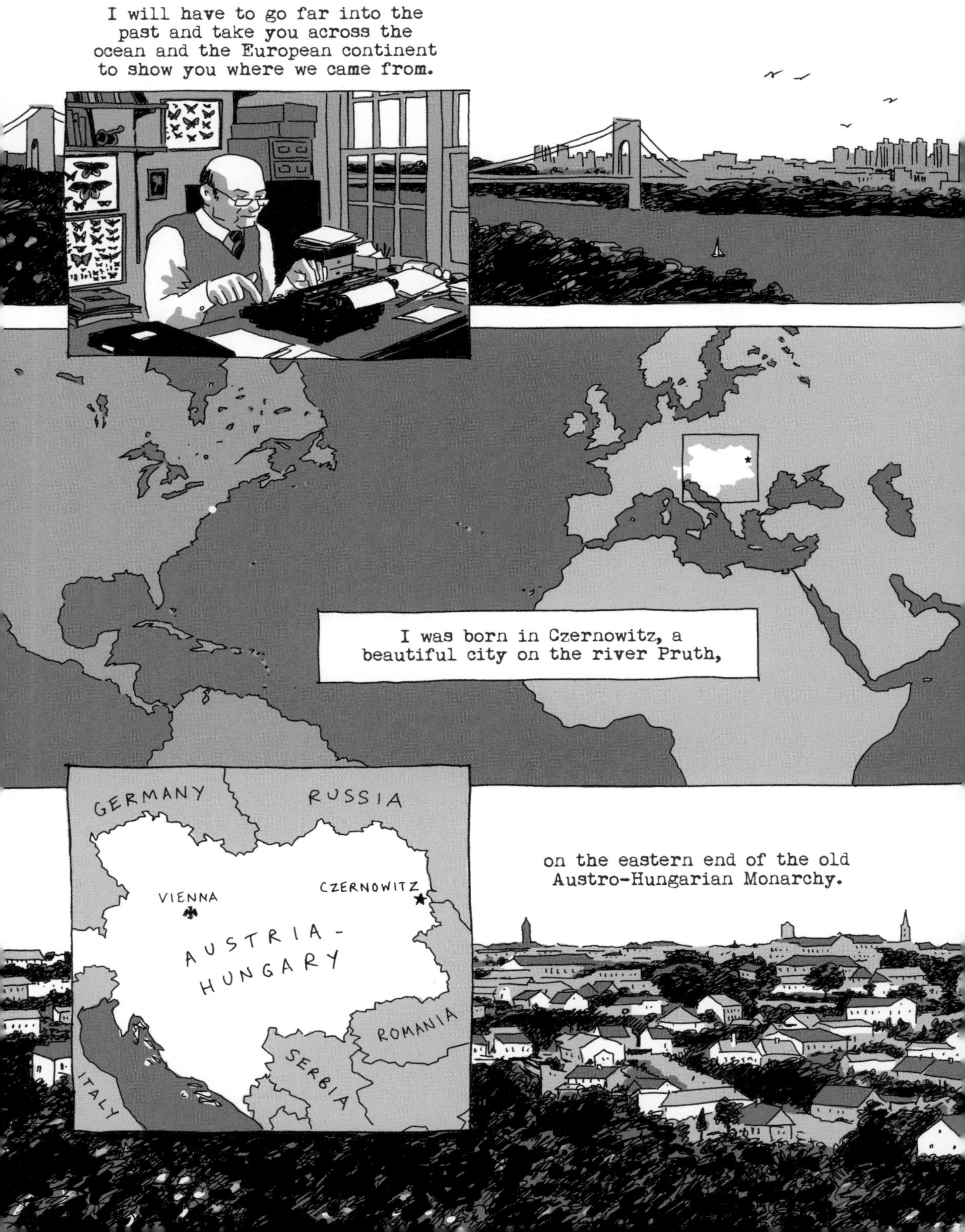
I will have to go far into the past and take you across the ocean and the European continent to show you where we came from.
I was born in Czernowitz, a beautiful city on the river Pruth,
GERMANY
RUSSIA
VIENNA
CZERNOWITZ
AUSTRIA-HUNGARY
ROMANIA
SERBIA
ITALY
on the eastern end of the old Austro-Hungarian Monarchy.

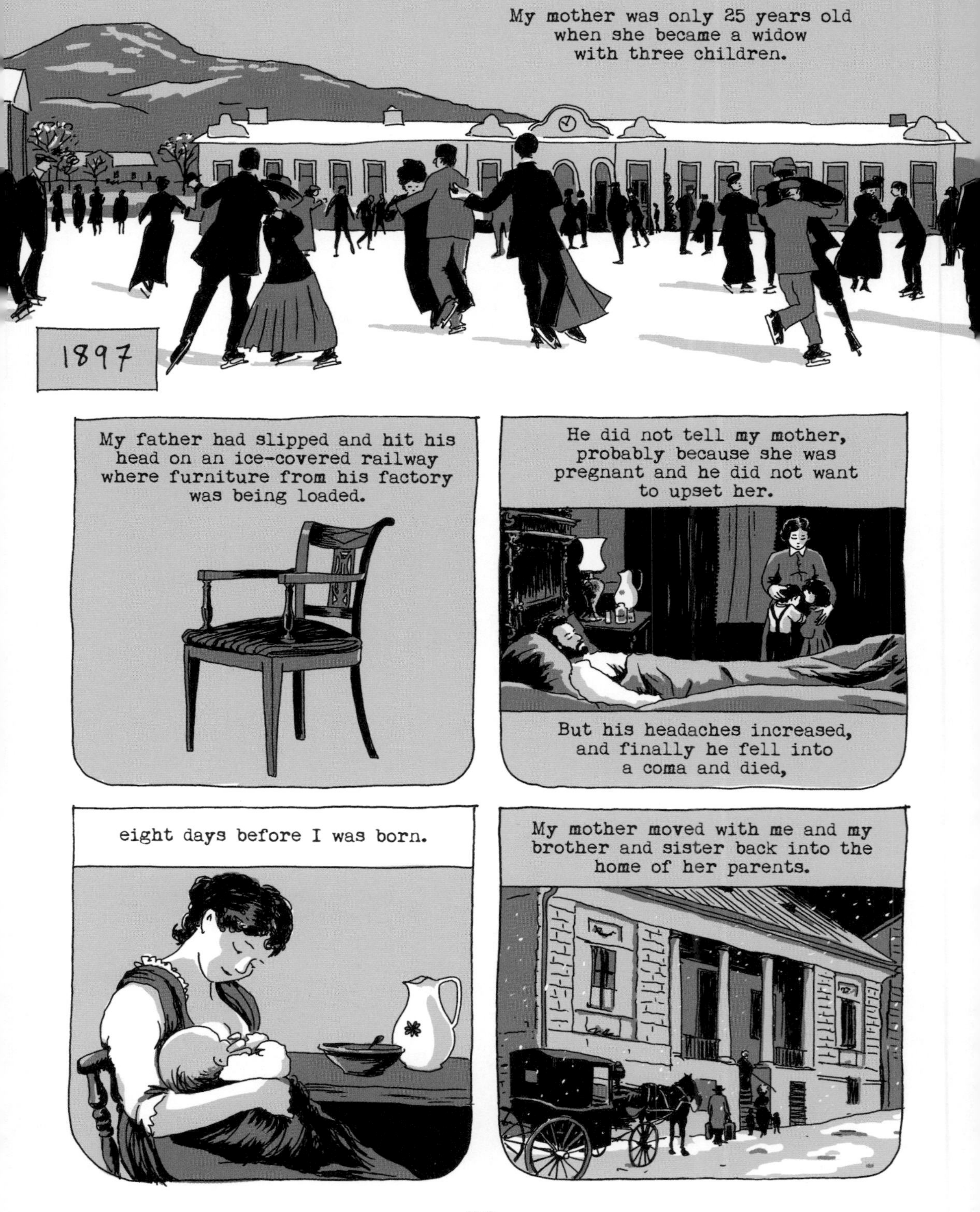
My mother was only 25 years old when she became a widow with three children.
1897
My father had slipped and hit his head on an ice-covered railway where furniture from his factory was being loaded.
He did not tell my mother, probably because she was pregnant and he did not want to upset her.
But his headaches increased, and finally he fell into a coma and died,
eight days before I was born.
My mother moved with me and my brother and sister back into the home of her parents.

We lived near the old Turkish bridge. Our grammar school was on the corner of our street, so we did not have to go far.

Our grandfather had a grocery shop in the center of the city.

The official language was German. The population was mixed, with Poles, Turks, Romanians, Hungarians, Ukrainians (who were generally called Ruthenians),

and quite a lot of Jews (about 35%). Jews had already for many decades equal rights with others.

In school, we studied German literature, Latin, and Greek, the same education that was being taught in Vienna.

Check out this photo of Papi when he was 15. He looks just like Ethan!

Brooklyn December 2016

109

Life Drawing

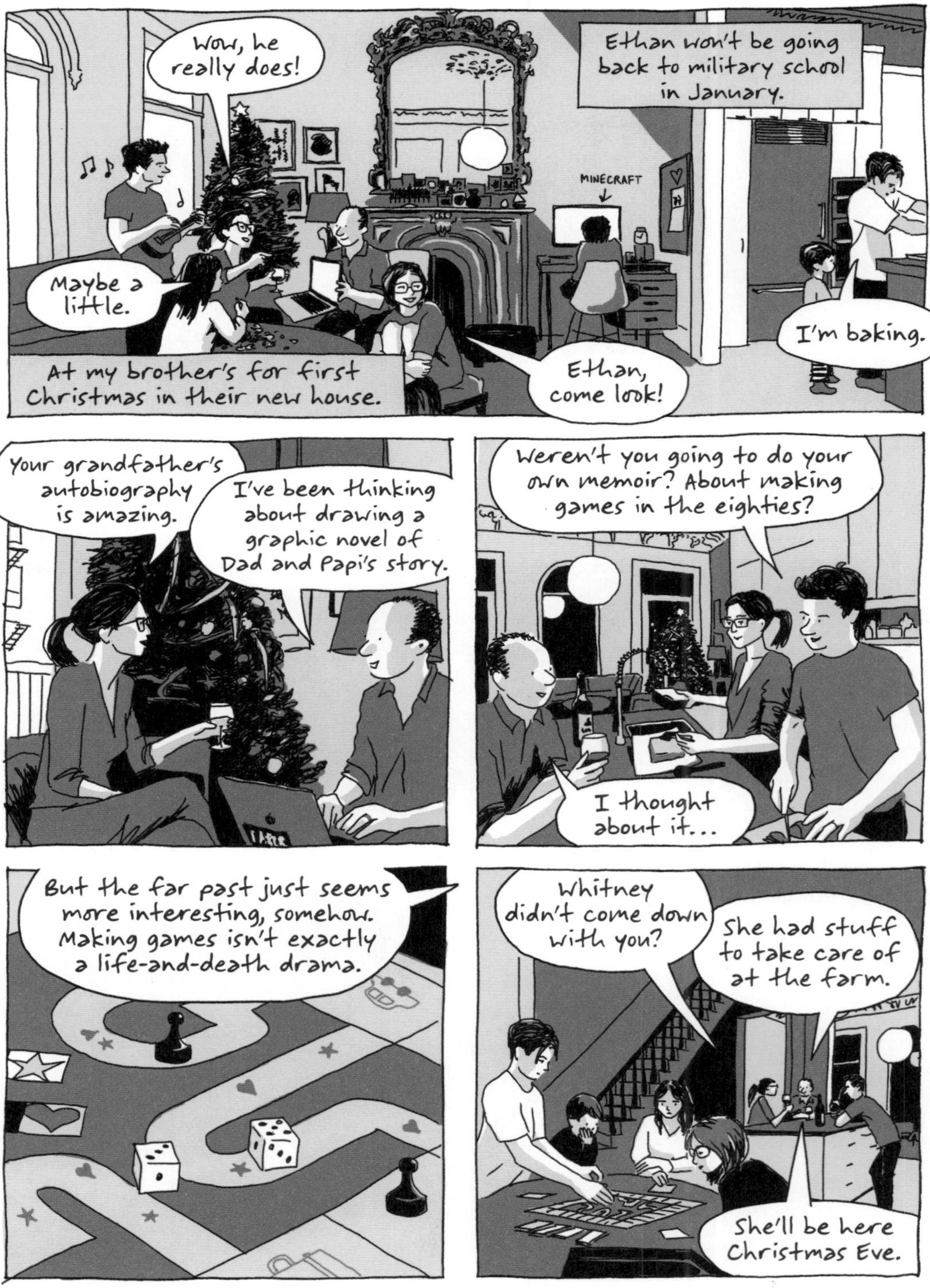

At my brother's for first Christmas in their new house.
Maybe a little.
Wow, he really does!
MINECRAFT
Ethan, come look!
Ethan won't be going back to military school in January.
I'm baking.
Your grandfather's autobiography is amazing.
I've been thinking about drawing a graphic novel of Dad and Papi's story.
Weren't you going to do your own memoir? About making games in the eighties?
I thought about it...
But the far past just seems more interesting, somehow. Making games isn't exactly a life-and-death drama.
Whitney didn't come down with you?
She had stuff to take care of at the farm.
She'll be here Christmas Eve.

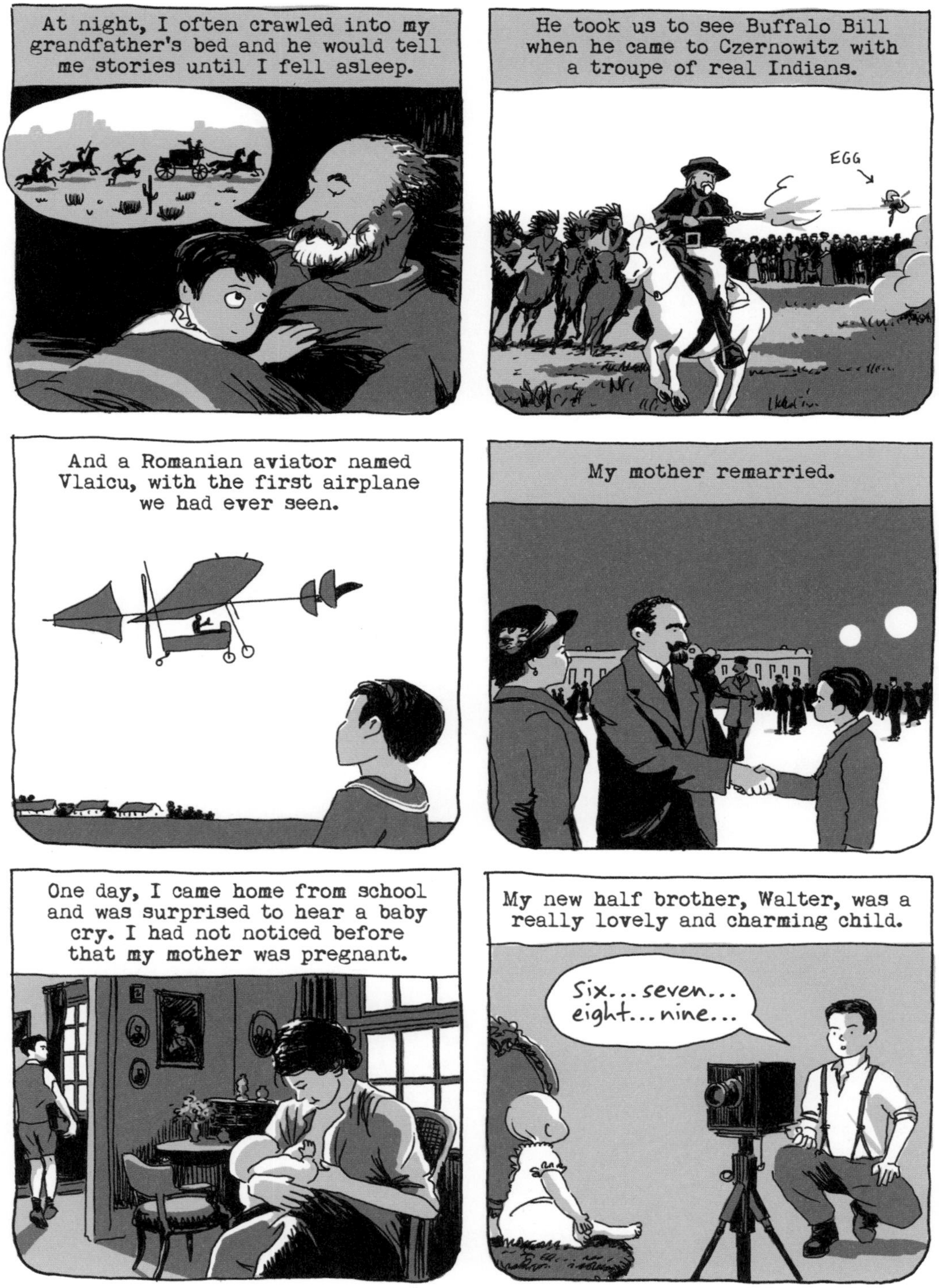
At night, I often crawled into my grandfather's bed and he would tell me stories until I fell asleep.
He took us to see Buffalo Bill when he came to Czernowitz with a troupe of real Indians.
EGG
And a Romanian aviator named Vlaicu, with the first airplane we had ever seen.
My mother remarried.
One day, I came home from school and was surprised to hear a baby cry. I had not noticed before that my mother was pregnant.
My new half brother, Walter, was a really lovely and charming child.
Six... seven... eight... nine...

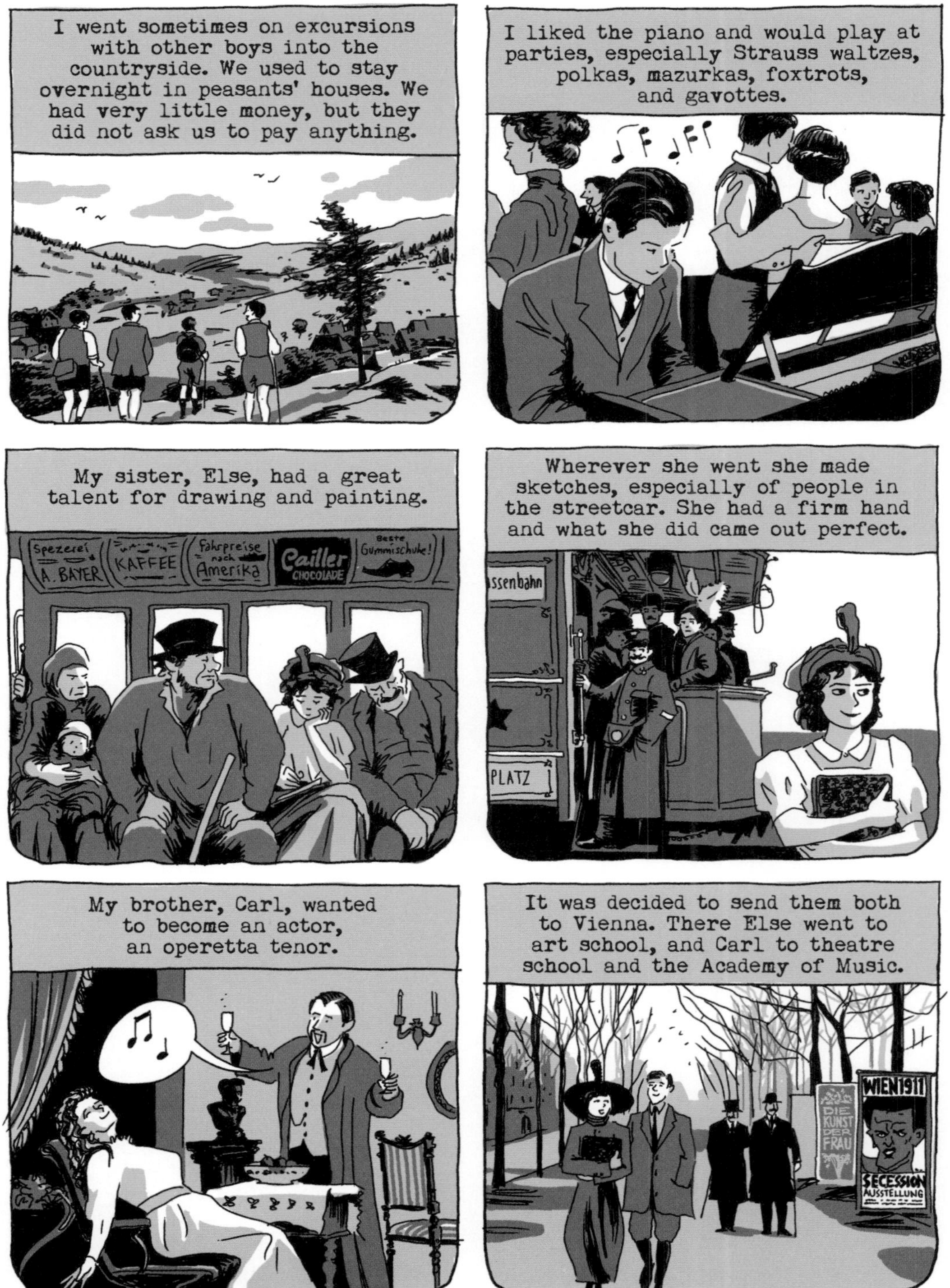
I went sometimes on excursions with other boys into the countryside. We used to stay overnight in peasants' houses. We had very little money, but they did not ask us to pay anything.
I liked the piano and would play at parties, especially Strauss waltzes, polkas, mazurkas, foxtrots, and gavottes.
My sister, Else, had a great talent for drawing and painting.
Spezerei A. BAYER
KAFFEE
Fahrpreise nach Amerika
Cailler CHOCOLADE
Beste Gummischuhe!
Wherever she went she made sketches, especially of people in the streetcar. She had a firm hand and what she did came out perfect.
ssenbahn
PLATZ
My brother, Carl, wanted to become an actor, an operetta tenor.
It was decided to send them both to Vienna. There Else went to art school, and Carl to theatre school and the Academy of Music.
DIE KUNST DER FRAU
WIEN 1911
SECESSION AUSSTELLUNG

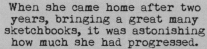

When she came home after two years, bringing a great many sketchbooks, it was astonishing how much she had progressed.

1912

I just realized...

Papi's sister, Else, was studying art in Vienna at the same time as Hitler.

Huh.

...Around the time Uncle Joji bought those watercolors.

That's crazy.

She got into art school, Hitler didn't...

They could have met!

Hey... Are you drawing me??

Maybe.

Long Distance

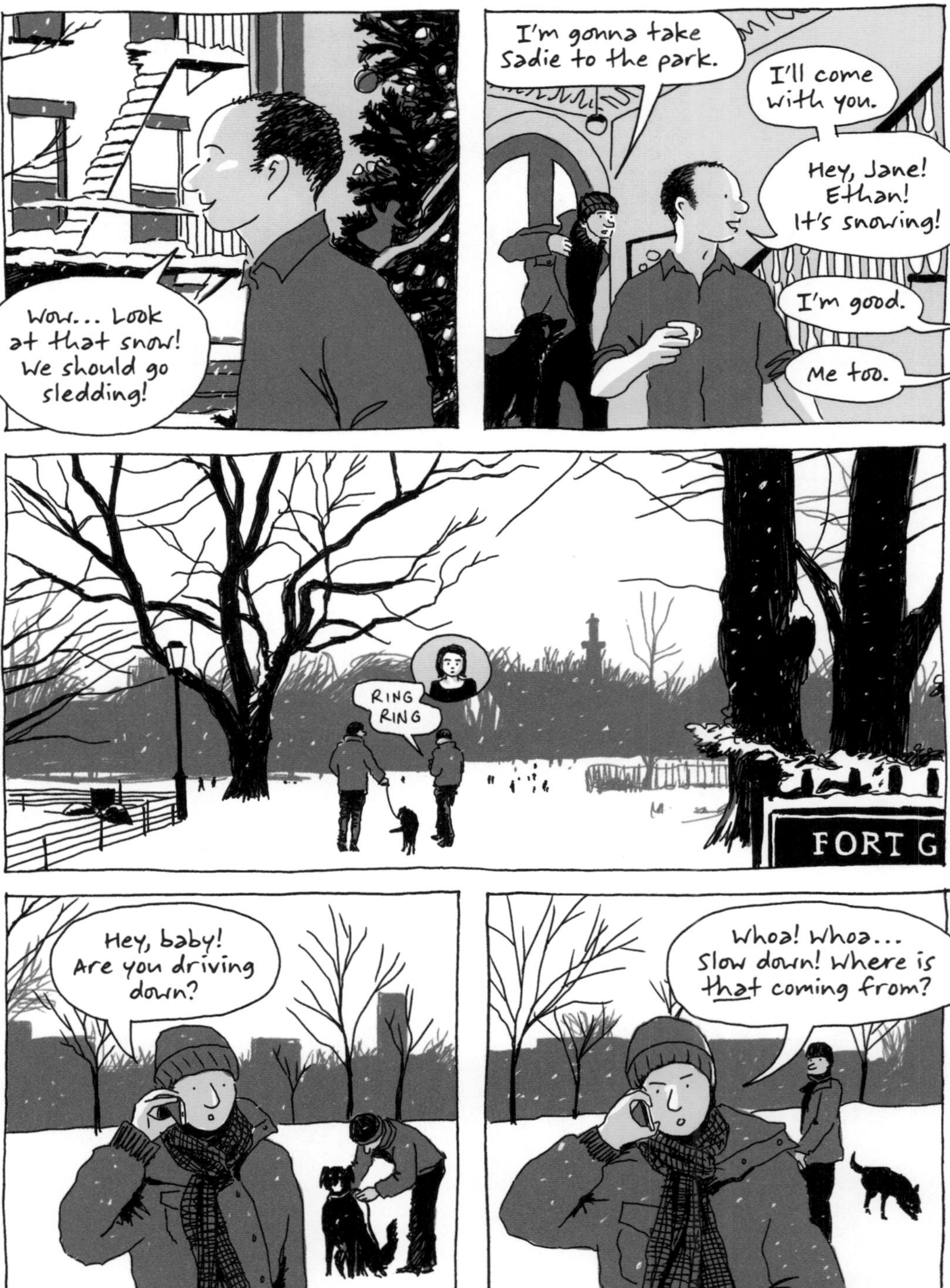
Wow... Look at that snow! We should go sledding!
I'm gonna take Sadie to the park.
I'll come with you.
Hey, Jane! Ethan! It's snowing!
I'm good.
Me too.
RING RING
FORT G
Hey, baby! Are you driving down?
Whoa! Whoa... Slow down! Where is that coming from?

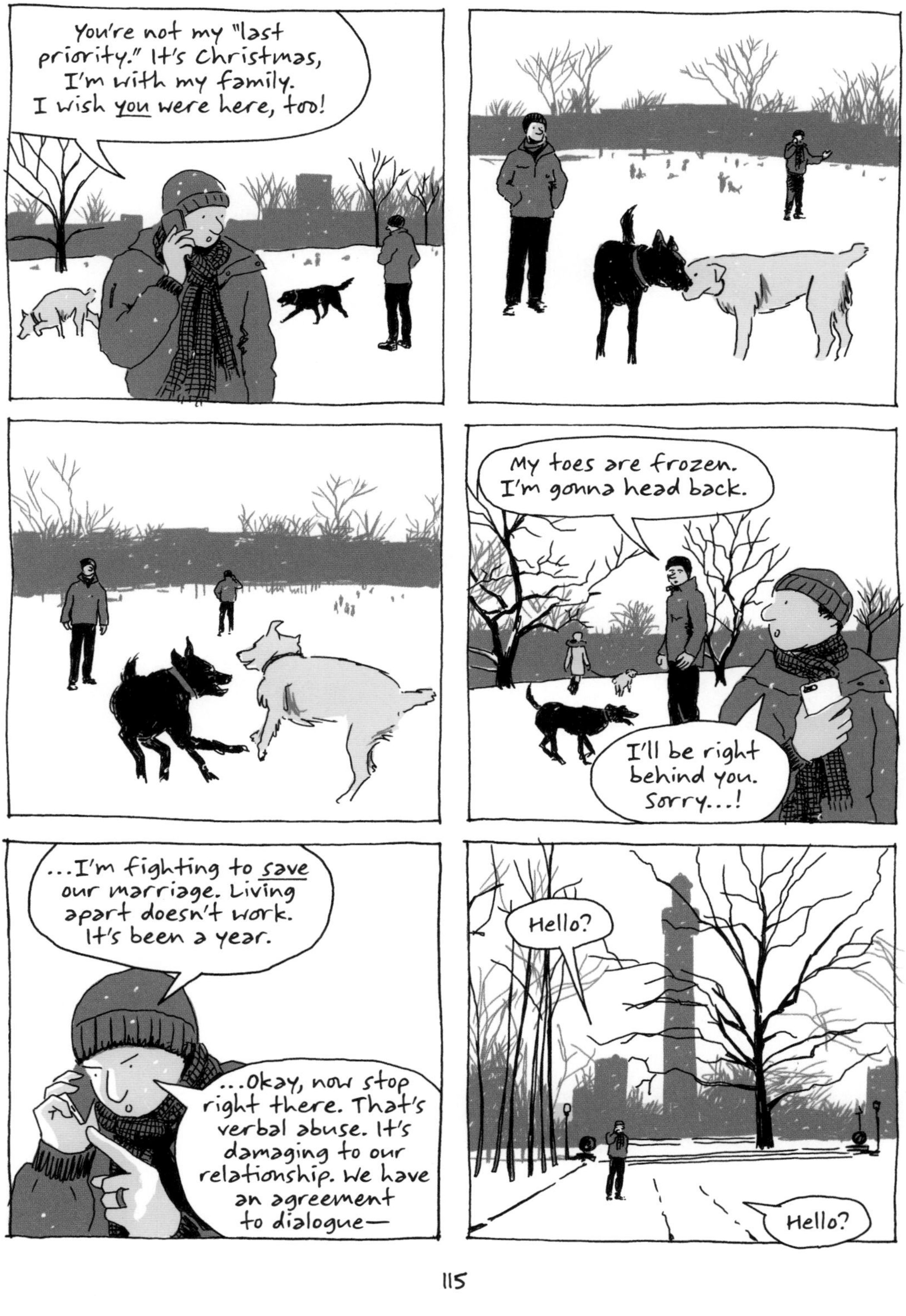

You're not my "last priority." It's Christmas, I'm with my family. I wish you were here, too!
My toes are frozen. I'm gonna head back.
I'll be right behind you. Sorry...!
...I'm fighting to save our marriage. Living apart doesn't work. It's been a year.
...Okay, now stop right there. That's verbal abuse. It's damaging to our relationship. We have an agreement to dialogue—
Hello?
Hello?

Reeds

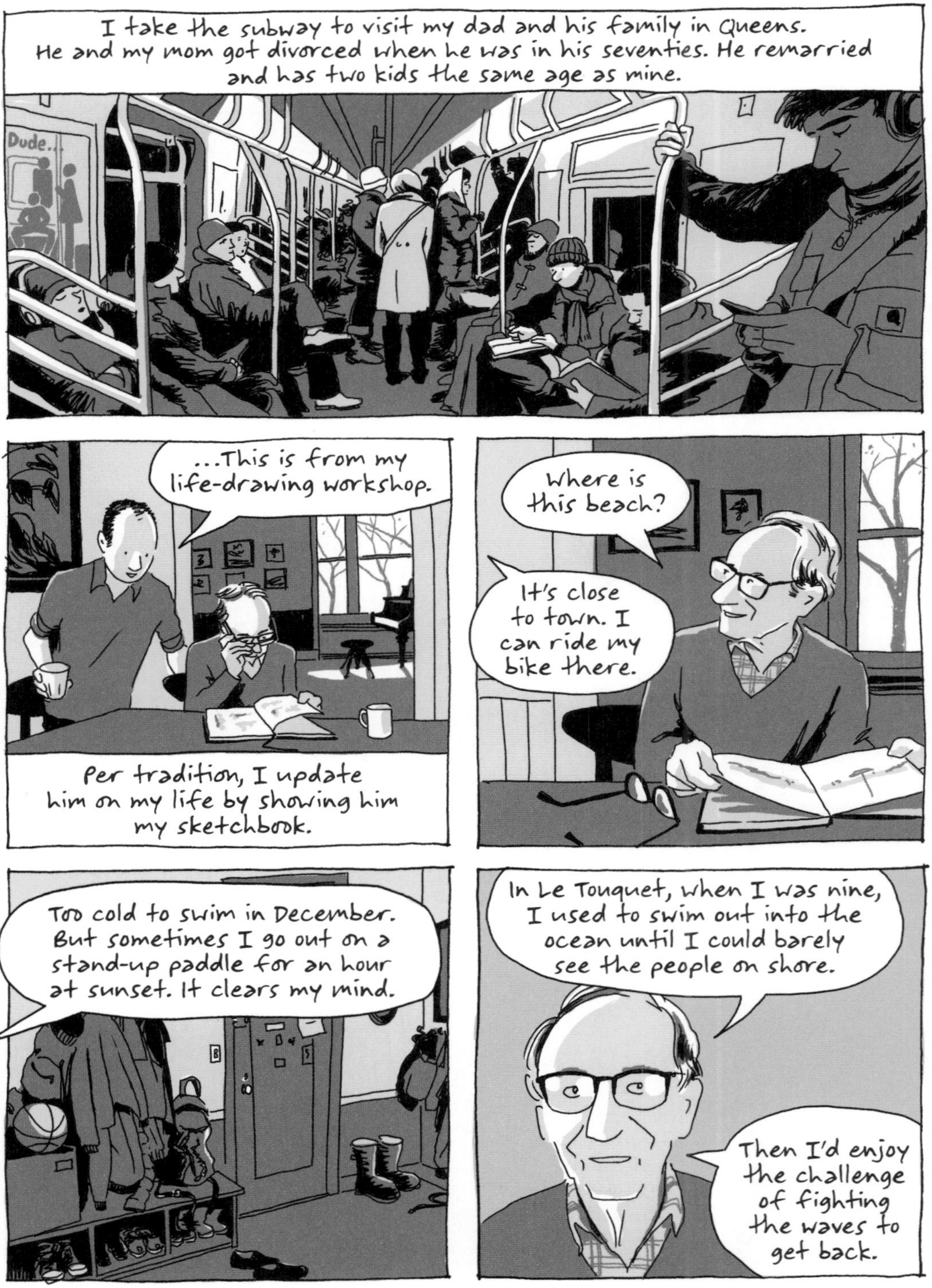

I take the subway to visit my dad and his family in Queens. He and my mom got divorced when he was in his seventies. He remarried and has two kids the same age as mine.
Dude...
...This is from my life-drawing workshop.
Per tradition, I update him on my life by showing him my sketchbook.
Where is this beach?
It's close to town. I can ride my bike there.
Too cold to swim in December. But sometimes I go out on a stand-up paddle for an hour at sunset. It clears my mind.
In Le Touquet, when I was nine, I used to swim out into the ocean until I could barely see the people on shore.
Then I'd enjoy the challenge of fighting the waves to get back.

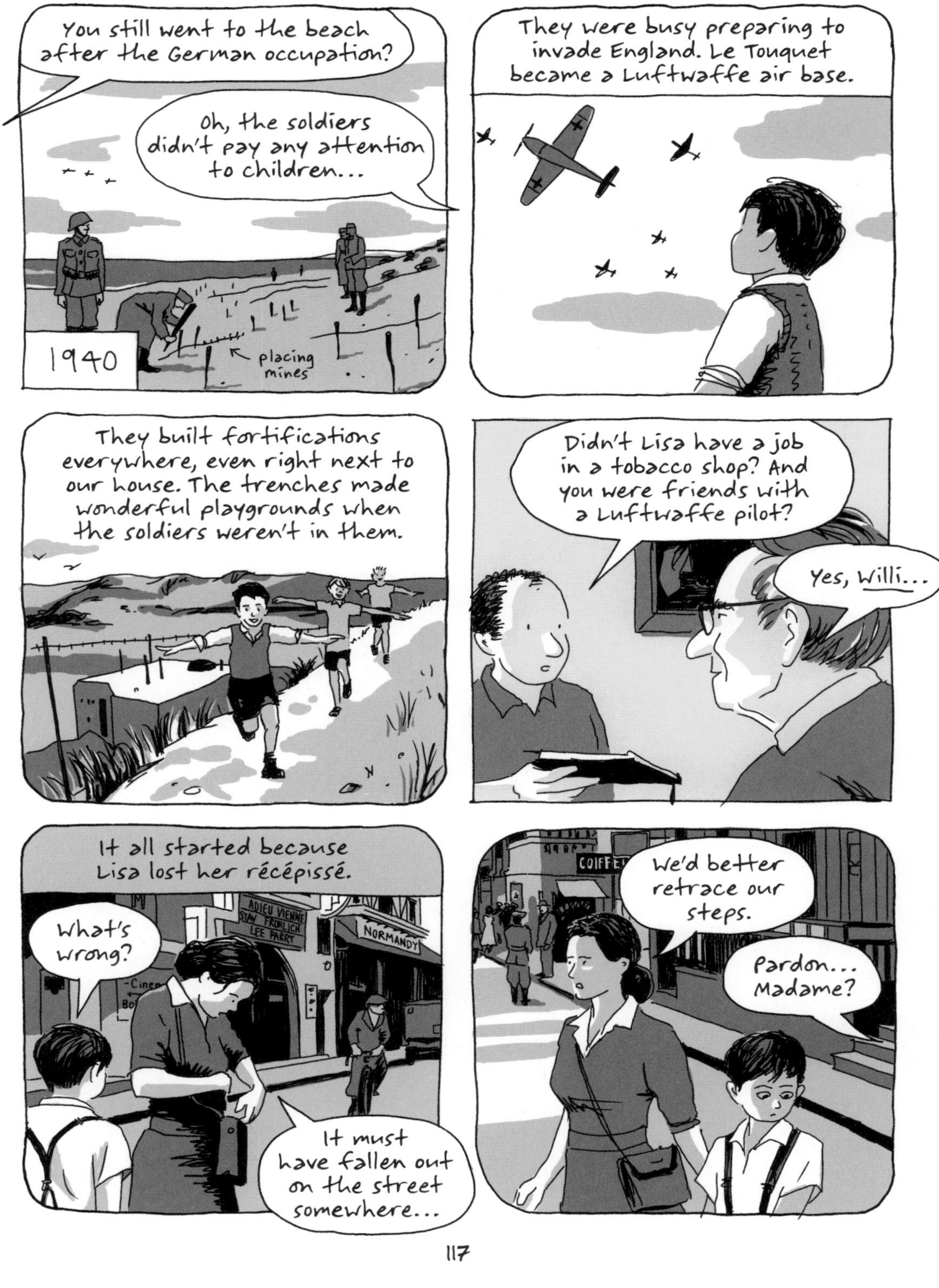
You still went to the beach after the German occupation?
Oh, the soldiers didn't pay any attention to children...
1940
placing mines
They were busy preparing to invade England. Le Touquet became a Luftwaffe air base.
They built fortifications everywhere, even right next to our house. The trenches made wonderful playgrounds when the soldiers weren't in them.
Didn't Lisa have a job in a tobacco shop? And you were friends with a Luftwaffe pilot?
Yes, Willi...
It all started because Lisa lost her récépissé.
ADIEU VIENNE
LEE PARRY
NORMANDY
What's wrong?
It must have fallen out on the street somewhere...
COIFFE
We'd better retrace our steps.
Pardon... Madame?

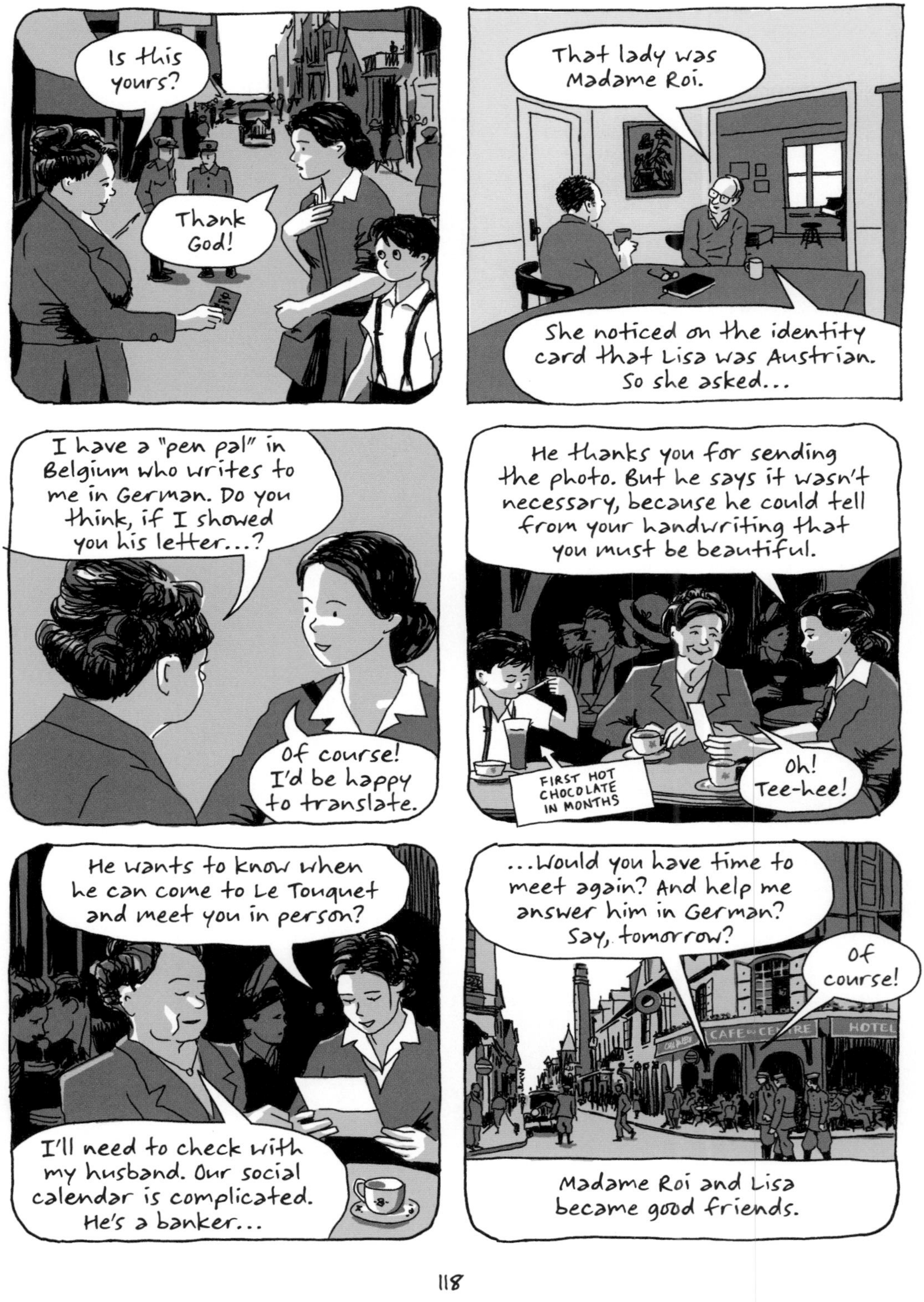
Is this yours?
Thank God!
That lady was Madame Roi.
She noticed on the identity card that Lisa was Austrian. So she asked...
I have a "pen pal" in Belgium who writes to me in German. Do you think, if I showed you his letter...?
Of course! I'd be happy to translate.
He thanks you for sending the photo. But he says it wasn't necessary, because he could tell from your handwriting that you must be beautiful.
FIRST HOT CHOCOLATE IN MONTHS
Oh! Tee-hee!
He wants to know when he can come to Le Touquet and meet you in person?
I'll need to check with my husband. Our social calendar is complicated. He's a banker...
...Would you have time to meet again? And help me answer him in German? Say, tomorrow?
Of course!
CAFE DU CENTRE
HOTEL
Madame Roi and Lisa became good friends.

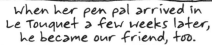
When her pen pal arrived in Le Touquet a few weeks later, he became our friend, too.

He was a Jewish refugee from Vienna, like us. His name was Philip Baer.

Is his name "Baer" because he's so hairy?

Ha ha! It should be!

His romance with Madame Roi didn't last long.

It soon became obvious that he preferred Lisa.

Awkward!

Oh, Madame Roi took it with good humor...

Everyone who met Lisa loved her.

She had really remarkable social skills. She always knew just what to do and say in every situation.

I didn't like Baer, though. And he didn't like me.

...gib mir einen Kuss...

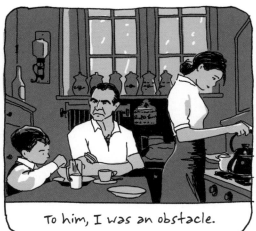
To him, I was an obstacle.

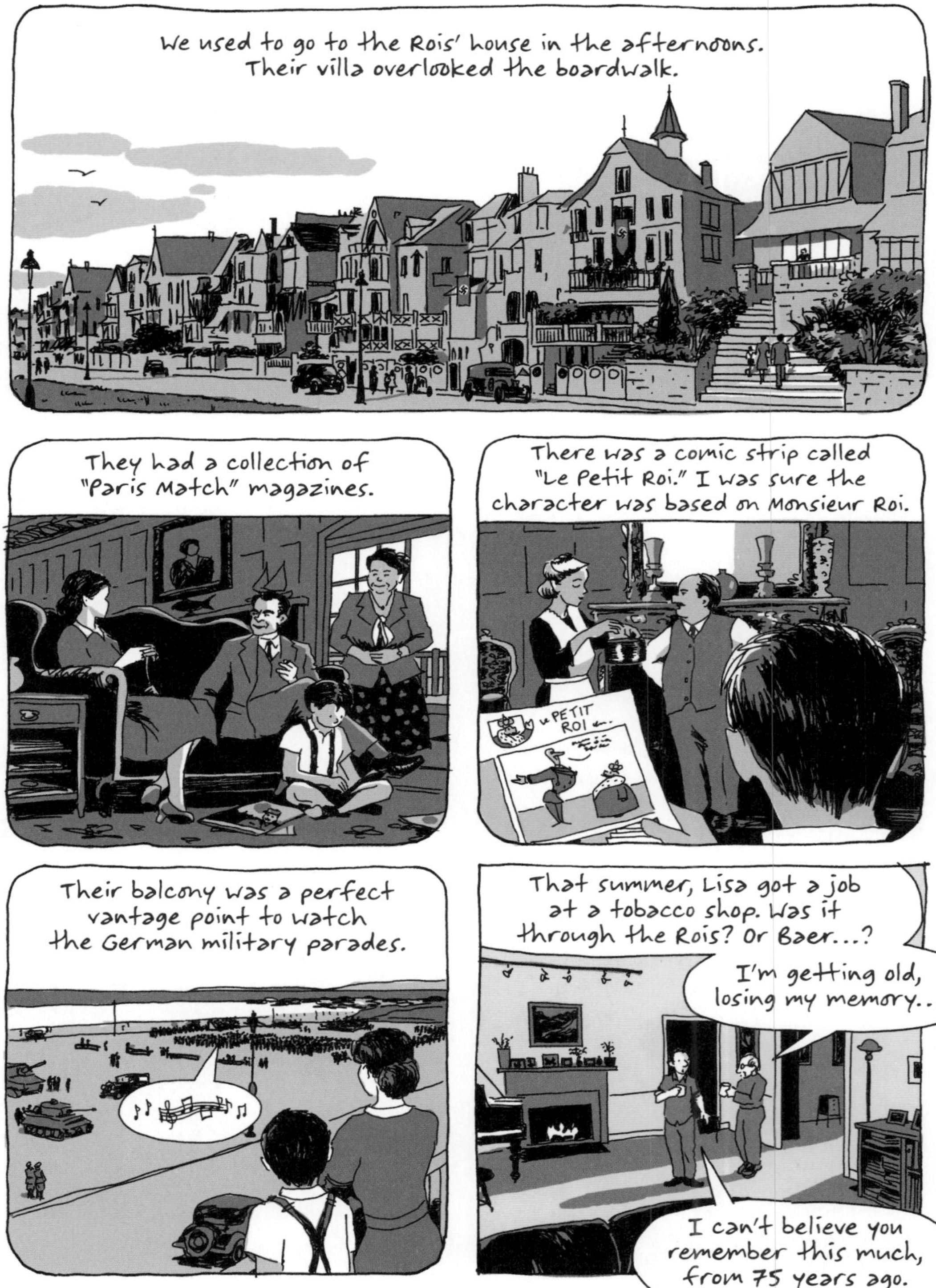
We used to go to the Rois' house in the afternoons. Their villa overlooked the boardwalk.
They had a collection of "Paris Match" magazines.
There was a comic strip called "Le Petit Roi." I was sure the character was based on Monsieur Roi.
Le PETIT ROI
Their balcony was a perfect vantage point to watch the German military parades.
That summer, Lisa got a job at a tobacco shop. Was it through the Rois? Or Baer...?
I'm getting old, losing my memory...
I can't believe you remember this much, from 75 years ago.

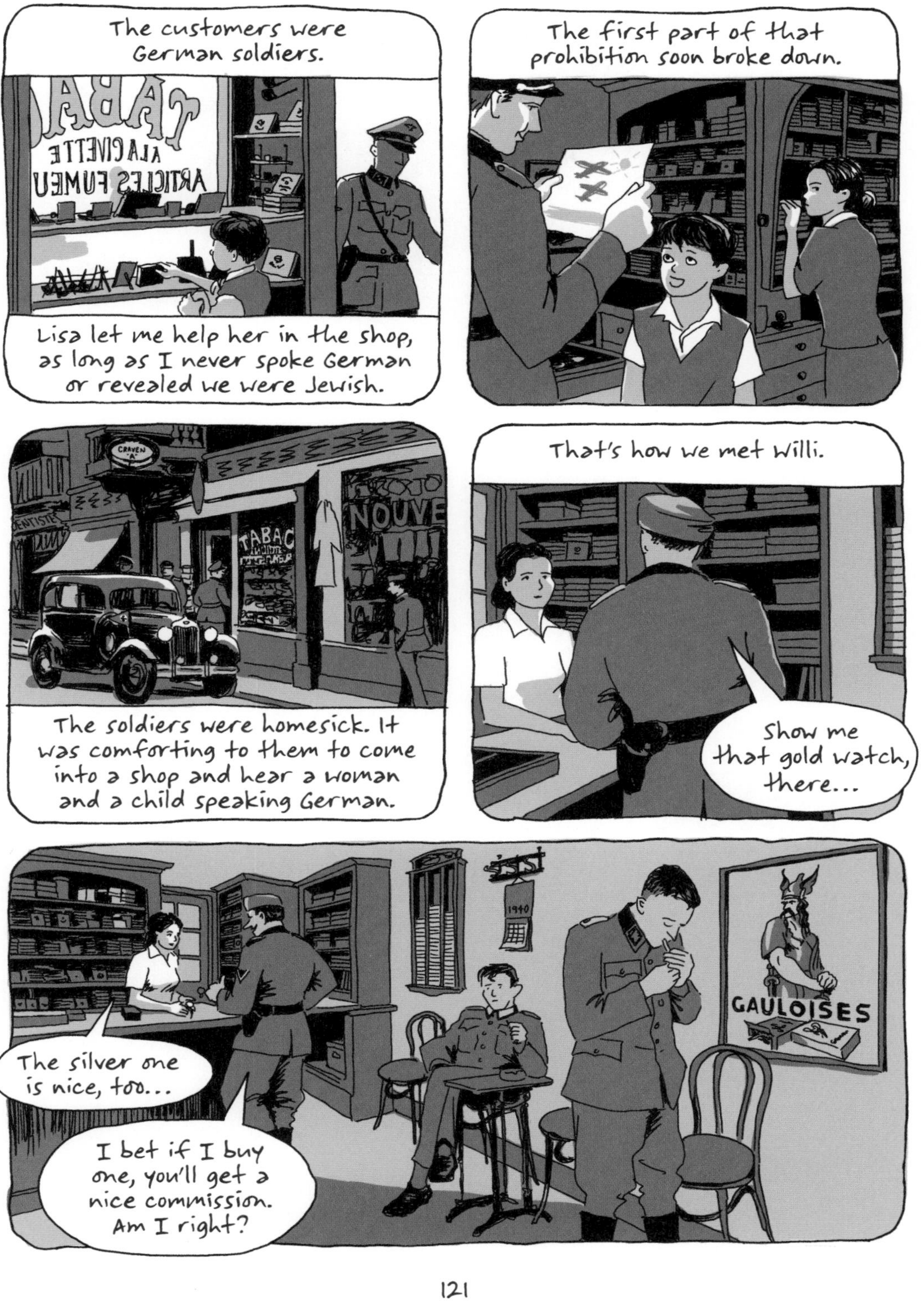
The customers were German soldiers.
TABAC
A LA CIVETTE
ARTICLES FUMEU
Lisa let me help her in the shop, as long as I never spoke German or revealed we were Jewish.
The first part of that prohibition soon broke down.
CRAVEN "A"
DENTISTE
TABAC
NOUVE
The soldiers were homesick. It was comforting to them to come into a shop and hear a woman and a child speaking German.
That's how we met Willi.
Show me that gold watch, there...
1940
GAULOISES
The silver one is nice, too...
I bet if I buy one, you'll get a nice commission. Am I right?

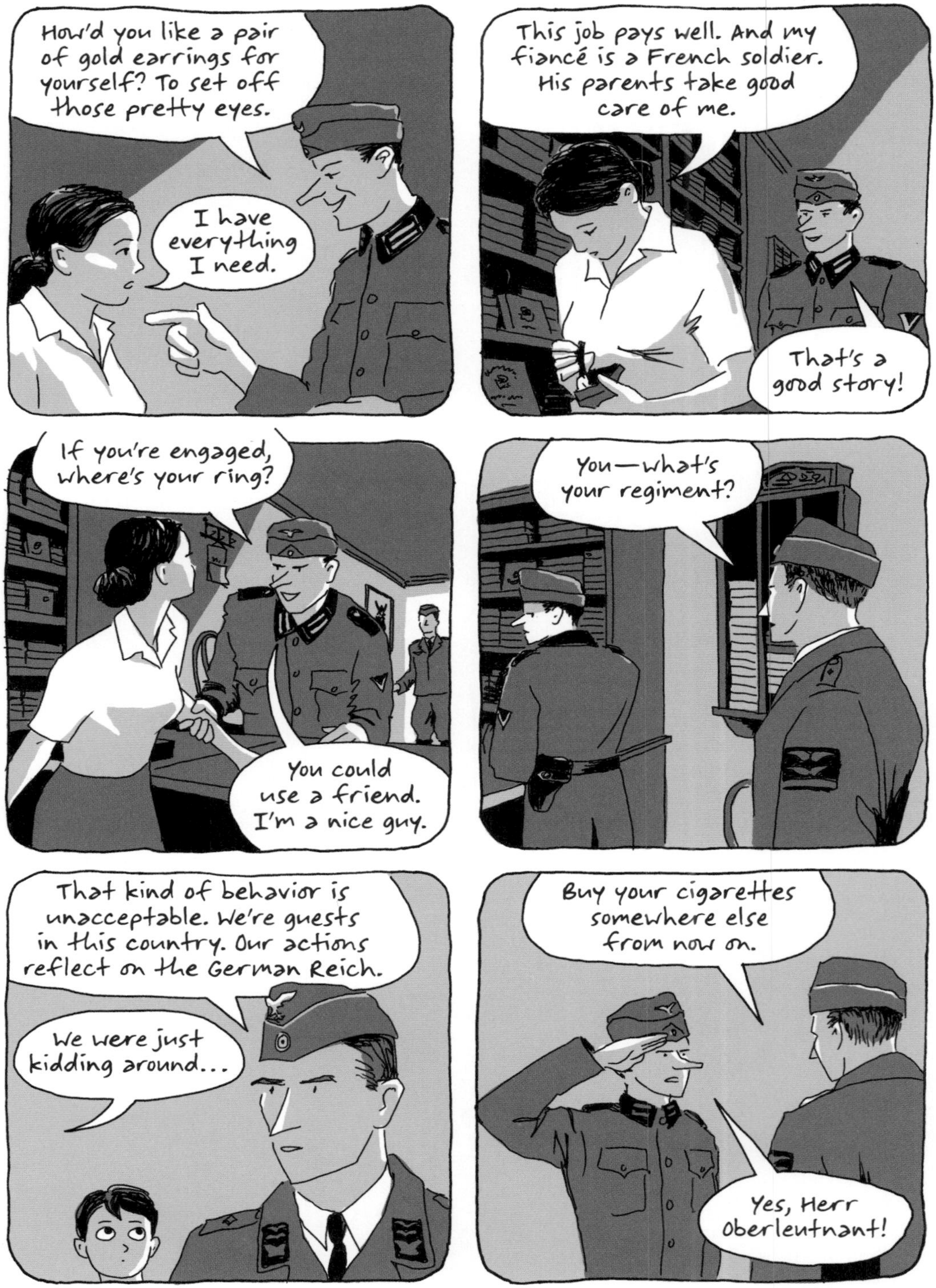
How'd you like a pair of gold earrings for yourself? To set off those pretty eyes.
I have everything I need.
This job pays well. And my fiancé is a French soldier. His parents take good care of me.
That's a good story!
If you're engaged, where's your ring?
You could use a friend. I'm a nice guy.
You—what's your regiment?
That kind of behavior is unacceptable. We're guests in this country. Our actions reflect on the German Reich.
We were just kidding around...
Buy your cigarettes somewhere else from now on.
Yes, Herr Oberleutnant!

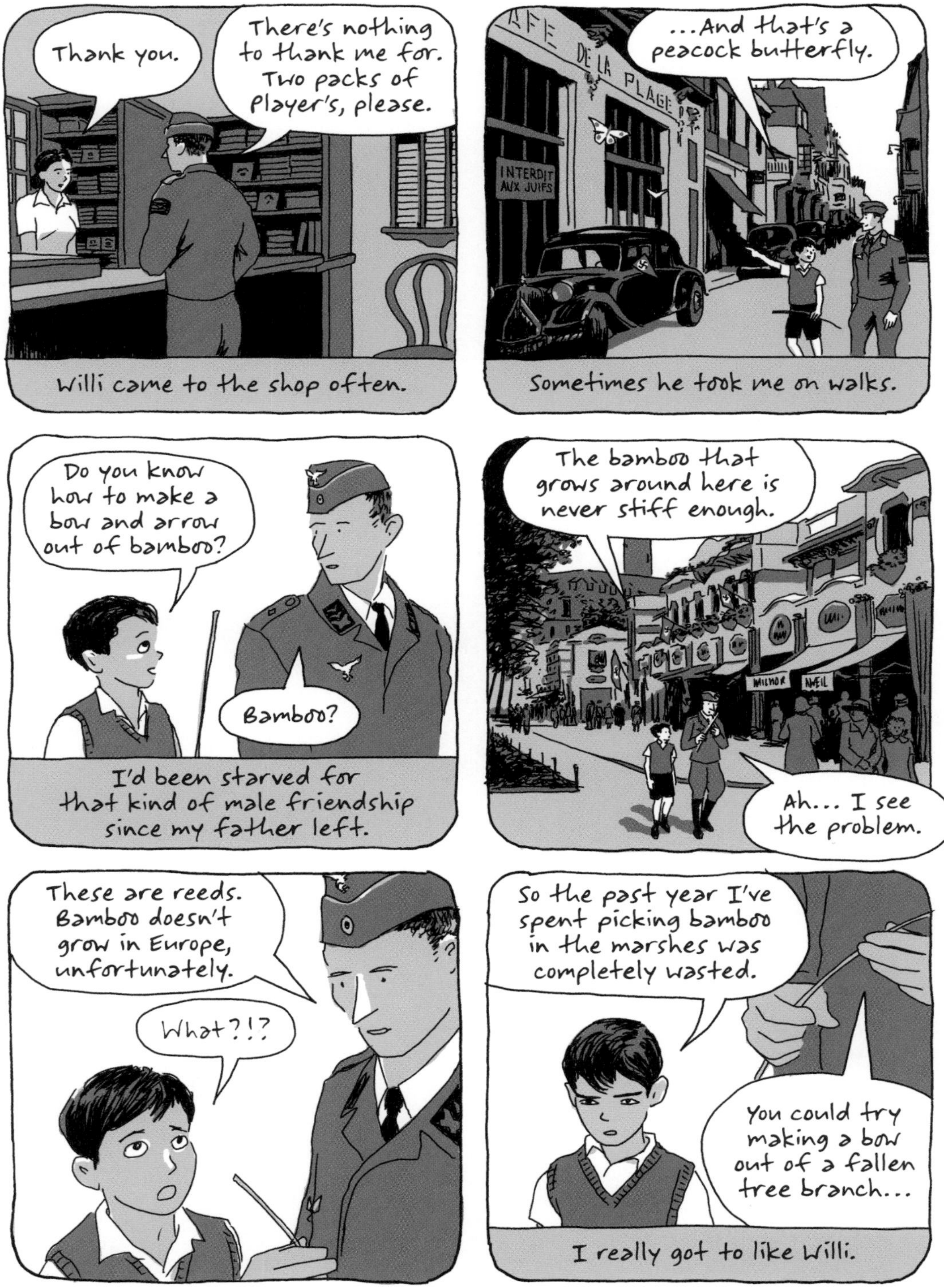
Thank you.
There's nothing to thank me for. Two packs of Player's, please.
Willi came to the shop often.
AFE DE LA PLAGE
INTERDIT AUX JUIFS
...And that's a peacock butterfly.
Sometimes he took me on walks.
Do you know how to make a bow and arrow out of bamboo?
Bamboo?
I'd been starved for that kind of male friendship since my father left.
The bamboo that grows around here is never stiff enough.
Ah... I see the problem.
These are reeds. Bamboo doesn't grow in Europe, unfortunately.
What?!?
So the past year I've spent picking bamboo in the marshes was completely wasted.
You could try making a bow out of a fallen tree branch...
I really got to like Willi.

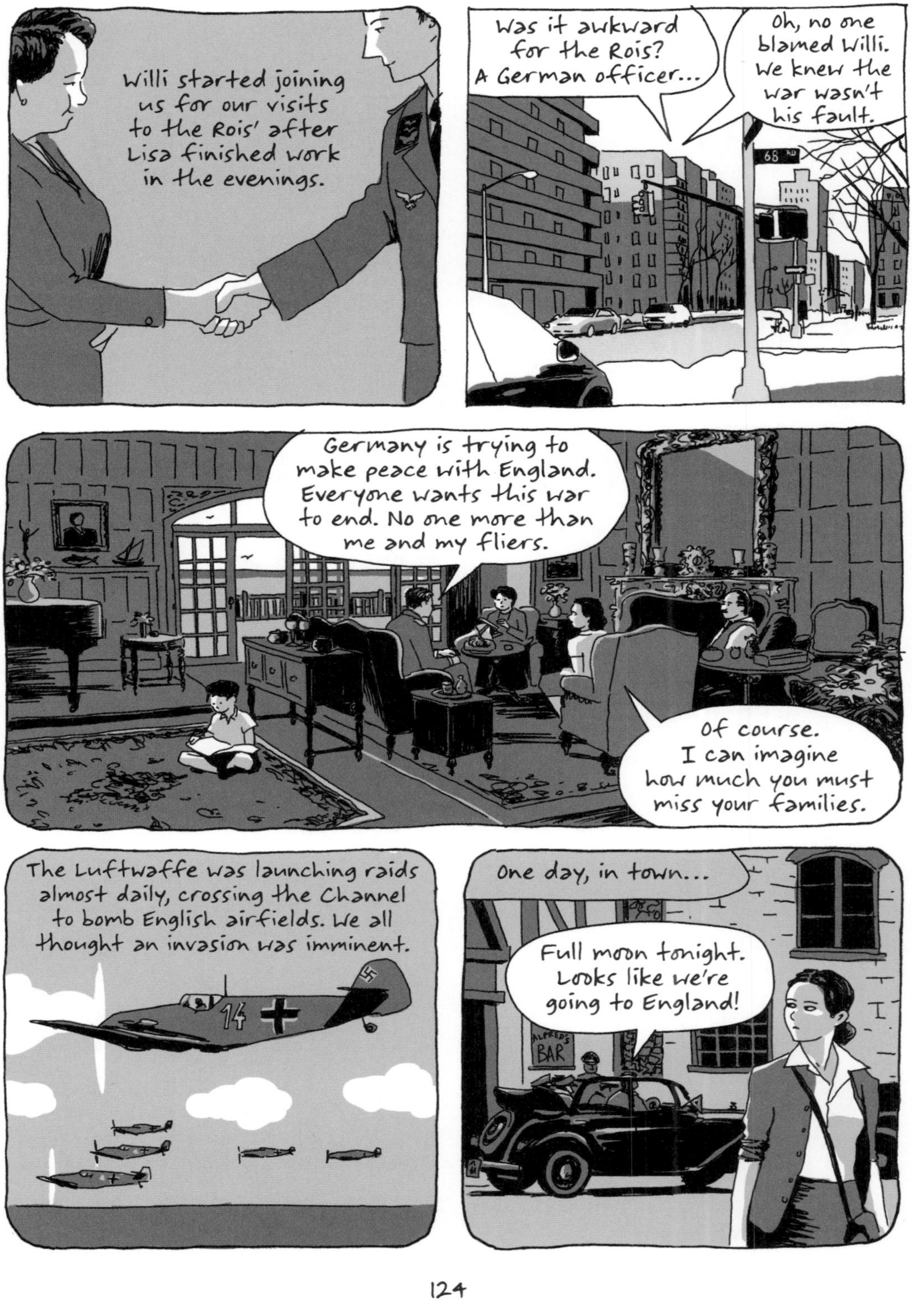
Willi started joining us for our visits to the Rois' after Lisa finished work in the evenings.
Was it awkward for the Rois? A German officer...
Oh, no one blamed Willi. We knew the war wasn't his fault.
68 RD
Germany is trying to make peace with England. Everyone wants this war to end. No one more than me and my fliers.
Of course. I can imagine how much you must miss your families.
The Luftwaffe was launching raids almost daily, crossing the Channel to bomb English airfields. We all thought an invasion was imminent.
14
One day, in town...
Full moon tonight. Looks like we're going to England!
ALFRED'S BAR

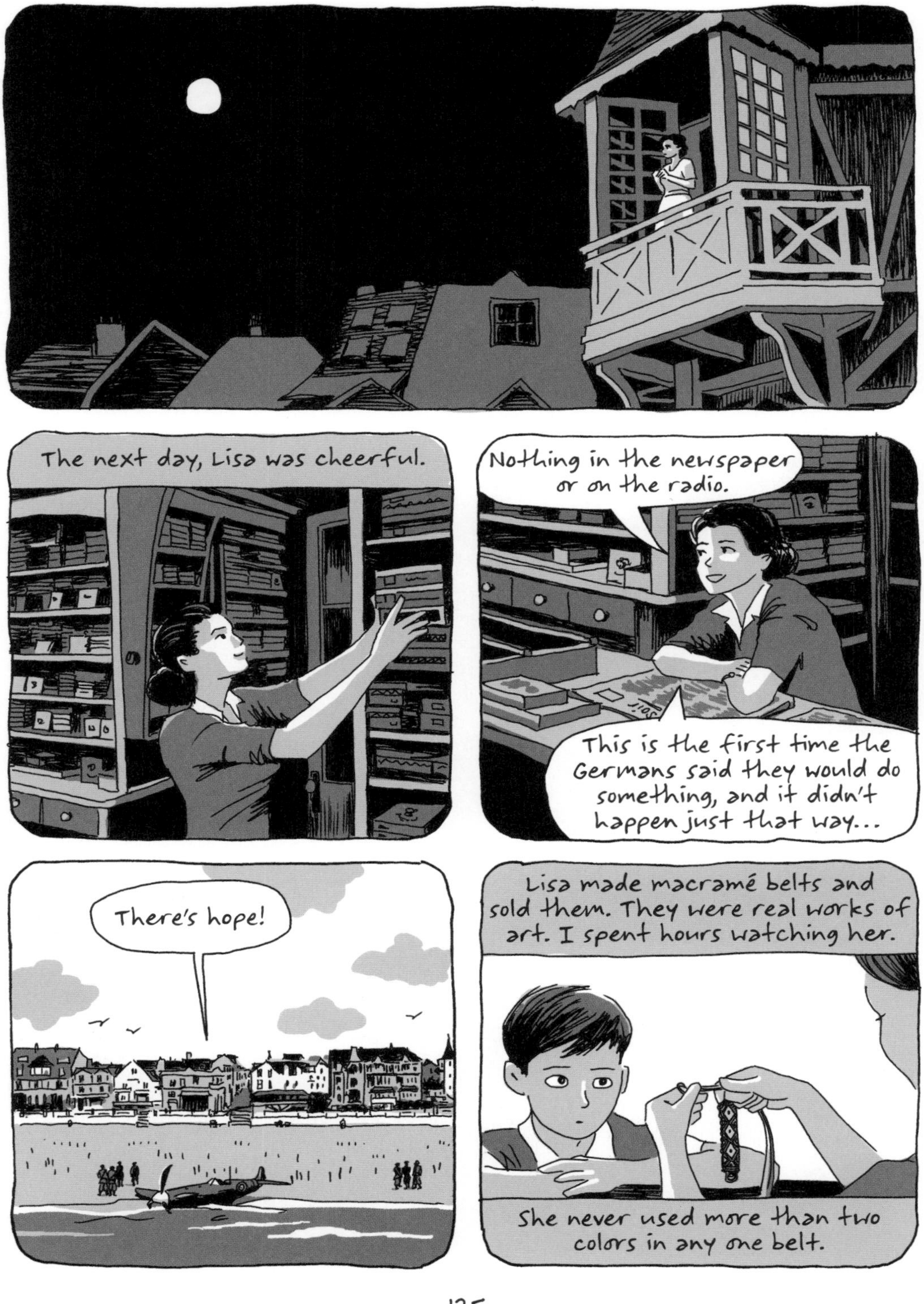
The next day, Lisa was cheerful.
Nothing in the newspaper or on the radio.
This is the first time the Germans said they would do something, and it didn't happen just that way...
There's hope!
Lisa made macramé belts and sold them. They were real works of art. I spent hours watching her.
She never used more than two colors in any one belt.

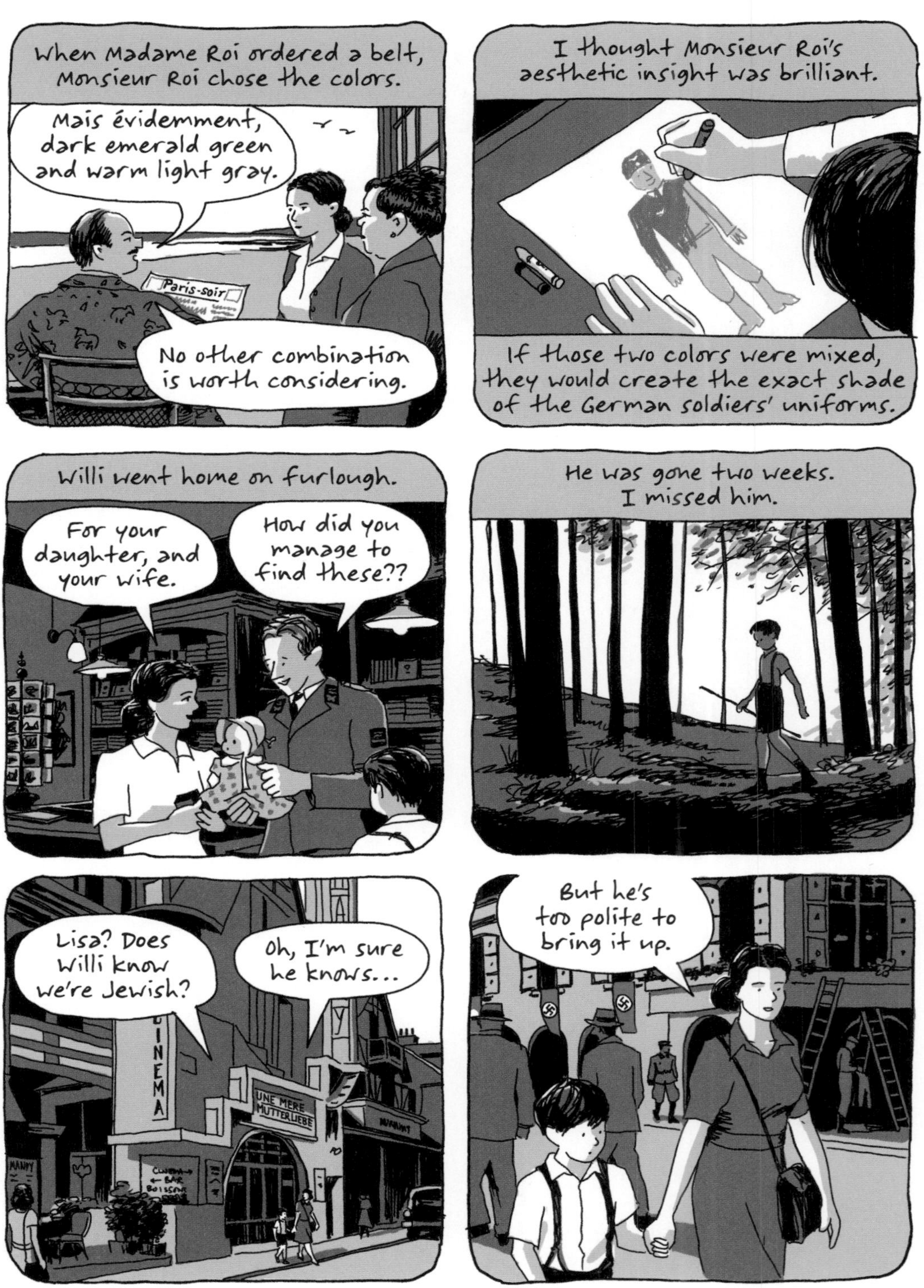
When Madame Roi ordered a belt, Monsieur Roi chose the colors.
Mais évidemment, dark emerald green and warm light gray.
Paris-soir
No other combination is worth considering.
I thought Monsieur Roi's aesthetic insight was brilliant.
If those two colors were mixed, they would create the exact shade of the German soldiers' uniforms.
Willi went home on furlough.
For your daughter, and your wife.
How did you manage to find these??
He was gone two weeks. I missed him.
Lisa? Does Willi know we're Jewish?
Oh, I'm sure he knows...
CINEMA
UNE MERE
MUTTERLIEBE
But he's too polite to bring it up.

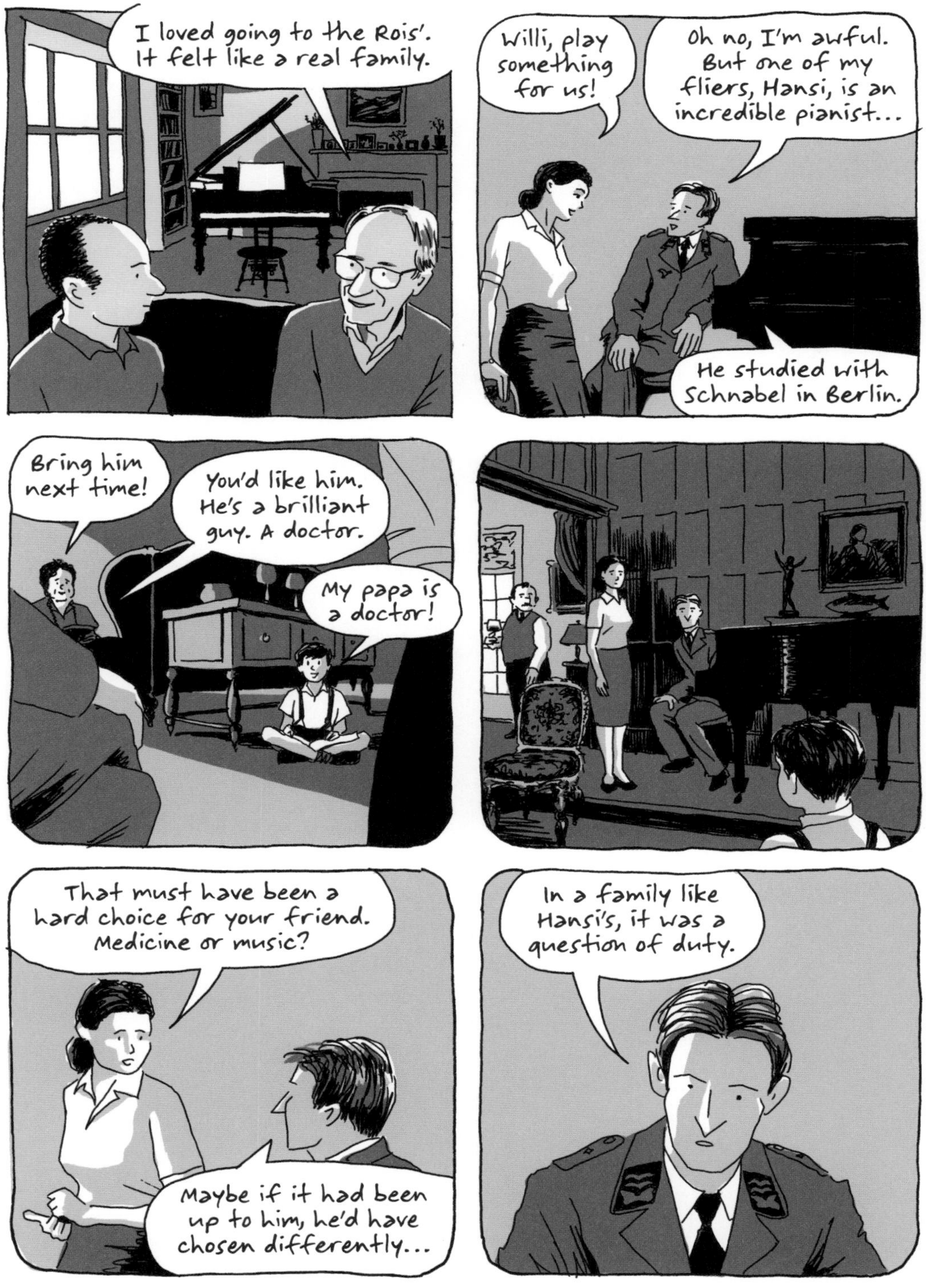
I loved going to the Rois'. It felt like a real family.
Willi, play something for us!
Oh no, I'm awful. But one of my fliers, Hansi, is an incredible pianist...
He studied with Schnabel in Berlin.
Bring him next time!
You'd like him. He's a brilliant guy. A doctor.
My papa is a doctor!
That must have been a hard choice for your friend. Medicine or music?
Maybe if it had been up to him, he'd have chosen differently...
In a family like Hansi's, it was a question of duty.

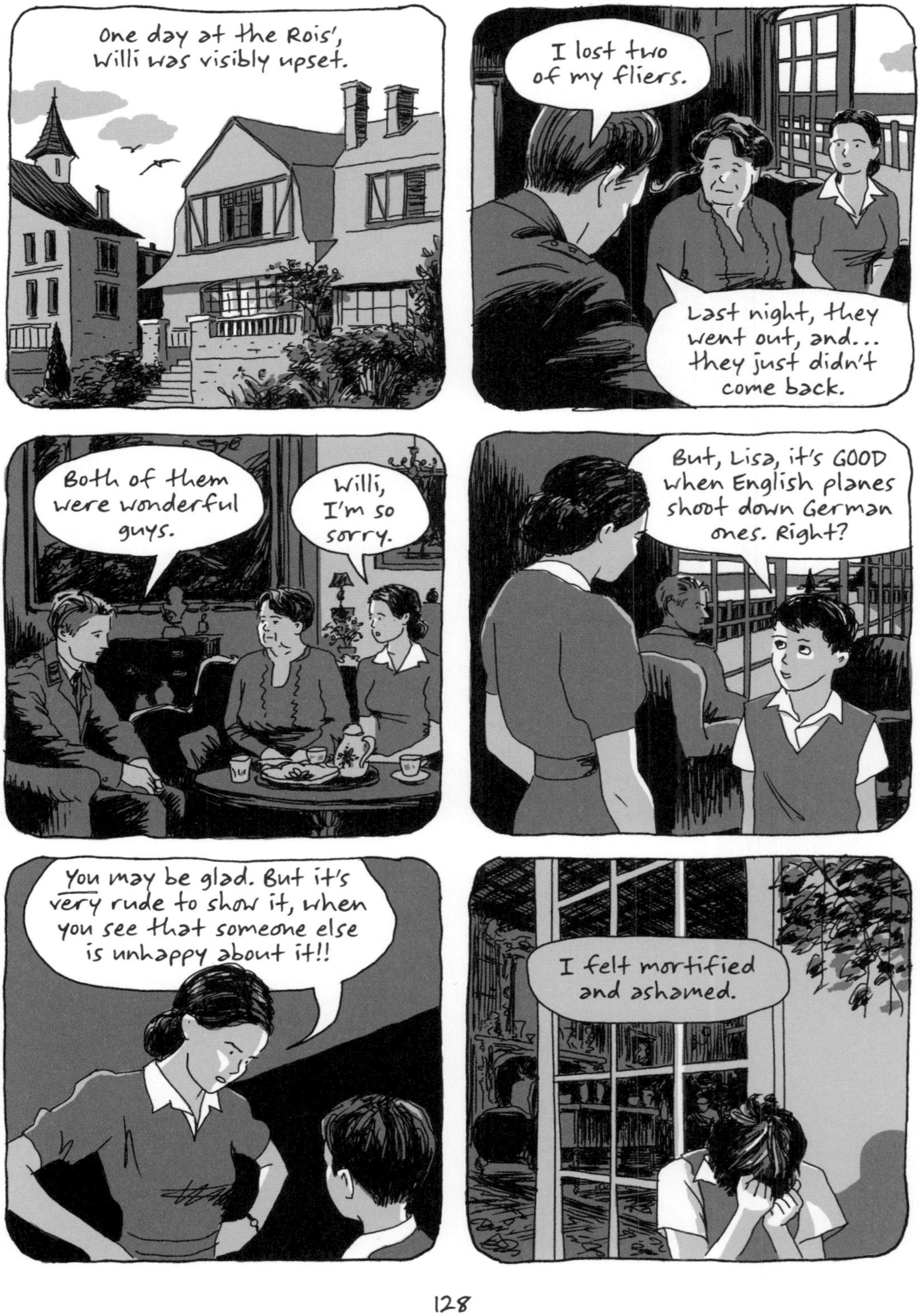
One day at the Rois', Willi was visibly upset.
I lost two of my fliers.
Last night, they went out, and... they just didn't come back.
Both of them were wonderful guys.
Willi, I'm so sorry.
But, Lisa, it's GOOD when English planes shoot down German ones. Right?
You may be glad. But it's very rude to show it, when you see that someone else is unhappy about it!!
I felt mortified and ashamed.

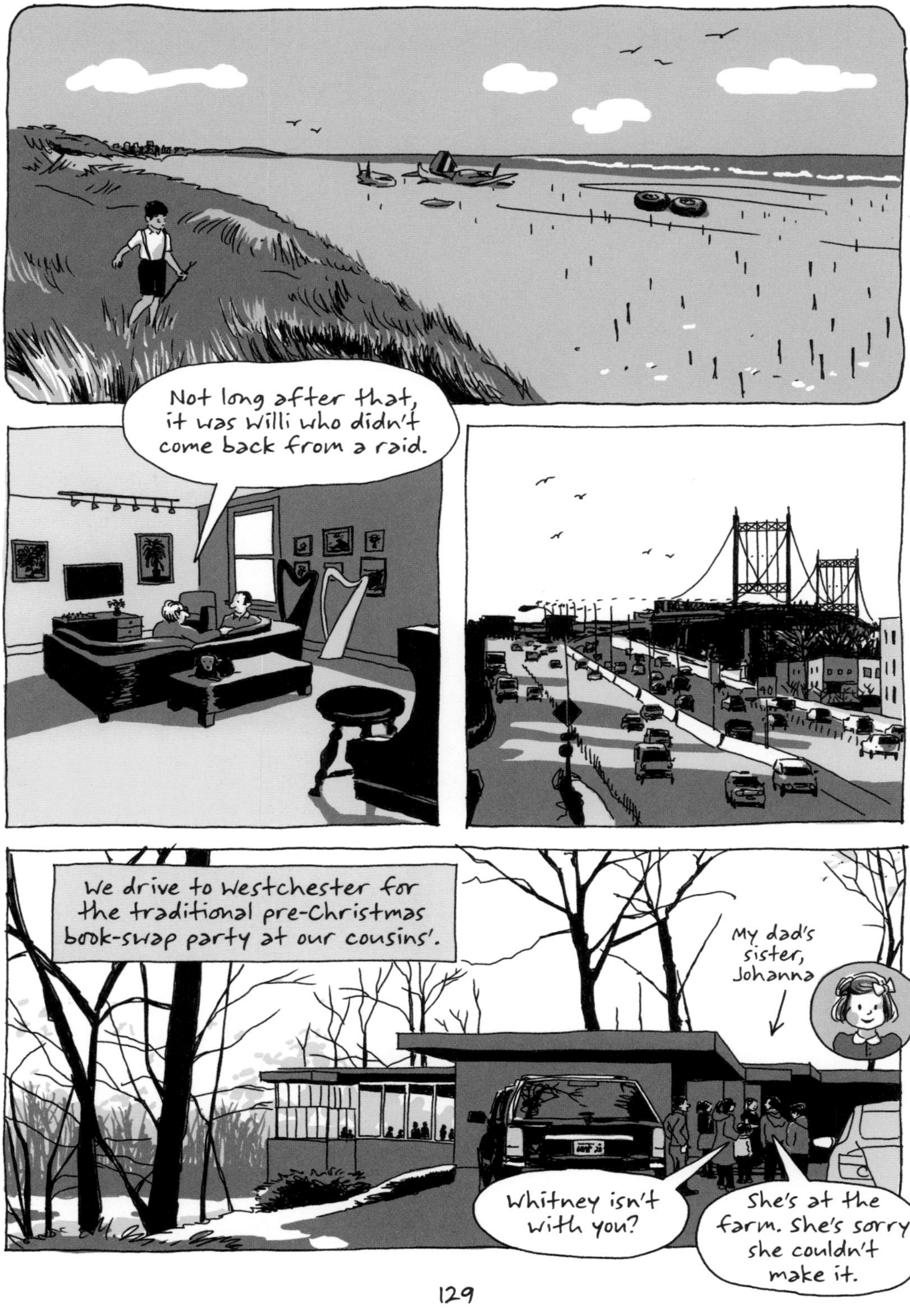
Not long after that, it was Willi who didn't come back from a raid.
We drive to Westchester for the traditional pre-Christmas book-swap party at our cousins'.
My dad's sister, Johanna
Whitney isn't with you?
She's at the farm. She's sorry she couldn't make it.

Silk Road

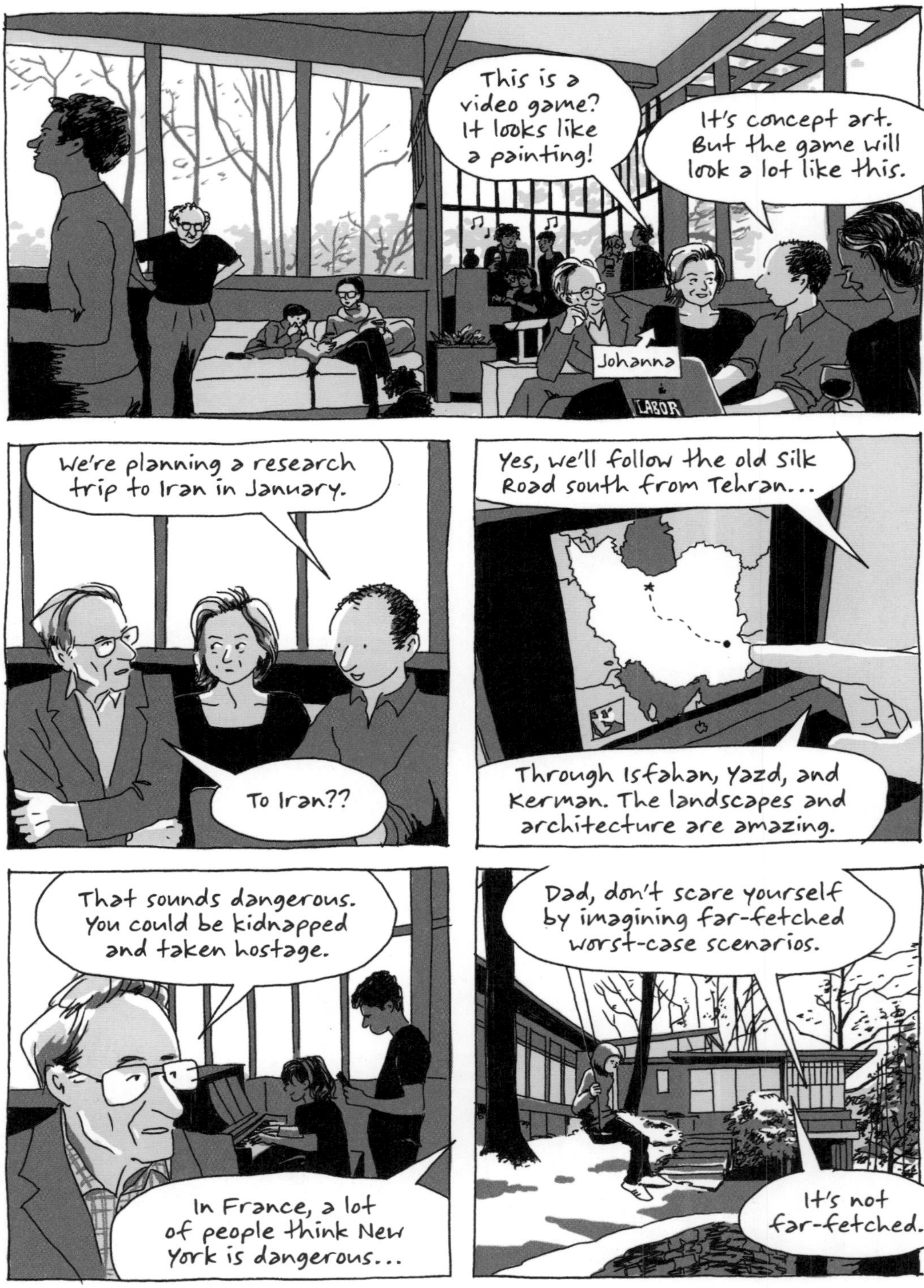
This is a video game? It looks like a painting!
It's concept art. But the game will look a lot like this.
Johanna
LABOR
We're planning a research trip to Iran in January.
To Iran??
Yes, we'll follow the old Silk Road south from Tehran...
Through Isfahan, Yazd, and Kerman. The landscapes and architecture are amazing.
That sounds dangerous. You could be kidnapped and taken hostage.
In France, a lot of people think New York is dangerous...
Dad, don't scare yourself by imagining far-fetched worst-case scenarios.
It's not far-fetched.

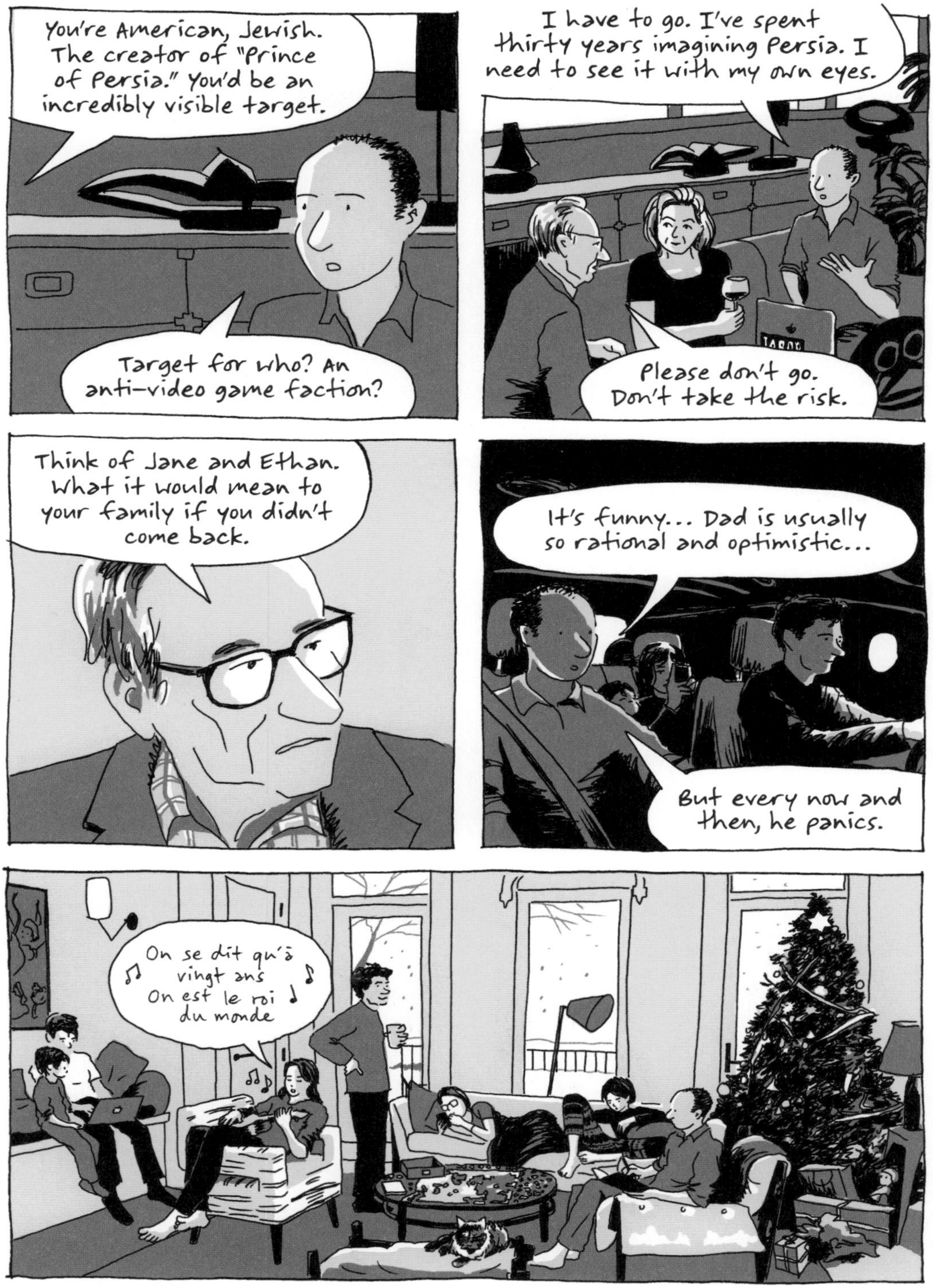
You're American, Jewish. The creator of "Prince of Persia." You'd be an incredibly visible target.
Target for who? An anti-video game faction?
I have to go. I've spent thirty years imagining Persia. I need to see it with my own eyes.
Please don't go. Don't take the risk.
Think of Jane and Ethan. What it would mean to your family if you didn't come back.
It's funny... Dad is usually so rational and optimistic...
But every now and then, he panics.
On se dit qu'à vingt ans On est le roi du monde

Storm

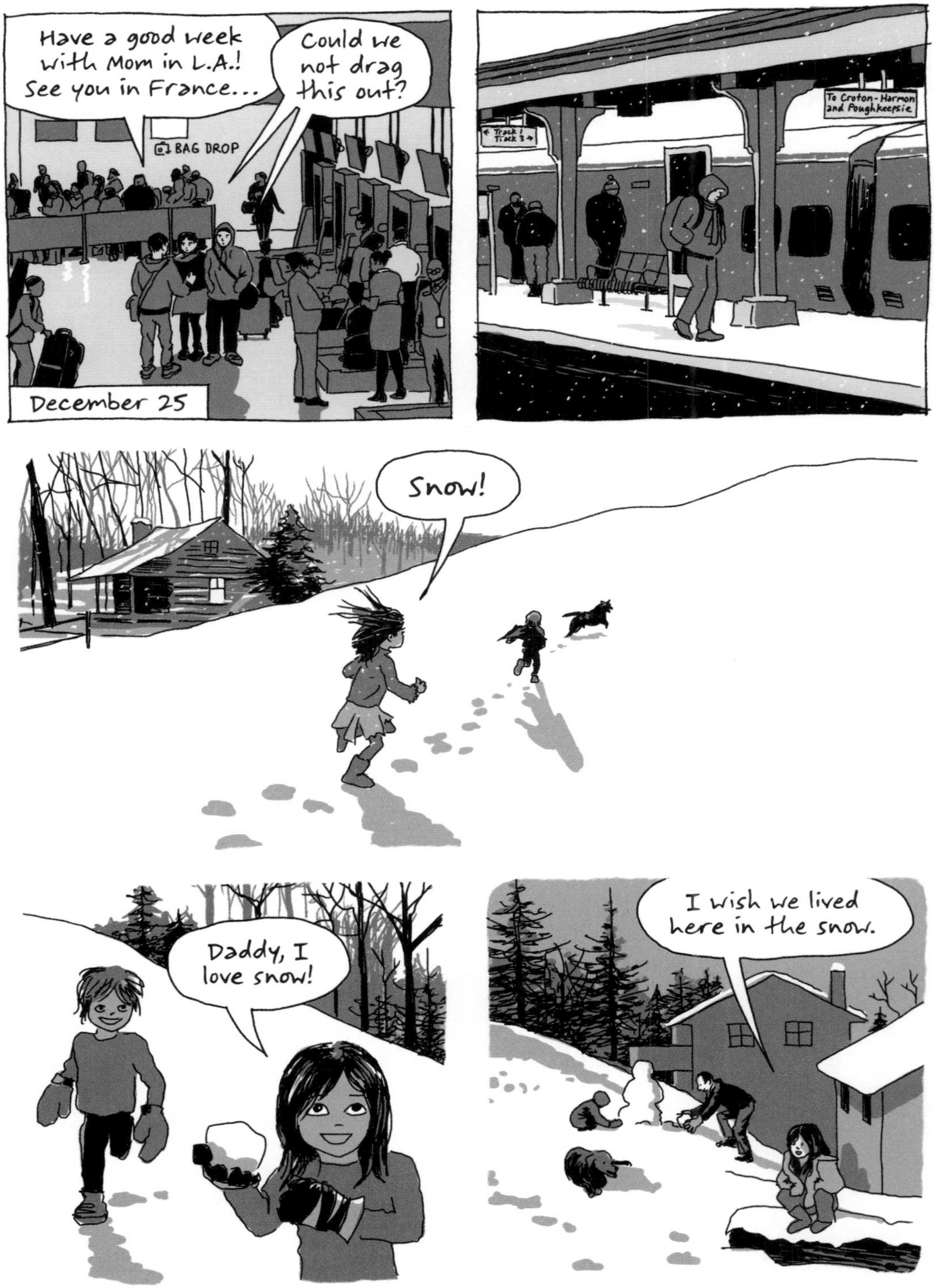

Have a good week with Mom in L.A.! See you in France...
Could we not drag this out?
BAG DROP
December 25
To Croton-Harmon and Poughkeepsie
Track 1
Track 3
Snow!
Daddy, I love snow!
I wish we lived here in the snow.

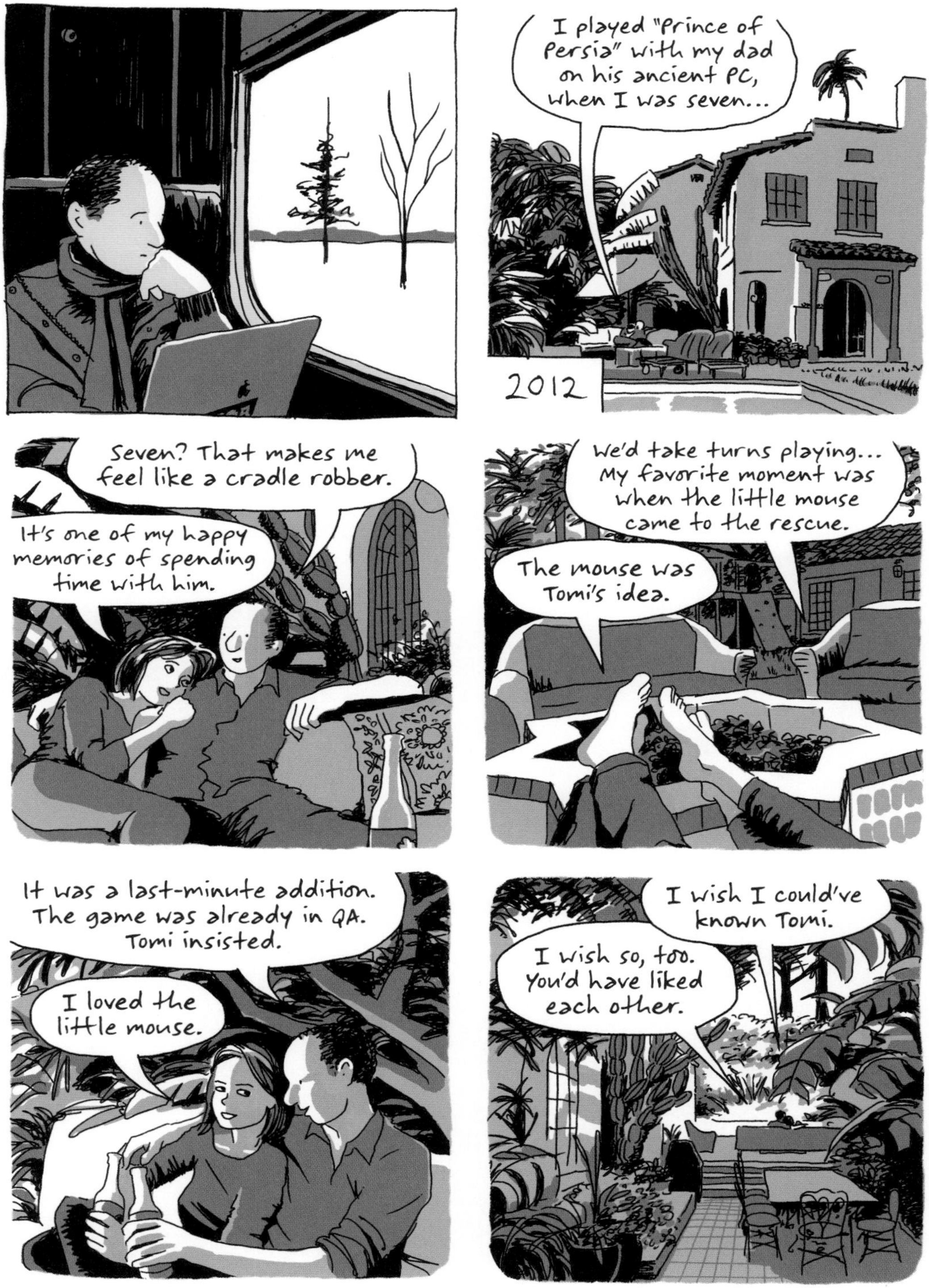
I played "Prince of Persia" with my dad on his ancient PC, when I was seven...
2012
Seven? That makes me feel like a cradle robber.
It's one of my happy memories of spending time with him.
We'd take turns playing... My favorite moment was when the little mouse came to the rescue.
The mouse was Tomi's idea.
It was a last-minute addition. The game was already in QA. Tomi insisted.
I loved the little mouse.
I wish I could've known Tomi.
I wish so, too. You'd have liked each other.

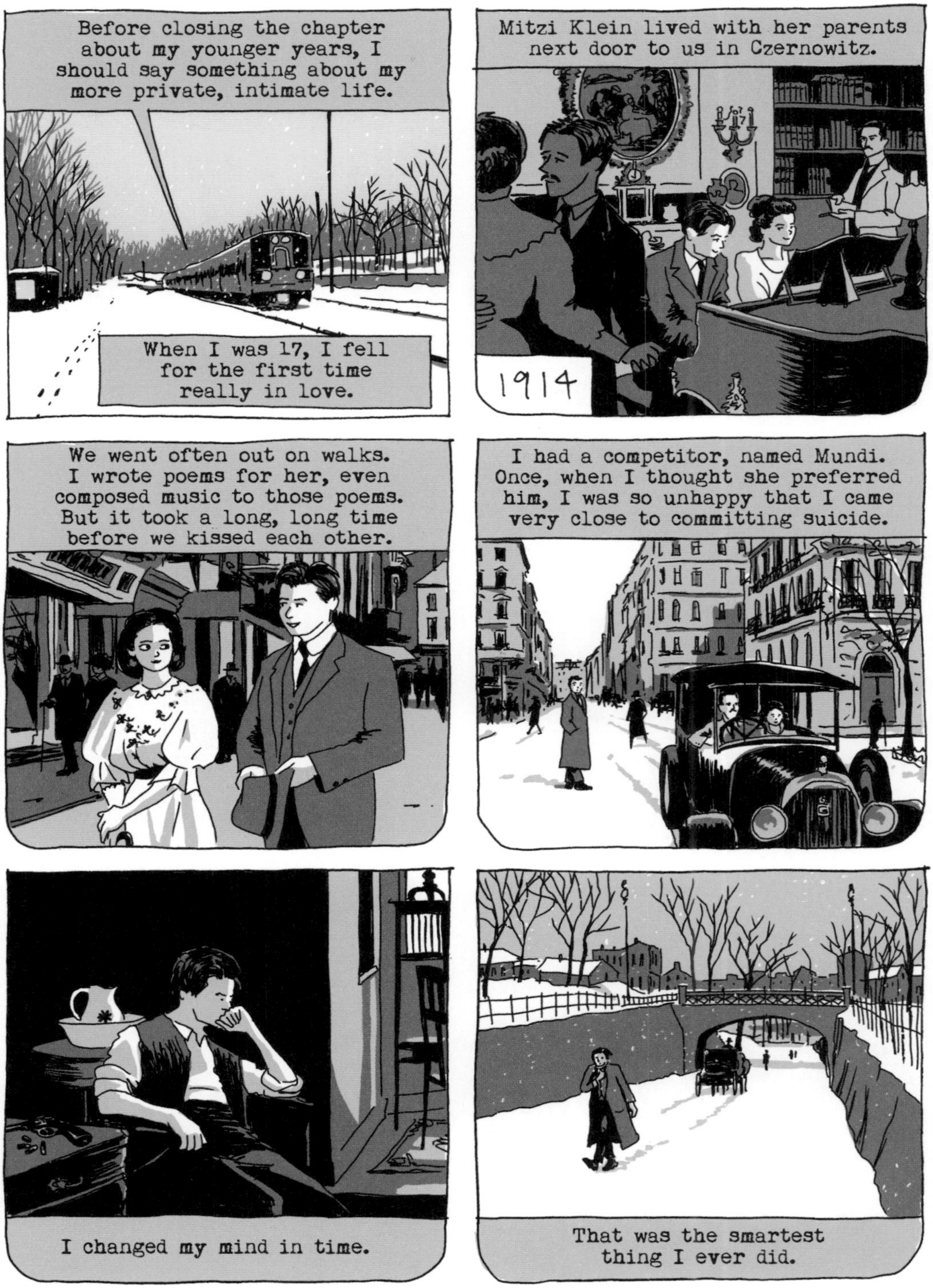
Before closing the chapter about my younger years, I should say something about my more private, intimate life.
When I was 17, I fell for the first time really in love.
Mitzi Klein lived with her parents next door to us in Czernowitz.
1914
We went often out on walks. I wrote poems for her, even composed music to those poems. But it took a long, long time before we kissed each other.
I had a competitor, named Mundi. Once, when I thought she preferred him, I was so unhappy that I came very close to committing suicide.
I changed my mind in time.
That was the smartest thing I ever did.

Two days before New Year's Eve, Whitney and I agree to divorce.

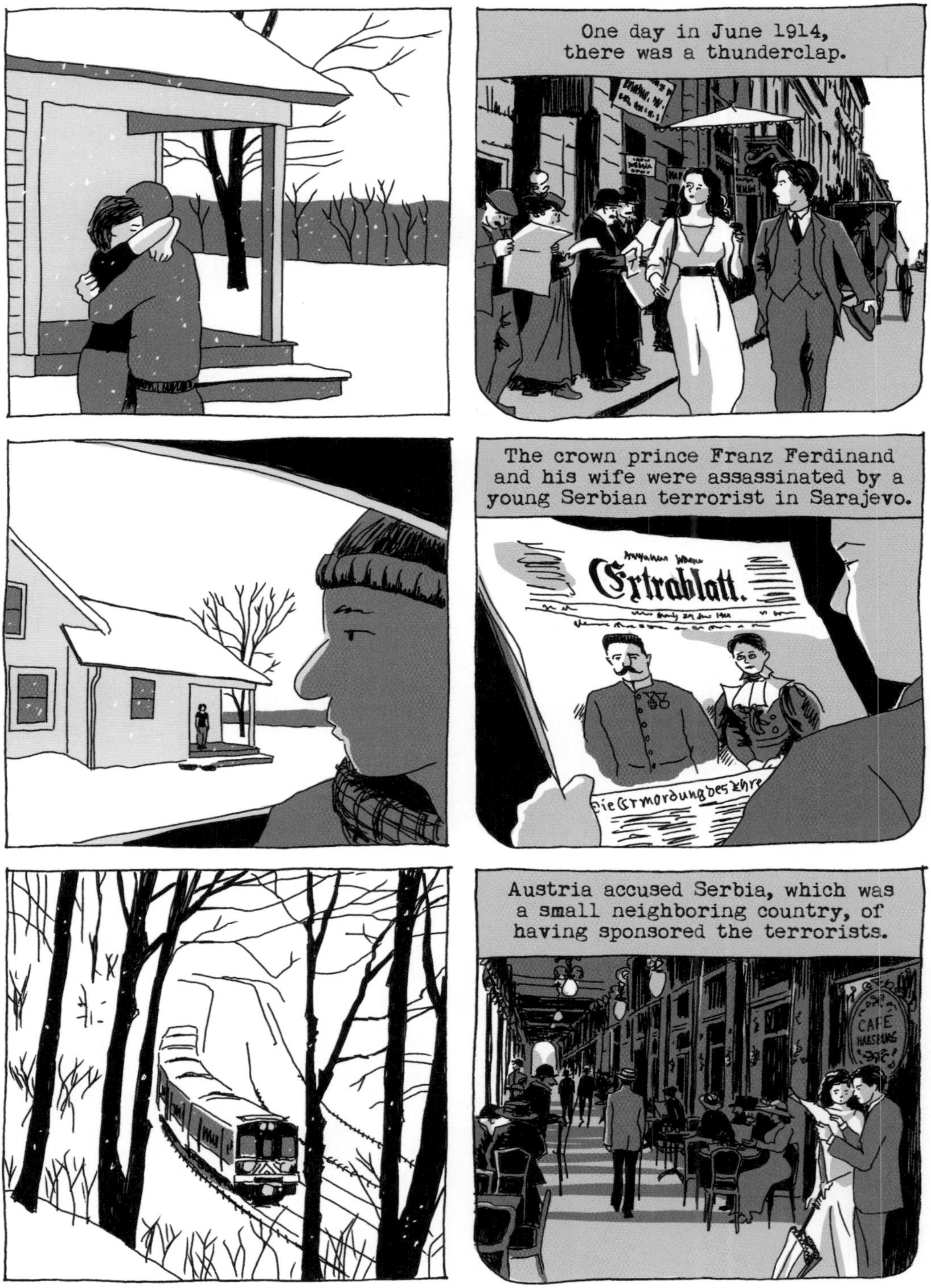
One day in June 1914, there was a thunderclap.
The crown prince Franz Ferdinand and his wife were assassinated by a young Serbian terrorist in Sarajevo.
Extrablatt.
Austria accused Serbia, which was a small neighboring country, of having sponsored the terrorists.
CAFÉ HABSBURG

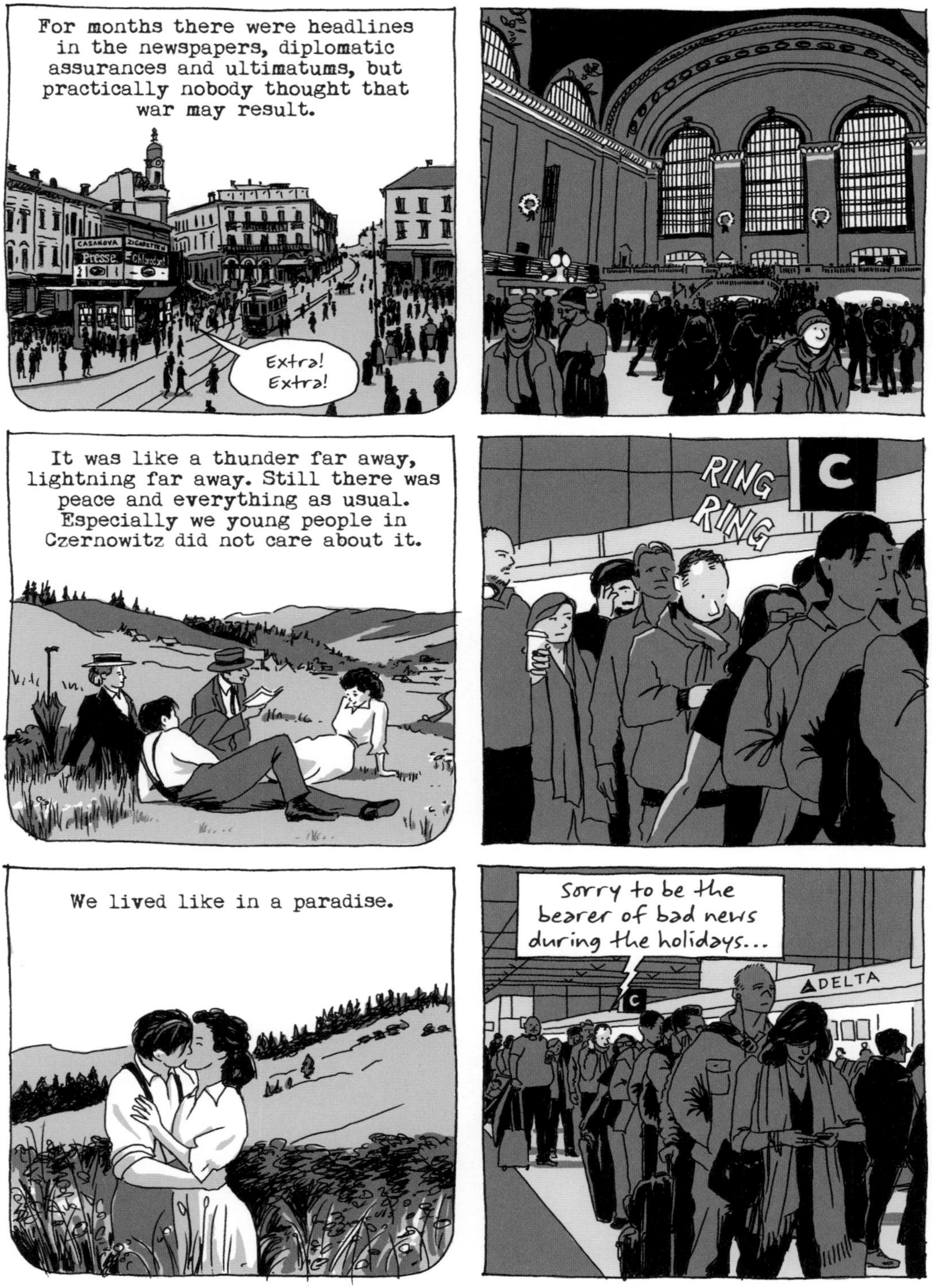
For months there were headlines in the newspapers, diplomatic assurances and ultimatums, but practically nobody thought that war may result.
CASANOVA
Presse
Extra! Extra!
It was like a thunder far away, lightning far away. Still there was peace and everything as usual. Especially we young people in Czernowitz did not care about it.
RING RING
C
We lived like in a paradise.
Sorry to be the bearer of bad news during the holidays...
C
DELTA

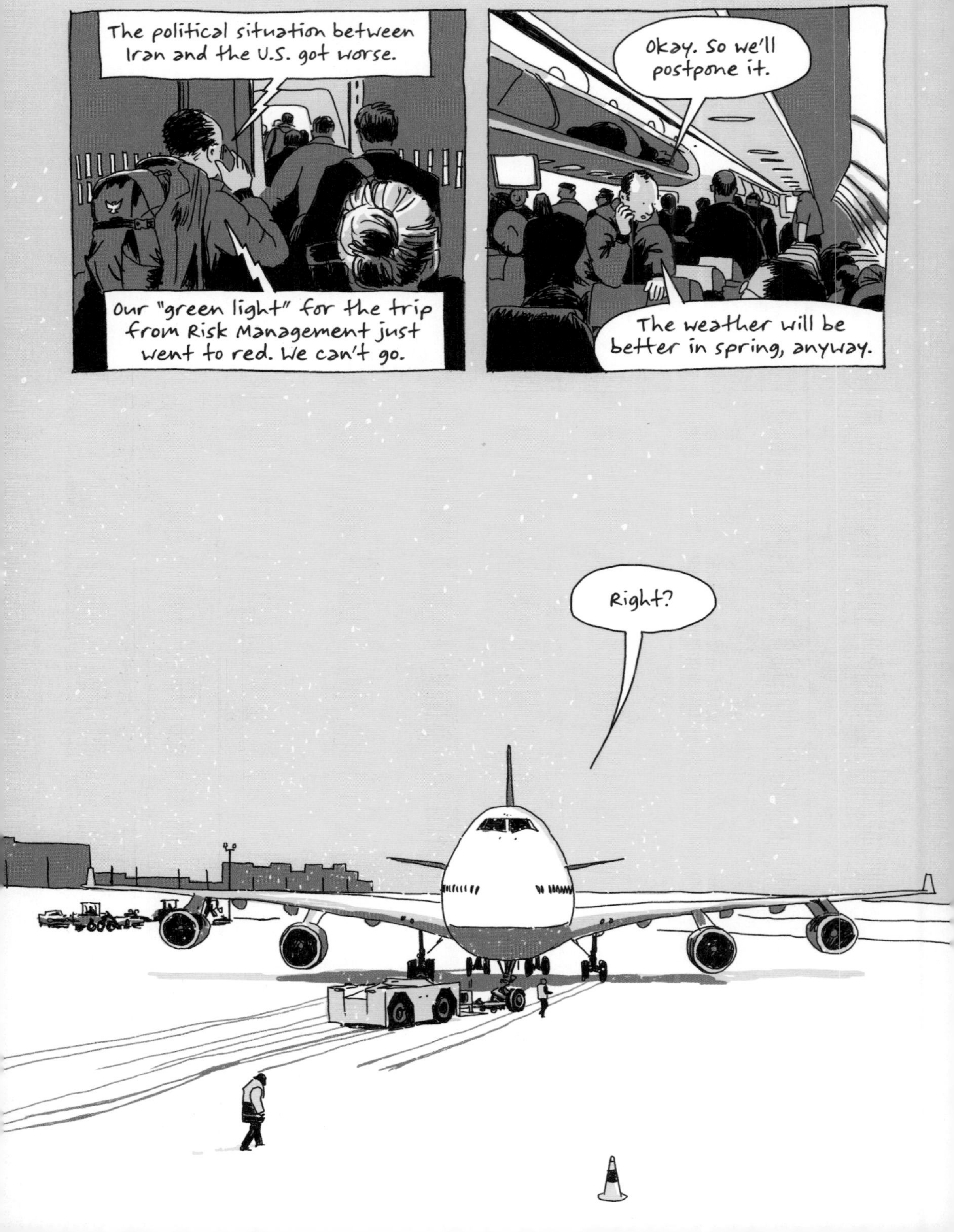
The political situation between Iran and the U.S. got worse.
Our "green light" for the trip from Risk Management just went to red. We can't go.
Okay. So we'll postpone it.
The weather will be better in spring, anyway.
Right?

Chapter 5

The Witch

Adolf Mechner, age 20
Italy, 1918

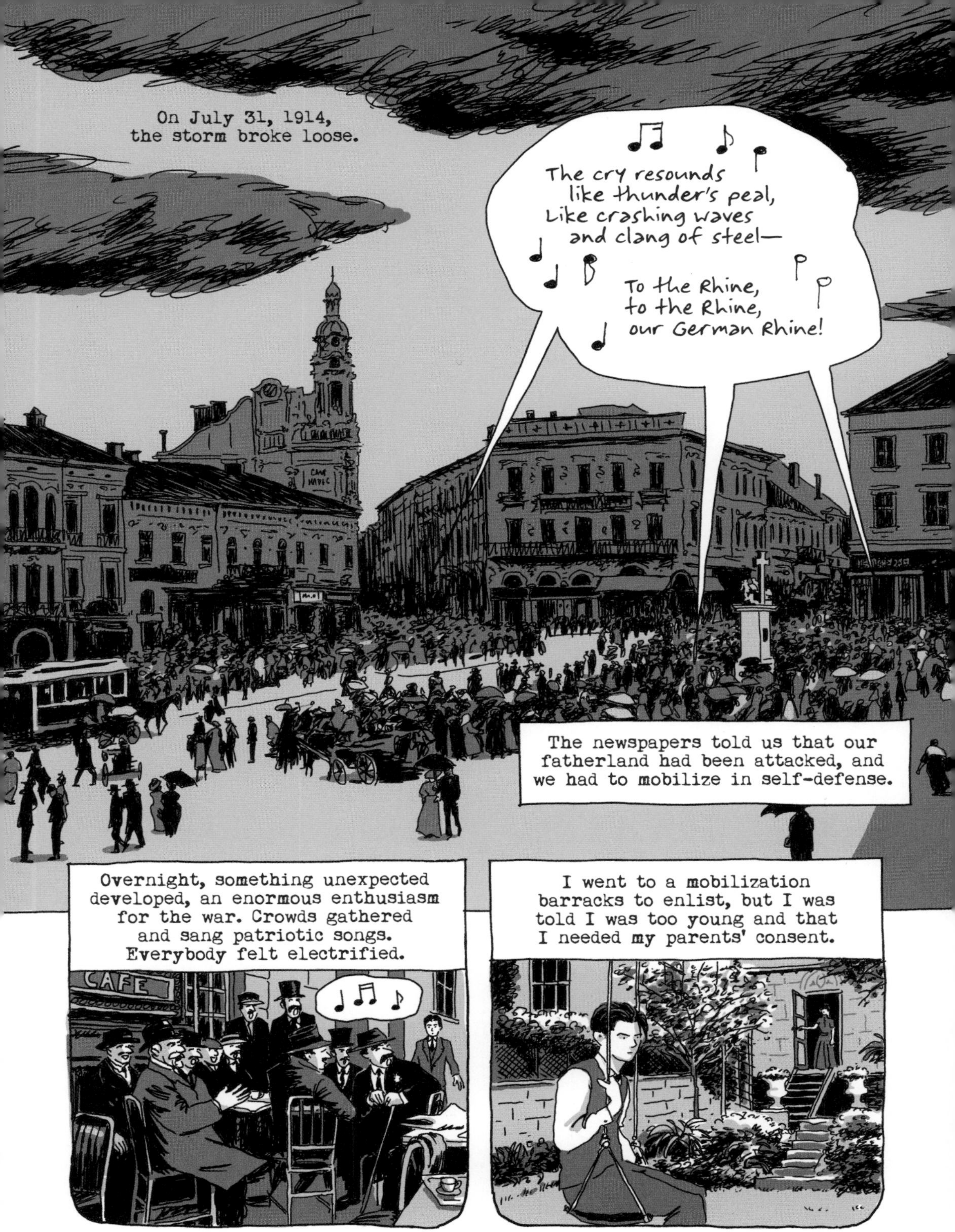
On July 31, 1914, the storm broke loose.
The cry resounds like thunder's peal, Like crashing waves and clang of steel— To the Rhine, to the Rhine, our German Rhine!
The newspapers told us that our fatherland had been attacked, and we had to mobilize in self-defense.
Overnight, something unexpected developed, an enormous enthusiasm for the war. Crowds gathered and sang patriotic songs. Everybody felt electrified.
CAFE
I went to a mobilization barracks to enlist, but I was told I was too young and that I needed my parents' consent.

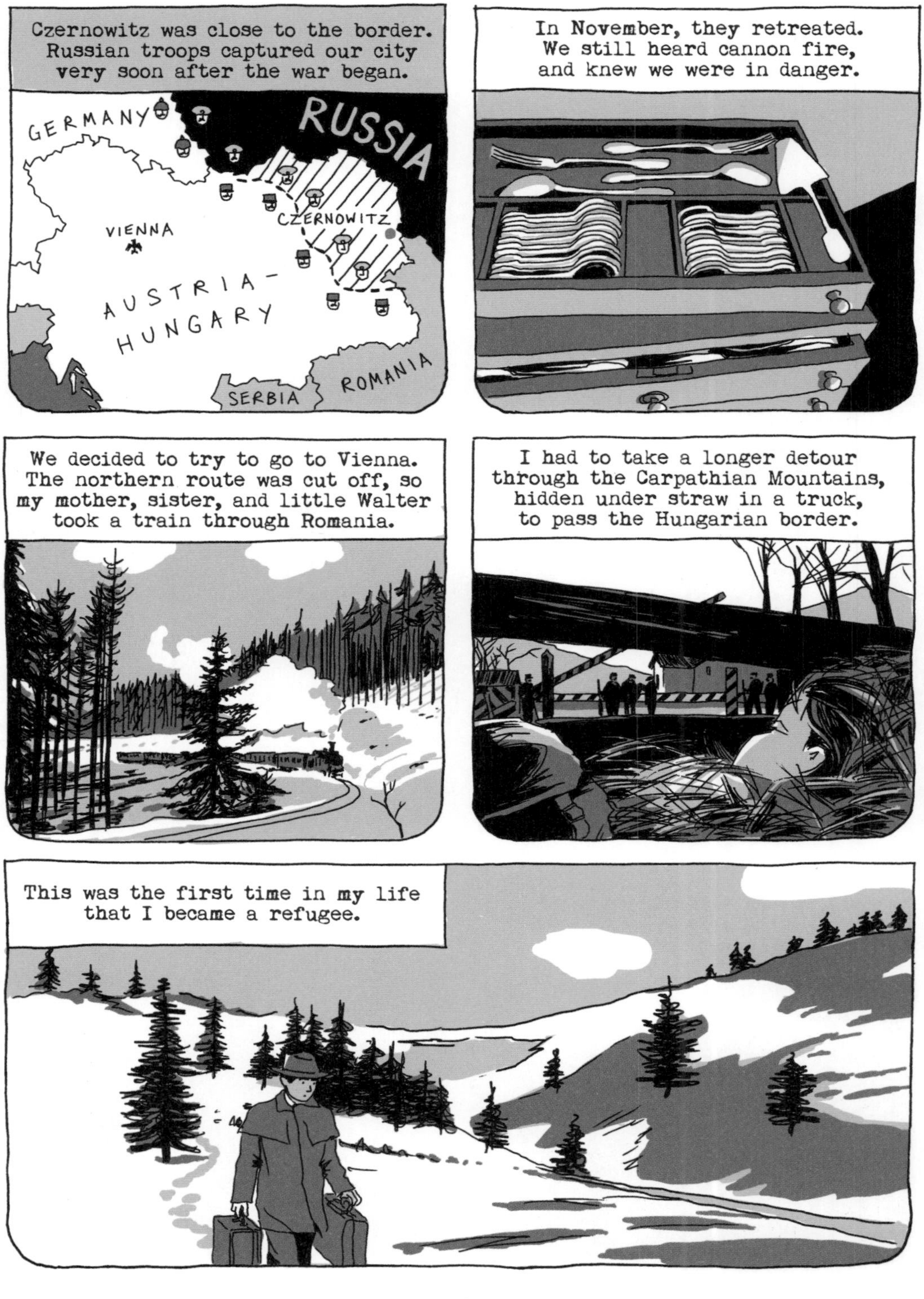
Czernowitz was close to the border. Russian troops captured our city very soon after the war began.
GERMANY
RUSSIA
VIENNA
CZERNOWITZ
AUSTRIA-HUNGARY
SERBIA
ROMANIA
In November, they retreated. We still heard cannon fire, and knew we were in danger.
We decided to try to go to Vienna. The northern route was cut off, so my mother, sister, and little Walter took a train through Romania.
I had to take a longer detour through the Carpathian Mountains, hidden under straw in a truck, to pass the Hungarian border.
This was the first time in my life that I became a refugee.

Eighteen

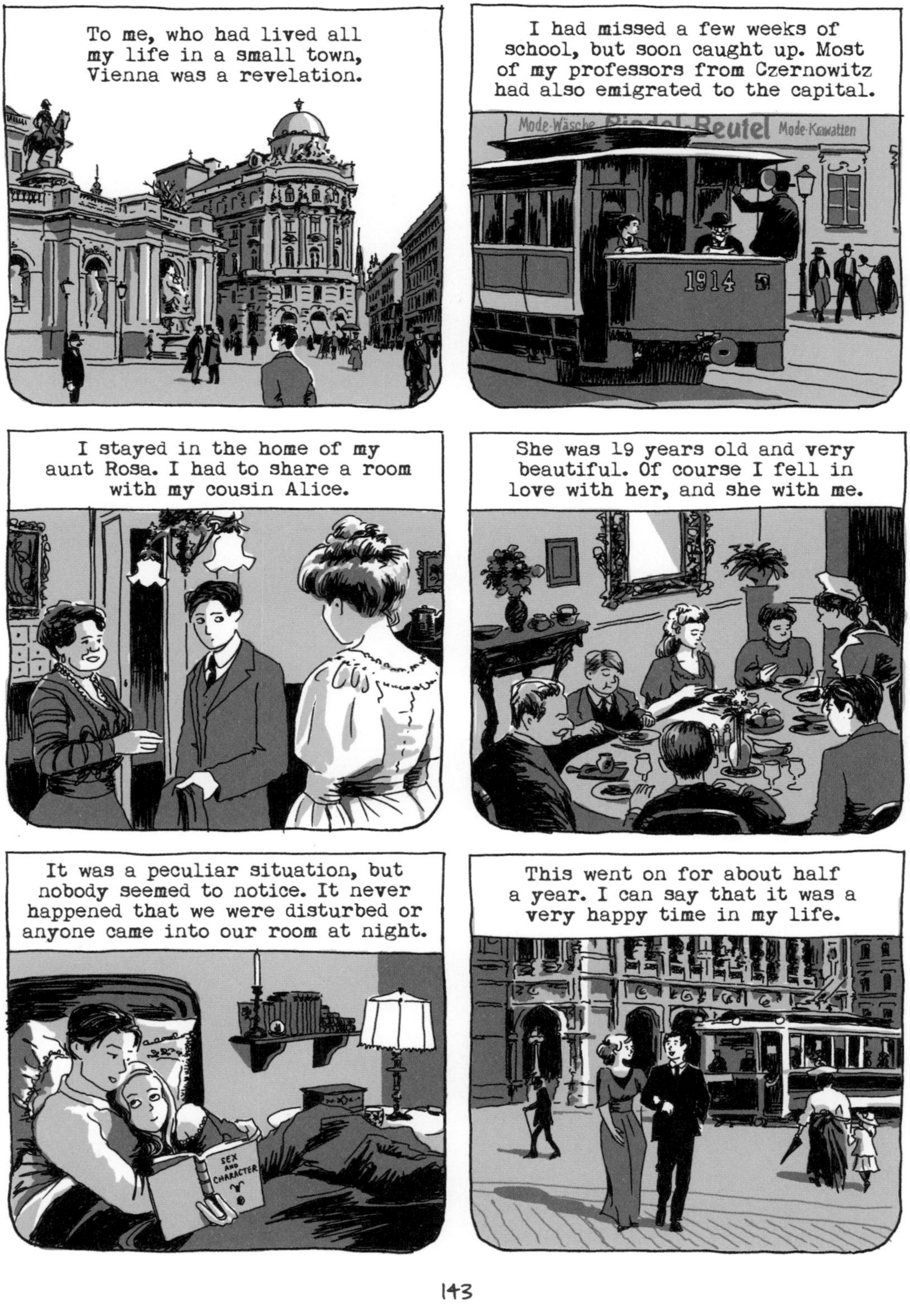
To me, who had lived all my life in a small town, Vienna was a revelation.
I had missed a few weeks of school, but soon caught up. Most of my professors from Czernowitz had also emigrated to the capital.
Mode-Wäsche
Beutel
Mode-Krawatten
1914
I stayed in the home of my aunt Rosa. I had to share a room with my cousin Alice.
She was 19 years old and very beautiful. Of course I fell in love with her, and she with me.
It was a peculiar situation, but nobody seemed to notice. It never happened that we were disturbed or anyone came into our room at night.
SEX AND CHARACTER
This went on for about half a year. I can say that it was a very happy time in my life.

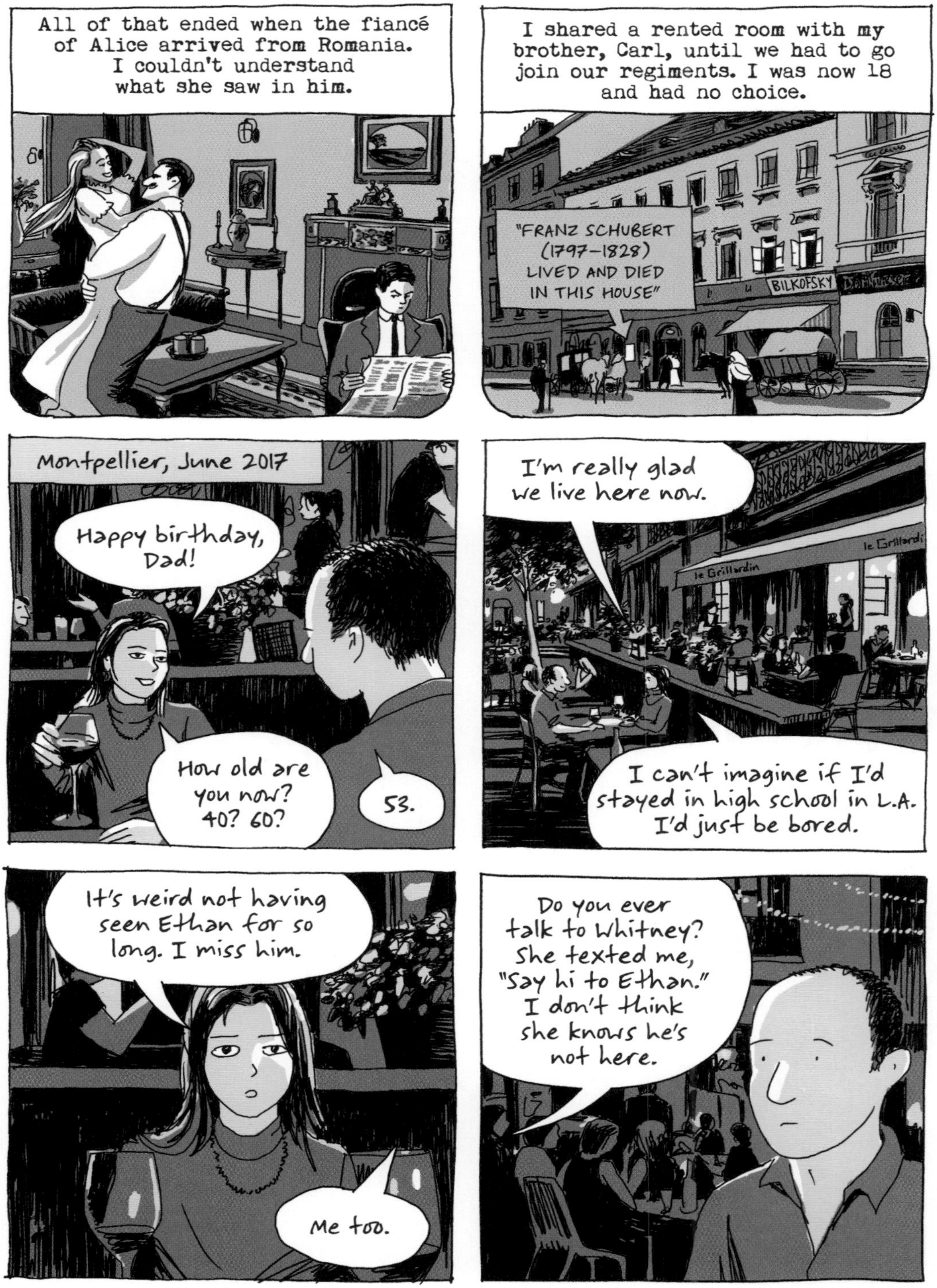
All of that ended when the fiancé of Alice arrived from Romania. I couldn't understand what she saw in him.
I shared a rented room with my brother, Carl, until we had to go join our regiments. I was now 18 and had no choice.
"FRANZ SCHUBERT (1797–1828) LIVED AND DIED IN THIS HOUSE"
BILKOFSKY
Montpellier, June 2017
Happy birthday, Dad!
How old are you now? 40? 60?
53.
I'm really glad we live here now.
le Grillardin
I can't imagine if I'd stayed in high school in L.A. I'd just be bored.
It's weird not having seen Ethan for so long. I miss him.
Me too.
Do you ever talk to Whitney? She texted me, "Say hi to Ethan." I don't think she knows he's not here.

Transfer

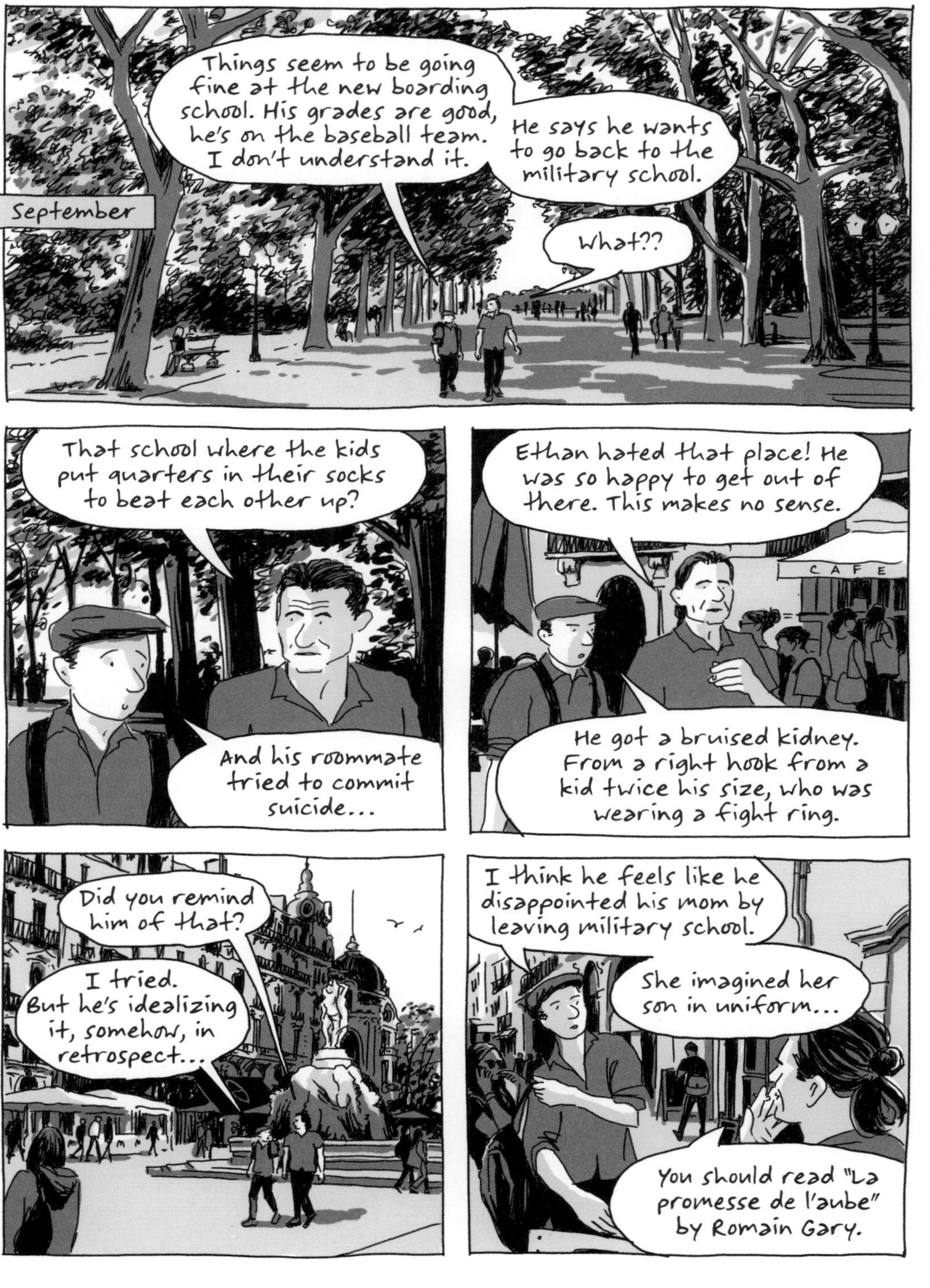
September
Things seem to be going fine at the new boarding school. His grades are good, he's on the baseball team. I don't understand it.
He says he wants to go back to the military school.
What??
That school where the kids put quarters in their socks to beat each other up?
And his roommate tried to commit suicide...
Ethan hated that place! He was so happy to get out of there. This makes no sense.
CAFE
He got a bruised kidney. From a right hook from a kid twice his size, who was wearing a fight ring.
Did you remind him of that?
I tried. But he's idealizing it, somehow, in retrospect...
I think he feels like he disappointed his mom by leaving military school.
She imagined her son in uniform...
You should read "La promesse de l'aube" by Romain Gary.

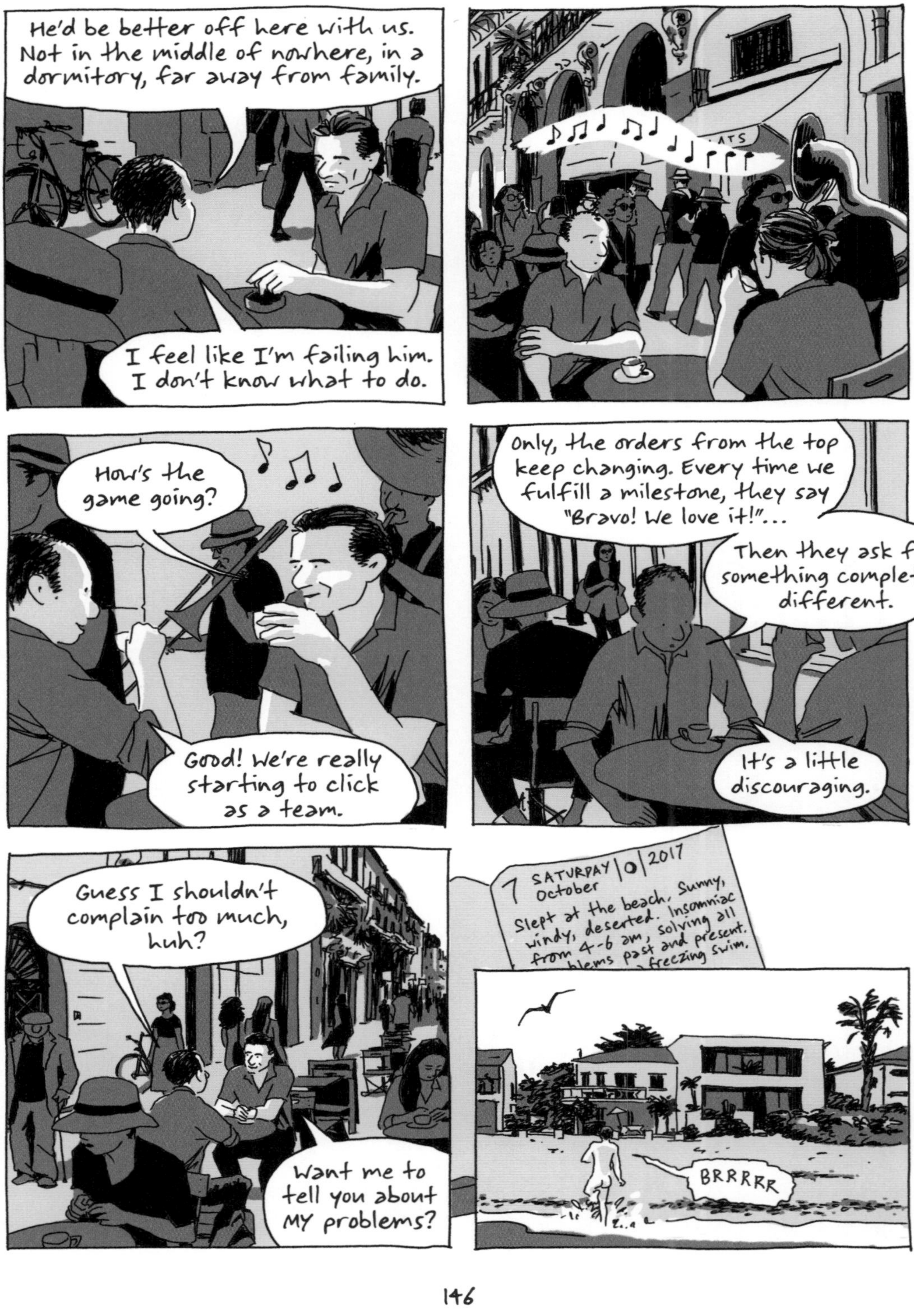
He'd be better off here with us. Not in the middle of nowhere, in a dormitory, far away from family.
I feel like I'm failing him. I don't know what to do.
How's the game going?
Good! We're really starting to click as a team.
Only, the orders from the top keep changing. Every time we fulfill a milestone, they say "Bravo! We love it!"...
Then they ask for something completely different.
It's a little discouraging.
Guess I shouldn't complain too much, huh?
Want me to tell you about MY problems?
7 SATURDAY October 10 2017
Slept at the beach. Sunny, windy, deserted. Insomniac from 4-6 am, solving all blems past and present. freezing swim.
BRRRRR

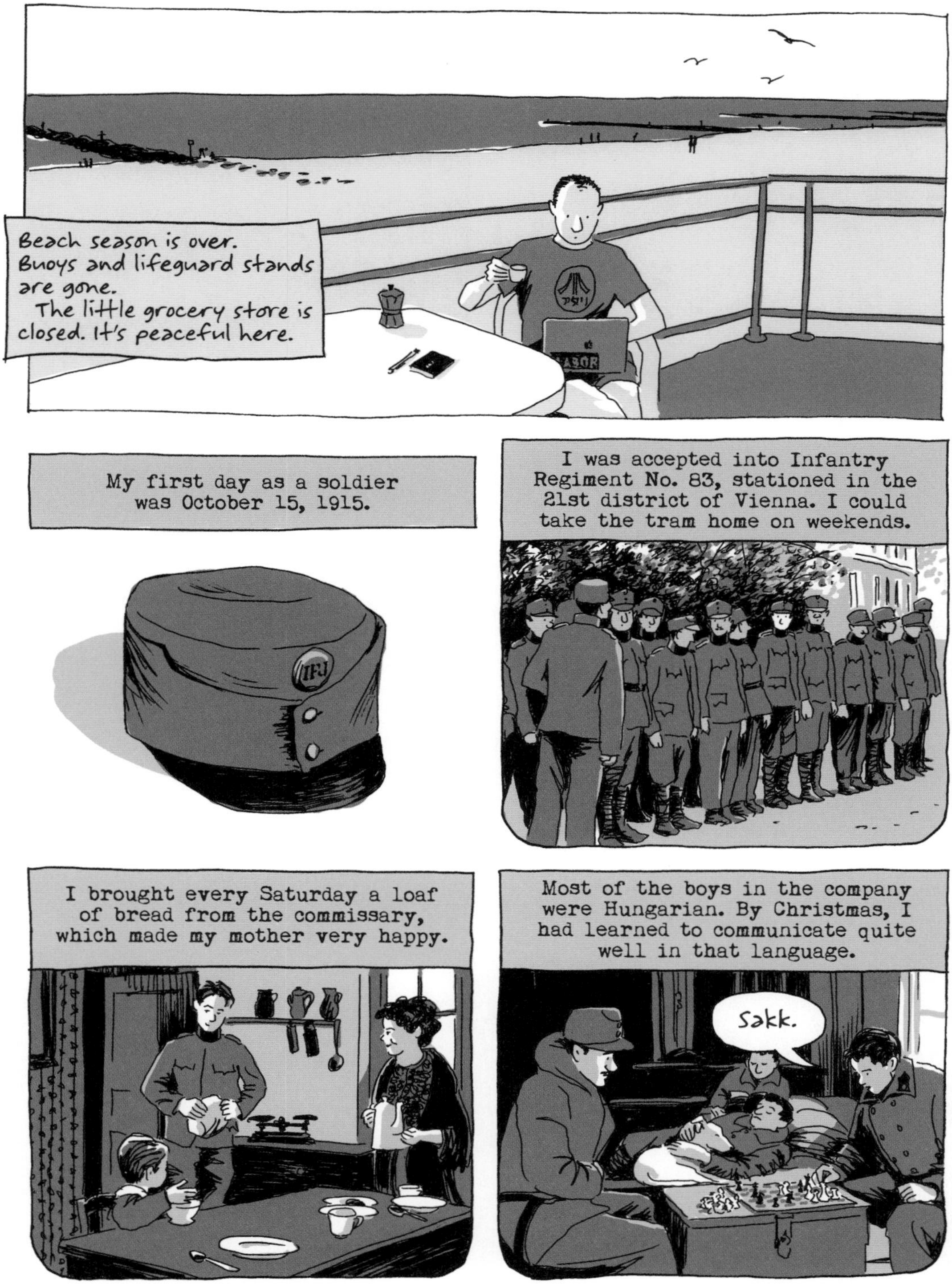
Beach season is over. Buoys and lifeguard stands are gone. The little grocery store is closed. It's peaceful here.
My first day as a soldier was October 15, 1915.
I was accepted into Infantry Regiment No. 83, stationed in the 21st district of Vienna. I could take the tram home on weekends.
I brought every Saturday a loaf of bread from the commissary, which made my mother very happy.
Most of the boys in the company were Hungarian. By Christmas, I had learned to communicate quite well in that language.
Sakk.

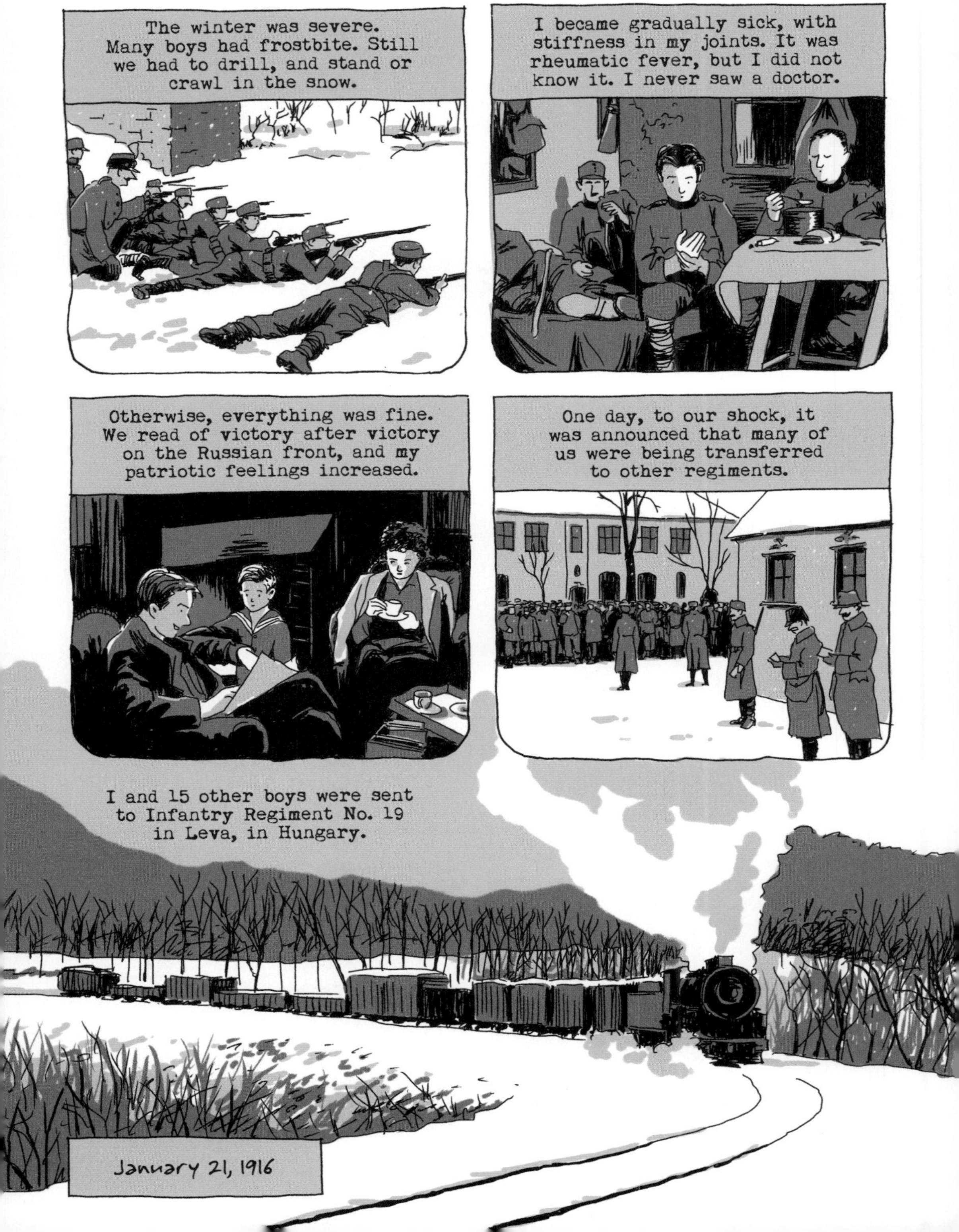
The winter was severe. Many boys had frostbite. Still we had to drill, and stand or crawl in the snow.
I became gradually sick, with stiffness in my joints. It was rheumatic fever, but I did not know it. I never saw a doctor.
Otherwise, everything was fine. We read of victory after victory on the Russian front, and my patriotic feelings increased.
One day, to our shock, it was announced that many of us were being transferred to other regiments.
I and 15 other boys were sent to Infantry Regiment No. 19 in Leva, in Hungary.
January 21, 1916

Barracks

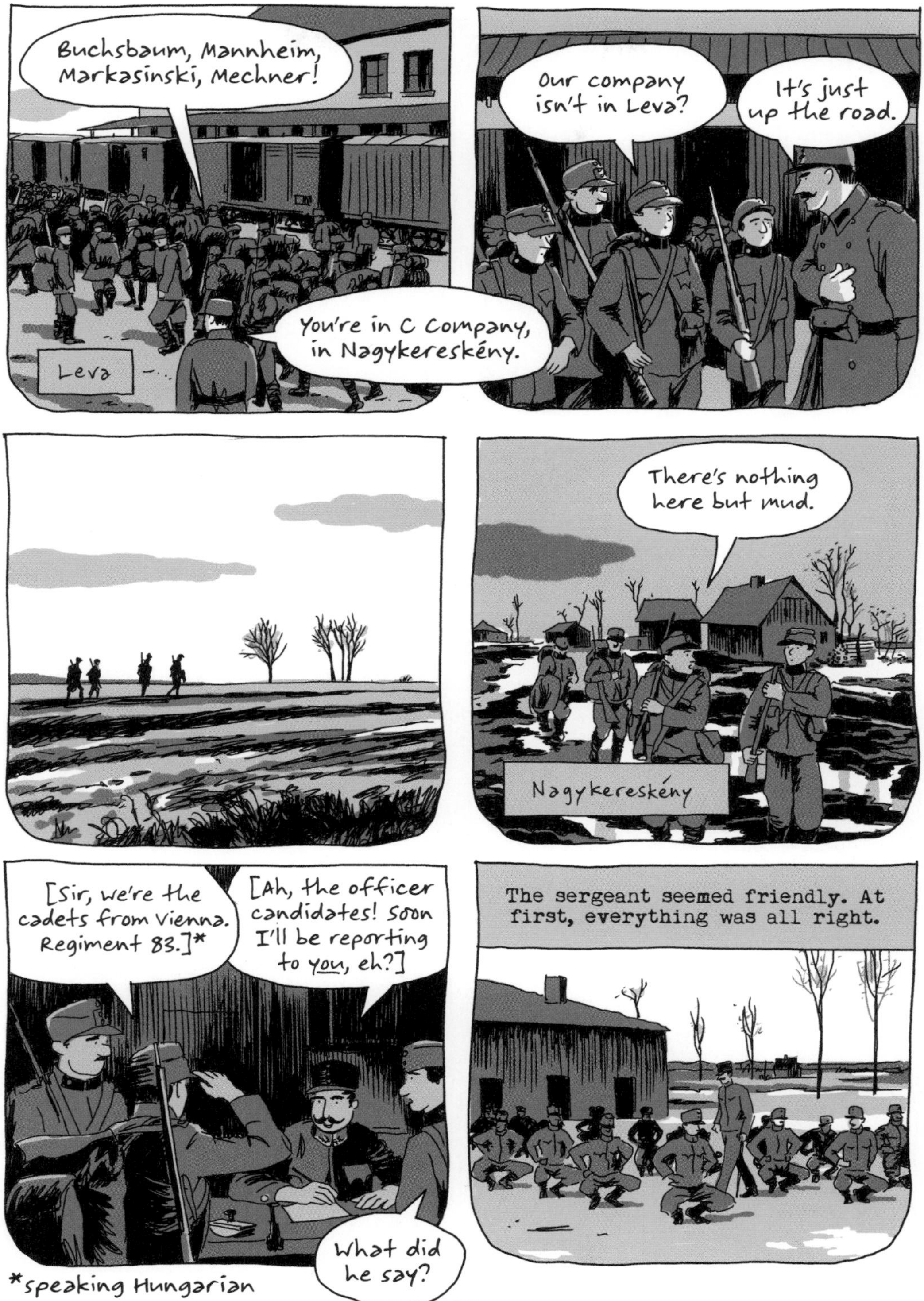

Buchsbaum, Mannheim, Markasinski, Mechner!
You're in C Company, in Nagykereskény.
Leva
Our company isn't in Leva?
It's just up the road.
There's nothing here but mud.
Nagykereskény
[Sir, we're the cadets from Vienna. Regiment 83.]*
[Ah, the officer candidates! Soon I'll be reporting to you, eh?]
What did he say?
*speaking Hungarian
The sergeant seemed friendly. At first, everything was all right.

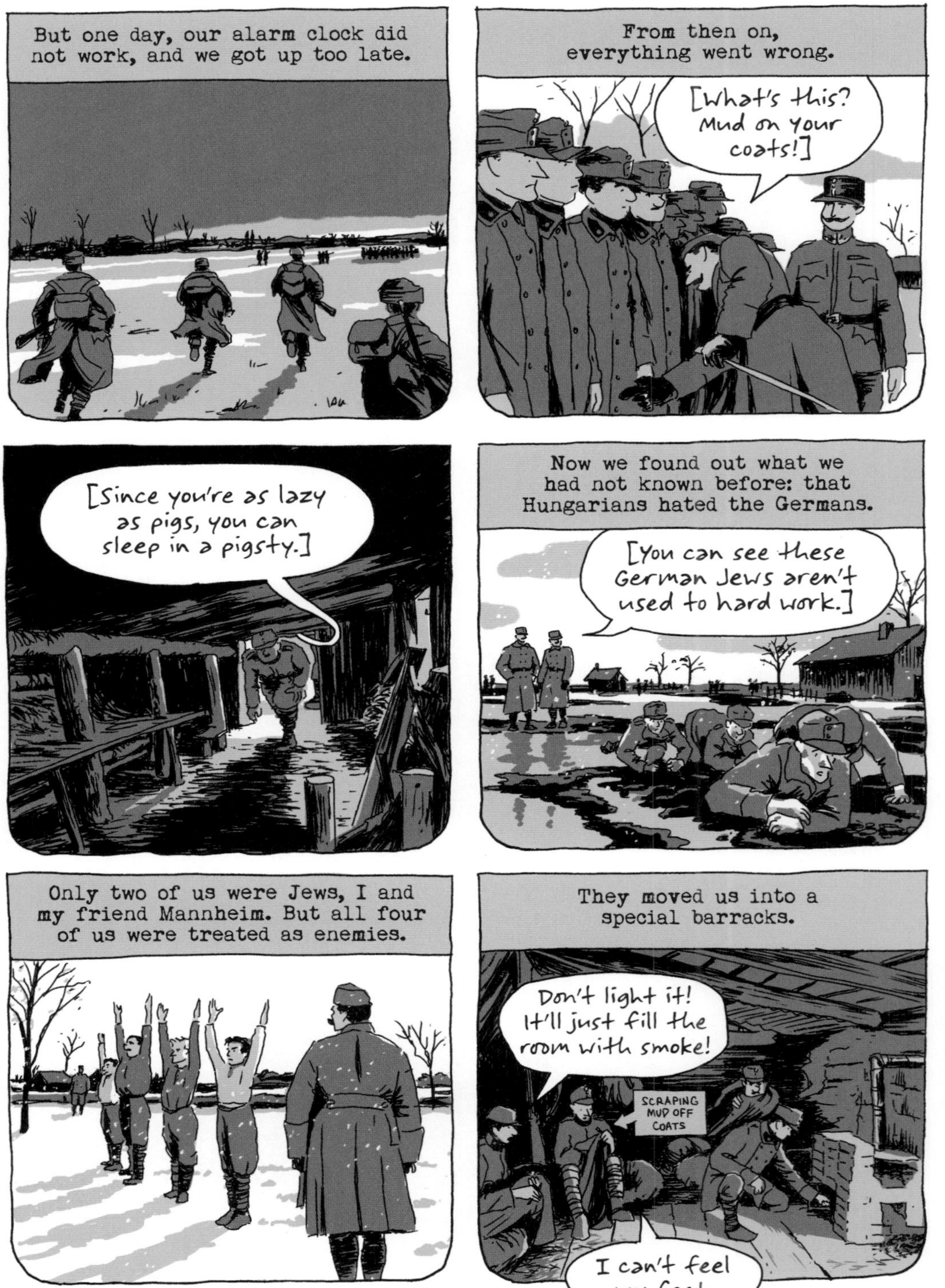

But one day, our alarm clock did not work, and we got up too late.
From then on, everything went wrong.
[What's this? Mud on your coats!]
[Since you're as lazy as pigs, you can sleep in a pigsty.]
Now we found out what we had not known before: that Hungarians hated the Germans.
[You can see these German Jews aren't used to hard work.]
Only two of us were Jews, I and my friend Mannheim. But all four of us were treated as enemies.
They moved us into a special barracks.
Don't light it! It'll just fill the room with smoke!
SCRAPING MUD OFF COATS
I can't feel my feet.

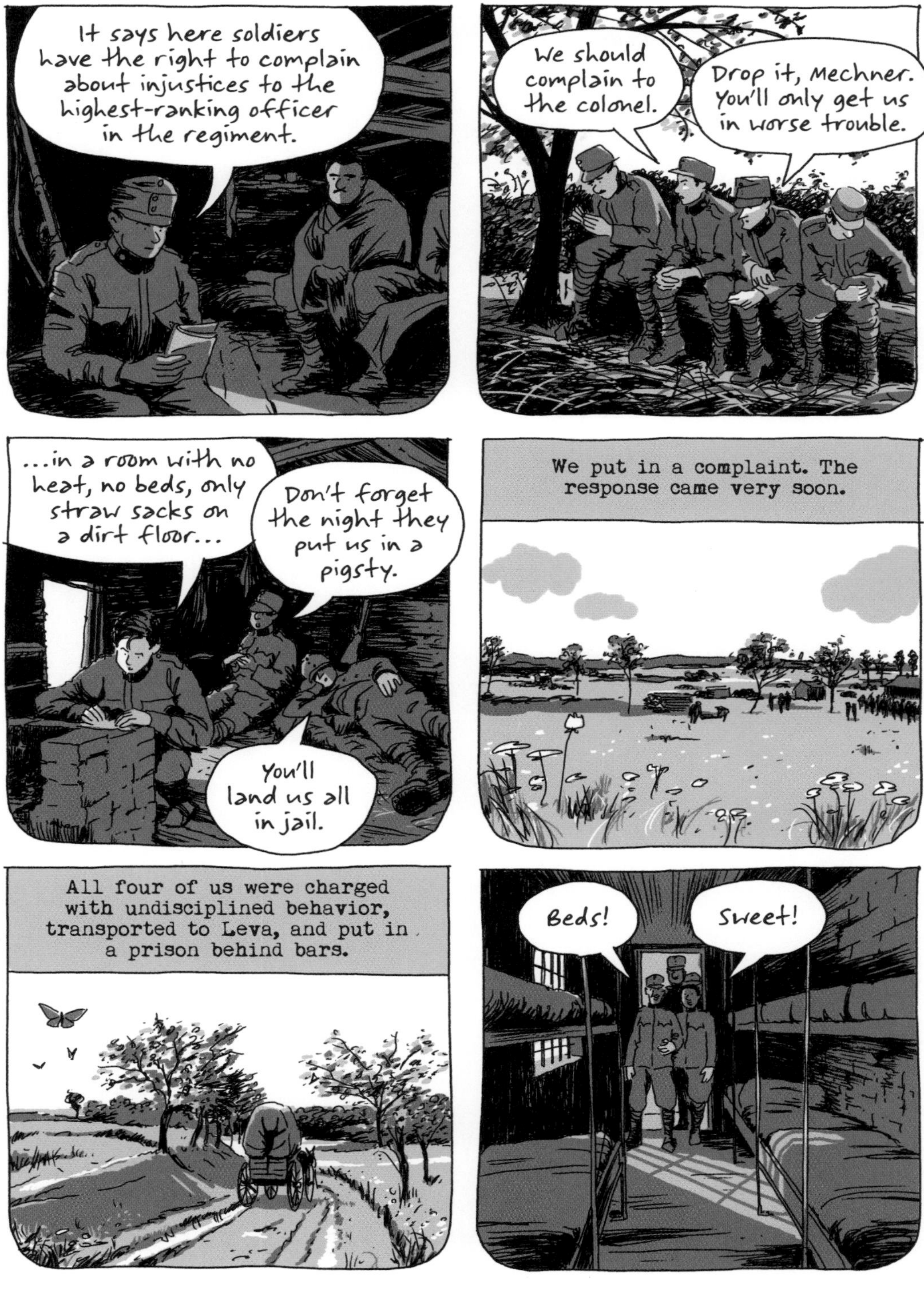
It says here soldiers have the right to complain about injustices to the highest-ranking officer in the regiment.
We should complain to the colonel.
Drop it, Mechner. You'll only get us in worse trouble.
...in a room with no heat, no beds, only straw sacks on a dirt floor...
Don't forget the night they put us in a pigsty.
You'll land us all in jail.
We put in a complaint. The response came very soon.
All four of us were charged with undisciplined behavior, transported to Leva, and put in a prison behind bars.
Beds!
Sweet!

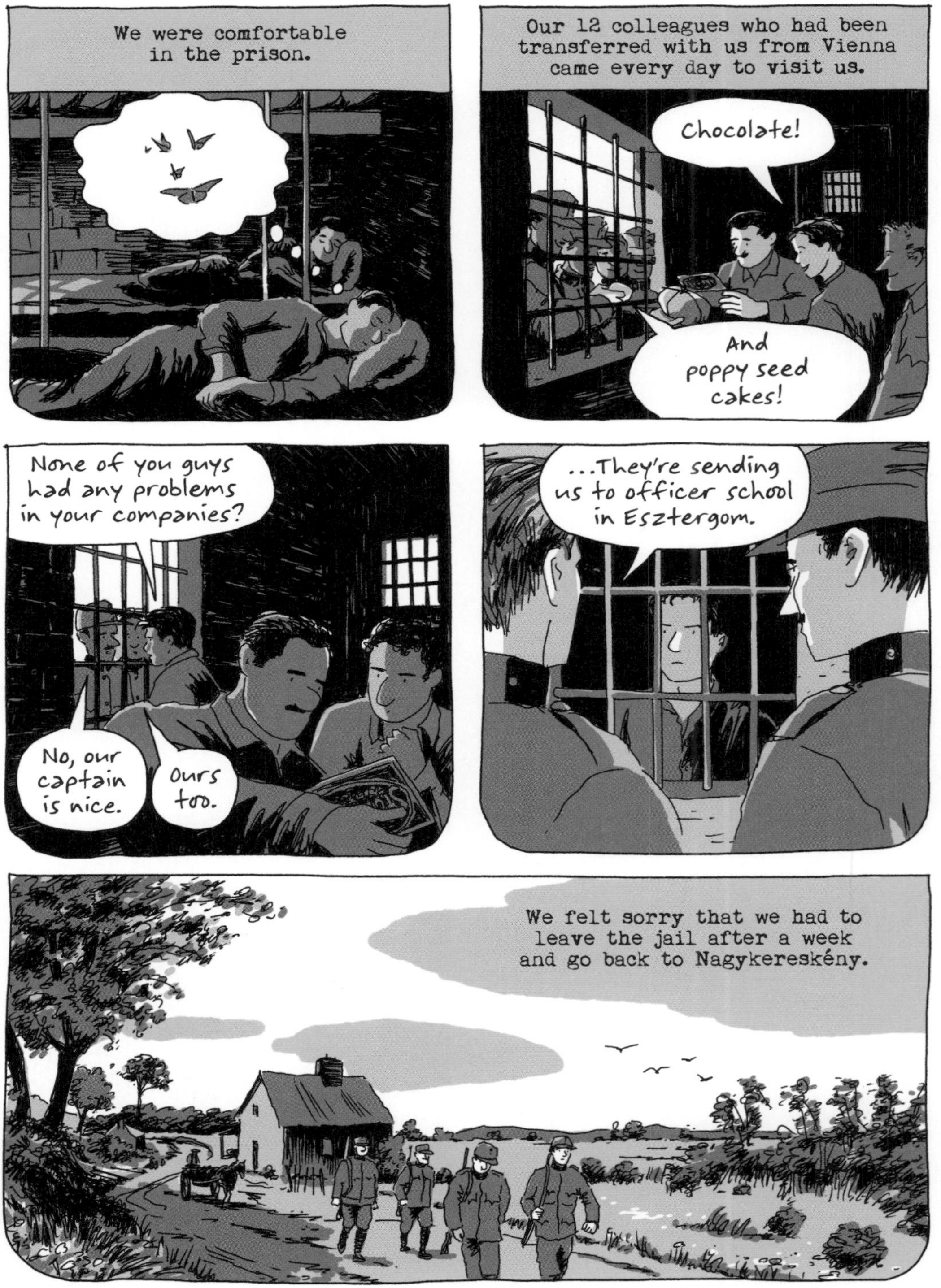
We were comfortable in the prison.
Our 12 colleagues who had been transferred with us from Vienna came every day to visit us.
Chocolate!
And poppy seed cakes!
None of you guys had any problems in your companies?
No, our captain is nice.
Ours too.
...They're sending us to officer school in Esztergom.
We felt sorry that we had to leave the jail after a week and go back to Nagykereskény.

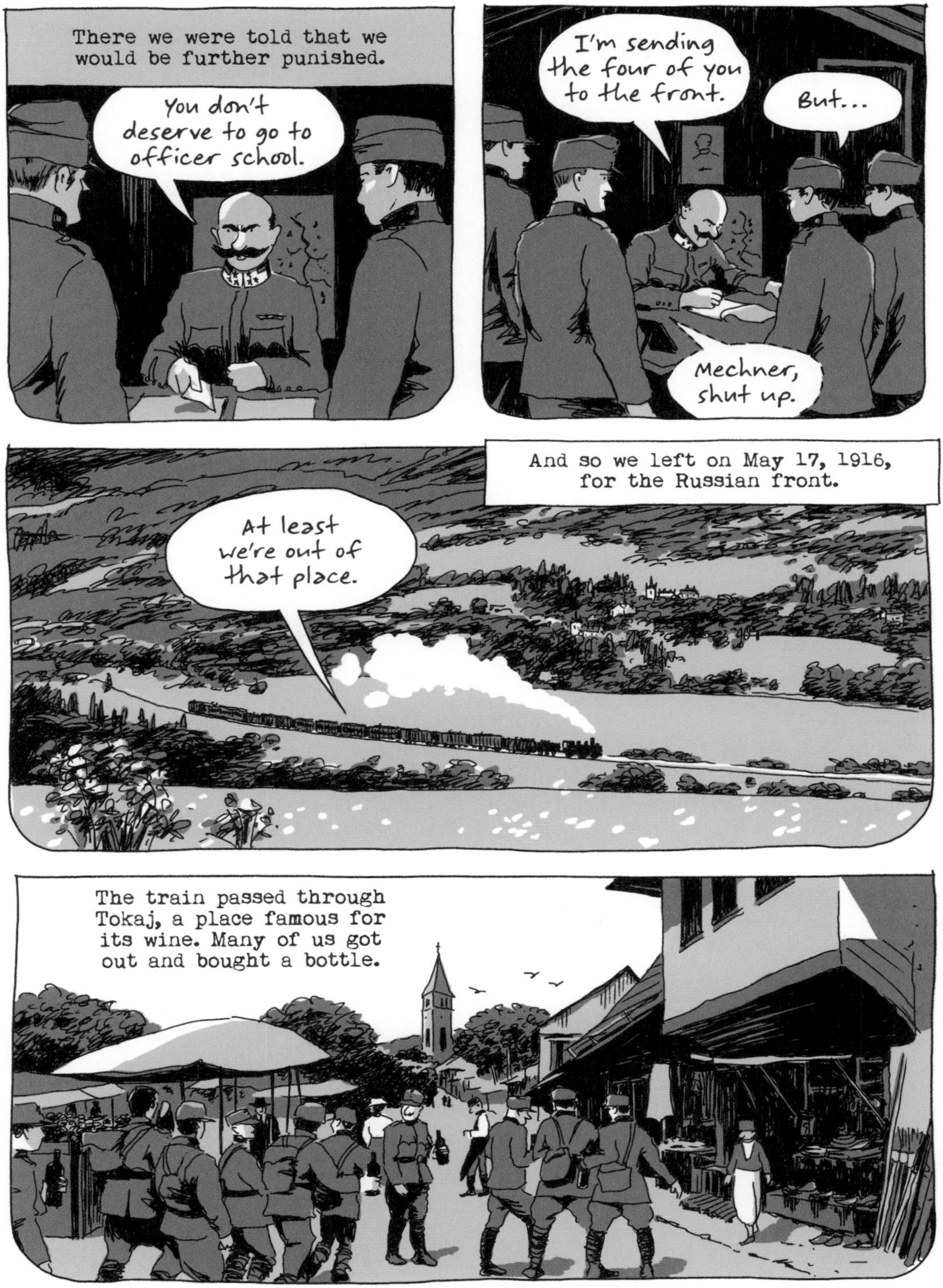
There we were told that we would be further punished.
You don't deserve to go to officer school.
I'm sending the four of you to the front.
But...
Mechner, shut up.
And so we left on May 17, 1916, for the Russian front.
At least we're out of that place.
The train passed through Tokaj, a place famous for its wine. Many of us got out and bought a bottle.

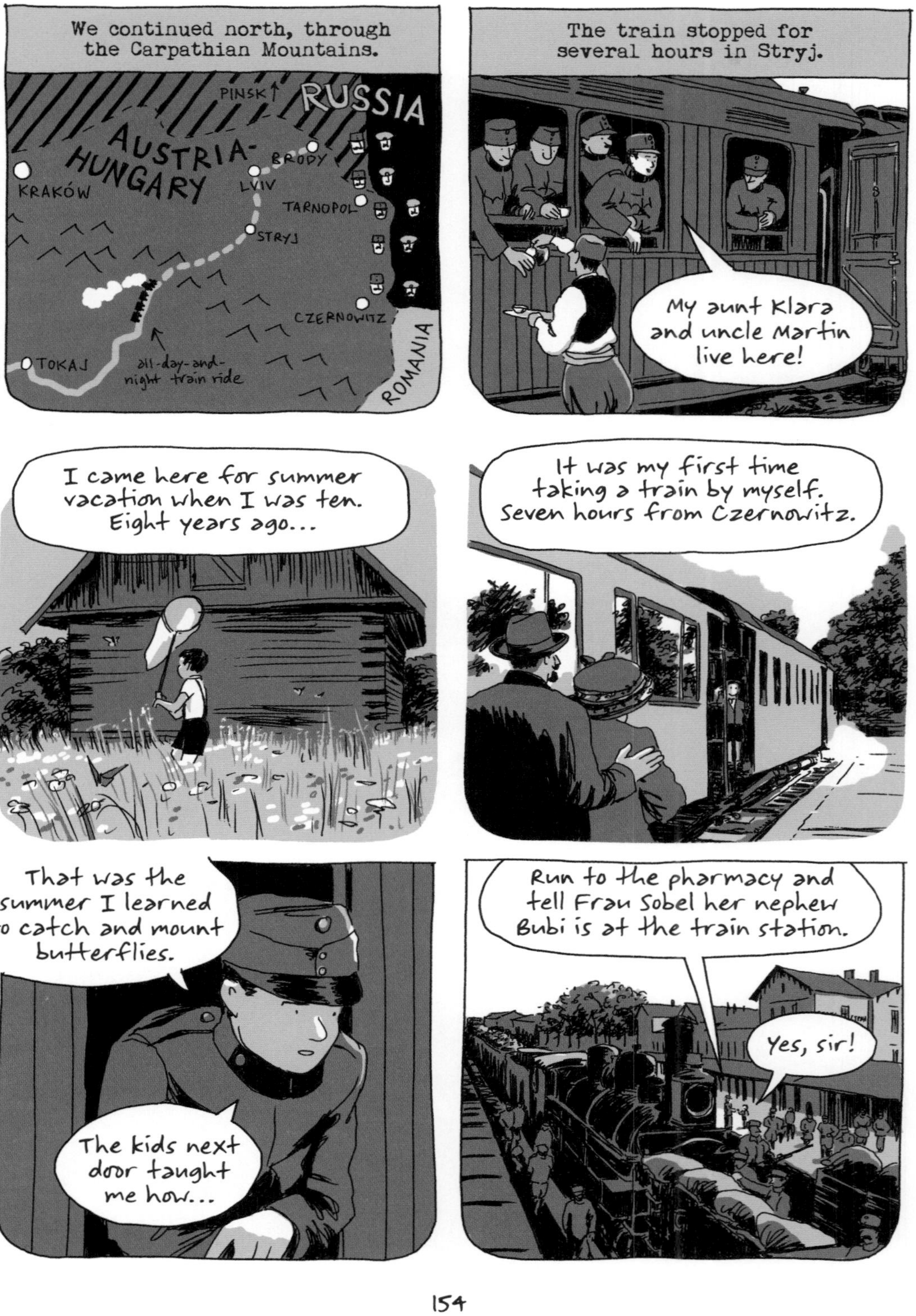
We continued north, through the Carpathian Mountains.
PINSK
RUSSIA
AUSTRIA-HUNGARY
BRODY
KRAKÓW
LVIV
TARNOPOL
STRYJ
CZERNOWITZ
TOKAJ
all-day-and-night train ride
ROMANIA
The train stopped for several hours in Stryj.
My aunt Klara and uncle Martin live here!
I came here for summer vacation when I was ten. Eight years ago...
It was my first time taking a train by myself. Seven hours from Czernowitz.
That was the summer I learned to catch and mount butterflies.
The kids next door taught me how...
Run to the pharmacy and tell Frau Sobel her nephew Bubi is at the train station.
Yes, sir!

The Russian Front

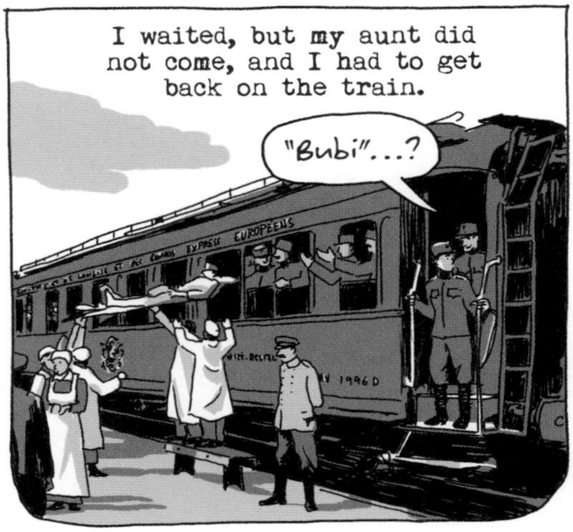
I waited, but my aunt did not come, and I had to get back on the train.
"Bubi"...?

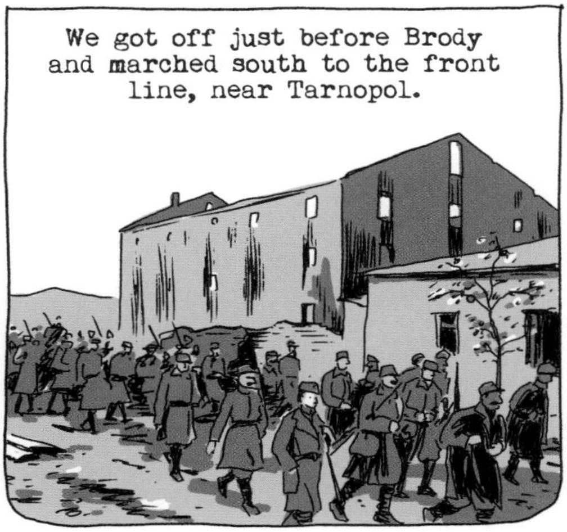
We got off just before Brody and marched south to the front line, near Tarnopol.

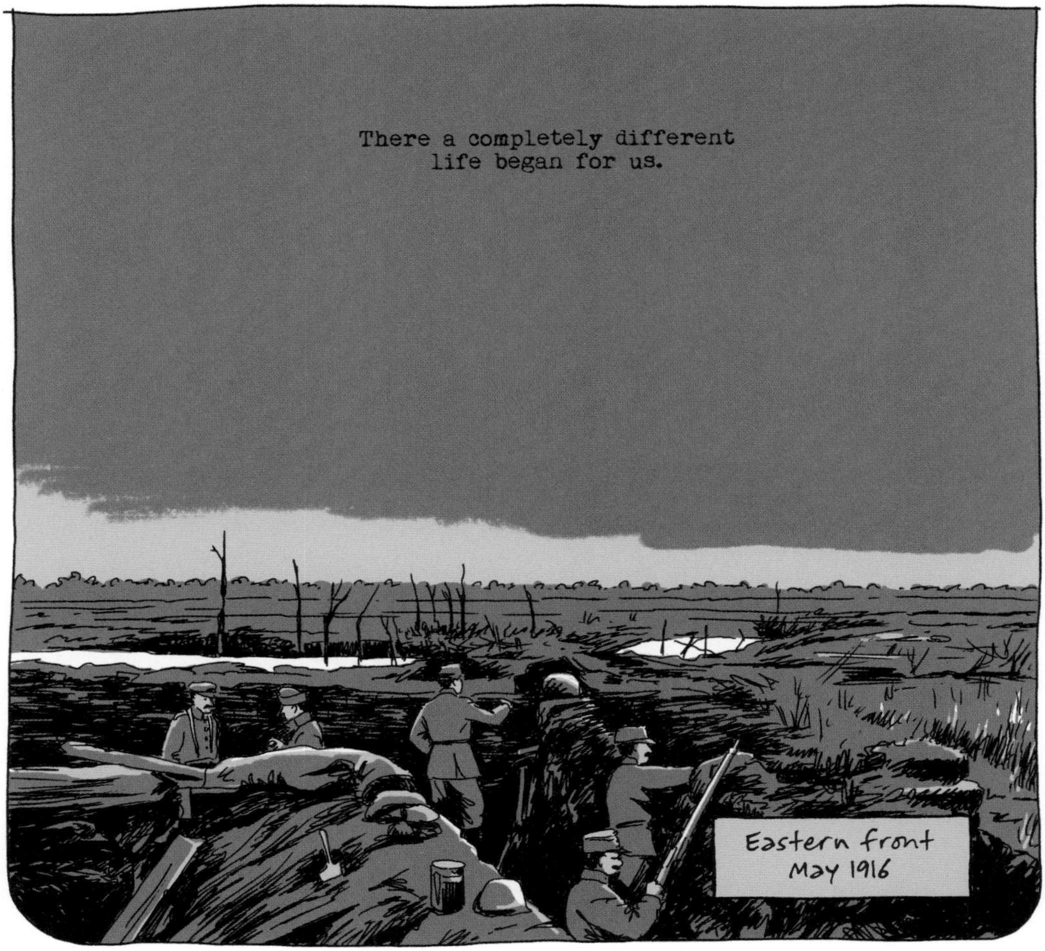
There a completely different life began for us.
Eastern front May 1916

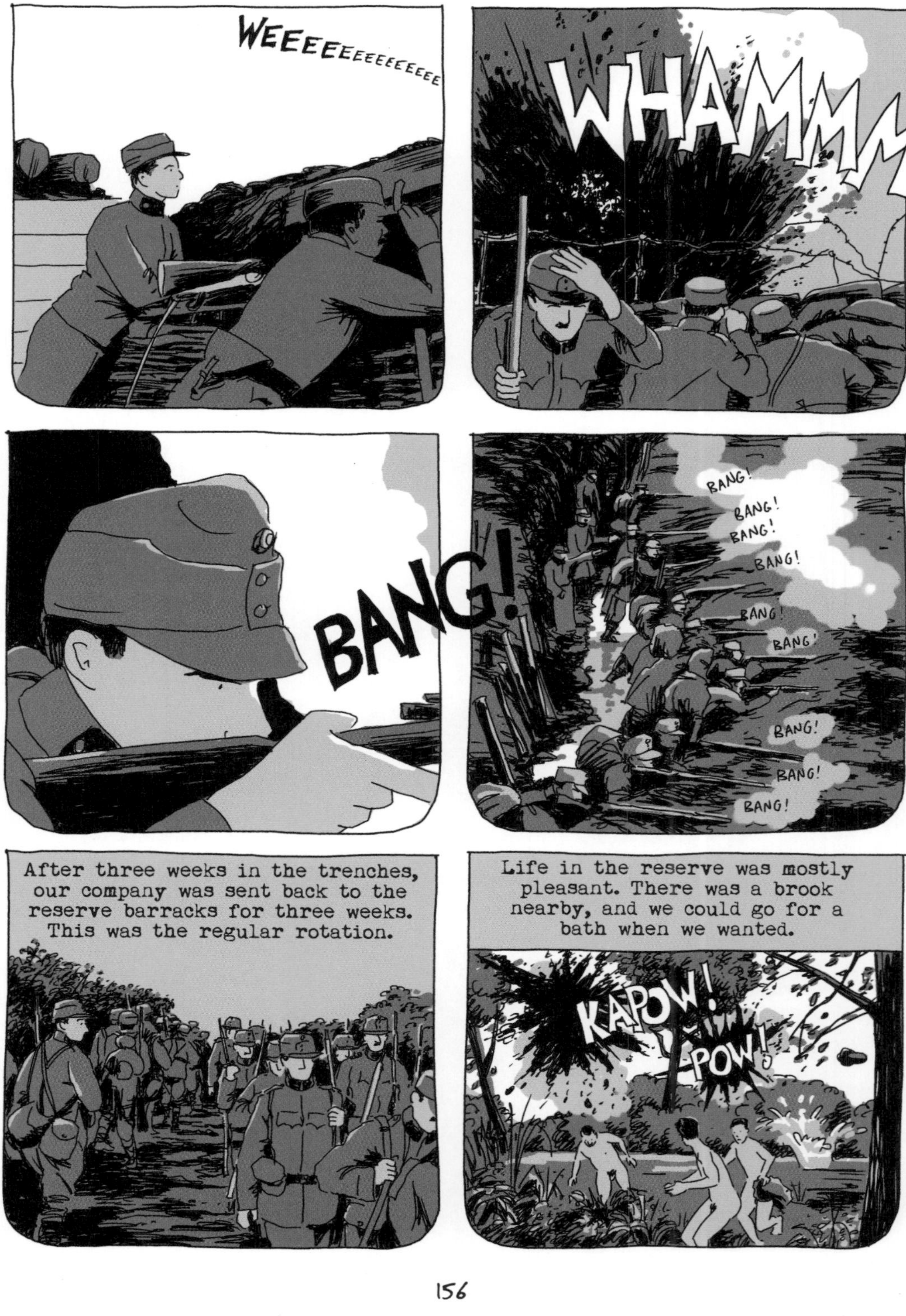
WEEEEEEEEEEEEEE
WHAMMM
BANG!
BANG!
BANG!
BANG!
BANG!
BANG!
BANG!
BANG!
BANG!
BANG!
After three weeks in the trenches, our company was sent back to the reserve barracks for three weeks. This was the regular rotation.
Life in the reserve was mostly pleasant. There was a brook nearby, and we could go for a bath when we wanted.
KAPOW!
POW!

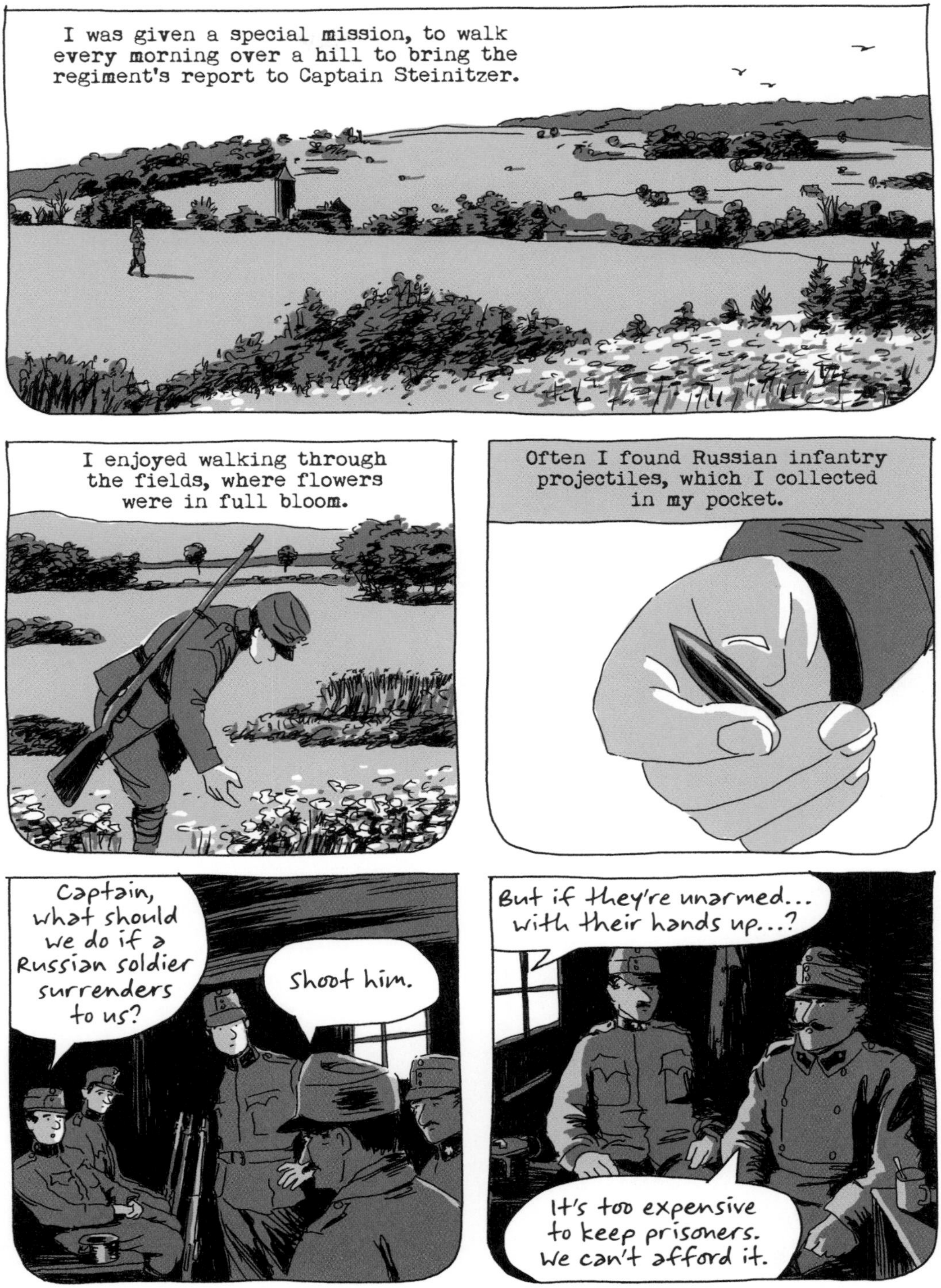
I was given a special mission, to walk every morning over a hill to bring the regiment's report to Captain Steinitzer.
I enjoyed walking through the fields, where flowers were in full bloom.
Often I found Russian infantry projectiles, which I collected in my pocket.
Captain, what should we do if a Russian soldier surrenders to us?
Shoot him.
But if they're unarmed... with their hands up...?
It's too expensive to keep prisoners. We can't afford it.

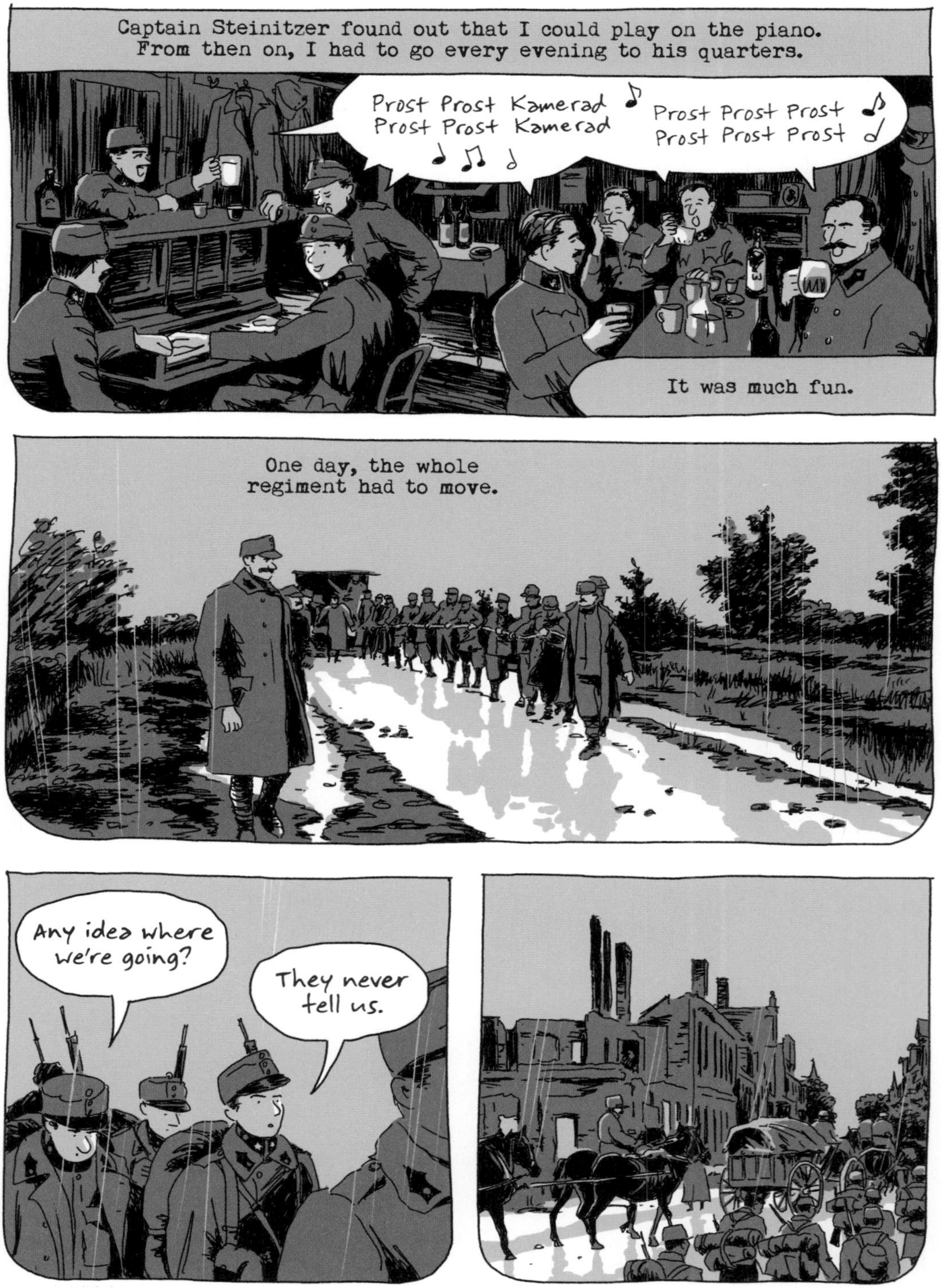
Captain Steinitzer found out that I could play on the piano. From then on, I had to go every evening to his quarters.
Prost Prost Kamerad Prost Prost Kamerad
Prost Prost Prost Prost Prost Prost
It was much fun.
One day, the whole regiment had to move.
Any idea where we're going?
They never tell us.

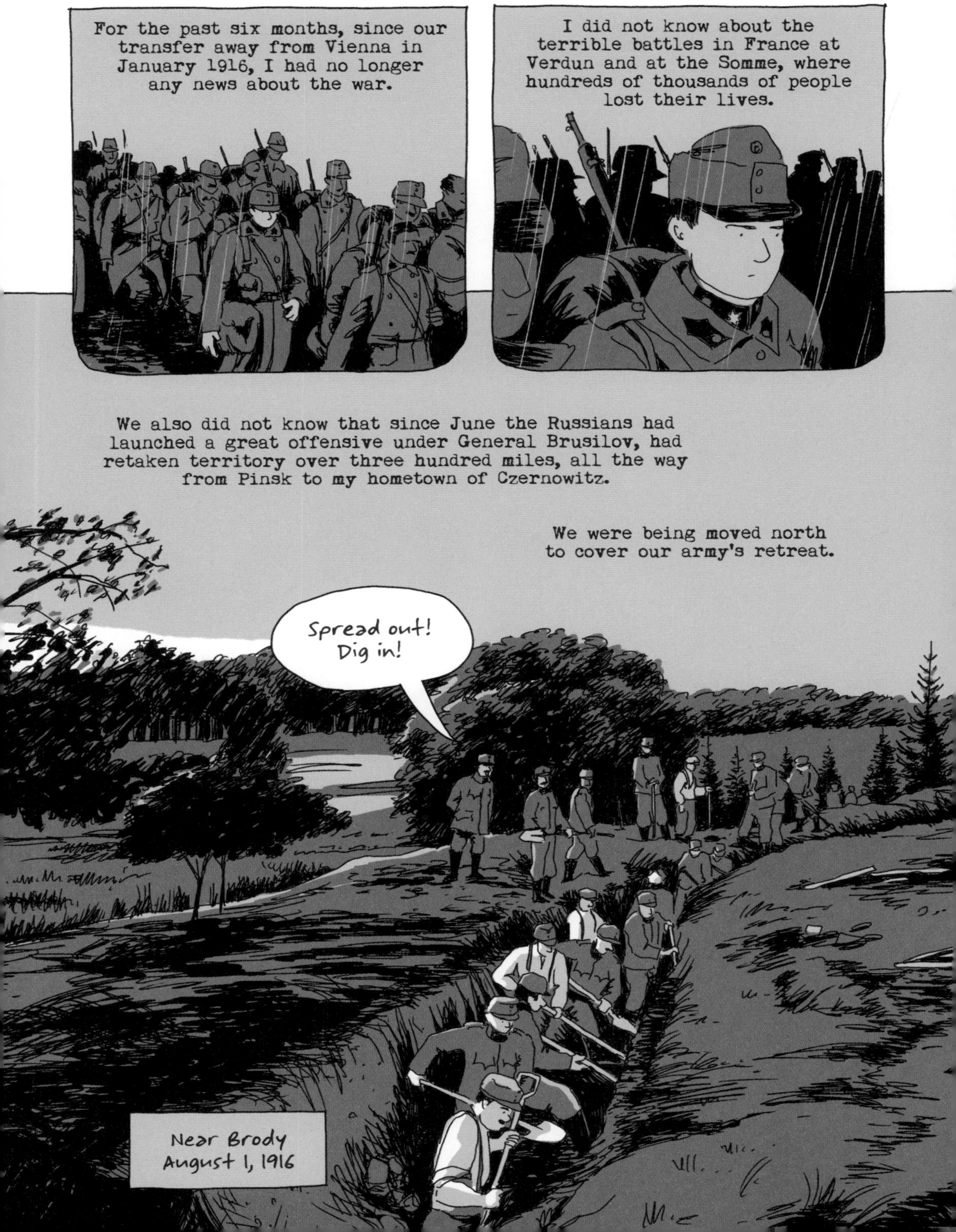
For the past six months, since our transfer away from Vienna in January 1916, I had no longer any news about the war.
I did not know about the terrible battles in France at Verdun and at the Somme, where hundreds of thousands of people lost their lives.
We also did not know that since June the Russians had launched a great offensive under General Brusilov, had retaken territory over three hundred miles, all the way from Pinsk to my hometown of Czernowitz.
We were being moved north to cover our army's retreat.
Spread out! Dig in!
Near Brody
August 1, 1916

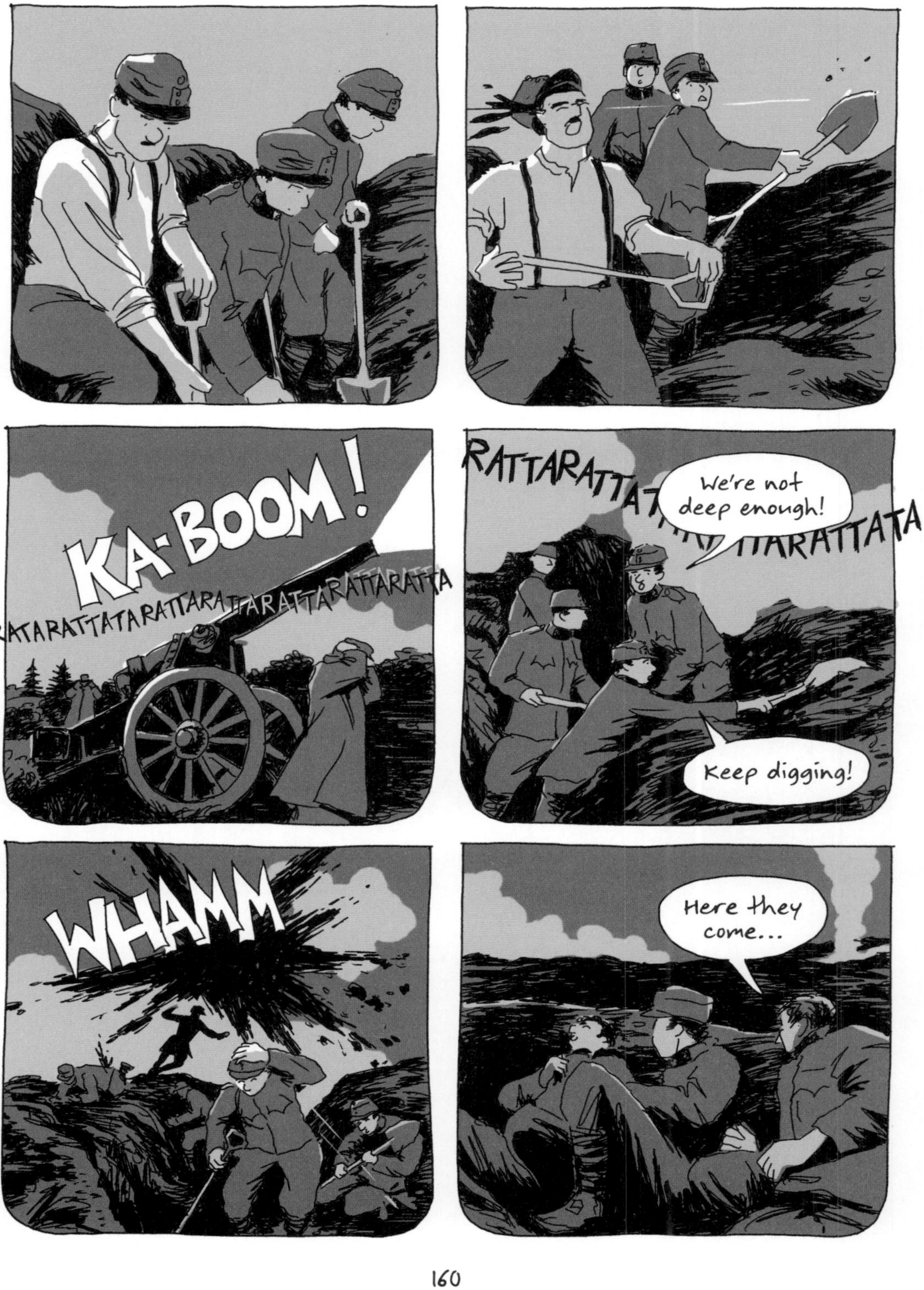
KA-BOOM!
RATARATTATARATTARATTARATTARATTARATTA
RATTARATTATA
We're not deep enough!
TTARATTATA
Keep digging!
WHAMM
Here they come...

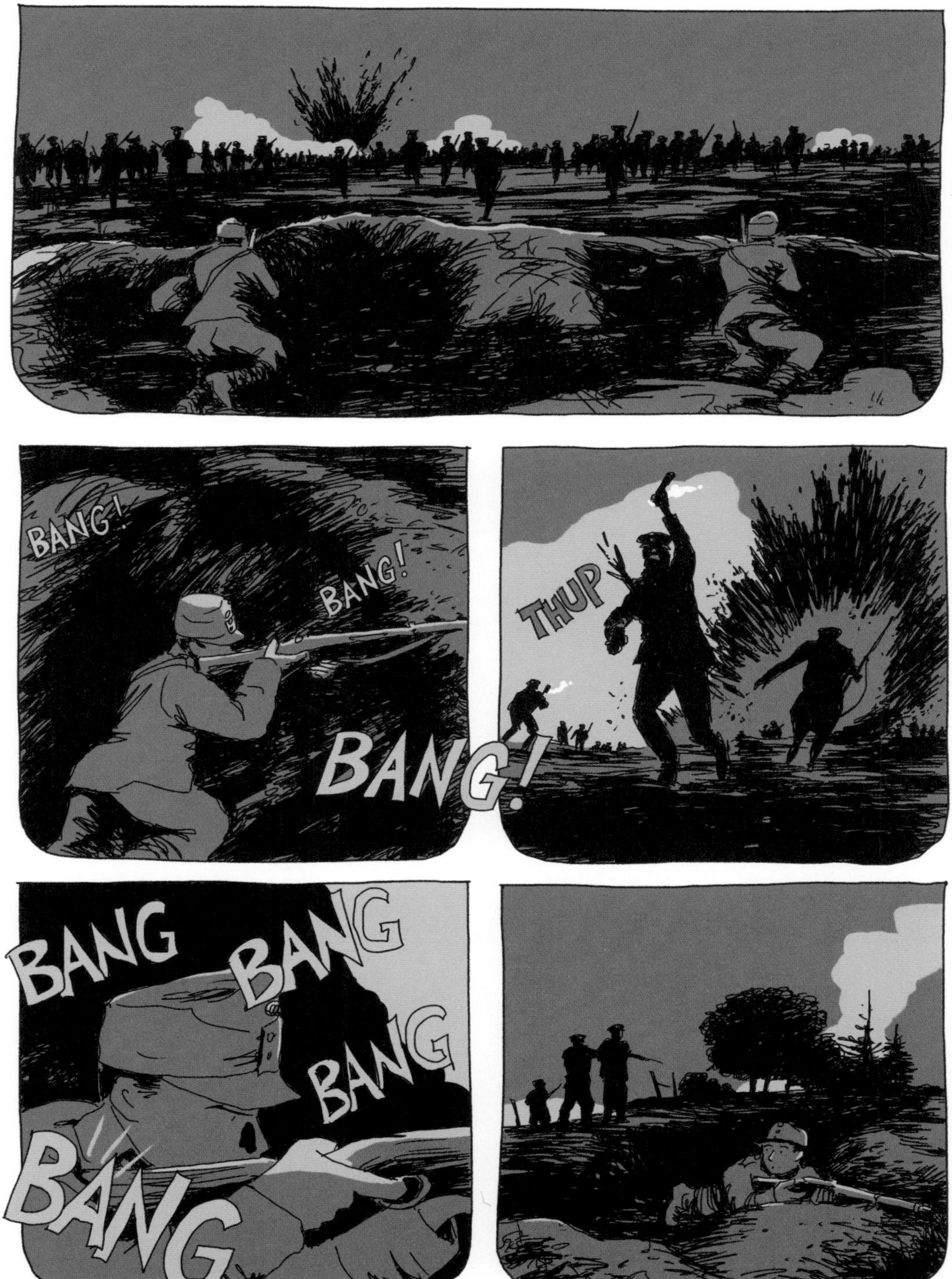
BANG!
BANG!
BANG!
THUP
BANG
BANG
BANG
BANG

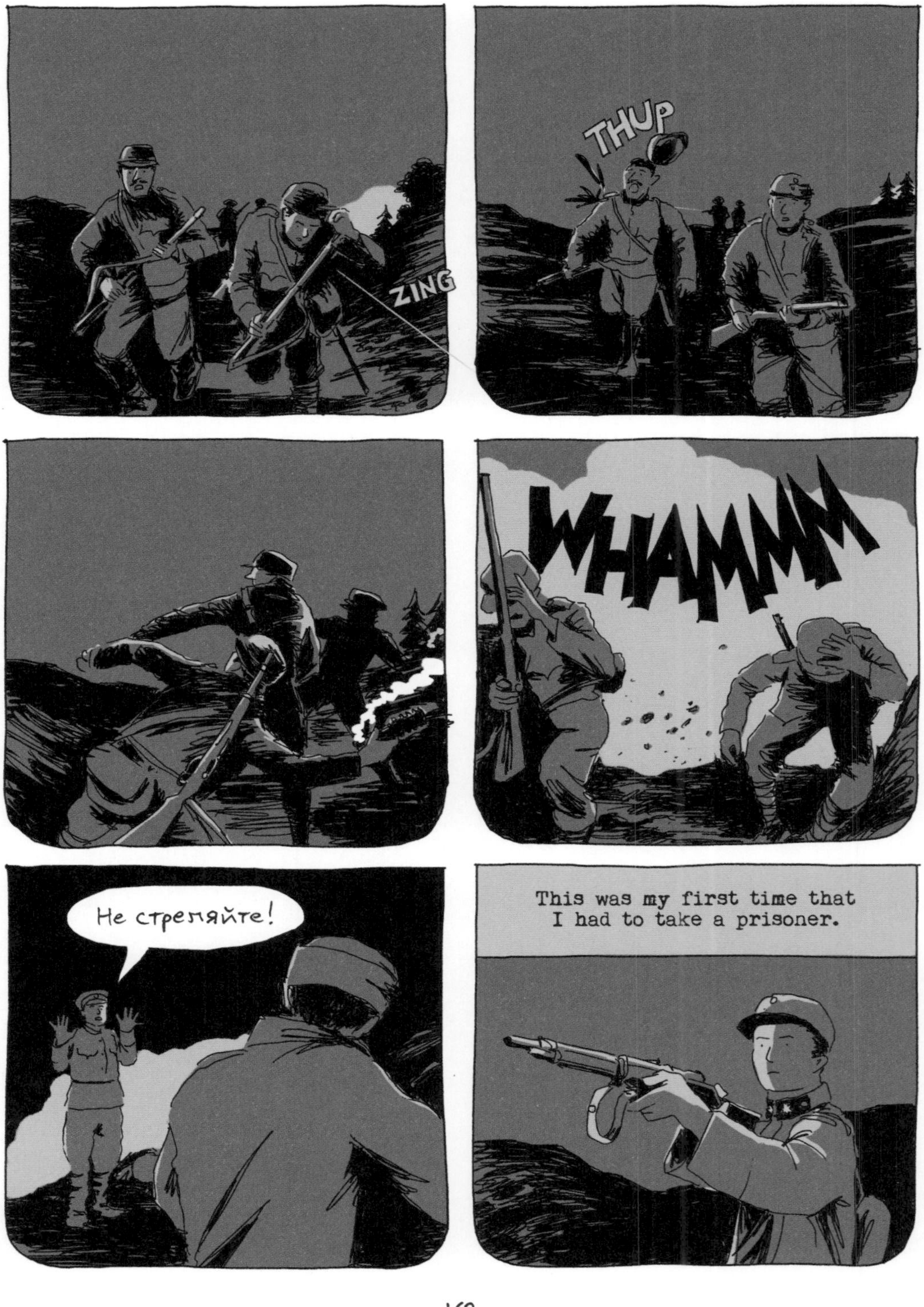
ZING
THUP
WHAMMM
Не стреляйте!
This was my first time that
I had to take a prisoner.

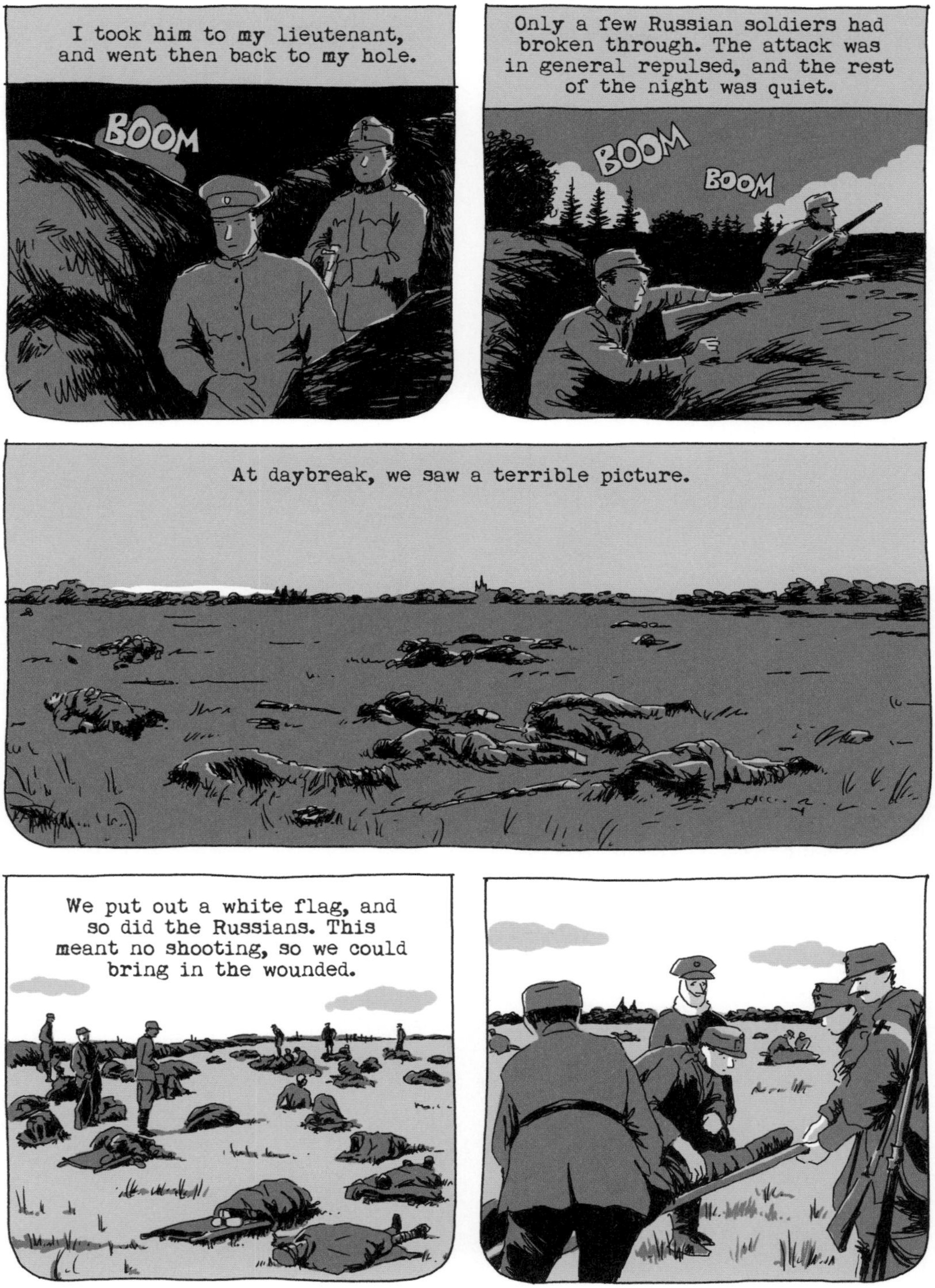
I took him to my lieutenant, and went then back to my hole.
BOOM
Only a few Russian soldiers had broken through. The attack was in general repulsed, and the rest of the night was quiet.
BOOM
BOOM
At daybreak, we saw a terrible picture.
We put out a white flag, and so did the Russians. This meant no shooting, so we could bring in the wounded.

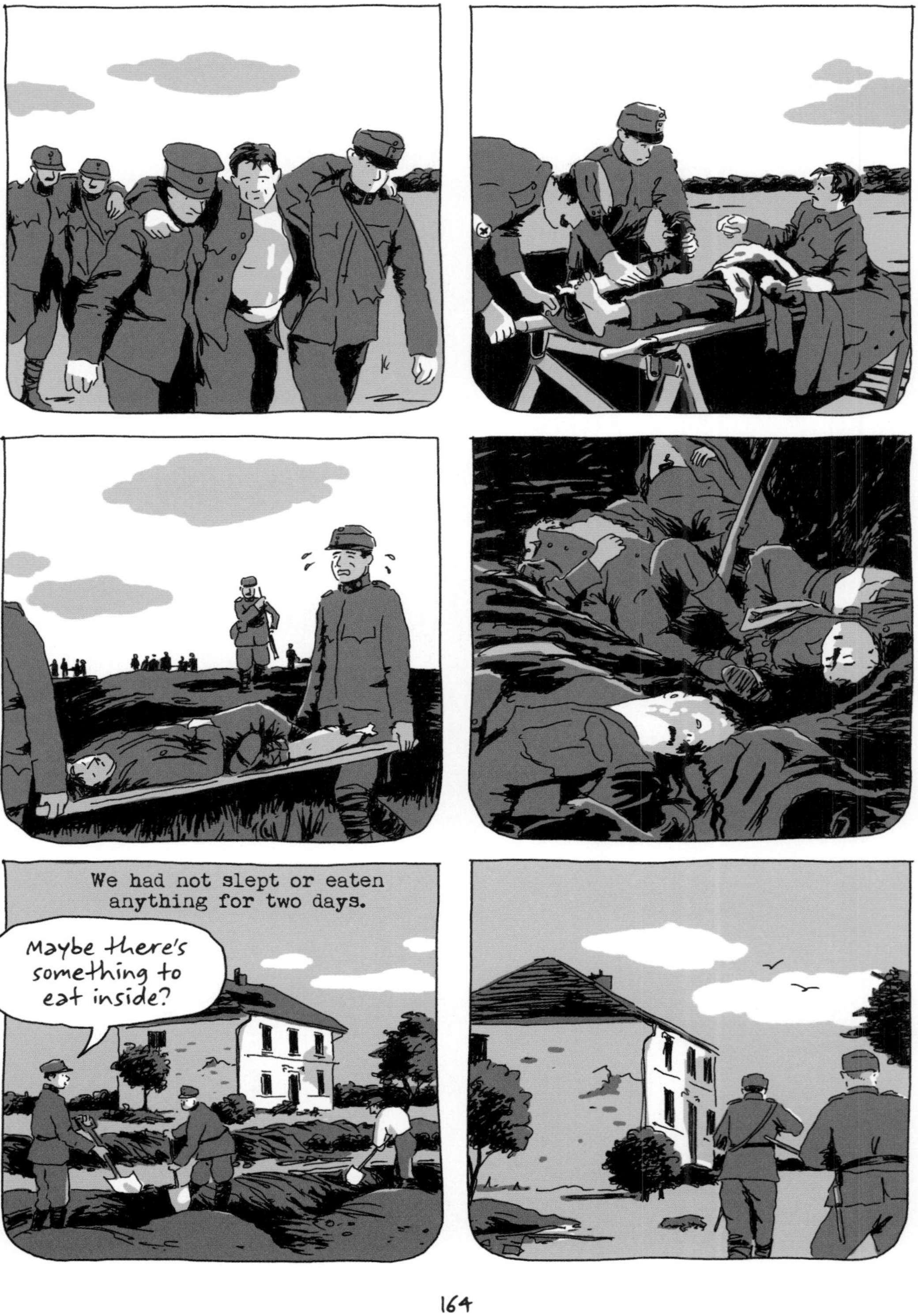
We had not slept or eaten anything for two days.
Maybe there's something to eat inside?

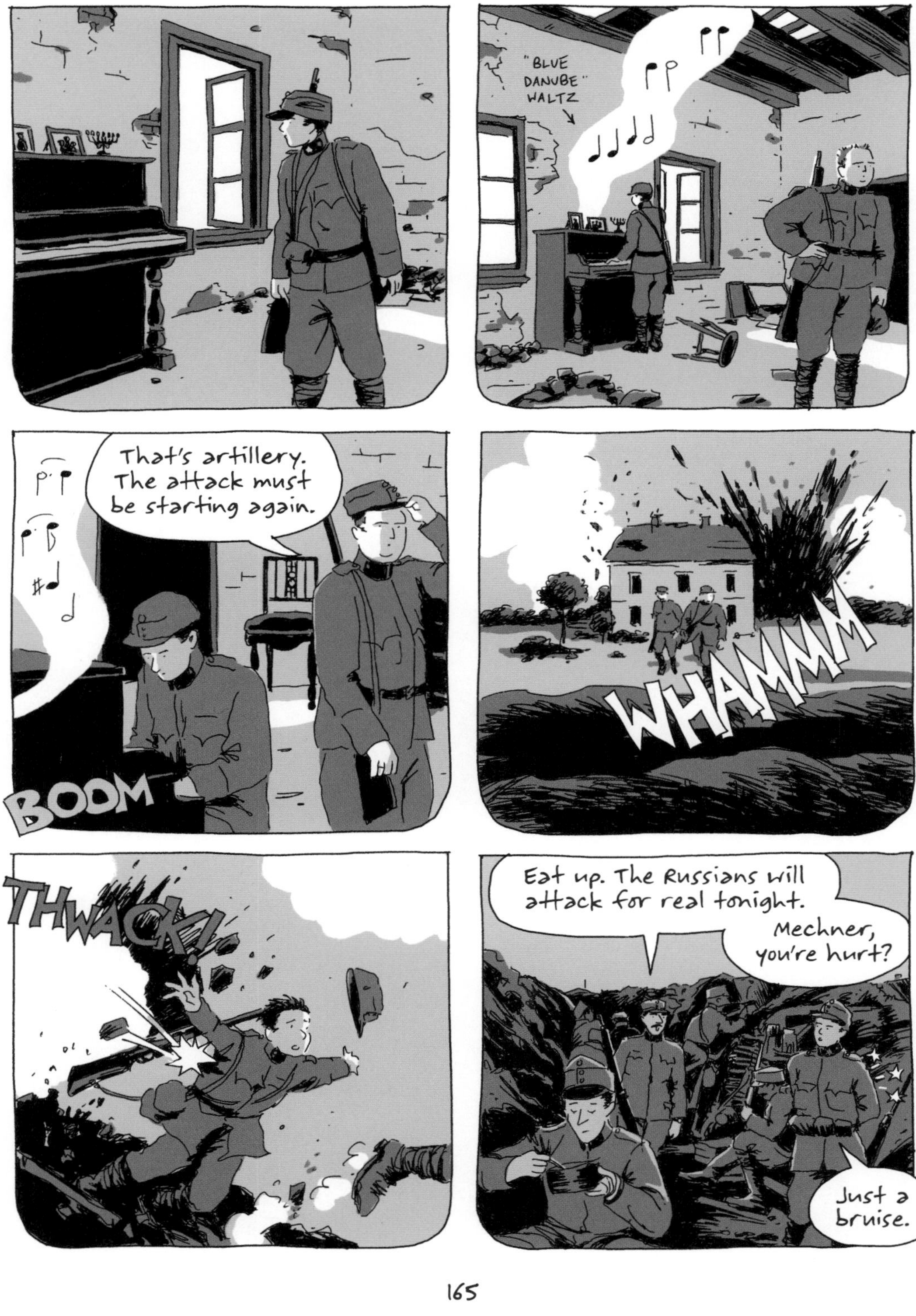
"BLUE DANUBE" WALTZ
That's artillery. The attack must be starting again.
BOOM
WHAMMM
THWACK!
Eat up. The Russians will attack for real tonight.
Mechner, you're hurt?
Just a bruise.

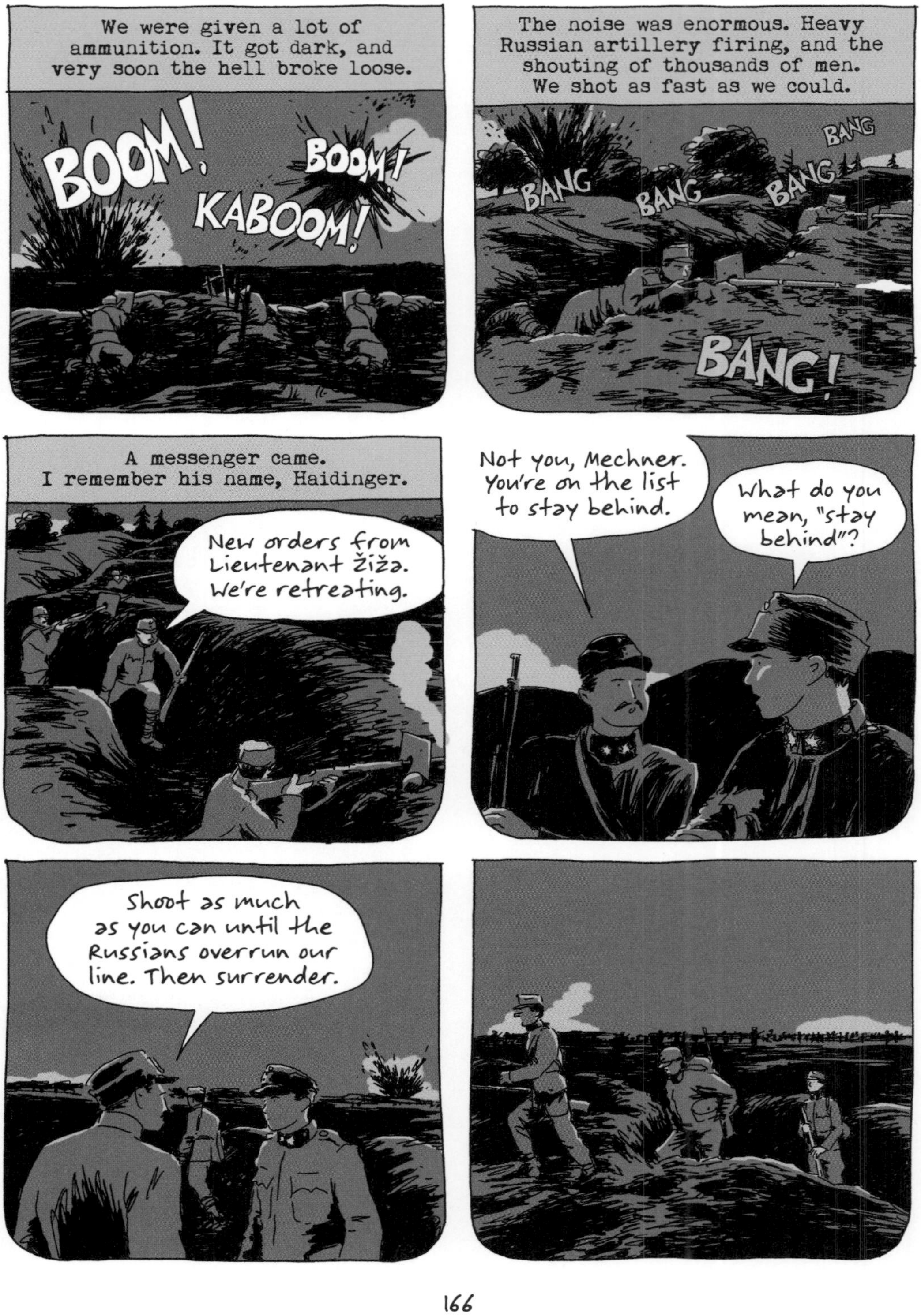
We were given a lot of ammunition. It got dark, and very soon the hell broke loose.
BOOM!
BOOM!
KABOOM!
The noise was enormous. Heavy Russian artillery firing, and the shouting of thousands of men. We shot as fast as we could.
BANG
BANG
BANG
BANG
BANG!
A messenger came. I remember his name, Haidinger.
New orders from Lieutenant Žiža. We're retreating.
Not you, Mechner. You're on the list to stay behind.
What do you mean, "stay behind"?
Shoot as much as you can until the Russians overrun our line. Then surrender.

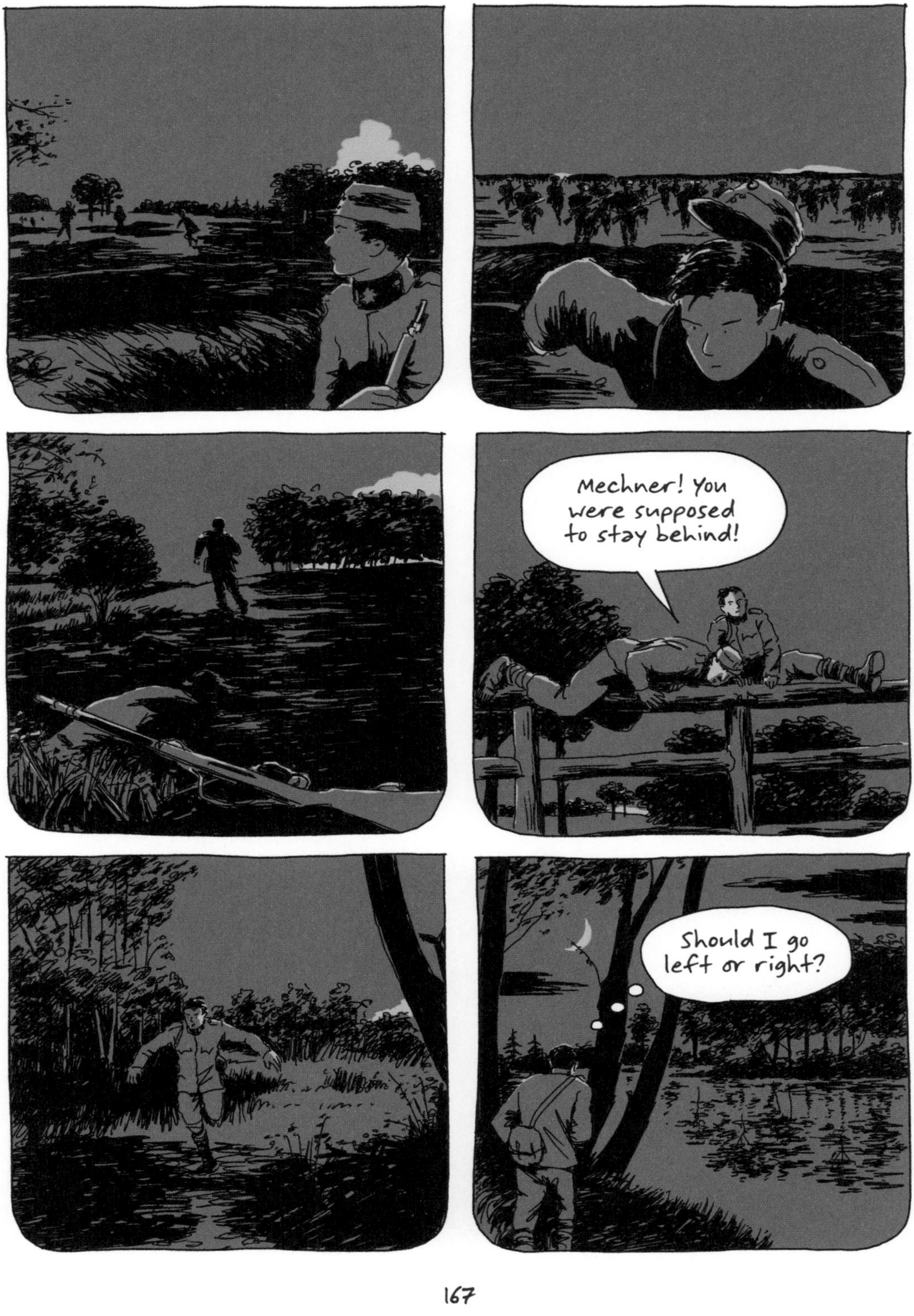
Mechner! You were supposed to stay behind!
Should I go left or right?

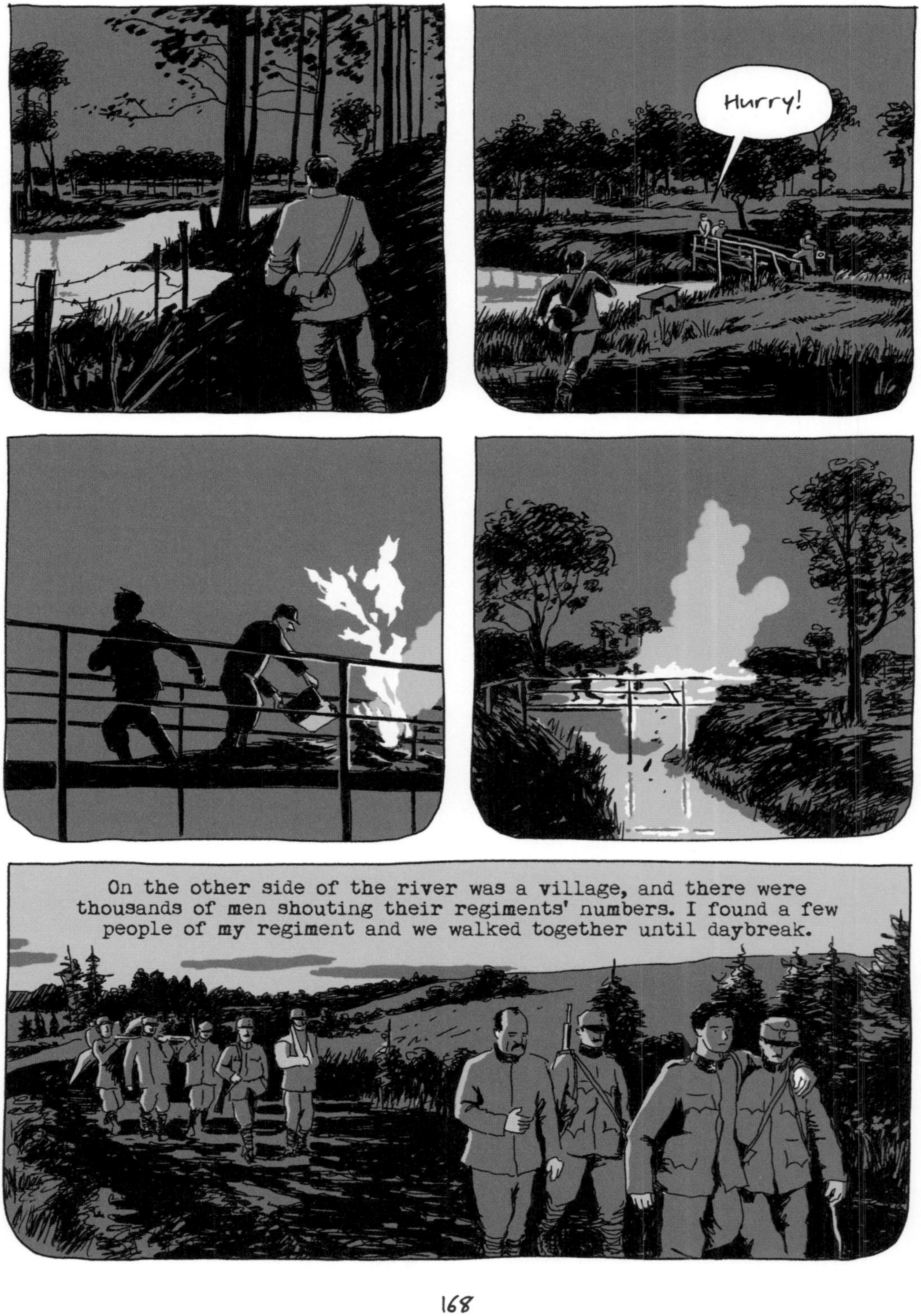
Hurry!
On the other side of the river was a village, and there were thousands of men shouting their regiments' numbers. I found a few people of my regiment and we walked together until daybreak.

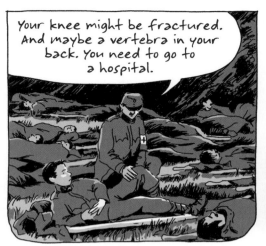

Your knee might be fractured. And maybe a vertebra in your back. You need to go to a hospital.

I was taken to Zabłotce and put in a railway car, which took us to a hospital in Przemyśl.

There was a man in the car who was supposed to take care of the wounded.

That he was a thief, I found out when we arrived at the hospital and I opened my knapsack.

My watch...

My knife!

Name and regiment?

Adolf Mechner. Infantry Regiment No. 83, Vienna.

I had had enough of the Infantry Regiment No. 19.

Cold Water

I was told by people who shared the room with me that I often cried and yelled out in my sleep. I believed them, since I had every night bad dreams.

My back and knee were only severely sprained, not broken. They needed beds for more serious cases, so I was soon discharged.

They sent me back to my regiment in Vienna, with a recommendation for four months of rest and twice-weekly cold-water treatments.

August 1916

I was happy to be home.

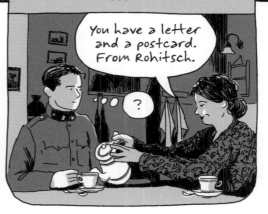

You have a letter and a postcard. From Rohitsch.

?

Mitzi...

My sister, Else, was now engaged, and had converted to Lutheranism.

You should come to church with us on Sunday.

Mhm.

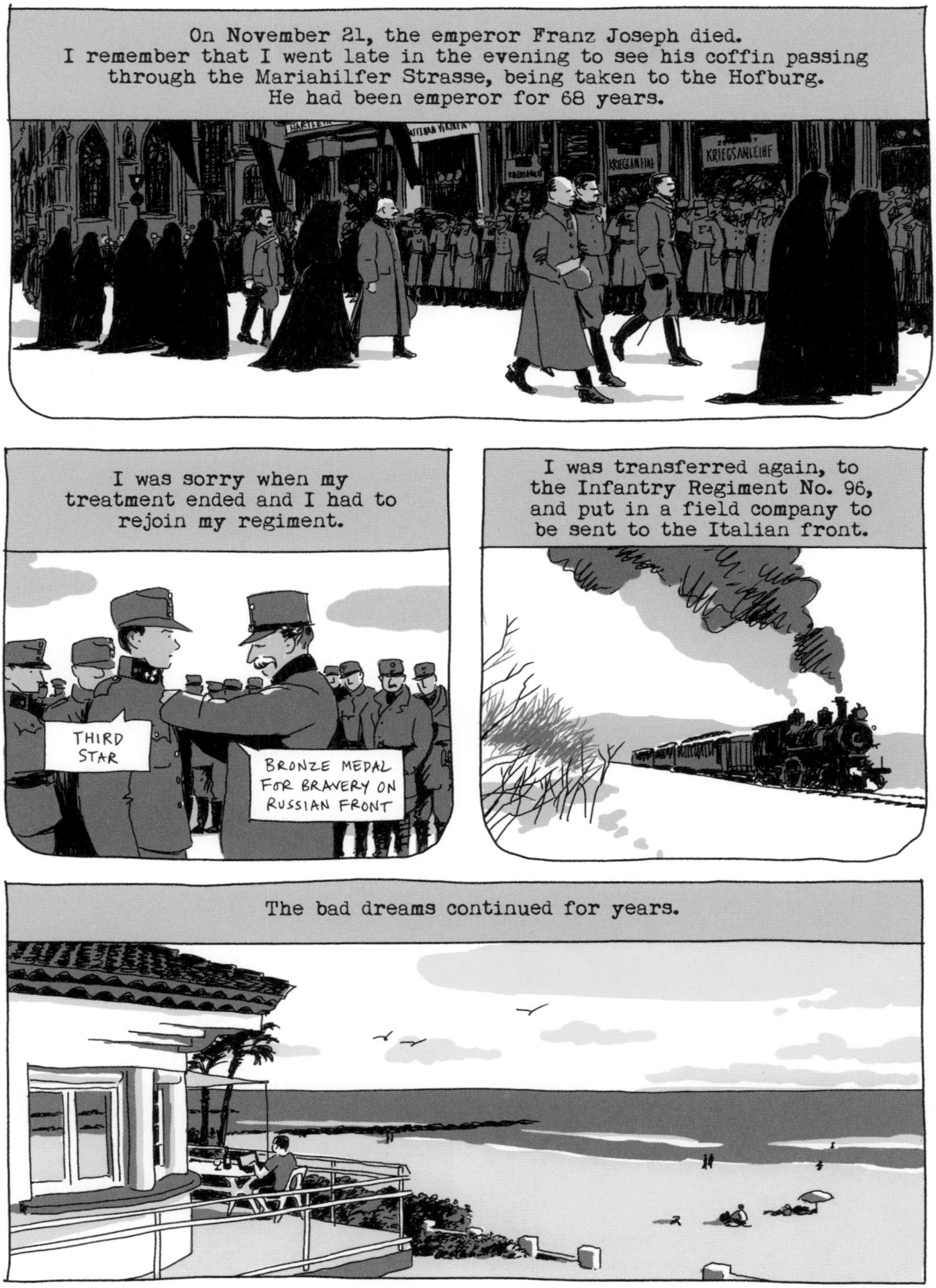
On November 21, the emperor Franz Joseph died.
I remember that I went late in the evening to see his coffin passing through the Mariahilfer Strasse, being taken to the Hofburg.
He had been emperor for 68 years.
I was sorry when my treatment ended and I had to rejoin my regiment.
THIRD STAR
BRONZE MEDAL FOR BRAVERY ON RUSSIAN FRONT
I was transferred again, to the Infantry Regiment No. 96, and put in a field company to be sent to the Italian front.
The bad dreams continued for years.

The Italian Front

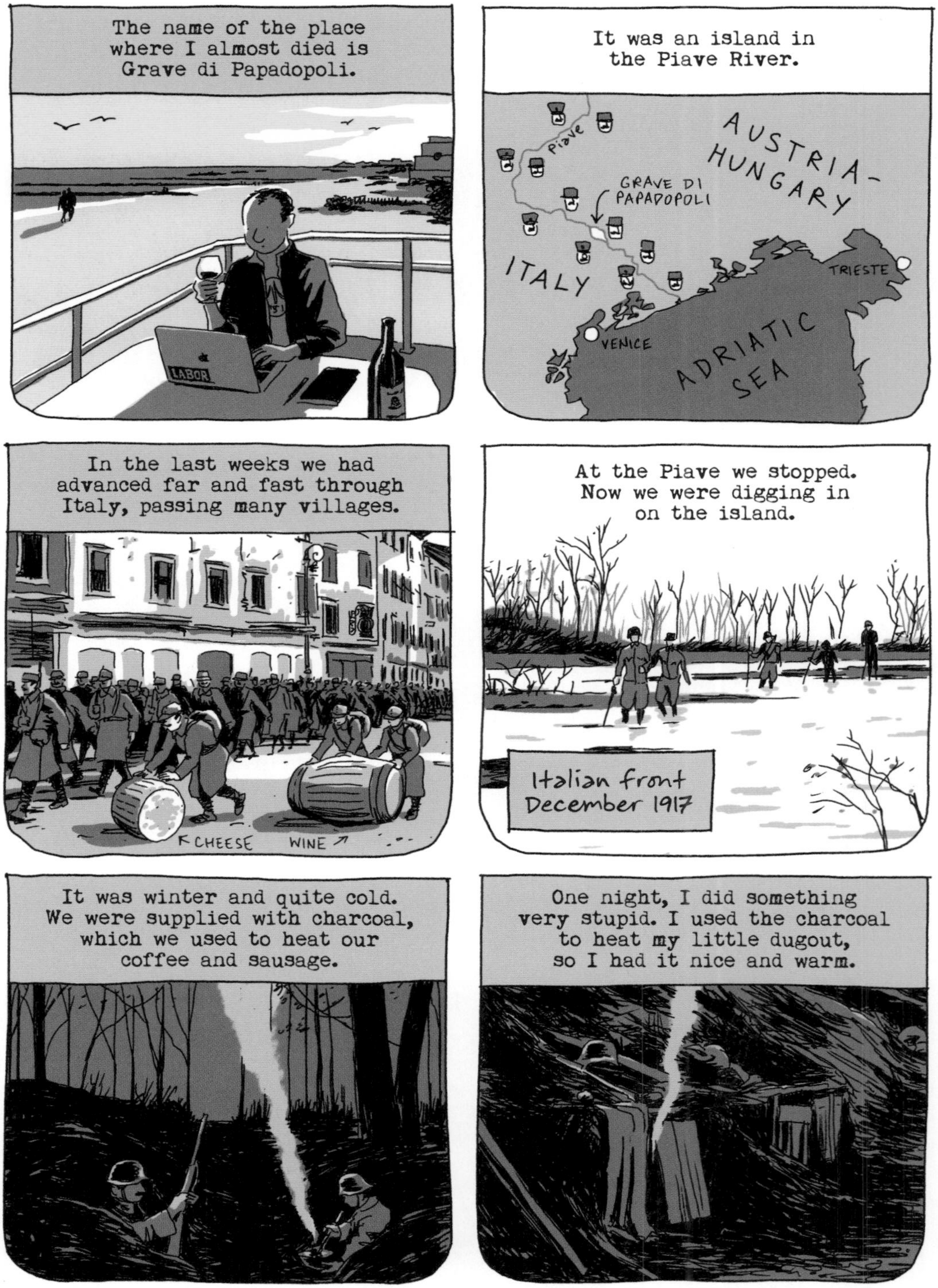
The name of the place where I almost died is Grave di Papadopoli.
LABOR
It was an island in the Piave River.
Piave
AUSTRIA-HUNGARY
GRAVE DI PAPADOPOLI
ITALY
TRIESTE
VENICE
ADRIATIC SEA
In the last weeks we had advanced far and fast through Italy, passing many villages.
CHEESE
WINE
At the Piave we stopped. Now we were digging in on the island.
Italian front December 1917
It was winter and quite cold. We were supplied with charcoal, which we used to heat our coffee and sausage.
One night, I did something very stupid. I used the charcoal to heat my little dugout, so I had it nice and warm.

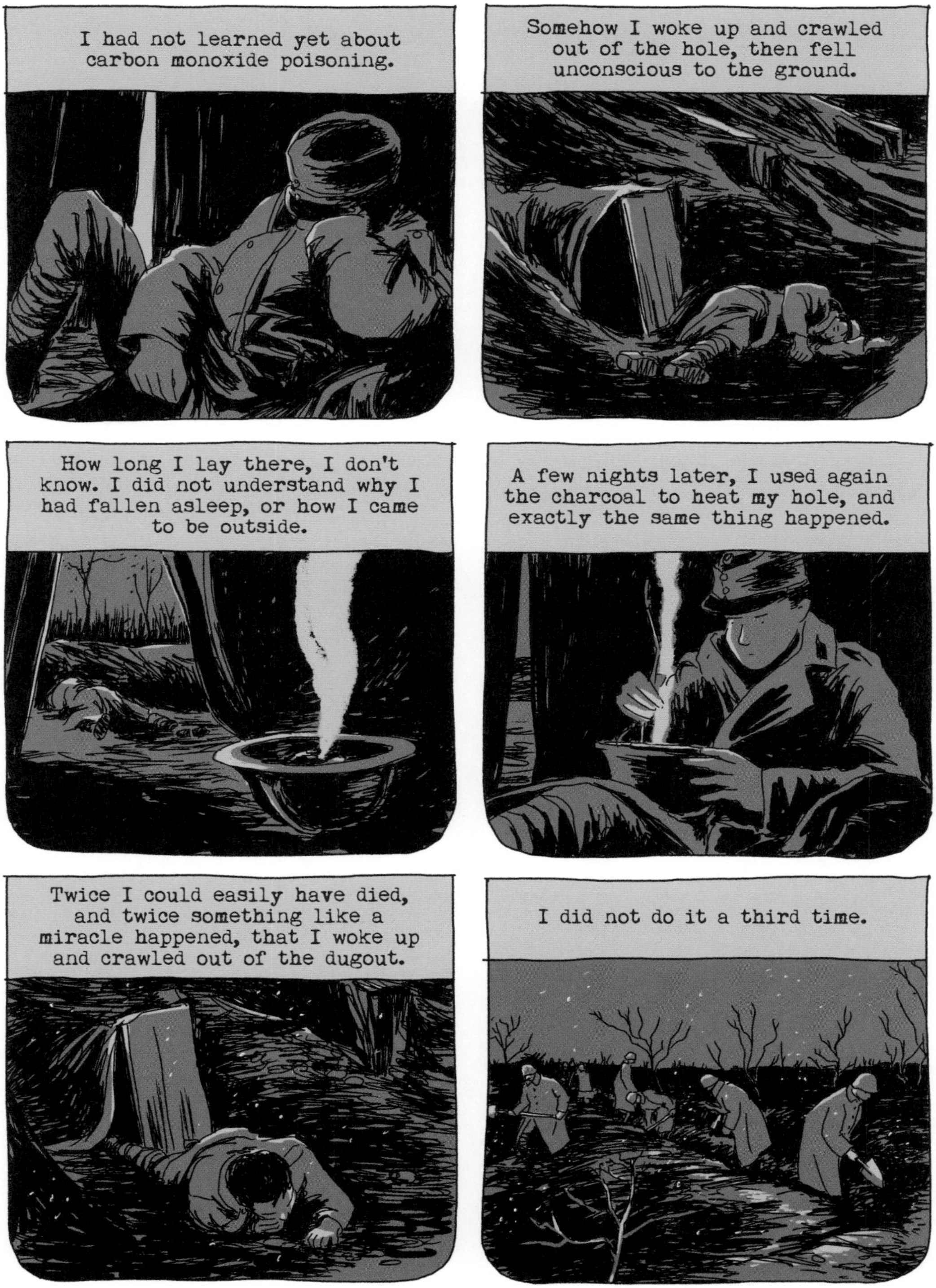
I had not learned yet about carbon monoxide poisoning.
Somehow I woke up and crawled out of the hole, then fell unconscious to the ground.
How long I lay there, I don't know. I did not understand why I had fallen asleep, or how I came to be outside.
A few nights later, I used again the charcoal to heat my hole, and exactly the same thing happened.
Twice I could easily have died, and twice something like a miracle happened, that I woke up and crawled out of the dugout.
I did not do it a third time.

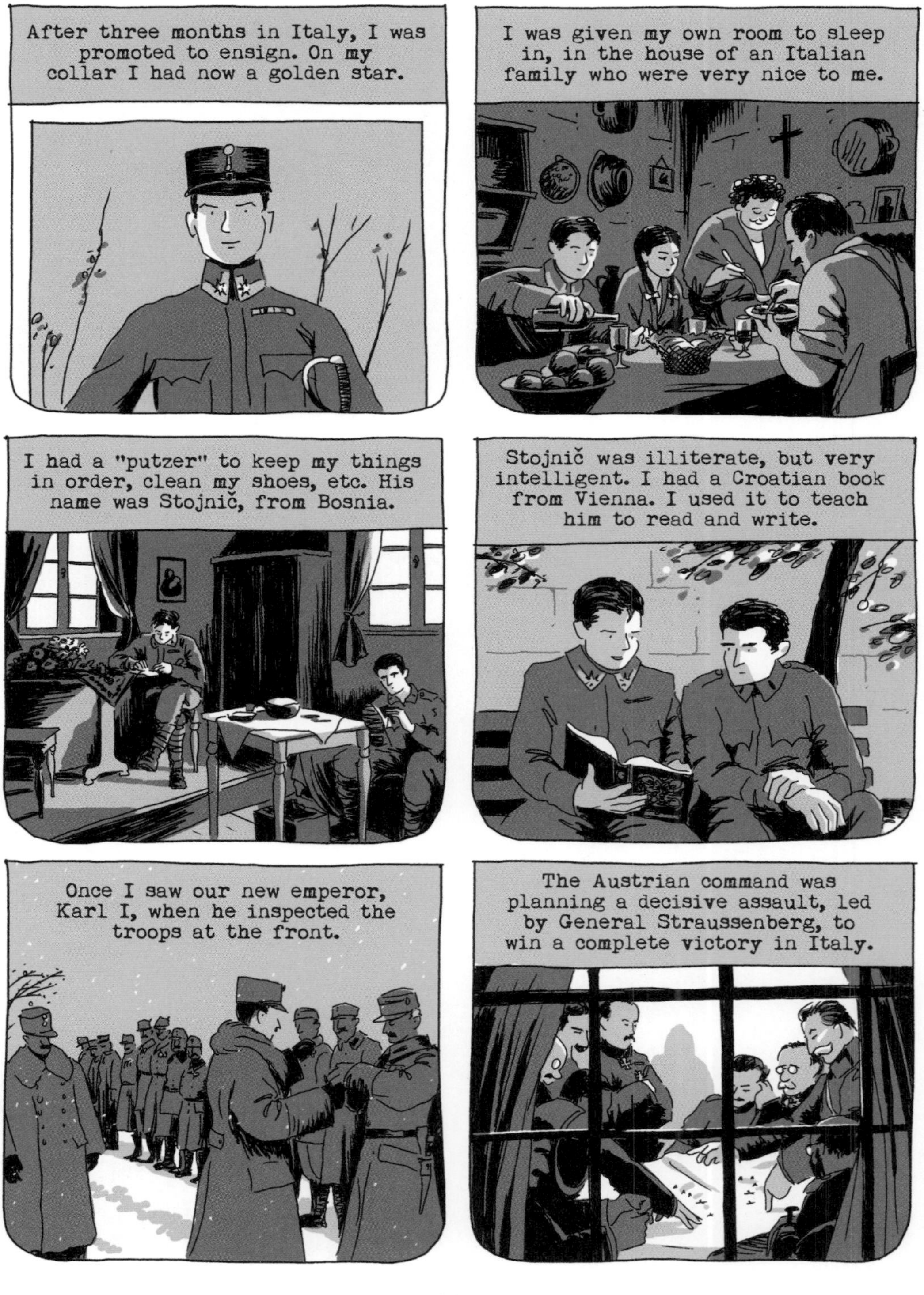
After three months in Italy, I was promoted to ensign. On my collar I had now a golden star.
I was given my own room to sleep in, in the house of an Italian family who were very nice to me.
I had a "putzer" to keep my things in order, clean my shoes, etc. His name was Stojnič, from Bosnia.
Stojnič was illiterate, but very intelligent. I had a Croatian book from Vienna. I used it to teach him to read and write.
Once I saw our new emperor, Karl I, when he inspected the troops at the front.
The Austrian command was planning a decisive assault, led by General Straussenberg, to win a complete victory in Italy.

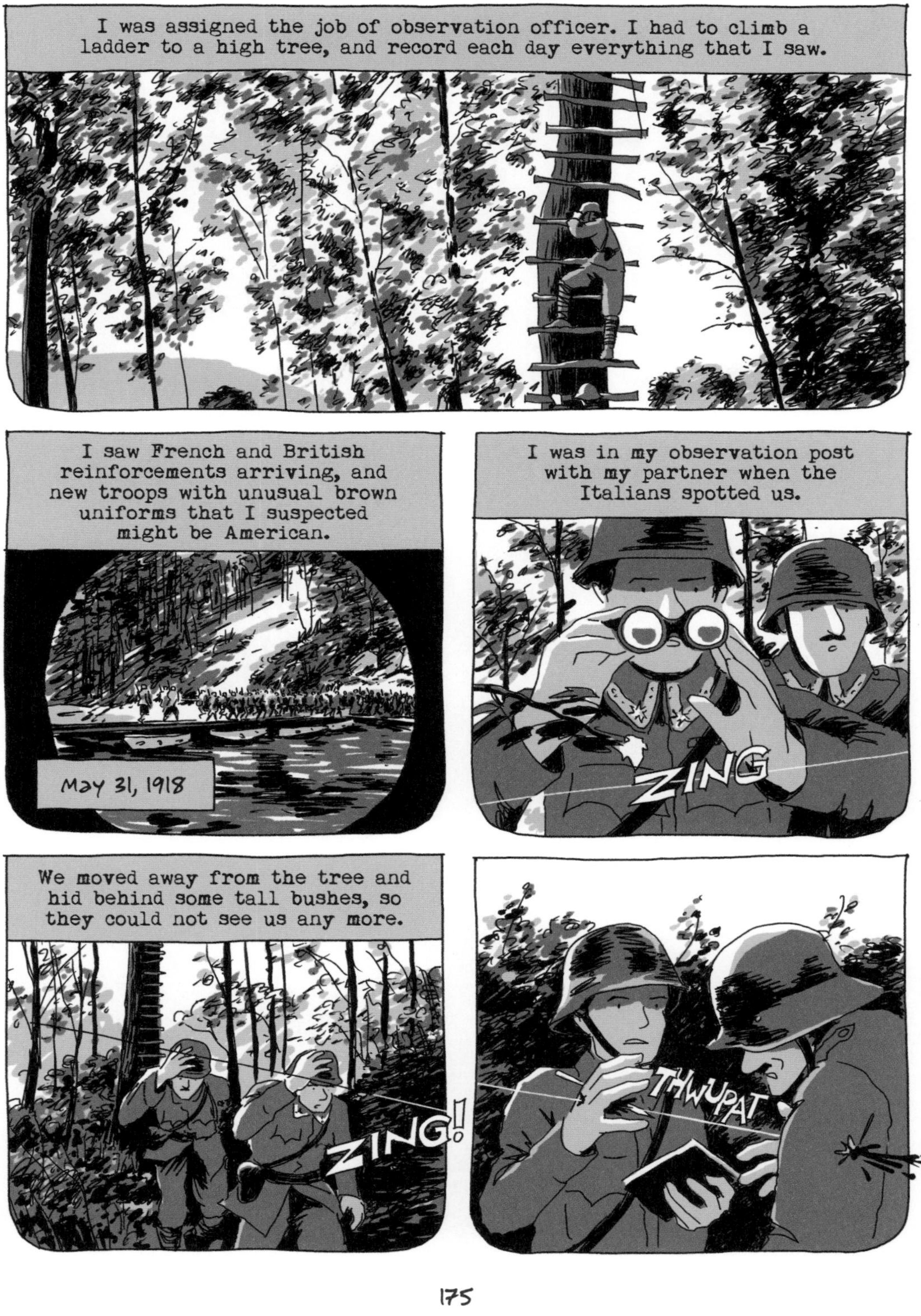
I was assigned the job of observation officer. I had to climb a ladder to a high tree, and record each day everything that I saw.
I saw French and British reinforcements arriving, and new troops with unusual brown uniforms that I suspected might be American.
May 31, 1918
I was in my observation post with my partner when the Italians spotted us.
ZING
We moved away from the tree and hid behind some tall bushes, so they could not see us any more.
ZING!
THWUPAT

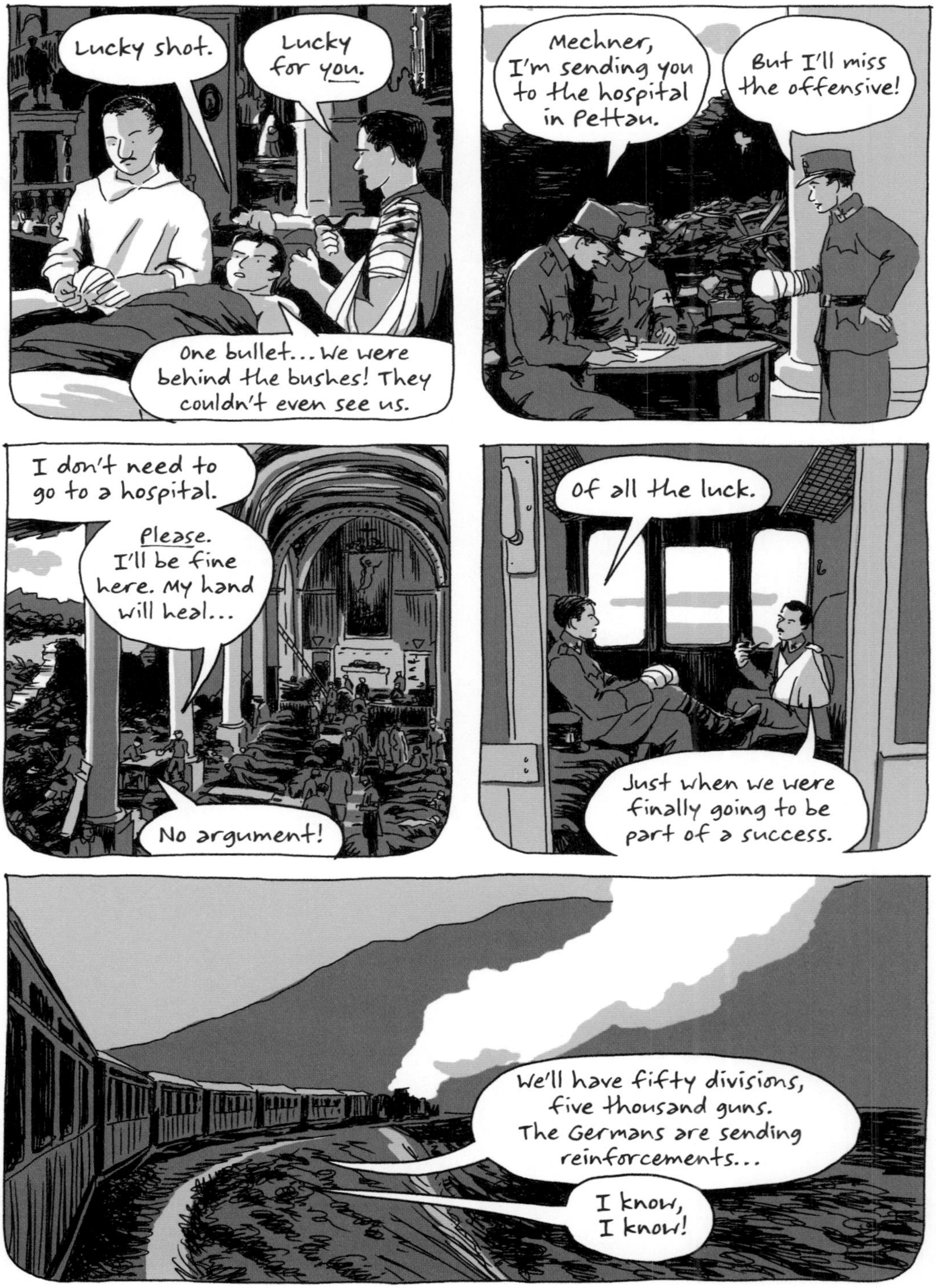
Lucky shot.
Lucky for you.
One bullet... We were behind the bushes! They couldn't even see us.
Mechner, I'm sending you to the hospital in Pettau.
But I'll miss the offensive!
I don't need to go to a hospital.
Please. I'll be fine here. My hand will heal...
No argument!
Of all the luck.
Just when we were finally going to be part of a success.
We'll have fifty divisions, five thousand guns. The Germans are sending reinforcements...
I know, I know!

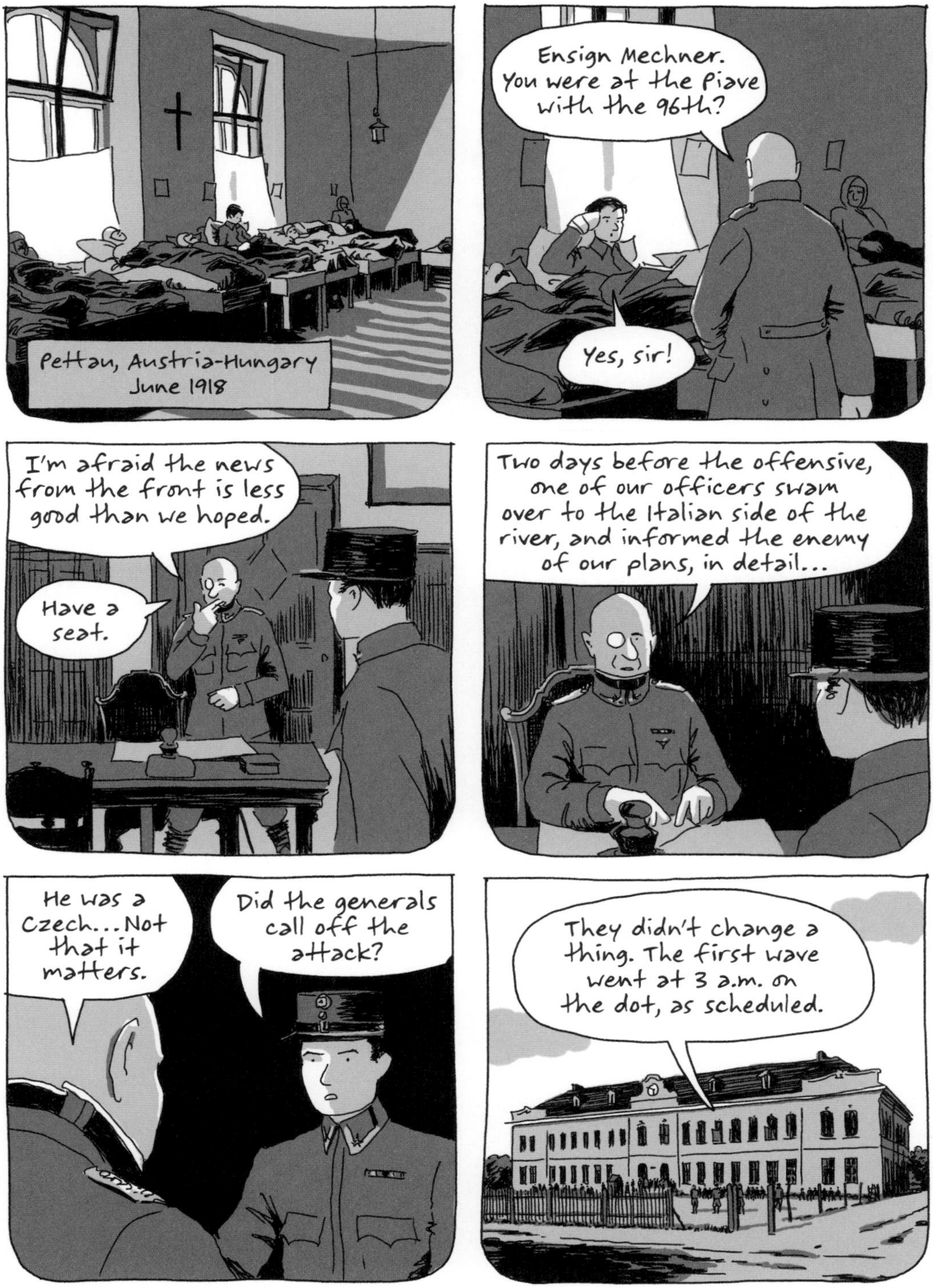

Pettau, Austria-Hungary
June 1918
Ensign Mechner. You were at the Piave with the 96th?
Yes, sir!
I'm afraid the news from the front is less good than we hoped.
Have a seat.
Two days before the offensive, one of our officers swam over to the Italian side of the river, and informed the enemy of our plans, in detail...
He was a Czech...Not that it matters.
Did the generals call off the attack?
They didn't change a thing. The first wave went at 3 a.m. on the dot, as scheduled.

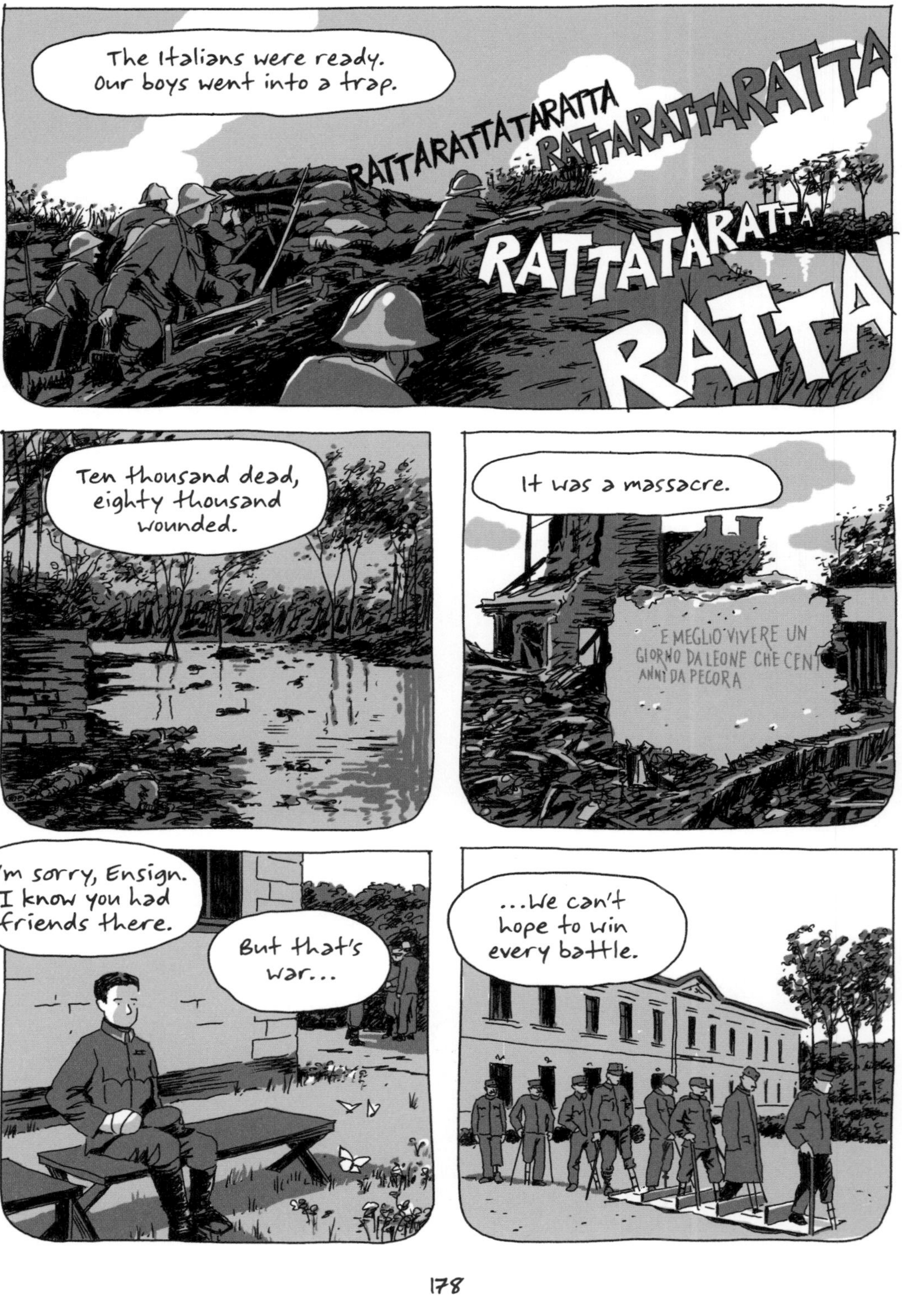

The Italians were ready. Our boys went into a trap.
RATTARATTATARATTA
RATTARATTARATTA
RATTATARATTA
RATTATARATTA
RATTA
Ten thousand dead, eighty thousand wounded.
It was a massacre.
E MEGLIO VIVERE UN GIORNO DA LEONE CHE CENT ANNI DA PECORA
I'm sorry, Ensign. I know you had friends there.
But that's war...
...We can't hope to win every battle.

Cliffhanger

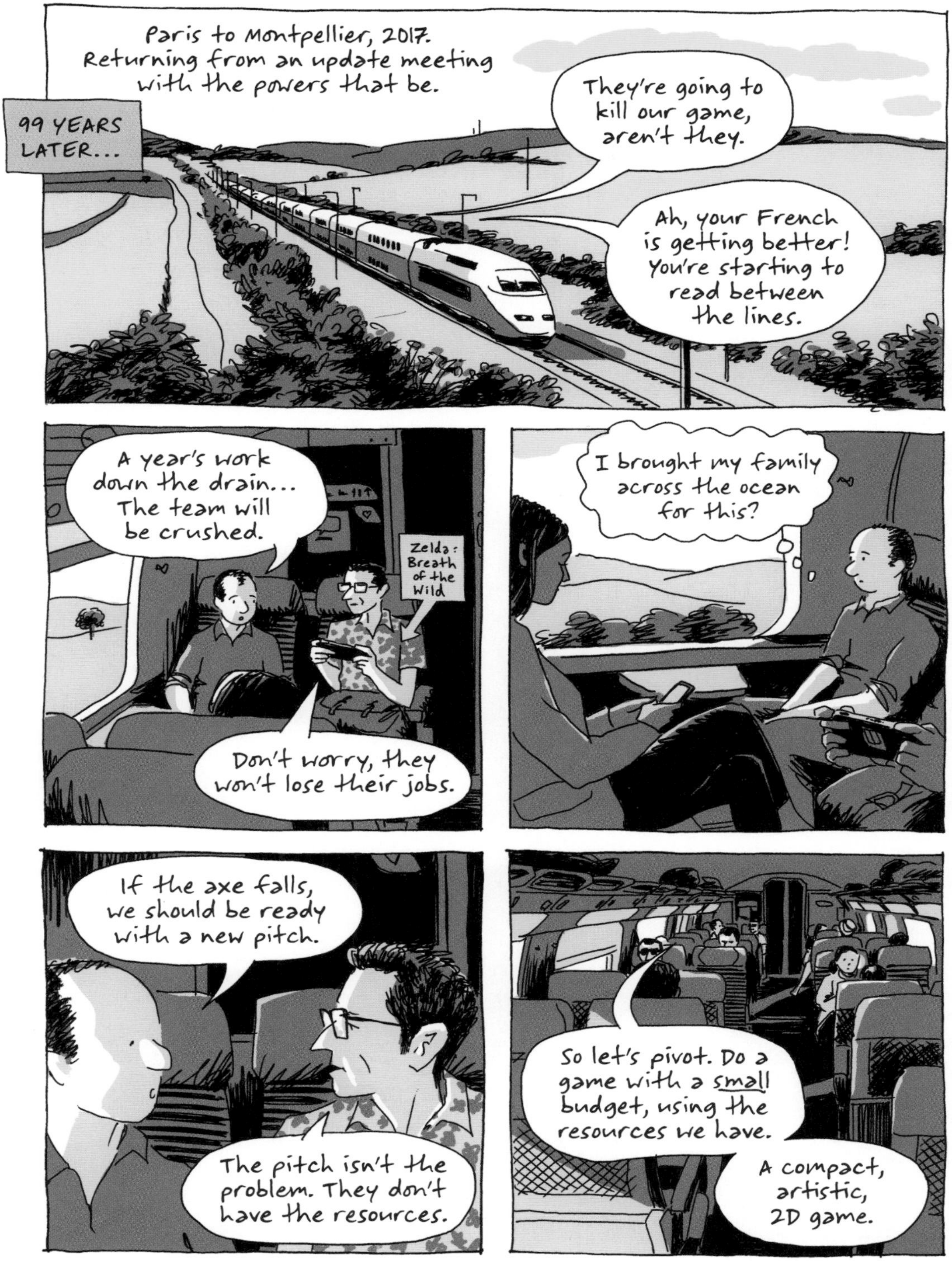
Paris to Montpellier, 2017. Returning from an update meeting with the powers that be.
99 YEARS LATER...
They're going to kill our game, aren't they.
Ah, your French is getting better! You're starting to read between the lines.
A year's work down the drain... The team will be crushed.
Zelda: Breath of the Wild
Don't worry, they won't lose their jobs.
I brought my family across the ocean for this?
If the axe falls, we should be ready with a new pitch.
The pitch isn't the problem. They don't have the resources.
So let's pivot. Do a game with a small budget, using the resources we have.
A compact, artistic, 2D game.

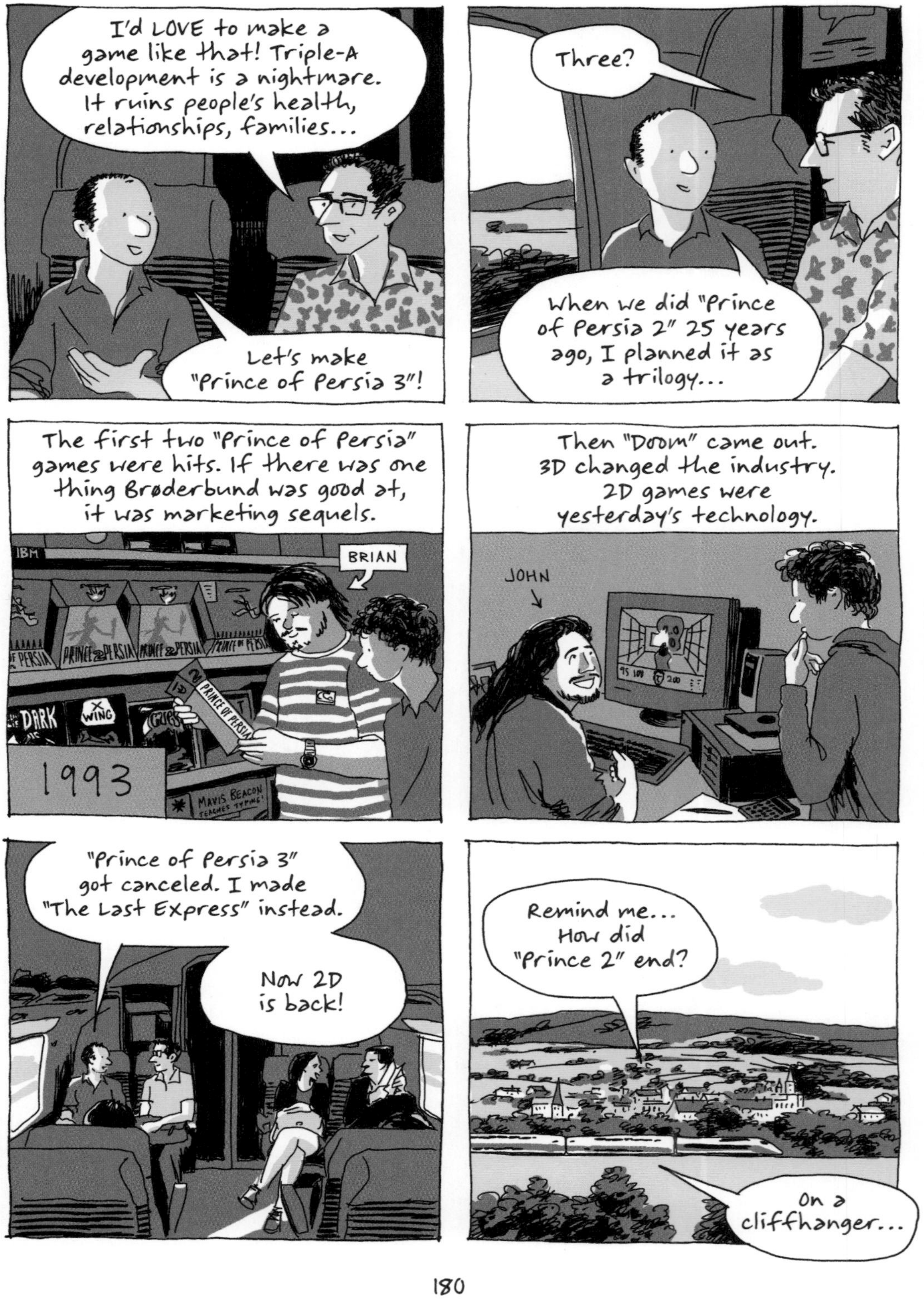
I'd LOVE to make a game like that! Triple-A development is a nightmare. It ruins people's health, relationships, families...
Let's make "Prince of Persia 3"!
Three?
When we did "Prince of Persia 2" 25 years ago, I planned it as a trilogy...
The first two "Prince of Persia" games were hits. If there was one thing Brøderbund was good at, it was marketing sequels.
BRIAN
IBM
PRINCE OF PERSIA
X WING
DARK
1993
MAVIS BEACON TEACHES TYPING!
Then "Doom" came out. 3D changed the industry. 2D games were yesterday's technology.
JOHN
"Prince of Persia 3" got canceled. I made "The Last Express" instead.
Now 2D is back!
Remind me... How did "Prince 2" end?
On a cliffhanger...

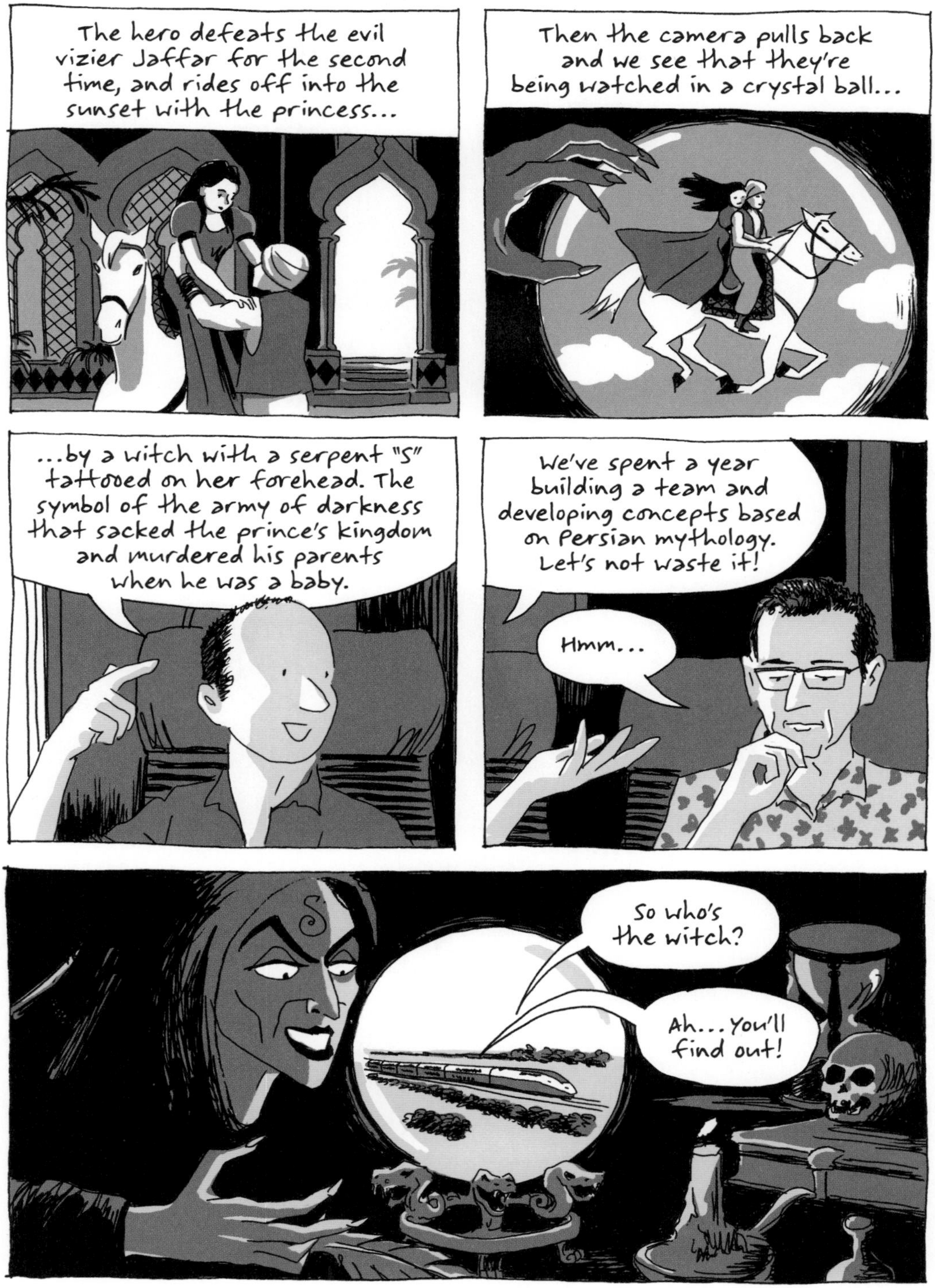
The hero defeats the evil vizier Jaffar for the second time, and rides off into the sunset with the princess...
Then the camera pulls back and we see that they're being watched in a crystal ball...
...by a witch with a serpent "S" tattooed on her forehead. The symbol of the army of darkness that sacked the prince's kingdom and murdered his parents when he was a baby.
We've spent a year building a team and developing concepts based on Persian mythology. Let's not waste it!
Hmm...
So who's the witch?
Ah... You'll find out!

Day Trip

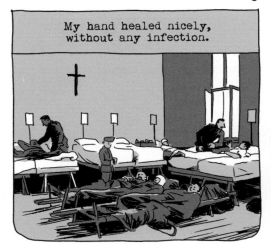

My hand healed nicely, without any infection.

One day, I looked at the map and realized that my hospital was...

Not far from Rohitsch!

Mitzi wrote to me from there...

Without asking the hospital commander for permission, I went to the train station and bought a ticket to Rohitsch.

Mitzi!

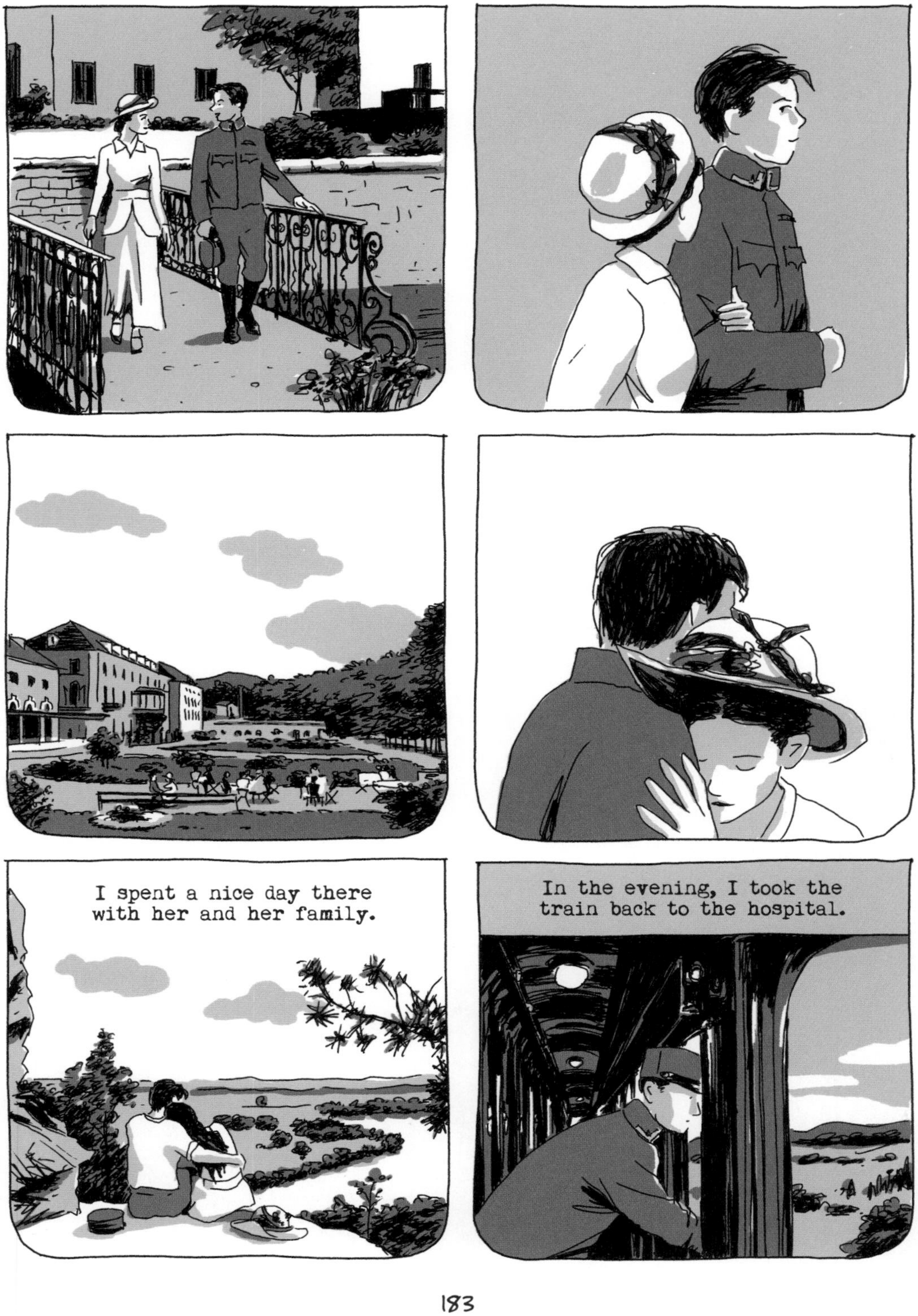
I spent a nice day there with her and her family.
In the evening, I took the train back to the hospital.

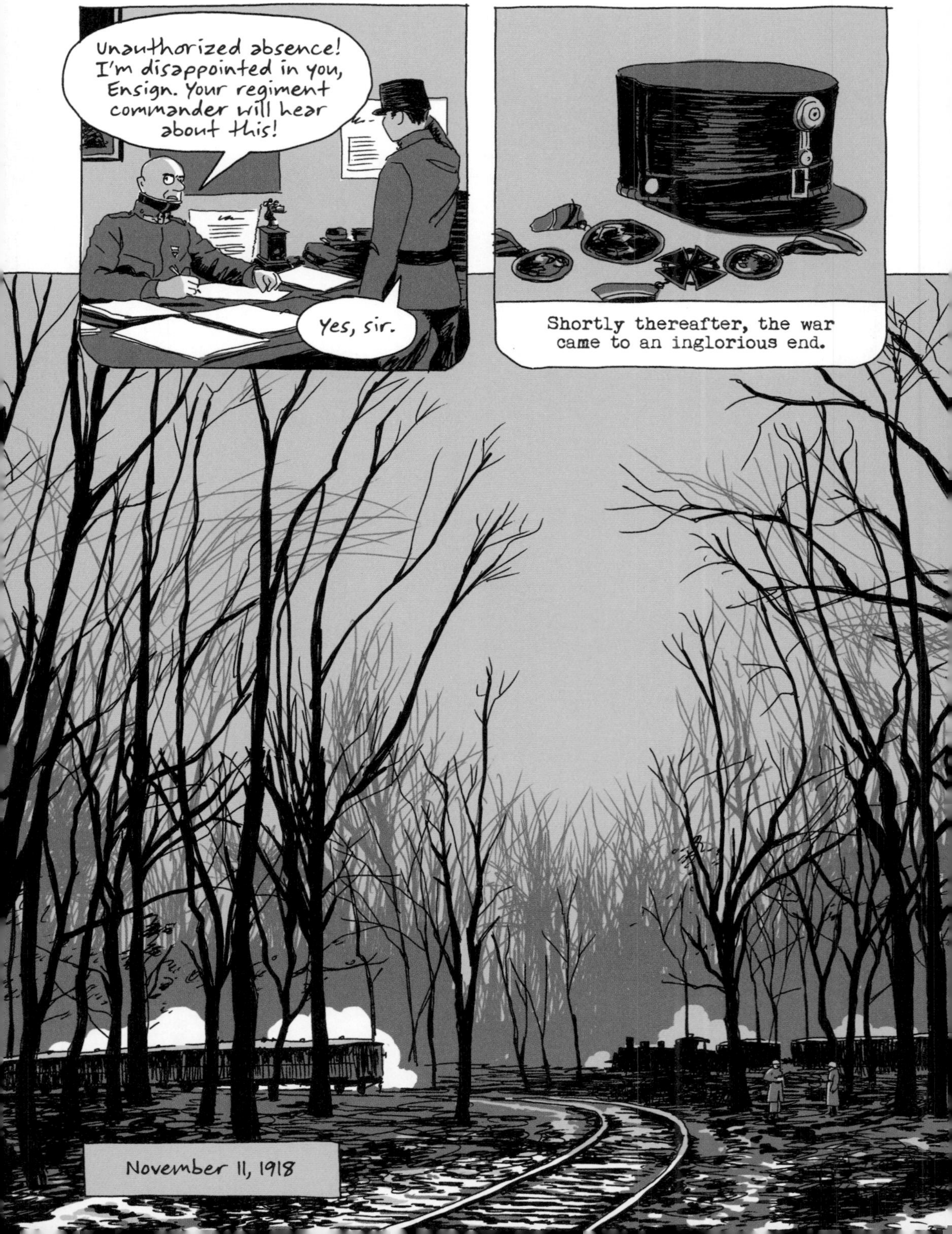
Unauthorized absence! I'm disappointed in you, Ensign. Your regiment commander will hear about this!
Yes, sir.
Shortly thereafter, the war came to an inglorious end.
November 11, 1918

Chapter 6

The Princess

Lisa Ziegler
Date unknown

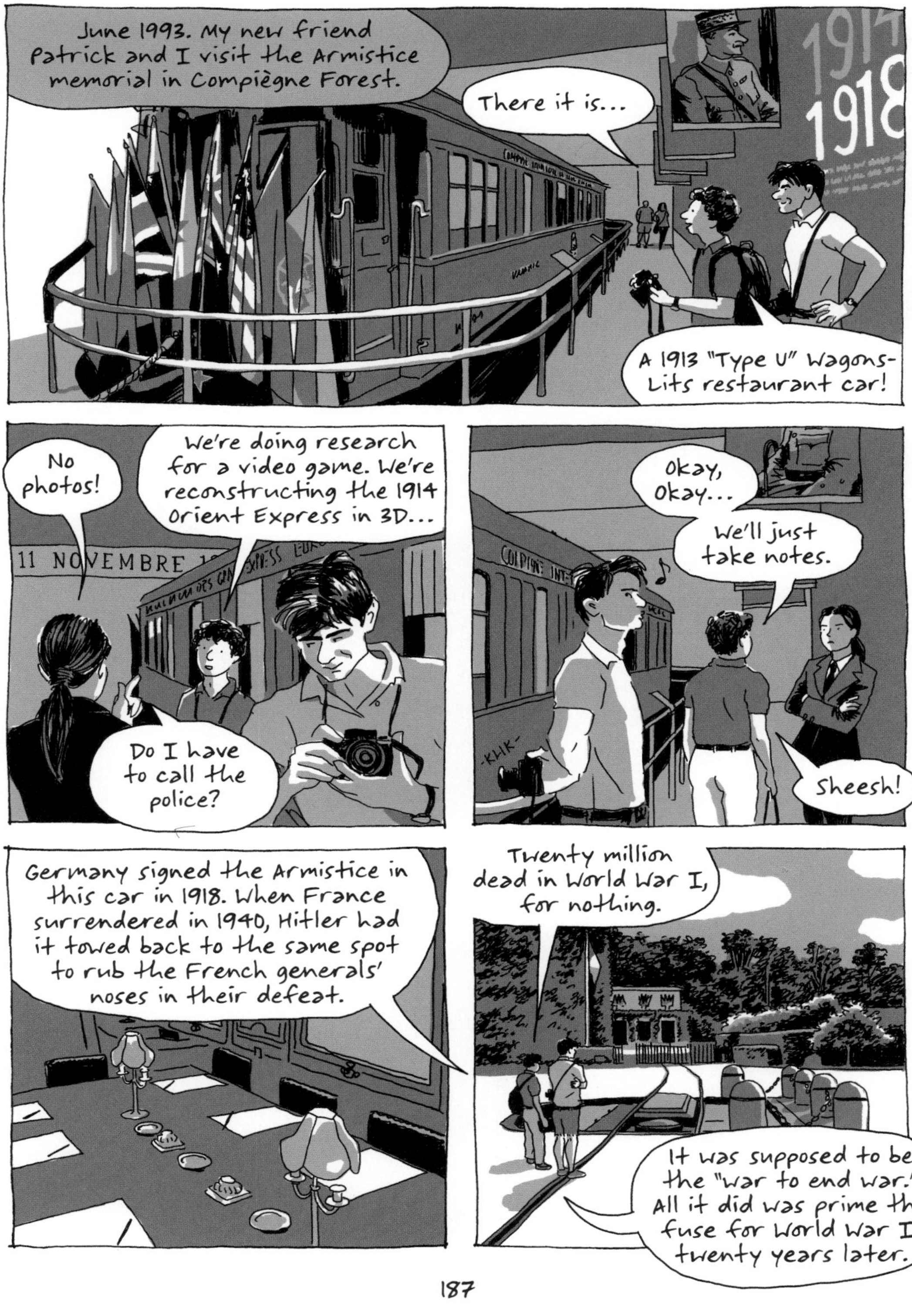
June 1993. My new friend Patrick and I visit the Armistice memorial in Compiègne Forest.
There it is...
1914
1918
A 1913 "Type U" Wagons-Lits restaurant car!
No photos!
We're doing research for a video game. We're reconstructing the 1914 Orient Express in 3D...
11 NOVEMBRE 1
Do I have to call the police?
Okay, Okay...
We'll just take notes.
-KLIK-
Sheesh!
Germany signed the Armistice in this car in 1918. When France surrendered in 1940, Hitler had it towed back to the same spot to rub the French generals' noses in their defeat.
Twenty million dead in World War I, for nothing.
It was supposed to be the "war to end war." All it did was prime the fuse for World War II twenty years later.

Willi's Friends

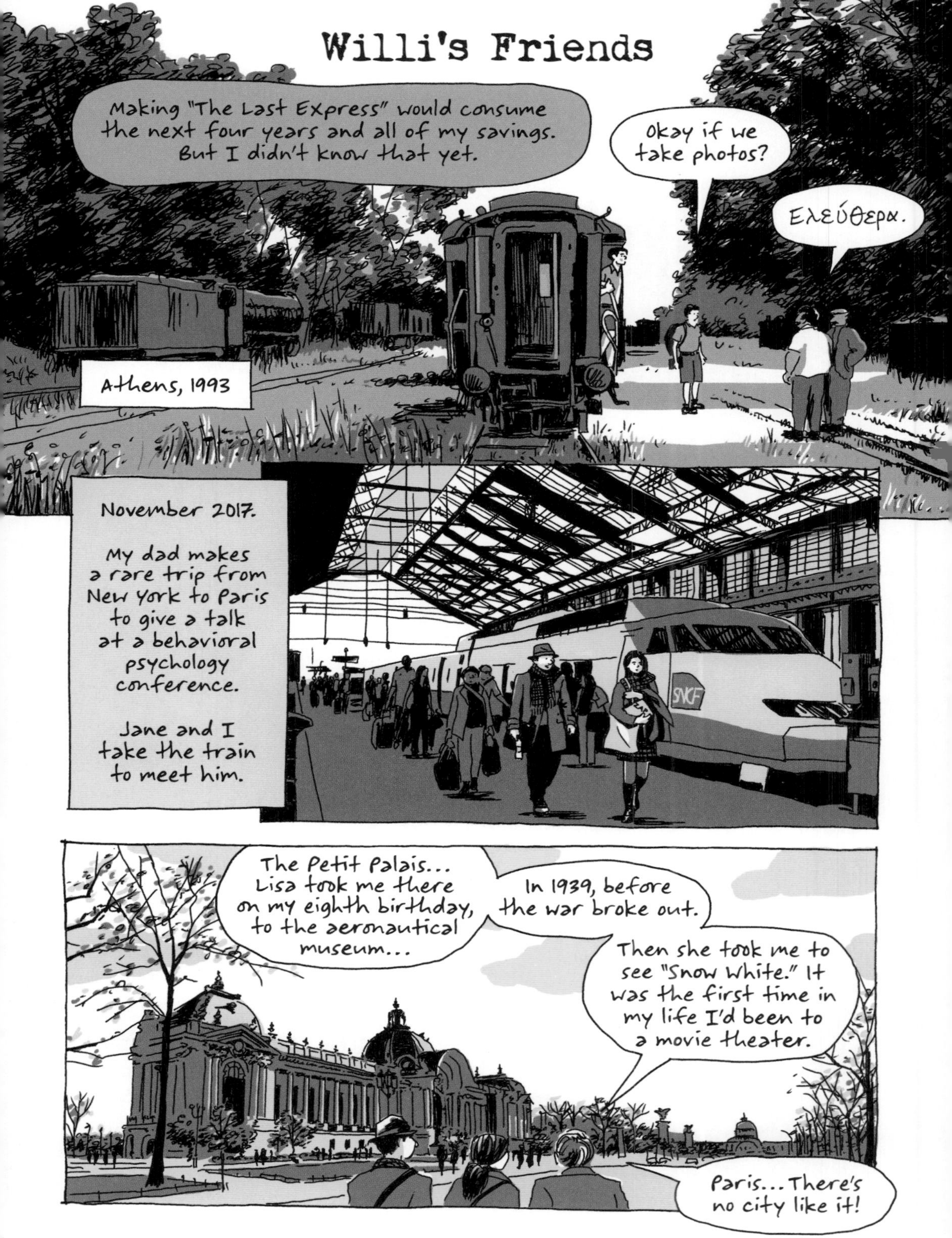
Making "The Last Express" would consume the next four years and all of my savings. But I didn't know that yet.
Okay if we take photos?
Ελεύθερα.
Athens, 1993
November 2017.
My dad makes a rare trip from New York to Paris to give a talk at a behavioral psychology conference.
Jane and I take the train to meet him.
SNCF
The Petit Palais... Lisa took me there on my eighth birthday, to the aeronautical museum...
In 1939, before the war broke out.
Then she took me to see "Snow White." It was the first time in my life I'd been to a movie theater.
Paris... There's no city like it!

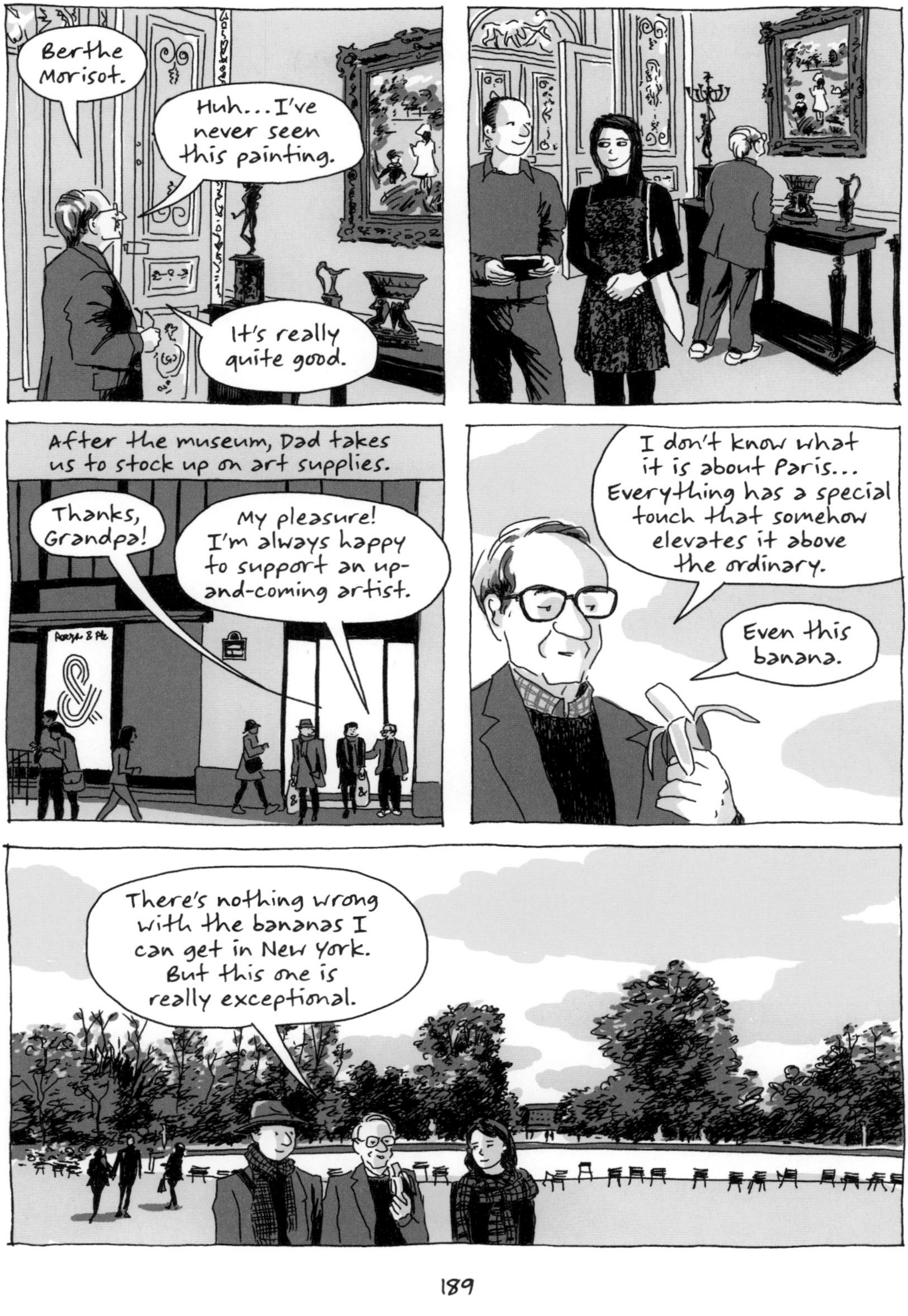
Berthe Morisot.
Huh... I've never seen this painting.
It's really quite good.
After the museum, Dad takes us to stock up on art supplies.
Thanks, Grandpa!
My pleasure! I'm always happy to support an up-and-coming artist.
I don't know what it is about Paris... Everything has a special touch that somehow elevates it above the ordinary.
Even this banana.
There's nothing wrong with the bananas I can get in New York. But this one is really exceptional.

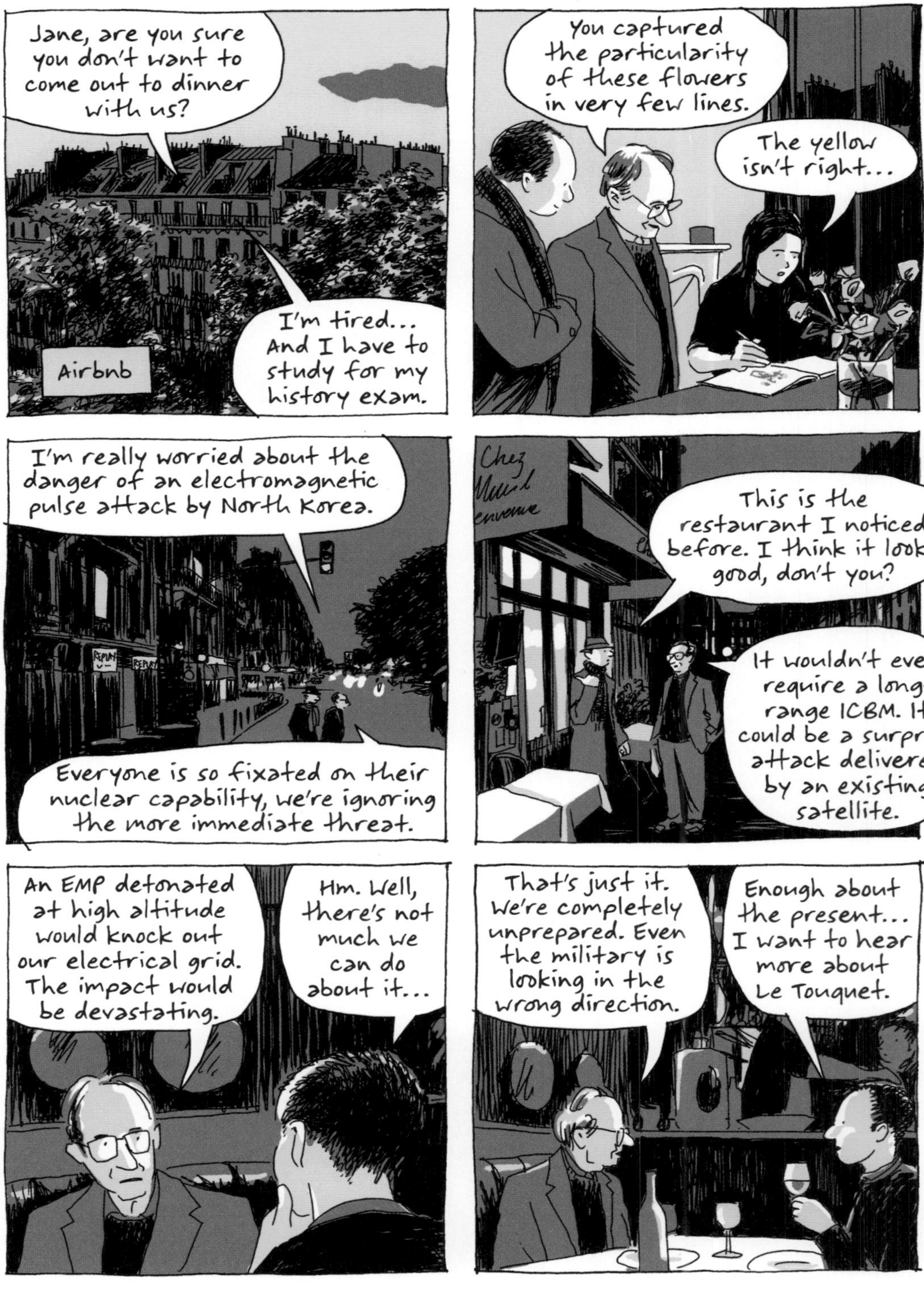
Jane, are you sure you don't want to come out to dinner with us?
Airbnb
I'm tired... And I have to study for my history exam.
You captured the particularity of these flowers in very few lines.
The yellow isn't right...
I'm really worried about the danger of an electromagnetic pulse attack by North Korea.
Everyone is so fixated on their nuclear capability, we're ignoring the more immediate threat.
This is the restaurant I noticed before. I think it looks good, don't you?
It wouldn't even require a long-range ICBM. It could be a surprise attack delivered by an existing satellite.
An EMP detonated at high altitude would knock out our electrical grid. The impact would be devastating.
Hm. Well, there's not much we can do about it...
That's just it. We're completely unprepared. Even the military is looking in the wrong direction.
Enough about the present... I want to hear more about Le Touquet.

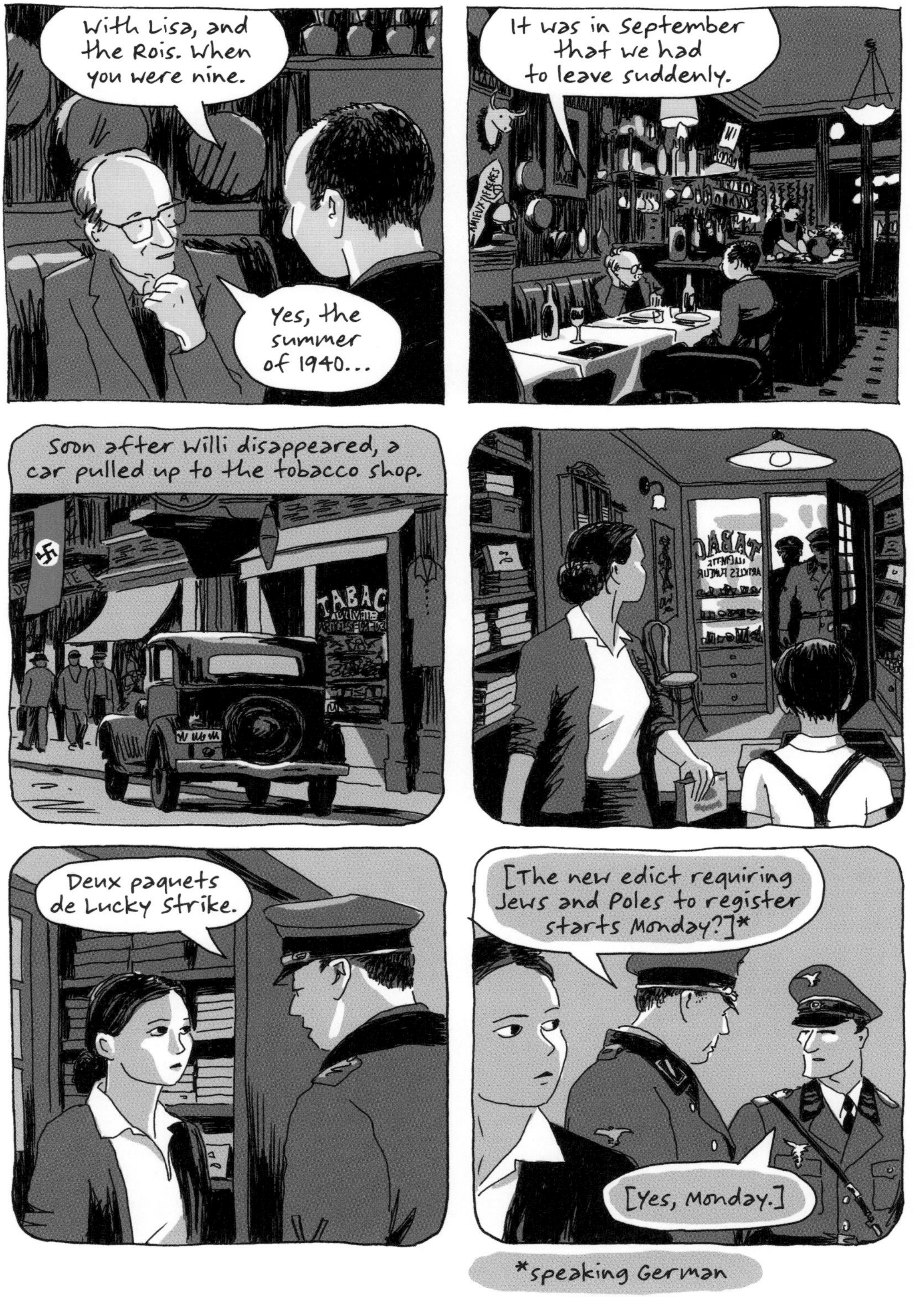
With Lisa, and the Rois. When you were nine.
Yes, the summer of 1940...
It was in September that we had to leave suddenly.
Soon after Willi disappeared, a car pulled up to the tobacco shop.
TABAC
Deux paquets de Lucky Strike.
[The new edict requiring Jews and Poles to register starts Monday?]*
[Yes, Monday.]
*speaking German

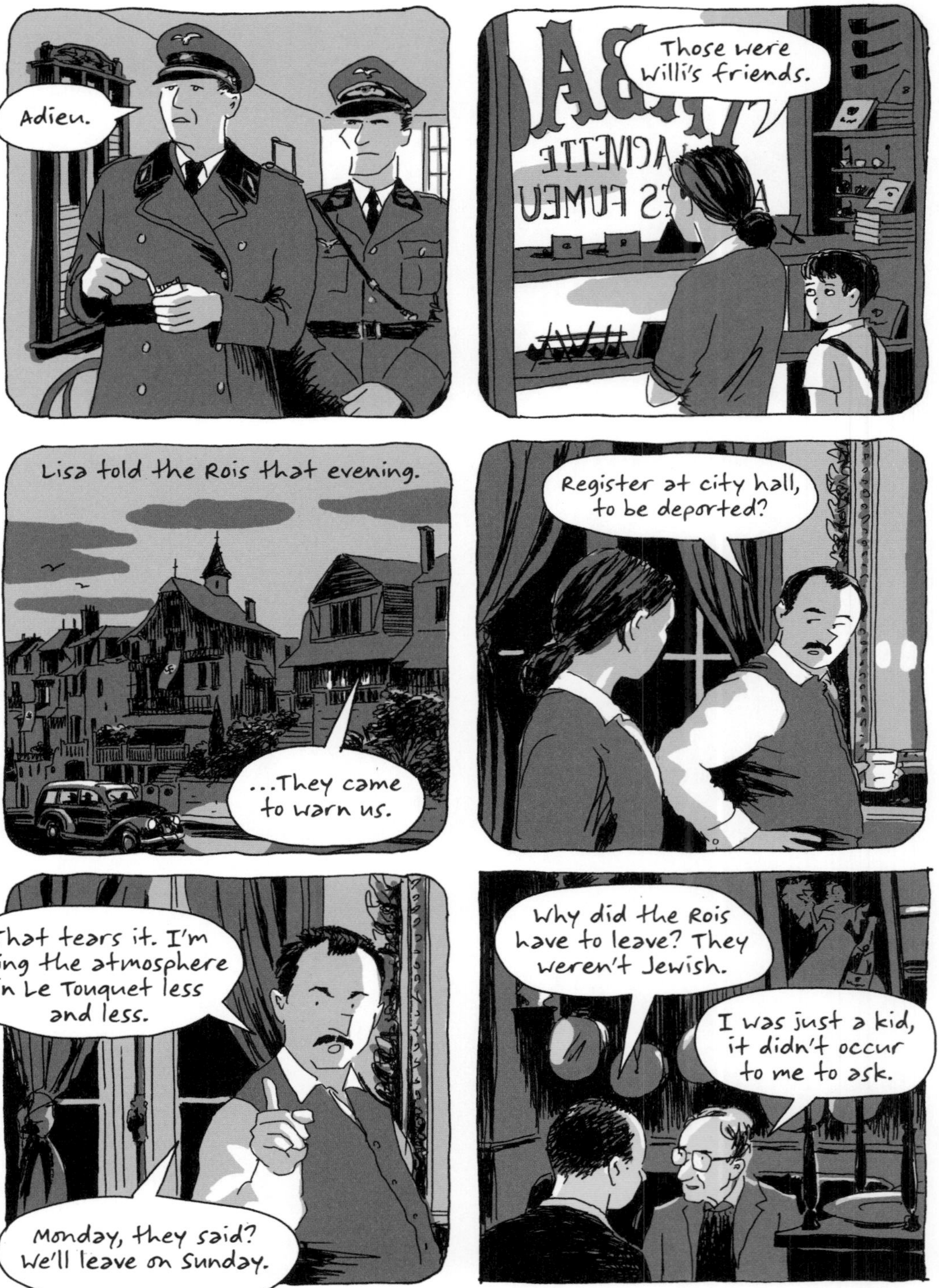
Adieu.
Those were Willi's friends.
Lisa told the Rois that evening.
...They came to warn us.
Register at city hall, to be deported?
That tears it. I'm liking the atmosphere in Le Touquet less and less.
Monday, they said? We'll leave on Sunday.
Why did the Rois have to leave? They weren't Jewish.
I was just a kid, it didn't occur to me to ask.

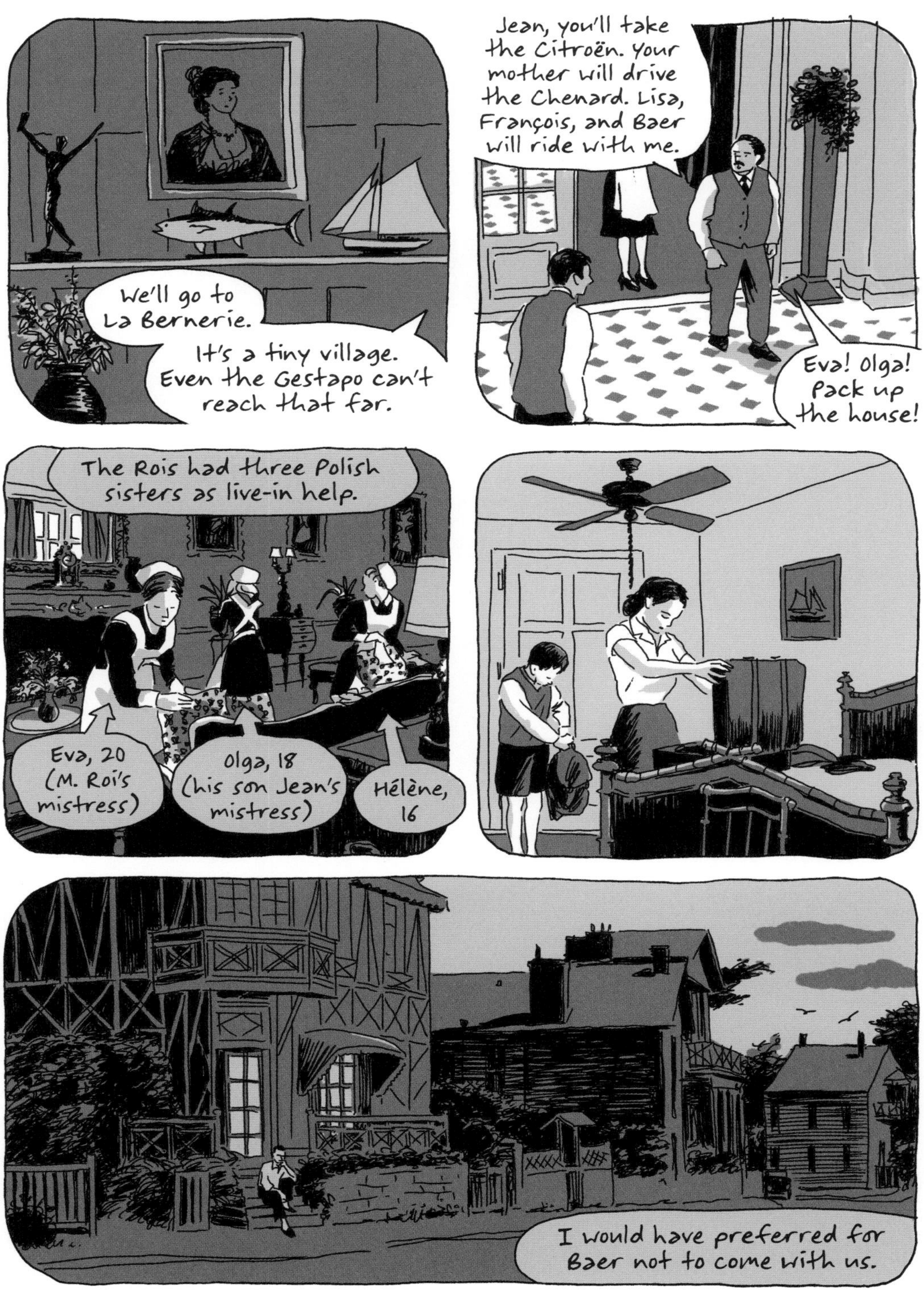
We'll go to La Bernerie.
It's a tiny village. Even the Gestapo can't reach that far.
Jean, you'll take the Citroën. Your mother will drive the Chenard. Lisa, François, and Baer will ride with me.
Eva! Olga! Pack up the house!
The Rois had three Polish sisters as live-in help.
Eva, 20 (M. Roi's mistress)
Olga, 18 (his son Jean's mistress)
Hélène, 16
I would have preferred for Baer not to come with us.

Road Trip

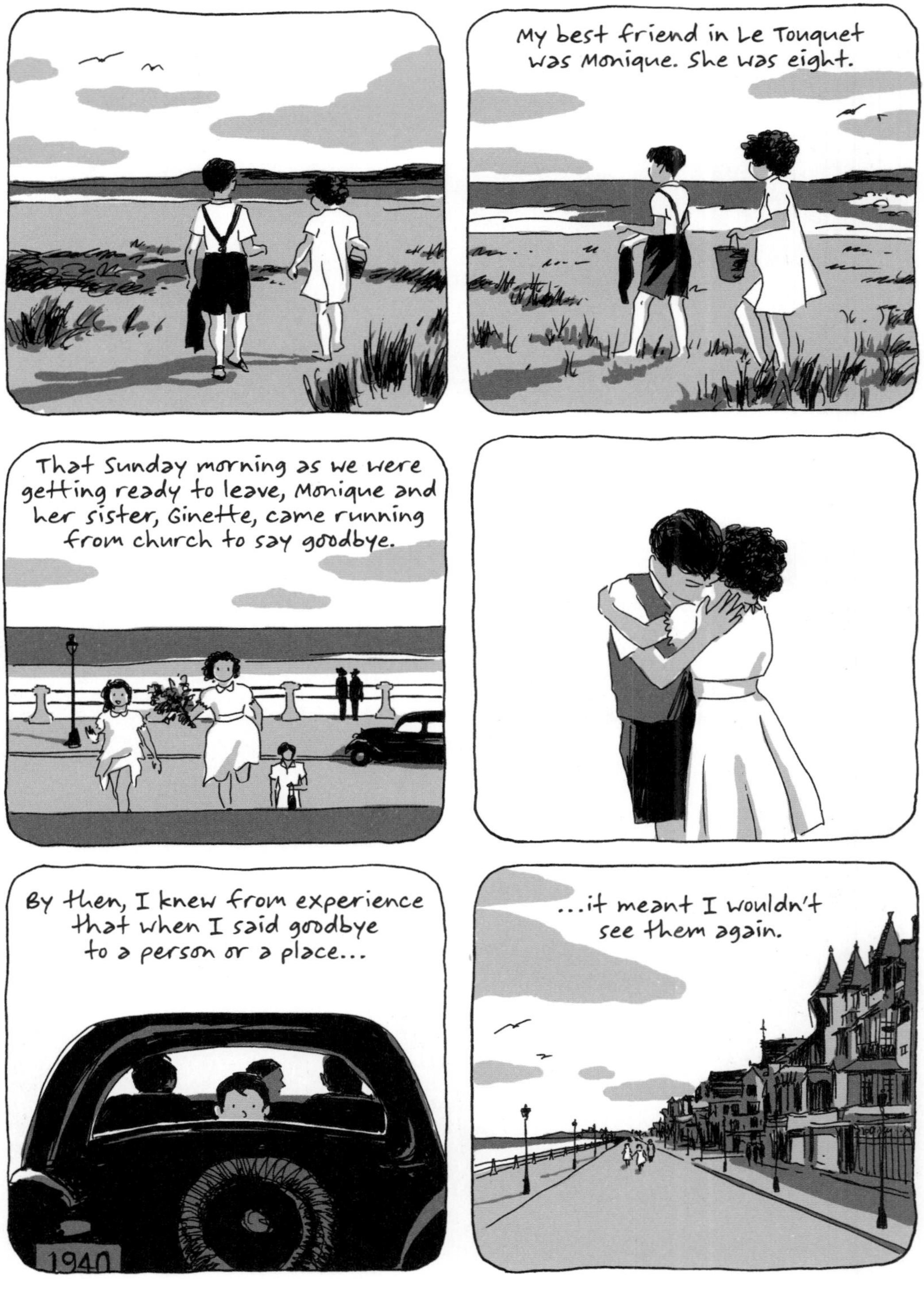

My best friend in Le Touquet was Monique. She was eight.
That Sunday morning as we were getting ready to leave, Monique and her sister, Ginette, came running from church to say goodbye.
By then, I knew from experience that when I said goodbye to a person or a place...
1940
...it meant I wouldn't see them again.

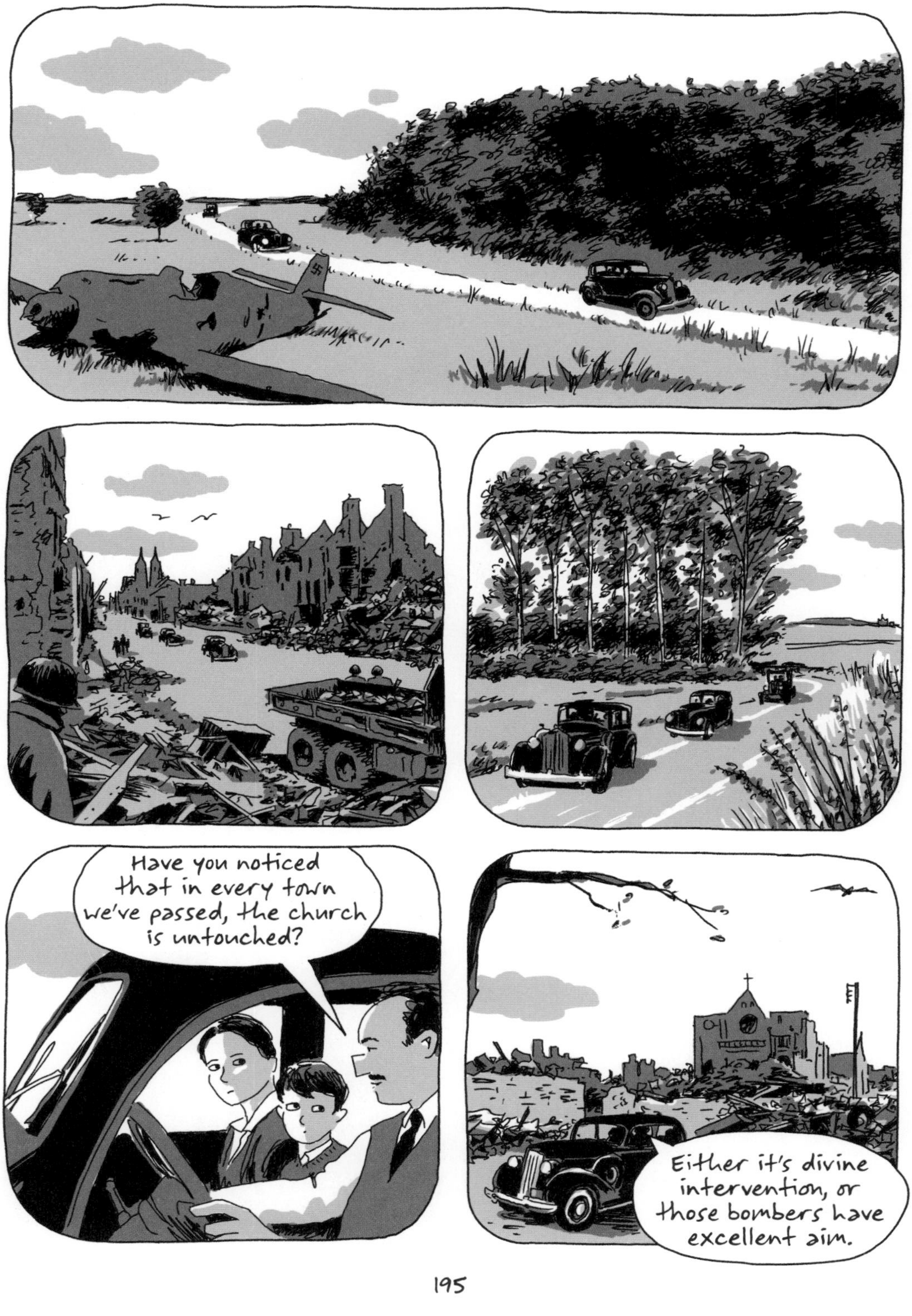
Have you noticed that in every town we've passed, the church is untouched?
Either it's divine intervention, or those bombers have excellent aim.

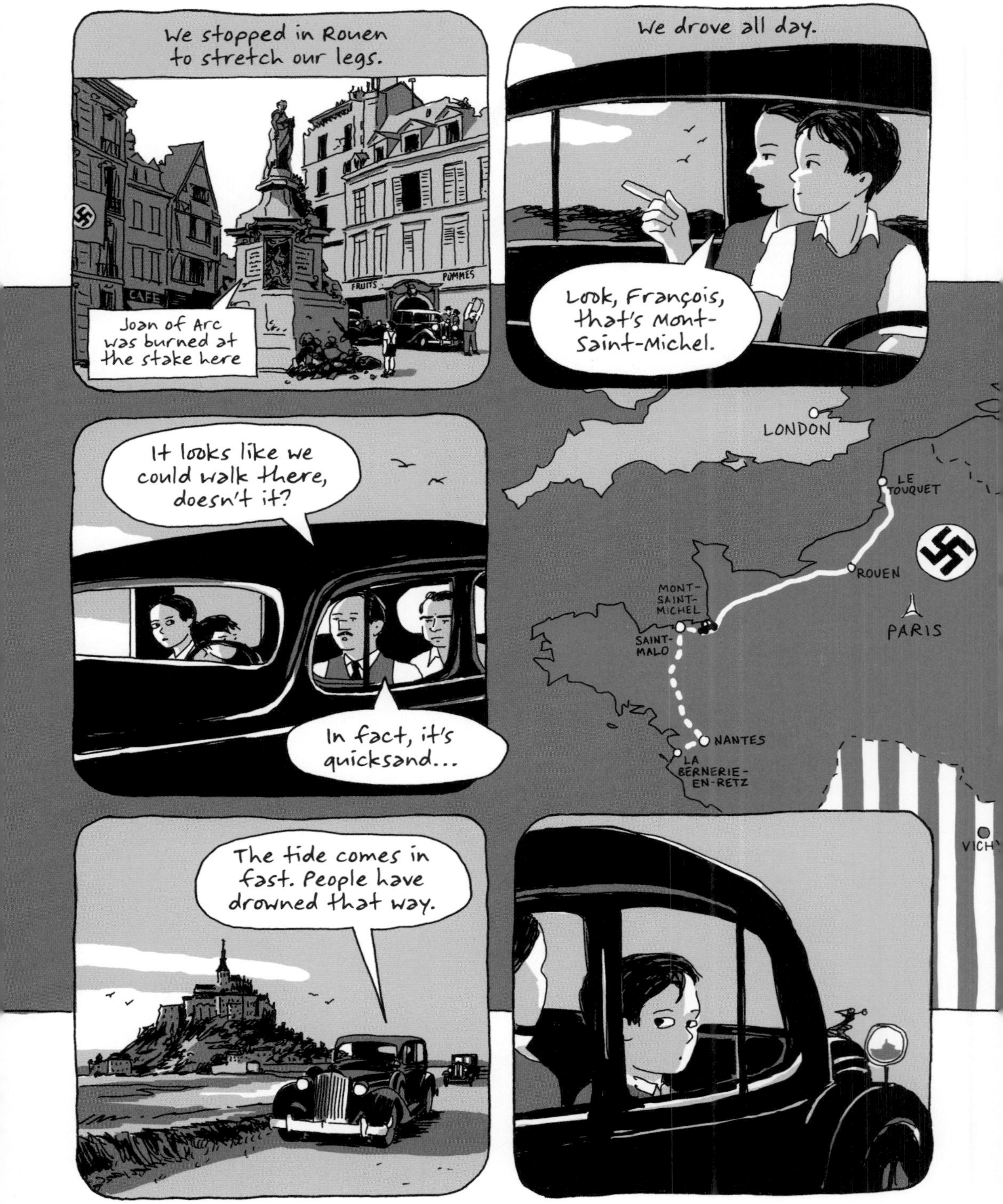
We stopped in Rouen to stretch our legs.
CAFE
FRUITS
POMMES
Joan of Arc was burned at the stake here
We drove all day.
Look, François, that's Mont-Saint-Michel.
It looks like we could walk there, doesn't it?
In fact, it's quicksand...
LONDON
LE TOUQUET
ROUEN
PARIS
MONT-SAINT-MICHEL
SAINT-MALO
NANTES
LA BERNERIE-EN-RETZ
The tide comes in fast. People have drowned that way.

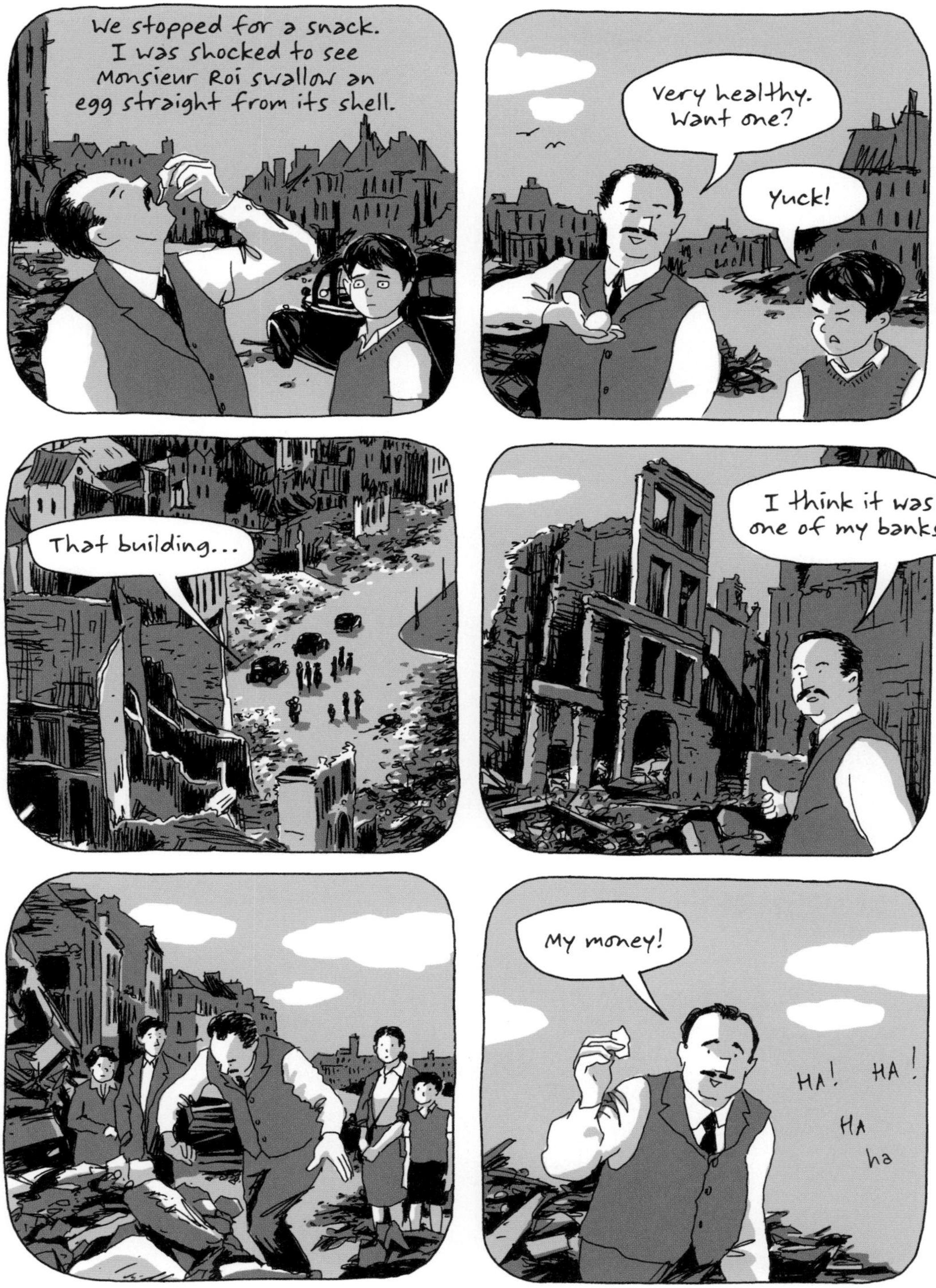
We stopped for a snack. I was shocked to see Monsieur Roi swallow an egg straight from its shell.
Very healthy. Want one?
Yuck!
That building...
I think it was one of my banks.
My money!
HA! HA!
HA
ha

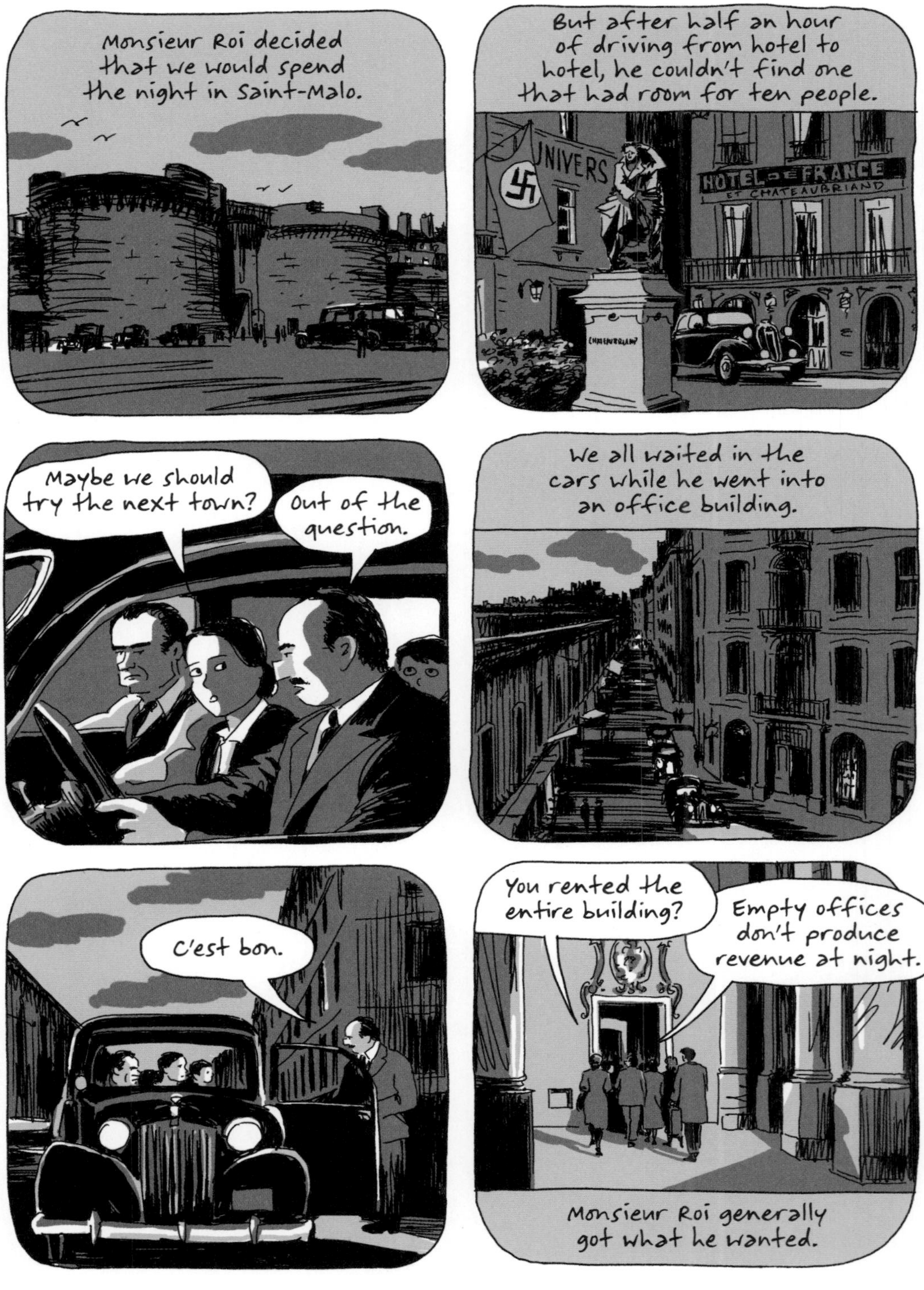
Monsieur Roi decided that we would spend the night in Saint-Malo.
But after half an hour of driving from hotel to hotel, he couldn't find one that had room for ten people.
UNIVERS
HOTEL DE FRANCE
ET CHATEAUBRIAND
Maybe we should try the next town?
Out of the question.
We all waited in the cars while he went into an office building.
C'est bon.
You rented the entire building?
Empty offices don't produce revenue at night.
Monsieur Roi generally got what he wanted.

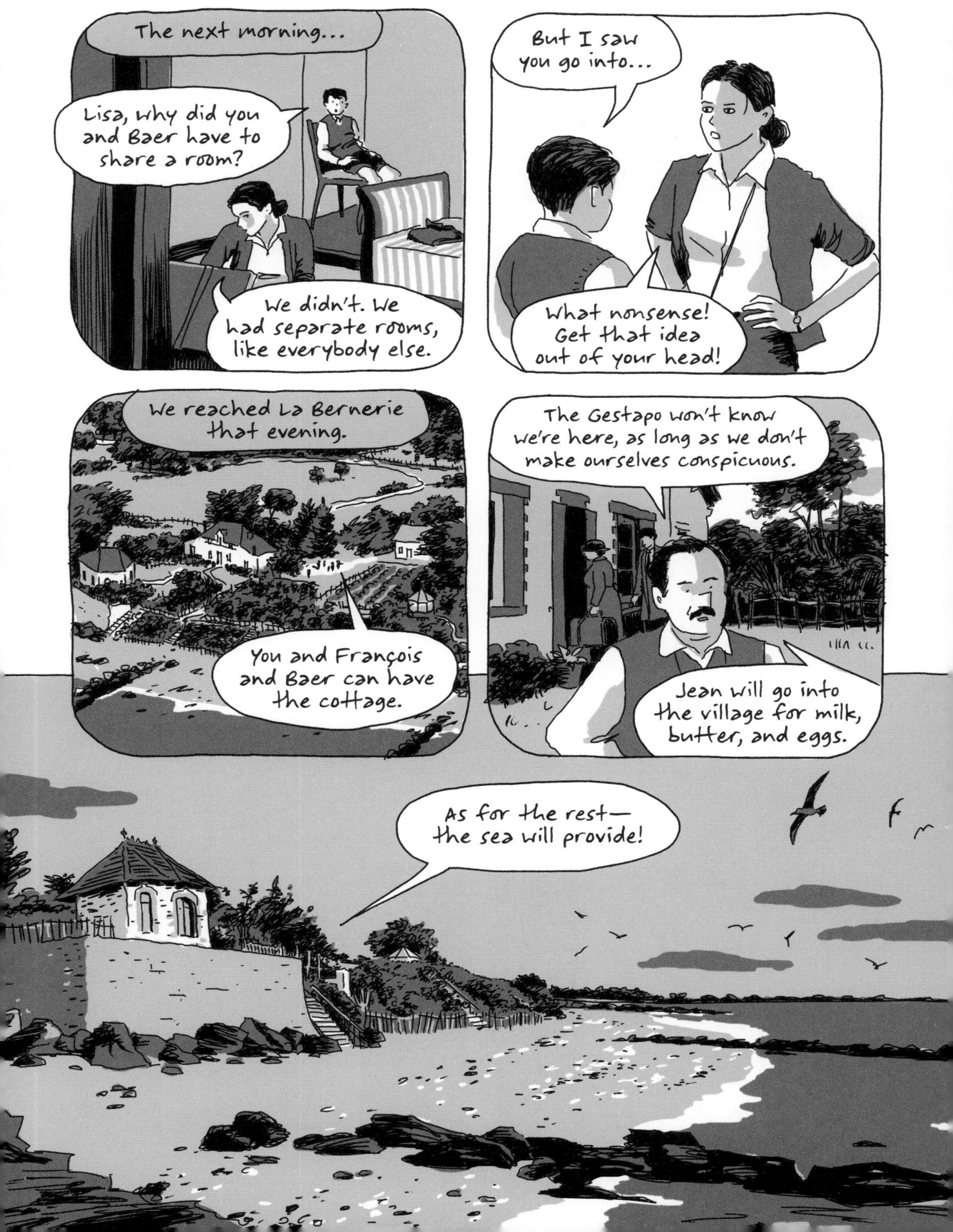
The next morning...
Lisa, why did you and Baer have to share a room?
We didn't. We had separate rooms, like everybody else.
But I saw you go into...
What nonsense! Get that idea out of your head!
We reached La Bernerie that evening.
You and François and Baer can have the cottage.
The Gestapo won't know we're here, as long as we don't make ourselves conspicuous.
Jean will go into the village for milk, butter, and eggs.
As for the rest— the sea will provide!

Wanderer

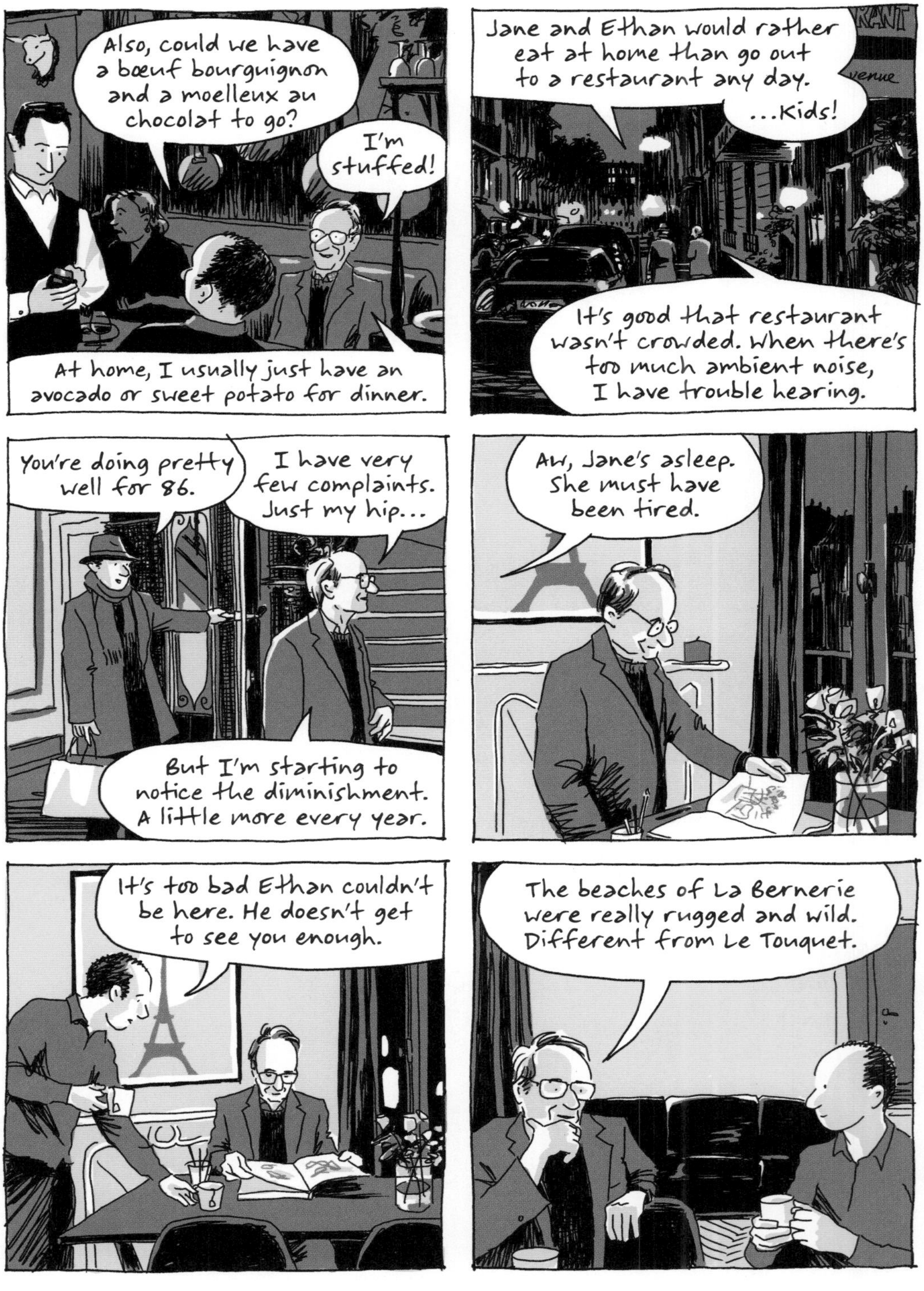
Also, could we have a bœuf bourguignon and a moelleux au chocolat to go?
I'm stuffed!
At home, I usually just have an avocado or sweet potato for dinner.
Jane and Ethan would rather eat at home than go out to a restaurant any day.
...Kids!
It's good that restaurant wasn't crowded. When there's too much ambient noise, I have trouble hearing.
You're doing pretty well for 86.
I have very few complaints. Just my hip...
But I'm starting to notice the diminishment. A little more every year.
Aw, Jane's asleep. She must have been tired.
It's too bad Ethan couldn't be here. He doesn't get to see you enough.
The beaches of La Bernerie were really rugged and wild. Different from Le Touquet.

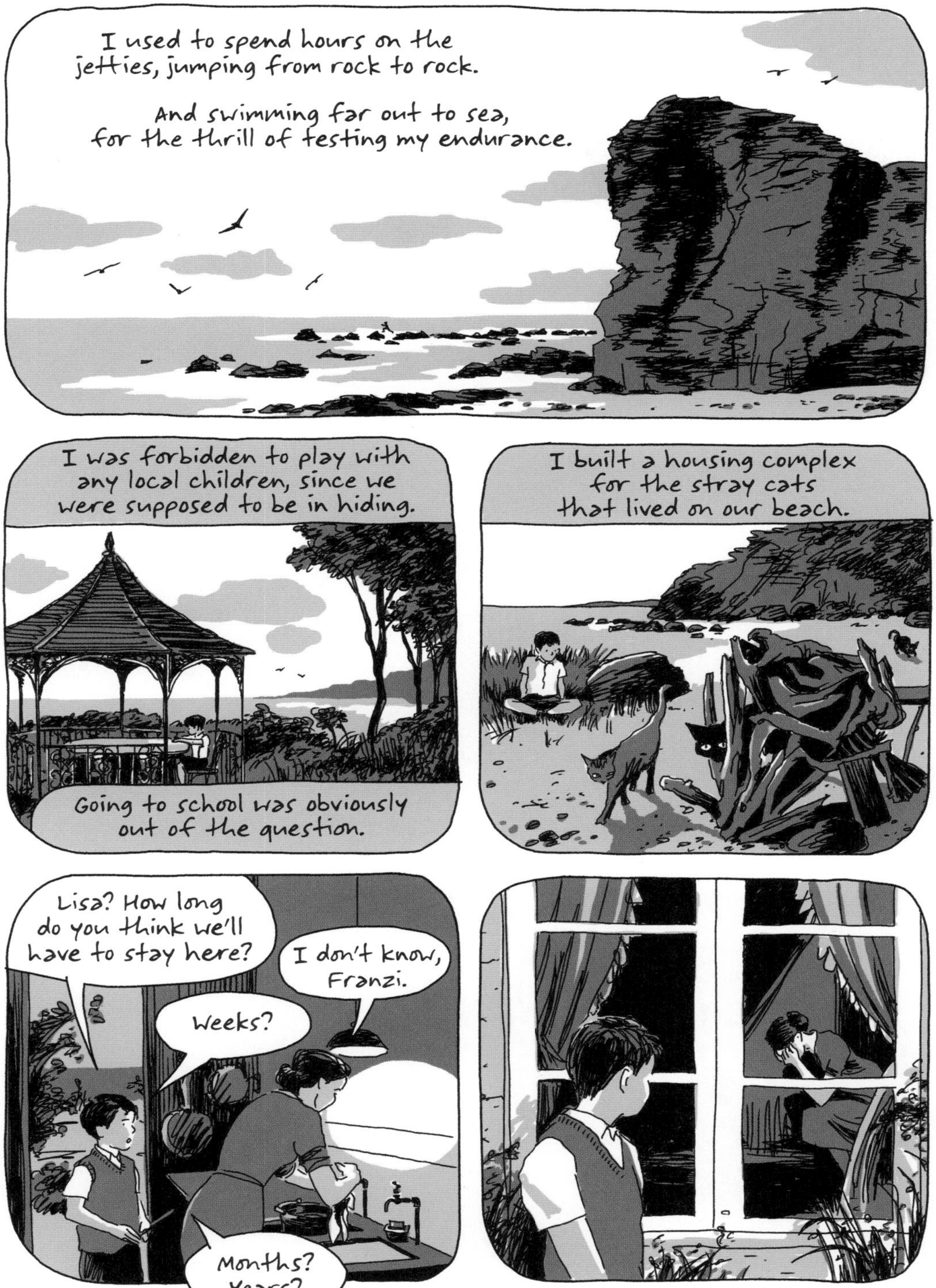
I used to spend hours on the jetties, jumping from rock to rock.
And swimming far out to sea, for the thrill of testing my endurance.
I was forbidden to play with any local children, since we were supposed to be in hiding.
Going to school was obviously out of the question.
I built a housing complex for the stray cats that lived on our beach.
Lisa? How long do you think we'll have to stay here?
I don't know, Franzi.
Weeks?
Months? Years?

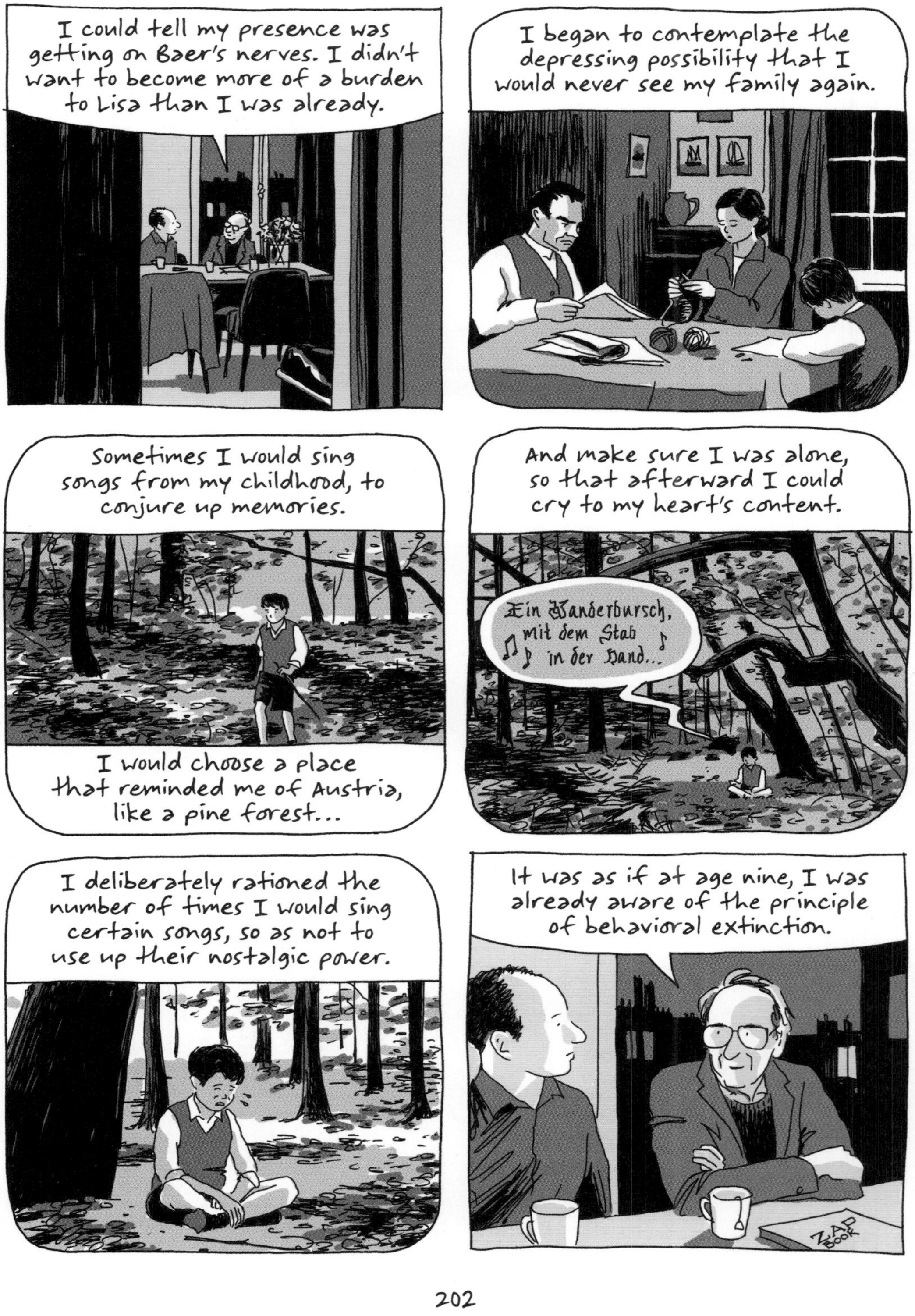
I could tell my presence was getting on Baer's nerves. I didn't want to become more of a burden to Lisa than I was already.
I began to contemplate the depressing possibility that I would never see my family again.
Sometimes I would sing songs from my childhood, to conjure up memories.
I would choose a place that reminded me of Austria, like a pine forest...
And make sure I was alone, so that afterward I could cry to my heart's content.
Ein Wanderbursch, mit dem Stab in der Hand...
I deliberately rationed the number of times I would sing certain songs, so as not to use up their nostalgic power.
It was as if at age nine, I was already aware of the principle of behavioral extinction.

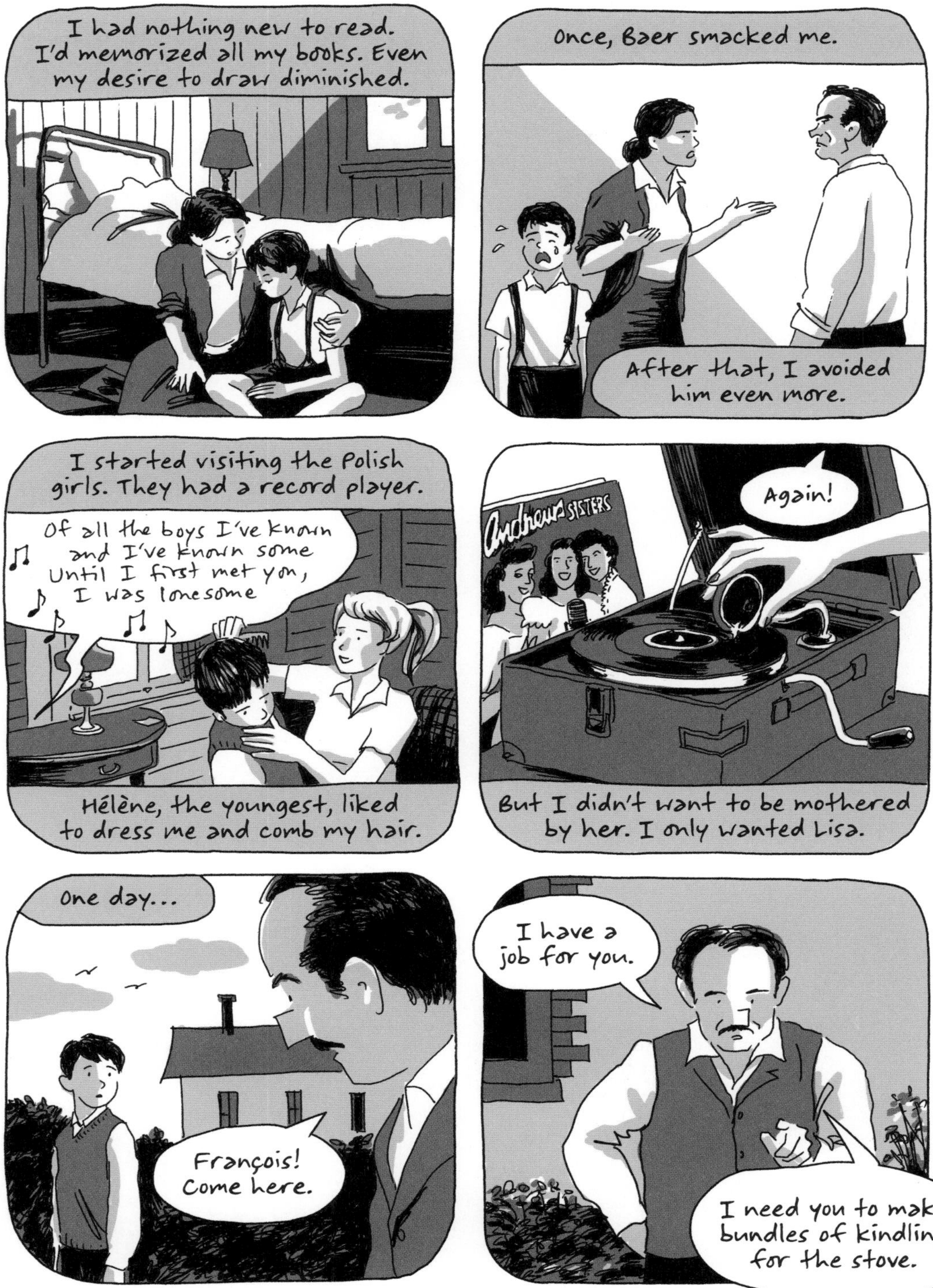
I had nothing new to read. I'd memorized all my books. Even my desire to draw diminished.
Once, Baer smacked me.
After that, I avoided him even more.
I started visiting the Polish girls. They had a record player.
Of all the boys I've known and I've known some Until I first met you, I was lonesome
Hélène, the youngest, liked to dress me and comb my hair.
Andrews SISTERS
Again!
But I didn't want to be mothered by her. I only wanted Lisa.
One day...
François! Come here.
I have a job for you.
I need you to make bundles of kindling for the stove.

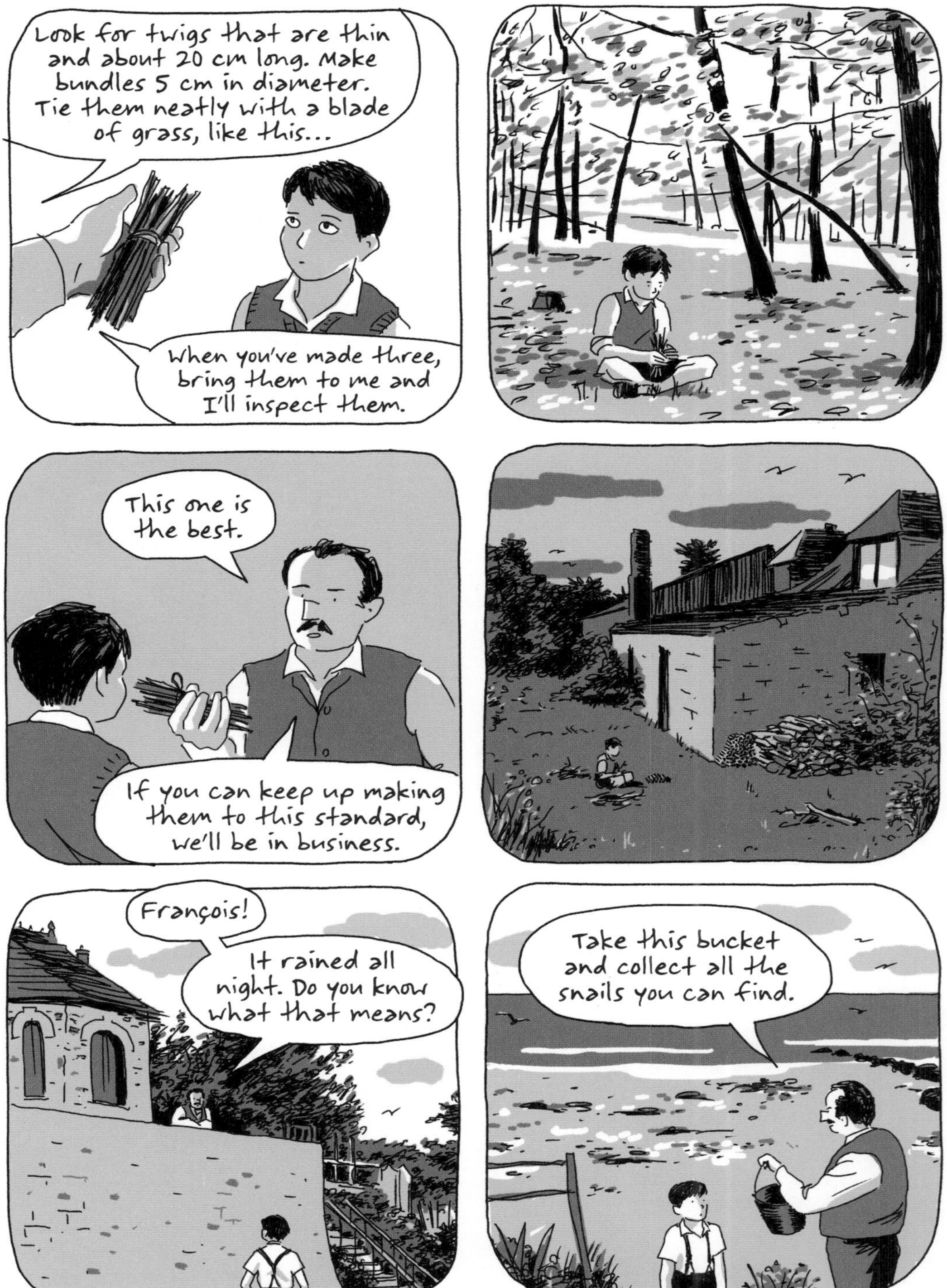

Look for twigs that are thin and about 20 cm long. Make bundles 5 cm in diameter. Tie them neatly with a blade of grass, like this...
When you've made three, bring them to me and I'll inspect them.
This one is the best.
If you can keep up making them to this standard, we'll be in business.
François!
It rained all night. Do you know what that means?
Take this bucket and collect all the snails you can find.

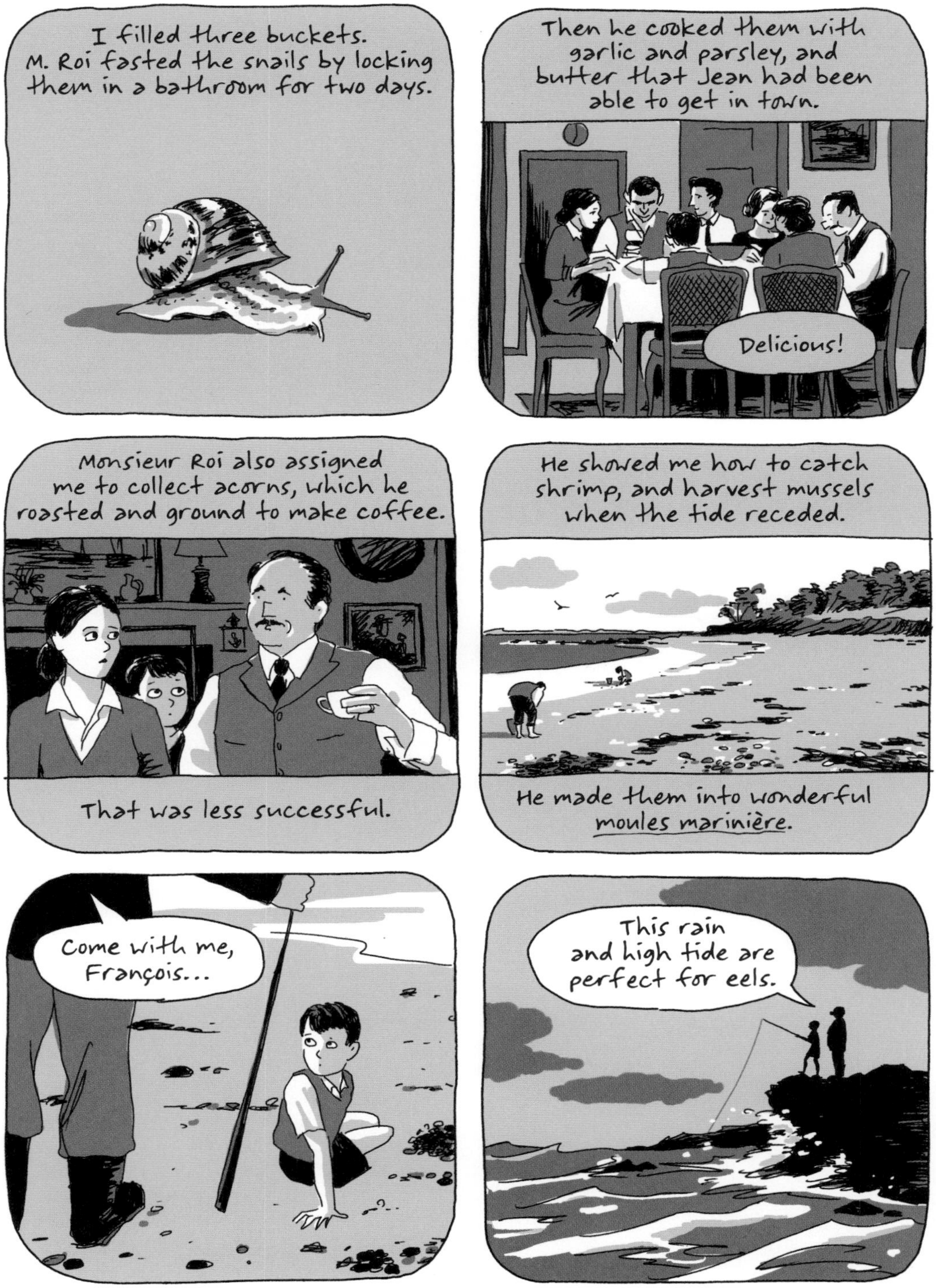
I filled three buckets. M. Roi fasted the snails by locking them in a bathroom for two days.
Then he cooked them with garlic and parsley, and butter that Jean had been able to get in town.
Delicious!
Monsieur Roi also assigned me to collect acorns, which he roasted and ground to make coffee.
That was less successful.
He showed me how to catch shrimp, and harvest mussels when the tide receded.
He made them into wonderful moules marinière.
Come with me, François...
This rain and high tide are perfect for eels.

Slickers

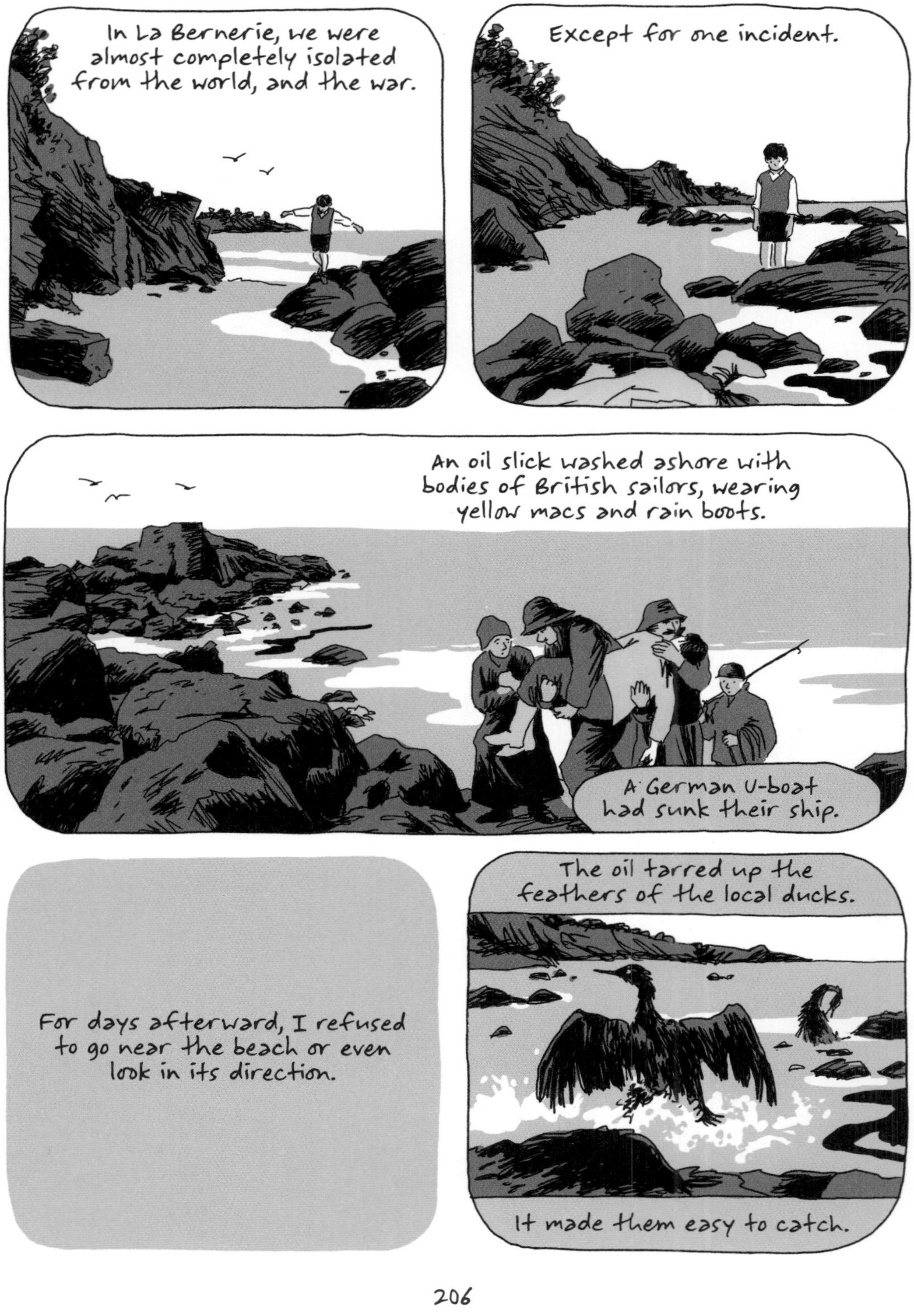
In La Bernerie, we were almost completely isolated from the world, and the war.
Except for one incident.
An oil slick washed ashore with bodies of British sailors, wearing yellow macs and rain boots.
A German U-boat had sunk their ship.
For days afterward, I refused to go near the beach or even look in its direction.
The oil tarred up the feathers of the local ducks.
It made them easy to catch.

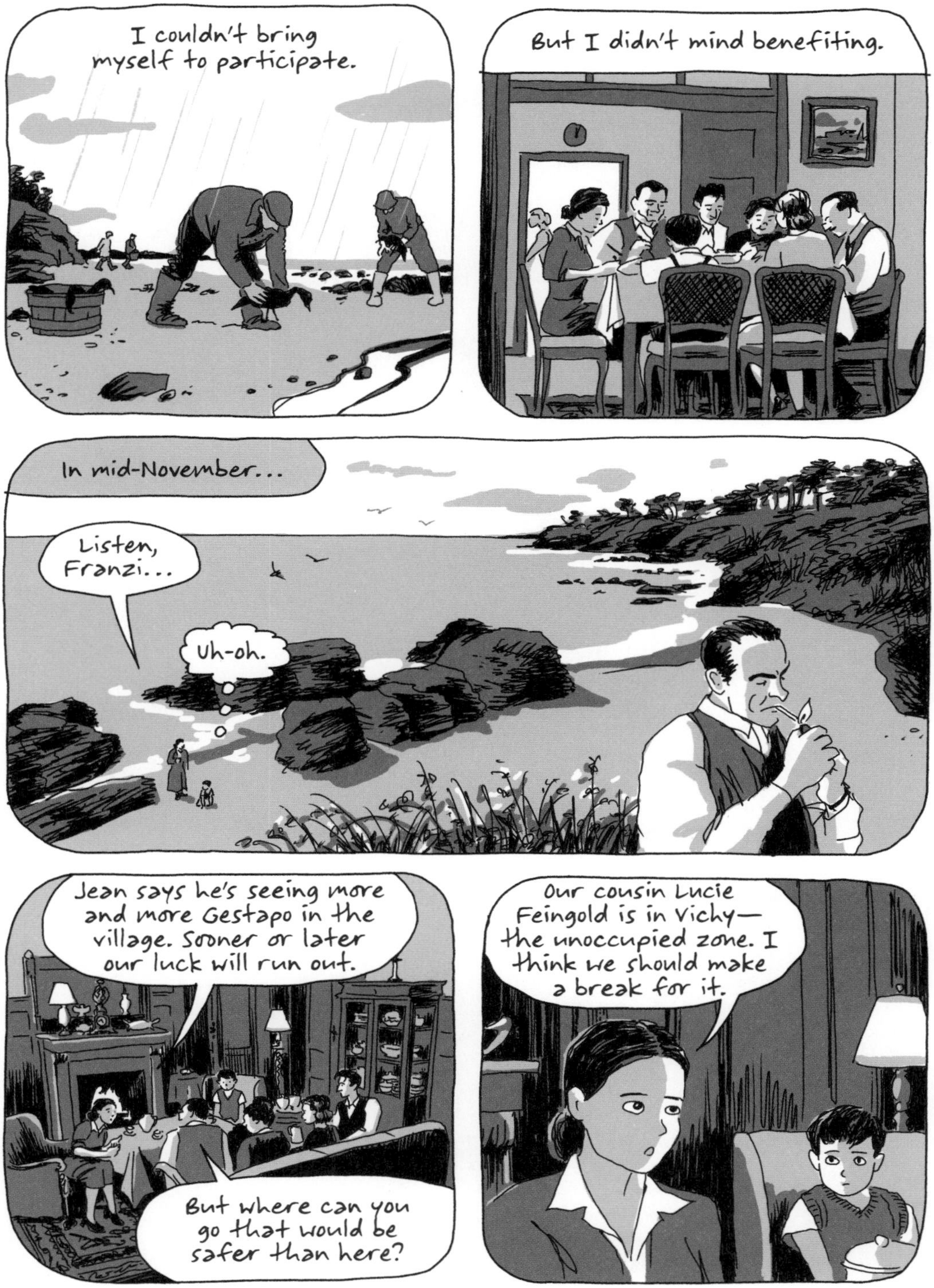
I couldn't bring myself to participate.
But I didn't mind benefiting.
In mid-November...
Listen, Franzi...
Uh-oh.
Jean says he's seeing more and more Gestapo in the village. Sooner or later our luck will run out.
But where can you go that would be safer than here?
Our cousin Lucie Feingold is in Vichy— the unoccupied zone. I think we should make a break for it.

Rothschild

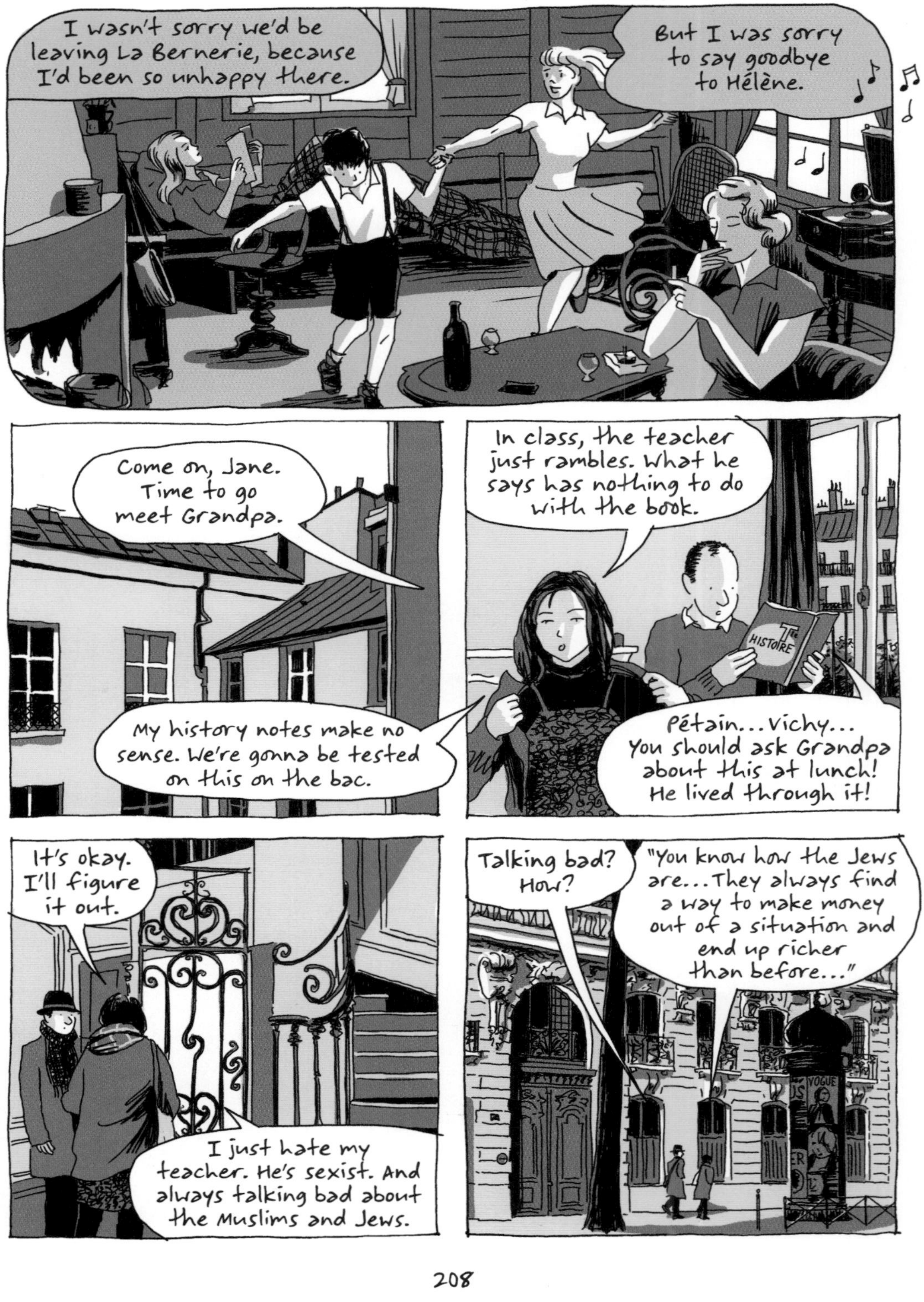
I wasn't sorry we'd be leaving La Bernerie, because I'd been so unhappy there.
But I was sorry to say goodbye to Hélène.
Come on, Jane. Time to go meet Grandpa.
My history notes make no sense. We're gonna be tested on this on the bac.
In class, the teacher just rambles. What he says has nothing to do with the book.
HISTOIRE
Pétain... Vichy... You should ask Grandpa about this at lunch! He lived through it!
It's okay. I'll figure it out.
I just hate my teacher. He's sexist. And always talking bad about the Muslims and Jews.
Talking bad? How?
"You know how the Jews are... They always find a way to make money out of a situation and end up richer than before..."
VOGUE

Did you say something?

Yes! I raised my hand and said: "That's not cool!"

And?

I got sent to the directrice. She said not to worry about it.

He's worse about Muslims. The two Algerian boys always get mad and argue with him, and he sends them out of the classroom.

That's outrageous!! And he's not even teaching you history!

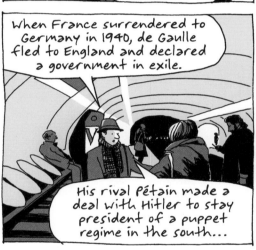

When France surrendered to Germany in 1940, de Gaulle fled to England and declared a government in exile.

His rival Pétain made a deal with Hitler to stay president of a puppet regime in the south...

...while the Nazis occupied the rest of France and tried to crush the resistance.

LE TOUQUET

PARIS

NANTES

LA BERNERIE-EN-RETZ

VICHY

"FREE ZONE"

ITALY

NICE

MONTPELLIER

SPAIN

Pétain was a French hero from the last war, so he had credibility.

That's what my teacher said. Pétain was a hero... He kept France free.

Ha ha! I see where you got confused. Pétain led the "Free Zone"...which served the Nazis. De Gaulle was "Free France," which was AGAINST the Nazis.

I thought de Gaulle and Pétain were on the same side?

It's in my notes: "De Gaulle was the sword of France. Pétain was the shield."

Your teacher said that?!?

There's Grandpa. Good...I'm starving!

Dad, Jane is learning about Vichy France in school. Tell her how you went there.

To Vichy?

It's okay, Dad. We can talk about something else.

First we had to go to Paris and request a travel permit from the German authorities.

That meant putting ourselves in the hands of the Gestapo.

The Rois tried to talk Lisa out of it. They said it was too dangerous.

Madame Roi drove us to the train station in Nantes. We had lunch there, in the most elegant restaurant I'd ever seen.

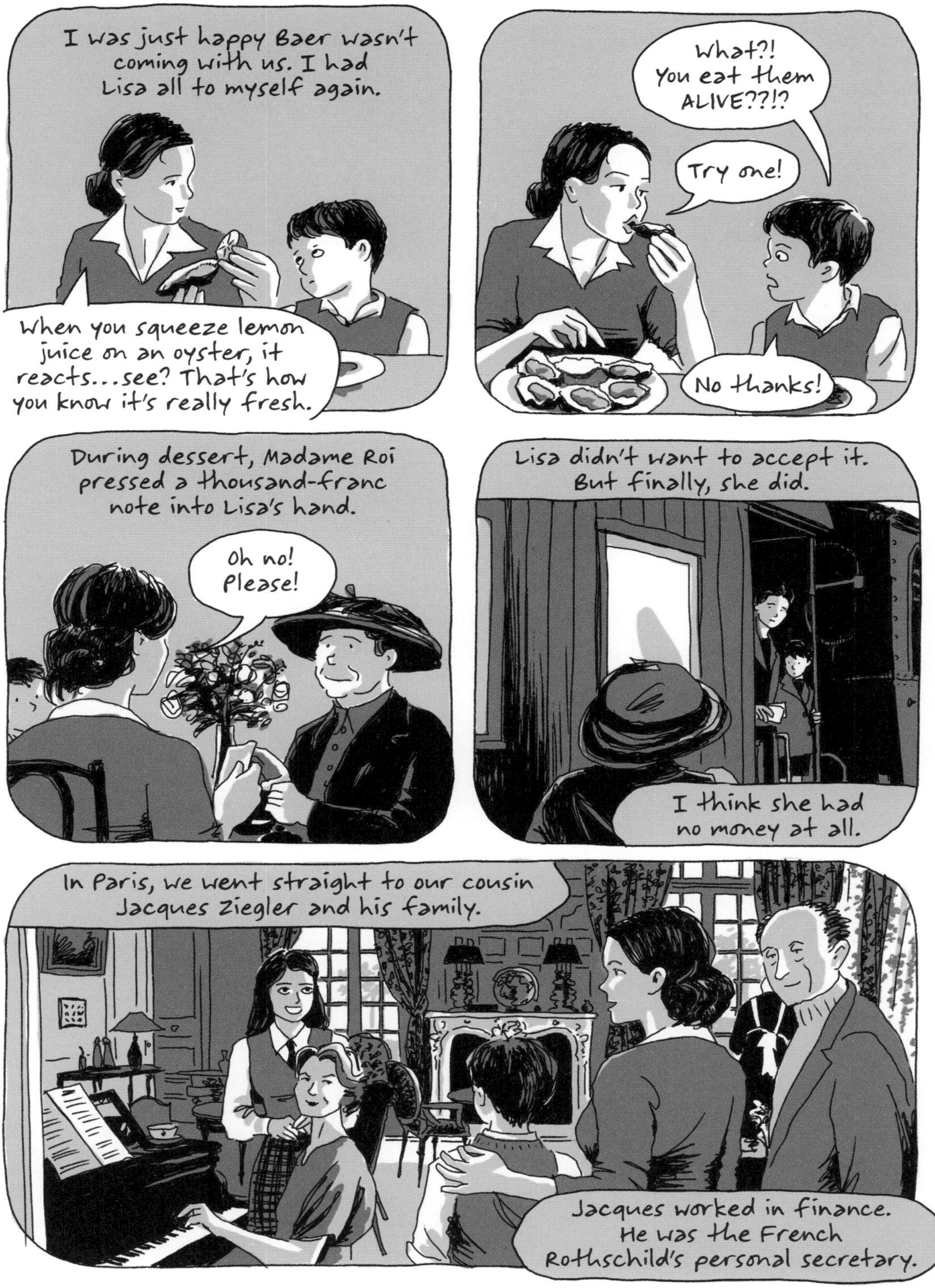
I was just happy Baer wasn't coming with us. I had Lisa all to myself again.
When you squeeze lemon juice on an oyster, it reacts...see? That's how you know it's really fresh.
What?! You eat them ALIVE??!?
Try one!
No thanks!
During dessert, Madame Roi pressed a thousand-franc note into Lisa's hand.
Oh no! Please!
Lisa didn't want to accept it. But finally, she did.
I think she had no money at all.
In Paris, we went straight to our cousin Jacques Ziegler and his family.
Jacques worked in finance. He was the French Rothschild's personal secretary.

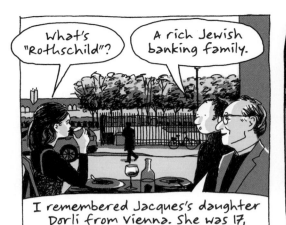

What's "Rothschild"?

A rich Jewish banking family.

I remembered Jacques's daughter Dorli from Vienna. She was 17, extremely bright, and beautiful...

I loved staying with the Zieglers. To be back in a warm, happy, German-speaking home was like heaven for me.

I fell in love with Dorli.

Every time she asked me to play Battleship, my heart would jump.

B-7.

Touché... Coulé!

Lisa stayed somewhere else. I think she didn't want Jacques and his family to be put at risk in case her plan to get a travel permit from the Gestapo went wrong.

We didn't see her for ten days.

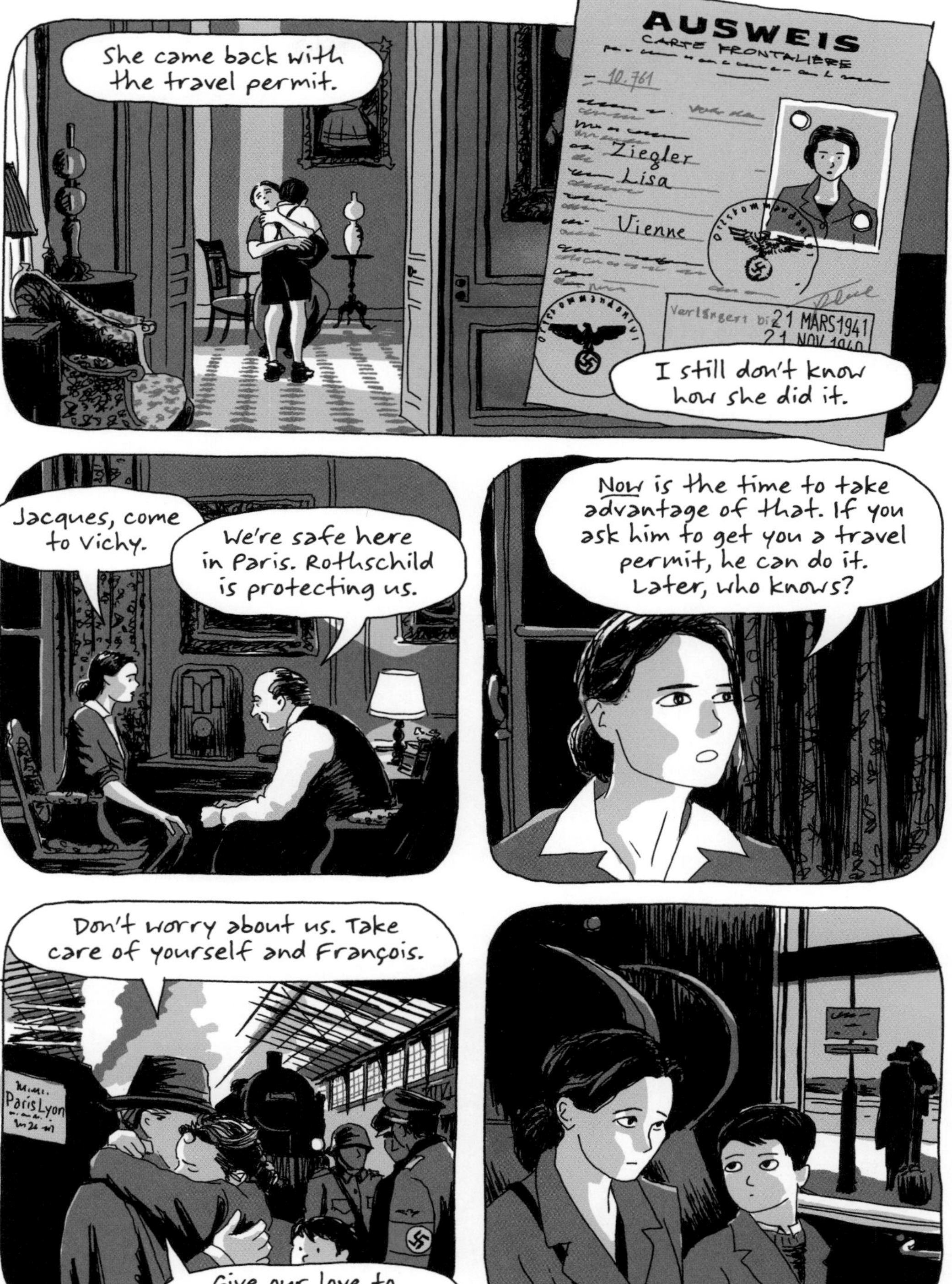
She came back with the travel permit.
AUSWEIS
CARTE FRONTALIERE
10.761
Ziegler
Lisa
Vienne
Verlängert bis 21 MARS 1941
I still don't know how she did it.
Jacques, come to Vichy.
We're safe here in Paris. Rothschild is protecting us.
Now is the time to take advantage of that. If you ask him to get you a travel permit, he can do it. Later, who knows?
Don't worry about us. Take care of yourself and François.
Paris Lyon
Give our love to Lucie. This will end and we'll be together again soon.

Gare de Lyon

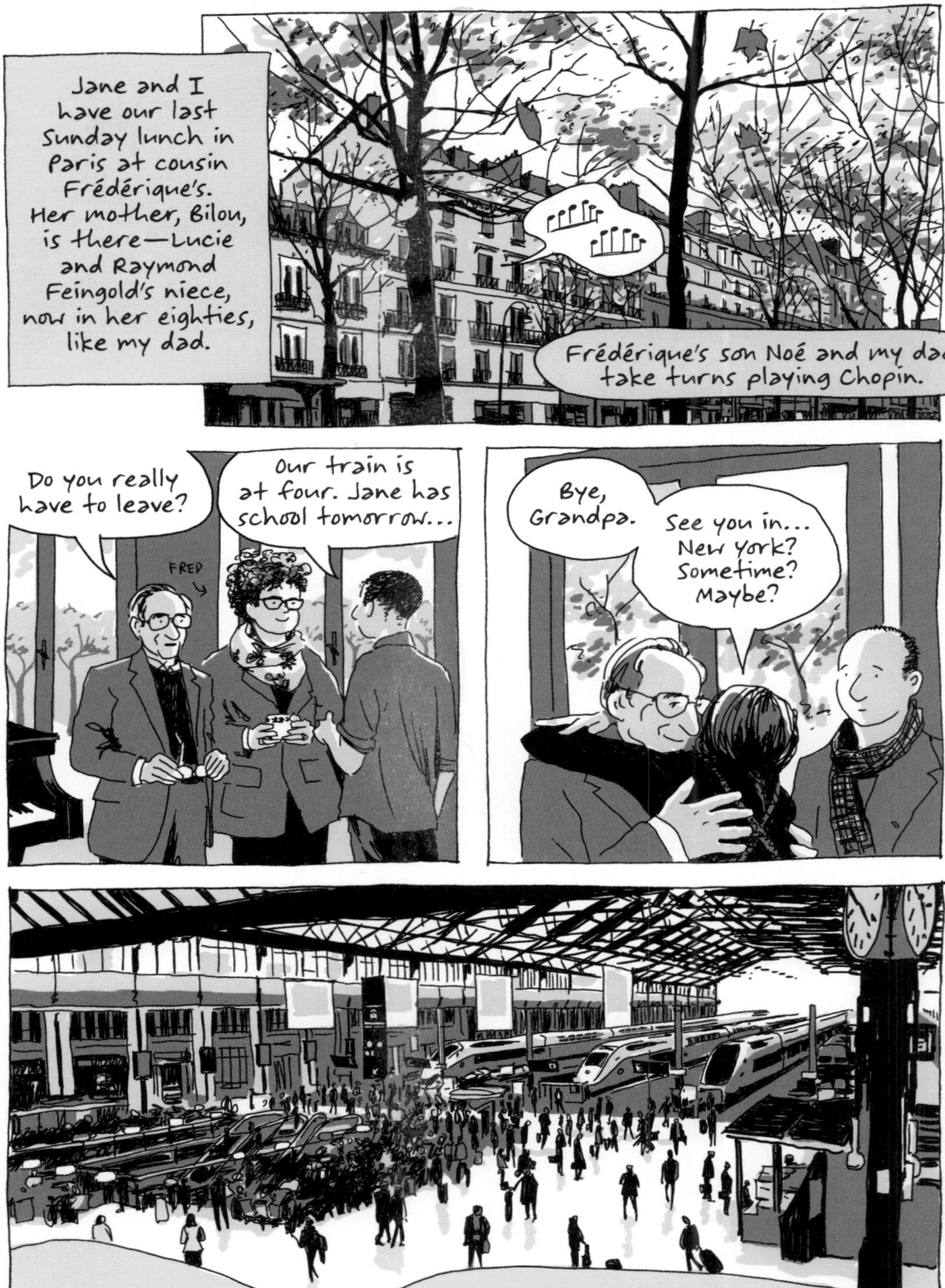

Jane and I have our last Sunday lunch in Paris at cousin Frédérique's. Her mother, Bilou, is there—Lucie and Raymond Feingold's niece, now in her eighties, like my dad.
Frédérique's son Noé and my dad take turns playing Chopin.
Do you really have to leave?
Our train is at four. Jane has school tomorrow...
FRED
Bye, Grandpa.
See you in... New York? Sometime? Maybe?

ATTENTION AU PAS
CHARENTON
FRANÇAIS!
Venez à moi avec confiance
LABO
What are you working on?
A PowerPoint presentation.
To pitch the new game.

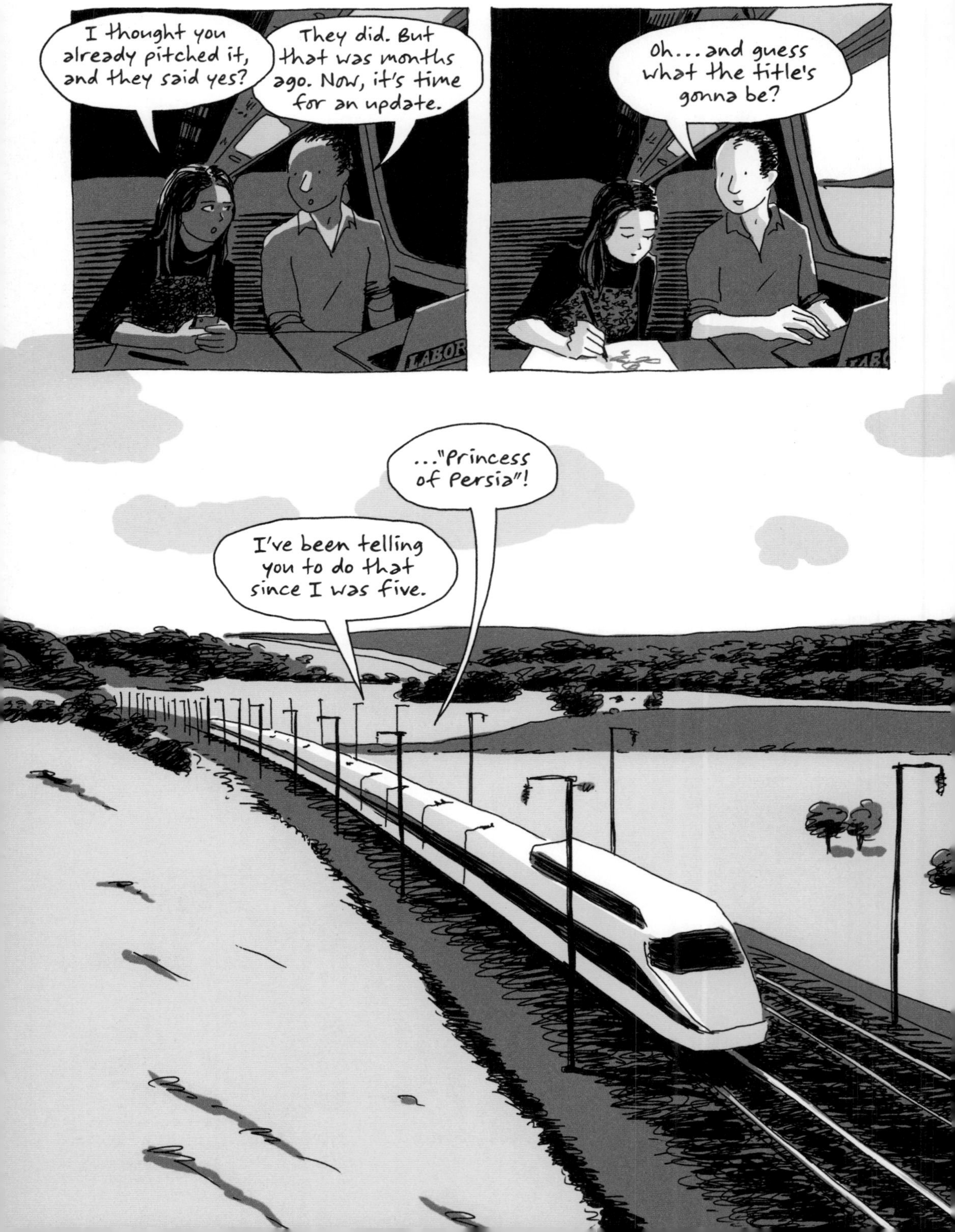
I thought you already pitched it, and they said yes?
They did. But that was months ago. Now, it's time for an update.
LABOR
Oh... and guess what the title's gonna be?
LABO
..."Princess of Persia"!
I've been telling you to do that since I was five.

Chapter 7

Passover

Lisa Ziegler, Paul Rosegg,
and Franz Mechner
Nice, 1941

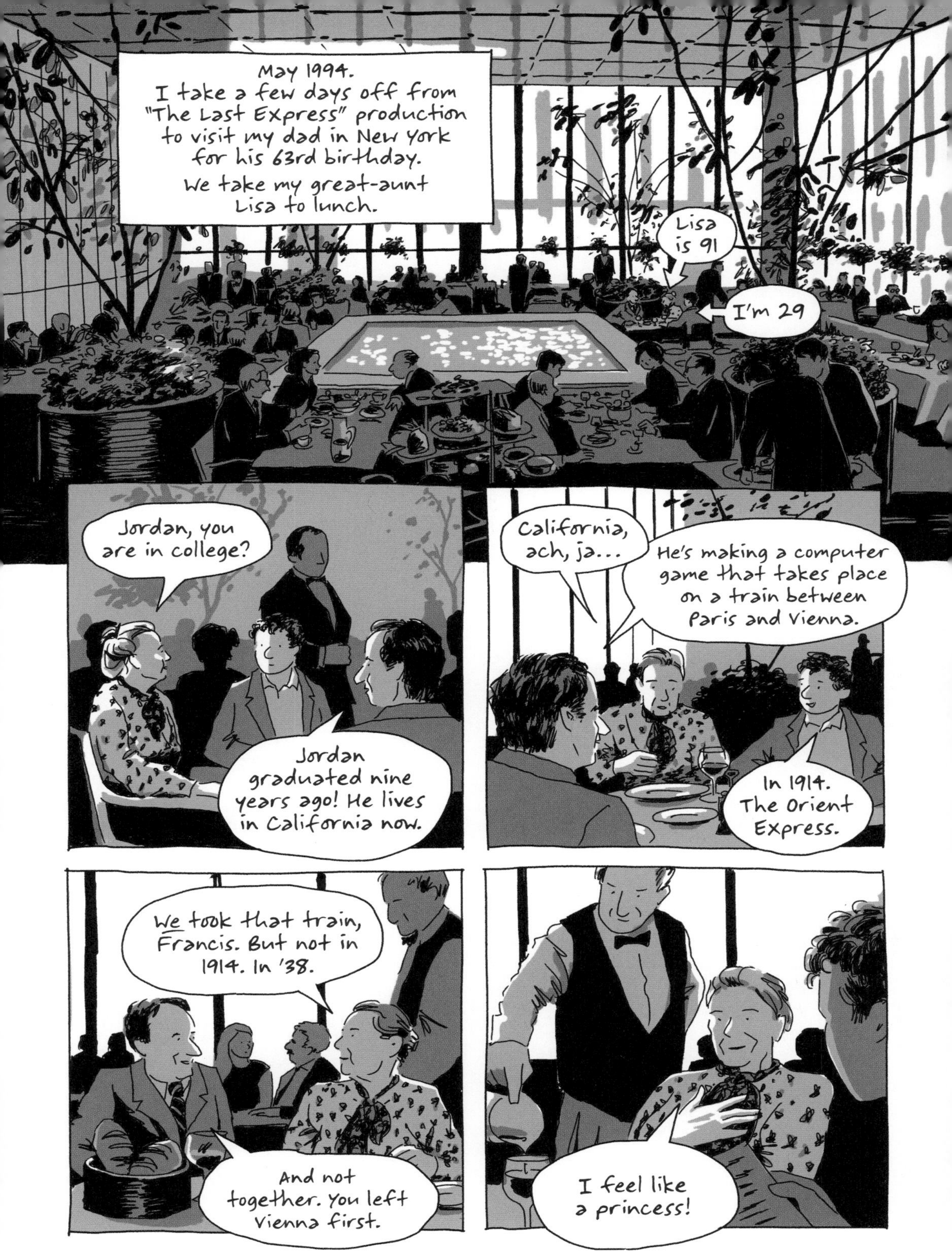

May 1994. I take a few days off from "The Last Express" production to visit my dad in New York for his 63rd birthday.
We take my great-aunt Lisa to lunch.
Lisa is 91
I'm 29
Jordan, you are in college?
Jordan graduated nine years ago! He lives in California now.
California, ach, ja...
He's making a computer game that takes place on a train between Paris and Vienna.
In 1914. The Orient Express.
We took that train, Francis. But not in 1914. In '38.
And not together. You left Vienna first.
I feel like a princess!

Dachshunds

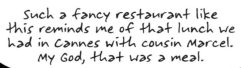

Such a fancy restaurant like this reminds me of that lunch we had in Cannes with cousin Marcel. My God, that was a meal.

I remember it well! In 1941...

Everybody was hungry. You couldn't buy food, it was all going to the Germans. I couldn't believe such a restaurant would still exist.

You went to Cannes? During the occupation?

...I was just there last summer for a film festival with my friend George!

Cannes was in the unoccupied zone. First we went to the capital—Vichy.

Vichy was cold, cold...

The heating oil was going to the Germans, too.

We had a bottle of benzene in our hotel room. One night, it froze solid.

What's benzene's freezing point again...?

The only room in the hotel that was warm was the lobby. So everybody was there all the time.

It was only refugees in that hotel.

HOTEL CALIDUS

BANQUE

CREDIT LYONNAIS

CAFE - RESTAURANT

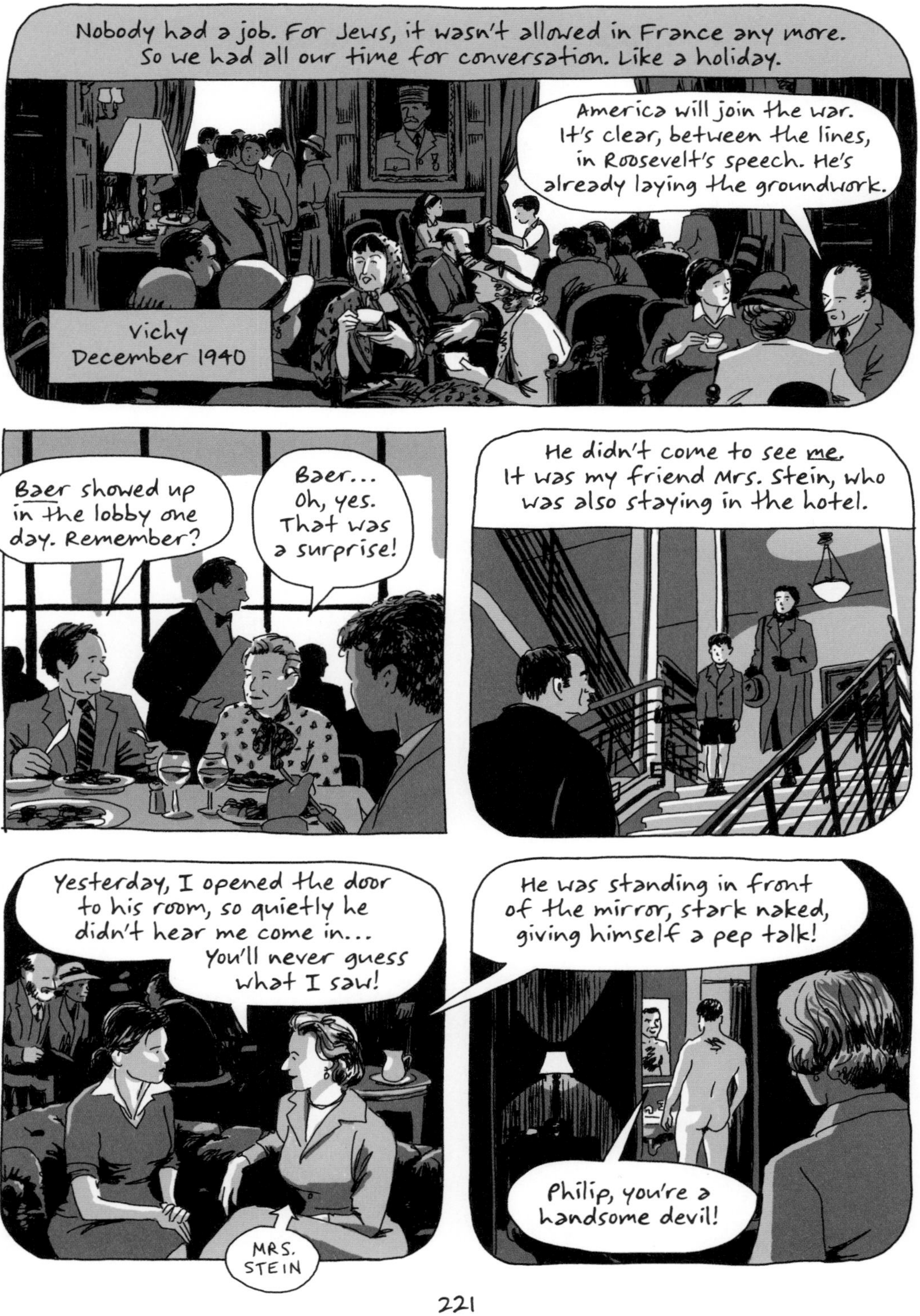
Nobody had a job. For Jews, it wasn't allowed in France any more. So we had all our time for conversation. Like a holiday.
America will join the war. It's clear, between the lines, in Roosevelt's speech. He's already laying the groundwork.
Vichy December 1940
Baer showed up in the lobby one day. Remember?
Baer... Oh, yes. That was a surprise!
He didn't come to see me. It was my friend Mrs. Stein, who was also staying in the hotel.
Yesterday, I opened the door to his room, so quietly he didn't hear me come in... You'll never guess what I saw!
MRS. STEIN
He was standing in front of the mirror, stark naked, giving himself a pep talk!
Philip, you're a handsome devil!

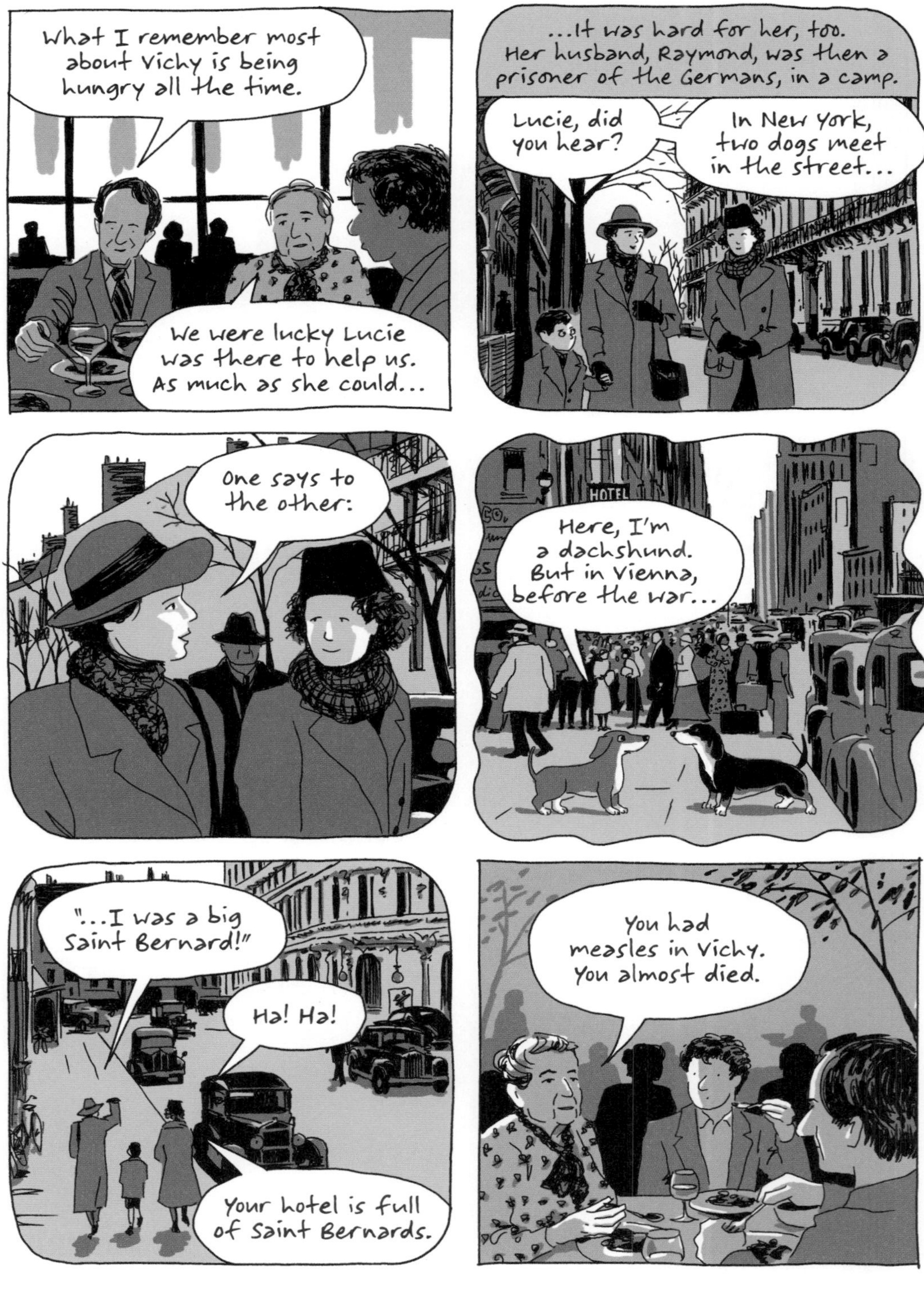
What I remember most about Vichy is being hungry all the time.
We were lucky Lucie was there to help us. As much as she could...
...It was hard for her, too. Her husband, Raymond, was then a prisoner of the Germans, in a camp.
Lucie, did you hear?
In New York, two dogs meet in the street...
One says to the other:
HOTEL
Here, I'm a dachshund. But in Vienna, before the war...
"...I was a big Saint Bernard!"
Ha! Ha!
Your hotel is full of Saint Bernards.
You had measles in Vichy. You almost died.

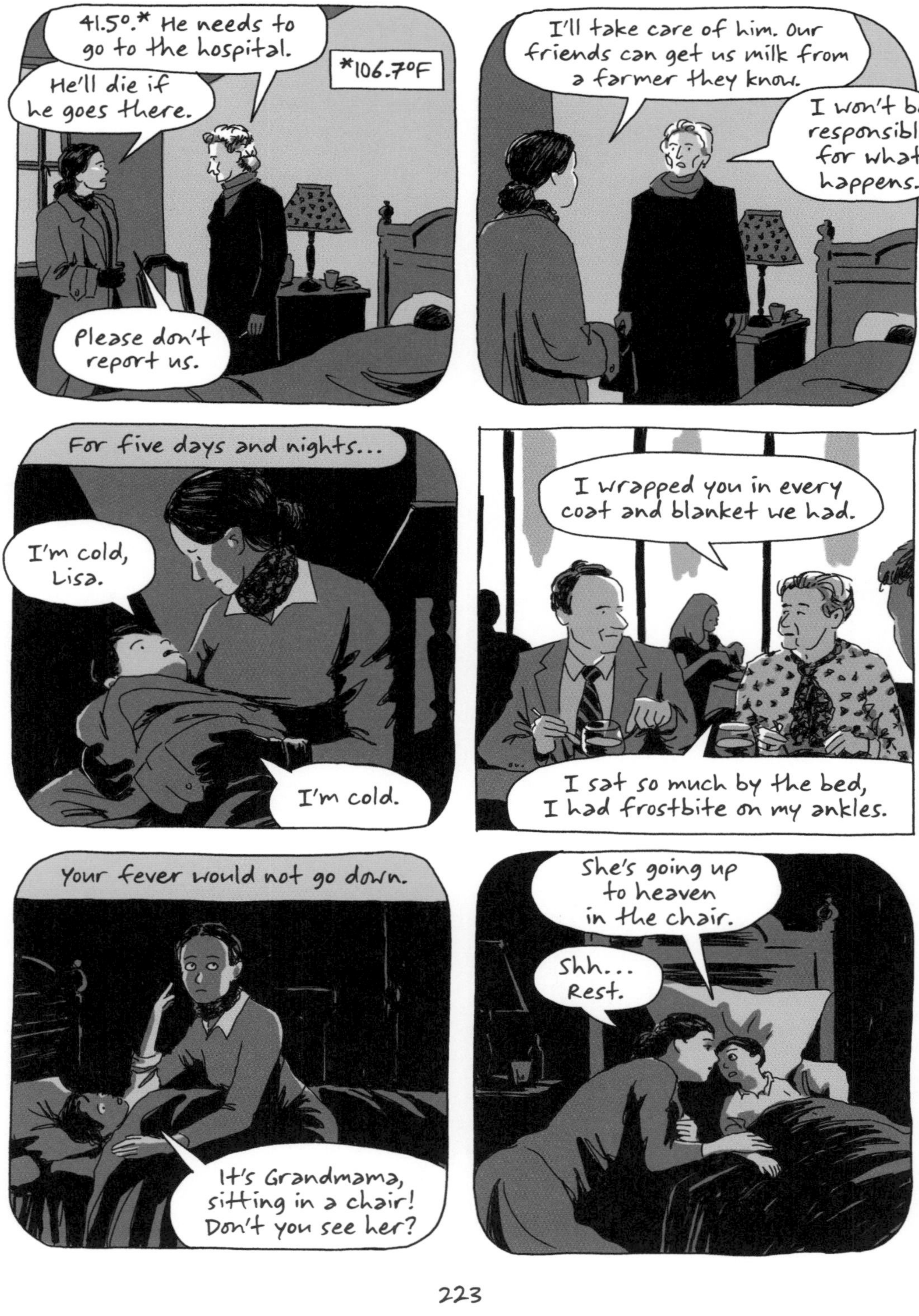
41.5°.* He needs to go to the hospital.
*106.7°F
He'll die if he goes there.
Please don't report us.
I'll take care of him. Our friends can get us milk from a farmer they know.
I won't be responsible for what happens.
For five days and nights...
I'm cold, Lisa.
I'm cold.
I wrapped you in every coat and blanket we had.
I sat so much by the bed, I had frostbite on my ankles.
Your fever would not go down.
It's Grandmama, sitting in a chair! Don't you see her?
She's going up to heaven in the chair.
Shh... Rest.

New Year's Eve

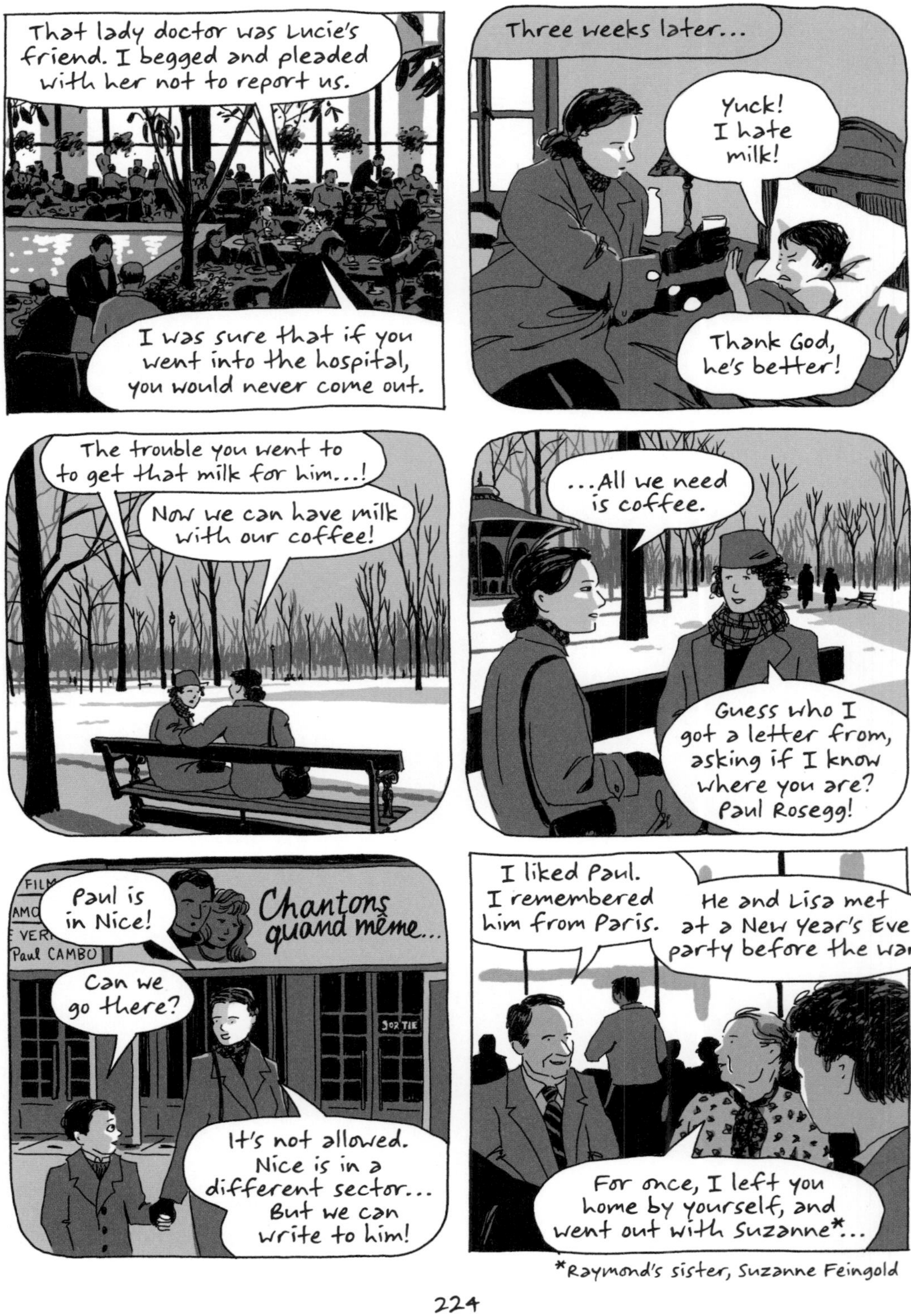

That lady doctor was Lucie's friend. I begged and pleaded with her not to report us.
I was sure that if you went into the hospital, you would never come out.
Three weeks later...
Yuck! I hate milk!
Thank God, he's better!
The trouble you went to to get that milk for him...!
Now we can have milk with our coffee!
...All we need is coffee.
Guess who I got a letter from, asking if I know where you are? Paul Rosegg!
Chantons quand même...
Paul CAMBO
SORTIE
Paul is in Nice!
Can we go there?
It's not allowed. Nice is in a different sector... But we can write to him!
I liked Paul. I remembered him from Paris.
He and Lisa met at a New Year's Eve party before the war.
For once, I left you home by yourself, and went out with Suzanne*...

*Raymond's sister, Suzanne Feingold

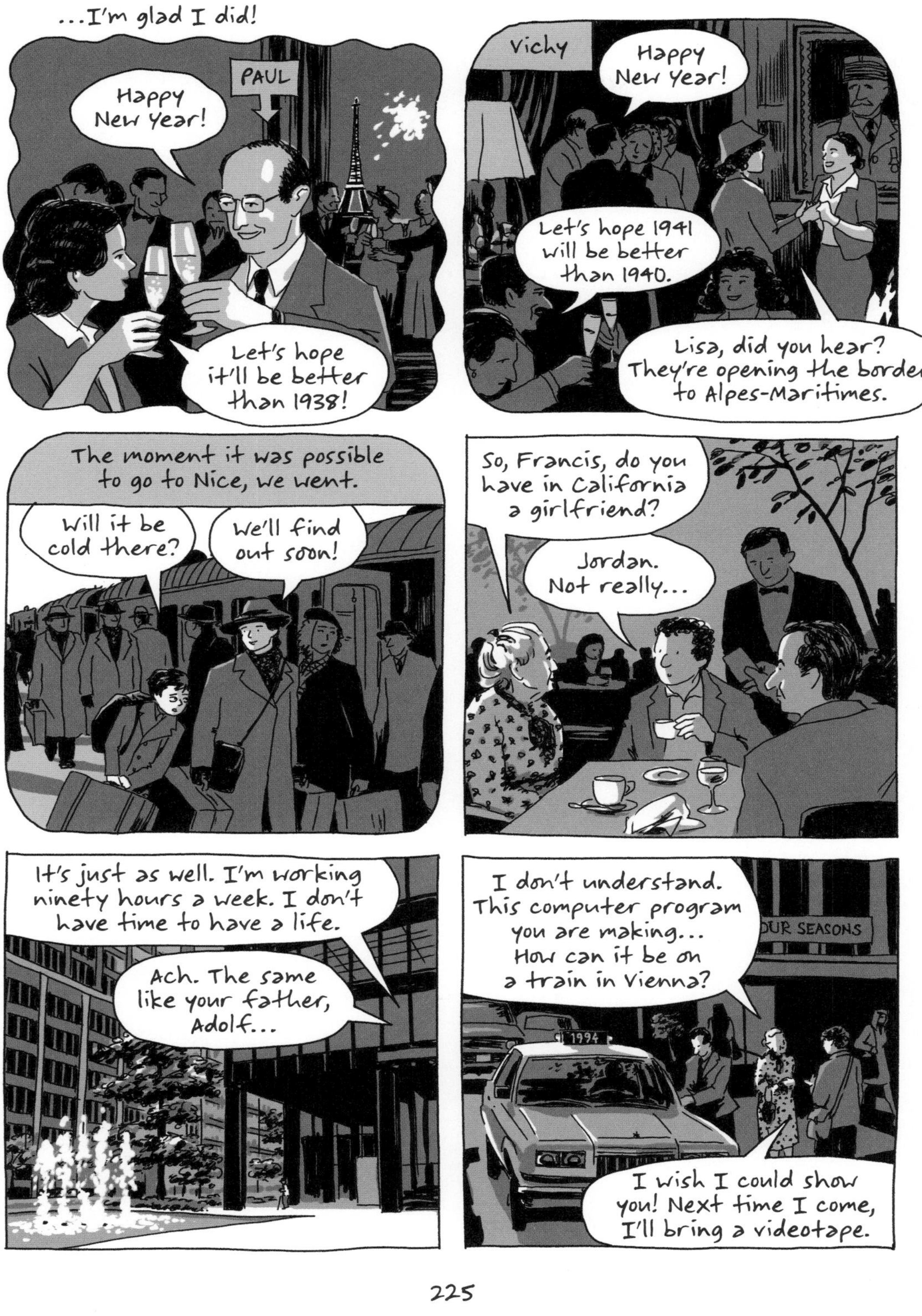
...I'm glad I did!
PAUL
Happy New Year!
Let's hope it'll be better than 1938!
Vichy
Happy New Year!
Let's hope 1941 will be better than 1940.
Lisa, did you hear? They're opening the border to Alpes-Maritimes.
The moment it was possible to go to Nice, we went.
Will it be cold there?
We'll find out soon!
So, Francis, do you have in California a girlfriend?
Jordan. Not really...
It's just as well. I'm working ninety hours a week. I don't have time to have a life.
Ach. The same like your father, Adolf...
I don't understand. This computer program you are making... How can it be on a train in Vienna?
OUR SEASONS
1994
I wish I could show you! Next time I come, I'll bring a videotape.

Gambit

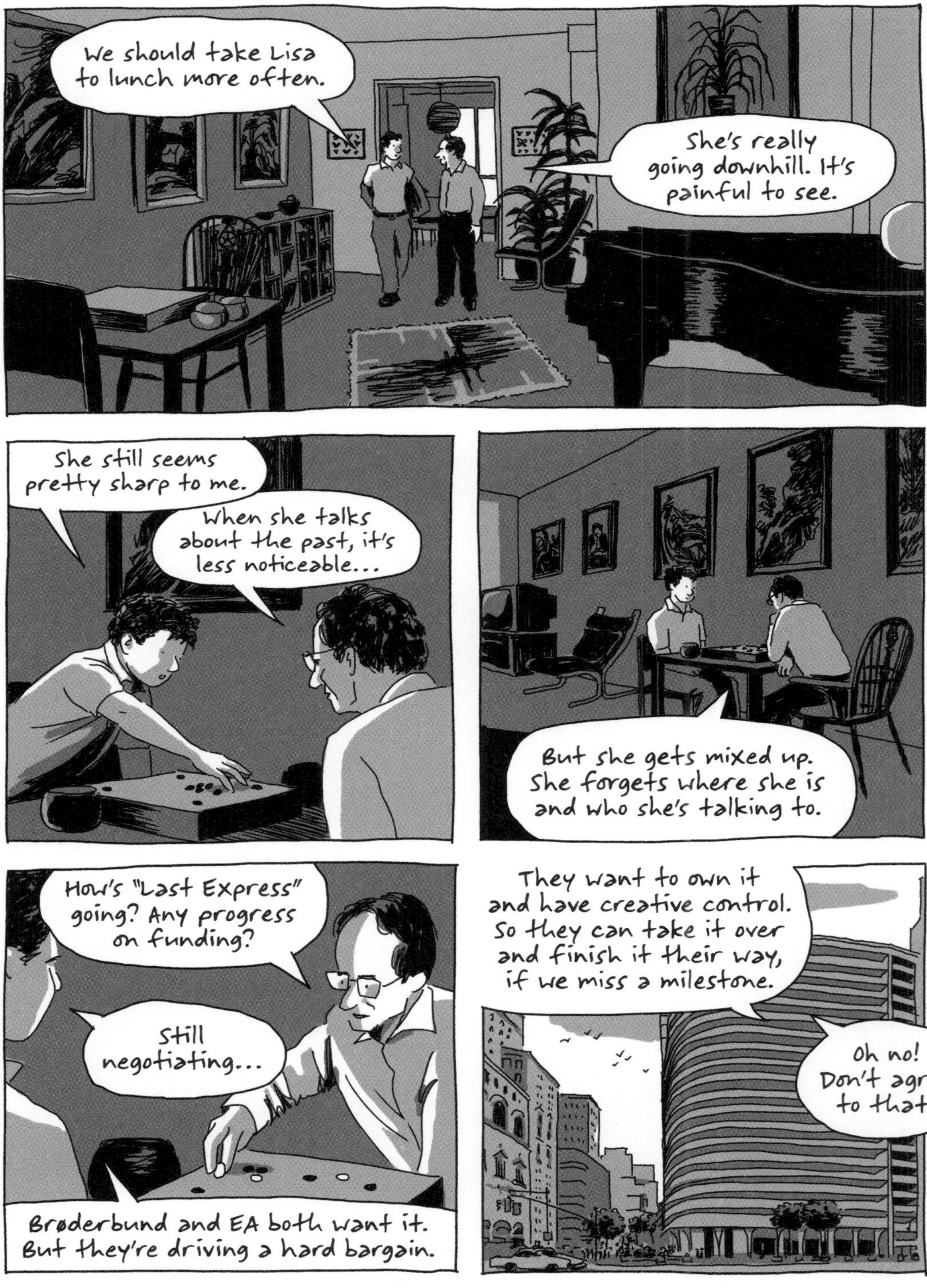
We should take Lisa to lunch more often.
She's really going downhill. It's painful to see.
She still seems pretty sharp to me.
When she talks about the past, it's less noticeable...
But she gets mixed up. She forgets where she is and who she's talking to.
How's "Last Express" going? Any progress on funding?
Still negotiating...
Brøderbund and EA both want it. But they're driving a hard bargain.
They want to own it and have creative control. So they can take it over and finish it their way, if we miss a milestone.
Oh no! Don't agree to that!

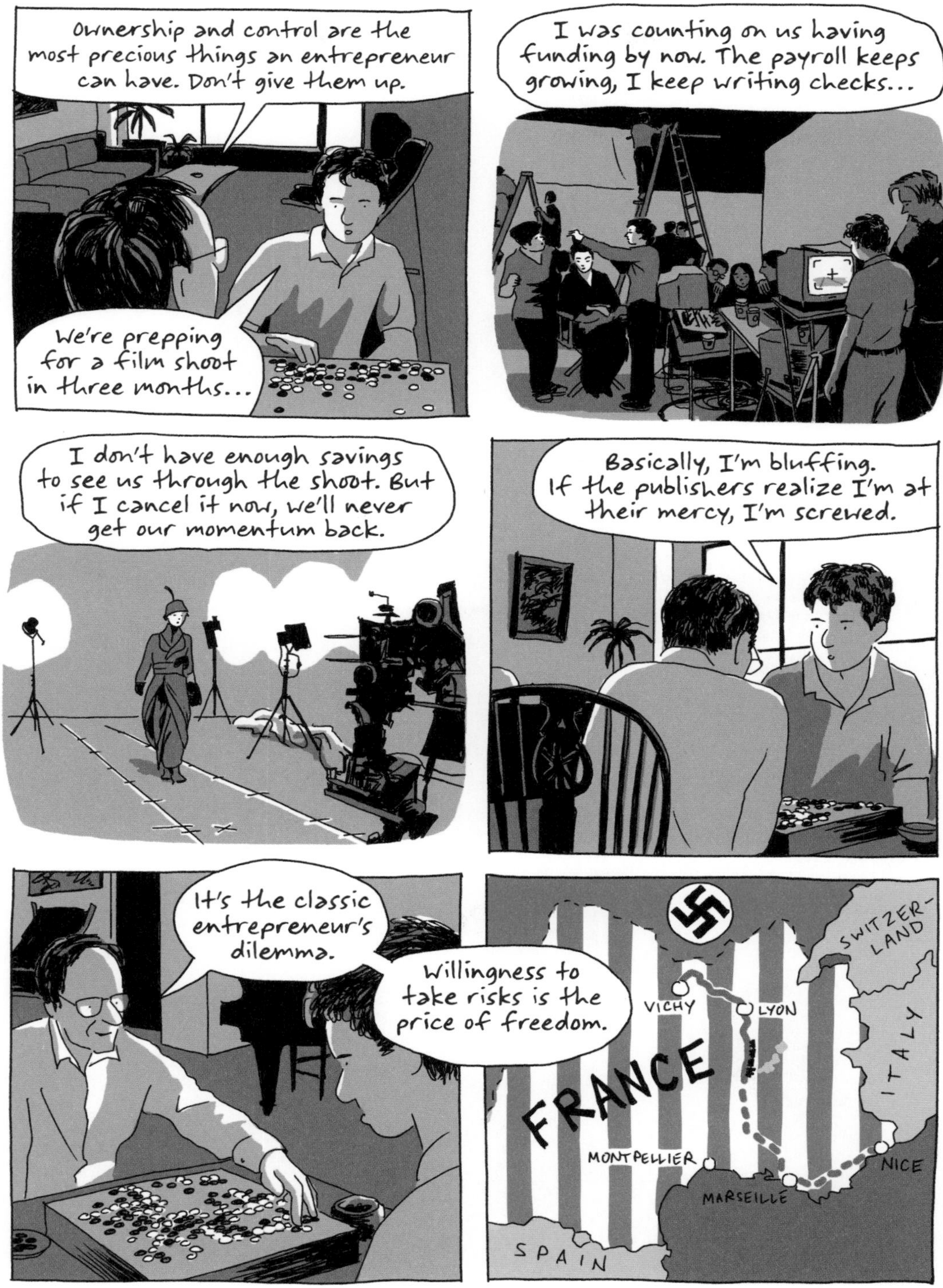
Ownership and control are the most precious things an entrepreneur can have. Don't give them up.
We're prepping for a film shoot in three months...
I was counting on us having funding by now. The payroll keeps growing, I keep writing checks...
I don't have enough savings to see us through the shoot. But if I cancel it now, we'll never get our momentum back.
Basically, I'm bluffing. If the publishers realize I'm at their mercy, I'm screwed.
It's the classic entrepreneur's dilemma.
Willingness to take risks is the price of freedom.
SWITZERLAND
VICHY
LYON
FRANCE
ITALY
MONTPELLIER
NICE
MARSEILLE
SPAIN

Côte d'Azur

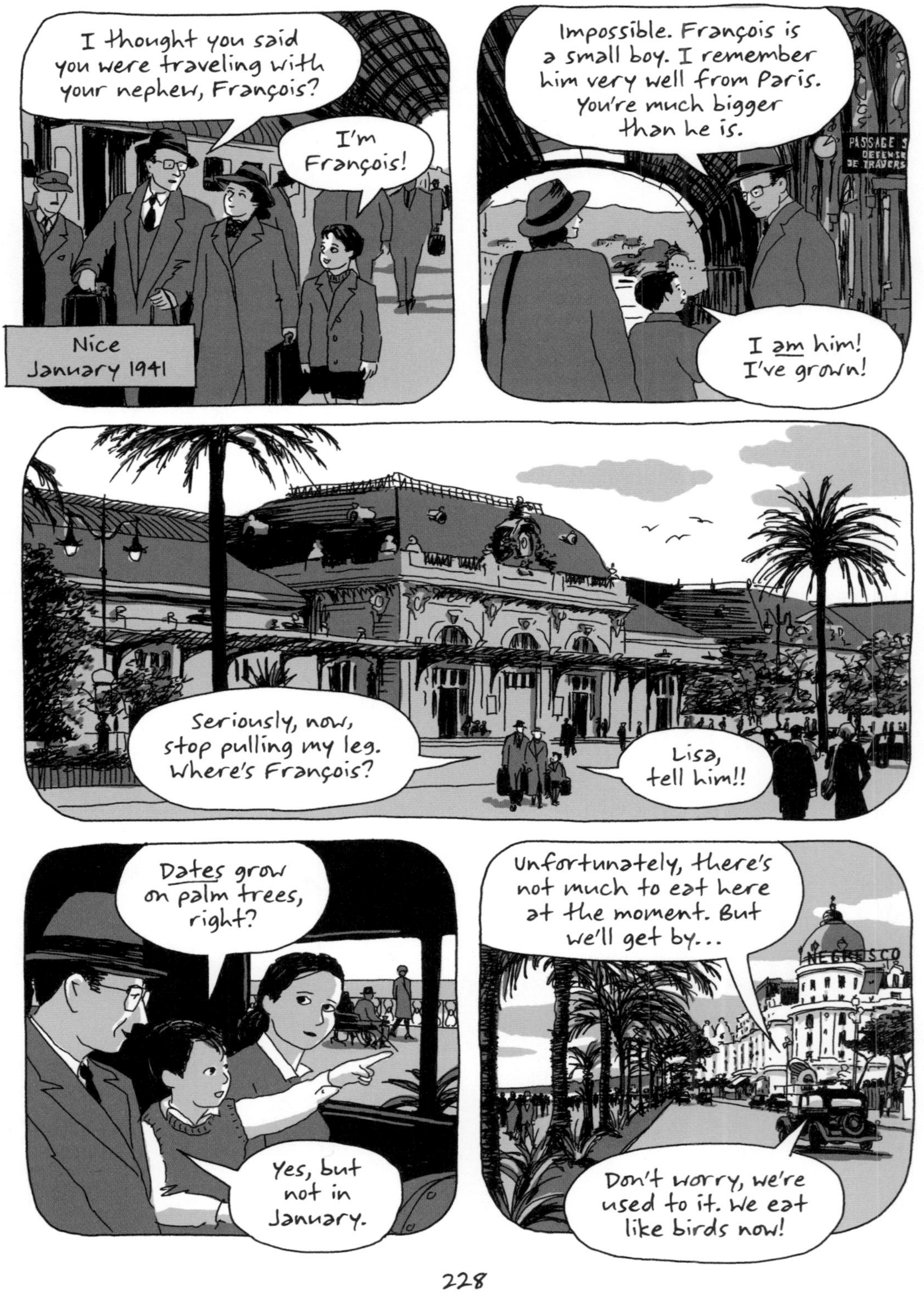

I thought you said you were traveling with your nephew, François?
I'm François!
Nice
January 1941
Impossible. François is a small boy. I remember him very well from Paris. You're much bigger than he is.
PASSAGE S
DEFENSE DE TRAVERS
I am him! I've grown!
Seriously, now, stop pulling my leg. Where's François?
Lisa, tell him!!
Dates grow on palm trees, right?
Yes, but not in January.
Unfortunately, there's not much to eat here at the moment. But we'll get by...
NEGRESCO
Don't worry, we're used to it. We eat like birds now!

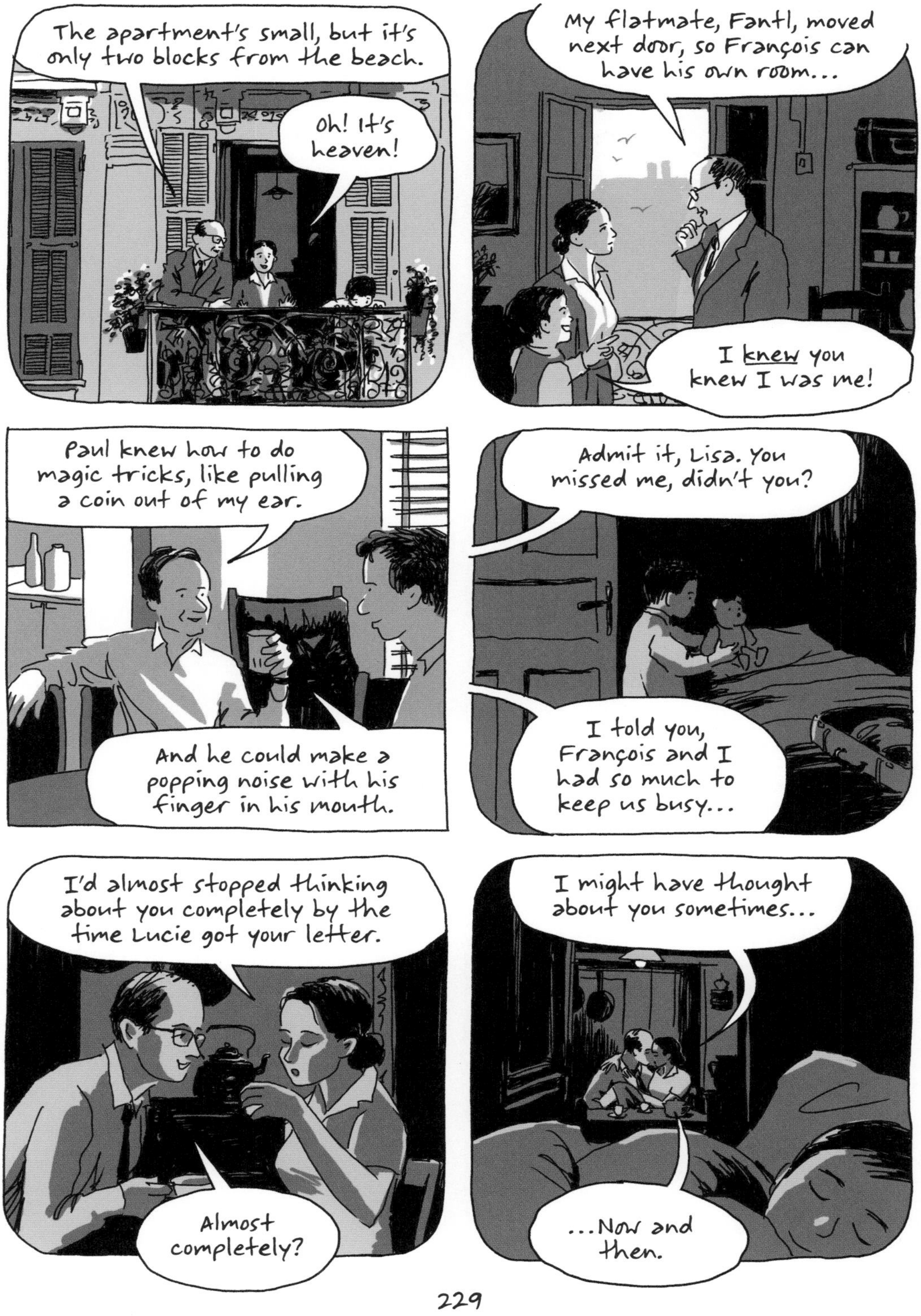
The apartment's small, but it's only two blocks from the beach.
Oh! It's heaven!
My flatmate, Fantl, moved next door, so François can have his own room...
I knew you knew I was me!
Paul knew how to do magic tricks, like pulling a coin out of my ear.
And he could make a popping noise with his finger in his mouth.
Admit it, Lisa. You missed me, didn't you?
I told you, François and I had so much to keep us busy...
I'd almost stopped thinking about you completely by the time Lucie got your letter.
Almost completely?
I might have thought about you sometimes...
...Now and then.

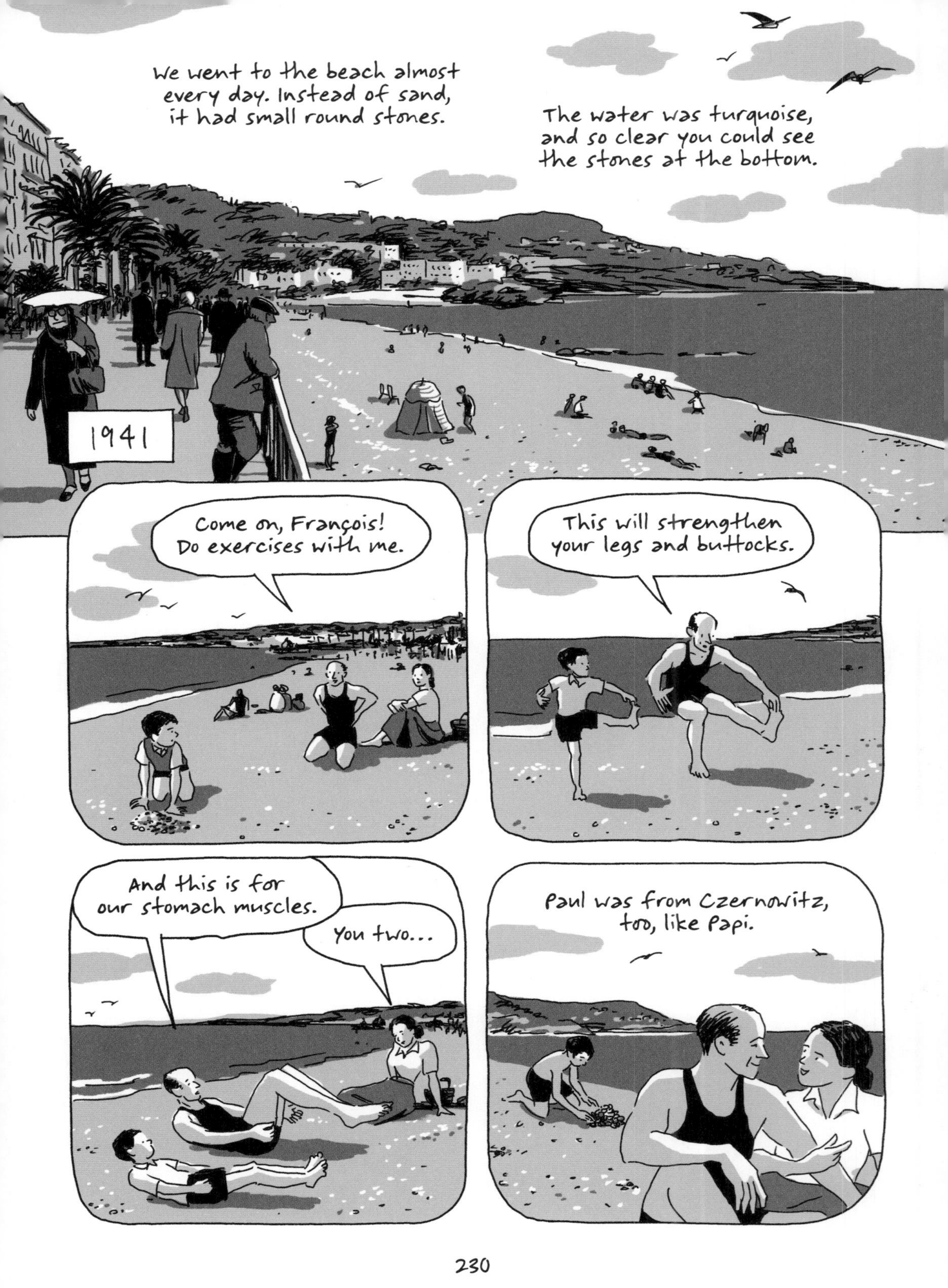
We went to the beach almost every day. Instead of sand, it had small round stones.
The water was turquoise, and so clear you could see the stones at the bottom.
1941
Come on, François! Do exercises with me.
This will strengthen your legs and buttocks.
And this is for our stomach muscles.
You two...
Paul was from Czernowitz, too, like Papi.

I resumed my old habit of swimming out to sea, as far as I dared...

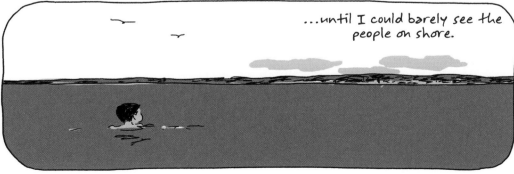

...until I could barely see the people on shore.

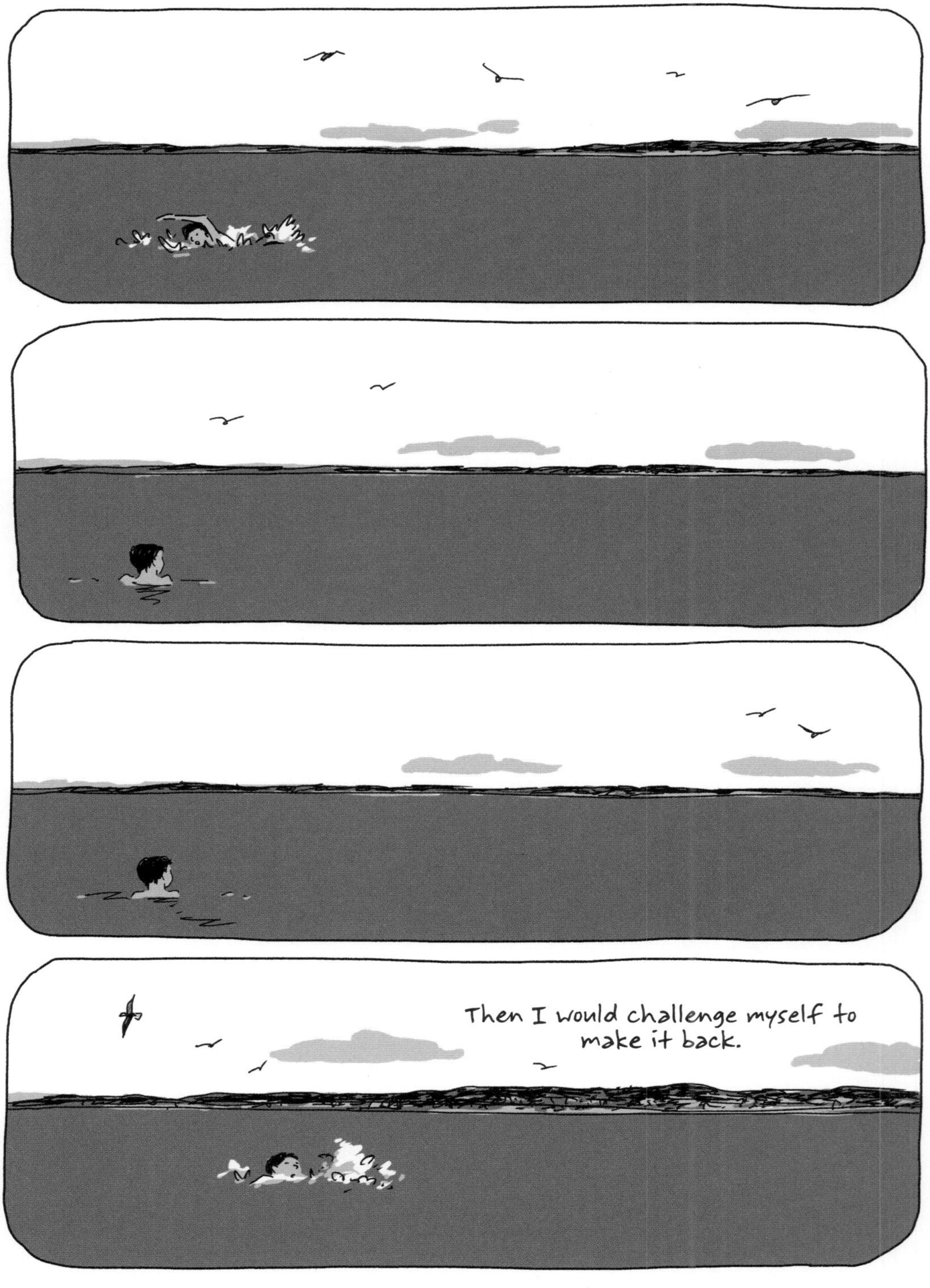
Then I would challenge myself to make it back.

Criminal Life

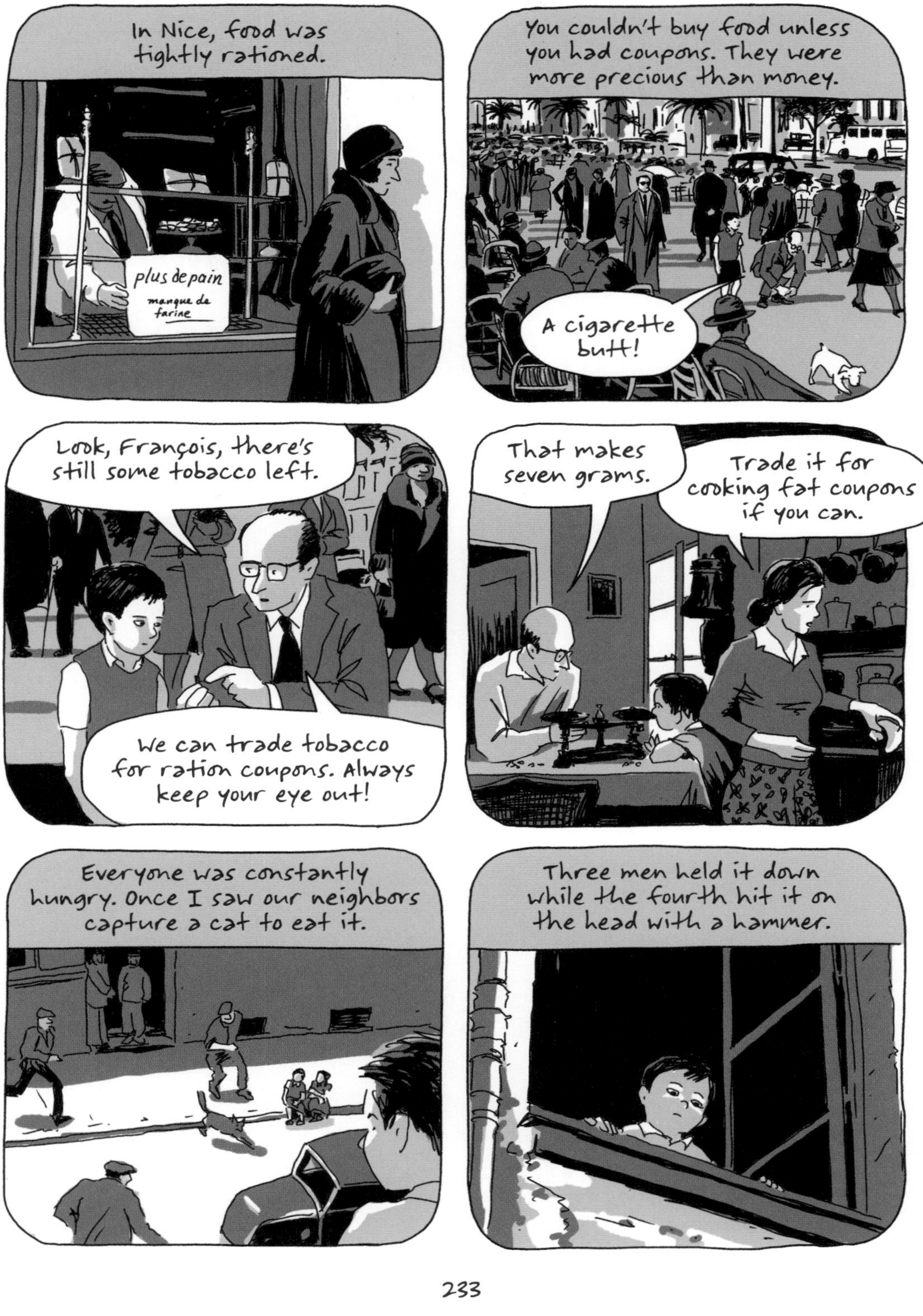
In Nice, food was tightly rationed.
plus de pain
manque de farine
You couldn't buy food unless you had coupons. They were more precious than money.
A cigarette butt!
Look, François, there's still some tobacco left.
We can trade tobacco for ration coupons. Always keep your eye out!
That makes seven grams.
Trade it for cooking fat coupons if you can.
Everyone was constantly hungry. Once I saw our neighbors capture a cat to eat it.
Three men held it down while the fourth hit it on the head with a hammer.

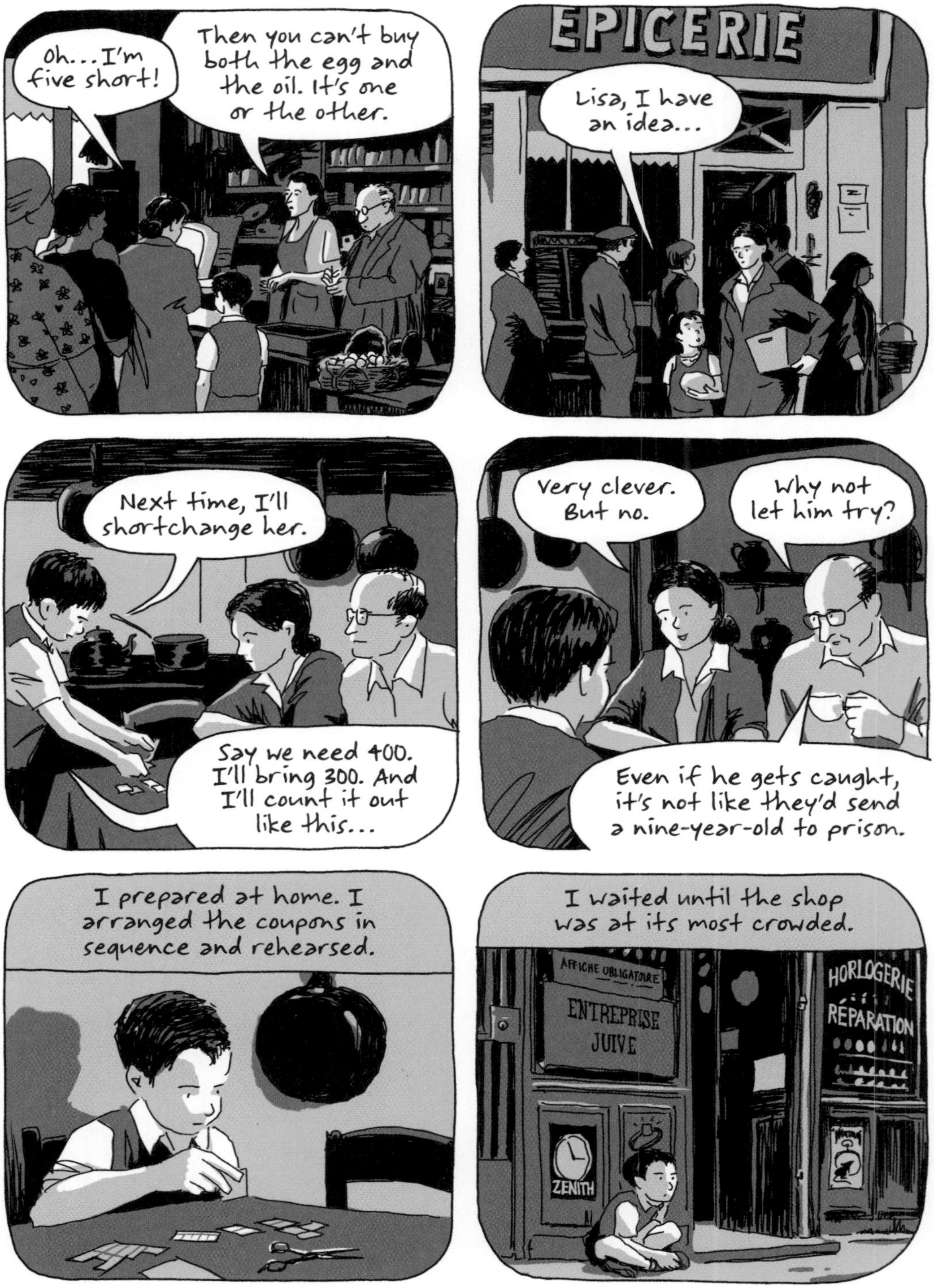
Oh...I'm five short!
Then you can't buy both the egg and the oil. It's one or the other.
EPICERIE
Lisa, I have an idea...
Next time, I'll shortchange her.
Say we need 400. I'll bring 300. And I'll count it out like this...
Very clever. But no.
Why not let him try?
Even if he gets caught, it's not like they'd send a nine-year-old to prison.
I prepared at home. I arranged the coupons in sequence and rehearsed.
I waited until the shop was at its most crowded.
AFFICHE OBLIGATOIRE
ENTREPRISE JUIVE
HORLOGERIE
RÉPARATION
ZENITH

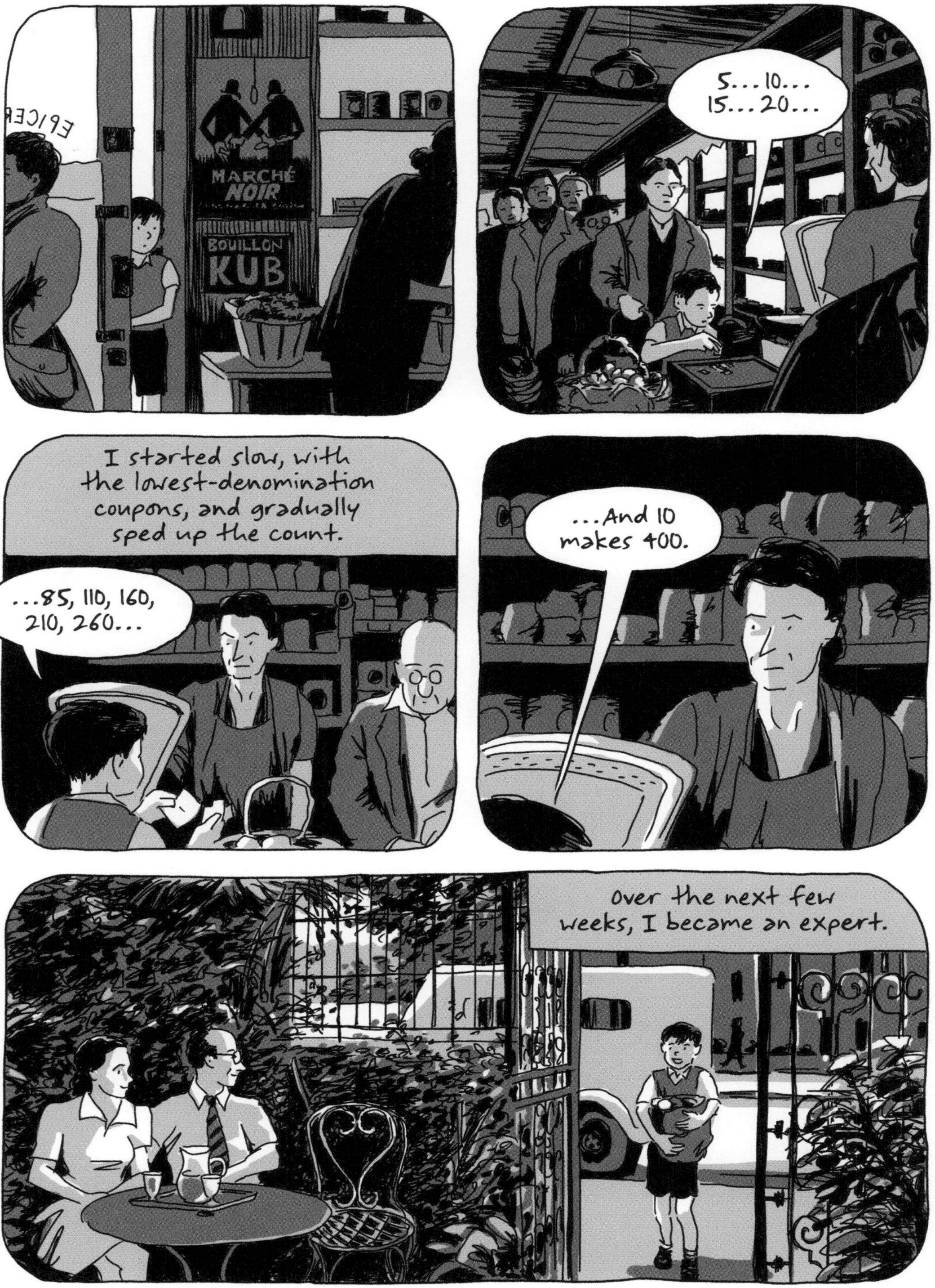
MARCHÉ NOIR
BOUILLON KUB
5...10... 15...20...
I started slow, with the lowest-denomination coupons, and gradually sped up the count.
...85, 110, 160, 210, 260...
...And 10 makes 400.
Over the next few weeks, I became an expert.

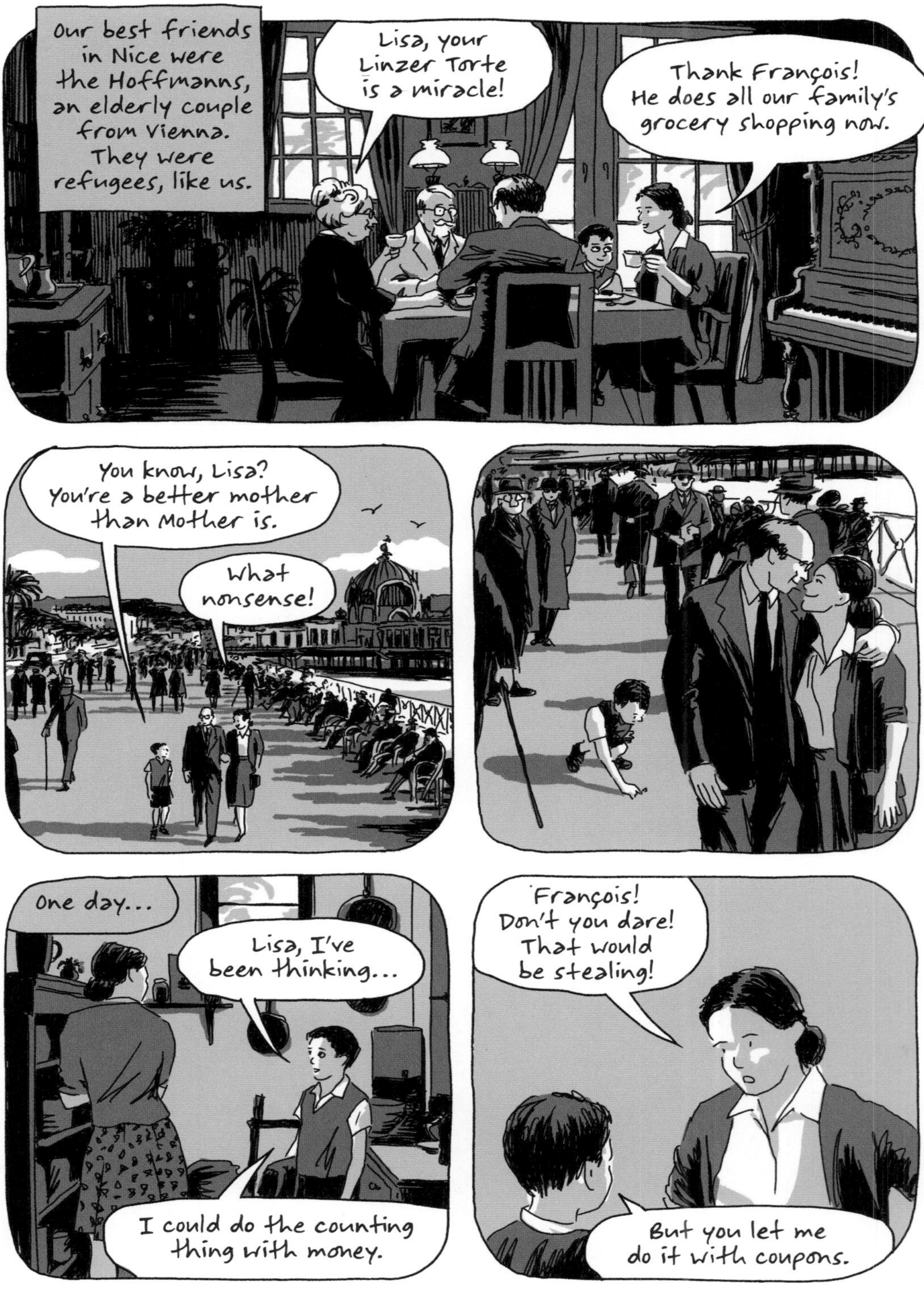
Our best friends in Nice were the Hoffmanns, an elderly couple from Vienna. They were refugees, like us.
Lisa, your Linzer Torte is a miracle!
Thank François! He does all our family's grocery shopping now.
You know, Lisa? You're a better mother than Mother is.
What nonsense!
One day...
Lisa, I've been thinking...
I could do the counting thing with money.
François! Don't you dare! That would be stealing!
But you let me do it with coupons.

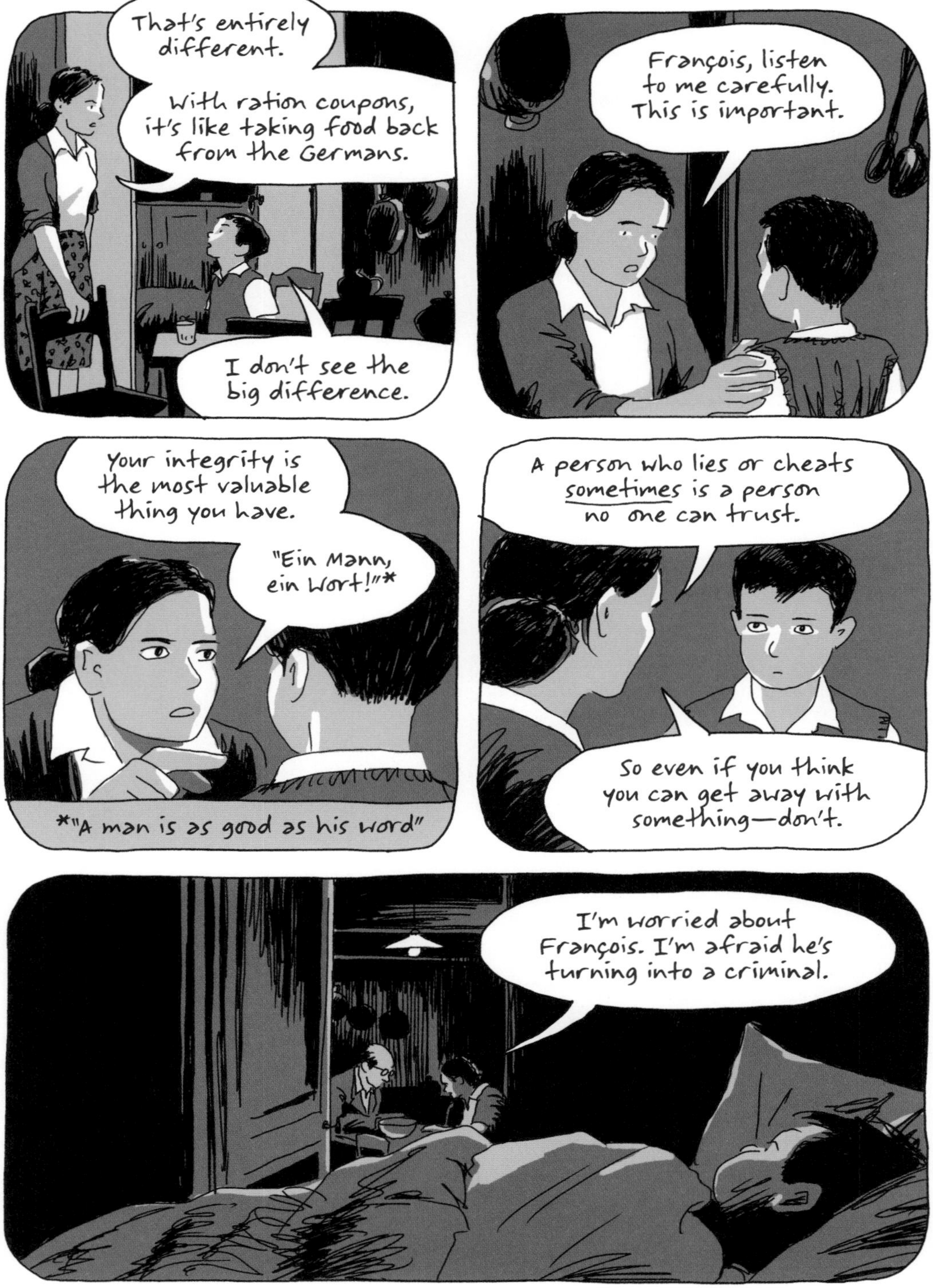
That's entirely different.
With ration coupons, it's like taking food back from the Germans.
I don't see the big difference.
François, listen to me carefully. This is important.
Your integrity is the most valuable thing you have.
"Ein Mann, ein Wort!"*
*"A man is as good as his word"
A person who lies or cheats sometimes is a person no one can trust.
So even if you think you can get away with something—don't.
I'm worried about François. I'm afraid he's turning into a criminal.

Stamp Collectors

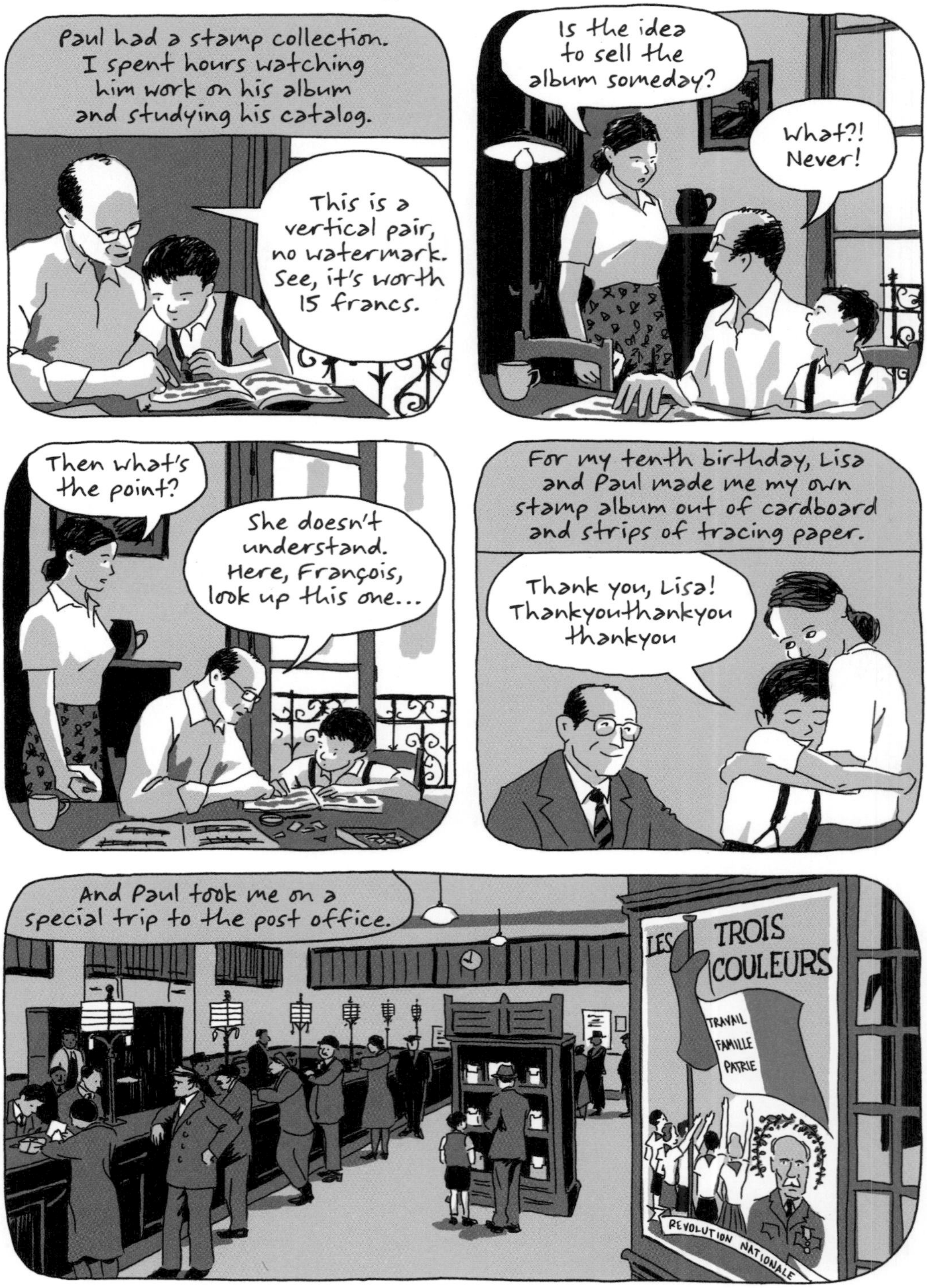

Paul had a stamp collection. I spent hours watching him work on his album and studying his catalog.
This is a vertical pair, no watermark. See, it's worth 15 francs.
Is the idea to sell the album someday?
What?! Never!
Then what's the point?
She doesn't understand. Here, François, look up this one...
For my tenth birthday, Lisa and Paul made me my own stamp album out of cardboard and strips of tracing paper.
Thank you, Lisa! Thankyouthankyou thankyou
And Paul took me on a special trip to the post office.
LES TROIS COULEURS
TRAVAIL
FAMILLE
PATRIE
REVOLUTION NATIONALE

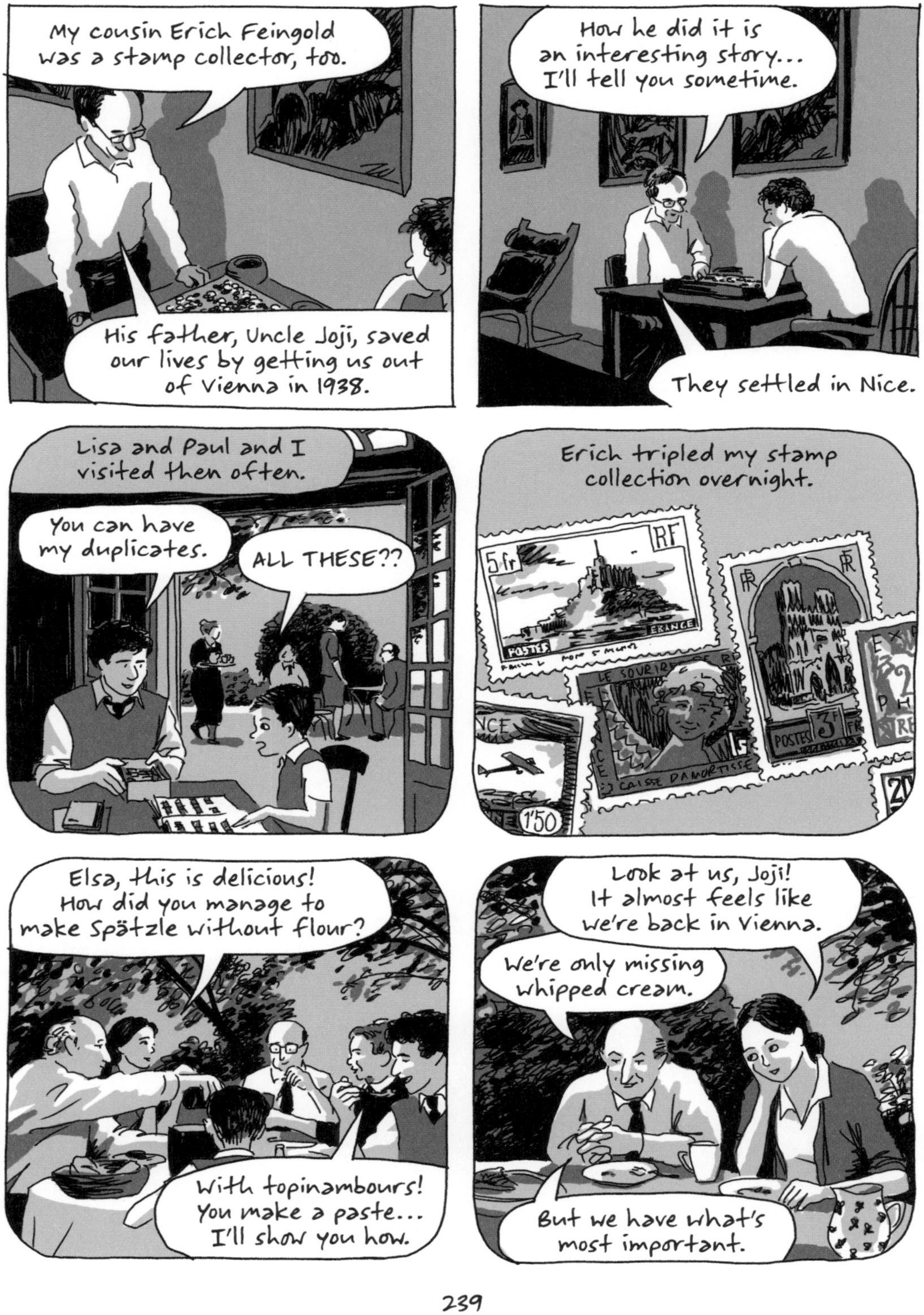
My cousin Erich Feingold was a stamp collector, too.
His father, Uncle Joji, saved our lives by getting us out of Vienna in 1938.
How he did it is an interesting story... I'll tell you sometime.
They settled in Nice.
Lisa and Paul and I visited then often.
You can have my duplicates.
ALL THESE??
Erich tripled my stamp collection overnight.
Elsa, this is delicious! How did you manage to make Spätzle without flour?
With topinambours! You make a paste... I'll show you how.
Look at us, Joji! It almost feels like we're back in Vienna.
We're only missing whipped cream.
But we have what's most important.

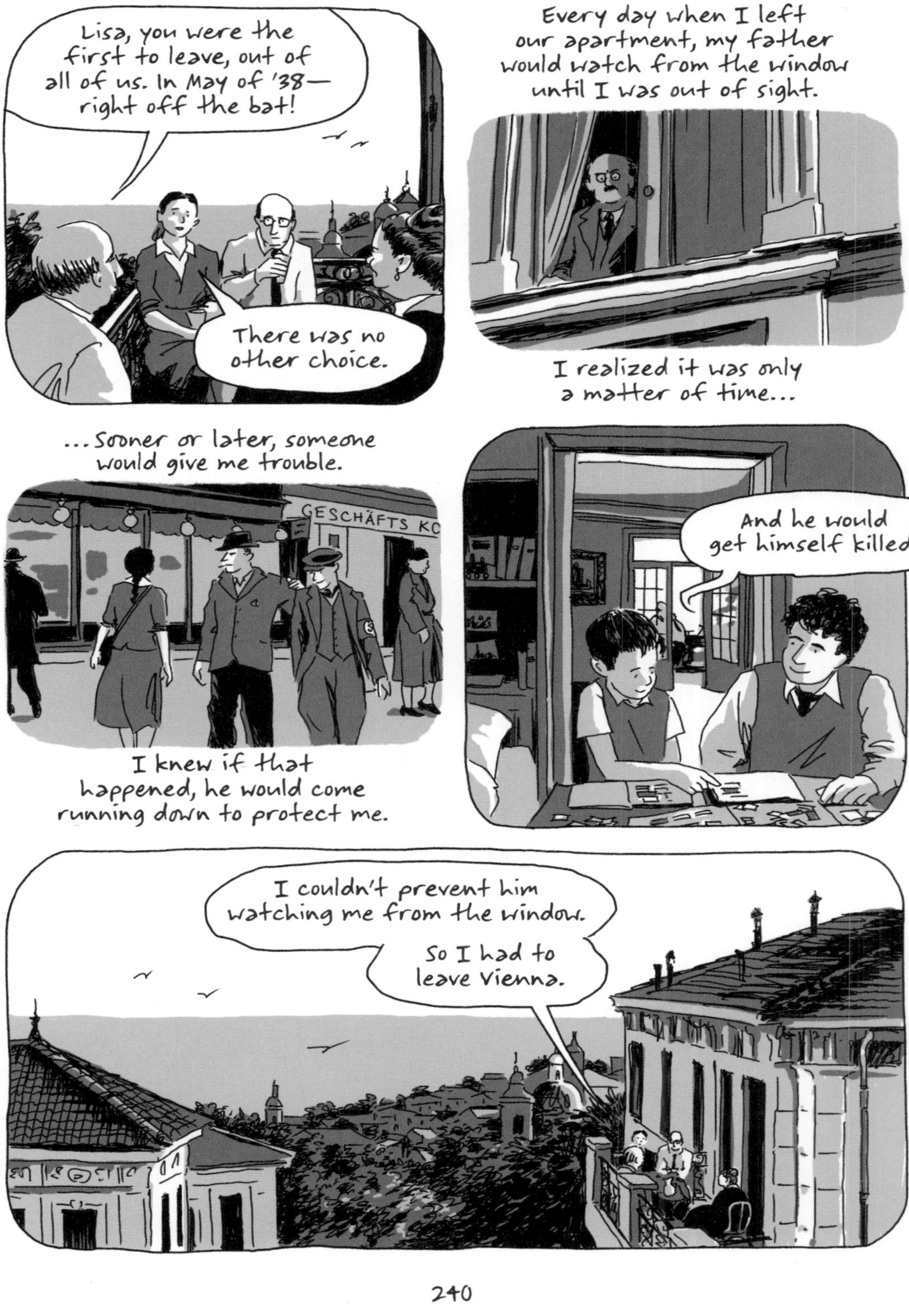
Lisa, you were the first to leave, out of all of us. In May of '38— right off the bat!
There was no other choice.
Every day when I left our apartment, my father would watch from the window until I was out of sight.
I realized it was only a matter of time...
...Sooner or later, someone would give me trouble.
GESCHÄFTS KO
I knew if that happened, he would come running down to protect me.
And he would get himself killed.
I couldn't prevent him watching me from the window.
So I had to leave Vienna.

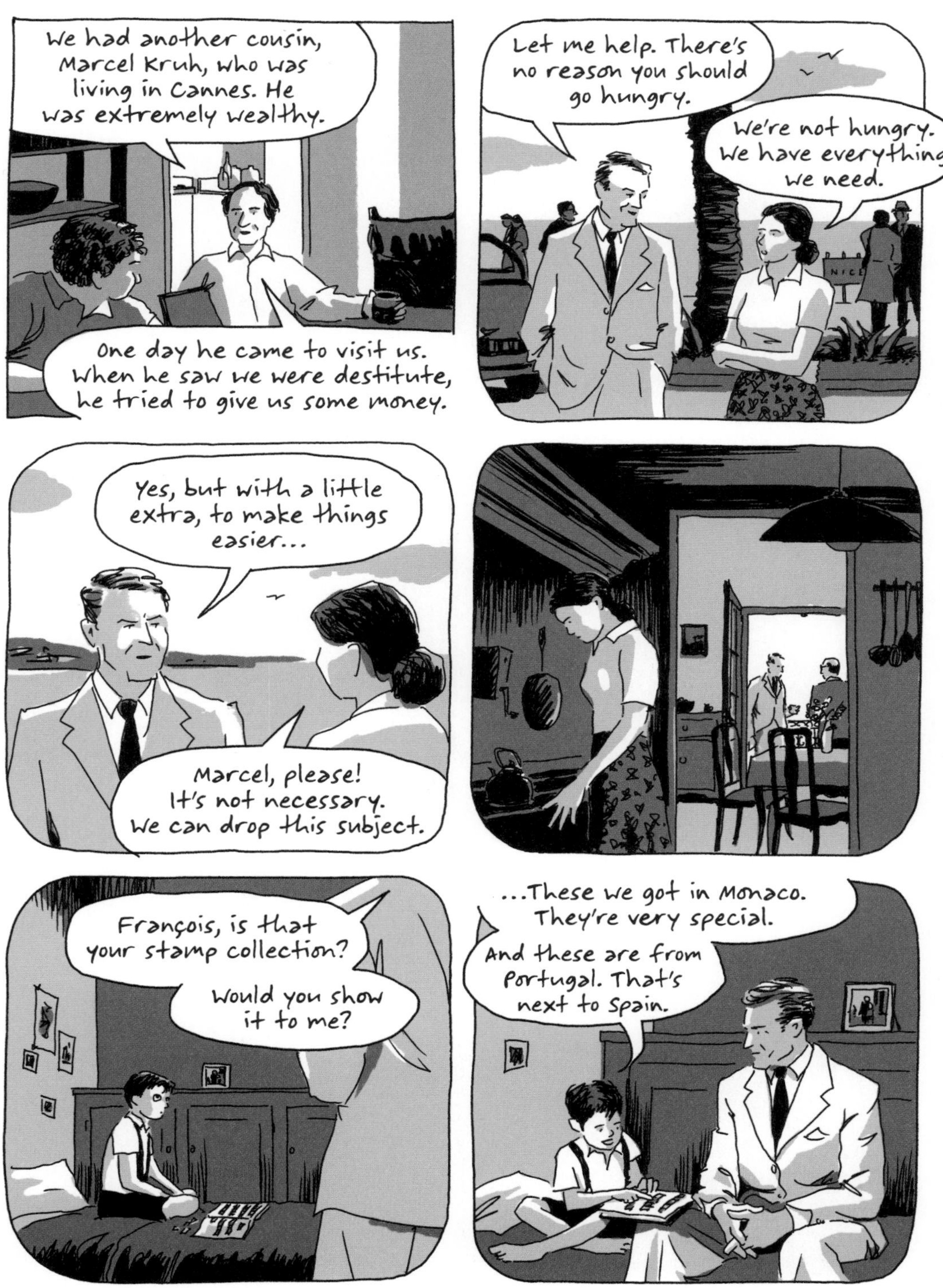
We had another cousin, Marcel Kruh, who was living in Cannes. He was extremely wealthy.
One day he came to visit us. When he saw we were destitute, he tried to give us some money.
Let me help. There's no reason you should go hungry.
We're not hungry. We have everything we need.
NICE
Yes, but with a little extra, to make things easier...
Marcel, please! It's not necessary. We can drop this subject.
François, is that your stamp collection?
Would you show it to me?
...These we got in Monaco. They're very special.
And these are from Portugal. That's next to Spain.

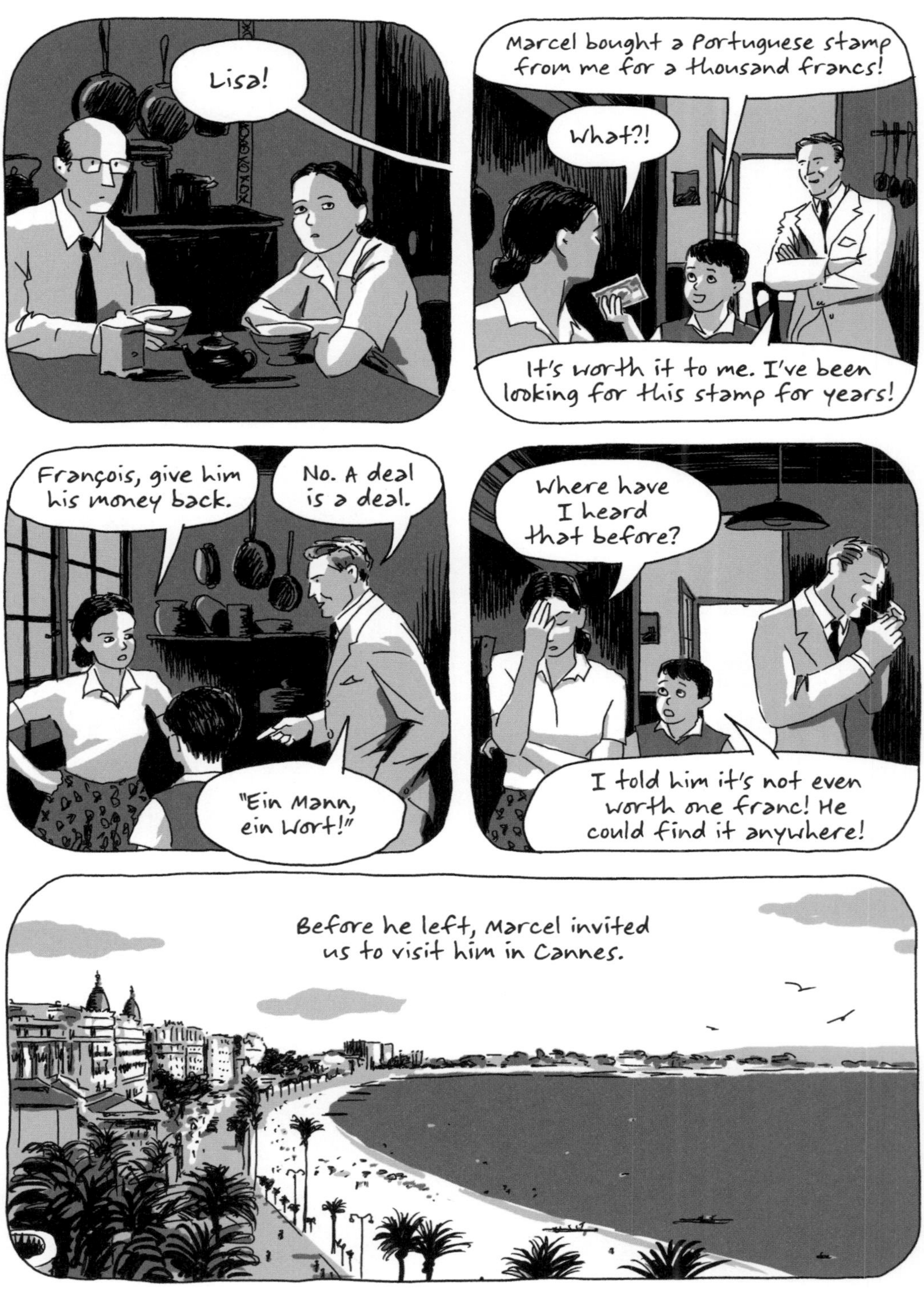
Lisa!
Marcel bought a Portuguese stamp from me for a thousand francs!
What?!
It's worth it to me. I've been looking for this stamp for years!
François, give him his money back.
No. A deal is a deal.
"Ein Mann, ein Wort!"
Where have I heard that before?
I told him it's not even worth one franc! He could find it anywhere!
Before he left, Marcel invited us to visit him in Cannes.

A Peach

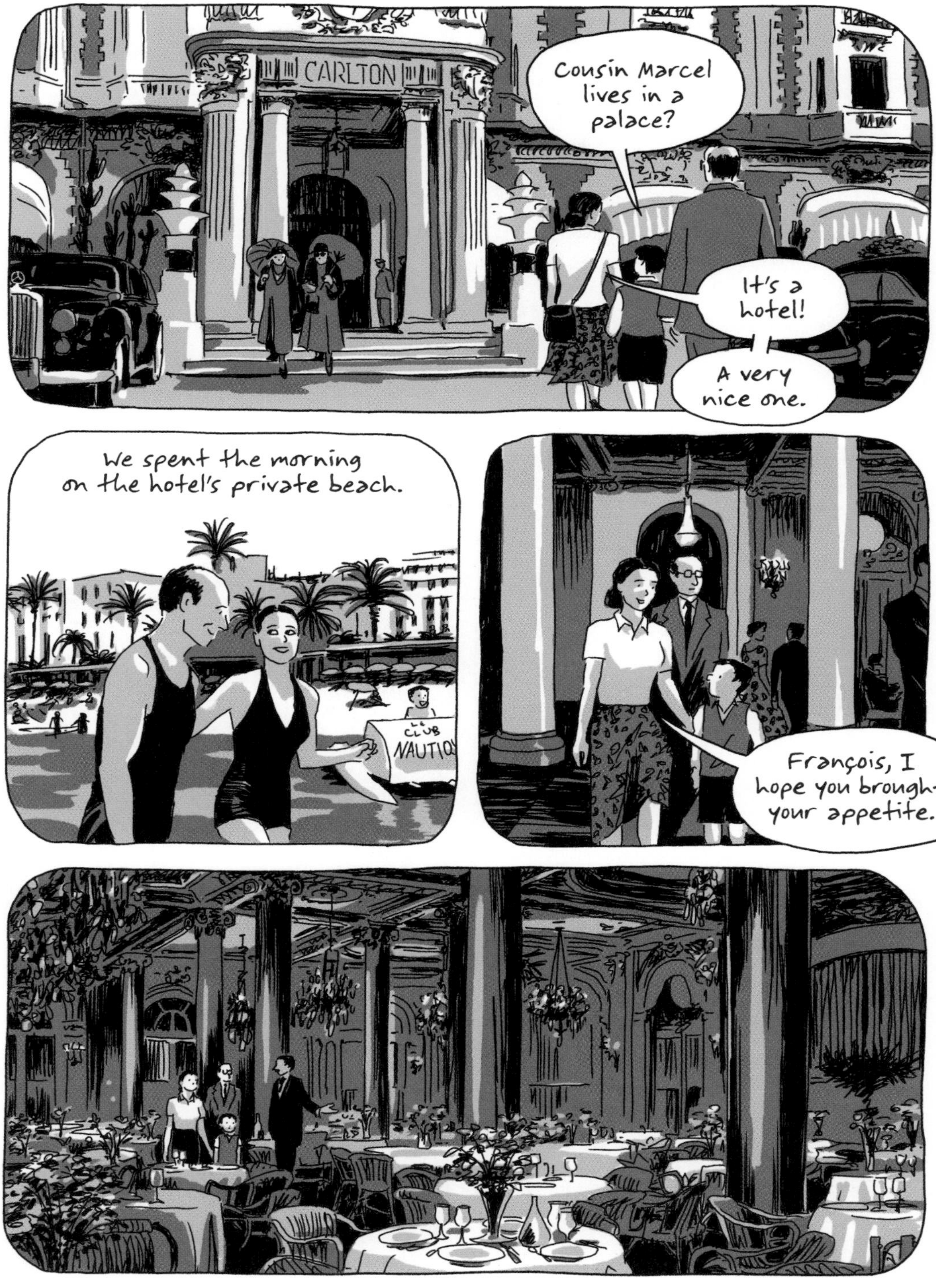
CARLTON
Cousin Marcel lives in a palace?
It's a hotel!
A very nice one.
We spent the morning on the hotel's private beach.
François, I hope you brought your appetite.

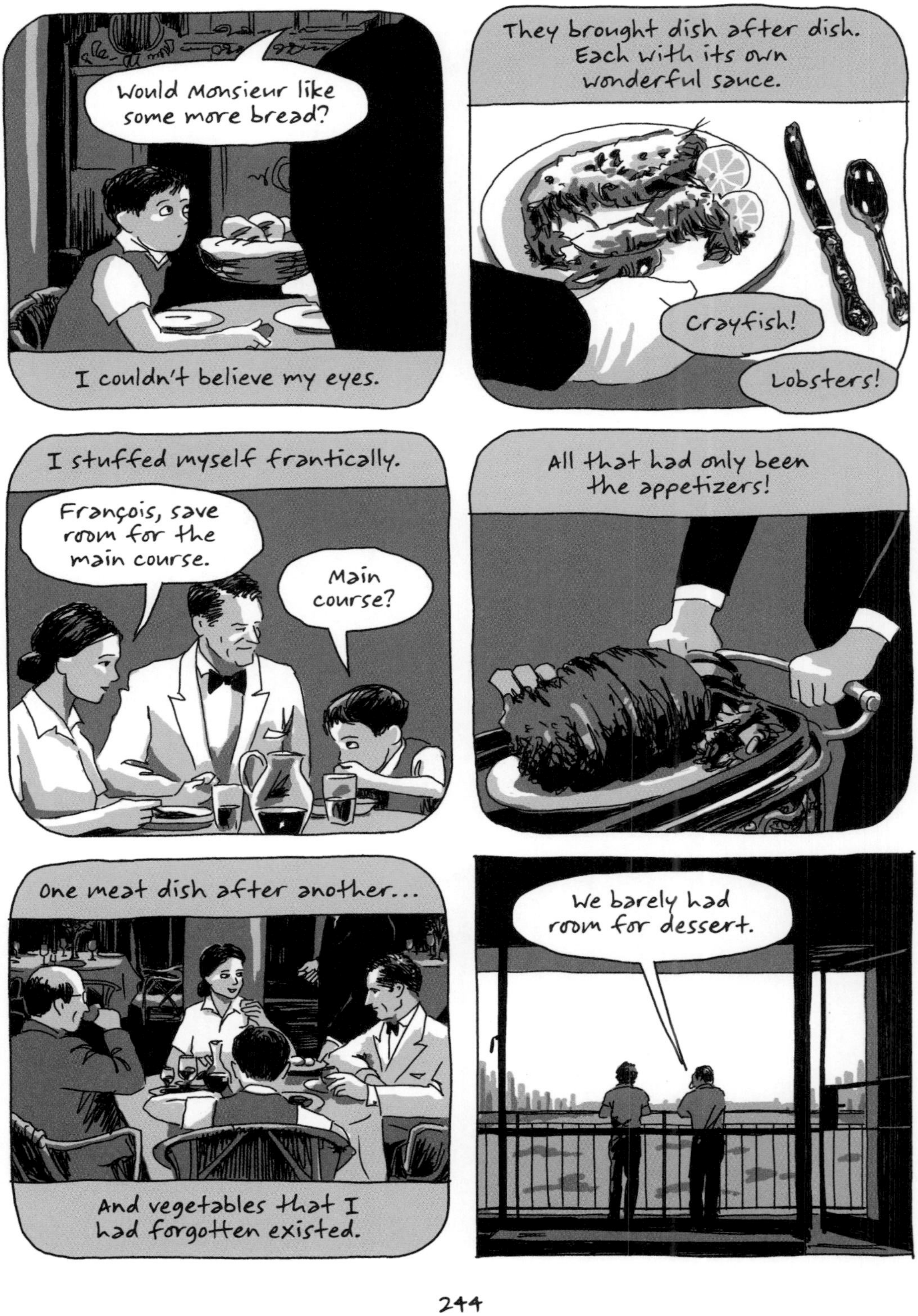
Would Monsieur like some more bread?
I couldn't believe my eyes.
They brought dish after dish. Each with its own wonderful sauce.
Crayfish!
Lobsters!
I stuffed myself frantically.
François, save room for the main course.
Main course?
All that had only been the appetizers!
One meat dish after another...
And vegetables that I had forgotten existed.
We barely had room for dessert.

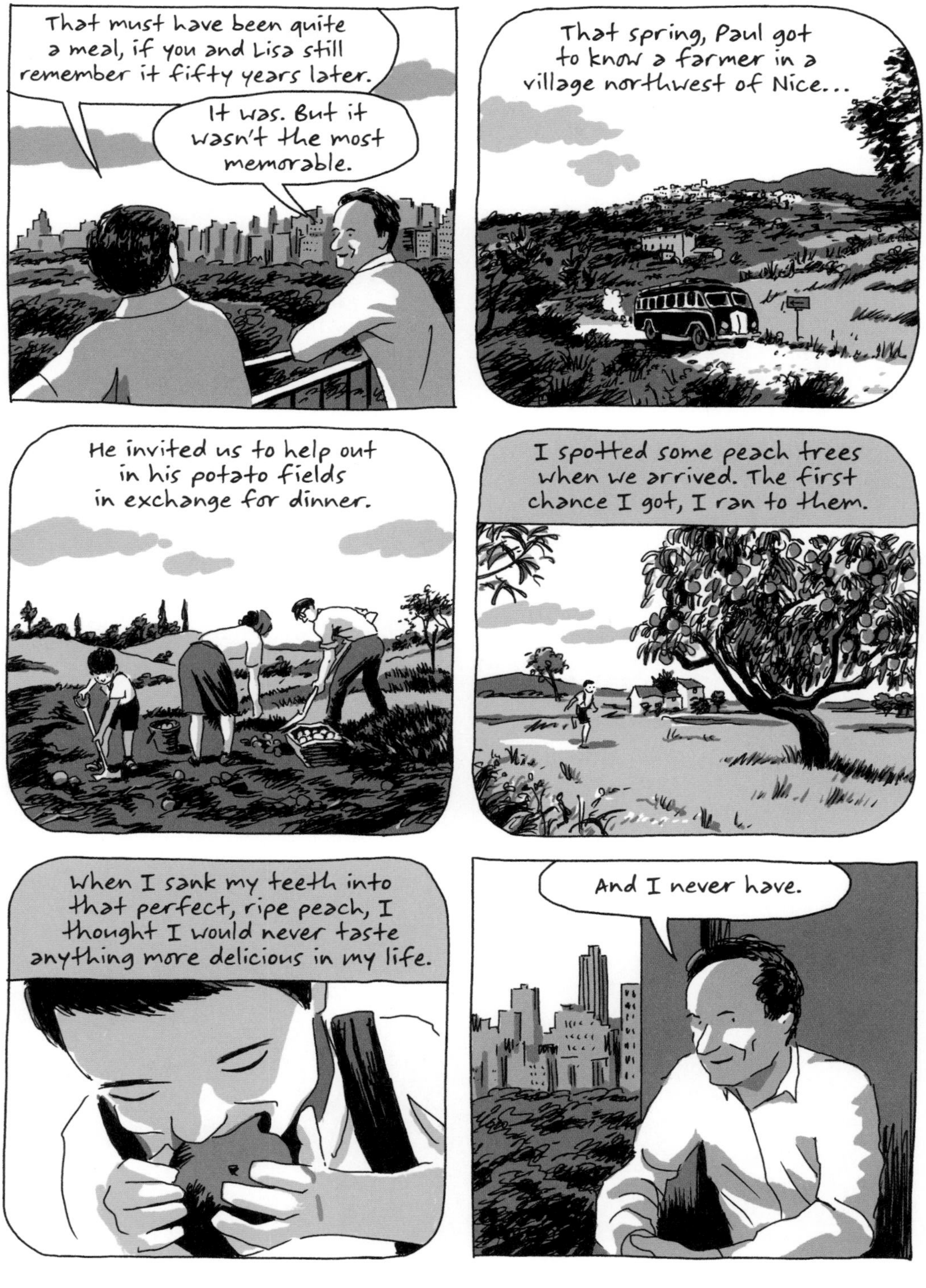
That must have been quite a meal, if you and Lisa still remember it fifty years later.
It was. But it wasn't the most memorable.
That spring, Paul got to know a farmer in a village northwest of Nice...
He invited us to help out in his potato fields in exchange for dinner.
I spotted some peach trees when we arrived. The first chance I got, I ran to them.
When I sank my teeth into that perfect, ripe peach, I thought I would never taste anything more delicious in my life.
And I never have.

Descendance

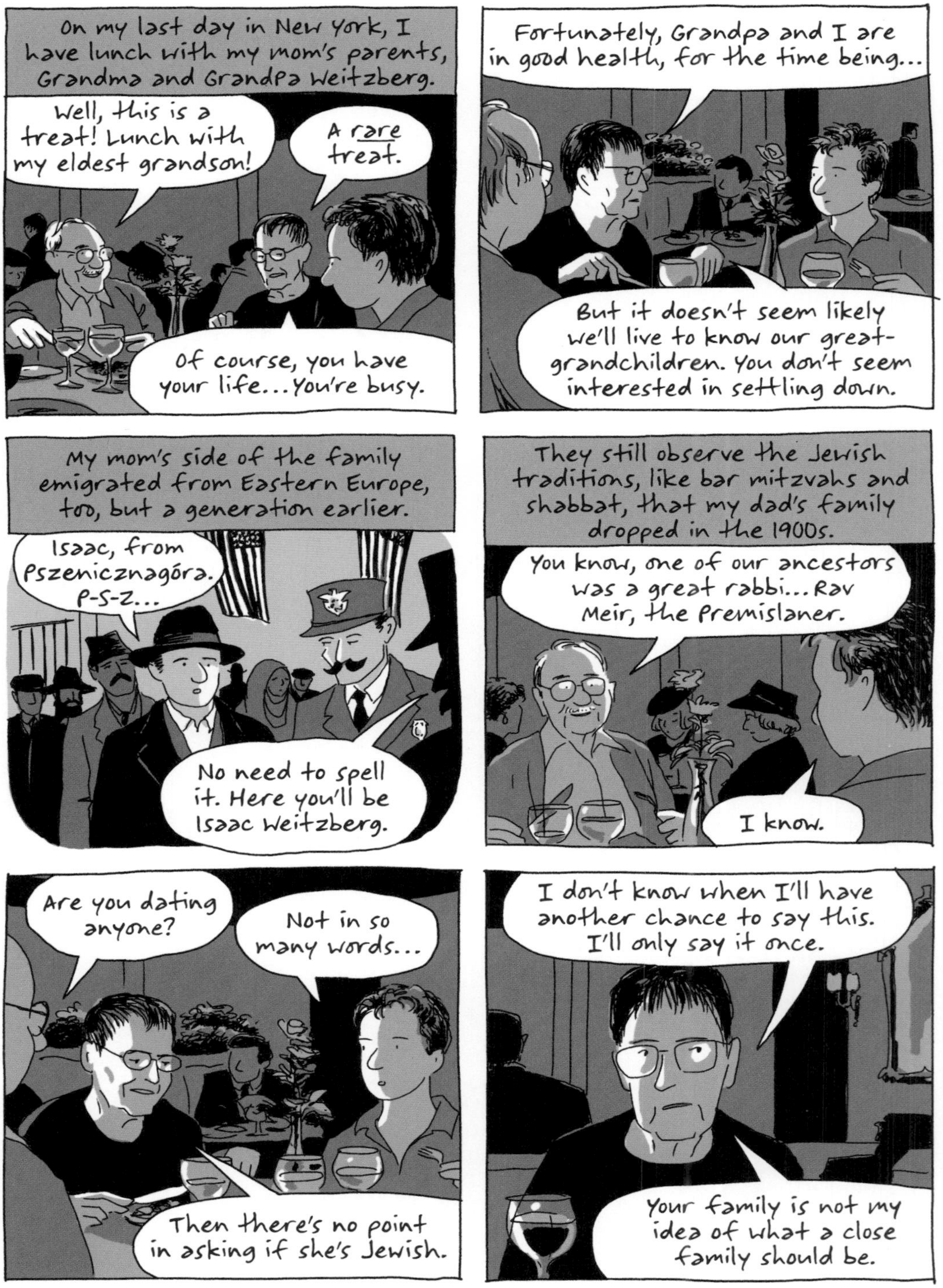

On my last day in New York, I have lunch with my mom's parents, Grandma and Grandpa Weitzberg.
Well, this is a treat! Lunch with my eldest grandson!
A rare treat.
Of course, you have your life... You're busy.
Fortunately, Grandpa and I are in good health, for the time being...
But it doesn't seem likely we'll live to know our great-grandchildren. You don't seem interested in settling down.
My mom's side of the family emigrated from Eastern Europe, too, but a generation earlier.
Isaac, from Pszenicznagóra. P-S-Z...
No need to spell it. Here you'll be Isaac Weitzberg.
They still observe the Jewish traditions, like bar mitzvahs and shabbat, that my dad's family dropped in the 1900s.
You know, one of our ancestors was a great rabbi... Rav Meir, the Premislaner.
I know.
Are you dating anyone?
Not in so many words...
Then there's no point in asking if she's Jewish.
I don't know when I'll have another chance to say this. I'll only say it once.
Your family is not my idea of what a close family should be.

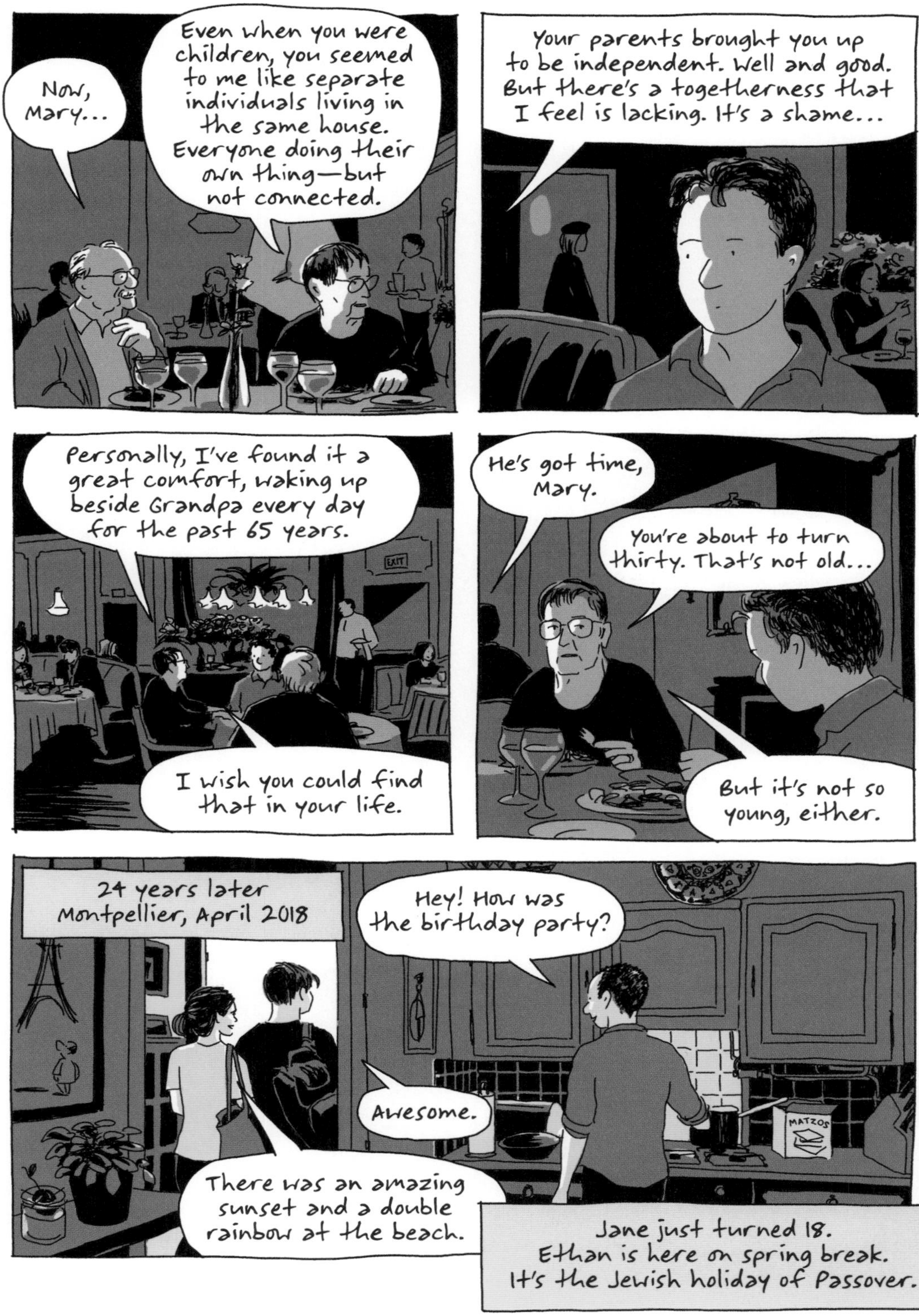
Now, Mary...
Even when you were children, you seemed to me like separate individuals living in the same house. Everyone doing their own thing—but not connected.
Your parents brought you up to be independent. Well and good. But there's a togetherness that I feel is lacking. It's a shame...
Personally, I've found it a great comfort, waking up beside Grandpa every day for the past 65 years.
EXIT
I wish you could find that in your life.
He's got time, Mary.
You're about to turn thirty. That's not old...
But it's not so young, either.
24 years later
Montpellier, April 2018
Hey! How was the birthday party?
Awesome.
There was an amazing sunset and a double rainbow at the beach.
MATZOS
Jane just turned 18.
Ethan is here on spring break.
It's the Jewish holiday of Passover.

Missiles

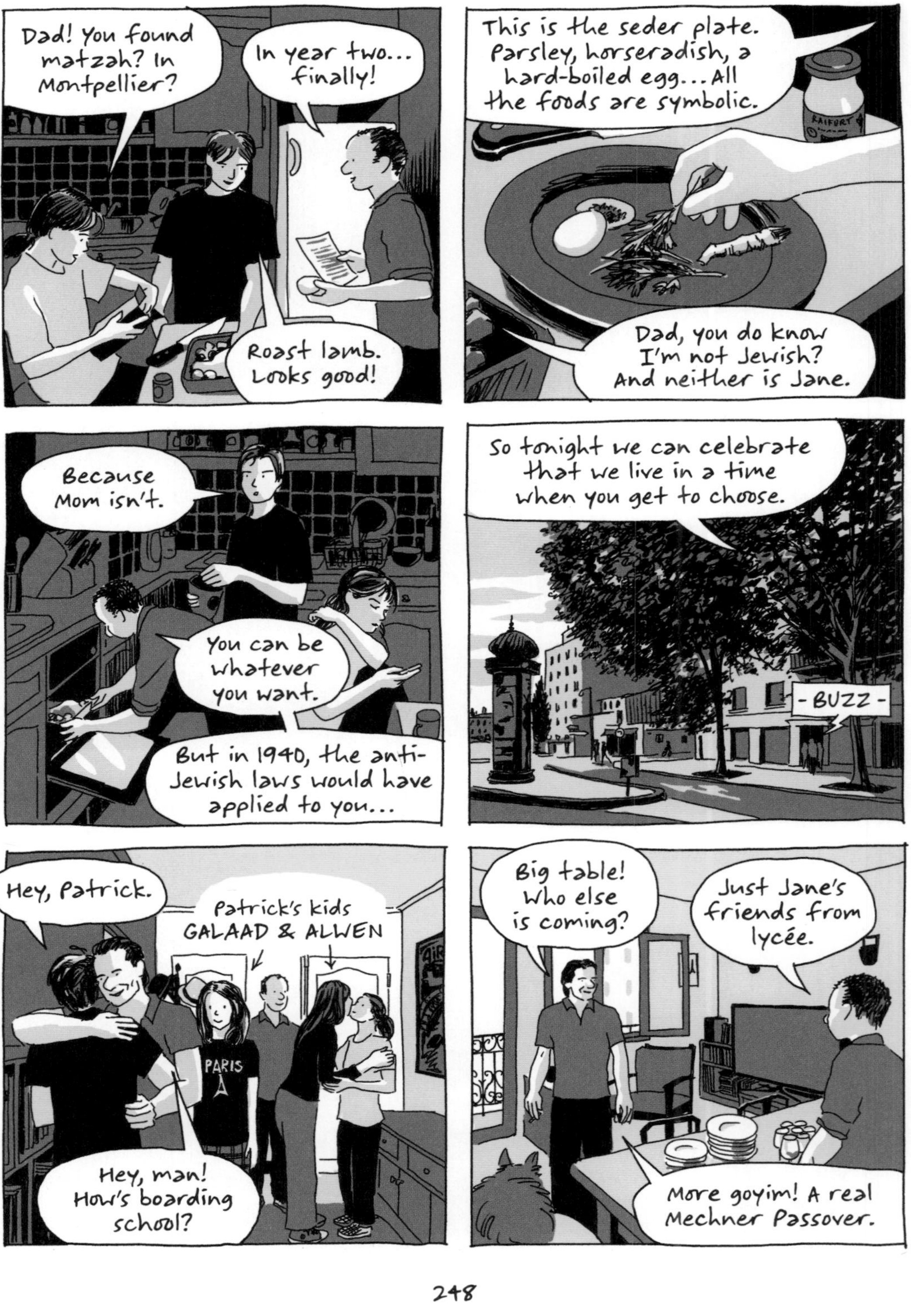
Dad! You found matzah? In Montpellier?
In year two... finally!
Roast lamb. Looks good!
This is the seder plate. Parsley, horseradish, a hard-boiled egg... All the foods are symbolic.
RAIFORT
Dad, you do know I'm not Jewish? And neither is Jane.
Because Mom isn't.
You can be whatever you want.
But in 1940, the anti-Jewish laws would have applied to you...
So tonight we can celebrate that we live in a time when you get to choose.
- BUZZ -
Hey, Patrick.
Patrick's kids GALAAD & ALWEN
PARIS
Hey, man! How's boarding school?
Big table! Who else is coming?
Just Jane's friends from lycée.
More goyim! A real Mechner Passover.

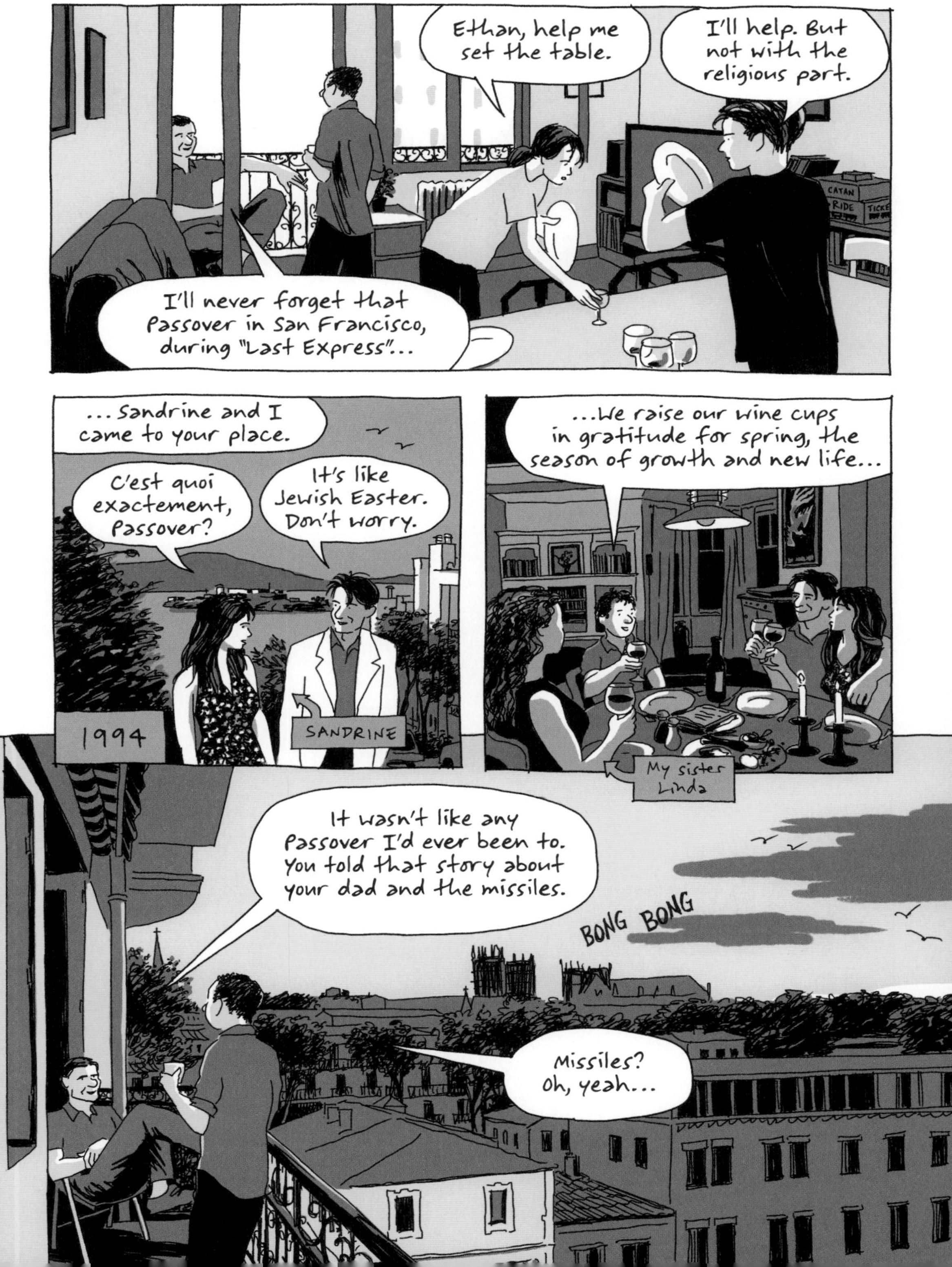

Ethan, help me set the table.
I'll help. But not with the religious part.
CATAN
RIDE
TICKE
I'll never forget that Passover in San Francisco, during "Last Express"...
...Sandrine and I came to your place.
C'est quoi exactement, Passover?
It's like Jewish Easter. Don't worry.
1994
SANDRINE
...We raise our wine cups in gratitude for spring, the season of growth and new life...
My sister Linda
It wasn't like any Passover I'd ever been to. You told that story about your dad and the missiles.
BONG BONG
Missiles? Oh, yeah...

My dad's been telling that story at Passover since we were kids.

"Why is this night different from all other nights?"

1972

"On other nights, we eat any kind of bread. Why, on this night, do we eat only matzah?"

David

Linda

Me

I know the answer.

The Jews left Egypt in such a hurry, they didn't wait for the dough to rise. Because Pharaoh might have changed his mind and not let them go. So they'd have stayed slaves, blah blah blah...

Grandpa Weitzberg

Let's not get ahead of ourselves...

This is the part where we read the questions. We'll answer them later.

Emily

But they're the same questions as last year.

Why can't we say the answers now, if we already know them?

Jordan actually raises an interesting question.

Here we go...

Let's follow the order in the Haggadah,* then you'll see.

Why did our ancestors design this holiday in such a way that we repeat the same questions, in the same words, every year?

*Hebrew guidebook to Passover

250

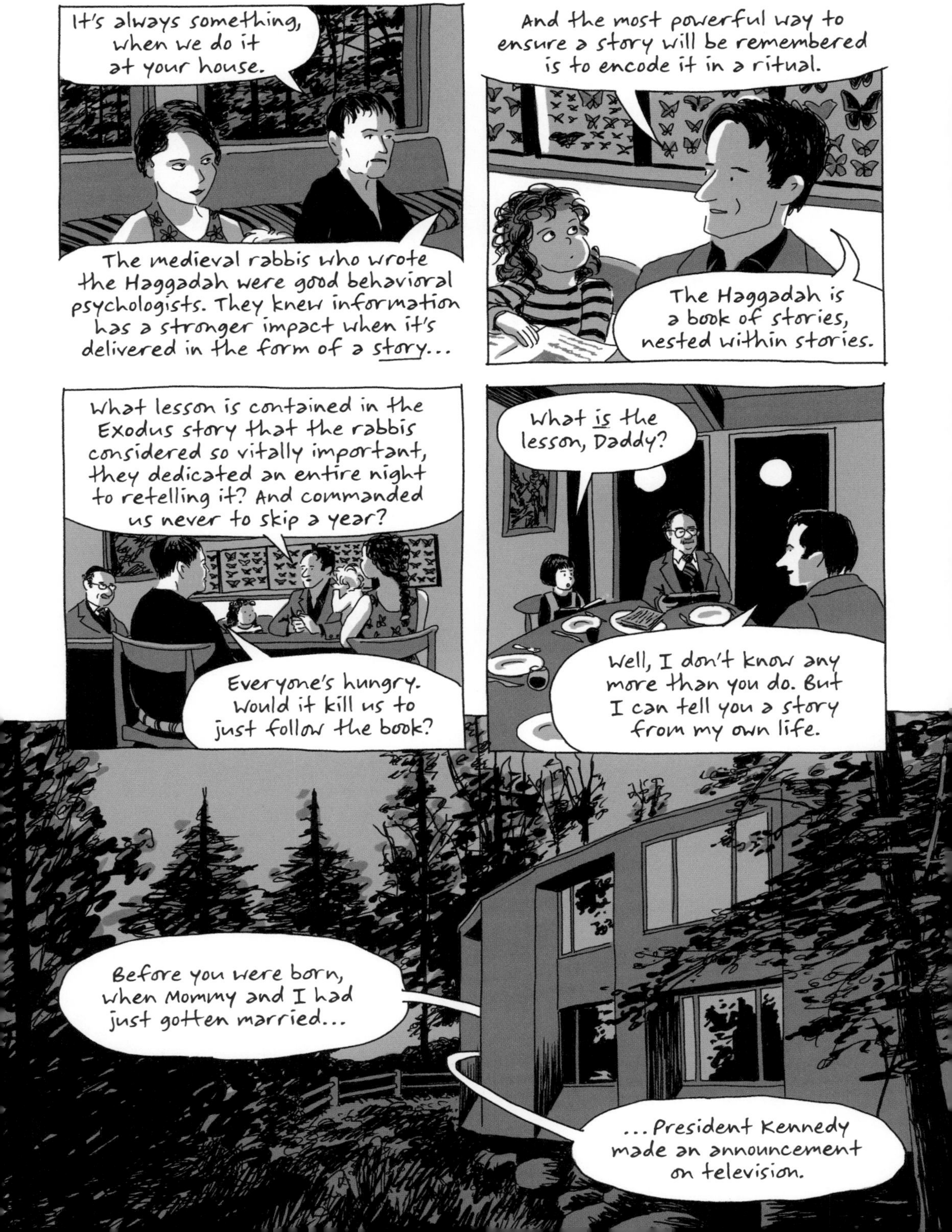
It's always something, when we do it at your house.
The medieval rabbis who wrote the Haggadah were good behavioral psychologists. They knew information has a stronger impact when it's delivered in the form of a story...
And the most powerful way to ensure a story will be remembered is to encode it in a ritual.
The Haggadah is a book of stories, nested within stories.
What lesson is contained in the Exodus story that the rabbis considered so vitally important, they dedicated an entire night to retelling it? And commanded us never to skip a year?
Everyone's hungry. Would it kill us to just follow the book?
What is the lesson, Daddy?
Well, I don't know any more than you do. But I can tell you a story from my own life.
Before you were born, when Mommy and I had just gotten married...
...President Kennedy made an announcement on television.

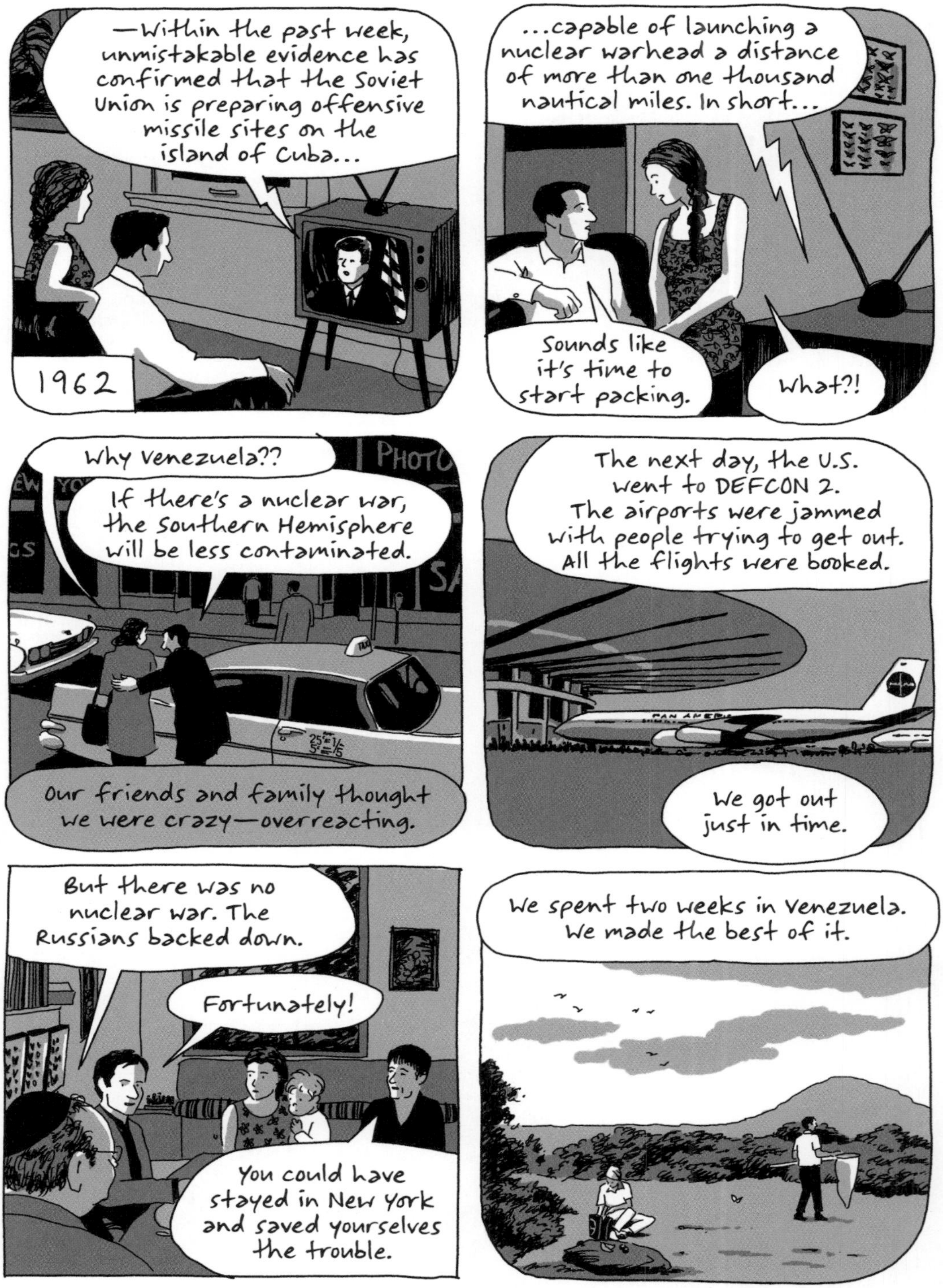
—Within the past week, unmistakable evidence has confirmed that the Soviet Union is preparing offensive missile sites on the island of Cuba...
1962
...capable of launching a nuclear warhead a distance of more than one thousand nautical miles. In short...
Sounds like it's time to start packing.
What?!
Why Venezuela??
If there's a nuclear war, the Southern Hemisphere will be less contaminated.
PHOTO
Our friends and family thought we were crazy—overreacting.
The next day, the U.S. went to DEFCON 2. The airports were jammed with people trying to get out. All the flights were booked.
We got out just in time.
But there was no nuclear war. The Russians backed down.
Fortunately!
You could have stayed in New York and saved yourselves the trouble.
We spent two weeks in Venezuela. We made the best of it.

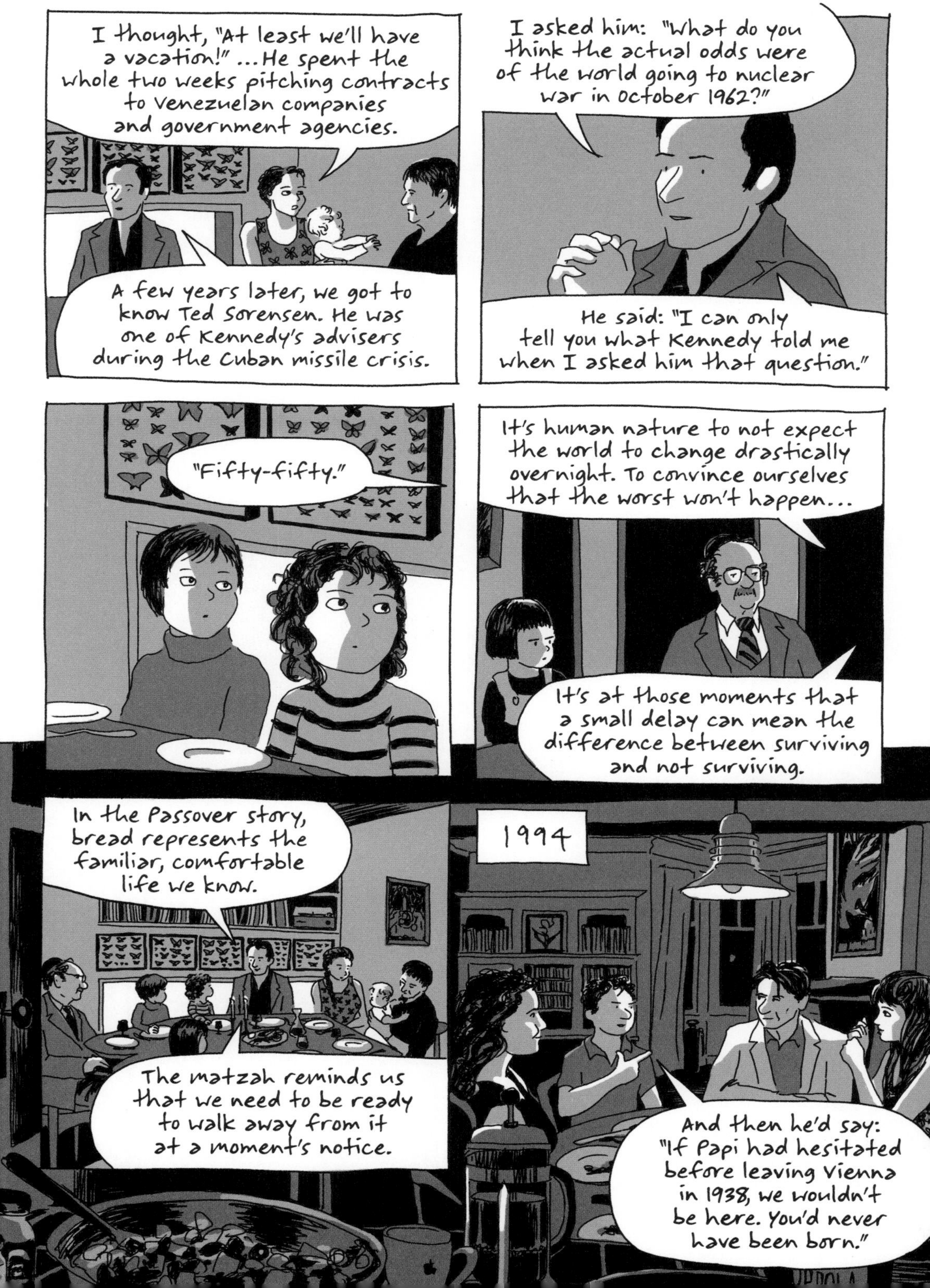
I thought, "At least we'll have a vacation!" ...He spent the whole two weeks pitching contracts to Venezuelan companies and government agencies.
A few years later, we got to know Ted Sorensen. He was one of Kennedy's advisers during the Cuban missile crisis.
I asked him: "What do you think the actual odds were of the world going to nuclear war in October 1962?"
He said: "I can only tell you what Kennedy told me when I asked him that question."
"Fifty-fifty."
It's human nature to not expect the world to change drastically overnight. To convince ourselves that the worst won't happen...
It's at those moments that a small delay can mean the difference between surviving and not surviving.
In the Passover story, bread represents the familiar, comfortable life we know.
The matzah reminds us that we need to be ready to walk away from it at a moment's notice.
1994
And then he'd say: "If Papi had hesitated before leaving Vienna in 1938, we wouldn't be here. You'd never have been born."

Bread

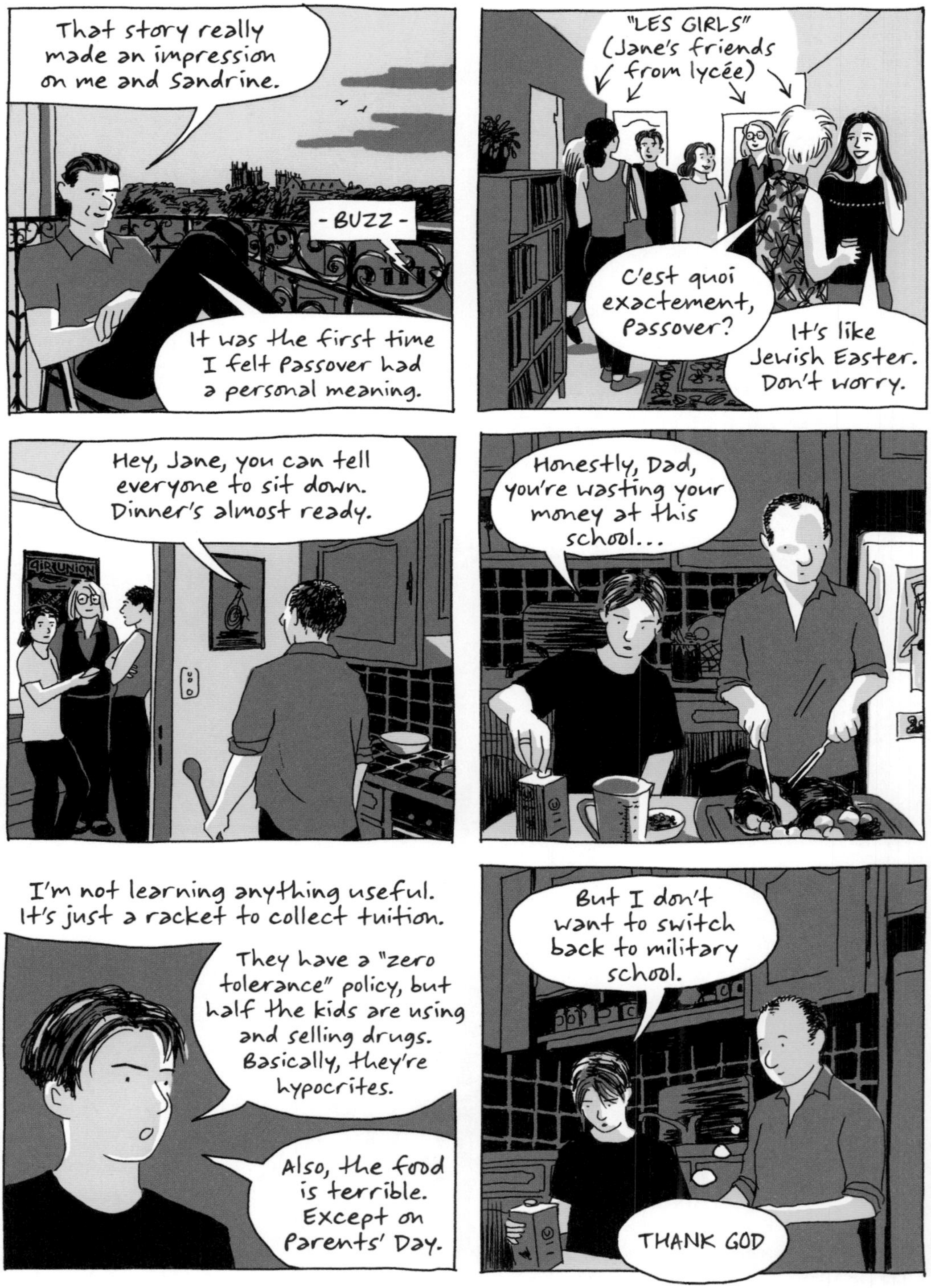
That story really made an impression on me and Sandrine.
-BUZZ-
It was the first time I felt Passover had a personal meaning.
"LES GIRLS" (Jane's friends from lycée)
C'est quoi exactement, Passover?
It's like Jewish Easter. Don't worry.
Hey, Jane, you can tell everyone to sit down. Dinner's almost ready.
Honestly, Dad, you're wasting your money at this school...
I'm not learning anything useful. It's just a racket to collect tuition.
They have a "zero tolerance" policy, but half the kids are using and selling drugs. Basically, they're hypocrites.
Also, the food is terrible. Except on Parents' Day.
But I don't want to switch back to military school.
THANK GOD

It feels good being back here.

Maybe I could come in the summer... Like, for a month?

First, we light the candles. The light symbolizes life, knowledge, and learning...

Then we raise our wine cups in gratitude for nature's bounty, the fruit of the vine.

Next, we eat a sprig of parsley— symbol of spring and new growth.

You dip it in salt water.

Sérieux?

Dip it twice. We'll ask why in a minute...

The matzah comes next, Dad. You don't need the book to tell you that.

I'm just double-checking to make sure I don't skip a step...

The broken piece is the "afikomen." He's going to hide it.

And we have to look for it.

SNAP

Oh, like Easter eggs!

Now, the matzah!

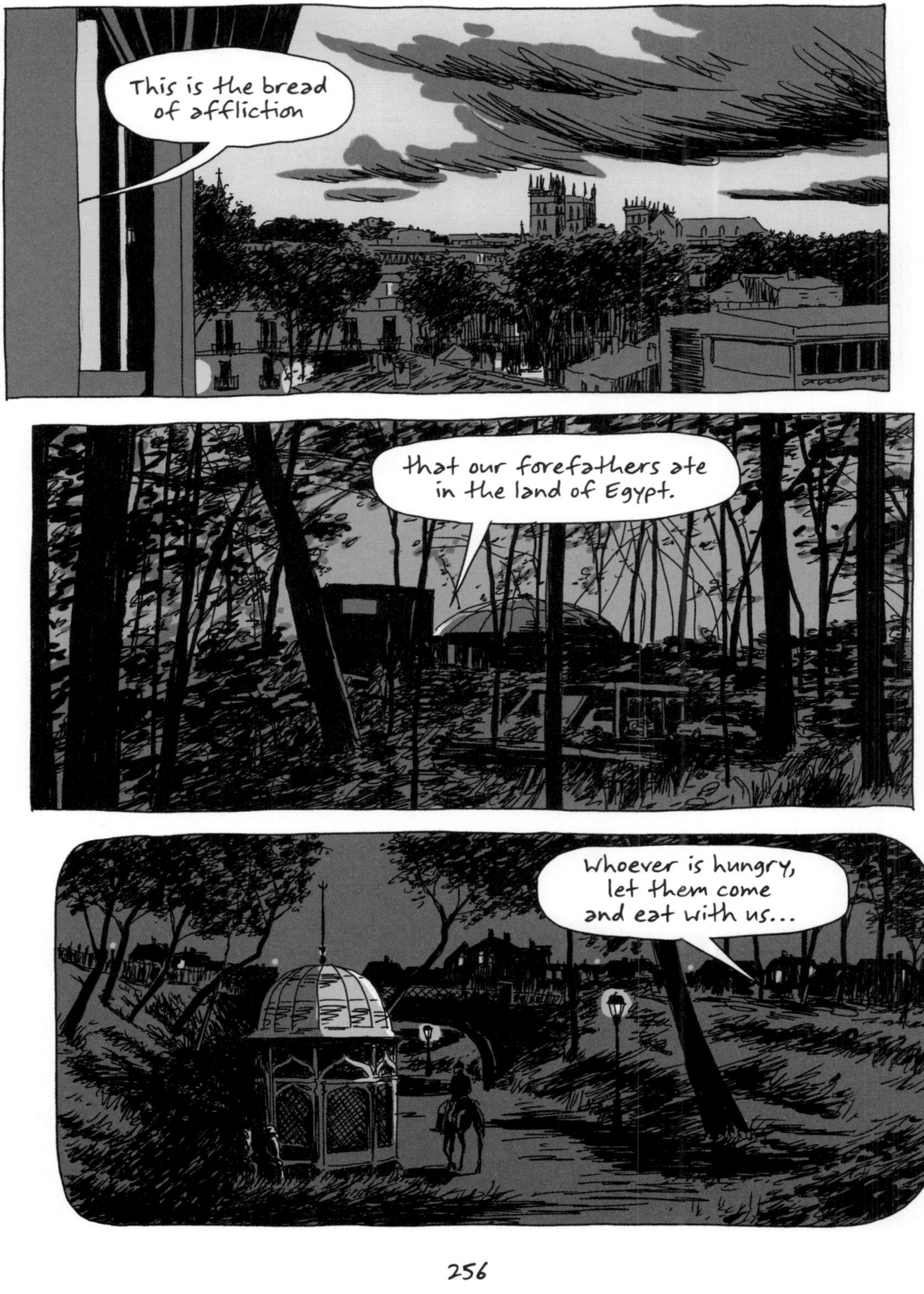
This is the bread of affliction
that our forefathers ate in the land of Egypt.
Whoever is hungry, let them come and eat with us...

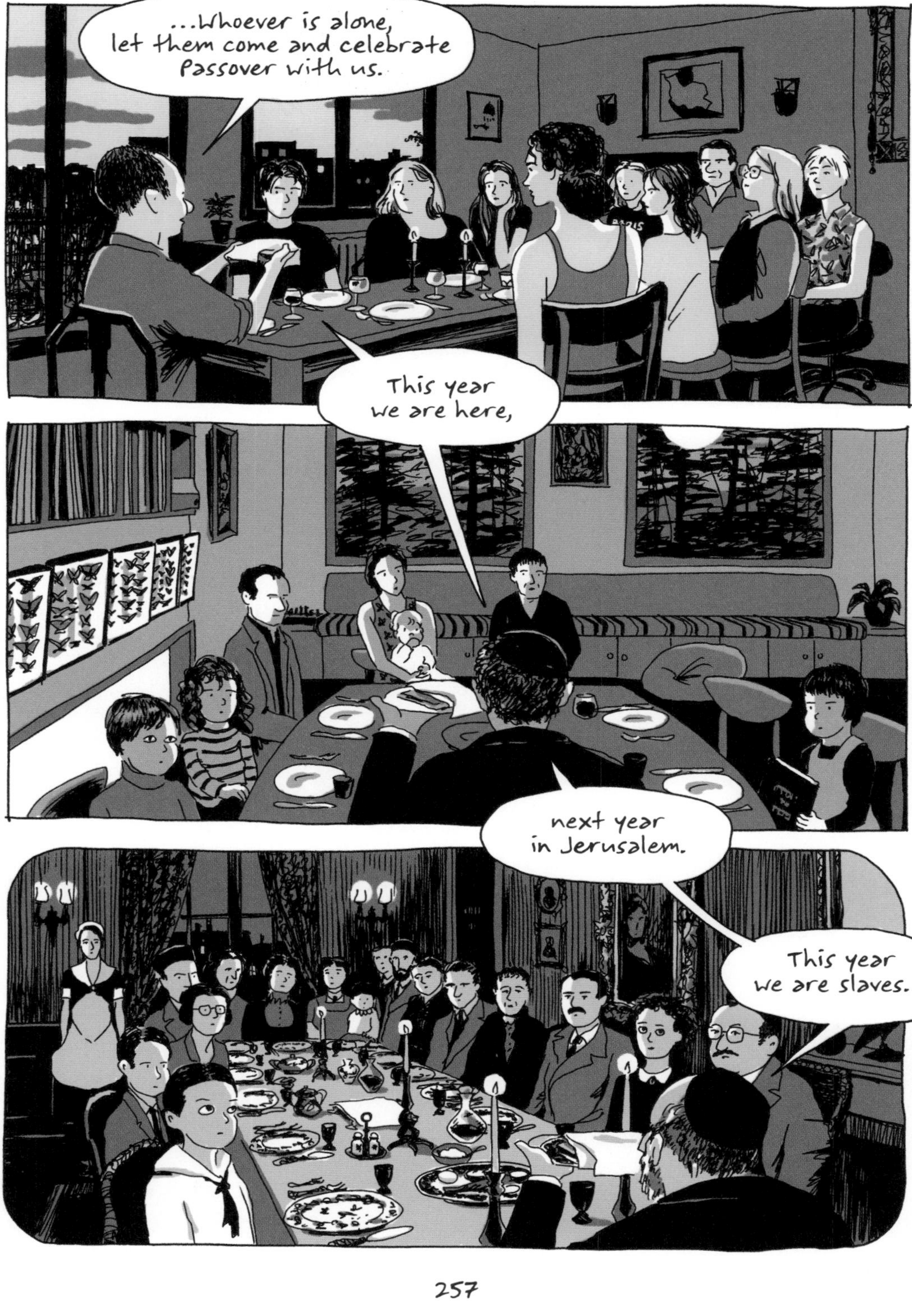
...Whoever is alone, let them come and celebrate Passover with us.
This year we are here,
next year in Jerusalem.
This year we are slaves...

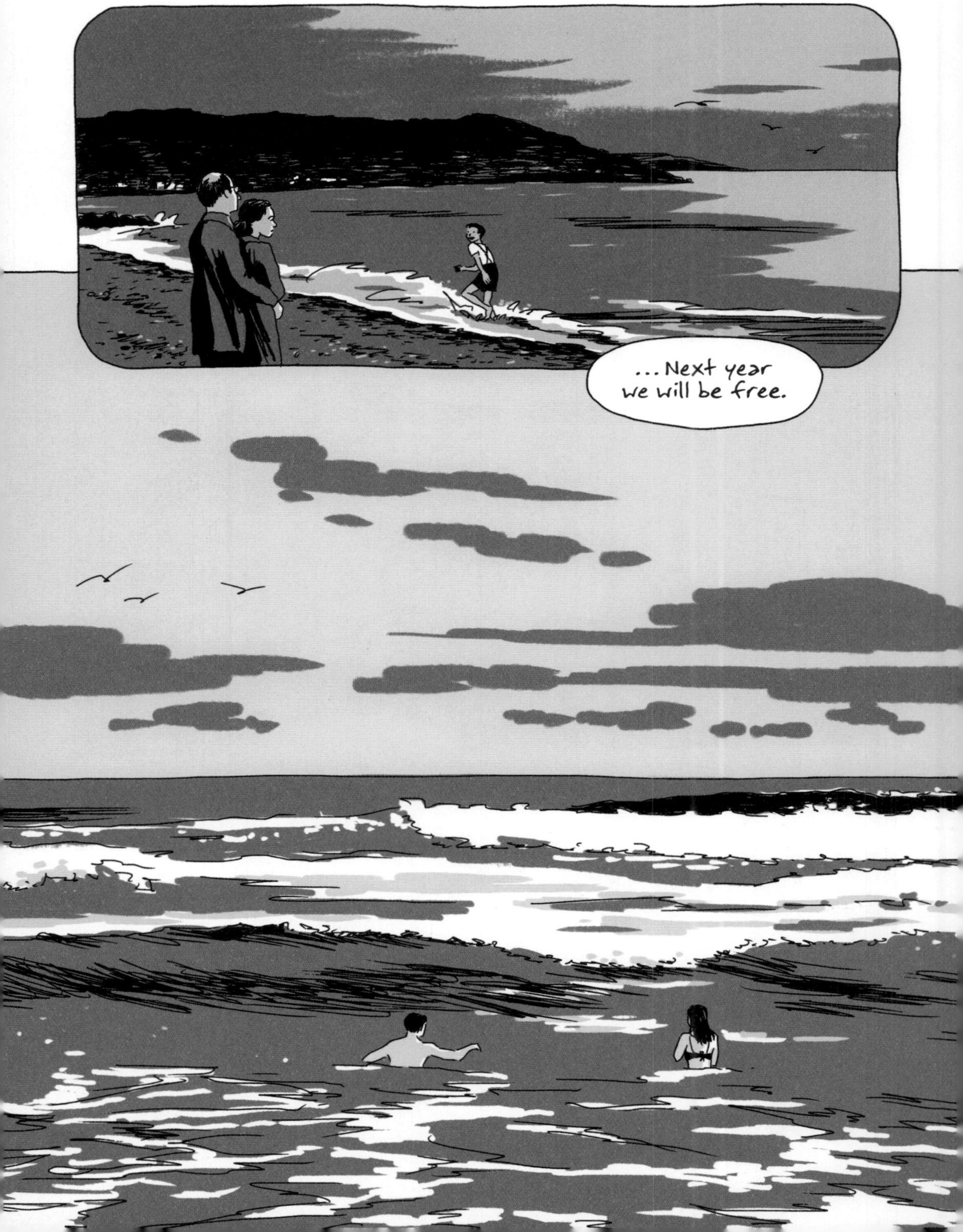
...Next year we will be free.

Chapter 8

Arriving

Benjamin and Regina Ziegler
Vienna, 1938

Lisa died in February 1995. Her memorial service was in New York.

I missed it.

After three years in production, "The Last Express" was two years behind schedule.

San Francisco 1996

I'd spent all my "Prince of Persia" royalties and run through our publisher advances.

The payroll I was struggling to meet every two weeks included my best friends. We were on board this runaway train together.

Patrick ran the 3D graphics department. His girlfriend, Sandrine, had moved from France to be with him.

ALWEN who will be 22 in 2018

Robert, my programmer pal from Brøderbund Apple II days, was technical director.

Two babies born so far, and we're not even in beta!

Tomi co-wrote the script with me.

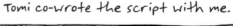

PARIS EST

1/43

A.F.A.C

un train cache l'autre!

261

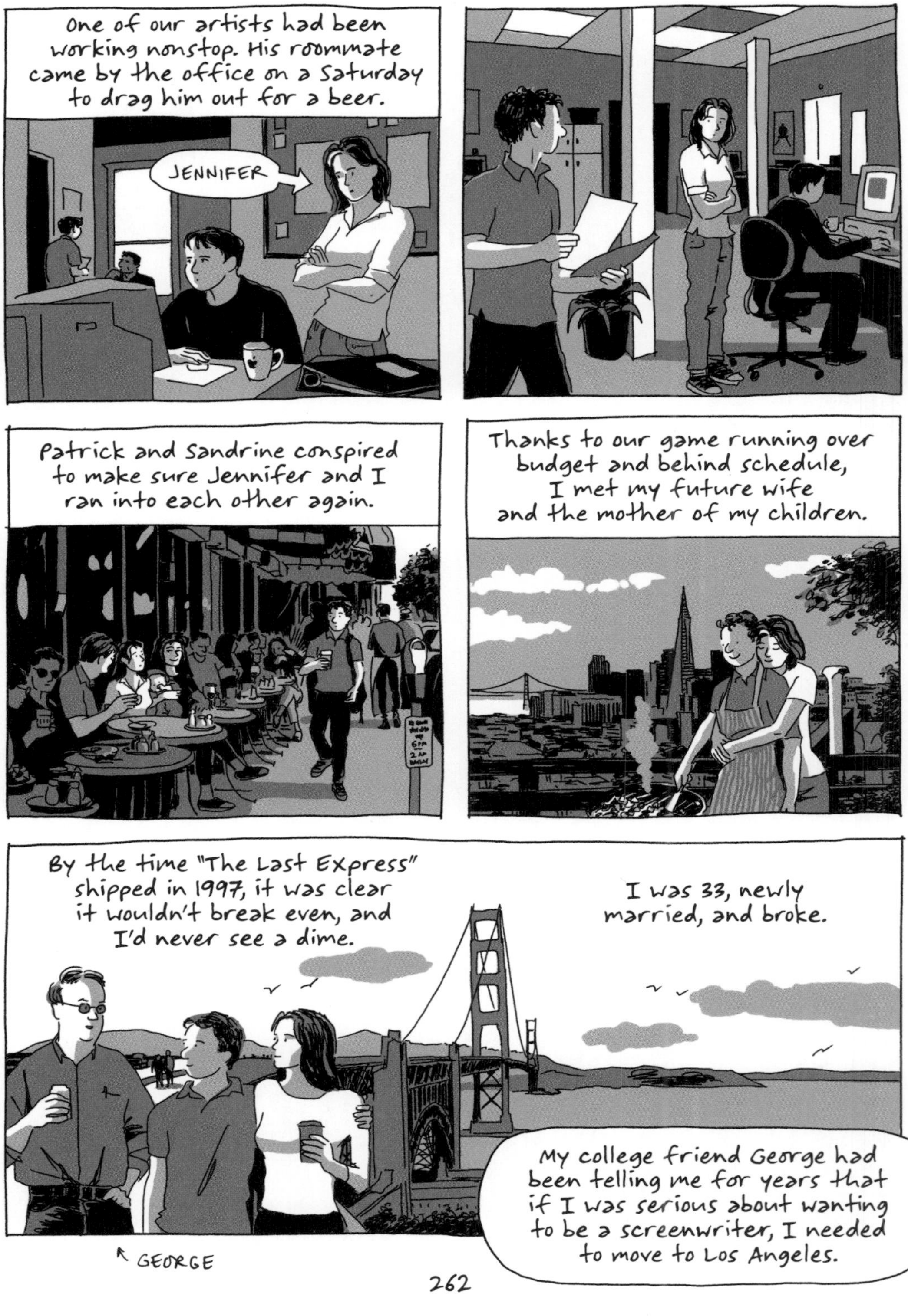
One of our artists had been working nonstop. His roommate came by the office on a Saturday to drag him out for a beer.
JENNIFER
Patrick and Sandrine conspired to make sure Jennifer and I ran into each other again.
Thanks to our game running over budget and behind schedule, I met my future wife and the mother of my children.
By the time "The Last Express" shipped in 1997, it was clear it wouldn't break even, and I'd never see a dime.
I was 33, newly married, and broke.
My college friend George had been telling me for years that if I was serious about wanting to be a screenwriter, I needed to move to Los Angeles.
GEORGE

Dagger

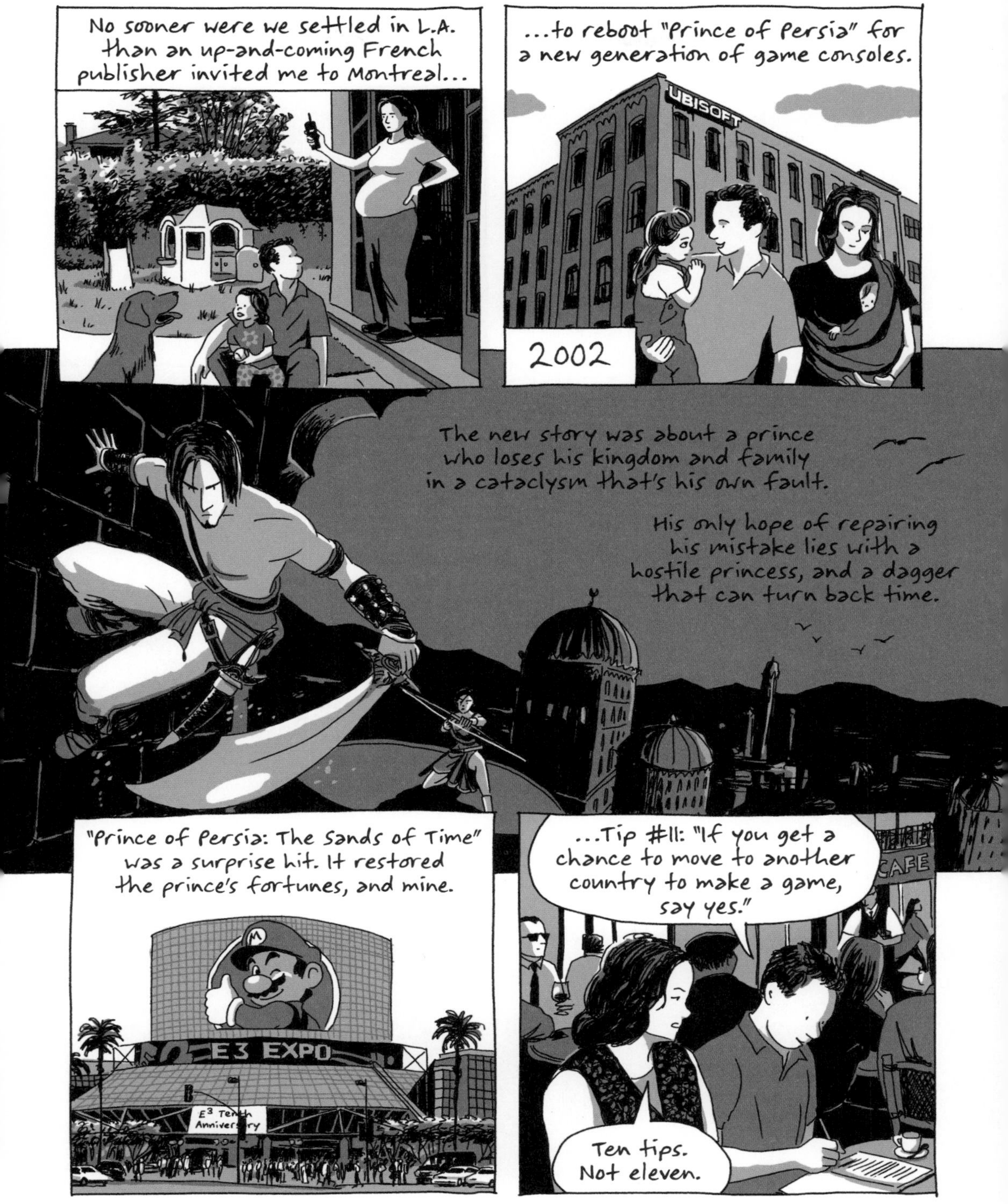
No sooner were we settled in L.A. than an up-and-coming French publisher invited me to Montreal...
...to reboot "Prince of Persia" for a new generation of game consoles.
UBISOFT
2002
The new story was about a prince who loses his kingdom and family in a cataclysm that's his own fault.
His only hope of repairing his mistake lies with a hostile princess, and a dagger that can turn back time.
"Prince of Persia: The Sands of Time" was a surprise hit. It restored the prince's fortunes, and mine.
E3 EXPO
...Tip #11: "If you get a chance to move to another country to make a game, say yes."
CAFE
Ten tips. Not eleven.

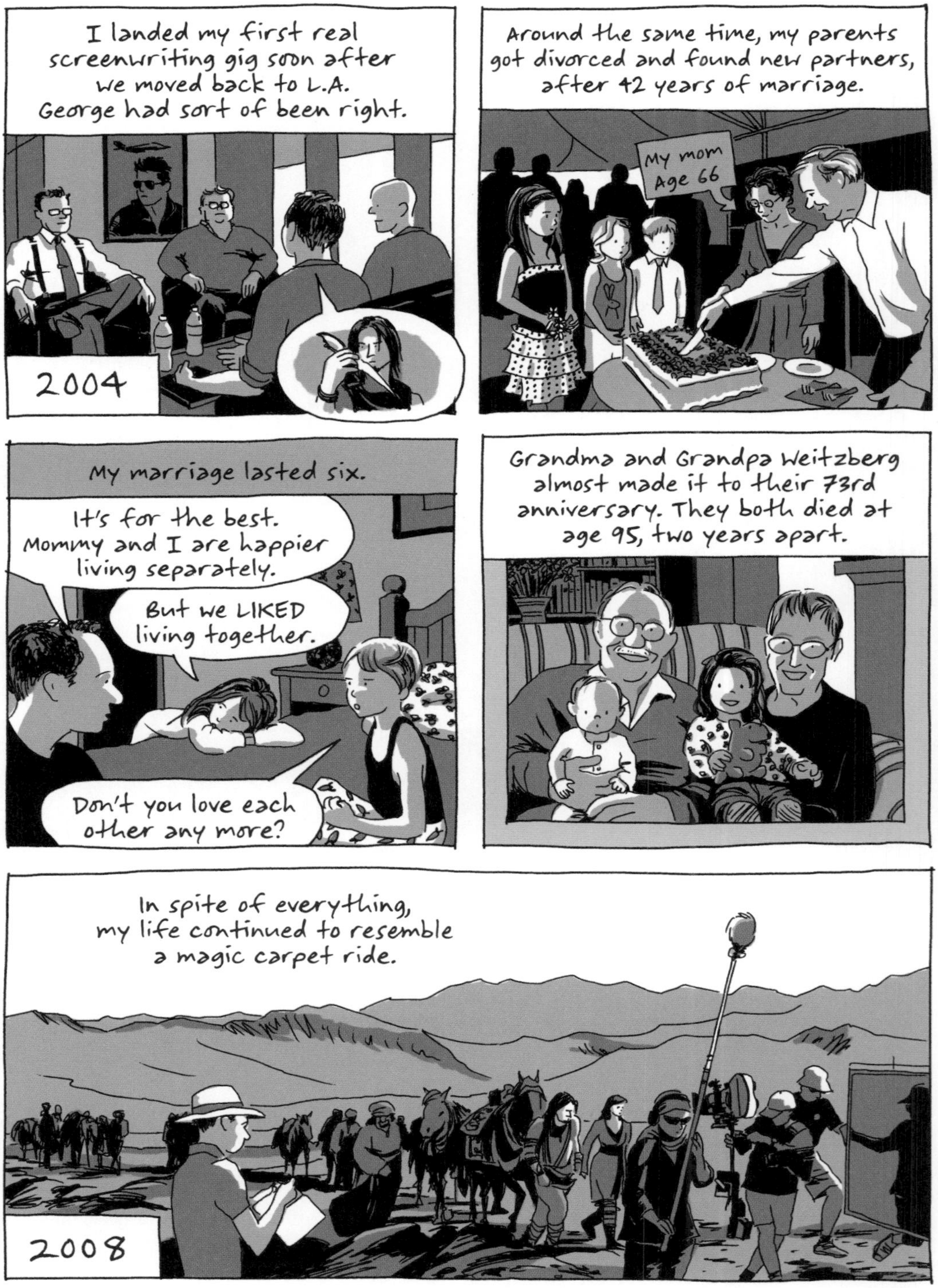

I landed my first real screenwriting gig soon after we moved back to L.A. George had sort of been right.
2004
Around the same time, my parents got divorced and found new partners, after 42 years of marriage.
My mom Age 66
My marriage lasted six.
It's for the best. Mommy and I are happier living separately.
But we LIKED living together.
Don't you love each other any more?
Grandma and Grandpa Weitzberg almost made it to their 73rd anniversary. They both died at age 95, two years apart.
In spite of everything, my life continued to resemble a magic carpet ride.
2008

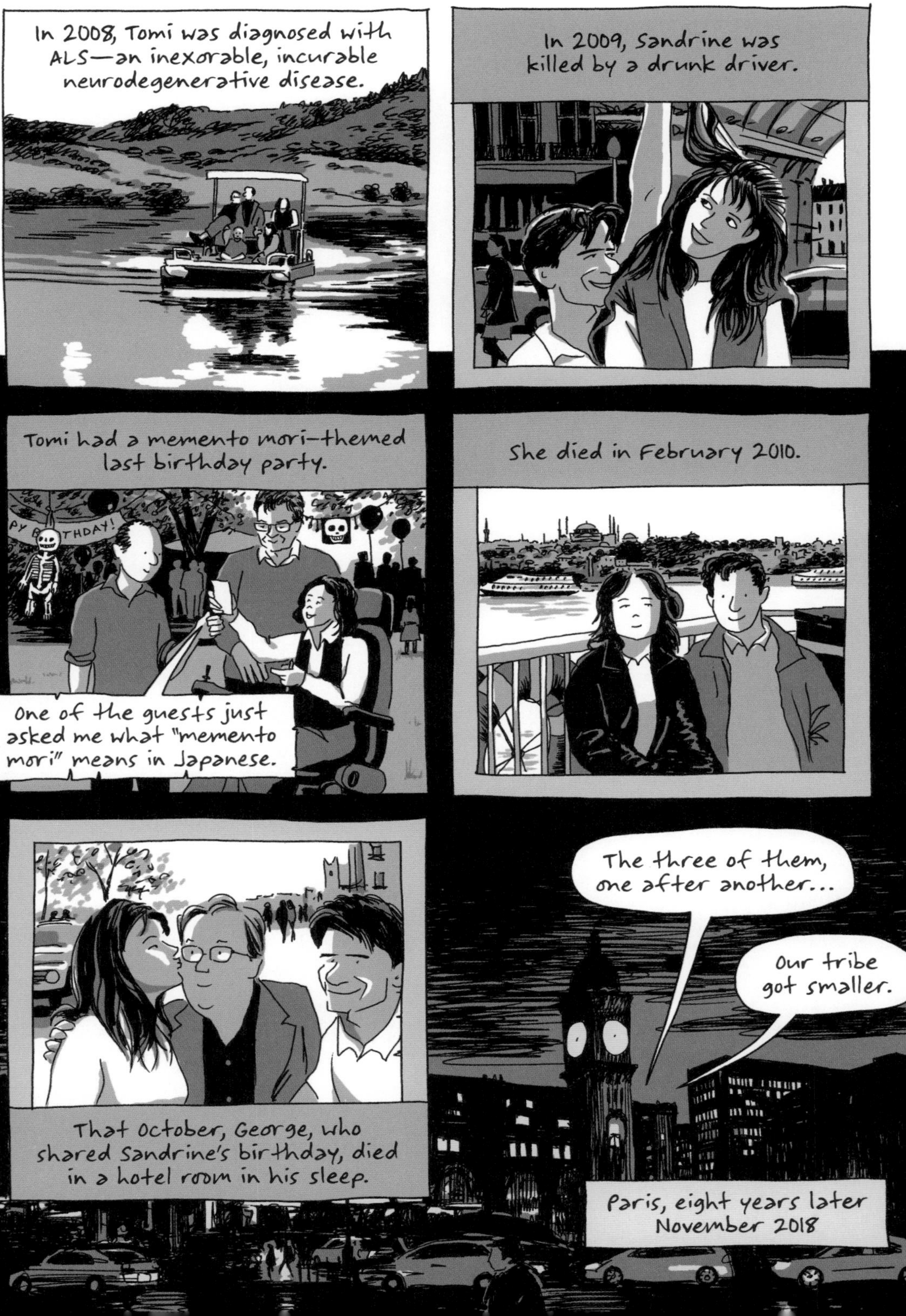
In 2008, Tomi was diagnosed with ALS—an inexorable, incurable neurodegenerative disease.
In 2009, Sandrine was killed by a drunk driver.
Tomi had a memento mori–themed last birthday party.
PY B THDAY!
One of the guests just asked me what "memento mori" means in Japanese.
She died in February 2010.
That October, George, who shared Sandrine's birthday, died in a hotel room in his sleep.
The three of them, one after another...
Our tribe got smaller.
Paris, eight years later
November 2018

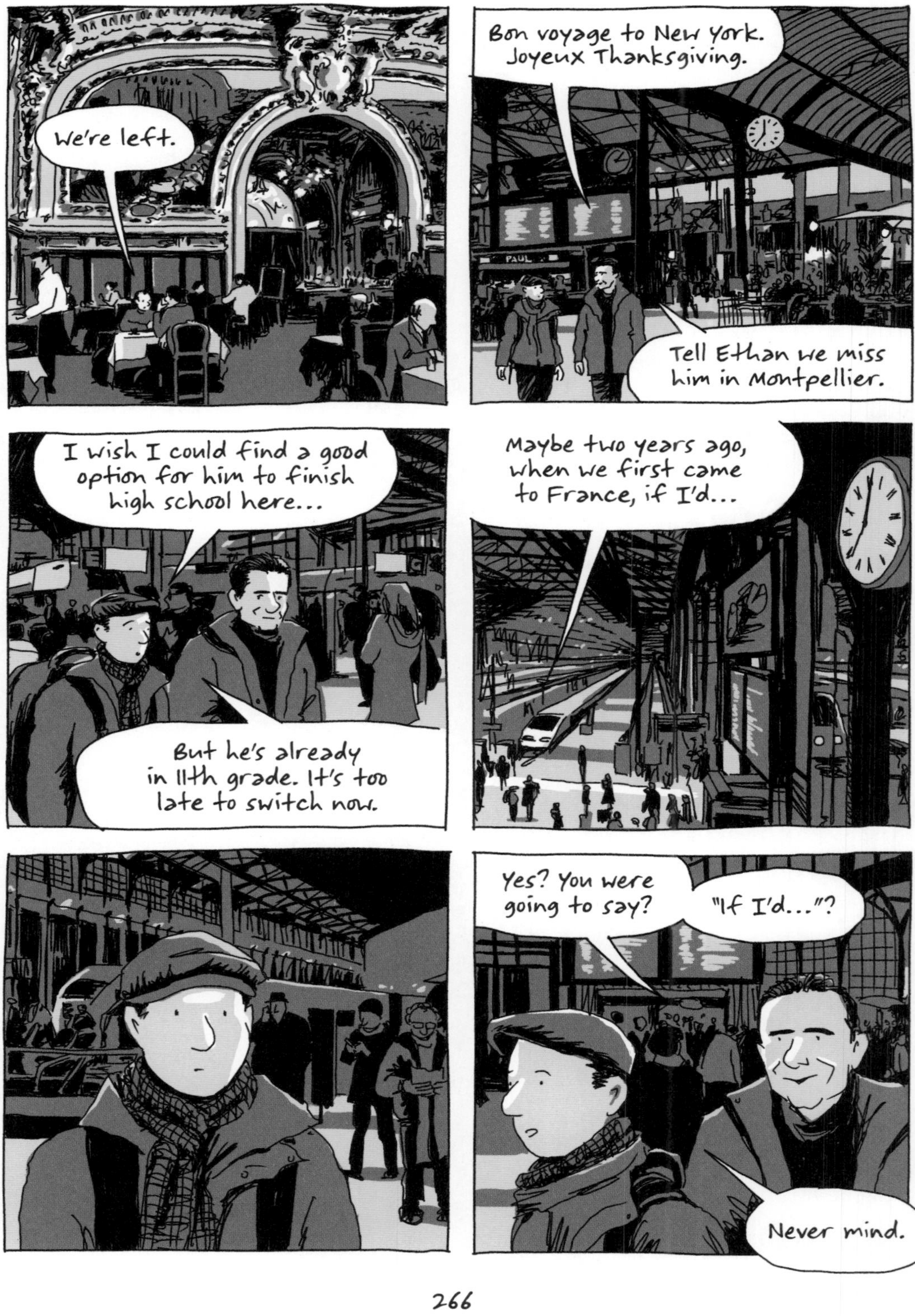
We're left.
Bon voyage to New York. Joyeux Thanksgiving.
Tell Ethan we miss him in Montpellier.
I wish I could find a good option for him to finish high school here...
But he's already in 11th grade. It's too late to switch now.
Maybe two years ago, when we first came to France, if I'd...
Yes? You were going to say?
"If I'd..."?
Never mind.

Grandfather

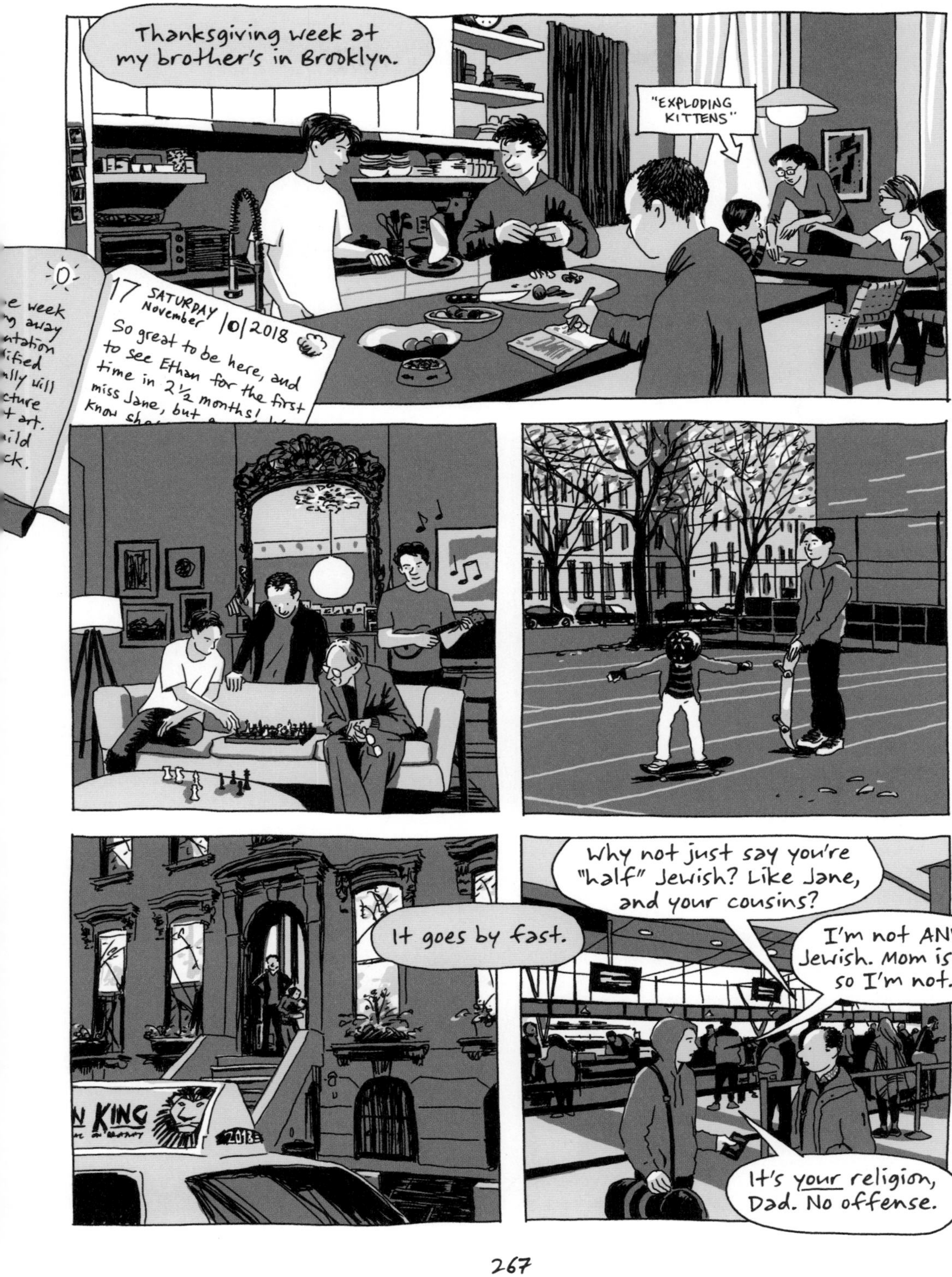
Thanksgiving week at my brother's in Brooklyn.
"EXPLODING KITTENS"
17 SATURDAY November |0| 2018
So great to be here, and to see Ethan for the first time in 2½ months! miss Jane, but
It goes by fast.
Why not just say you're "half" Jewish? Like Jane, and your cousins?
I'm not ANY Jewish. Mom isn't, so I'm not.
It's your religion, Dad. No offense.

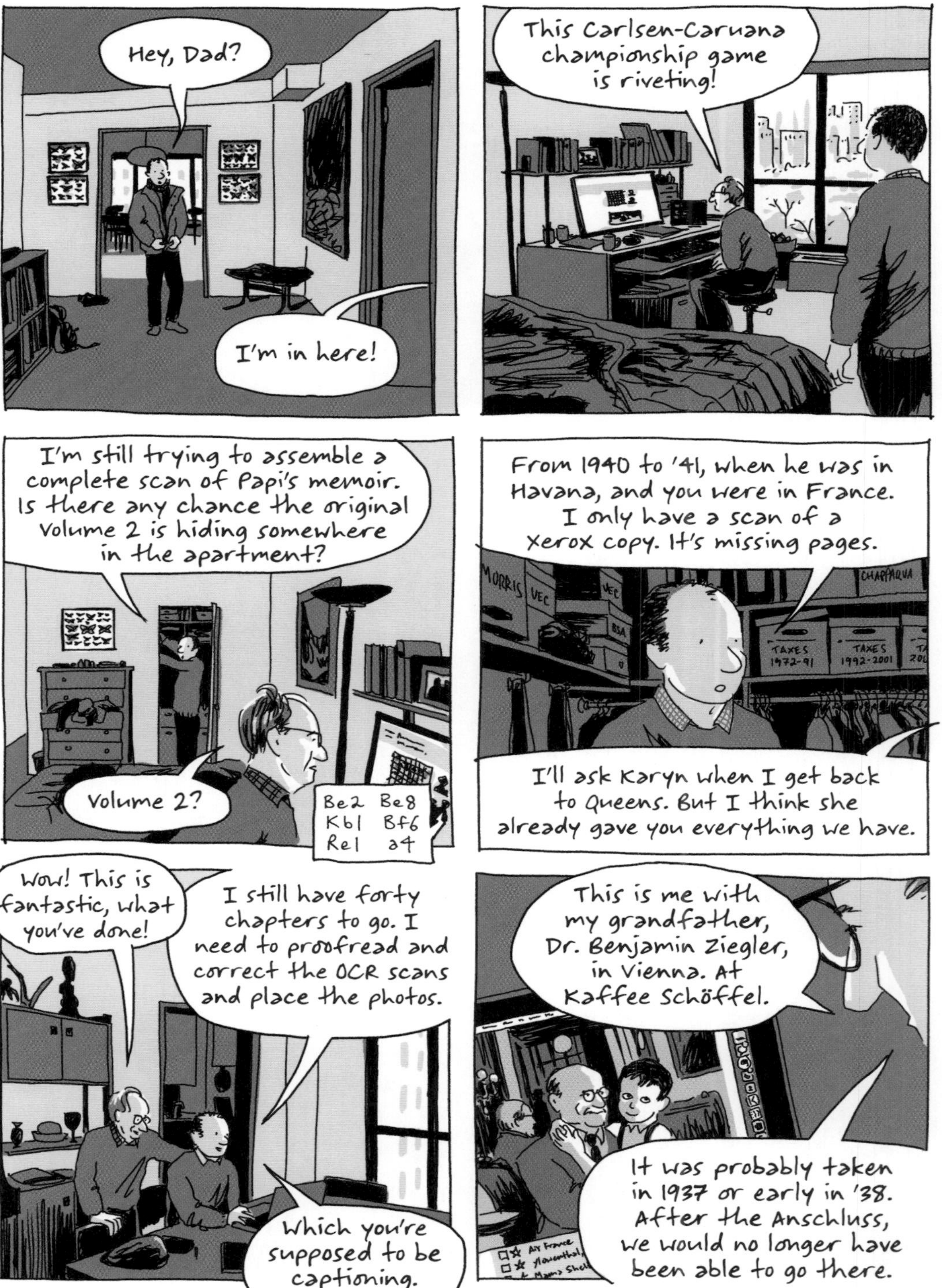

Hey, Dad?
I'm in here!
This Carlsen-Caruana championship game is riveting!
I'm still trying to assemble a complete scan of Papi's memoir. Is there any chance the original Volume 2 is hiding somewhere in the apartment?
Volume 2?
Be2 Be8
Kb1 Bf6
Re1 a4
From 1940 to '41, when he was in Havana, and you were in France. I only have a scan of a Xerox copy. It's missing pages.
MORRIS
VEC
VEC
BSA
CHAPPAQUA
TAXES 1972-91
TAXES 1992-2001
I'll ask Karyn when I get back to Queens. But I think she already gave you everything we have.
Wow! This is fantastic, what you've done!
I still have forty chapters to go. I need to proofread and correct the OCR scans and place the photos.
Which you're supposed to be captioning. Remember?
This is me with my grandfather, Dr. Benjamin Ziegler, in Vienna. At Kaffee Schöffel.
It was probably taken in 1937 or early in '38. After the Anschluss, we would no longer have been able to go there.

He used to take me with him on house calls.

1937

And to coffeehouses where we would sit for hours with his friends.

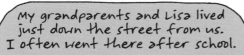

My grandparents and Lisa lived just down the street from us. I often went there after school.

Lisa, play the "Radetzky March"!

Again?!

Take your coat! It's freezing out!

Cold is good for the circulation.

Grandmother was twenty years younger than Grandfather.

With the chess and the Schöffel, you'll turn him into a coffeehouse bum!

She had 6 brothers and sisters and Grandfather had 17.

So my mother and Lisa had more than one hundred first cousins.

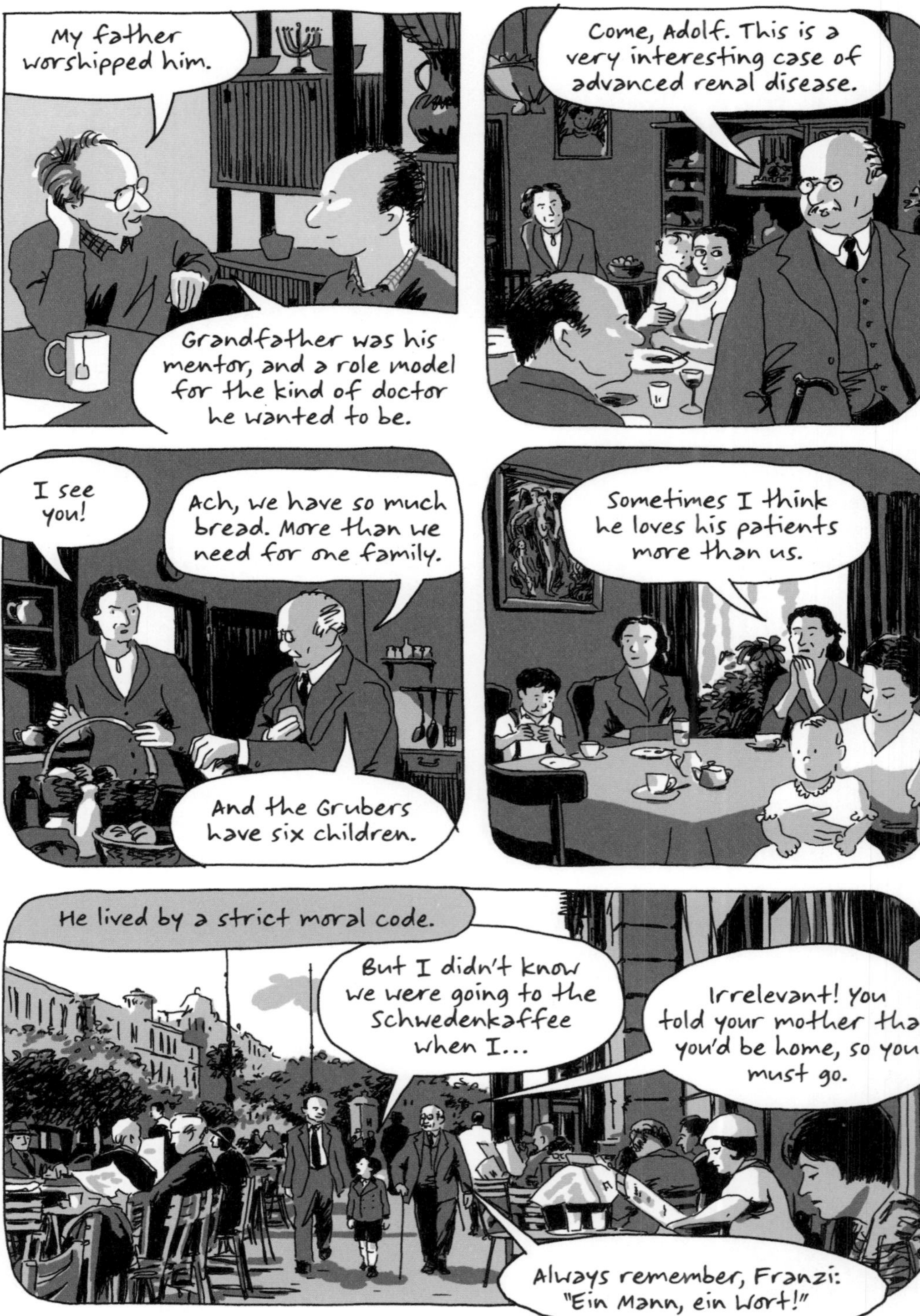
My father worshipped him.
Grandfather was his mentor, and a role model for the kind of doctor he wanted to be.
Come, Adolf. This is a very interesting case of advanced renal disease.
I see you!
Ach, we have so much bread. More than we need for one family.
And the Grubers have six children.
Sometimes I think he loves his patients more than us.
He lived by a strict moral code.
But I didn't know we were going to the Schwedenkaffee when I...
Irrelevant! You told your mother that you'd be home, so you must go.
Always remember, Franzi: "Ein Mann, ein Wort!"

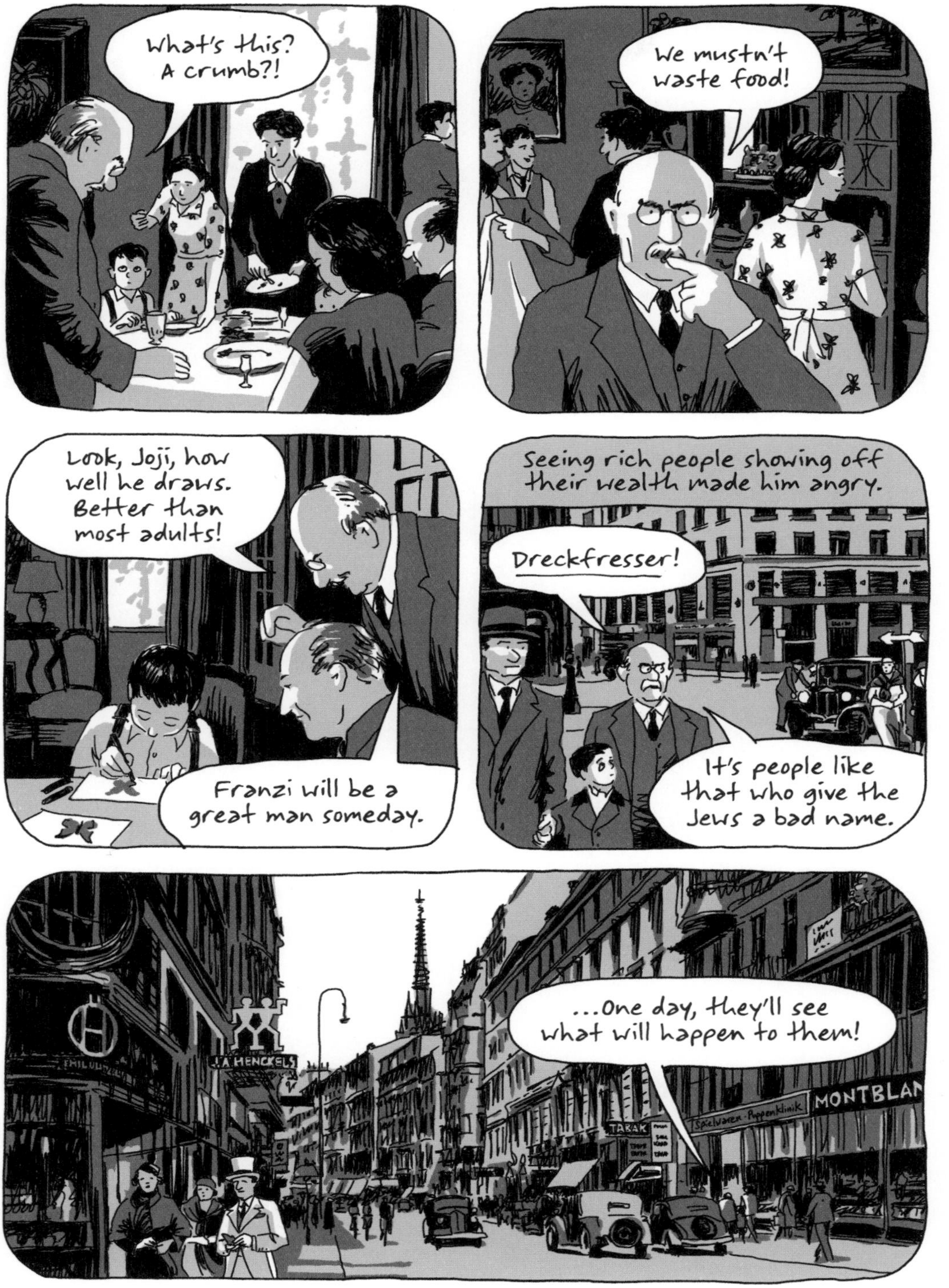
What's this? A crumb?!
We mustn't waste food!
Look, Joji, how well he draws. Better than most adults!
Franzi will be a great man someday.
Seeing rich people showing off their wealth made him angry.
Dreckfresser!
It's people like that who give the Jews a bad name.
J.A. HENCKELS
TABAK
Spielwaren-Puppenklinik
MONTBLAN
...One day, they'll see what will happen to them!

Schoolyard

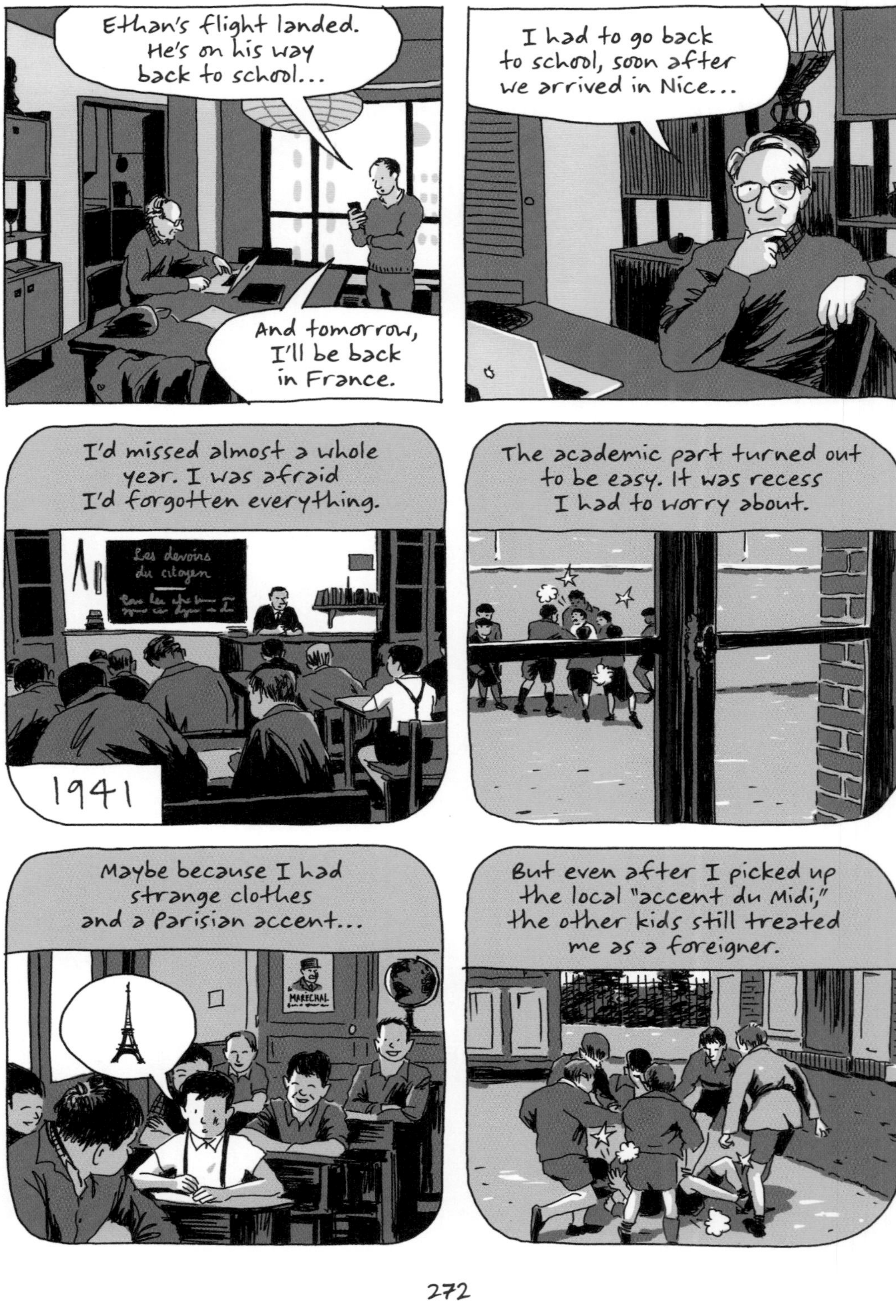

Ethan's flight landed. He's on his way back to school...
And tomorrow, I'll be back in France.
I had to go back to school, soon after we arrived in Nice...
I'd missed almost a whole year. I was afraid I'd forgotten everything.
Les devoirs du citoyen
1941
The academic part turned out to be easy. It was recess I had to worry about.
Maybe because I had strange clothes and a Parisian accent...
MARÉCHAL
But even after I picked up the local "accent du Midi," the other kids still treated me as a foreigner.

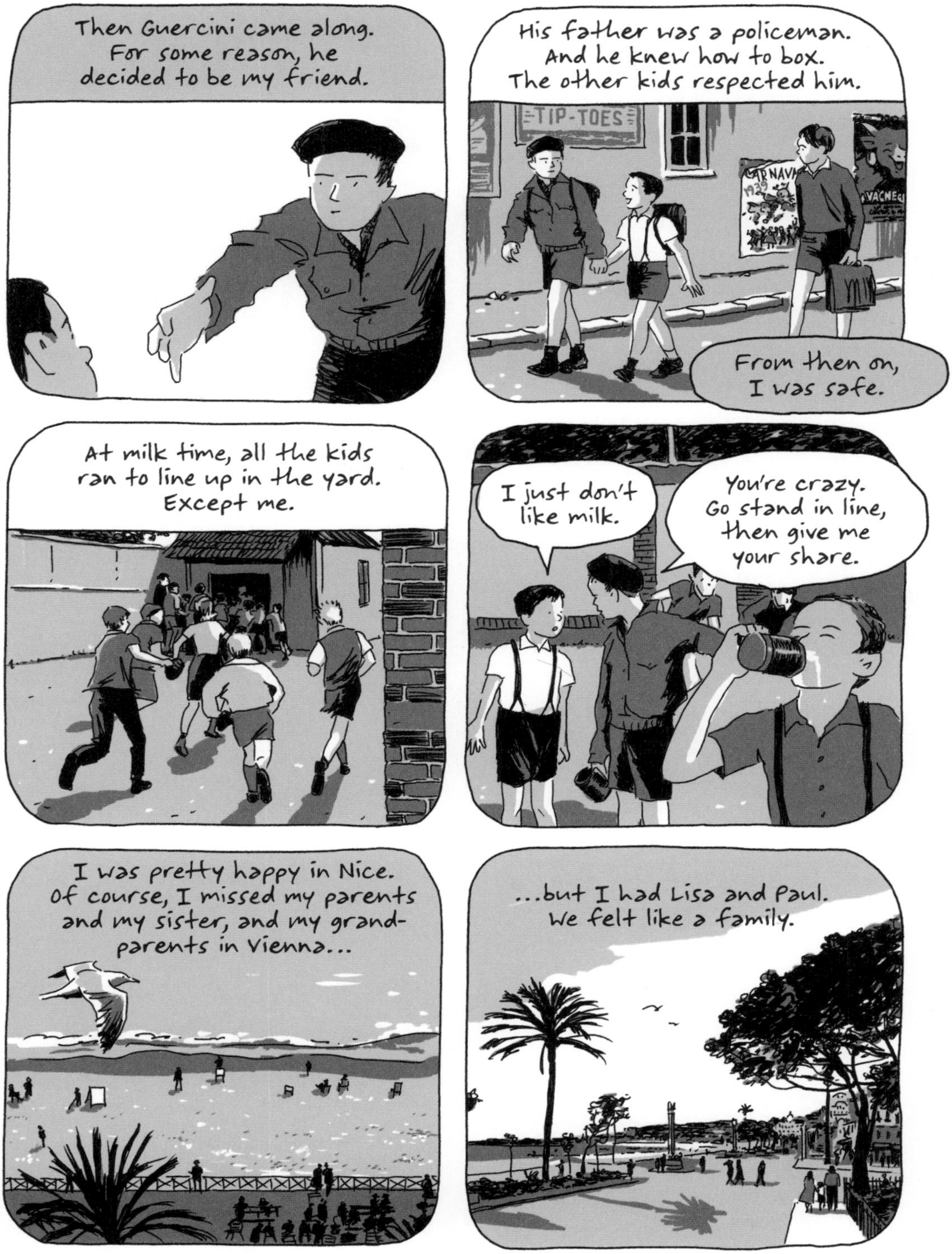
Then Guercini came along. For some reason, he decided to be my friend.
His father was a policeman. And he knew how to box. The other kids respected him.
TIP-TOES
From then on, I was safe.
At milk time, all the kids ran to line up in the yard. Except me.
I just don't like milk.
You're crazy. Go stand in line, then give me your share.
I was pretty happy in Nice. Of course, I missed my parents and my sister, and my grand-parents in Vienna...
...but I had Lisa and Paul. We felt like a family.

Motorcycle

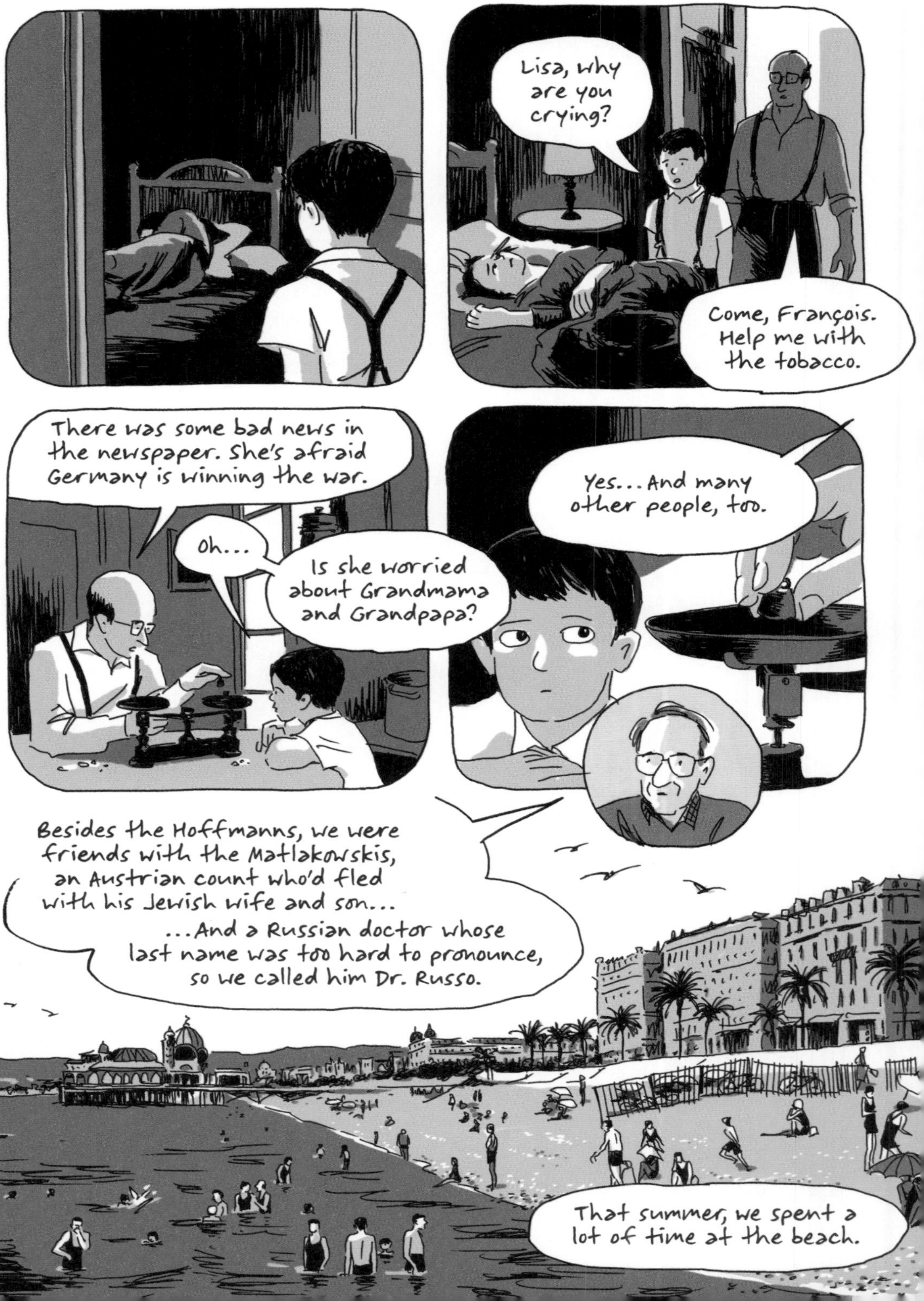
Lisa, why are you crying?
Come, François. Help me with the tobacco.
There was some bad news in the newspaper. She's afraid Germany is winning the war.
Oh...
Is she worried about Grandmama and Grandpapa?
Yes... And many other people, too.
Besides the Hoffmanns, we were friends with the Matlakowskis, an Austrian count who'd fled with his Jewish wife and son...
...And a Russian doctor whose last name was too hard to pronounce, so we called him Dr. Russo.
That summer, we spent a lot of time at the beach.

One day...

Another one.

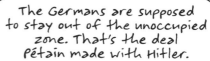

The Germans are supposed to stay out of the unoccupied zone. That's the deal Pétain made with Hitler.

There's nothing in the newspapers or on the radio.

One motorcycle... It might not mean anything.

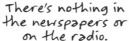

Two motorcycles.

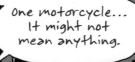

We've seen this before. In Le Touquet and La Bernerie. We know what comes next.

Nice is the end of the line. There's no place left for us to run to.

You're not saying anything helpful!

What should we do...

...sit here waiting for a miracle?

Extraction

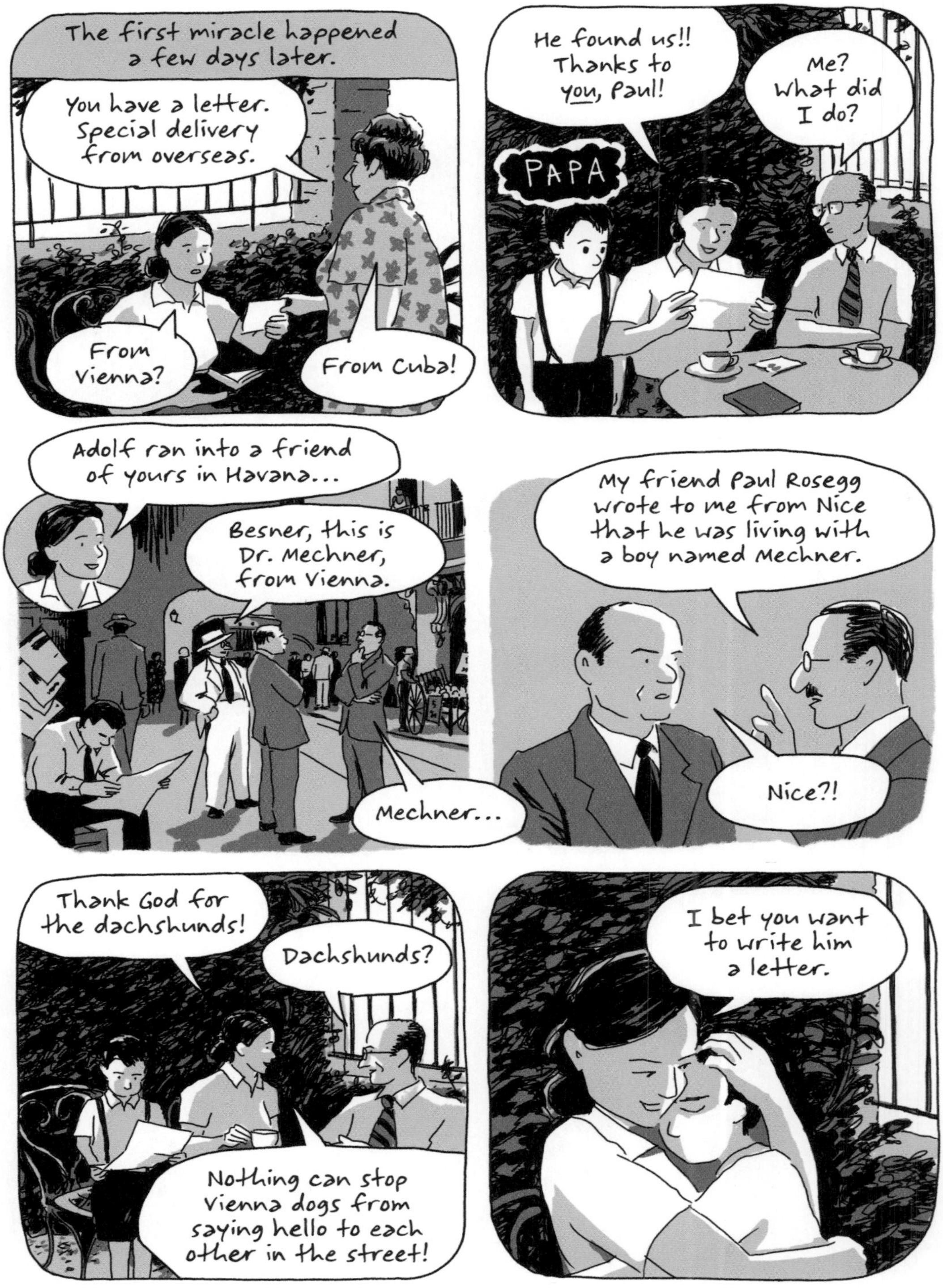

The first miracle happened a few days later.
You have a letter. Special delivery from overseas.
From Vienna?
From Cuba!
He found us!! Thanks to you, Paul!
PAPA
Me? What did I do?
Adolf ran into a friend of yours in Havana...
Besner, this is Dr. Mechner, from Vienna.
Mechner...
My friend Paul Rosegg wrote to me from Nice that he was living with a boy named Mechner.
Nice?!
Thank God for the dachshunds!
Dachshunds?
Nothing can stop Vienna dogs from saying hello to each other in the street!
I bet you want to write him a letter.

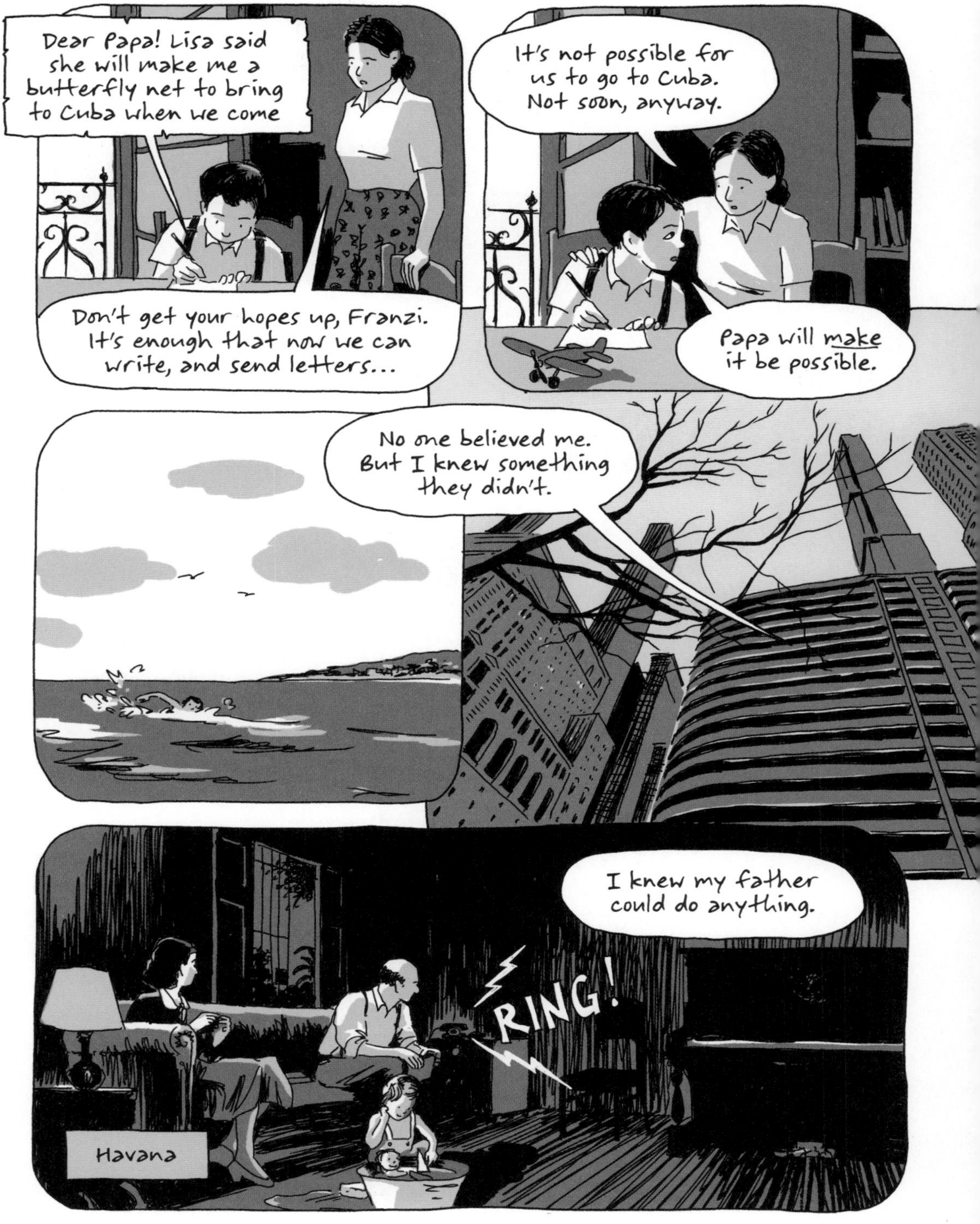
Dear Papa! Lisa said she will make me a butterfly net to bring to Cuba when we come
Don't get your hopes up, Franzi. It's enough that now we can write, and send letters...
It's not possible for us to go to Cuba. Not soon, anyway.
Papa will make it be possible.
No one believed me. But I knew something they didn't.
I knew my father could do anything.
RING!
Havana

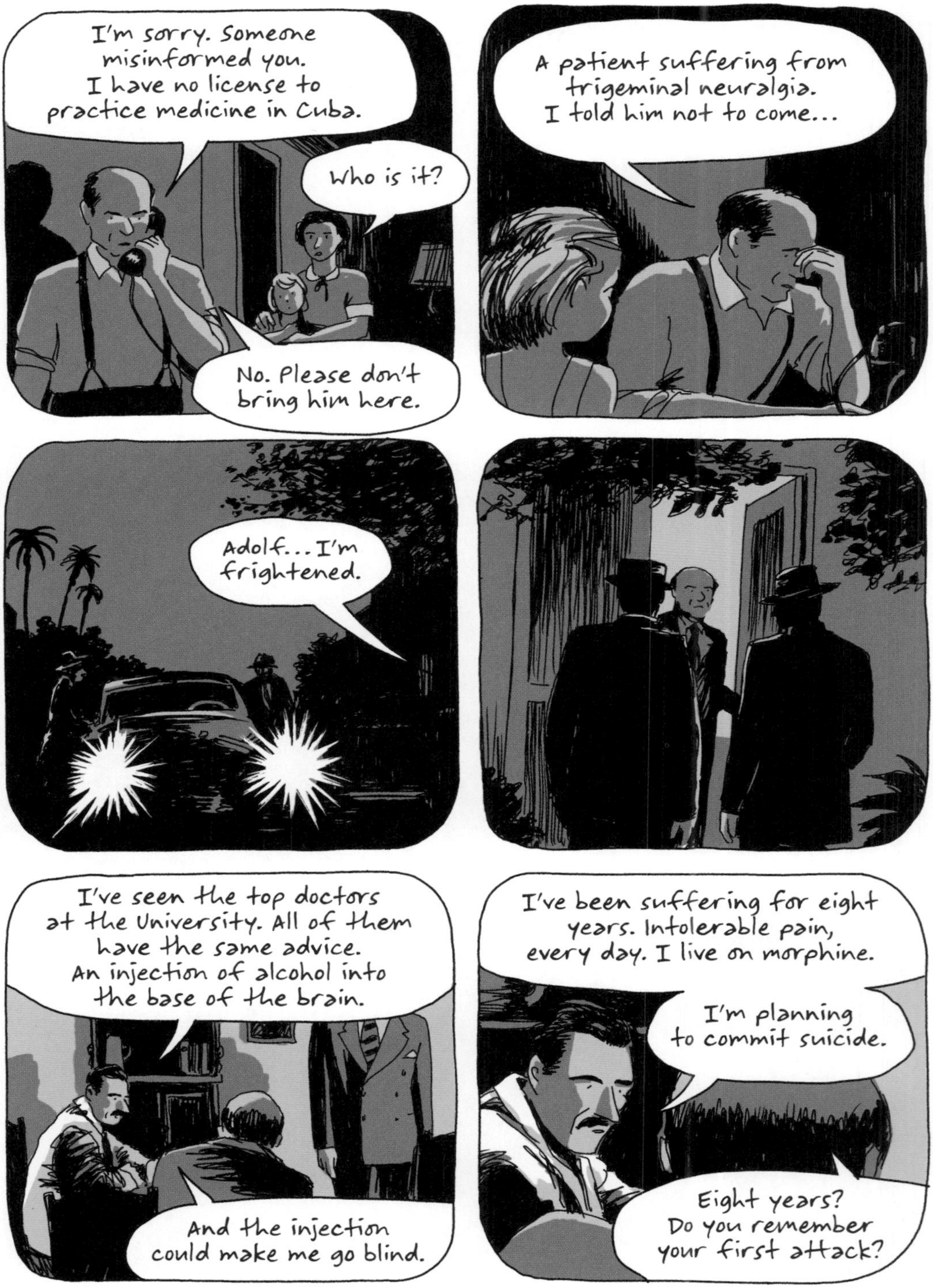
I'm sorry. Someone misinformed you. I have no license to practice medicine in Cuba.
Who is it?
No. Please don't bring him here.
A patient suffering from trigeminal neuralgia. I told him not to come...
Adolf... I'm frightened.
I've seen the top doctors at the University. All of them have the same advice. An injection of alcohol into the base of the brain.
And the injection could make me go blind.
I've been suffering for eight years. Intolerable pain, every day. I live on morphine.
I'm planning to commit suicide.
Eight years? Do you remember your first attack?

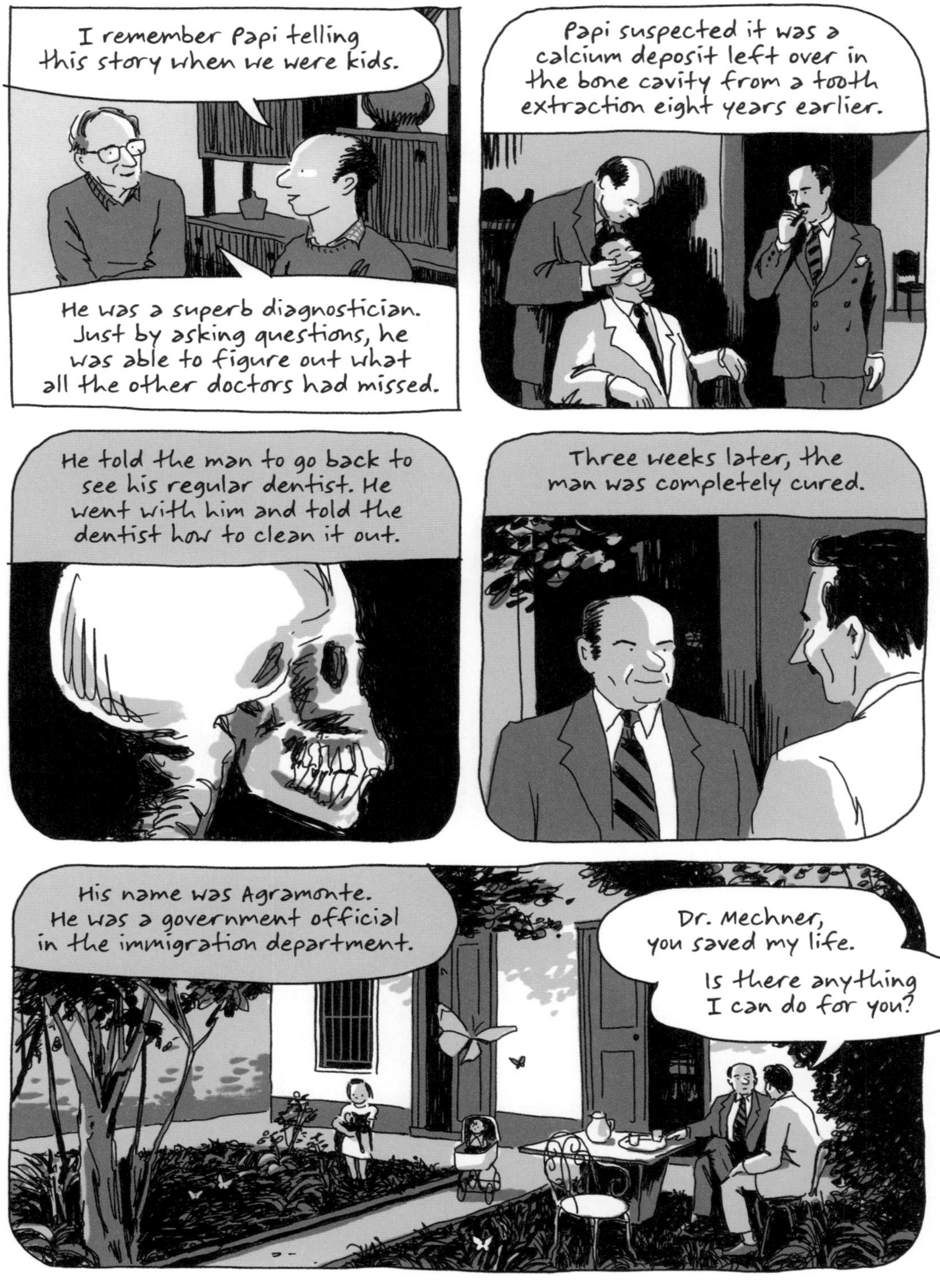
I remember Papi telling this story when we were kids.
He was a superb diagnostician. Just by asking questions, he was able to figure out what all the other doctors had missed.
Papi suspected it was a calcium deposit left over in the bone cavity from a tooth extraction eight years earlier.
He told the man to go back to see his regular dentist. He went with him and told the dentist how to clean it out.
Three weeks later, the man was completely cured.
His name was Agramonte. He was a government official in the immigration department.
Dr. Mechner, you saved my life.
Is there anything I can do for you?

Last Boat

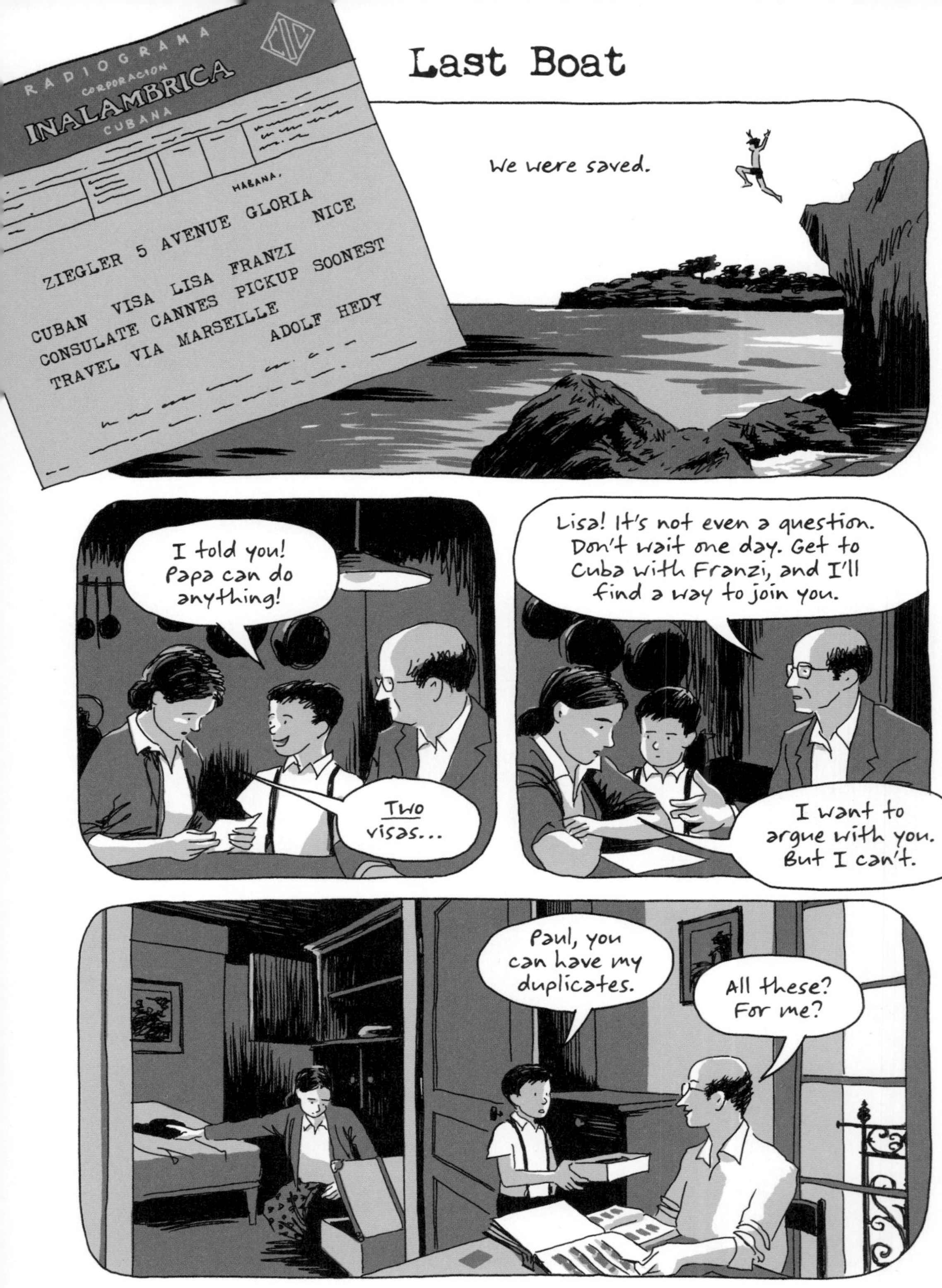

RADIOGRAMA
CORPORACION
INALAMBRICA
CUBANA
HABANA.
ZIEGLER 5 AVENUE GLORIA NICE
CUBAN VISA LISA FRANZI
CONSULATE CANNES PICKUP SOONEST
TRAVEL VIA MARSEILLE
ADOLF HEDY
We were saved.
I told you! Papa can do anything!
Two visas...
Lisa! It's not even a question. Don't wait one day. Get to Cuba with Franzi, and I'll find a way to join you.
I want to argue with you. But I can't.
Paul, you can have my duplicates.
All these? For me?

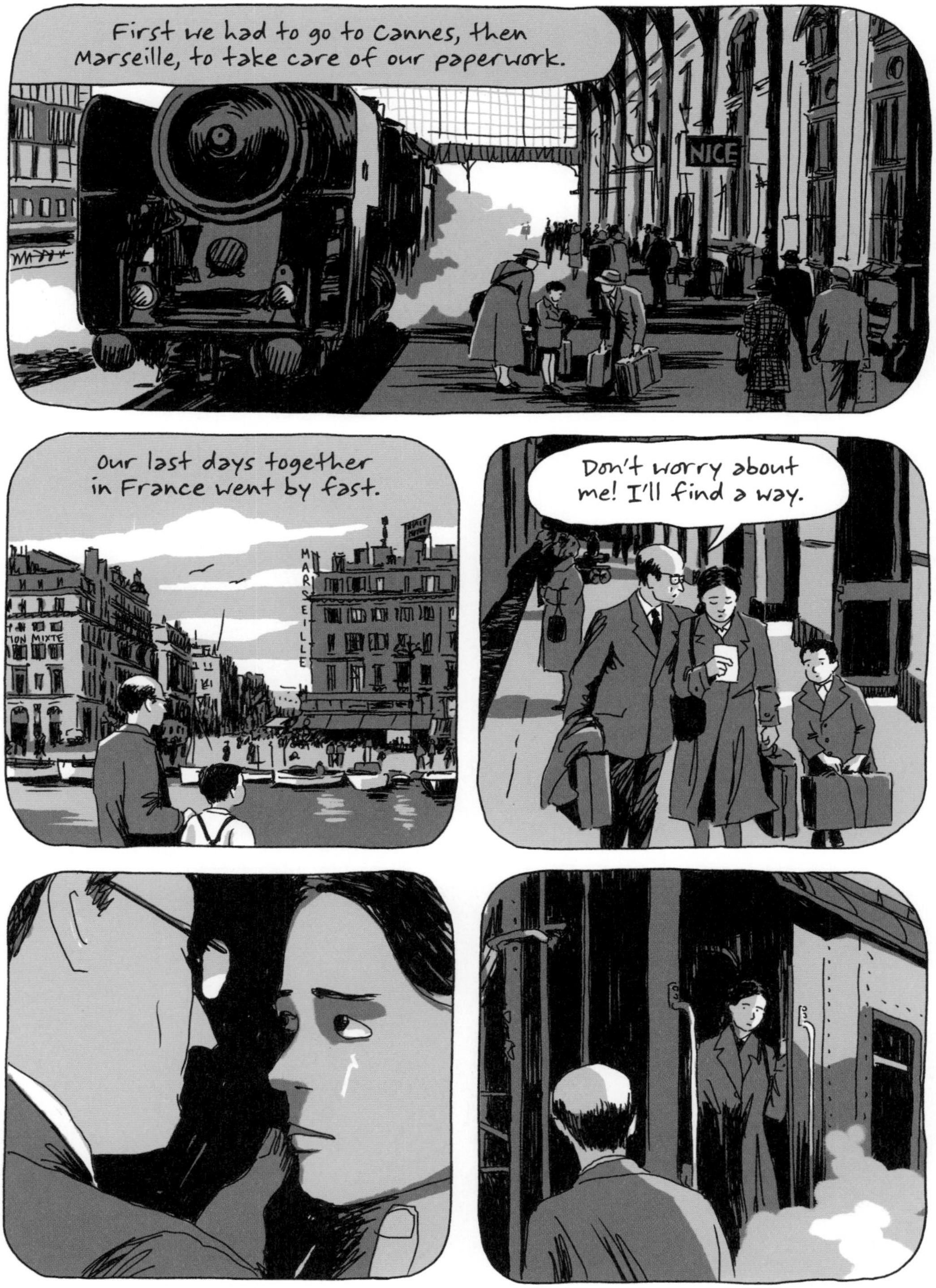
First we had to go to Cannes, then Marseille, to take care of our paperwork.
NICE
Our last days together in France went by fast.
MARSEILLE
Don't worry about me! I'll find a way.

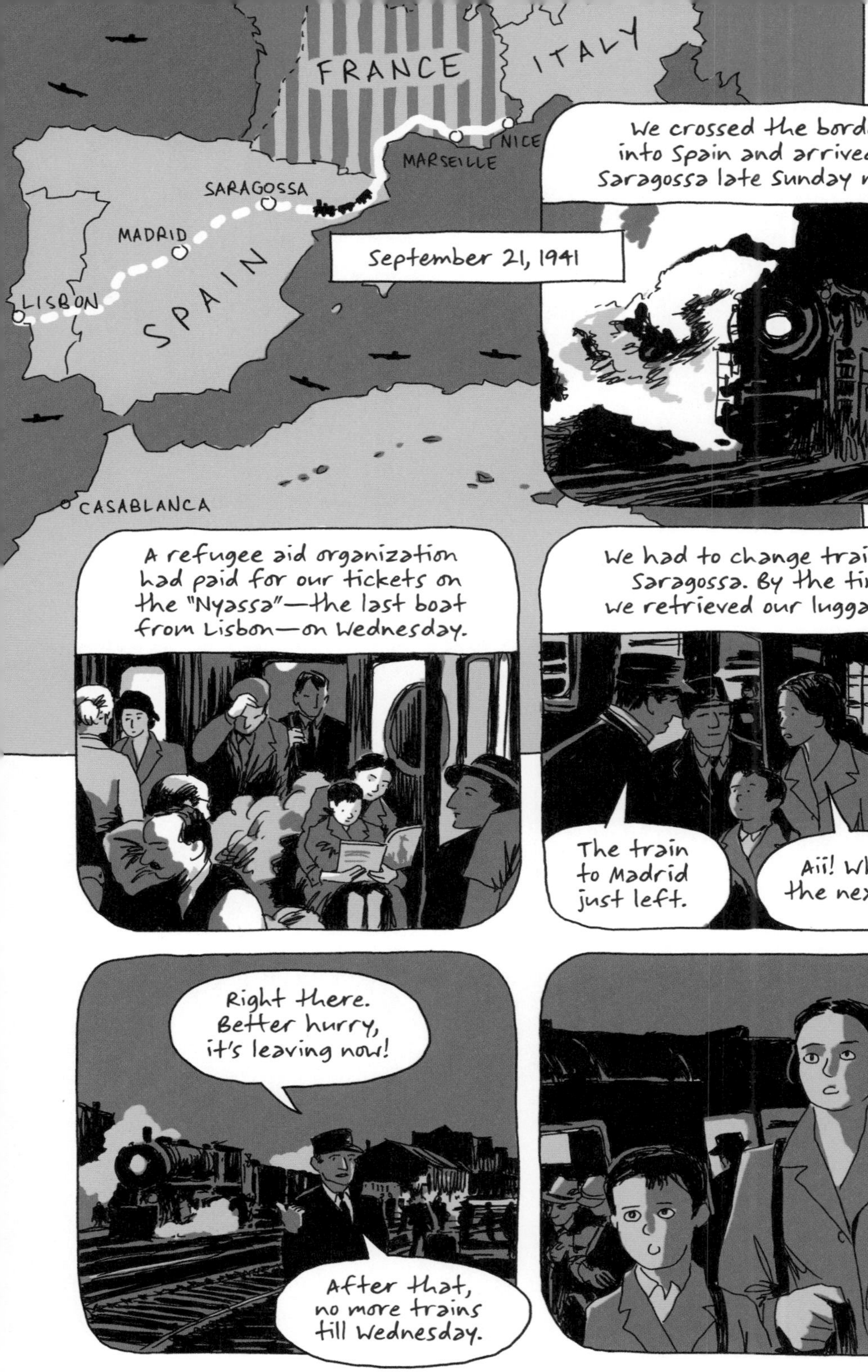
FRANCE
ITALY
NICE
MARSEILLE
SARAGOSSA
MADRID
SPAIN
LISBON
CASABLANCA
September 21, 1941
We crossed the border into Spain and arrived in Saragossa late Sunday night.
A refugee aid organization had paid for our tickets on the "Nyassa"—the last boat from Lisbon—on Wednesday.
We had to change trains in Saragossa. By the time we retrieved our luggage...
The train to Madrid just left.
Aii! When is the next one?
Right there. Better hurry, it's leaving now!
After that, no more trains till Wednesday.

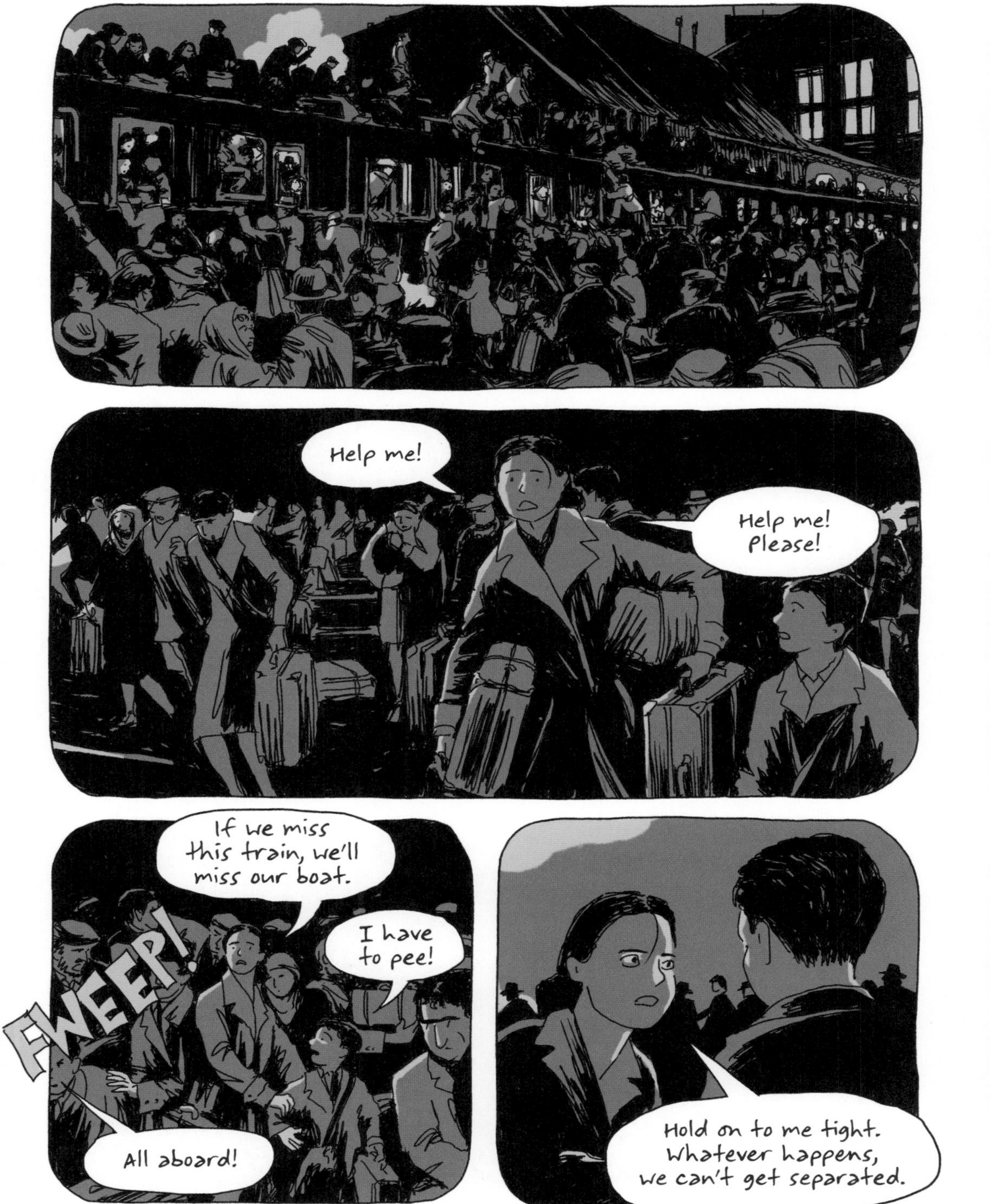
Help me!
Help me! Please!
If we miss this train, we'll miss our boat.
I have to pee!
FWEEP!
All aboard!
Hold on to me tight. Whatever happens, we can't get separated.

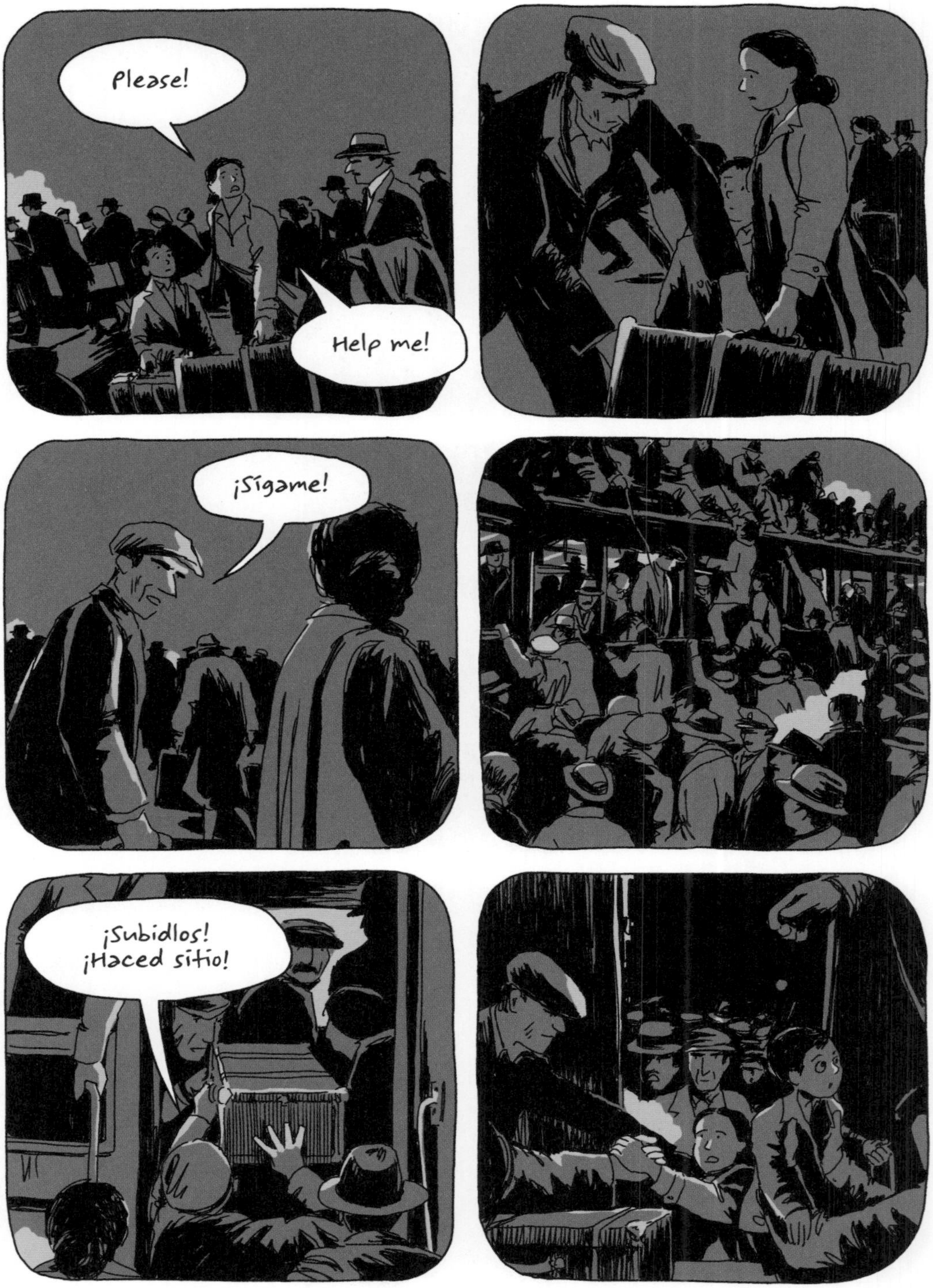
Please!
Help me!
¡Sígame!
¡Subidlos!
¡Haced sitio!

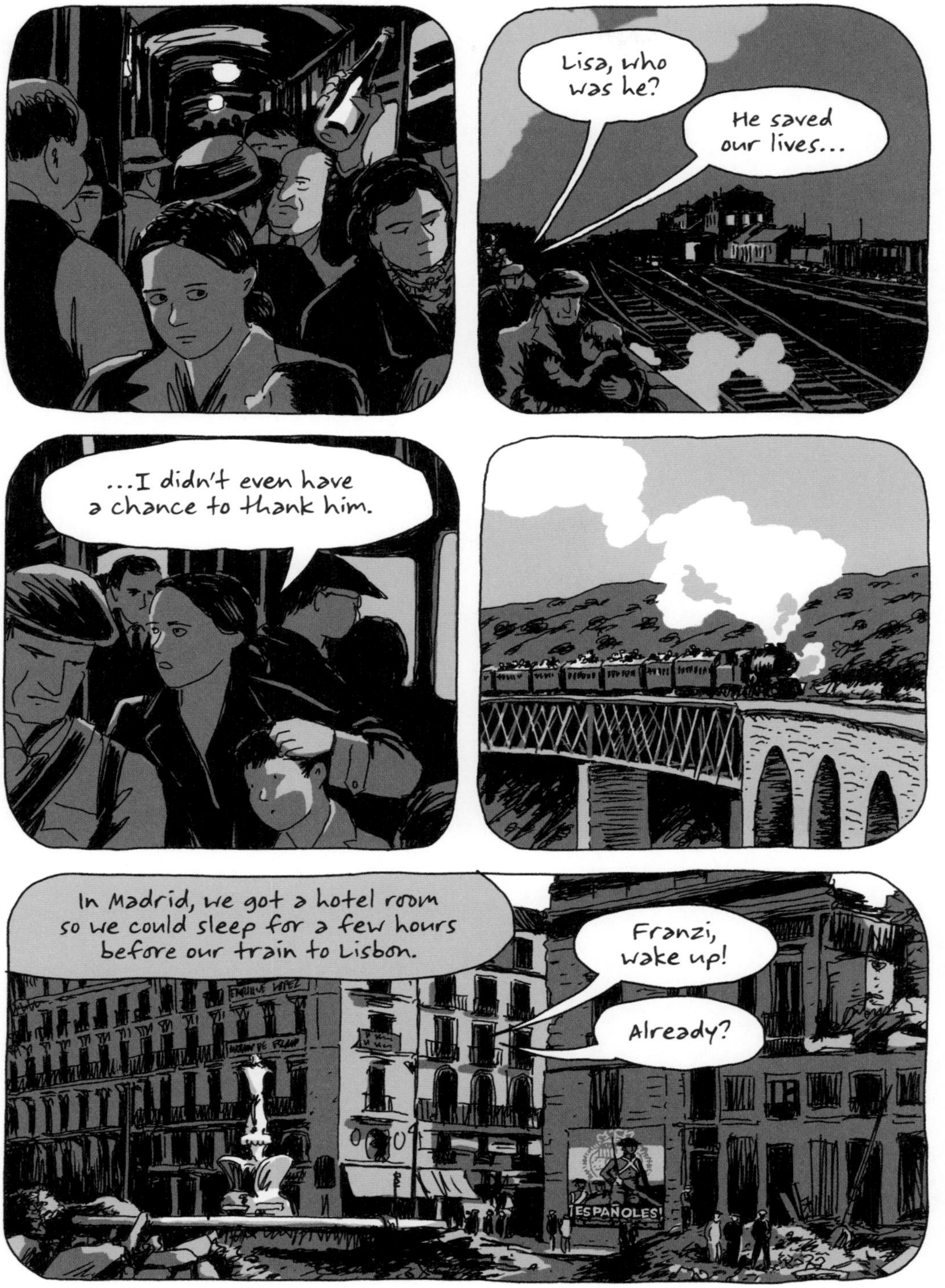
Lisa, who was he?
He saved our lives...
...I didn't even have a chance to thank him.
In Madrid, we got a hotel room so we could sleep for a few hours before our train to Lisbon.
Franzi, wake up!
Already?
¡ESPAÑOLES!

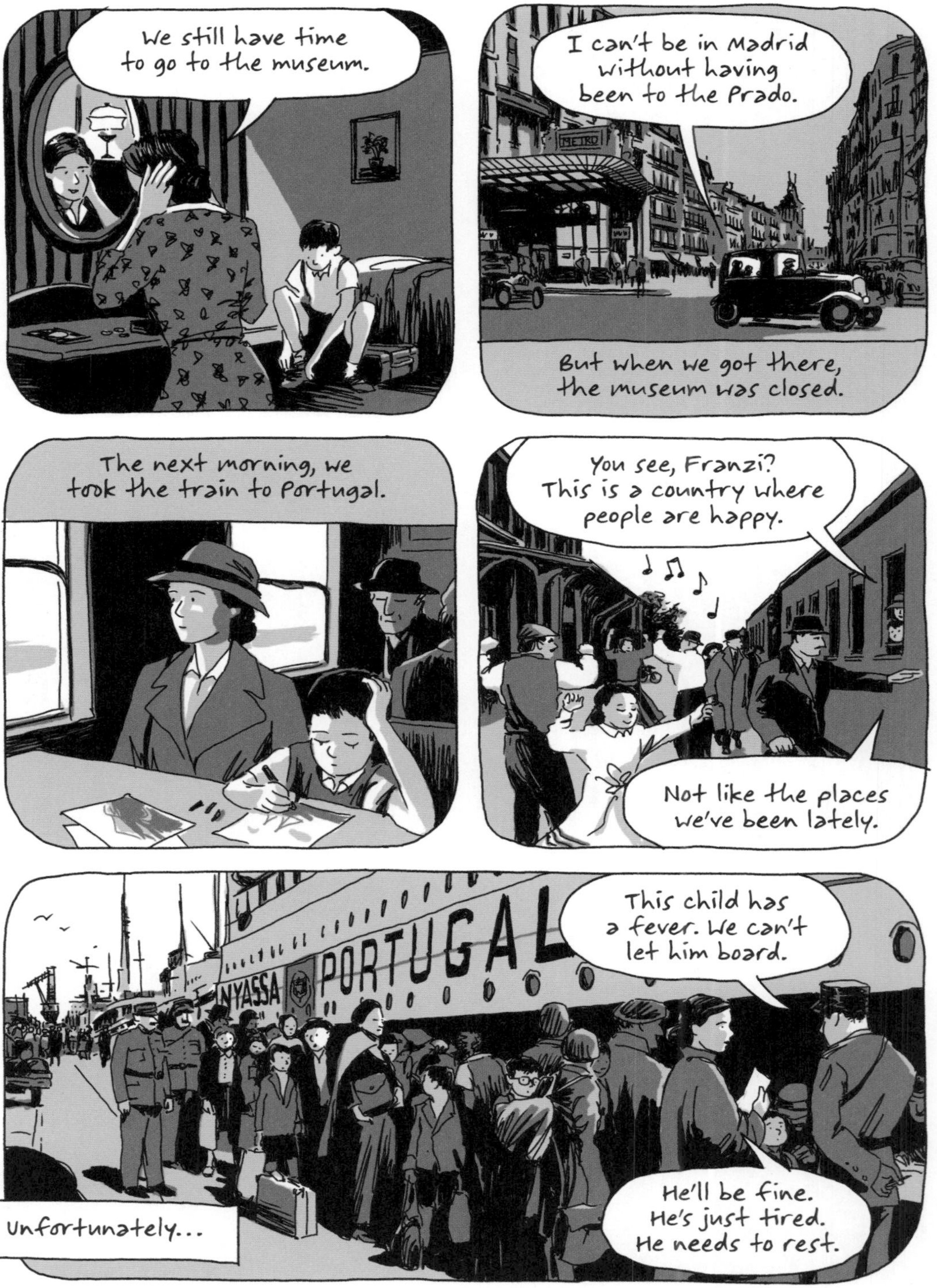
We still have time to go to the museum.
I can't be in Madrid without having been to the Prado.
METRO
But when we got there, the museum was closed.
The next morning, we took the train to Portugal.
You see, Franzi? This is a country where people are happy.
Not like the places we've been lately.
NYASSA
PORTUGAL
This child has a fever. We can't let him board.
Unfortunately...
He'll be fine. He's just tired. He needs to rest.

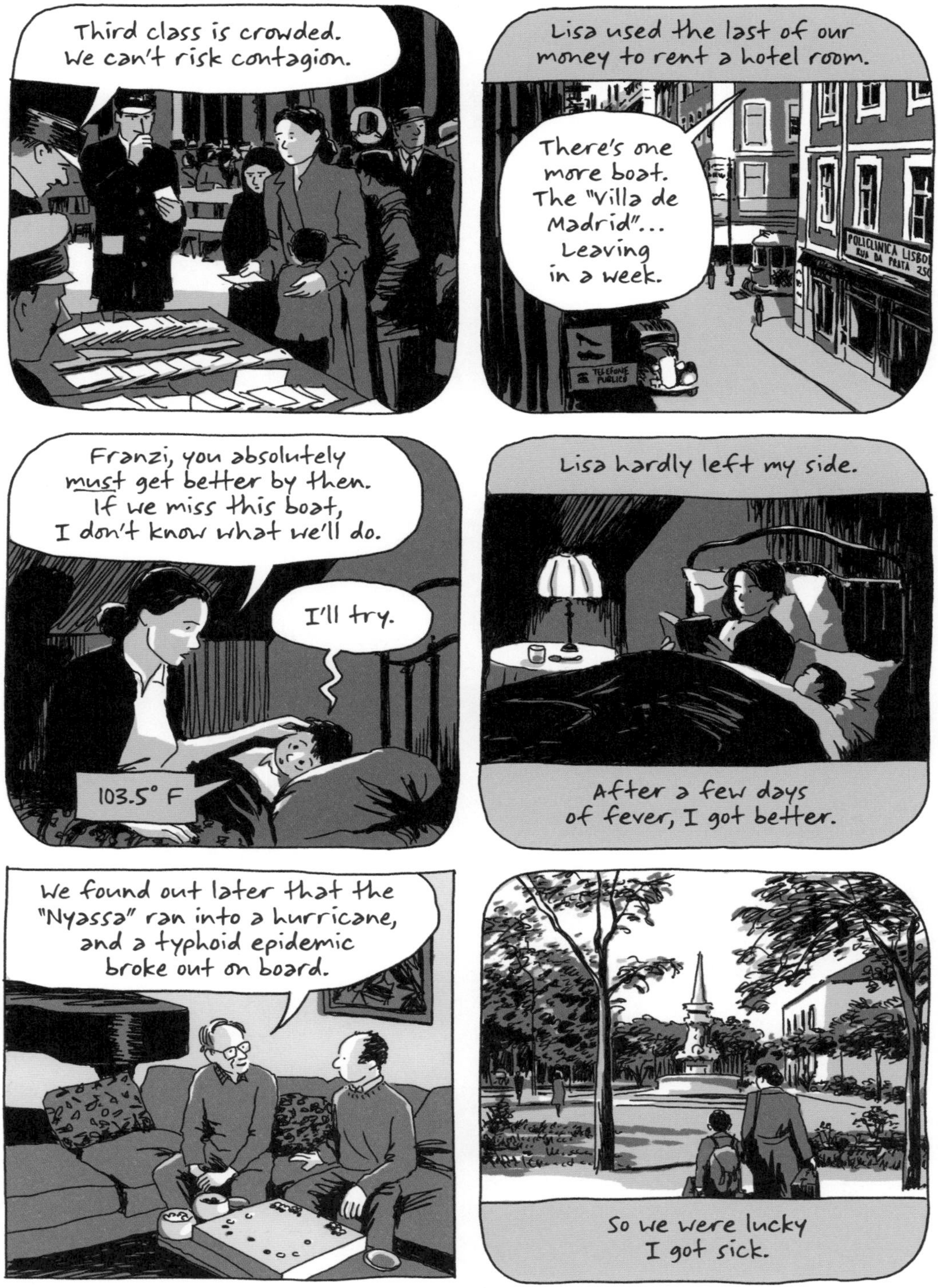
Third class is crowded. We can't risk contagion.
Lisa used the last of our money to rent a hotel room.
There's one more boat. The "Villa de Madrid"... Leaving in a week.
TELEFONE PUBLICO
Franzi, you absolutely must get better by then. If we miss this boat, I don't know what we'll do.
I'll try.
103.5° F
Lisa hardly left my side.
After a few days of fever, I got better.
We found out later that the "Nyassa" ran into a hurricane, and a typhoid epidemic broke out on board.
So we were lucky I got sick.

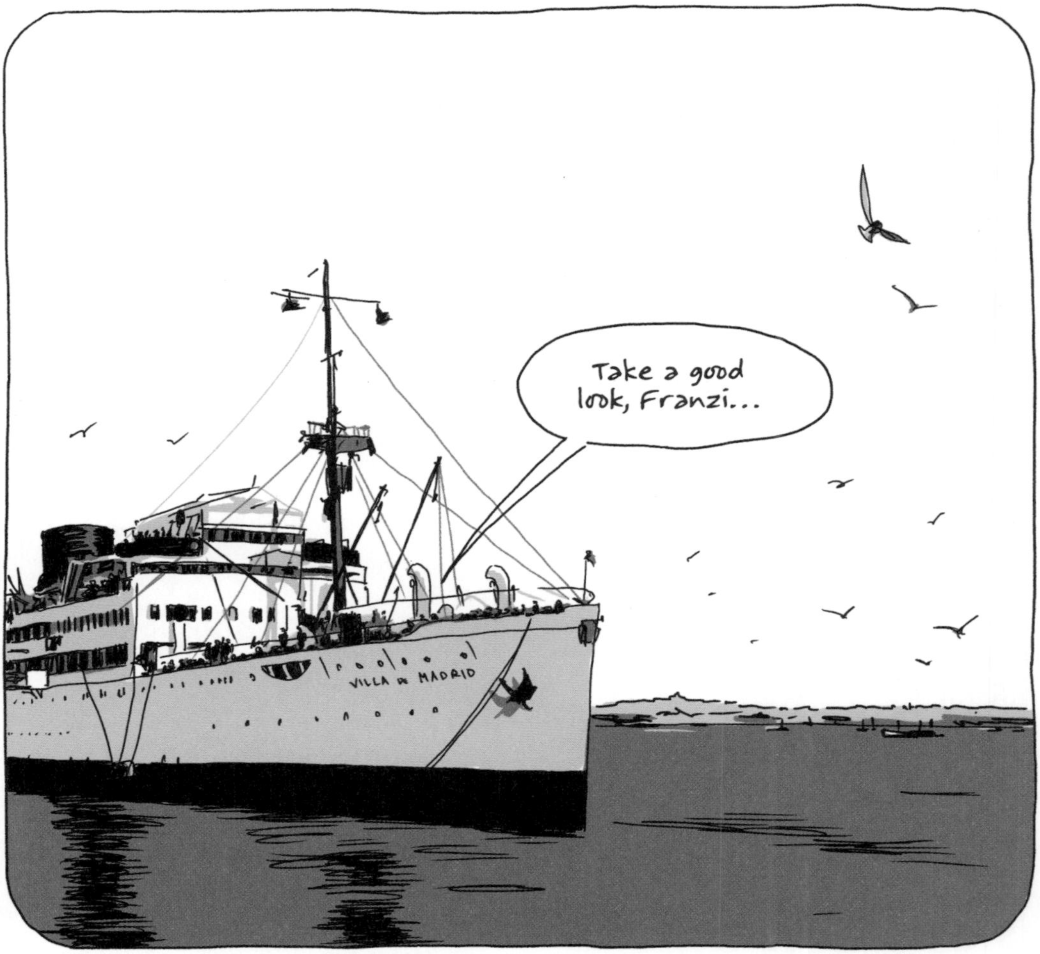
VILLA DE MADRID
Take a good look, Franzi...

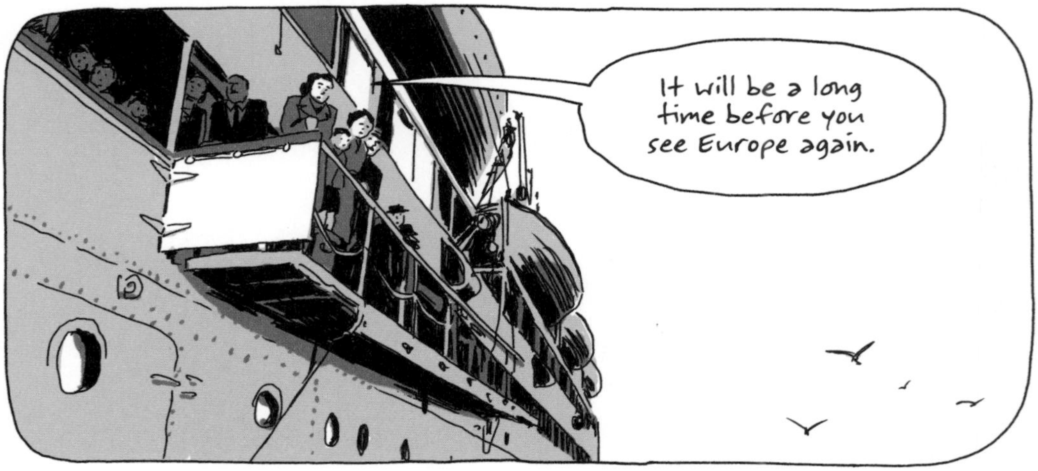
It will be a long time before you see Europe again.

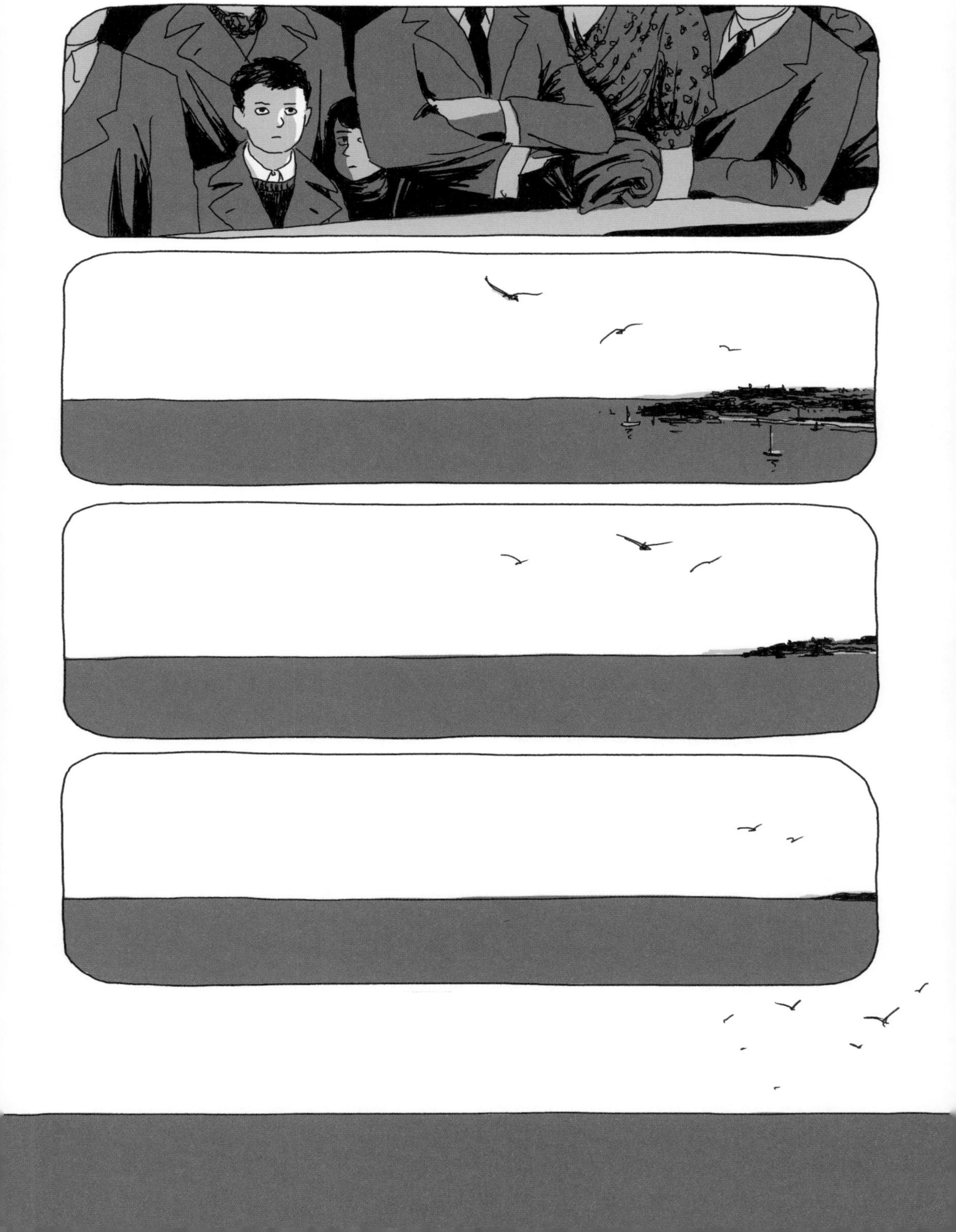

Postcard

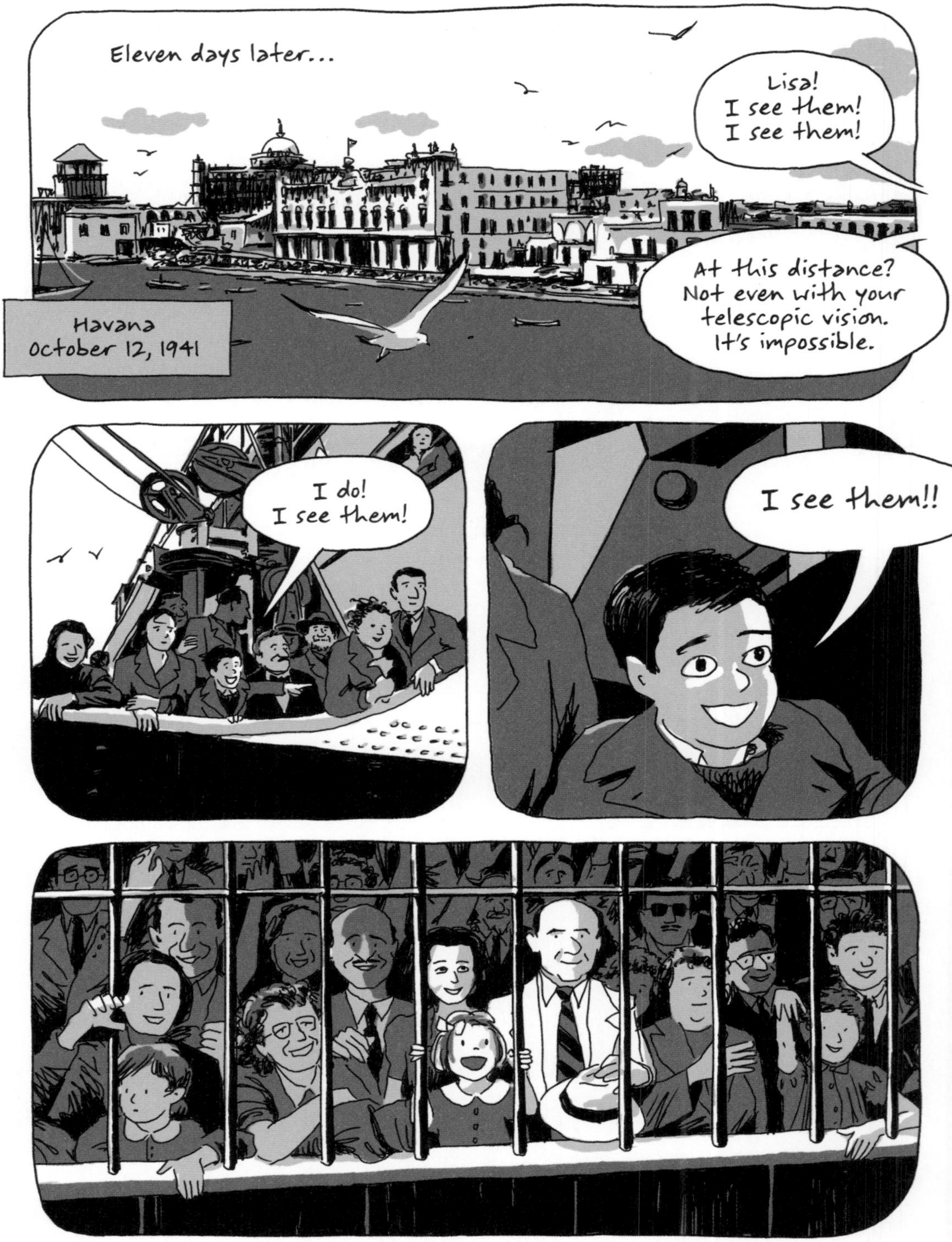
Eleven days later...
Havana
October 12, 1941
Lisa! I see them! I see them!
At this distance? Not even with your telescopic vision. It's impossible.
I do! I see them!
I see them!!

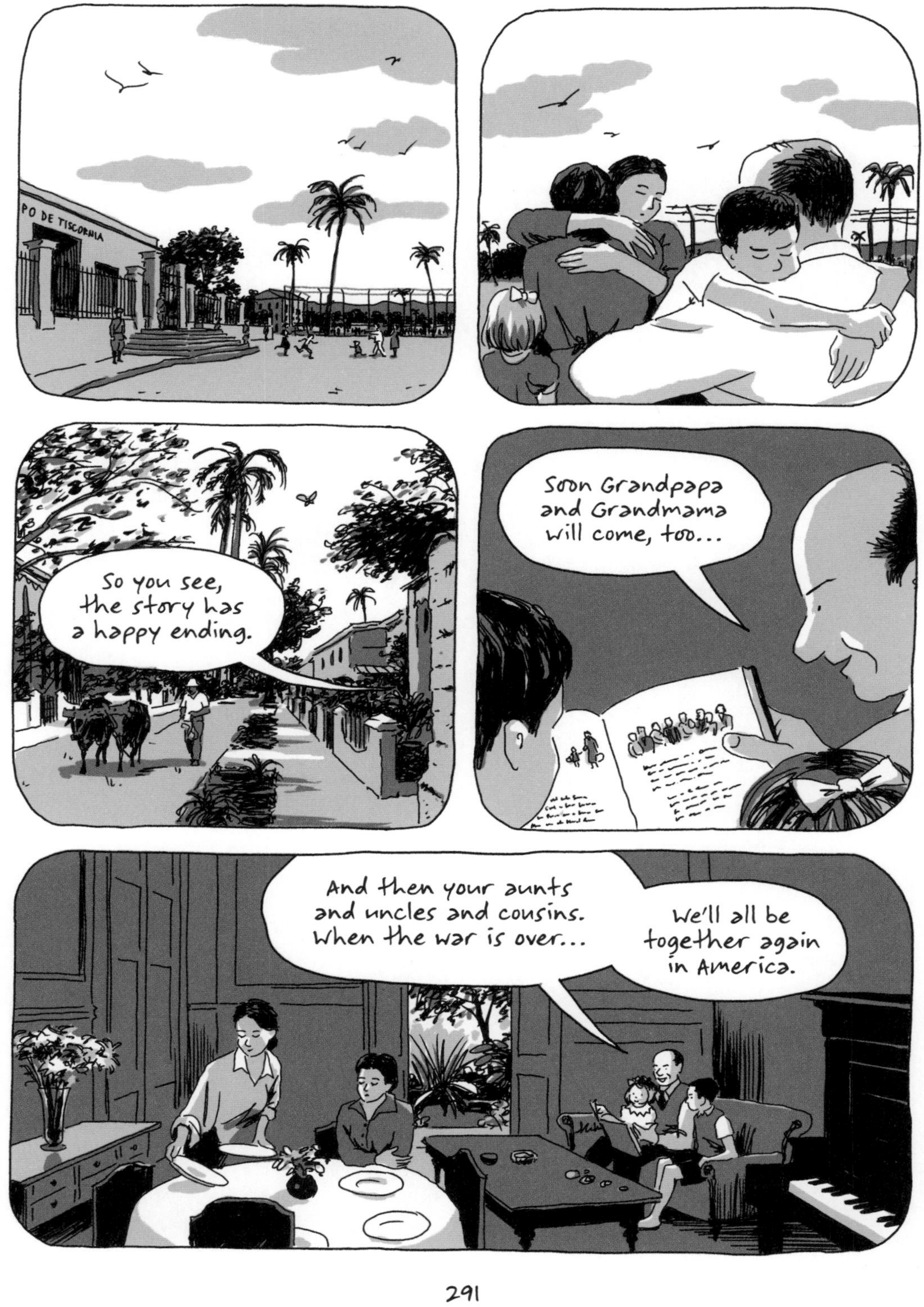
PO DE TISCORNIA
So you see, the story has a happy ending.
Soon Grandpapa and Grandmama will come, too...
And then your aunts and uncles and cousins. When the war is over...
We'll all be together again in America.

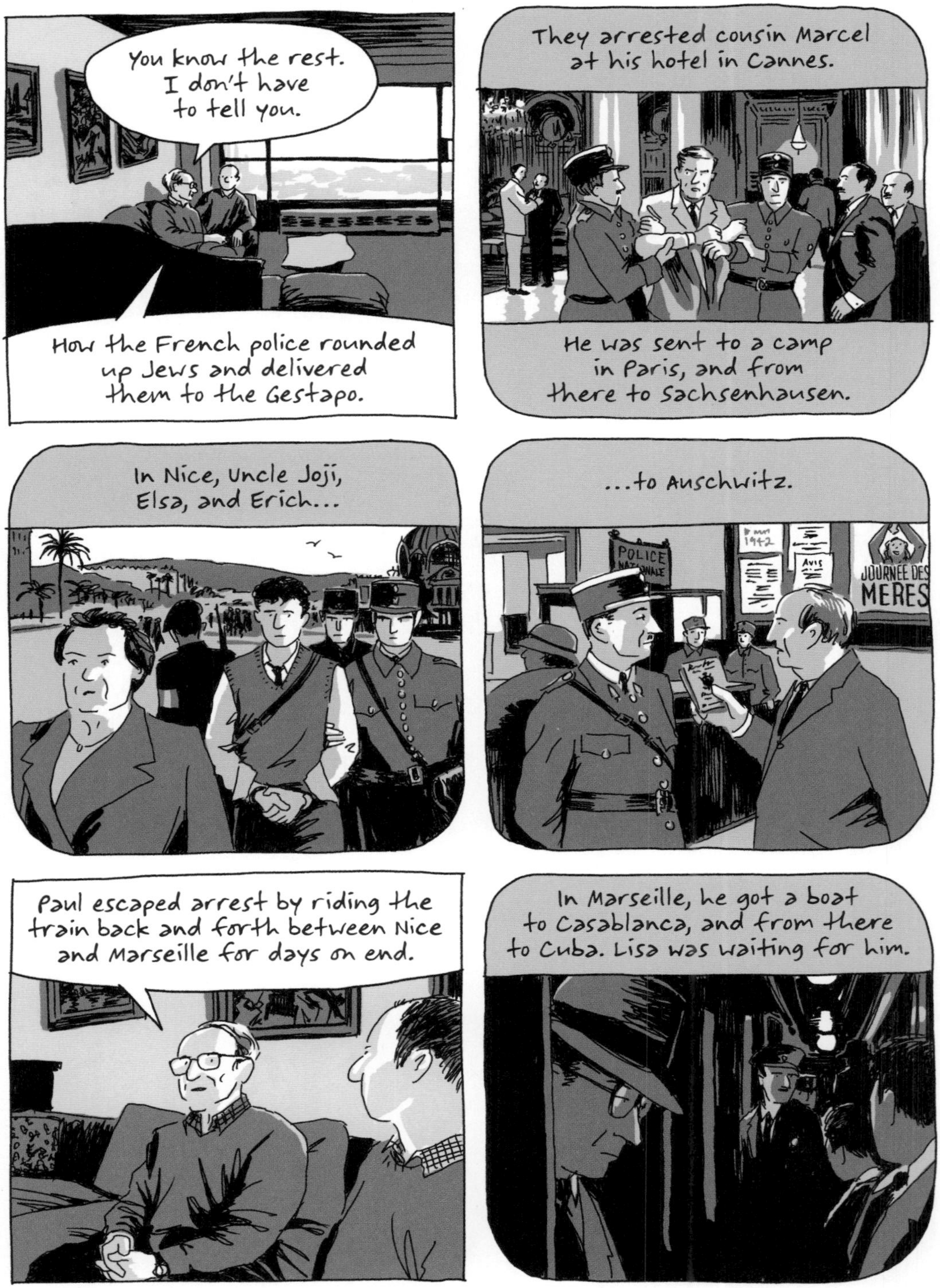
You know the rest. I don't have to tell you.
How the French police rounded up Jews and delivered them to the Gestapo.
They arrested cousin Marcel at his hotel in Cannes.
He was sent to a camp in Paris, and from there to Sachsenhausen.
In Nice, Uncle Joji, Elsa, and Erich...
...to Auschwitz.
POLICE
AVIS
JOURNÉE DES MERES
Paul escaped arrest by riding the train back and forth between Nice and Marseille for days on end.
In Marseille, he got a boat to Casablanca, and from there to Cuba. Lisa was waiting for him.

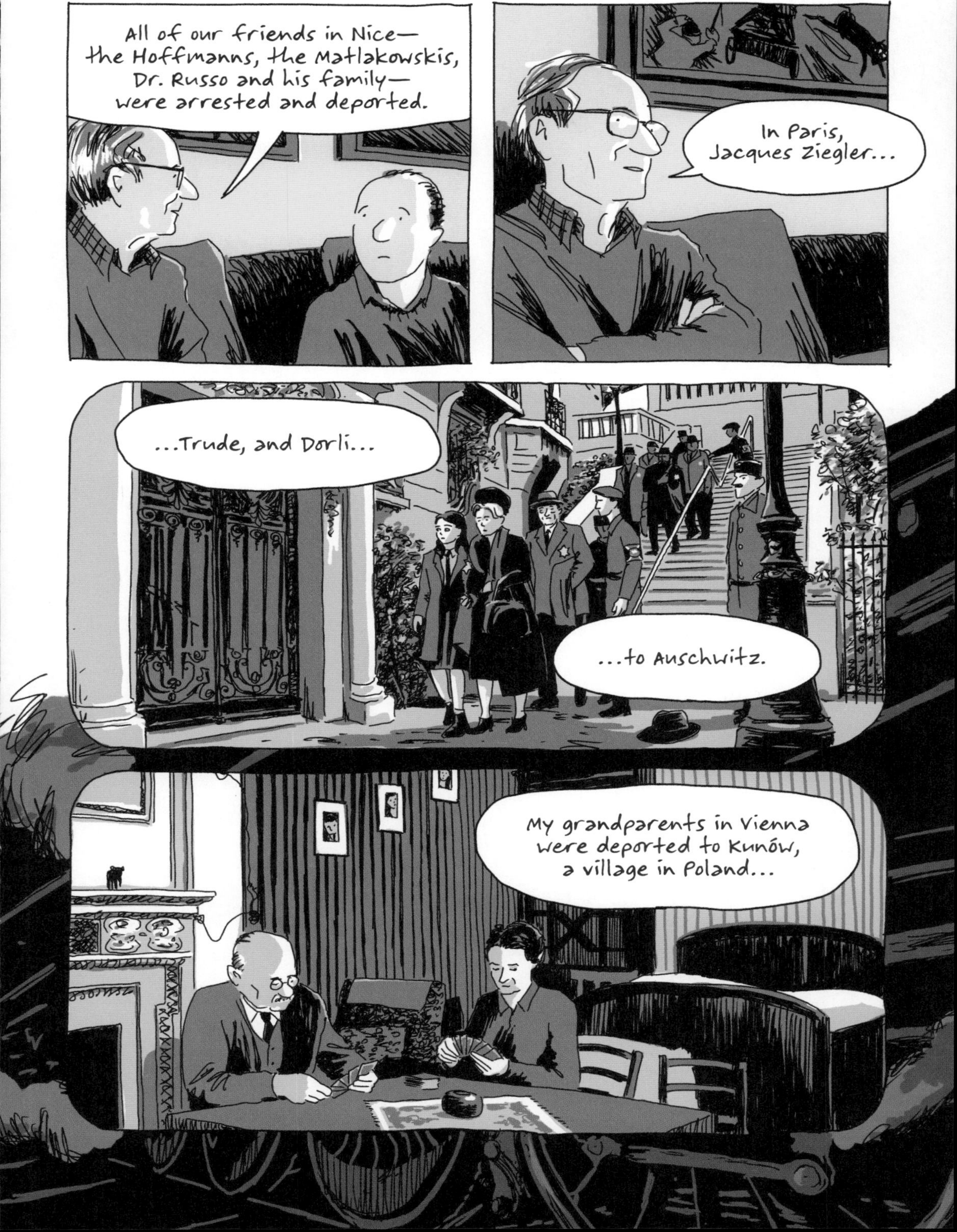
All of our friends in Nice— the Hoffmanns, the Matlakowskis, Dr. Russo and his family— were arrested and deported.
In Paris, Jacques Ziegler...
...Trude, and Dorli...
...to Auschwitz.
My grandparents in Vienna were deported to Kunów, a village in Poland...

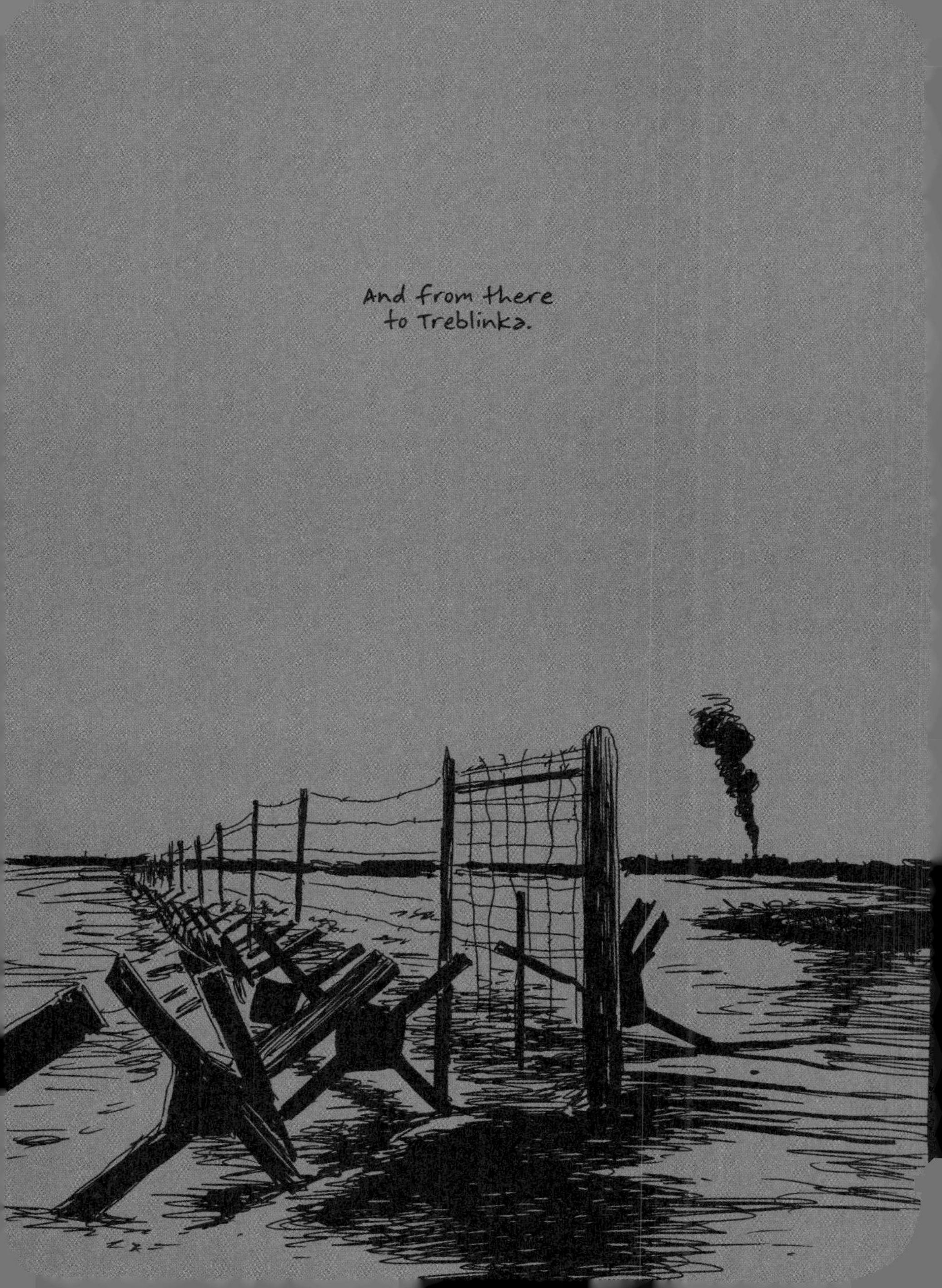
And from there
to Treblinka.

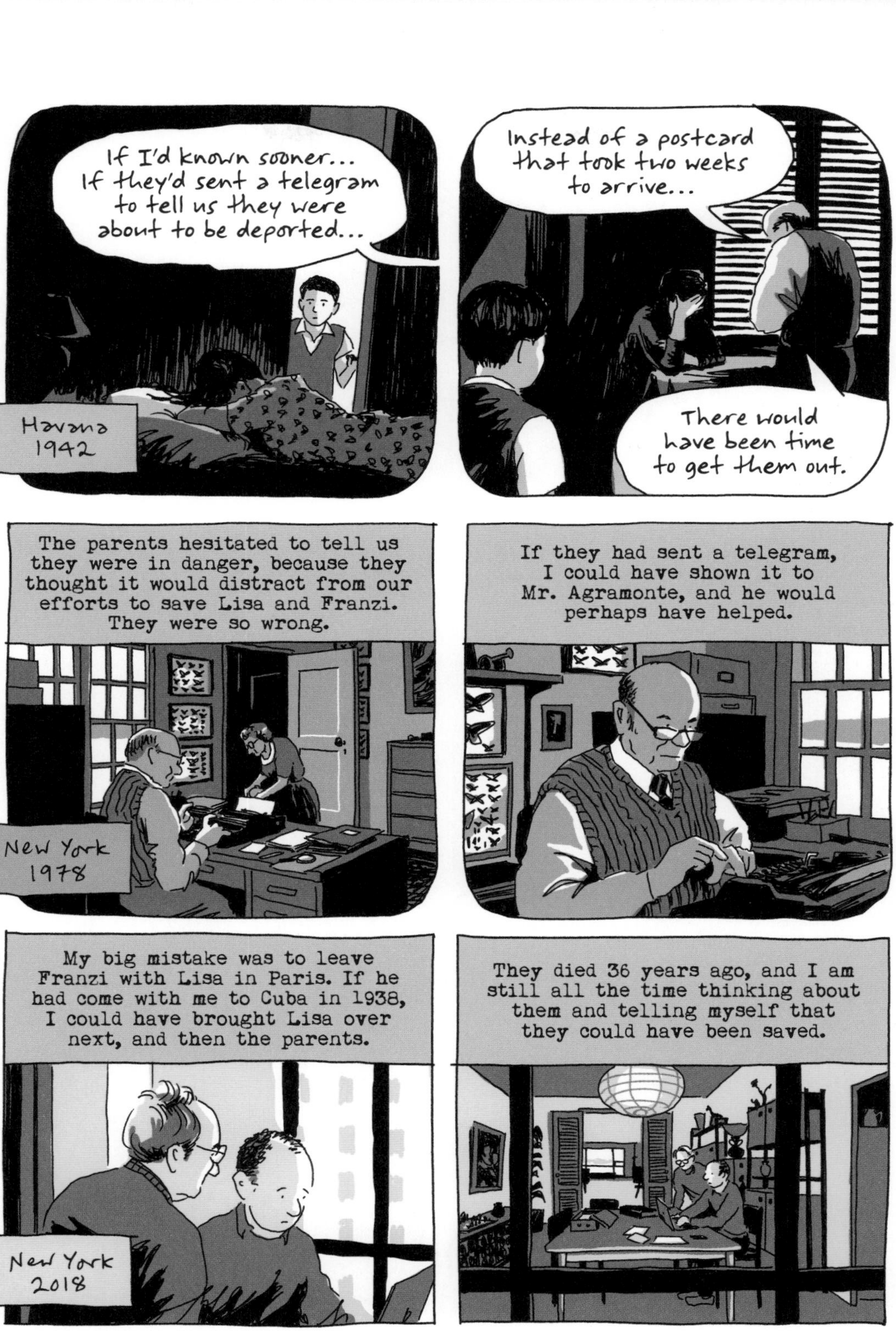
If I'd known sooner... If they'd sent a telegram to tell us they were about to be deported...
Havana 1942
Instead of a postcard that took two weeks to arrive...
There would have been time to get them out.
The parents hesitated to tell us they were in danger, because they thought it would distract from our efforts to save Lisa and Franzi. They were so wrong.
New York 1978
If they had sent a telegram, I could have shown it to Mr. Agramonte, and he would perhaps have helped.
My big mistake was to leave Franzi with Lisa in Paris. If he had come with me to Cuba in 1938, I could have brought Lisa over next, and then the parents.
New York 2018
They died 36 years ago, and I am still all the time thinking about them and telling myself that they could have been saved.

A Dream

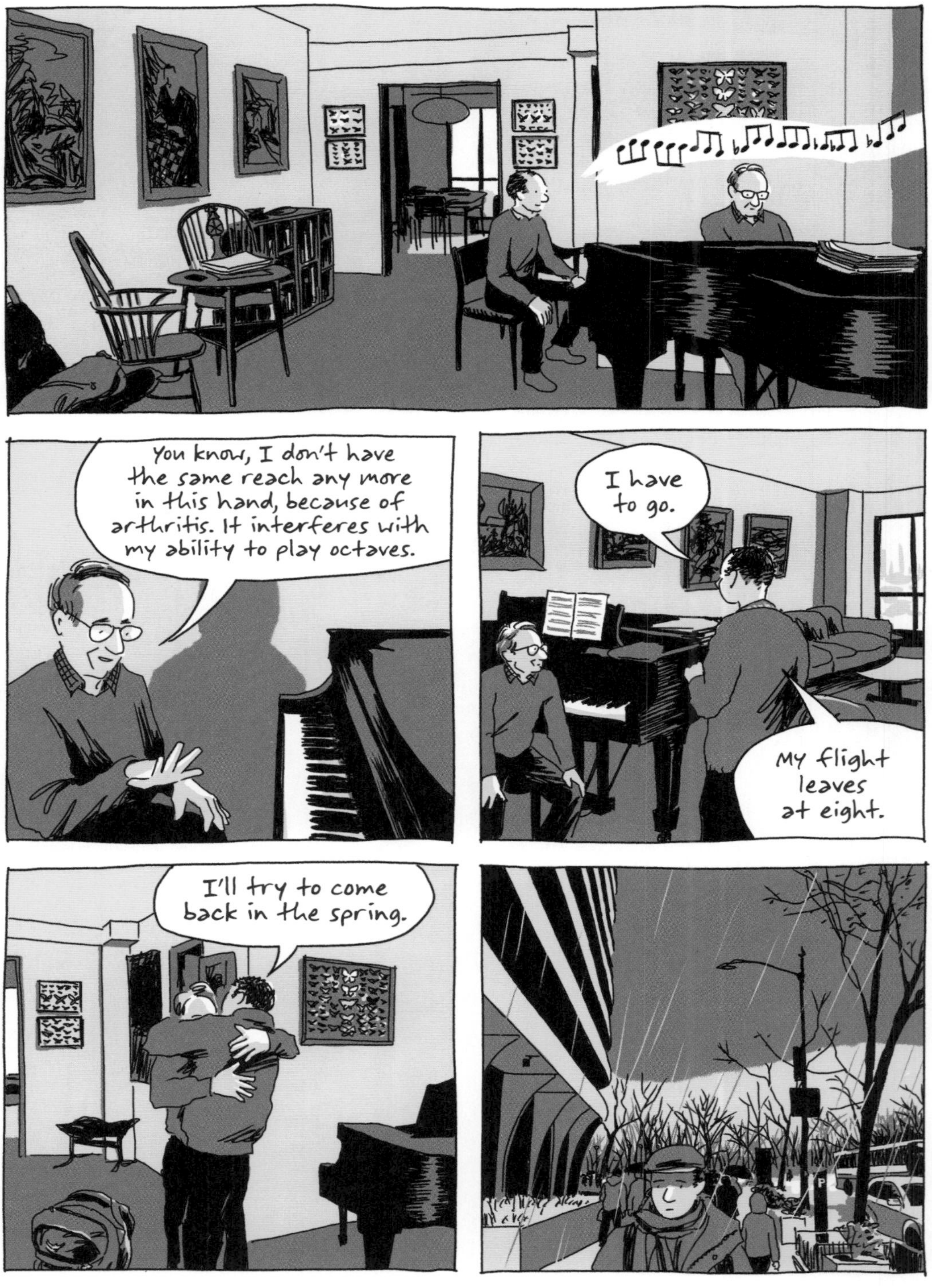
You know, I don't have the same reach any more in this hand, because of arthritis. It interferes with my ability to play octaves.
I have to go.
My flight leaves at eight.
I'll try to come back in the spring.

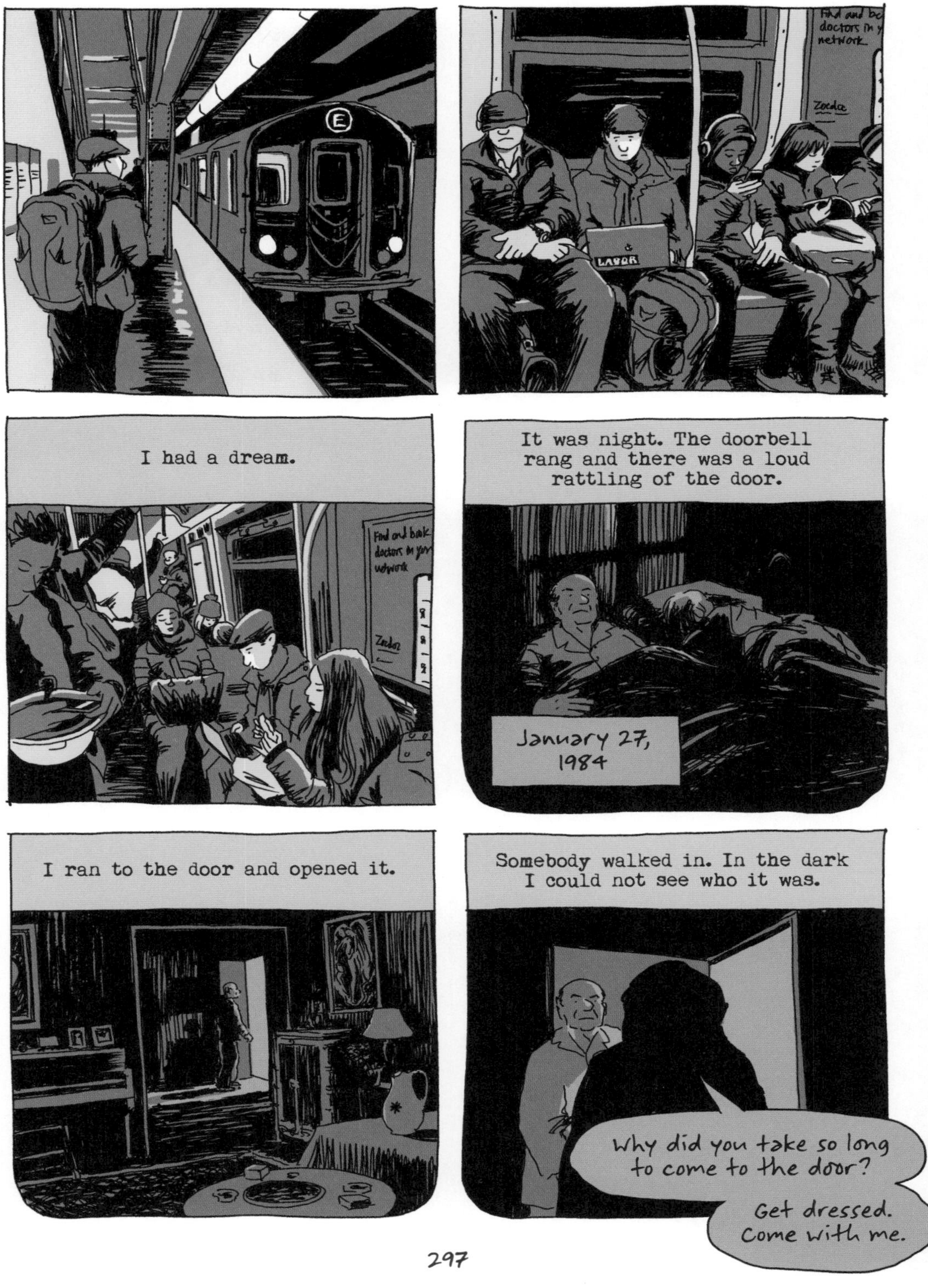
I had a dream.
It was night. The doorbell rang and there was a loud rattling of the door.
January 27, 1984
I ran to the door and opened it.
Somebody walked in. In the dark I could not see who it was.
Why did you take so long to come to the door?
Get dressed. Come with me.

I saw that he had no eyes,
only two dark holes.

Now I knew who he was.

I've been expecting
you for a long time.
But I'm not prepared.

Maybe you could
come back later?
Say, one year
from now...?

No, that
cannot be.

One week?

No.

Then just one day?
To put my things
in order.

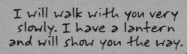

Do not be afraid.
It will be painless.

I will walk with you very
slowly. I have a lantern
and will show you the way.

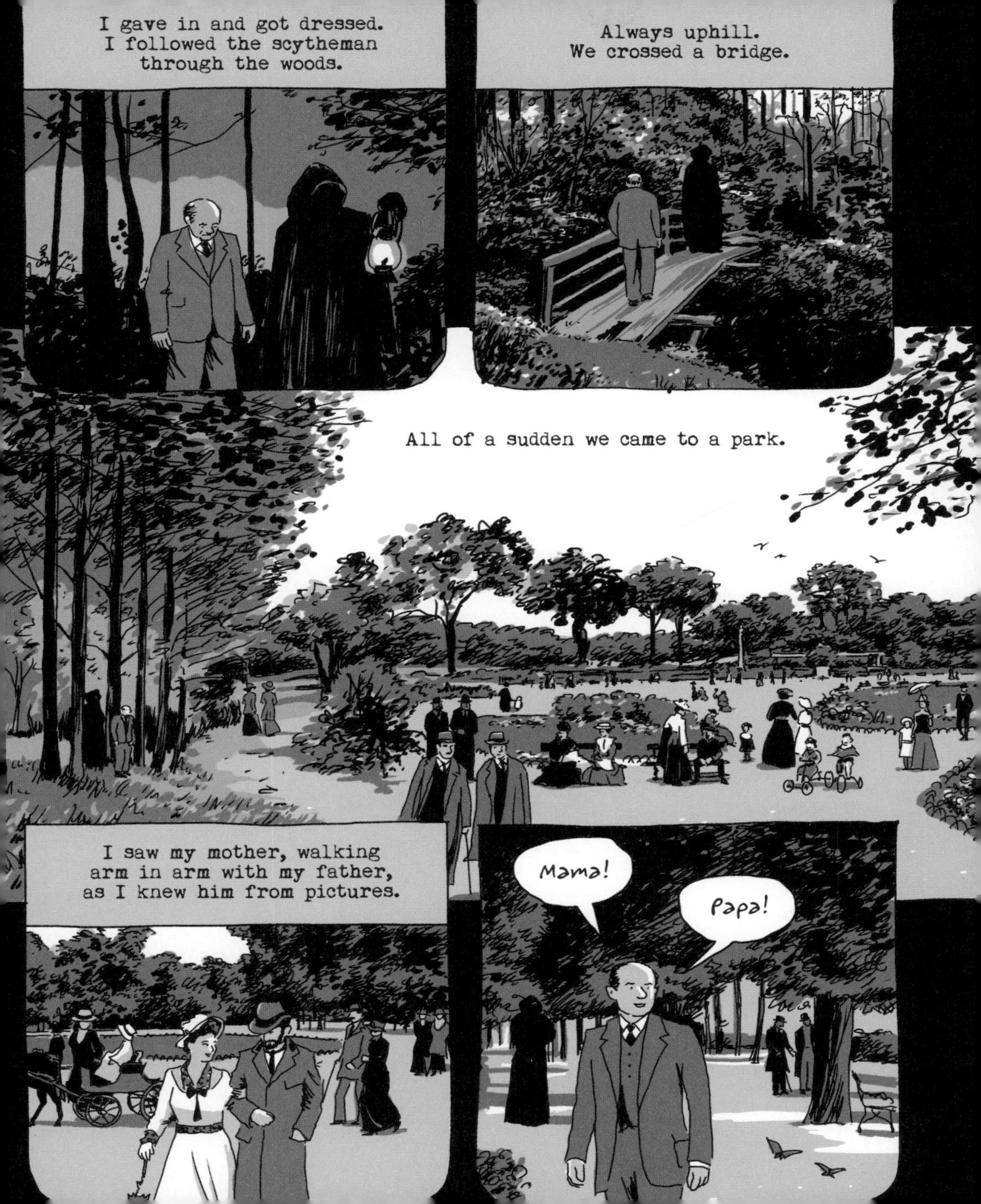
I gave in and got dressed. I followed the scytheman through the woods.
Always uphill. We crossed a bridge.
All of a sudden we came to a park.
I saw my mother, walking arm in arm with my father, as I knew him from pictures.
Mama!
Papa!

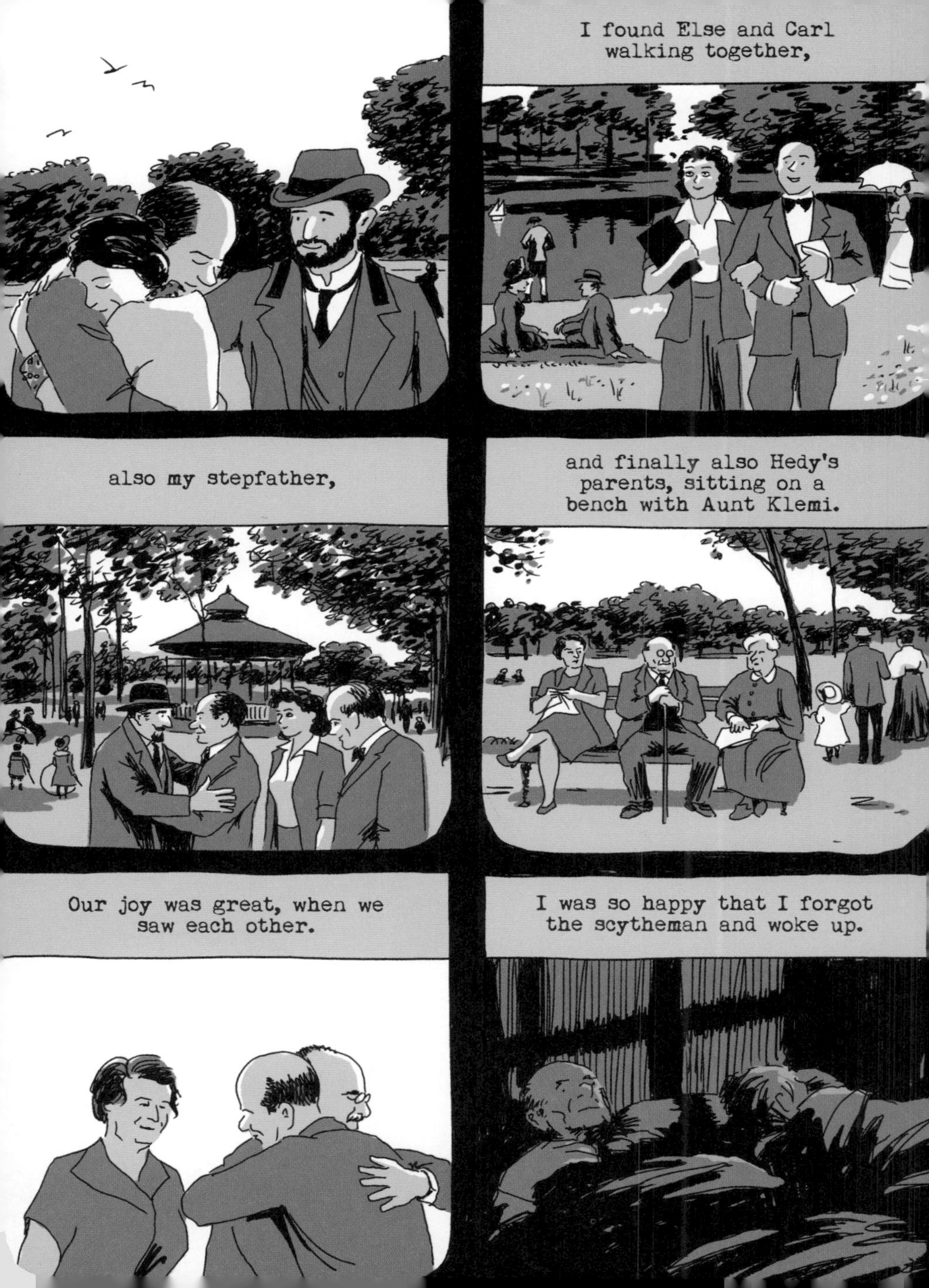
I found Else and Carl walking together,
also my stepfather,
and finally also Hedy's parents, sitting on a bench with Aunt Klemi.
Our joy was great, when we saw each other.
I was so happy that I forgot the scytheman and woke up.

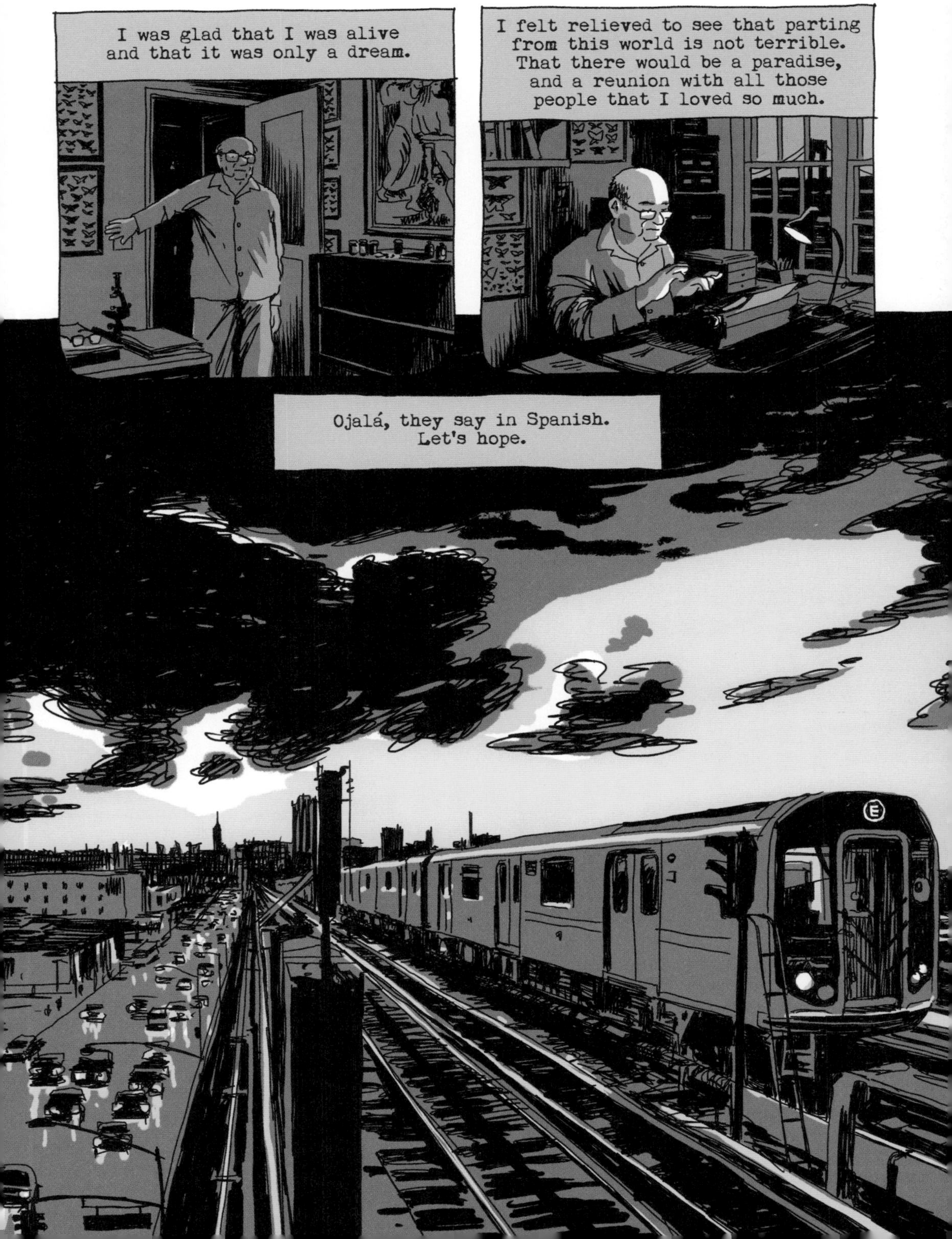
I was glad that I was alive and that it was only a dream.
I felt relieved to see that parting from this world is not terrible. That there would be a paradise, and a reunion with all those people that I loved so much.
Ojalá, they say in Spanish. Let's hope.
E

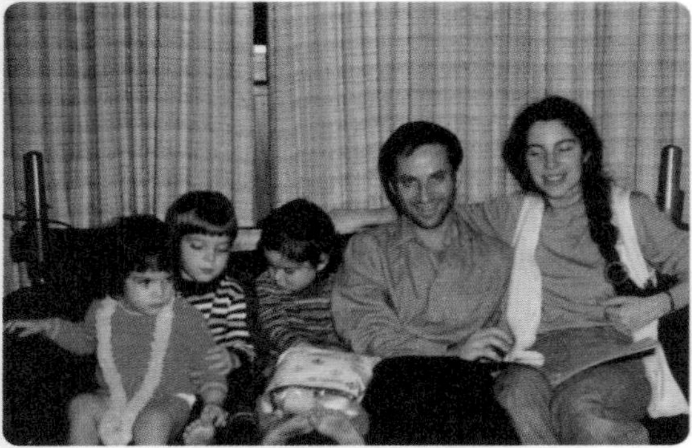

Emily, Jordan, Linda,
Francis, and Vicki Mechner
New York, 1970

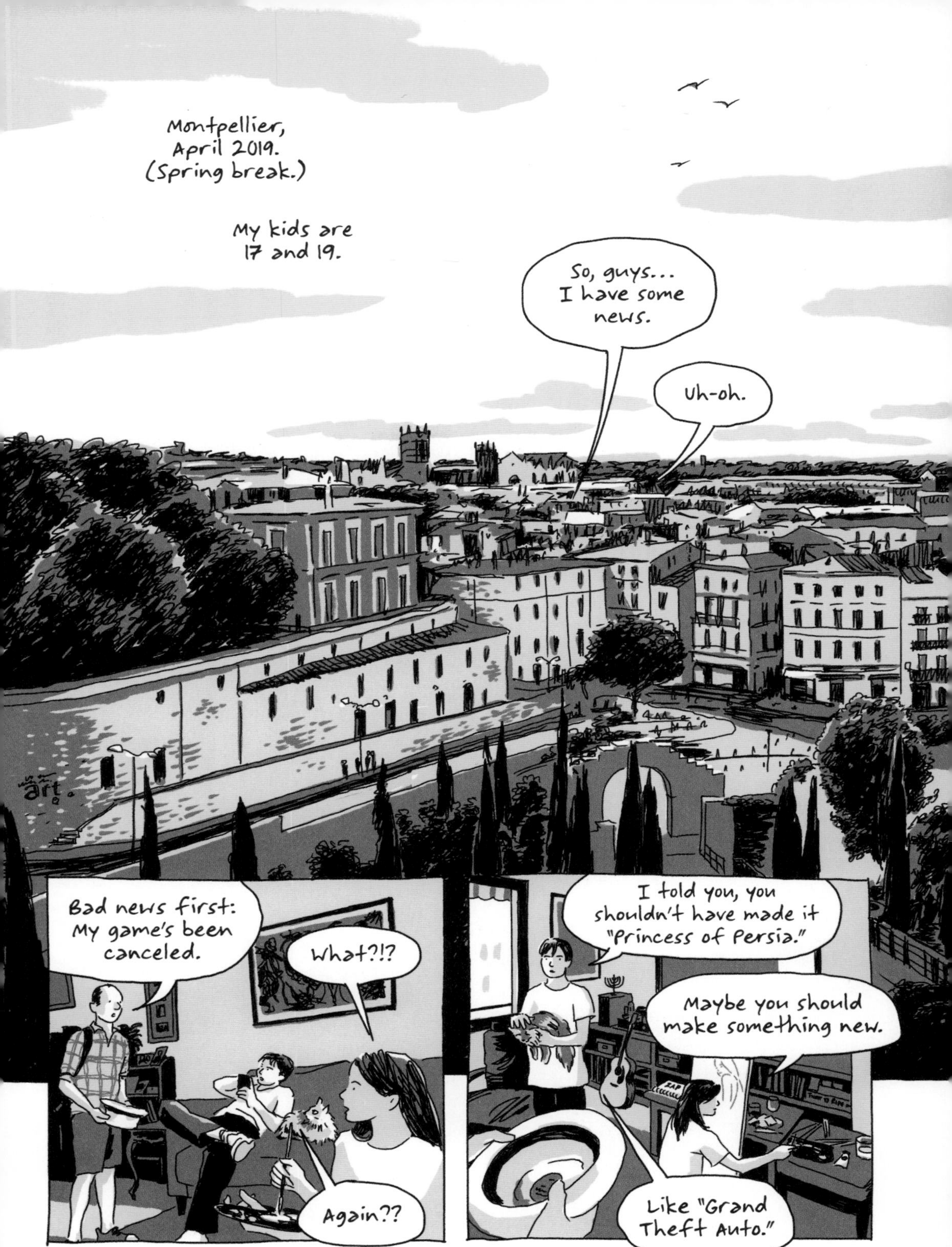
Montpellier, April 2019. (Spring break.)
My kids are 17 and 19.
So, guys... I have some news.
Uh-oh.
Bad news first: My game's been canceled.
What?!?
Again??
I told you, you shouldn't have made it "Princess of Persia."
Maybe you should make something new.
Like "Grand Theft Auto."

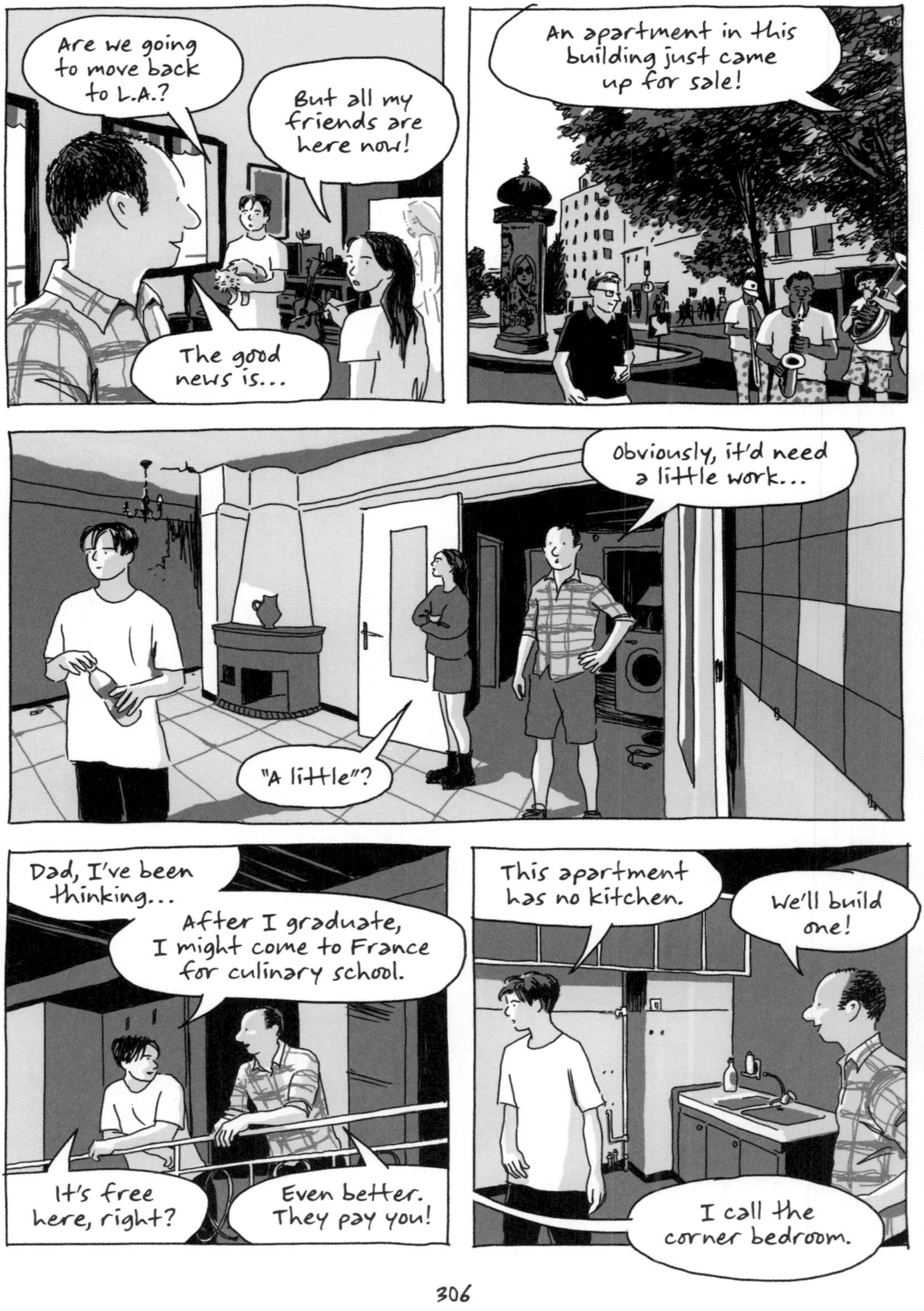
Are we going to move back to L.A.?
But all my friends are here now!
The good news is...
An apartment in this building just came up for sale!
Obviously, it'd need a little work...
"A little"?
Dad, I've been thinking...
After I graduate, I might come to France for culinary school.
It's free here, right?
Even better. They pay you!
This apartment has no kitchen.
We'll build one!
I call the corner bedroom.

Land of Opportunity

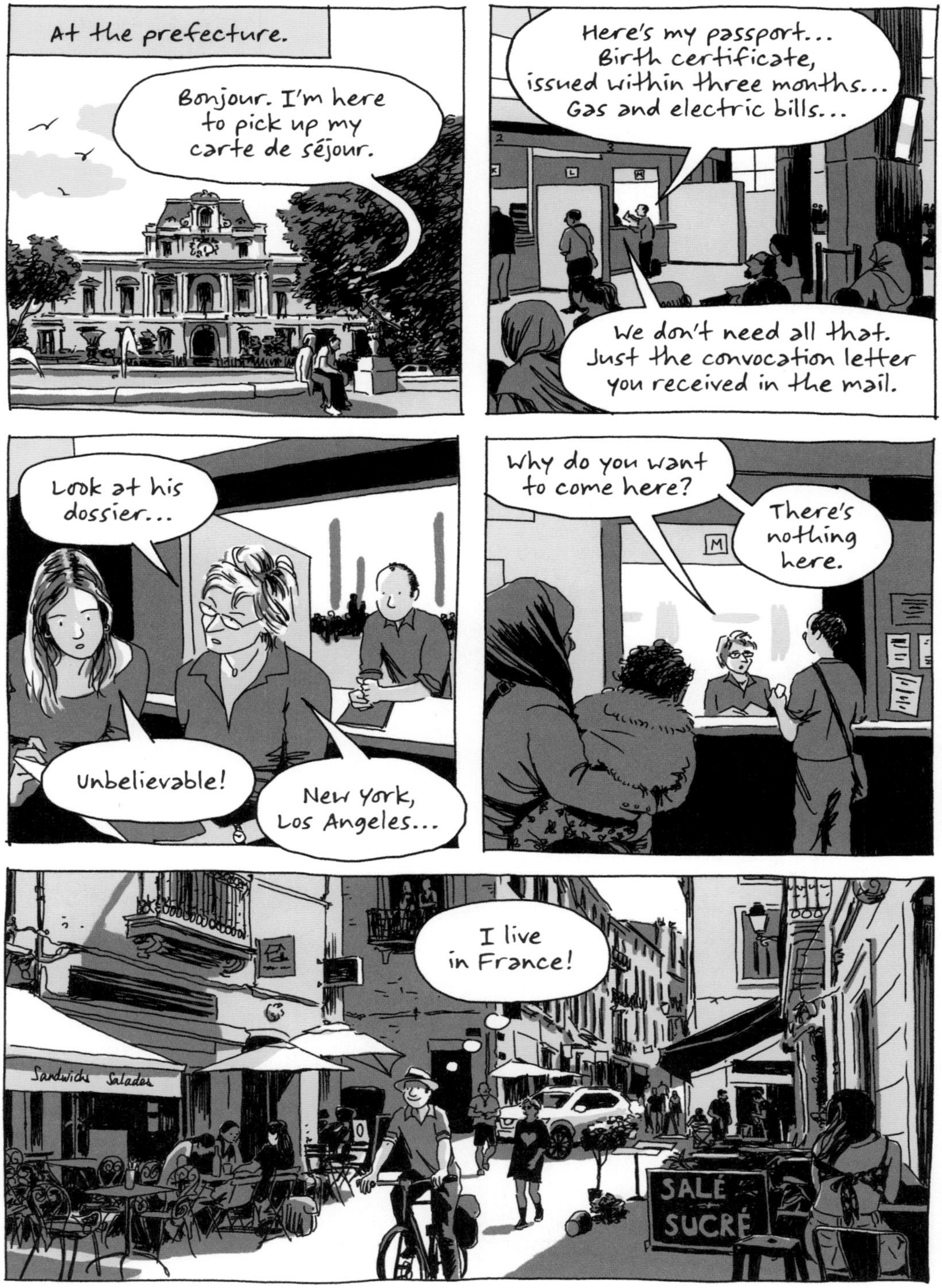
At the prefecture.
Bonjour. I'm here to pick up my carte de séjour.
Here's my passport... Birth certificate, issued within three months... Gas and electric bills...
We don't need all that. Just the convocation letter you received in the mail.
Look at his dossier...
Unbelievable!
New York, Los Angeles...
Why do you want to come here?
There's nothing here.
I live in France!
Sandwichs Salades
SALÉ SUCRÉ

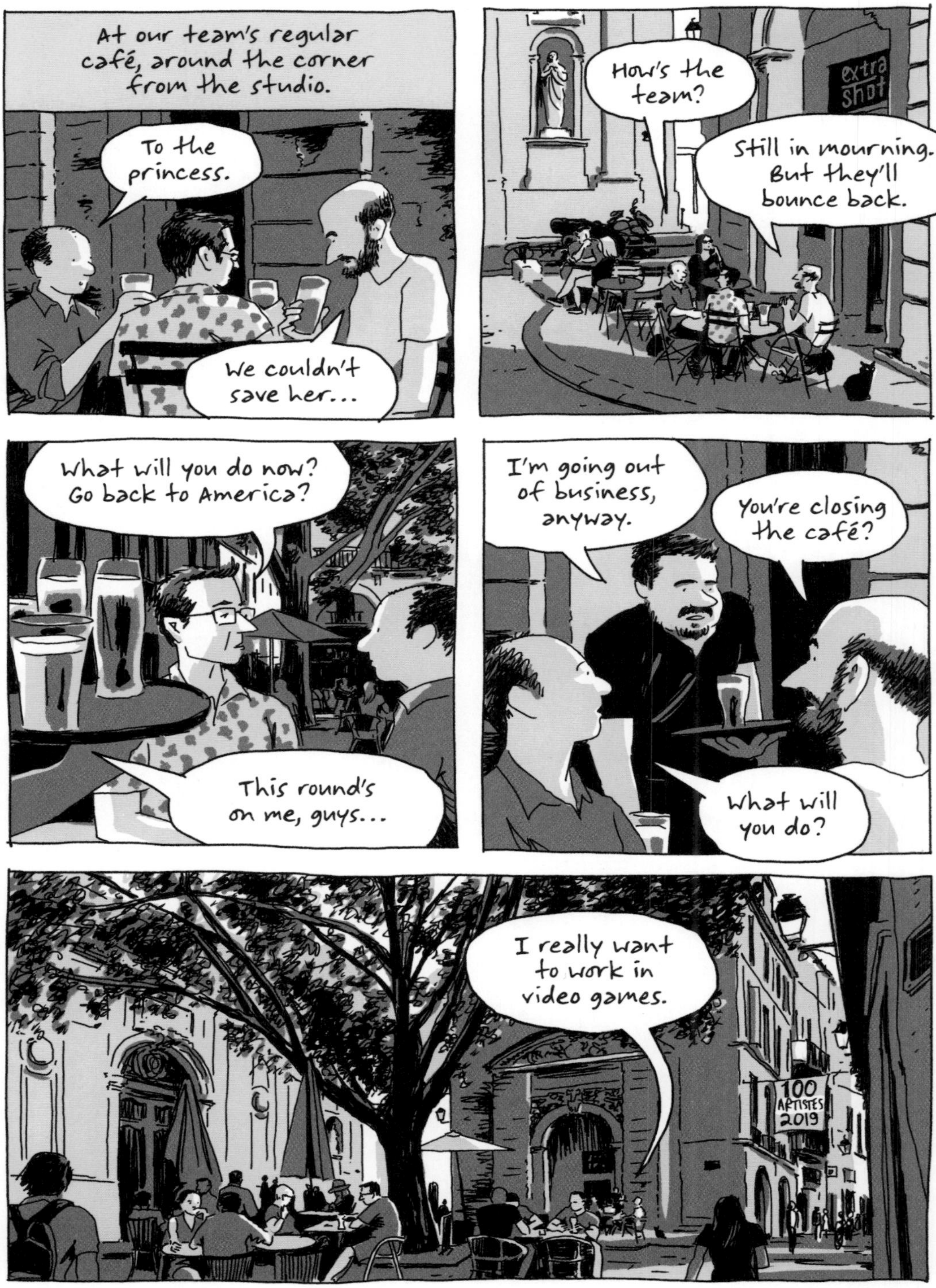
At our team's regular café, around the corner from the studio.
To the princess.
We couldn't save her...
How's the team?
extra shot
Still in mourning. But they'll bounce back.
What will you do now? Go back to America?
This round's on me, guys...
I'm going out of business, anyway.
You're closing the café?
What will you do?
I really want to work in video games.
100 ARTISTES 2019

White Mouse

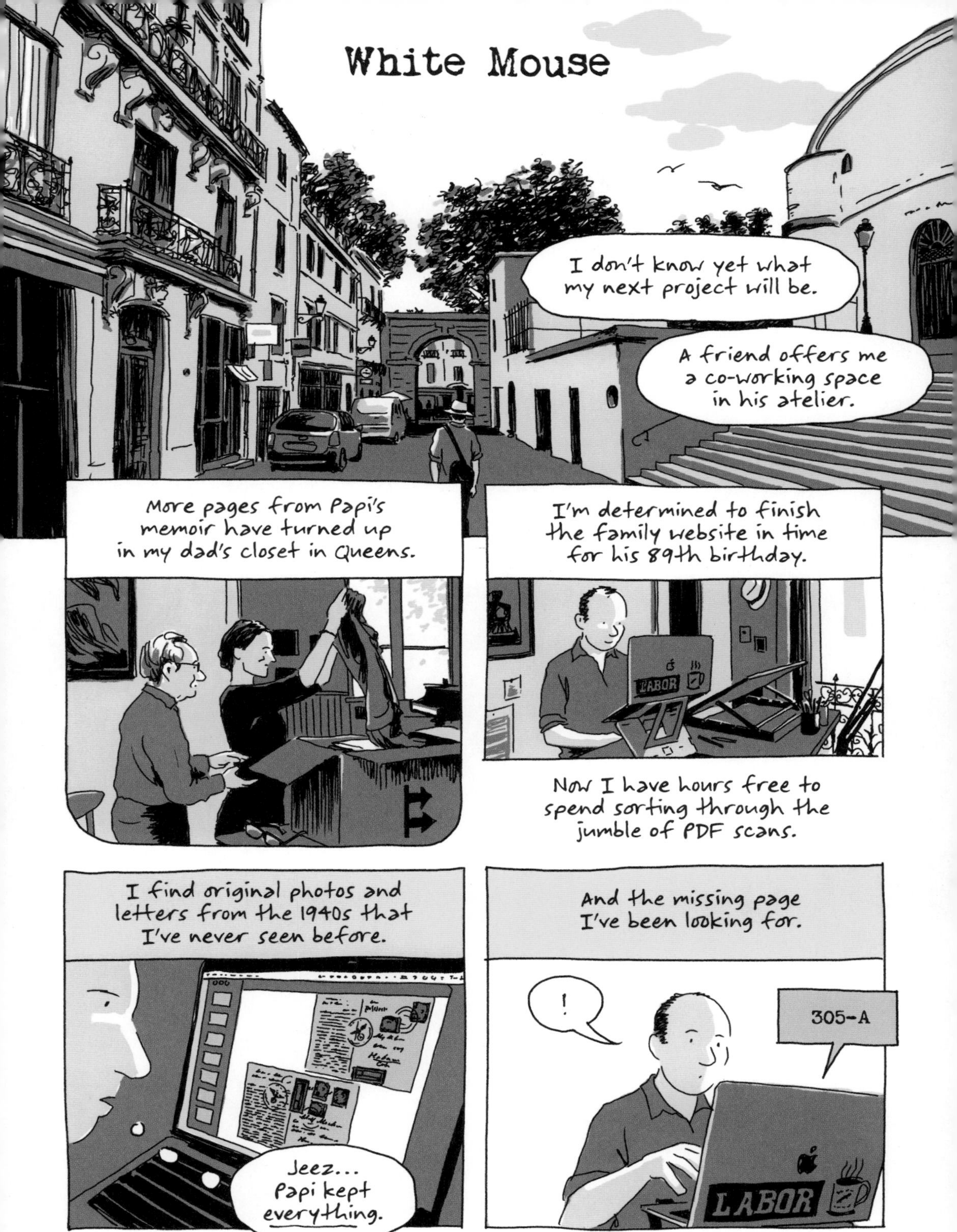
I don't know yet what my next project will be.
A friend offers me a co-working space in his atelier.
More pages from Papi's memoir have turned up in my dad's closet in Queens.
I'm determined to finish the family website in time for his 89th birthday.
LABOR
Now I have hours free to spend sorting through the jumble of PDF scans.
I find original photos and letters from the 1940s that I've never seen before.
Jeez... Papi kept everything.
And the missing page I've been looking for.
!
305-A
LABOR

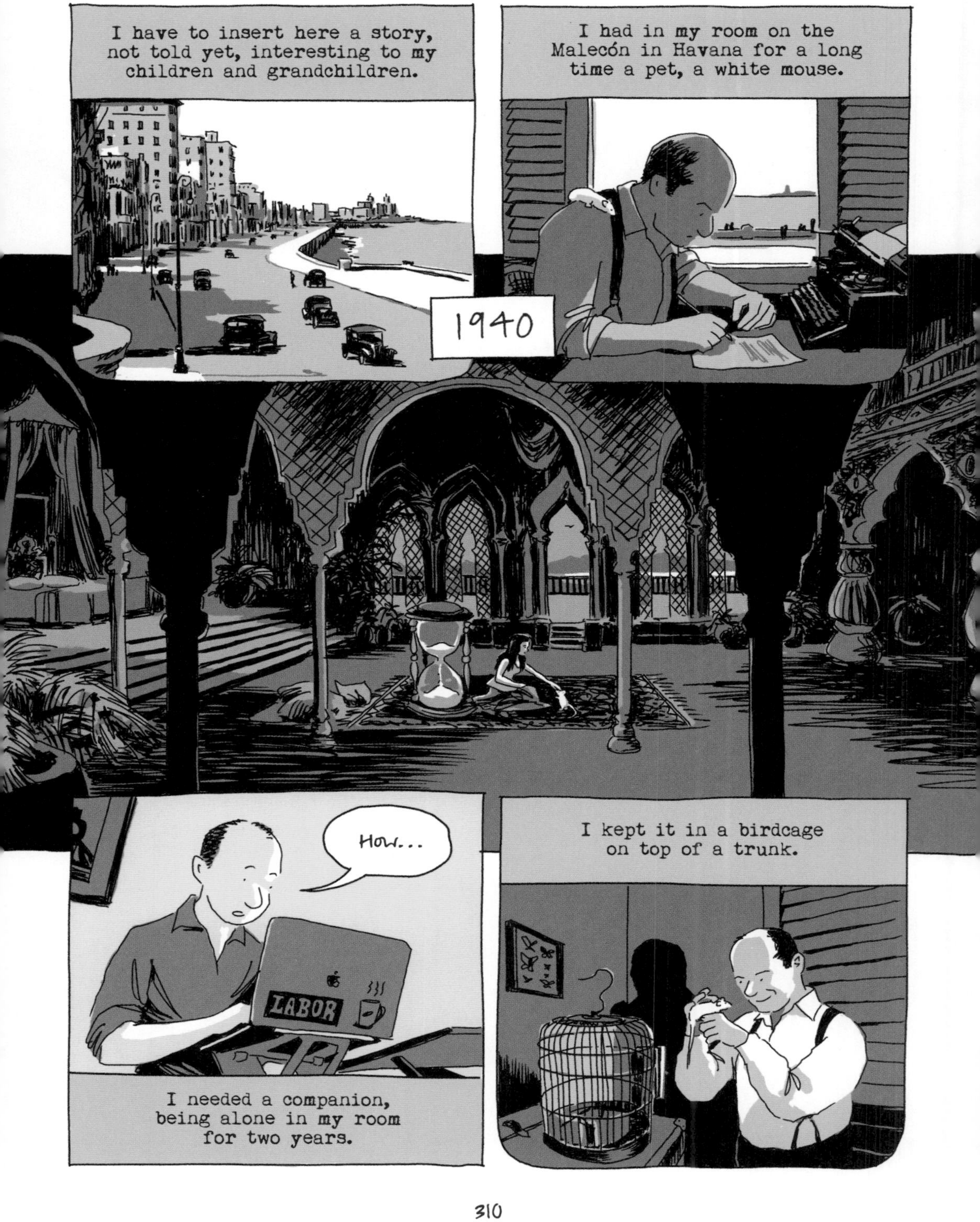
I have to insert here a story, not told yet, interesting to my children and grandchildren.
I had in my room on the Malecón in Havana for a long time a pet, a white mouse.
1940
How...
LABOR
I needed a companion, being alone in my room for two years.
I kept it in a birdcage on top of a trunk.

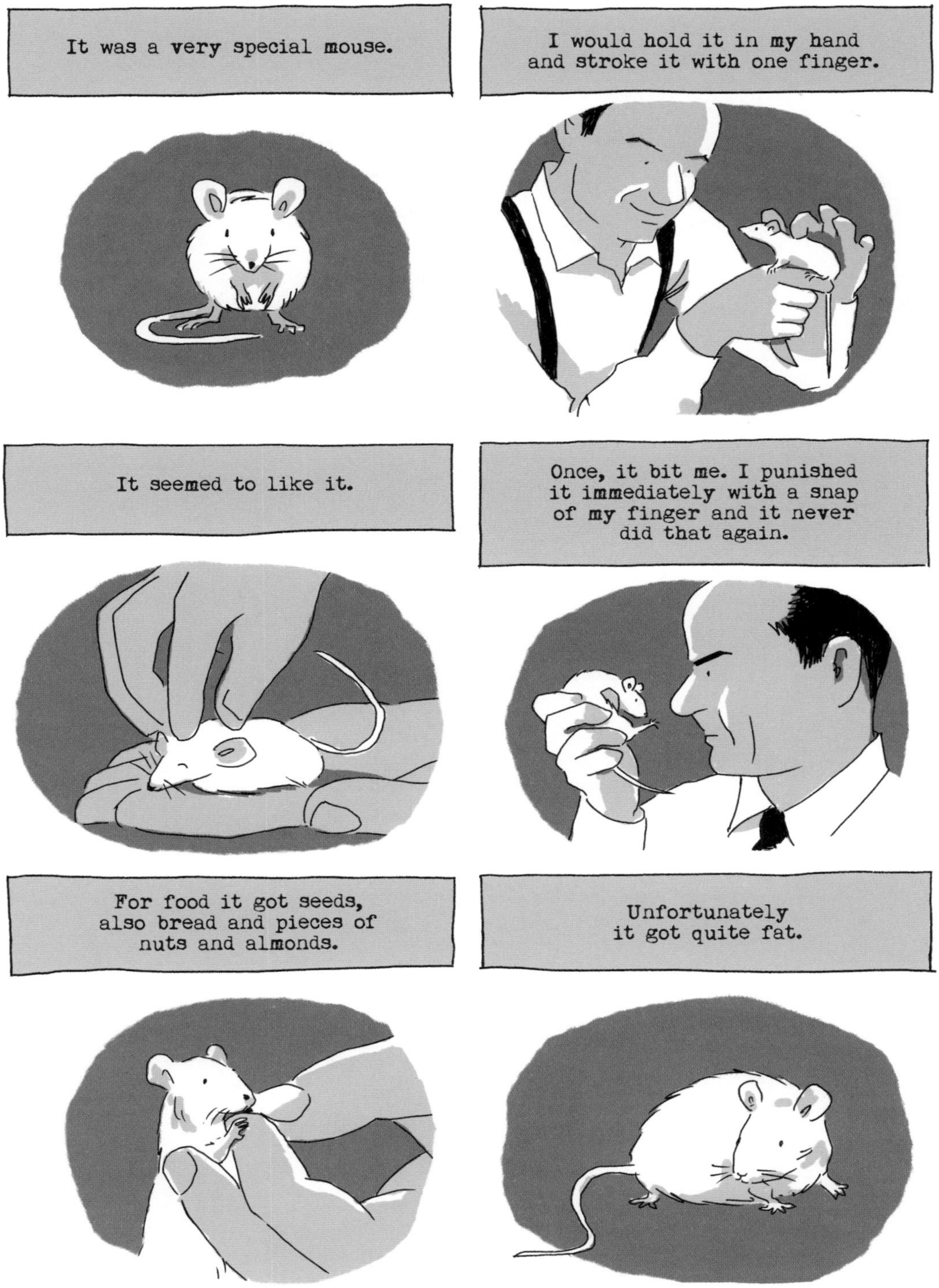
It was a very special mouse.
I would hold it in my hand and stroke it with one finger.
It seemed to like it.
Once, it bit me. I punished it immediately with a snap of my finger and it never did that again.
For food it got seeds, also bread and pieces of nuts and almonds.
Unfortunately it got quite fat.

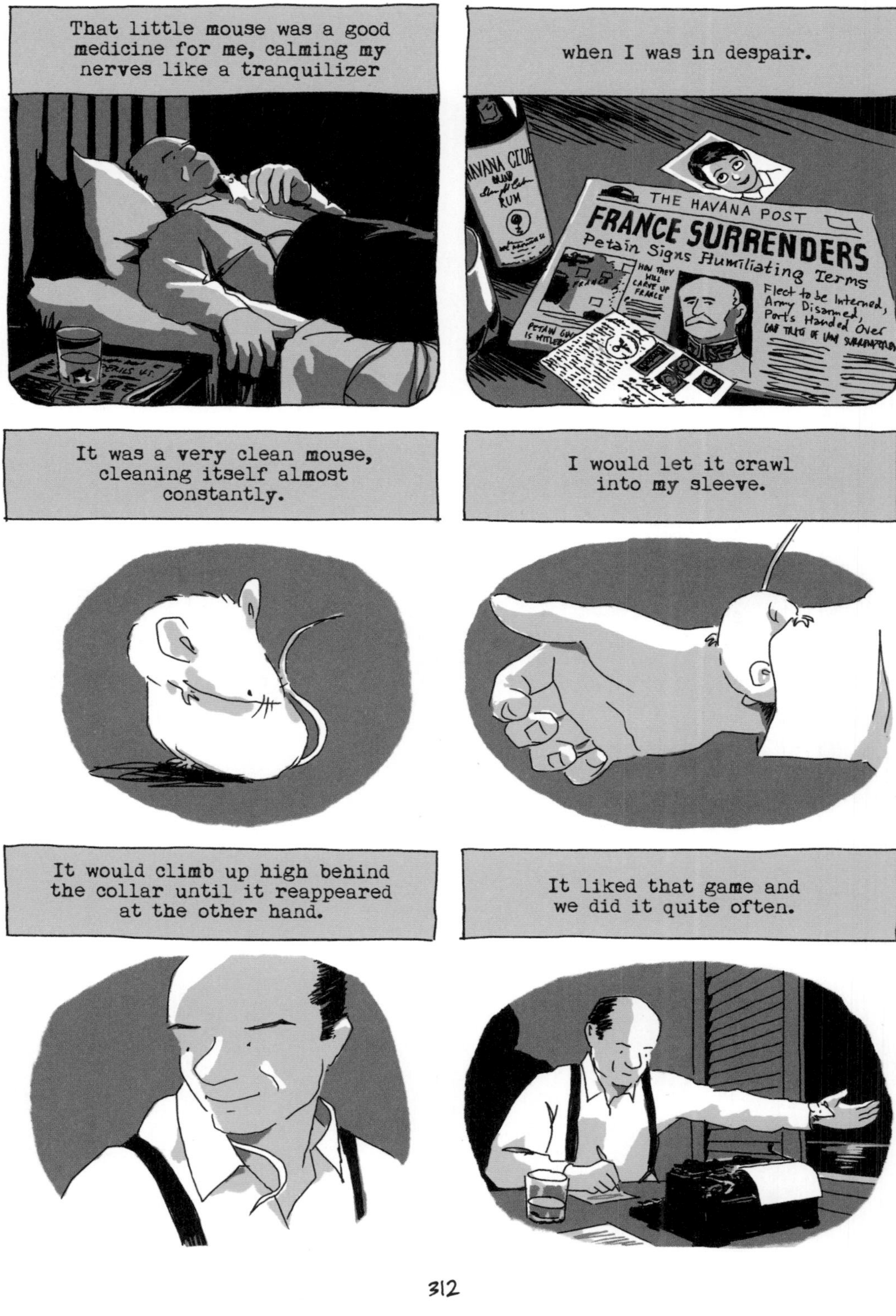
That little mouse was a good medicine for me, calming my nerves like a tranquilizer
when I was in despair.
HAVANA CLUB
RUM
THE HAVANA POST
FRANCE SURRENDERS
Petain Signs Humiliating Terms
Fleet to be Interned, Army Disarmed, Ports Handed Over
It was a very clean mouse, cleaning itself almost constantly.
I would let it crawl into my sleeve.
It would climb up high behind the collar until it reappeared at the other hand.
It liked that game and we did it quite often.

Pilgrimage

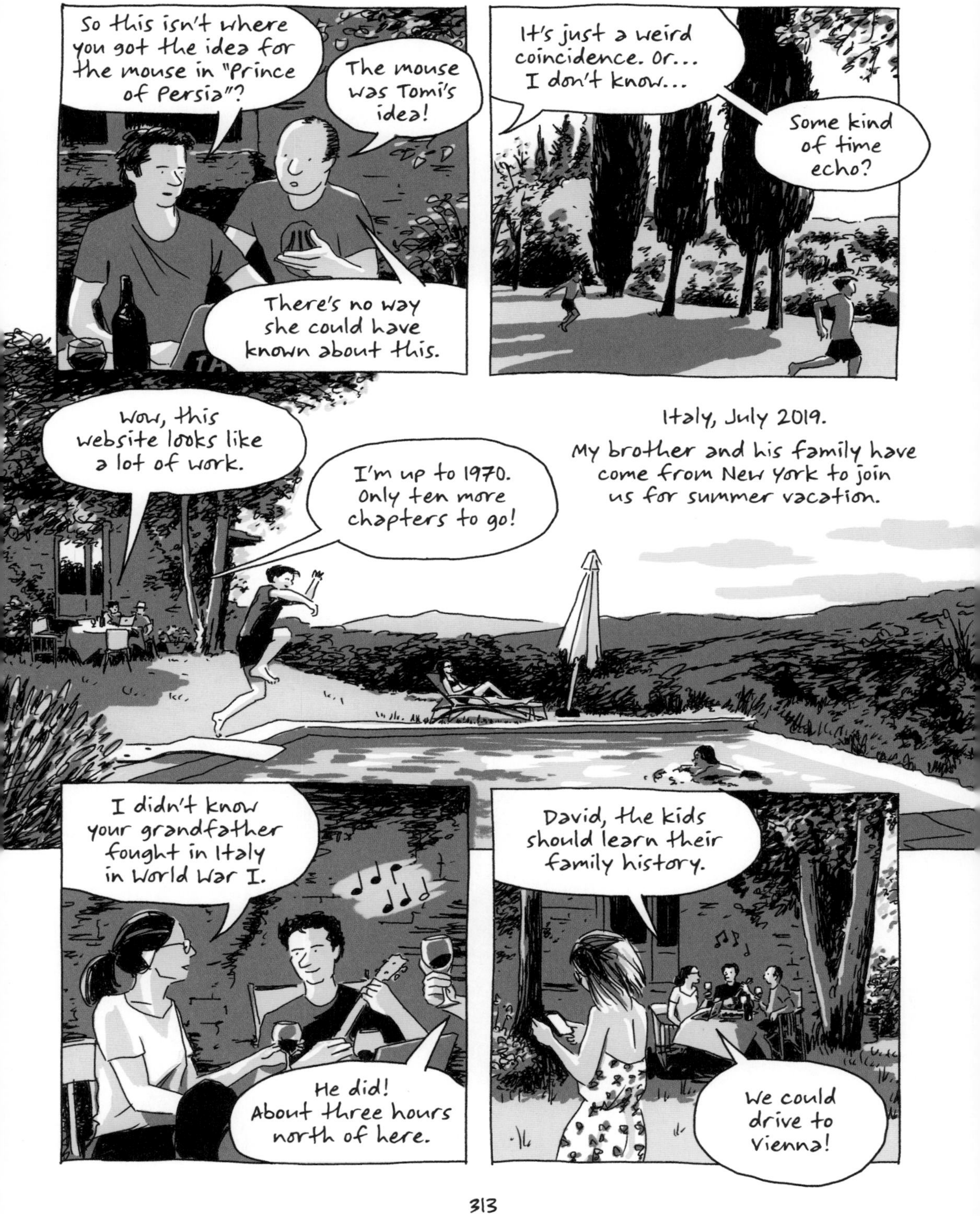

So this isn't where you got the idea for the mouse in "Prince of Persia"?
The mouse was Tomi's idea!
There's no way she could have known about this.
It's just a weird coincidence. Or... I don't know...
Some kind of time echo?
Wow, this website looks like a lot of work.
I'm up to 1970. Only ten more chapters to go!
Italy, July 2019.
My brother and his family have come from New York to join us for summer vacation.
I didn't know your grandfather fought in Italy in World War I.
He did! About three hours north of here.
David, the kids should learn their family history.
We could drive to Vienna!

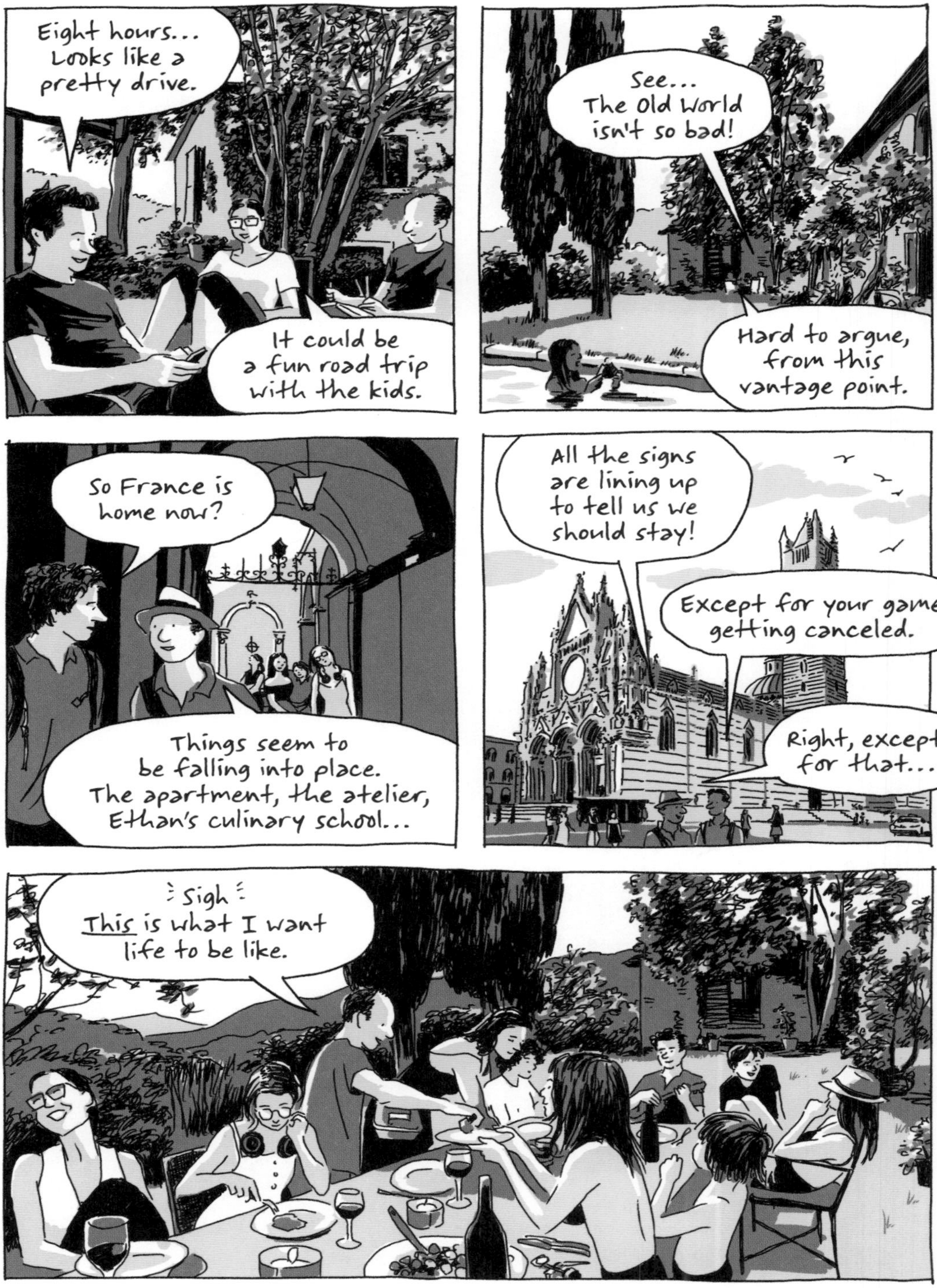
Eight hours... Looks like a pretty drive.
It could be a fun road trip with the kids.
See... The Old World isn't so bad!
Hard to argue, from this vantage point.
So France is home now?
Things seem to be falling into place. The apartment, the atelier, Ethan's culinary school...
All the signs are lining up to tell us we should stay!
Except for your game getting canceled.
Right, except for that...
Sigh
This is what I want life to be like.

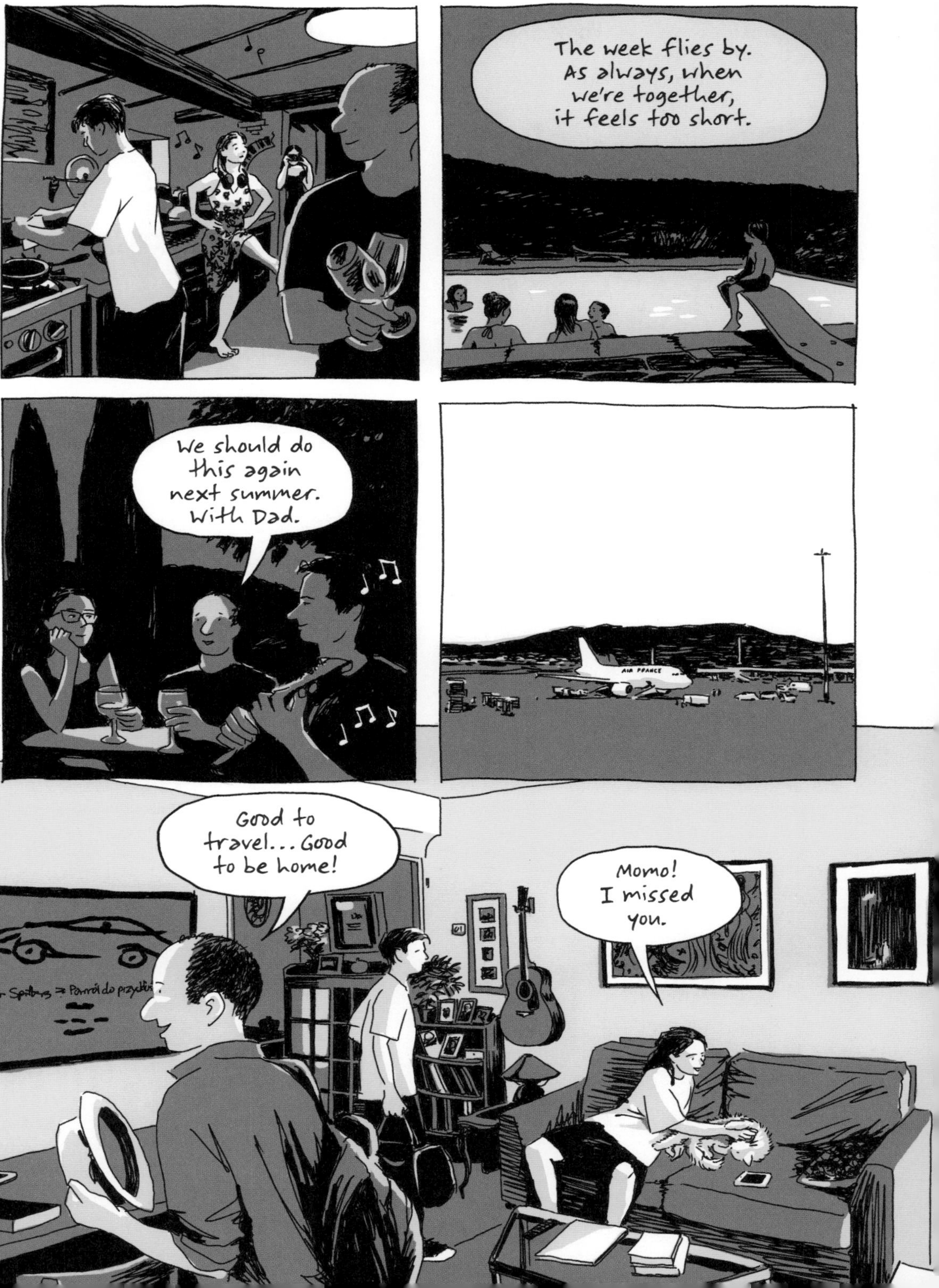
The week flies by. As always, when we're together, it feels too short.
We should do this again next summer. With Dad.
Good to travel... Good to be home!
Momo! I missed you.

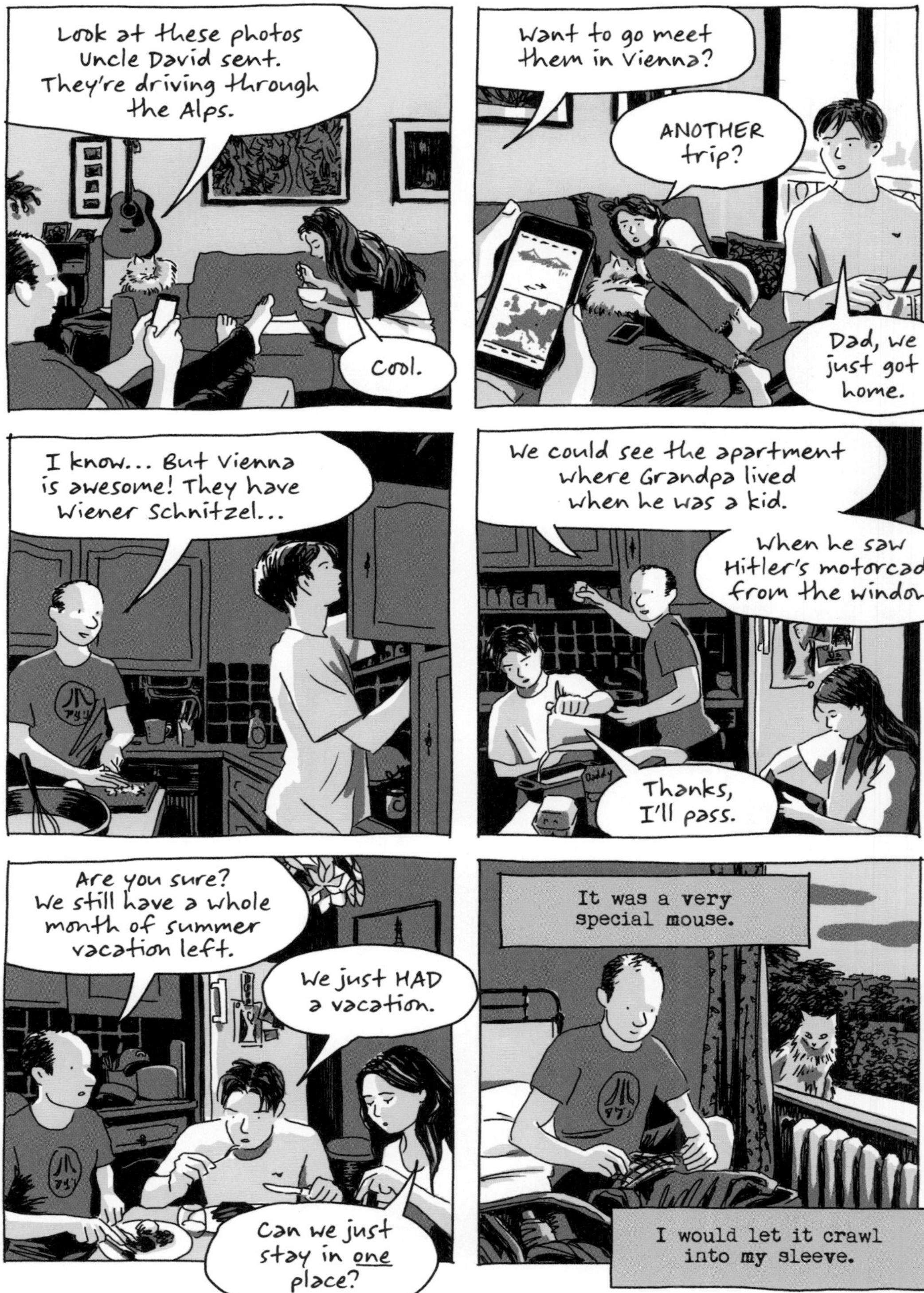
Look at these photos Uncle David sent. They're driving through the Alps.
Cool.
Want to go meet them in Vienna?
ANOTHER trip?
Dad, we just got home.
I know... But Vienna is awesome! They have Wiener Schnitzel...
We could see the apartment where Grandpa lived when he was a kid.
When he saw Hitler's motorcade from the window.
Thanks, I'll pass.
Are you sure? We still have a whole month of summer vacation left.
We just HAD a vacation.
Can we just stay in one place?
It was a very special mouse.
I would let it crawl into my sleeve.

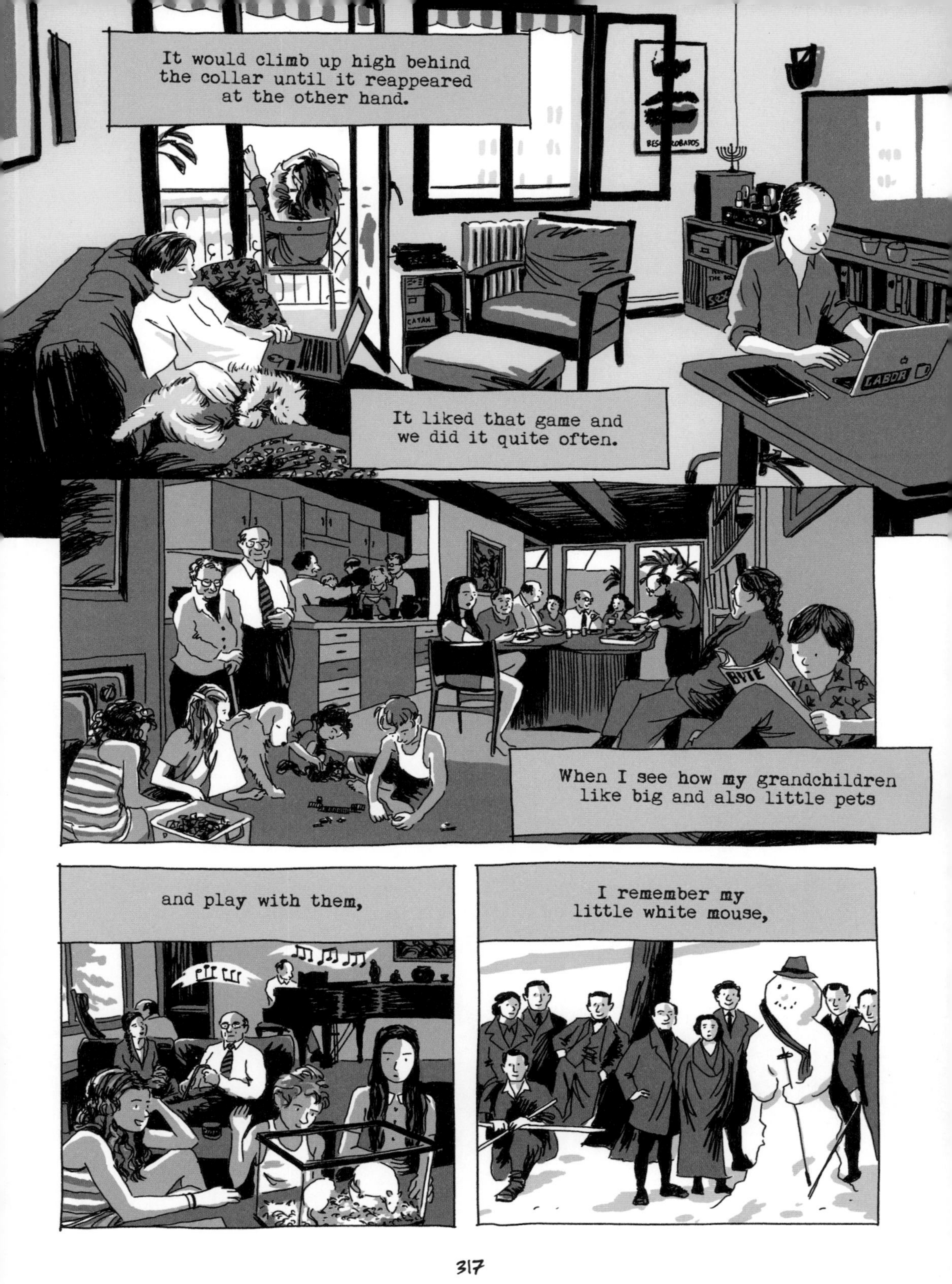
It would climb up high behind the collar until it reappeared at the other hand.
It liked that game and we did it quite often.
BYTE
When I see how my grandchildren like big and also little pets
and play with them,
I remember my little white mouse,

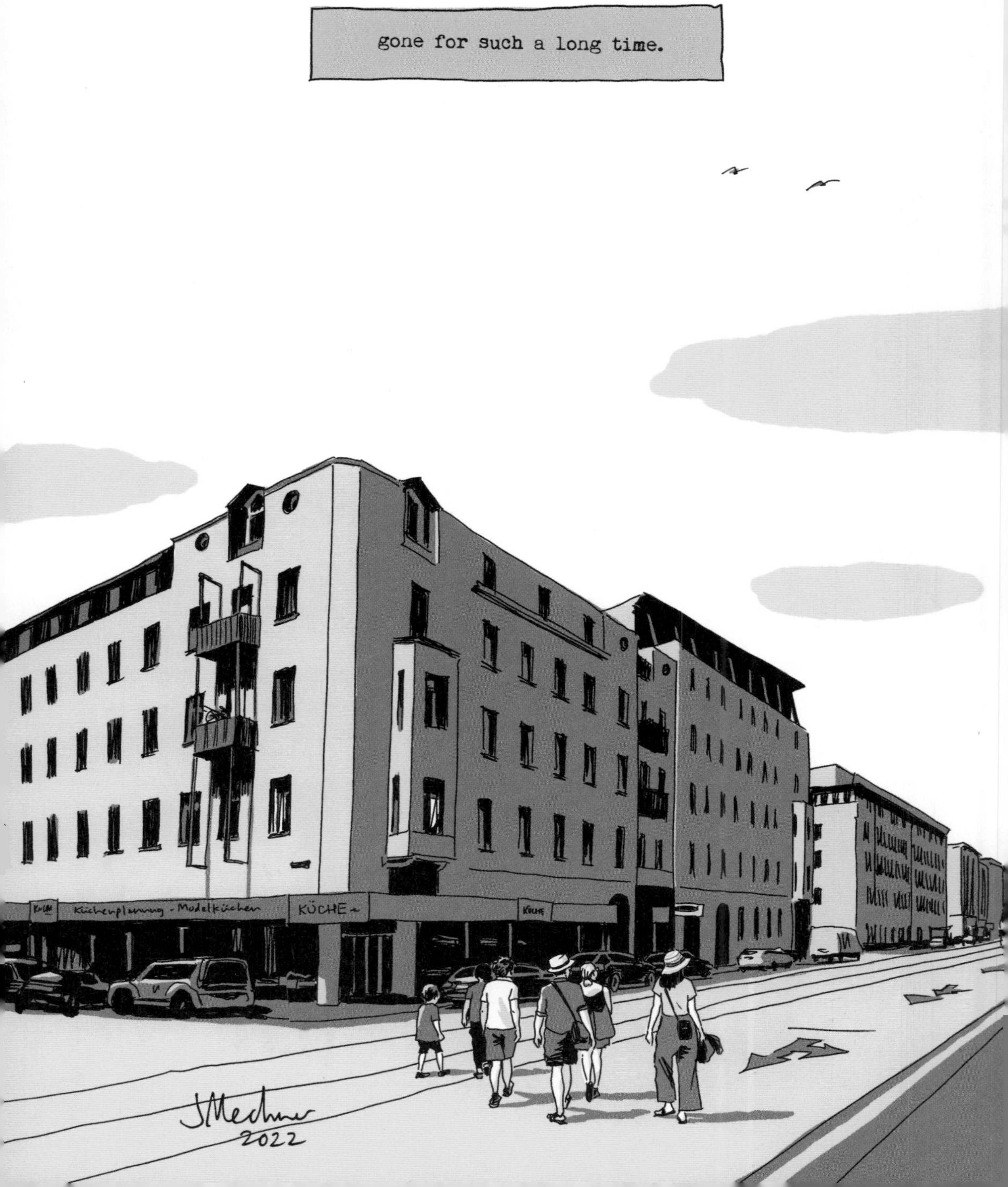
gone for such a long time.
Küchenplanung - Modelküchen
KÜCHE
2022

Acknowledgments

My inspiration and guiding force in making *Replay* was my grandfather Adolph Mechner, who wrote his autobiography at age 78 and encouraged his descendants to follow suit. My father, Francis Mechner, also shared his story in a written memoir and through countless conversations, patiently answering all my questions. I'm everlastingly grateful to them both, and to my great-aunt Lisa Rosegg; my aunt Johanna Cooper; and my mother, Vicki Mechner, who dug into their memories and photo archives to add their own perspectives to our family legacy. Their generosity, candor, and concern for accuracy set a standard I can only try to live up to.

I had the benefit of not one but two wonderful editorial teams on both sides of the Atlantic. My first editor, Lewis Trondheim, offered invaluable support and guidance in shaping *Replay* into coherent form, suggesting concrete improvements right up to the end. Tess Banta and Mark Siegel gave sensitive feedback that sharpened and enriched both the French and English editions. Robyn Chapman, Kirk Benshoff, and Sunny Lee at First Second joined efforts so seamlessly with their counterparts at Delcourt that I can't say which edition is the original. My deep thanks to all of them.

Special thanks to Nicolai Eberholst for generously sharing his expertise in World Wars I and II, Edgar Hauster for Czernowitz, Alain Holuigue for Le Touquet, Jean-Louis Vérisson for La Bernerie-en-Retz, and Erik Mombeeck for the pilots. Claude Seyrat, Fabien Delpiano, Stephanie Manfrini, John and Mary Ziegler, Frédérique Alexandre, Karyn Slutsky, Abraham Weitzberg, Ben Normark, Katie Taylor, Ana Tajder, Sophie, Jacqueline, and Peter Lillie, and more friends, photographers, memoirists, filmmakers, artists, and archivists than I can list helped me picture facets of our distant and less-distant past.

David and Katherine Mechner and Patrick Ladislav read and commented on drafts from the unique perspective of friends who'd lived through the blue and yellow timelines with me. Boaz Yakin, Bryan Seles, Olivier Vatine, Alex Puvilland, LeUyen Pham, Jane Mechner, Guy Delisle, and my atelier-mates at Association Satellites are among the fine artists who encouraged and helped me with craft-improving tips throughout *Replay*'s creation.

Above all, my heartfelt thanks to my children, Jane and Ethan, and to my family and friends who've graciously tolerated my cartoon portrayals of them through the years. This book couldn't exist without them, and neither could I.

For readers interested in the events or creative process behind *Replay*, I've created an online annex with commentary and resources:

jordanmechner.com/replay-annex